**Keep this book. ʏou will
need it and use it throughout
your career.**

About the American Hotel & Lodging Association (AH&LA)

Founded in 1910, AH&LA is the trade association representing the lodging industry in the United States. AH&LA is a federation of state lodging associations throughout the United States with 11,000 lodging properties worldwide as members. The association offers its members assistance with governmental affairs representation, communications, marketing, hospitality operations, training and education, technology issues, and more. For information, call 202-289-3100.

LODGING, the management magazine of AH&LA, is a "living textbook" for hospitality students that provides timely features, industry news, and vital lodging information.

About the American Hotel & Lodging Educational Institute (EI)

An affiliate of AH&LA, the Educational Institute is the world's largest source of quality training and educational materials for the lodging industry. EI develops textbooks and courses that are used in more than 1,200 colleges and universities worldwide, and also offers courses to individuals through its Distance Learning program. Hotels worldwide rely on EI for training resources that focus on every aspect of lodging operations. Industry-tested videos, CD-ROMs, seminars, and skills guides prepare employees at every skill level. EI also offers professional certification for the industry's top performers. For information about EI's products and services, call 800-349-0299 or 407-999-8100.

About the American Hotel & Lodging Educational Foundation (AH&LEF)

An affiliate of AH&LA, the American Hotel & Lodging Educational Foundation provides financial support that enhances the stability, prosperity, and growth of the lodging industry through educational and research programs. AH&LEF has awarded millions of dollars in scholarship funds for students pursuing higher education in hospitality management. AH&LEF has also funded research projects on topics important to the industry, including occupational safety and health, turnover and diversity, and best practices in the U.S. lodging industry. For more information, go to www.ahlef.org.

PURCHASING for FOOD SERVICE OPERATIONS

Educational Institute Books

UNIFORM SYSTEM OF ACCOUNTS FOR THE LODGING INDUSTRY
Tenth Revised Edition

WORLD OF RESORTS: FROM DEVELOPMENT TO MANAGEMENT
Third Edition
Chuck Yim Gee

PLANNING AND CONTROL FOR FOOD AND BEVERAGE OPERATIONS
Seventh Edition
Jack D. Ninemeier

UNDERSTANDING HOSPITALITY LAW
Fifth Edition
Jack P. Jefferies/Banks Brown

SUPERVISION IN THE HOSPITALITY INDUSTRY
Fourth Edition
Raphael R. Kavanaugh/Jack D. Ninemeier

MANAGEMENT OF FOOD AND BEVERAGE OPERATIONS
Fifth Edition
Jack D. Ninemeier

MANAGING FRONT OFFICE OPERATIONS
Eighth Edition
Michael L. Kasavana/Richard M. Brooks

MANAGING SERVICE IN FOOD AND BEVERAGE OPERATIONS
Fourth Edition
Ronald F. Cichy/Philip J. Hickey, Jr.

THE LODGING AND FOOD SERVICE INDUSTRY
Seventh Edition
Gerald W. Lattin

SECURITY AND LOSS PREVENTION MANAGEMENT
Second Edition
Raymond C. Ellis, Jr./David M. Stipanuk

HOSPITALITY INDUSTRY MANAGERIAL ACCOUNTING
Seventh Edition
Raymond S. Schmidgall

PURCHASING FOR FOOD SERVICE OPERATIONS
Ronald F. Cichy/Jeffery D Elsworth

MANAGING TECHNOLOGY IN THE HOSPITALITY INDUSTRY
Sixth Edition
Michael L. Kasavana

HOTEL AND RESTAURANT ACCOUNTING
Seventh Edition
Raymond Cote

ACCOUNTING FOR HOSPITALITY MANAGERS
Fifth Edition
Raymond Cote

CONVENTION MANAGEMENT AND SERVICE
Eighth Edition
Milton T. Astroff/James R. Abbey

HOSPITALITY SALES AND MARKETING
Fifth Edition
James R. Abbey

MANAGING HOUSEKEEPING OPERATIONS
Revised Third Edition
Aleta A. Nitschke/William D. Frye

HOSPITALITY TODAY: AN INTRODUCTION
Seventh Edition
Rocco M. Angelo/Andrew N. Vladimir

HOSPITALITY FACILITIES MANAGEMENT AND DESIGN
Third Edition
David M. Stipanuk

MANAGING HOSPITALITY HUMAN RESOURCES
Fifth Edition
Robert H. Woods, Misty M. Johanson, and Michael P. Sciarini

RETAIL MANAGEMENT FOR SPAS

HOSPITALITY INDUSTRY FINANCIAL ACCOUNTING
Third Edition
Raymond S. Schmidgall/James W. Damitio

INTERNATIONAL HOTELS: DEVELOPMENT & MANAGEMENT
Second Edition
Chuck Yim Gee

QUALITY SANITATION MANAGEMENT
Ronald F. Cichy

HOTEL INVESTMENTS: ISSUES & PERSPECTIVES
Fifth Edition
Edited by Lori E. Raleigh and Rachel J. Roginsky

LEADERSHIP AND MANAGEMENT IN THE HOSPITALITY INDUSTRY
Third Edition
Robert H. Woods/Judy Z. King

MARKETING IN THE HOSPITALITY INDUSTRY
Fifth Edition
Ronald A. Nykiel

UNIFORM SYSTEM OF ACCOUNTS FOR THE HEALTH, RACQUET AND SPORTSCLUB INDUSTRY

CONTEMPORARY CLUB MANAGEMENT
Second Edition
Edited by Joe Perdue for the Club Managers Association of America

RESORT CONDOMINIUM AND VACATION OWNERSHIP MANAGEMENT: A HOSPITALITY PERSPECTIVE
Robert A. Gentry/Pedro Mandoki/Jack Rush

ACCOUNTING FOR CLUB OPERATIONS
Raymond S. Schmidgall/James W. Damitio

TRAINING AND DEVELOPMENT FOR THE HOSPITALITY INDUSTRY
Debra F. Cannon/Catherine M. Gustafson

UNIFORM SYSTEM OF FINANCIAL REPORTING FOR CLUBS
Sixth Revised Edition

HOTEL ASSET MANAGEMENT: PRINCIPLES & PRACTICES
Second Edition
Edited by Greg Denton, Lori E. Raleigh, and A. J. Singh

MANAGING BEVERAGE OPERATIONS
Second Edition
Ronald F. Cichy/Lendal H. Kotschevar

FOOD SAFETY: MANAGING WITH THE HACCP SYSTEM
Second Edition
Ronald F. Cichy

UNIFORM SYSTEM OF FINANCIAL REPORTING FOR SPAS

FUNDAMENTALS OF DESTINATION MANAGEMENT AND MARKETING
Edited by Rich Harrill

ETHICS IN THE HOSPITALITY AND TOURISM INDUSTRY
Second Edition
Karen Lieberman/Bruce Nissen

SPA: A COMPREHENSIVE INTRODUCTION
Elizabeth M. Johnson/Bridgette M. Redman

HOSPITALITY 2015: THE FUTURE OF HOSPITALITY AND TRAVEL
Marvin Cetron/Fred DeMicco/Owen Davies

REVENUE MANAGEMENT: MAXIMIZING REVENUE IN HOSPITALITY OPERATIONS
Gabor Forgacs

FINANCIAL MANAGEMENT FOR SPAS
Raymond S. Schmidgall/John R. Korpi

01/12

PURCHASING for FOOD SERVICE OPERATIONS

Ronald F. Cichy, Ph.D., CFBE, CHA, CHE, NCE
Jeffery D Elsworth, Ph.D.

American
Hotel & Lodging
Educational Institute

Disclaimer

This publication is designed to provide accurate and authoritative information in regard to the subject matter covered. It is sold with the understanding that the publisher is not engaged in rendering legal, accounting, or other professional service. If legal advice or other expert assistance is required, the services of a competent professional person should be sought.

> — From the Declaration of Principles jointly adopted by the American Bar Association and a Committee of Publishers and Associations

The authors are solely responsible for the contents of this publication. All views expressed herein are solely those of the authors and do not necessarily reflect the views of the American Hotel & Lodging Educational Institute (the Institute) or the American Hotel & Lodging Association (AH&LA).

Nothing contained in this publication shall constitute a standard, an endorsement, or a recommendation of the Institute or AH&LA. The Institute and AH&LA disclaim any liability with respect to the use of any information, procedure, or product, or reliance thereon by any member of the hospitality industry.

Contents

DEDICATION

This book is dedicated to Dr. Anthony G. Marshall, CHA, former President of the Educational Institute, who identified a need and gave us the opportunity to work together on this book. *Requiescat in pace.* (May he rest in peace.)

This book is also dedicated to the members of our families—Shelley, Grace, John, and Lily Cichy, as well as Nancy, Nathan, and Molly Elsworth—who taught us to recognize the value proposition in our families.

Preface

Purchasing for Food Service Operations was written to present the basic purchasing essentials applicable to any food service operation. A theme throughout this book is value and the ways in which value is added by each member of the food service distribution channel, as well as by members of the management and staff team in the food service operation.

We address trends in purchasing, e-purchasing, and products as we give readers the tools and information they will need in their careers. We also present ethics from both the distributor's and the operator's perspectives. This book covers food security and defense issues, including bioterrorism, while including proven strategies for ensuring food safety.

In Chapter 1 we describe the importance of purchasing, identify the primary and secondary members in the food service distribution channel, and evaluate the value proposition that each member provides to the end user. We also discuss the forces affecting the distribution system. While detailing the process to assess a distributor partner, including the key performance indicators, we explain the key performance indicators of the food service distribution channel.

In Chapter 2 we identify the food service segments and distinguish among the different structures of food service organizations. We describe the food service process flow from menu planning to cleaning and maintenance, and explain the unique and common characteristics of the purchasing control point. After defining the customer, particularly with regard to lifestyle changes and the shift to healthier dining, we explain the roles of internal customers and how these staff members create and deliver value through purchasing. We also describe the essentials of food safety in a food service operation.

Chapter 3 details how purchasing contributes to managing for quality and the steps in the purchasing process. We describe the skills, knowledge, and behaviors required in effective purchasing staff members and managers. We also describe the ethics of operators and define the market, distributor, and internal areas of market research. The components of group purchasing are identified. Then we outline the basics of purchase specifications, pricing, and cost controls, including payment policies. This chapter also describes the process of ordering, including e-purchasing, and defines the security considerations of food service operations.

In Chapter 4 we identify the characteristics of distributor partners. We describe the process to select partners and outline the security considerations of distributors. This chapter also identifies the food safety and HACCP essentials for distributors and explains the essentials of ethics from a distributor's perspective. We also explain the role of distributors in helping food service operations to become more effective.

Chapter 5 covers the buyer-distributor relationship and details the ethics required in the relationship. This chapter also defines the essentials of the negotiation process between buyers and distributors. Chapter 6 identifies the quality, cost, and safety requirements at the receiving and storing control points. We also describe the procedures necessary for effective inventory controls. Chapter 7 explains the federal, state, and local food and commerce laws applicable to purchasing, and outlines requirements for purchasing contracts.

The remainder of the book focuses on specific products purchased by a food service operation. Chapter 8 covers meat products: beef, pork, veal and lamb. Chapter 9 details the requirements for fish and shellfish. Chapter 10 covers poultry, while Chapter 11 focuses on dairy and eggs. Chapter 12 covers produce, and Chapter 13 presents baked goods and grocery items. In Chapter 14 readers will find beverages, and in Chapter 15 they will find equipment, supplies, smallware, and services.

Acknowledgments

We would like to acknowledge the contributions of many highly talented collaborators on this project. Industry leaders who were members of the review committee included Dave Dow, Vice President, Gordon Food Service (retired); Gail F. Venrick, Director of Purchasing, Max & Erma's Restaurants, Inc.; Dennis P. Wells, Director of Purchasing, HDS Services; Jeff Darby, Vice President of Purchasing, RARE Hospitality International, Inc.; Roger Bing, Senior Director of Purchasing, Darden Restaurants; Marta Mittermaier, Purchasing Manager, Michigan State University Food Stores; Putnam Gibson, Houstons Restaurants; and Dieter Kadoke, Senior Vice President of Food and Beverage, Wyndham International.

Lena Loeffler and Nancy Elsworth assisted with the word processing of the manuscript. Research Assistants Mi Ran Kim, Ashley Saur, and Ann Doré helped us identify reference materials for the book. We also wish to thank the committed and dedicated members of the editorial and production team at the Educational Institute, and specifically Writer/Editor Jessica Miller, Senior Director of Academic Publications Tim Eaton, and Senior Vice President of Research and Development George Glazer.

Ronald F. Cichy
Okemos, Michigan

Jeffery D Elsworth
Okemos, Michigan

About the Authors

Ronald F. Cichy

Jeffery D Elsworth

Ronald F. Cichy, Ph.D., CFBE, CHA, CHE, NCE, is the director of and a professor in *The* School of Hospitality Business at Michigan State University, a position in which he has served his alma mater since 1988. Dr. Cichy's research has led to his identification as one of the 50 most influential scholars in hospitality management. He is a recognized pioneer researcher on the topics of leadership qualities, keys, and secrets, both in the United States and Japan, as well as the leadership essentials and the emotional intelligence of hospitality leaders.

In 2004, Dr. Cichy wrote *Food Safety: Managing the HACCP Process* and co-wrote *Managing Beverage Service* with Dr. Lendal Kotschevar. *Managing for Quality in the Hospitality Industry*, co-authored with John King, Jr., was published in 2005. The third edition of *Managing Service in Food and Beverage Operations*, co-authored with Phil Hickey, Jr., was published in 2005. He has co-authored his ninth book, *Purchasing for Food Service Operations*, with Dr. Jeffery D Elsworth.

Dr. Cichy is a frequent speaker at annual conferences, meetings, and institutes for businesses ranging from Fortune 500 companies to those in the hospitality industry. His lectures are both educational and entertaining, and include Strategic Values and Vision, Leading Change, Service Excellence, Personal Leadership, Organizational Leadership, and Team Building, Training, and the Emotionally Intelligent Leader. His insights come from decades of industry experience and working with top global service business leaders.

Dr. Cichy has delivered seminars and workshops in Australia, Canada, Europe, Japan, Mexico, and the United States. His work with executives from five continents has developed managers and leaders, team builders and trainers, and helped businesses become high-performance organizations. He has worked with Fortune 500 companies, including MASCO and General Motors, as well as the city of Detroit, Consumers Energy, Eagle Ottawa, Accident Fund Insurance Company of America, Toyota, Isuzu, National Automatic Merchandising Association, Michigan State Police Forensics Division, Radisson Hotels and Resorts, Club Managers Association of America, and the United States Air Force.

Dr. Cichy serves on the boards of several hospitality industry institutes, foundations, and associations. He is a member of the Board of Trustees of the American Hotel & Lodging Educational Foundation, and the Chairman of National Automatic Merchandising Association's Certification Commission. In 1999, the American Hotel & Lodging Educational Institute honored him as an Outstanding Hospitality Educator. In 2001, he was inducted into *The* School of Hospitality Business Alumni Association's Wall of Fame Class of Contributors. Dr. Cichy was named a 75th Anniversary Year Distinguished Alumnus of *The* School of Hospitality Business in 2002. In 2003, he was honored with the Broad College of Business Outstanding Alumni Award. In 2004, Dr. Cichy was inducted into the Manistee Catholic Central Alumni Association Hall of Fame. In 2006, Dr Cichy received the Anthony G. Marshall Award for long-term contributions to the hospitality industry.

Dr. Cichy is a Certified Hotel Administrator (CHA), Certified Hospitality Educator (CHE), Certified Food and Beverage Executive (CFBE), and NAMA Certified Executive (NCE). He is married to Shelley, and they are parents of two children, Grace and John. They reside in Okemos, Michigan with a yellow Labrador named Lily. Dr. Cichy is a member of the Society of American Magicians and the International Brotherhood of Magicians.

Jeffery D Elsworth, Ph.D., is an associate professor of Hospitality Business Entrepreneurship in *The* School of Hospitality Business at Michigan State University. He comes by his interest in food service operations honestly as he was a manager, general manager, and franchise trainer of managers for 20 years before turning to academics. Dr. Elsworth's experience in the restaurant industry gives him a unique perspective, which he uses in the classroom to teach his students the essential skills needed for success in the food service and hospitality industry.

Dr. Elsworth's research interests include hospitality entrepreneurship, food service purchasing, food service operations, food safety and food service inspection media reporting issues, hospitality wage determinants, and hospitality small-business finance issues. He has written, and won awards for, several scholarly papers on these and other subjects, and has worked as a food service consultant. He has conducted presentations for several government-sponsored foreign trade agencies, the United States Air Force Services, and various trade organizations in the areas of restaurant operations, menu trends, and food safety issues.

Dr. Elsworth is the faculty leader of the Hospitality Business Entrepreneurship specialization in *The* School of Hospitality Business. He teaches courses in hospitality business entrepreneurship; food and beverage management; facilities maintenance and systems management; food safety, nutrition, and controls; and food service facility planning and design. He also teaches a food service industry module for the graduate-level Food Protection and Defense course offered by Michigan State University's Food Safety and Toxicology Center. He has also taught courses in quantity food production systems, food service operations, and food service equipment.

Dr. Elsworth is a member of the National Restaurant Association, Michigan Restaurant Association, Foodservice Consultants Society International, the International Council on Hotel, Restaurant and Institutional Education, and the International Council of Shopping Centers. Dr. Elsworth earned his B.S., M.S., and Ph.D. degrees in Hospitality and Tourism Management from Purdue University in West Lafayette, Indiana. Dr. Elsworth resides in Okemos, Michigan, with his wife Nancy, daughter Molly, and son Nathan.

Chapter 1 Outline

The Importance of Purchasing
    A Brief History of Purchasing
    An Entrepreneurial Focus
    Purchasing Food, Beverages, Supplies,
      and Services
    Purchasing Considerations
Food Service Distribution Channel
   Members
    Touch Points for Customers and
      Products/Services
    Sources
    Manufacturers
    Distributors
    Food Service Operators
    Importers
    Sales and Marketing Agents
    On-Line Specialty Houses
    Alliances and Group Purchasing
      Organizations
    Value Each Member Brings to the
      Channel
    Food Safety and Defense
Forces Affecting the Distribution System
    Ethics
    Economic Forces
    Legal Forces
    Political Forces
    Technology
    Other Forces
Value Proposition that Each Member
   Provides to the End User
    Value Proposition
Assessing a Distributor Partner
    Physical Assessment
    Service Assessment
Key Performance Indicators in the
   Distribution Channel
Necessary Checks and Balances

Competencies

1. Describe the importance of purchasing. (pp. 3–9)

2. Identify the primary and secondary members in the food service distribution channel. (pp. 9–15)

3. Describe the forces affecting the distribution system. (pp. 15–19)

4. Evaluate the value proposition that each member provides to the end user. (pp. 19–21)

5. Detail the process to assess a distributor partner, including the role of key performance indicators. (pp. 21–22)

6. Explain the key performance indicators that food service operators can use to leverage their purchasing proposals. (p. 22)

7. Describe the necessary checks and balances in distributor relationships. (pp. 22–23)

Purchasing in the Food Service Distribution Channel

THE ROLE OF PURCHASING in the food service distribution channel has evolved and changed over the past several decades. At their fundamental level, purchasing functions help the food service operation survive and thrive by ensuring that the required food, beverages, supplies, equipment, and services are present when needed. These assets in the form of products and services are enhanced through the addition of value and contribute to the profitability and viability of the operation. The assets a food service organization will purchase can be determined only after asking and answering two essential questions:

* Who are our customers?
* What are these customers' requirements?

Customers can vary from food service operation to food service operation, and their requirements can vary based on individual needs, wants, and expectations. The basic goal of purchasing in the food service distribution channel is to satisfy customers' requirements.

The Importance of Purchasing

In the past, the skills of purchasing staff were often underutilized in that the role of purchasing staff was viewed as simply clerical. In other words, those responsible for purchasing were focused on spending as little as necessary to purchase the best possible products and services. In this view, purchasing was often categorized as a staff or service function that simply supported those who created and delivered products and services through the **food service distribution channel.** Purchasing staff often simply picked up the telephone and placed an order. Sometimes, the quality, quantity, and price of that order were left for the distributor to decide.

Today, purchasing is held in higher regard in that its many activities are tied to the organization's mission and vision. This strategic view is essential throughout the food service distribution channel as each member of the channel adds value and, ultimately, enhances the food service operation's ability to deliver customers' requirements.

A Brief History of Purchasing

The food service distribution channel has its roots in retail food distribution. In the 1920s and 1930s, large retail food chains such as A&P (Great Atlantic and Pacific Tea Company) and Safeway began. To compete, smaller independent grocery store owners formed cooperatives. IGA (Independent Grocers Alliance) was the first.

The chains and cooperatives competed directly with each other. Each discovered ways to produce and handle their products at a lower cost, including:

- Operating manufacturing or packing plants.

- Creating their own private labels by contracting directly with a product packer or packing the product themselves.

- Developing efficiently operated retail outlets in prime locations.

- Enhancing efficiency by transporting products in large quantities, using in-transit storage warehouses, negotiating better prices, and/or building automated facilities to manage inventory.

As the chains and cooperatives captured more markets and a larger market share, independent grocers faced extinction. Their choices were to go out of business, become part of a cooperative, or market to a different set of customers. While these distributors were losing their traditional customer base in the late 1940s, dining out in the various food service segments was on the rise.

Restaurant companies, such as Howard Johnson, Elias Brothers, and Stouffer's, were beginning to develop into larger multi-unit organizations. Many of these organizations started their own commissaries, which were production and distribution systems. They produced unique products at lower costs than those available from outside the organization while enhancing quality control and providing reliable service. At this point in history, most distributors lacked the capacity to produce and deliver some of the food products an operation might need.

Then, in the 1950s, distributors formed nonprofit organizations to purchase products as a group. They obtained their products, often popular customer brands, from major food manufacturers. Even though each distributor that joined the group remained independent, they were able to purchase products more competitively due to the power of group purchasing. Examples of these buying groups include NIFDA (National Institutional Food Distributors Association), CODE (Continental Organization of Distributor Enterprises), North American Food Services, Frosty Acres, and Nugget Distributors.

The other market force that emerged in the 1950s was quick-service restaurant chains. At first, traditional distributors met their purchasing needs. As these quick-service chains grew, their requirements increased and they were able to develop their own manufacturing and distribution channels, demand that distributors give them exclusive facilities, and dictate policy. Because of the relatively large volume of products that these chains were purchasing, they often required that the distributors sold them products priced on a cost-plus basis. The distributor's revenue was based on return on investment.

Quick-service chains, as well as hotel chains with full-service restaurants, achieved dramatic growth due to franchising. The organization that sold the franchise, known as the franchisor, to the franchisee often provided "equipment packages," ranging from individual pieces of equipment to complete, ready-to-operate systems to equip an entire kitchen. Some of the franchisors sold products to franchisees on a cost pass-through basis or through a separate profit-making division.

Today, products are distributed to food service operations in six basic ways:

1. Large national and/or regional organizations with broad product lines that serve a wide range of customers

2. Large national and/or regional organizations with relatively narrow product lines that serve specific customers or market segments

3. Distribution organizations owned or directed by large hospitality companies. In some cases, these organizations sell to operations outside of their owner's company.

4. Commissary systems used by many regional chains to distribute products ranging from basic commodities to ready-to-use products

5. Local specialty houses that distribute specific products (e.g., produce)

6. Local independent full-line distributors

Primary members in the food service distribution channel are the manufacturer and the distributor. Secondary members include sales and marketing agents (sometimes referred to as brokers), importers, on-line specialty houses, alliances, and purchasing groups. Each member will be discussed in more detail later in this chapter.

An Entrepreneurial Focus

An **entrepreneur** is someone who owns a business. Both the lodging and food service industries were built by entrepreneurs who saw an opportunity to transform products they obtained into products customers wanted by adding value to the products *as perceived by the customers or guests*. In today's lodging or food service organization, the owner frequently is not the manager. Yet, if the manager can think like an owner, the organization is well on its way to identifying the requirements (needs, wants, and expectations) of its customers and satisfying those requirements. Some qualities of thinking like an owner are presented in Exhibit 1.

Entrepreneurs focus on delivering value to their customers. Even though a manager may not actually own the food service business, there are a number of advantages to this person thinking like an owner:

- The availability and cost of products and services will be evaluated before they are purchased.

- The demand for and sales price of products and services will be determined before they are offered for sale.

Exhibit 1   Top Ten Qualities of Those Who Think Like an Owner

Ranking	Quality
1.	Meets commitments
2.	Honesty
3.	Conviction
4.	Communicates effectively
5.	Perseverance
6.	Attracted to challenge
7. (tie)	Attracted to risk
7. (tie)	Knowledge of financial numbers
7. (tie)	Curiosity
10.	Organized

Source: Jeffery D Elsworth, Jeff A. Beck, and Ronald F. Cichy, "Thinking Like an Owner." Adapted from in-progress research.

- The effect on the bottom line (i.e., profitability in commercial food service operations or surplus of revenue over expenses in other food service operations) will be assessed before the products and services are sold.

- And, most importantly, ways to maximize value received by the food service operation *and* value delivered to and perceived by the operation's customers through the products and services purchased will be evaluated before the actual sale.

Each of these leads to a determination of the correct food, beverages, supplies, and services to produce. When combined, the entrepreneur (whether the owner or a manager within an organization owned by someone else) enhances the value of the organization for its customers.

Purchasing Food, Beverages, Supplies, and Services

So far in our consideration of the importance of purchasing, we have reviewed a brief history and focused on the importance of entrepreneurial qualities in food service owners and managers. Perhaps it goes without saying, but entrepreneurs can benefit by becoming aware of what chain food service organizations implement in terms of purchasing and other processes, and adapting, modifying, and adopting these practices in their own operations.

Fundamentally, a food service operation must purchase, store, prepare, and serve food and beverage products that best satisfy those being served. Doing so means being in tune with the requirements of those being served and how they assess value. Whether food, beverages, supplies, or services are being purchased, value is a primary consideration.

Before value can be defined, the function of what is being purchased must be carefully defined. Consider the purchase of tomatoes, a food product that has hundreds of potential uses in a food service operation. If the tomatoes are to be prepared by slicing for display on a make-your-own-sandwich buffet at lunch, a different tomato will be required than if the tomato is to be used to prepare the chef's specialty lasagna. In the first case, the tomato must be fresh and firm enough to withstand the slicing and holding requirements. In the second case, the tomato is likely canned, and may even be in the form of tomato sauce for the lasagna recipe. Of course, the function is always based on customers' requirements.

Once the function is defined, the various options for purchasing can be assessed. This time, consider ketchup. Raw tomatoes could be purchased, prepared, and cooked into a specialty ketchup, unique to the individual food service operation; however, the time and effort required to transform the raw tomatoes into ketchup may not be valuable *as perceived by the operation's customers*.

Continuing with the ketchup example, bulk forms (i.e., #10 cans) of ketchup could be purchased and displayed on guests' tables in unique dispensers or dispensed from a bulk dispenser in a quick-service operation. Alternatively, ketchup could be purchased in individual bottles that can be present on guests' tables or delivered to guests, when requested, by the servers. This may add value if the guests are able to read a recognizable and preferred brand name on the ketchup bottle. Another option is to purchase ketchup in individual portion-controlled packets, again with the brand name printed on each packet.

In each case, the ketchup's function may be the same (i.e., to flavor whatever food product it is added to), but the value may vary based on the form in which the product is purchased. It has been suggested that the **value** of any food, beverage, supply, or service purchased can be determined by five factors:

- Quality
- Service
- Availability
- Information
- Price

As was noted earlier, quality depends on customer requirements. Perceived **quality** on the part of customers is one of the most important factors in purchasing. Quality is not what a product is, but what it does—that is, how it meets those requirements. Specifications help carefully define quality.

Service is affected by ordering procedures and delivery schedules. With equipment purchases, service also includes installation, and maintenance and repair. Service is strongly influenced by the relationship built between the operator and the distributor. Relationships based on honesty, fairness, and integrity lead to credibility, which can enhance service.

Availability is influenced in some cases by seasonality (e.g., fresh cherries from northern Michigan), but more often by the purchasing power of the distributor. When a distributor purchases in larger volumes, availability is usually enhanced.

Information is power, and information in the food service distribution channel includes ideas provided by the distributor, menu-consulting services, different options based on the function of what is being purchased, and educational seminars offered for professional development.

Price is based on the intended use of what is being purchased. The lowest price is not necessarily the best price, because price should be based on exactly what is specified. In summary, value is received when the quality, service, availability, information, and price are all evaluated and the purchasing decisions are made based on customers' requirements.

Purchasing Considerations

The role of value in purchasing was presented in the previous section. Purchasing is more relevant from a strategic perspective in a food service operation today than it was in the past. The objectives of purchasing must be tied to the organization's values and mission and vision.

For example, if an organization values reducing expenses and boosting profitability, it is more likely to purchase products based on price. The negotiation of the lowest price during the procurement process will become a primary focus for such an organization.

In contrast, consider an organization that values and wants to focus on product dependability. Here, purchasing considerations of risk management (i.e., food safety for food products) and continuous improvement would be more important. A third organization may value information in its mission to become the leader above all of its competitors. This food service organization may concentrate on competitive intelligence, including a SWOT (Strengths, Weaknesses, Opportunities, Threats) analysis and the use of technology to gain a competitive edge.

When purchasing is viewed strategically, it helps establish a relationship with the organization's distributors so they, too, can contribute to achieving the mission and vision of the food service operation. Take the example presented earlier of an operation wanting to control and reduce costs and thereby increase profits. When distributors are clear about this strategy, they will be able to recommend lower cost product alternatives to the operator. They understand that if the operation's food cost percentage can be lowered by one or two percentage points, it can have a huge impact on the operation's bottom line. So, too, these distributors can assist the operator in lowering labor costs by suggesting that ready-made, ready-to-serve products are purchased when this makes sense and adds value. Purchasing strategies impact both the operation's food costs and labor costs.

Sometimes it makes sense from the operation's perspective to have purchasing both decentralized and centralized at the same time. Consider a chain of casual-dining restaurants. Fresh produce may be purchased from a local specialty house, while beef products may be combined and centralized. This gives the chain the buying power it needs for strategic, high-volume purchases, while it yields to local managers of individual units the purchasing of products that make sense at the local level. The chain gains critical intelligence through corporate procurement and remains a quality resource to the local food service general manager. At the same time, the local GM can address critical availability and shelf life challenges

Exhibit 2   Food Service Distribution Channel Members

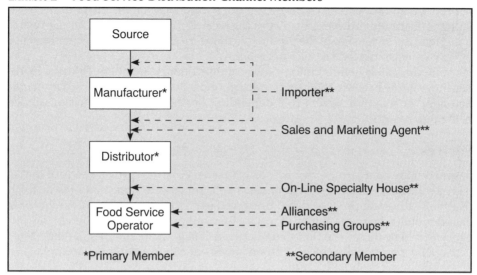

by purchasing produce locally. This combination maximizes value for the individual restaurant, as well as for the chain.

Larger food service organizations have integrated purchasing and quality assurance. Darden Restaurants, Inc., for example, drives quality through its purchasing organization. This is apparent in its decisions to not purchase caged veal and checking that sources of dairy products have humanitarian standards in place. Darden utilizes regular distributor audits on the food service distribution channel members. The Darden rating system for these members includes a rating by Darden's purchasing group on criteria including quality, service, innovation, cost, and diversity. The ranking takes place twice a year and has become an industry model.

Food Service Distribution Channel Members

There are both primary and secondary members in the food service distribution channel. Primary members include manufacturers and distributors. Secondary members include importers, sales and marketing agents, on-line specialty houses, alliances, and group purchasing organizations (GPOs). Each food or beverage product, supply, or service must begin with a source.

Touch Points for Customers and Products/Services

The food service distribution channel as illustrated in Exhibit 2 is a simplification of the movement of food and beverage products, supplies, and services from the source to the food service operation. In the illustration, the arrow represents movement and a point where customers and products/services touch. For example, the arrow between the distributor and the food service operator shows the movement of products and services from the distributor's warehouse on the distributor's truck with the distributor's driver to arrival at the receiving area of the food service operation. Here, the ownership of the products is transferred from the distributor member of the channel to the food service operation.

The channel is divided into primary and secondary members. Primary members have a role in every food service distribution channel, while secondary members may or may not have a role depending on the specific product or service being purchased.

Sources

A **source** may be a farmer, rancher, or harvester. A farmer grows produce that is then available to manufacturers to sell fresh, processed, and ready-to-eat fresh (e.g., cut lettuce), or processed and preserved (e.g., canned or frozen). A rancher is an individual who raises animals for slaughter and processing. Included in this category would be those who raise farm-raised fish (e.g., salmon, catfish). A harvester is one who intentionally catches certain species of fish (e.g., tilapia, salmon).

Manufacturers

A **manufacturer** changes raw materials into a form useful to a food service operation. Live animals (e.g., chickens) are processed into a form closer to what a food service operator needs (e.g., boneless chicken breasts, chicken wings). Frozen raw beef may be processed into ground beef patties. Manufacturers are sometimes called distributors since they supply distributors with products that can more easily be sold by food service operators.

Distributors

A **distributor** purchases, stores, sells, and delivers products and supplies to food service operators. A distributor may also sell services (e.g., hood cleaning, menu design consulting) to a food service operator. A distributor owns the products and supplies before they are sold to the food service operator.

Food Service Operators

The **food service operator** may be a freestanding restaurant, a restaurant within a lodging property, or an on-site (i.e., noncommercial or managed services, such as those found in healthcare, business, and industry) food service operation. The food service operator purchases products, supplies, and services and, in the case of products, resells them to the operation's customers, guests (lodging), or members (private clubs). The supplies and services usually are purchased to help the operator better offer his or her products for sale. Supplies include disposable containers for foods prepared to go, cleaning and sanitizing chemicals for tableware, and linen napkins that the lodging property launders for use in its main dining room. Services include Internet Web page servers, cleaning and sanitizing of the kitchen, and snow removal from the parking lot.

Importers

An **importer** is a secondary member of the food service distribution channel. Not all food service operators deal with importers. However, with the strong proliferation of global sourcing, the distribution channel has become more complex with international regulations and exchange rates. Importers may either help secure products from an international source for a manufacturer or may help obtain products manufactured in another country for a distributor.

Sales and Marketing Agents

A **sales and marketing agent** used to be referred to as a broker. The sales and marketing agent usually represents a manufacturer's line of products by promoting it to various distributors. Because sales and marketing agents do not actually purchase products and services from manufacturers, their focus is on helping the distributor's sales force sell the products, supplies, and services that the agent represents to food service operators. Some sales and marketing agents work directly with food service operators in tandem with the distributor's sales representatives.

On-Line Specialty Houses

This secondary member of the food service distribution channel has relatively narrow product lines for specific customers or market segments. Perhaps the best example of a **specialty house** is one that sells fresh produce. Another example is a specialty house that sells only meat products. In the case of the produce specialty house, food service operators used to purchase all their produce in unprocessed forms and then have to process it in their kitchens. With the dwindling sources of qualified affordable kitchen labor, many operators today purchase fresh cut produce.

Alliances and Group Purchasing Organizations

Two other secondary members of the channel continue to become more important today: **alliances** and **group purchasing organizations**. While "alliance" usually refers to nonprofit organizations such as those found in health care, "group purchasing organization" usually refers to for-profit businesses (e.g., franchisees). The goal of both is the same: to combine purchasing power and lower the per-unit cost while monitoring or raising quality and service levels. This goal is achieved by combining purchasing for a number of food service operations and using a common source for products, supplies, and services. Members of alliances and group purchasing organizations can obtain economies of scale with local distributors.

Value Each Member Brings to the Channel

Quite simply, a source adds value by transforming raw materials into products usable by the manufacturer. Thus, seeds are grown into wheat that a manufacturer can transform into flour and then pastries for a breakfast menu. Another source will harvest saltwater fish from the ocean for a manufacturer to process into canned

Exhibit 3   Manufacturer Web Site Recipe Ideas

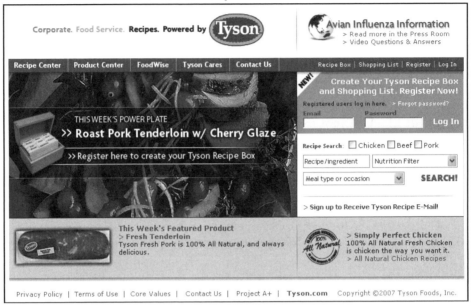

Source: www.tyson.com/recipes.

tuna. Sometimes, this harvester is also a manufacturer (when fish is harvested at sea and processed on that same ship before it reaches shore, for example).

The manufacturer further transforms what the source has initially provided into a form that is even closer to what the food service operator wants and can use. Heifers and steers are transported from the source to the feedlot, fed a nutritious diet, slaughtered, and fabricated into wholesale and retail cuts of beef. Sometimes, these products are further processed by manufacturers into corned beef, canned beef stew, or frozen chili with beef. The manufacturer supplies products and services that more closely represent the forms needed by the distributor.

Manufacturers also provide information value. As Exhibit 3 shows, the Tyson Foods Web site offers a number of recipe ideas and new ways to use its products. Other manufacturers have Web sites with similar ideas for their products and services. These ideas help food service operators become and stay competitive.

The distributor physically takes possession of food and beverage products and supplies, and, in many cases, creates the services purchased as they are requested by food service operators. By transporting products and supplies from the manufacturer to storage in the distributor's warehouse to the receiving area of the food service operation, when they are needed, a distributor adds both place (location) and time value. In addition, the distributor may change the form of a product (bulk heads of lettuce processed into ready-to-eat salads). Distributors also add a fourth form of value—information, in the form of menu ideas, purchasing volume reports, recipes, and marketing/promotional materials.

Distributors can enhance place, time, form, and information value for food service operators by:

- Understanding the food service operation's unique features (including menu).

- Carefully avoiding overselling both in person and on the telephone.

- Showing specific ways that the operator can reduce costs, improve quality, and/or enhance service for its customers.

- Brainstorming with the operator ways that both organizations can help each other meet their requirements.

- Assessing regularly the performance of distributor sales representatives and ways to continue to improve.

The assessment and continuous improvement strategies need to focus on ways to add value. This can only happen if the distributor takes the time to learn about the food service operation and its customers' requirements.

Importers that deal with European products must meet all European Union (EU) standards, which can be higher than United States standards. The formation of the EU has given European manufacturers a newfound strength through the benefits of a common currency, as well as free trade practices. China is also actively pursuing the sales of its products in North America. You might think about importers as adding value by linking the expertise and services from other countries to the end user. Some large organizations are addressing these challenges by retaining third-party outsourced providers of imports, rather than taking the time and making the investment to build an internal structure within the food service operation.

The sales and marketing agent also provides time and place value by connecting manufacturers with distributors. Some agents interface with food service operators often through the distributor's sales representatives. Sales and marketing agents also provide value in the form of information about how to utilize, promote and benefit from the manufacturers products and services. Sometimes this information is used to train distributors' sales representatives; other times it is shared directly with food service operators. This value takes the form of support services from manufacturers. As food service customers' requirements have become more varied, these value-added services have enhanced performance of food service operations in terms of customer satisfaction and profitability.

On-line specialty houses add value much like distributors do, but they are focused more clearly on a limited number of product categories. Sometimes these specialty houses provide the opportunity for more face-to-face interaction between the food service purchaser and the house's sales representative because the organization is smaller and more focused on a particular product niche. In other cases, additional value is added for smaller operators in the form of more frequent deliveries and smaller product minimums required for each delivery. In addition, sometimes these specialty houses have more staff expertise because they offer fewer products in their lines and can become experts on those products. For example, these on-line specialty houses may be better able to fabricate a specific specialty steak that could become a signature menu item in an independent food service operation. This flexibility could add value for the smaller restaurateur who is trying to compete with chain restaurants. Increasingly, specialty houses, as well as distributors, do not view themselves as sellers of products and services. Rather, they see themselves as providing solutions to food service operators. These solutions include a combination of product knowledge and the specialization of the products in the particular operation.

Alliances and buying groups aggregate their purchasing power to obtain better pricing for their members. Sometimes these group purchasing organizations negotiate directly with manufacturers to determine the delivered price of products to members. Starting as regional cooperatives, some GPOs are now national procurement networks with billions of dollars in purchasing power. Their growth has stemmed from the need to contain costs in food service operations. In some cases, the GPOs or alliances have helped on-site food service operations remain self-operated at a time when there is increasing pressure to hire a contract food service provider. This is of value to those who wish to continue to self-operate.

Alliances and GPOs negotiate rebates from manufacturers that benefit the food service operation by lowering the cost per unit of products or services or supplies purchased. Often the cost of a product's sales and marketing is built into the cost to the distributors from the manufacturer. This cost, ultimately, is passed on to the food service operation in the form of higher product, supply, or service costs. Since distributors operate on relatively low profit margins, alliances and GPOs help manufacturers to reduce costs by ensuring critical volume levels. Alliances and GPOs often negotiate cost-plus distribution contracts with distributors.

Food Safety and Defense

Food safety and food defense are related considerations in the food service distribution channel. The goal of all members of the channel is to provide food and beverage products that are safe for human consumption. Critical to ensuring food safety is the use of the **Hazard Analysis and Critical Control Point (HACCP) risk-management system**. Once food safety hazards are identified, the process can be designed to control the critical points to reduce or eliminate food safety hazards. A comprehensive HACCP system establishes and monitors food safety controls for people, products, equipment, and inventory. Maintaining the temperature requirements for chilled and frozen food products as they move from the manufacturer to the distributor to the food service operation is just one example of how HACCP is applied.

Operators must also consider staff-member safety in the preparation of food and beverage products. When products (e.g., salad ingredients) are purchased fresh cut rather than in whole forms, accident claims from kitchen staff who have cut themselves may be reduced. Similarly, the number of burns may be reduced if products that used to be prepared from scratch (e.g., breaded fish fillets) are purchased ready made. While the cost per unit of the product may be higher, perhaps the overall cost to the food service operation, including staff-member accident insurance and claims, could be reduced.

Food defense includes all the preventative steps that are taken in the distribution channel to prevent intentional contamination of the food supply. Many manufacturers now keep their loading docks under electronic surveillance, distributors lock storage areas for delivery trucks, and food service operations require that all fresh produce be delivered in sealed containers and verify that these containers have not had their integrity compromised during transportation through the supply chain.

Forces Affecting the Distribution System

Forces affecting the food service distribution channel include ethical, economic, legal, political, and technological developments. While these are the main forces affecting the channel today, other forces may emerge in the future to impact the channel.

Ethics

We will begin by identifying some of the ethical issues facing those involved in purchasing. **Ethics** is presented first because of the heightened focus on ethics in business in general and because of the many ethical decisions that must be made in a food service operation, particularly in purchasing. Ethics is, fundamentally, about doing the right thing, about walking the walk, and about building personal and organizational credibility. **Credibility** is built on dependability—being able to rely on the person, product, or organization; accountability—being able to identify and solve problems and learn from mistakes; and responsibility—being able to consistently carry out necessary actions and nurture and build personal and organizational reputations.

Purchasing professionals are expected to leverage their organizations' buying power, but how much is ethical before it goes over the top? These professionals must balance being effective purchasers against destroying relationships in the industry. The impact of group purchasing organizations has affected buying power leverage.

Ethical issues in purchasing are influenced by a number of external groups, including activists (e.g., animal rights, endangered species, environmental concerns, human rights), government (e.g., regulations covering agriculture and food), labor unions (health, safety, workers' rights), media outlets, religious groups and churches, society at large, and trade associations. Once ethical issues are raised by any of these groups, it is expected that the food service operator will respond with information. Partners in the distribution channel—manufacturers and distributors—can often help answer specific questions.

Of course, the individuals responsible for the various activities in the channel must behave ethically. Ethical behavior is tied to credibility, character, and communication. Credible individuals are honest and they lead by example. Character relates to a person's values and the way that the individual acts and behaves. Those with character do what they say they will do and keep promises. A purchasing professional with character has straightforward honesty, based on mutual trust. Purchasing professionals must communicate with sincerity. The communications process requires more active listening than talking. Communication must be believable based on a genuine and authentic approach.

In order for an organization to address ethics, people in the organization must have the required information to make ethical decisions. In addition, the organization must make everyone aware of and then reward ethical behavior and actions. In the case of distributors, it is ethical to comply with what has been specified and agreed to in the food service operation's purchasing program. Sometimes distributors specify an ethics compliance program as a prerequisite for working with a chain.

For ethics to be addressed, individuals must understand how acting ethically affects them personally, as well as how their actions affect the organization. What is a distributor's obligation to its food service customers when it learns of a recall program by one of its manufacturers? The fundamental response has to include rapidly informing food service operators of ways to address food safety issues, centered around the recalled product.

Economic Forces

Economic forces in the food service distribution channel relate to supply and demand of basic commodities, manufactured products, and created services. Basic laws of supply and demand are in play when the weather conditions cause a drop in the fresh strawberry crop in Mexico and this results in higher prices for strawberries delivered to a food service operator. Similarly, when the catch of soft shell crabs exceeds demand, the price to the food service operator would be expected to decline. Economic forces also affect the prices that manufacturers charge distributors and, ultimately, the prices that distributors and operators negotiate and agree upon.

Economic forces impact the channel in other ways. If a food service operation can more accurately plan and forecast demand and quantities of intended purchases, purchasing costs can be reduced and cash flow improved. If the timing of orders and deliveries can coincide more with the operation's demand, then the cost per purchase order processed can be reduced. If forecasts are more accurate, fewer of the operation's assets will be tied up in inventory and the return on assets for the operation will be improved. If a prime distributor relationship is established so the majority of products and supplies purchased are placed with one full-line distributor, then we would expect that there would be a reduction in the unit cost for purchases, service to the operation would be enhanced, dependability in deliveries would be increased, planning and information sharing would be improved, improved business intelligence would be available by leveraging equipment data and technology, and a shift from purchasing as a transactional (i.e., place the order for the lowest cost) to a strategic set of skills and activities. All of these have economic impacts.

Legal Forces

Legal forces include local, state, national, and international laws affecting the channel. For example, the law of agency means that the person responsible for purchasing acts as an agent of the owner of the operation. That means the purchaser can legally obligate the owner when he or she signs contracts for the operation. Before a contract is signed, operations may be required to obtain bids detailing the proposed terms of the agreement. Bids may be informal and oral or more formal and in writing. Once a contract is signed, purchasers have an obligation to fulfill their part of the contract, including timely payment for products, supplies, and services purchased. In addition, members of the food service distribution channel are responsible for protecting the customers who purchase their products and services.

Political Forces

Increasingly, **political forces** impacting purchasing are global in nature since the food service distribution channel has become more international. In many cases, this has enhanced the role of importers in the channel. Globalization is not a short-term fad, but a long-term trend. While it began with products, now there are increasingly global sources of services as well.

The political retreat of communism and the surge in economic power of China and India have fueled changes in the global political landscape. Political strife in certain parts of the world have made developed countries more aware of and concerned about terrorism, particularly bioterrorism as it relates to the food service distribution channel. As a result of these political forces, food service operations and other organizations that depend on global delivery of products and services have had to conduct detailed risk assessments, often by product category and by country. These same businesses have had to develop written contingency plans in the event that the political climate changes in one of these countries, as well as including disaster recovery in some of these plans. Organizations that have moved to offshore outsourcing of products and services have examined their exposure to political risks.

Technology

In the digital age, technology has driven a shift in the importance of physical labor to that of information technology. Technology has increased the volume of available information exponentially, and technology is increasingly becoming a commodity itself.

While some say the Internet is a rich source of information, our responsibilities have changed to selecting, sorting, analyzing and using that Web-based information to make decisions. While technology is driving innovation, it is also diminishing some competitive advantages in purchasing since many operators now have readily available information that leads them to the lowest prices for products and services via the Internet and e-auctions (electronic auctions conducted on-line).

Technology is also changing the way that distribution takes place in the channel. Technological innovations have helped distributors optimize delivery-route planning, territory planning, dispatching and tracking trucks on the road, on-line self-scheduling for customers, bar code scanning for products loaded on the trucks and delivered to food service operations, and electronic signature capture when products are received at the food service operation.

This technology is increasing efficiency, reducing overtime, and saving money for the distributor. These savings may then be passed along to the operator. Other savings associated with this technology include reduced route-planning time, more on-time deliveries, and an increase in the number of deliveries per hour.

Additional technology forces include the insertion of electronic chips into chilled and frozen product boxes to monitor temperatures. Radio frequency identification (RFID), a more sophisticated technology than bar coding, offers distributors better inventory management, reduced data-entry times, and more accurate inventory tracking.

Other Forces

Two other forces are also affecting the food service distribution channel: corporate social responsibility and consolidation.

Consolidation has been occurring since the last century when members of the channel realized that they could obtain price leverage if they became larger. This consolidation has taken place by mergers and acquisitions between organizations. It is often easier for larger combined organizations to benefit from supply chain principles, such as strategic sourcing companies, global access to products and services, and a decline in domestic manufacturing, applied to the businesses. Some caution that although consolidation may yield short-term gains, it may drive out of business distributors who do not have a national presence and substantial technology capabilities. The result, they argue, will be just a handful of well-known national super-distributors, and a relatively small number of under-capitalized regional specialty houses.

This consolidation may be driven, in part, by food service purchasers who continue to reduce the number of distributors they deal with, often because the purchasing activities are becoming more centralized in those operations. Consolidation is also promoted when purchasers place heavy emphasis on large cost savings rather than stressing value over price. Some believe that the heavy focus on price reduces quality of service provided by distributors.

Consolidation also occurs when an individual distributor moves products in and out of its product mix. That is to say, this consolidation occurs when one brand (perhaps a house label offered by that distributor) is specified and then the distributor switches to another manufacturer, resulting in higher margins for the distributor and changed specifications for the operator. Due to consolidation, the distributor may want to eliminate one or two of the three choices offered for canned sliced peaches, for example. The distributor's original supreme private label peaches may have been 98-score, while the new private label peaches may only be 91-score. They may have very different sodium contents, which would be of concern to a dietitian in a healthcare food service operation. A way to avoid this potential problem is for the food service operator to specify a particular manufacturer's brand; in the case of sliced peaches, it may be Del Monte.

Corporate social responsibility is a second emerging force in purchasing. Purchasing decisions may have environmental impact issues, endangered species issues, and other issues that may be of concern to society as a whole. It is important to remember that food service operations function as integral parts of larger local communities. The viability of a food service operation in some communities depends, in part, on how the operators respond to ecological issues, whether they use exploitation to improve production, and whether they emphasize lower prices over responsible business practices. The diversity of the food service operation, as well as the distributors and manufacturers utilized as partners in the channel, may also impact how socially responsible the operation is perceived to be by customers, as well as the larger community.

Value Proposition that Each Member Provides to the End User

The end user in the food service distribution channel is the food service operation, whether it be lodging, freestanding, or on site. There are two considerations for the food service operator. First, what value does the operator provide to the guests, customers, or members who choose to spend their time and money in the operation? Second, what value does each member of the channel contribute to the value that the operator provides?

A hospitality operation provides form value when it serves a filet of Lake Superior Whitefish that has been broiled and presented with a special sauce created by the chef. The operation provides time value when it prepares and delivers a lunch entrée quickly and efficiently so a business meeting can continue uninterrupted.

The hospitality operation provides place value when it serves steamed whole Maine lobsters to guests at a seafood restaurant in a hotel in Cheyenne, Wyoming. The operation can also provide information value by explaining the nutrient and ingredient content to a guest who is concerned about weight loss or food allergies.

Value Proposition

In the 1990s, value-added services were promoted by manufacturers and distributors who tried to differentiate themselves from the competition. One such service was to optimize the processes in the food service distribution channel. Examples include the movement from face-to-face to Web-based ordering, the ability for distributors to provide operators with velocity reports indicating the volume of products purchased, and technology support for inventory-management systems.

While price is a consideration in most purchasing decisions, quality and value usually are more important. Nevertheless, purchases can sometimes be made on price alone when no value-added services are required from the distributor. In that case, the person responsible for purchasing can simply evaluate various distributors based only on price. This is called commodity purchasing.

Physical market forms are frequent value considerations in purchasing. Is it better to purchase heads of iceberg lettuce and process them into tossed salads or purchase a ready-to-eat processed lettuce mix? When the price of lettuce triples due to a shortage of lettuce from California, it may be higher value to purchase the lettuce mix containing less expensive ingredients. Many nutritionally conscious foods and convenience foods are alternative market forms with added value. Organic 100-percent pure carrot juice and squeezable strawberry spread are examples. While the strawberry spread may not be any healthier than other varieties, the squeezable packaging offers more convenience. French fries that have trans fats removed are market forms displacing some traditional fries made with hydrogenated oils.

Transportation adds place value to a food and beverage product or supply. Since fresh fruits are readily available during winter months in South America, North American food service operations are willing to pay a little more for this value. Customers, guests, and members of the operations are also willing to pay more for the place value.

Packaging as a source of value was already discussed with the squeezable strawberry spread in this section. The packaging of condiments in portion-controlled (PC) sizes is another example of how packaging adds value, in this case, for quick-service operators. A third example is vacuum packaging for fresh steaks. The packaging adds value because it delays spoilage and permits the operators to utilize the product over a longer period of time than without the packaging.

Branding adds value if customers see the branded item as unique or different from an unbranded item. If an organization is purchasing two different brands from two different distributors, it may be able to purchase a more expensive brand in higher volume from just one distributor and purchase a higher quality brand. Sometimes recognizable local brands can be utilized to enhance value for customers, guests, and members. For example, a local restaurant specializing in steaks and fresh seafood may successfully promote locally produced ice cream desserts that feature ice cream from a local entrepreneur. Some guests, customers, and members simply do not believe that the dining-out experience is complete without dessert. They also frequently purchase dessert wines and/or coffee (both with fairly high profit margins) to accompany their desserts. Branded desserts can enhance the perceived value of the dining experience.

To the food service operator, quality and price are clearly related to value. Given the same quality, as price increases, value drops. But if quality is constant, then as price drops, value goes up. Service also has an effect on quality and value. As service is enhanced and price remains the same, quality and value both increase. And, as quality and service both increase, value also goes up.

From the customer's perspective, sometimes the brand has a large influence on the perception of quality. It is possible to purchase several brands of soft drinks, some of which are recognizable by students attending universities around the country, others of which are not because they are local or regional brands. Customers are usually willing to pay more for recognizable brands because they know the product provides consistent quality.

Relationship management is the key to success in purchasing. Some have suggested that there ought to be a chief relationship officer sitting next to the chief financial officer and chief information officer in large organizations with huge volumes of products, supplies, and services provided. This is because the relationship has been identified as the new source of competition when purchasing professionals move from a transaction focus to a strategic focus. They do this by understanding the operation's business strategies and the effect that purchasing activities have on each strategy. The focus on relationship management is also important for smaller food service operators and entrepreneurs.

Assessing a Distributor Partner

Assessment of a distributor partner is an essential continuous improvement activity. Assessments provide regular feedback, both verbally and in writing. Assessments are helpful in determining the level of quality, and therefore, the value received from a distributor.

Physical Assessment

A **physical assessment** of a distributor may include a visit to its plant or other facilities, inspection of trucks, and other product-related considerations. A physical assessment usually is conducted by making regular visits to the distributor's facilities, as well as checking the condition of delivery trucks when they arrive at the food service operation's receiving area.

Regarding facilities, the main assessment concerns are the cleanliness and organization of the physical plant. Additional assessments might include the manufacturers with whom the distributor is doing business and the appearances and attitudes of the distributor's staff members. Security of trucks is important—trucks should be spot checked as they arrive at the receiving area in the food service operation. Are they clean? Do they maintain products at correct temperatures? Are the trucks well maintained? The products that the distributor has for sale also should be assessed. Are they the correct brands needed based on customer's requirements? Are they present in sufficient quantities?

Service Assessment

Coupled with an assessment of tangible items is a **service assessment** of the intangible value elements. Even though these are intangible, they can still be measured both verbally and with survey instruments. Of prime importance here are the differences between service in fact and service in perception. While regular fact-based assessments of service and value are essential to gauge the extent to which the distributor is delivering the required intangibles, it must be emphasized that the intangible aspects of service are really as perceived by those who receive the services. For example, if a distributor promises that deliveries will not be made during the busy lunch period, and the truck drives up to the receiving area at 11:45 A.M. just before the rush begins, the operator's perception is likely to be that the distributor has broken a service promise even though the driver arrived just before the lunch rush began. It is the service *as perceived by the operator*, not the driver, that must be assessed.

Assessments of both physical and service aspects of purchasing may take a variety of forms. Sometimes, formal surveys are preferred to capture the feedback in writing. These surveys may be quantitatively and qualitatively analyzed and the information shared with the distributor. Sometimes customer comments provide feedback useful to distributors. Other times, customer complaints and the resulting analysis can point to areas that the distributor can improve. These complaints can originate from either external customers (those who pay for the products and services sold by the food service operation) or internal customers (staff members). Other sources of assessments might include face-to-face discussions with distributor sales representatives and participation in new product tastings by the food service operator.

Key Performance Indicators in the Distribution Channel ——

Key performance indicators (KPIs) in the food service distribution channel help determine the effectiveness of the purchasing activities and processes. Key performance indicators will vary with the complexity of the channel and individual member within it. We will present examples of KPIs by focusing on the distributor.

We have already presented the assessments used for distributors in terms of physical and service considerations. In addition, some food service operators may value face-to-face time with the distribution company's owners (or principals if the company is publicly held). This strengthens the relationship and adds to service.

Knowledge of the distributor's disaster-response plan (e.g., what it will do if a tsunami strikes in the ocean near primary sources of shrimp) is another valuable KPI. If a food service operation has an unexpected demand for a particular product and runs out of that product, another KPI is the distributor's response to a request for an emergency delivery.

A number of tangible KPIs beyond those already detailed can be measured. Verification that the distributor uses HACCP principles is an essential KPI. The amount of food and beverage products and supplies, on-time deliveries, damage and spoilage of products and supplies, error ratios, and the integrity of the cold chain (i.e., chilled and frozen products handled, stored, and delivered at proper temperatures) are all product-related KPIs. Each can be tracked and measured.

Other KPIs help the food service operator better leverage purchasing proposals and maximize value for the operation. KPIs included in this category are accounts receivable and accounts payable, delivery times and frequency, required average order size, the availability of proprietary label products from the distributor, the way that special delivery requests are handled by the distributor, and whether all orders must be place electronically or if they can be placed face-to-face with a distributor's sales representative.

In many cases, a range of options are available when dealing with KPIs. In most instances, the selection of a particular option within a range has a cost associated with it. For example, if a food service operator wants more frequent deliveries, it may be necessary to increase the average order size. This increase comes at a cost in funds invested in inventory for the operator. In the case of emergency deliveries, the distributor may only be able to provide this service for operators who purchase the majority of their products, services, and supplies from that distributor.

In the case of accounts receivable by the distributor and accounts payable by the operator, consider paying the distributor weekly rather than every 30 days. In this case, the distributor may be willing to reduce the overall costs by as much as 1 percent, since more frequent accounts receivable mean better cash flow for the distributor. However, the operator must assess whether the increased processing costs (every week vs. once per month) are worth it, compared to the savings in the cost of products and supplies from that distributor.

Necessary Checks and Balances ——————————

It is prudent in any business transaction to have checks and balances that gauge how effectively resources are being used and value is being received. This is particularly true in purchasing, considering the volume of products, supplies, services, and funds involved. The role of purchasing professionals is to ensure that the optimal value is obtained for the funds and time spent. By utilizing proven purchasing processes, both an independent entrepreneur and a chain operator can help define requirements clearly; obtain the best prices, supplies, and services; and regularly assess the physical and service aspects of value.

The checks and balances begin by understanding the requirements of the customers. Sometimes these requirements are for external customers and they are more clearly defined by input from internal customers (staff members). Other times, the requirements are for internal customers and, again, their ideas and input are essential. An example of an external customer requirement may be the variety of premium vodka choices available in the food service operation's lounge and dining room. An example of an internal customer requirement may be the performance of detergent used to mop kitchen floors in heavy traffic areas.

Once requirements are understood, they must be transmitted into written specifications. In short, purchase specifications describe the required quality and how it will be assessed; the use of the product, service, or supply; a general product, supply, or service description; and any applicable special instructions to most clearly communicate requirements. Input for development of purchase specifications should come from staff members in food and beverage areas (who are most familiar with customer requirements), purchasing staff members, and distributors.

There are additional forms, both printed and electronic, used to provide the necessary checks and balances in purchasing. They include purchase orders, requisition forms, inventory forms, and purchase records.

Bottom-line invoice comparisons provide additional checks and balances in purchasing. Rather than comparing the price differences for each item from different distributors, the bottom-line invoice comparison begins by giving the exact same list of products, with specifications, to the competing distributors. Each is asked to provide a price for each item, which is not compared between the distributors, and a bottom-line total for the entire invoice. That way, the total cost to the food service operation can be compared. This is a particularly useful tool for smaller food service operators.

Quarterly business reviews are "snapshot" reviews of the performance of a distributor. They are sometimes used when there is a contract with a manufacturer (e.g., for New York strip steaks) and the distributor is only used for deliveries. These contracts are usually based on cost-plus pricing. The reviews permit the food service operator to manage and monitor the effectiveness of purchasing over a period of time.

🔑 Key Terms

alliance—An organization of nonprofit food service operators whose goal is to combine purchasing power and lower per-unit costs while monitoring or raising quality and service levels.

availability—A value factor that is determined by seasonality and the purchasing power of a distributor.

branding—A technique that adds value if customers see a branded item as unique or different from an unbranded item.

consolidation—A trend toward fewer, but larger food service distributors.

corporate social responsibility—An emerging force in purchasing that deals with an operation's impact on the community that surrounds it and society at large.

credibility—An organizational characteristic based on dependability, account-ability, and responsibility.

distributor—A food service distribution channel member that purchases, stores, sells, and delivers products and supplies to food service operators.

economic forces—Forces in the food service distribution channel that relate to supply and demand of basic commodities, manufactured products, and created services.

entrepreneur—Someone who owns a business.

ethics—A force in the food service distribution channel that is about doing the right thing, walking the walk, and building organizational credibility.

food service distribution channel—The path that products and services follow from their source to the end user. The channel includes both primary and second-ary members.

food service operator—A member of the food service distribution channel that purchases products, supplies, and services and, in the case of products, resells them to the operation's customers, guests, or members.

group purchasing organization—An organization of for-profit food service oper-ators whose goal is to combine purchasing power and lower per-unit costs while monitoring or raising quality and service levels.

Hazard Analysis and Critical Control Point (HACCP) risk-management sys-tem—A program to establish and monitor food safety controls for people, prod-ucts, equipment, and inventory.

importer—A secondary member of the food service distribution channel that helps secure products from an international source for a manufacturer or helps obtain products manufactured in another country for a distributor.

information—An element of value that distributors can provide in the form of education, training, menu consulting, and other services.

key performance indicators—Indicators used to measure the effectiveness of pur-chasing activities and processes.

legal forces—Local, state, national, and international laws that affect how food service operations conduct business.

manufacturer—A member of the food service distribution channel that changes raw materials into a form that is useful for food service operations.

packaging—Adding value to a product by selling it in ready-to-eat, portion-controlled, or other convenient forms.

physical assessment—A check on distributors that may include a visit to its plant or other facilities, inspection of trucks, and other product-related considerations.

physical market forms—The form in which products are delivered to food service operations.

political forces—Factors, such as terrorism, globalization, and outsourcing, that are related to the international nature of purchasing today.

price—An element of value that should be based on exactly how the product is being used. The lowest price is not always the best price.

relationship management—The key to success in purchasing as purchasers move from a transaction focus to a strategic focus.

sales and marketing agent—A member of the food service distribution channel that represents a manufacturer's line of products by promoting it to various distributors.

service—A value factor that is based on the relationship between the operator and the distributor and may include delivery schedules, ordering procedures, or repair and maintenance.

service assessment—A check on distributors that includes the intangible value elements of the purchasing process.

source—A member of the food service distribution channel that provides raw materials to manufacturers. Sources include ranchers, harvesters, and farmers.

specialty house—A secondary member of the food service distribution channel that has relatively narrow product lines for specific customers or market segments.

transportation—The addition of place value to a food and beverage product or supply.

value—An assessment of what a product or service is worth based on quality, service, availability, information, and price.

 # Review Questions

1. What are the two critical questions to ask and answer *before* purchasing?

2. What are the six basic ways that products are distributed to a food service operation?

3. What are the unique considerations in an entrepreneurial focus?

4. What are the five factors used to determine value for any food, beverage, supply, or service purchased?

5. Who are the primary and secondary members of the food service distribution channel? What is the role of each?

6. What are the food safety and food security concerns in the food service distribution channel?

7. What are the forces that affect the food service distribution channel, and how does each affect the channel?

8. What value does the food service operator provide to guests, customers, or members, and what value does each member of the food service distribution channel contribute to the value that the operator provides?

9. How is a food service distributor assessed by a food service operator?

10. What are key performance indicators (KPIs) in the food service distribution channel?

 ## References

Anonymous. "Global Trends in Ethical Foods: Fair Trade and Sustainability Go Mainstream" and "Management Briefing: Marketing Ethical Foods." *Just Food* (October 2004): p. 34.

Avery, Susan. "Purchasing Know How." *Purchasing Boston* 132, no. 10 (June 19, 2003): p. 37.

Carbone, Jim. "Expect More Value Add From Distributors." *Purchasing Boston* 132, no. 16 (October 23, 2003): pp. 39–43.

Hayes, Jack. "Purchasing: It's a Buyer's Market." *Nation's Restaurant News* 36, no. 32 (August 12, 2002): p. 76.

Newman, David. "How is Procurement Strategically Important to an Organization?" *Summit* (March 2005): pp. 10–11.

Porter, Anne Millen. "Containing Total Spending." *Purchasing Boston* (November 2003): pp. 31–38.

Rice, Amos. "What Purchasing Managers Expect from Distributors." *Foodservice Equipment & Supplies* 58, no. 5 (May 2005): p. 33.

 ## Internet Sites

For more information, visit the following Internet sites. Remember that Internet addresses can change without notice. If the site is no longer there, you can use a search engine to look for additional sites.

Commercial Foodservice Equipment
  Service Association
www.cfesa.com/resources/coe.htm

Food Insights
www.foodinsights.com/
foodpurchasing.htm

Food Service Idea Exchange
www.fsie.com/members.cfm

Foodservice Consultants International
  Code of Conduct
www.fcsi.org/ethics.html

Foodservice Distribution
www.distributionsite.net/s/
foodservice_distribution

Foodservice Equipment & Supplies
www.fesmag.com

Gateway to Government Food Safety
  Information
www.foodsafety.gov

International Foodservice Distributors
  Association
www.ifdaonline.org

USDA Food Security
www.fns.usda.gov/fsec

USDA HACCP Primer
http://vm.cfsan.fda.gov/~lrd/
haccp.html

Chapter 2 Outline

Competencies

1. Identify the food service segments. (pp. 29–32)

2. Contrast the different structures of food service organizations. (pp. 32–39)

3. Describe the food service process flow from menu planning to cleaning and maintenance. (pp. 39–47)

4. Describe the characteristics of the purchasing control point. (pp. 48–55)

5. Explain the importance of customer requirements, particularly in the context of lifestyle changes and the shift to healthier dining. (pp. 55–57)

6. Explain the role of the internal customer and how these staff members create and deliver value through purchasing. (pp. 57–58)

7. Describe the essentials of food safety in a food service operation. (pp. 58–64)

2

Food Service Operations

THE FOOD SERVICE INDUSTRY continues to enjoy phenomenal growth in terms of sales, number of units/operations, and percentage of potential customers who are increasingly dining out. The food service industry is also always looking for talented, energetic staff members who want to exceed guests' expectations. Many food service operators are optimistic about sales growth, growth in staffing levels, and increased capital expenditures. Capital expenditures include purchasing new equipment, or remodeling or expanding facilities.

Food Service Segments

Broadly classified, food service operations can be categorized as commercial operations or noncommercial operations. The categories are based on whether an organization maximizes profits through the sale of food and beverages (commercial) or minimizes expenses while providing nutritious meals (noncommercial). The two basic segments of food service operations are illustrated in Exhibit 1.

Commercial Food Service Operations

Commercial food service operations seek to maximize profits through the sale of food and beverages. Examples of commercial operations include freestanding restaurants, food service in lodging properties, and numerous other types of food service establishments.

Freestanding Eating and Drinking Places. Freestanding eating and drinking places can be independent operations, chain operations, or franchises. These organizational alternatives will be discussed later in the chapter. Freestanding eating and drinking places include white-tablecloth (high-check-average), casual-dining, family-service, and quick-service restaurants. They can provide indoor and/or outdoor table service and a wide variety of menu items. They may be open for only one meal period or for 24 hours daily. Some offer a "California style" menu, in which items that are usually served for breakfast, lunch, or dinner are offered at all times. Most white-tablecloth and many casual-dining restaurants serve alcoholic beverages.

Family-service operations offer "comfort foods" in a relaxed setting, typically without the availability of alcoholic beverages.

Quick-service restaurants have a limited variety of menu items. Typically, guests walk up to a service counter or drive up to a service window, order food,

Exhibit 1   Segments of the Food Service Industry

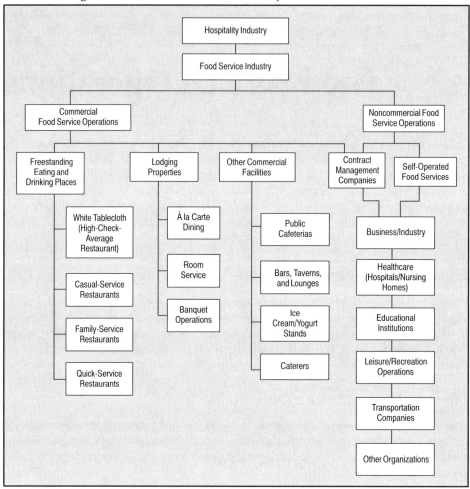

Source: Jack D. Ninemeier, *Management of Food and Beverage Operations,* 4th ed. (Lansing, Mich.: Educational Institute of the American Hotel & Lodging Association, 2005), p. 7.

and carry it to a table (if there is inside seating), consume the food in their car, or take it home or to work.

Lodging Food Service Operations. Food service operations are found in lodging properties ranging from the smallest bed-and-breakfast inns to the largest hotels. Just as with freestanding eating and drinking places, there are many types of hotel food service operations, such as à la carte dining in coffee shops, family restaurants, specialty restaurants, or gourmet rooms. Room service is frequently available, and many lodging properties also provide banquet services.

Historically, when hotels were classified according to food service, there were two types: full-service properties, which offered food and beverage services, and limited-service properties, which did not offer food and beverage services. Today, this distinction is blurred because some limited-service properties offer complimentary breakfast services, ranging from coffee, fruit, and simple pastry items to more extensive, hot breakfast items. Lobby food service is the term used to describe these offerings.

Many hoteliers realize that food and beverage departments cannot generate required profits on the basis of sales to in-house guests only. Extensive patronage from the local community is often necessary for hotel food and beverage operations to realize economic goals and hoteliers aggressively market to the community and compete with other food service operators in the area. This has led to the proliferation of street-entrance lodging food service operations.

Trends in lodging food services include use of in-room snack-and beverage dispensing equipment (mini bars), "take-up" orders (to the guestroom), deli-bar or other sandwich/snack service, and availability of pizza and beer through room service. Each of these services is designed to compete with food and beverage operations outside the hotel.

Other Commercial Facilities. Other commercial facilities include public cafeterias, bars, taverns, ice cream and frozen yogurt stands, and caterers. **Public cafeterias** are often similar to full-menu restaurants and lunchrooms because they offer a wide variety of menu items, but table service may be limited. **Bars, taverns, and lounges** serve alcoholic beverages, but typically offer limited or no food services. Ice cream and frozen yogurt stands offer primarily frozen dairy and related products. **Caterers** prepare meals for large or small banquets and may provide food service in on-or off-site locations.

Noncommercial Food Service Operations

Noncommercial food service operations exist in organizations for which providing food and beverage service is not the primary mission. Usually, but not always, noncommercial food service operations seek to minimize expenses while paying special attention to providing nutritious meals. Examples of institutions that provide food service include business/industry organizations, healthcare facilities, educational institutions, private clubs, leisure and recreation facilities, and transportation companies.

Traditionally, noncommercial food service operations have focused on nutrition and other noncommercial factors. After all, people in some of these facilities receive 100 percent of their daily food intake at the organization (hospital patients, for example). This makes it especially important to protect the health and well-being of those being served. Trained dietitians are often retained on a full-time or consulting basis. In some cases, dietitians actually manage the food service operations; in others, they assist operating managers.

Business/Industry Organizations. Food service programs for **business/industry organizations** range from vended services in manufacturing plants to gourmet dining facilities in the executive dining rooms of large banks, insurance companies, and other businesses. Food service programs for staff members can exist in almost any type of work situation. Sometimes programs are subsidized by employers who offer them as a fringe benefit to staff members. Factories and construction sites may serve a variety of products—hot dogs, sandwiches, and ice cream, for example.

Healthcare Facilities. Hospitals and extended-care facilities of all types make up an important part of the noncommercial food service segment. Some of these facilities are privately owned; others are managed by a government agency. In addition to acute-care hospitals where patients typically stay for only a short time and extended care facilities that provide long-term care for their residents, there are also **healthcare facilities** for the blind, for children without families, and for mentally and physically disabled people.

Educational Institutions. Food service for schools—public and private elementary and secondary schools and post-secondary schools (vocational schools, colleges, and universities)—is a big business. Some public school systems in large cities serve hundred of thousands of meals daily. Elementary and secondary schools may participate in the federally subsidized National School Lunch Program and other child-nutrition programs. In addition to traditional school lunches, school food service programs may include school breakfast, meals at community events, and senior citizen meals.

Private Clubs. Private clubs can be member-owned and governed by a board of directors elected by the members. Alternatively, they can be nonequity clubs that are owned by individuals or corporations. Country (golf) clubs, city clubs, athletic clubs, and military, tennis, and yacht clubs are examples of facilities that provide food and beverage (and other) service to members who pay an initiation fee, monthly charges, and membership dues.

Leisure and Recreation Facilities. Food service in theme parks, national and state parks, sports arenas and stadiums, and race tracks is a large and exciting part of noncommercial food service. Leisure operations that provide food service also include drive-in movie theaters, bowling centers, summer camps, and hunting lodges.

Transportation Companies. Food service offered in transportation terminals and on airplanes, trains, and ships are included in this segment. Services range from vended operations to sandwich and short-order preparation to extravagant gourmet meals. Since more people are traveling more frequently, an increase in this market segment is expected.

Other Noncommercial Food Service Operations. There are many other institutions that offer food service to people away from their homes, including prisons, military installations, religious organizations, and athletic facilities.

Structures of Food Service Operations

In addition to classifying food service operations by segments, food service operations may also be categorized by their structures or business models. Commercial food service operations are independent or chain restaurants or franchises.

Noncommercial food service operations are either on-site food or managed service (volume) operations.

Independents

An **independent operation** is owned by an owner or owners who have one or more operations that have no chain relationship. If multiple units are owned, menus may not be identical among operations, food purchase specifications may differ, operating procedures are varied, and there could be a number of other similarities and differences. These food services are frequently referred to as "entrepreneurial" operations. New operators are lured into the restaurant business for many reasons. "People have to eat—why shouldn't they eat at my place?" is a thought that has launched many restaurants. New entrepreneurs are further encouraged because many restaurants require relatively little capital to get started. Land, facilities, and equipment can be leased, and the minimal amount of inventory needed to open a restaurant can often be purchased on several weeks' credit. However, a large number of restaurants that open are not in business five years later, and the statistics work against independent operators.

In an industry increasingly dominated by chain restaurants and franchise operations, is there still a place for an independent operation? The answer is "yes." Entrepreneurs who can carefully target a market whose wants, needs, and expectations are not currently being met may be able to capture that market and prosper—if they consistently provide value and exceptional service for guests.

Chain Restaurants

Chain restaurants (also called brand restaurants) are part of a multi-unit organization. They often offer the same menu, purchase supplies and equipment cooperatively, and follow operating procedures that have been standardized for every restaurant in the chain. A chain restaurant may be owned by a parent company, a franchise company, or by a private owner or owners. There are many chain restaurants in the food service industry and their variety and number continue to grow.

Some people incorrectly believe that a chain and a franchise operation are the same. They are not. While a franchise operation is affiliated with a chain, a chain operation is not necessarily a franchise; it may be company-owned, for example.

What are the advantages of restaurant chains? Large chains can readily acquire cash, credit, and long-term leases on land and buildings. This is not as feasible for many independent operators. Chains can afford to make more mistakes than independent operators can and learn from those mistakes. Related to this is the ability of a chain to experiment with different menus, themes, designs, and operating procedures. After it discovers the correct "mix," the chain can develop a "package," including everything from menus to operating procedures, for use by all its operations. The independent operator has limited opportunities to undertake extensive experimentation.

Restaurant chains also have a personnel advantage. Chains can afford staff specialists who are experts in finance, construction, operations, and recipe development. Independent operators must handle most, if not all, of these responsibilities on their own.

Chains have another advantage from a control perspective. They are able to generate internal financial information that can be used as a basis of comparison among individual operations. Independent operators usually know how well their restaurants are doing, but are frequently unaware of how well their restaurants should be doing. A restaurant chain operating at many locations within a specific geographic area can more easily generate information that can be used to set revenue and cost goals, as well to as identify problems in specific operations and within those operating systems.

On the other hand, there are also disadvantages to restaurant chains. It can be difficult for chains to keep up with changing markets and economic conditions. As chains grow, a bureaucracy involving a large amount of paperwork, rules, and procedures can slow them down. Top management may lose the motivation to keep up, and what is best for the organization's guest might not always receive the highest priority.

Franchises

Franchises are a special category of chain operations. With a franchise, the **franchisee** (the owner of a specific food service operation) pays fees to a **franchisor** (or franchise company) in exchange for the right to use the name, building design, and business methods of the franchisor. Furthermore, the franchisee must agree to maintain the franchisor's business and quality standards. The franchisor expands its franchise chain by signing up franchisees. Franchisees are often local entrepreneurs with investment funds. However, large companies seeking investment options may also purchase a franchise.

The franchisee is usually responsible for generating funds to start the business. In addition to initial franchise fees, the franchisee may be required to pay royalty fees assessed on the basis of a specified percentage of revenue or other factors, as well as advertising costs, sign rental fees, and other costs such as stationery and food products. (It may be against the law to stipulate as part of the franchise agreement that the franchisee must buy products of any kind from the franchisor. The franchisor can, however, establish quality requirements that must be met by distributors providing products and services to the franchise.)

The benefits of owning or managing a food service franchise typically include:

- Start-up assistance.
- Company-sponsored training programs for management and training resource materials for staff members.
- National contributions toward local advertising campaigns.
- More revenue because of more extensive advertising, greater name recognition of the franchise chain, and the consistency of products and services among chain operations (guests know what to expect).
- Lower food costs due to volume purchasing by the chain.
- Tested operating procedures that specify how things should be done.
- Name recognition that often makes it easier to recruit new staff members.

Many food service franchisors and franchisees have been tremendously successful. When franchisors are successful, they can command high fees and there may be long waiting lists to buy a franchise. Often, the franchisees are screened, and there may be little choice in the areas (territories) that are available for purchase.

There are also disadvantages to owning or managing a food service franchise. The contract is often very restrictive. The franchisee has little choice about the style of operation, products served, services offered, and even methods of operation. The menu might be set, along with the décor, required furnishings, and production equipment. Since the franchise agreement is drawn up by the franchisor, the document generally favors the franchisor. The agreement may leave little room to negotiate. This causes problems if there are disagreements between the two parties. Most typically, a franchisee operates a unit such as a McDonald's or Subway in a freestanding building or in rented space to which the public has access (for example, in a shopping mall, hotel lobby, or airport terminal). However, some franchisees use a co-branding tactic in which, for example, two noncompeting brands share the same building, parking lot, and dining space. Co-branding is also a growth concept in hotel food service (a Radisson hotel with a T.G.I. Friday's restaurant inside or a Marriott hotel with a Starbucks in the lobby, for example).

On-Site and Managed Services Operations

Today, as pressures for cost containment accompany lower revenue and bottom lines, there is a need to manage **on-site food service operations** and **managed services** (volume) operations as professional businesses. An increasing number of organizations are using for-profit managed services companies to operate their food service programs. There are many advantages to their use:

- Large nationwide managed services companies have more resources to solve problems.

- Managed services companies can save money through effective negotiations with distributors for volume purchases.

- Managed services companies can often operate noncommercial food service programs at a lower cost than their self-operated counterparts.

- Institution administrators, trained in areas other than food service operations, can delegate food service responsibilities to professional managed services company. Large institutions often retain a "food service liaison" to represent them in initial negotiations and ongoing operations with managed services company personnel.

There are also potential disadvantages to using managed services companies:

- Some managed services companies may have too much control in matters that affect the public image of the institution, long-range operating plans, and other important issues.

- Some people dislike having a profit-making business involved in the operation of a healthcare, educational, or other noncommercial food service program.

- There may be concerns that a managed services company will decrease food and beverage quality.

- The organization may become dependent on the managed services company. What happens if the managed services company discontinues the contract? How long will it take to implement a self-operated program or find another managed services company?

Differing Classifications of Food Service Operations

Different organizations and publications tend to categorize food service operations in different ways. The most useful categorization will depend on what kind of information the reader needs. For example, the National Restaurant Association, in its annual "Restaurant Industry Food-and-Drink Sales" report uses the following system:

- Group 1—Commercial Restaurant Services (only for establishments with payroll)
  - Eating Places
    - Full-service restaurants (servers take the order while guests are seated and serve the order; guests pay after eating)
    - Limited-service (quick-service) restaurants (guests order at a cash register and pay before they eat)
    - Commercial cafeterias
    - Social caterers
    - Snack and nonalcoholic beverage bars
    - Bars and taverns
  - Managed Services (also referred to as on-site food service and food contractors)
    - Manufacturing and industrial plants
    - Commercial and office buildings
    - Hospitals and nursing homes
    - Colleges and universities
    - Primary and secondary schools
    - In-transit restaurant services (airlines)
    - Recreation and sports centers
  - Lodging Places
    - Hotel restaurants
    - Motel-hotel restaurants
    - Motel restaurants
    - Other accommodation restaurants

- Retail-host restaurants (restaurants in drug and proprietary stores, general merchandise stores, variety stores, food and grocery stores, gasoline service stations, and miscellaneous retailers)

- Recreation and sports (movies, bowling centers, recreation facilities, and sports centers)

- Mobile caterers

- Vending and non-store retailers (sales of hot foods, sandwiches, pastries, coffee, and other hot beverages)

- Group II—Noncommercial Restaurant Services (business, educational, governmental, or institutional organizations that operate their own restaurant services)

  - Employee restaurant services (industrial and commercial organizations, seagoing, and inland-waterway vessels)

  - Public and parochial elementary, secondary schools

  - Colleges and universities

  - Transportation

  - Hospitals (voluntary and proprietary hospitals, long-term general, TB, psychiatric hospitals, and state and local short-term hospitals and federal hospitals)

  - Nursing homes, homes for the aged, blind, orphans, and the mentally and physically disabled

  - Clubs, sporting, and recreational camps

  - Community centers

- Group III—Military Restaurant Services (Continental United States only)

  - Officers' and NCO clubs (open mess)

  - Military exchanges

In this classification, the NRA reports estimated food-and-drink sales, projected food-and-drink sales, percent change year-to-year, percent real growth change from year to year, and the compound annual growth rate for several years. See www.restaurant.org for more details.

Food service segments are presented using a second classification by *Nation's Restaurant News* magazine. *NRN* uses the following segments:

- Sandwich

- Contract

- Pizza

- Chicken

- Coffee

- Dinnerhouse

- Snack
- Family
- C-stores (convenience stores)
- Grill-buffet
- Hotel
- Bakery-café
- Theme park
- Fish QSRs
- Chinese QSRs
- Italian QSRs

NRN's segmentation of food service operations mixes primary products served by each operation (e.g., sandwiches, chicken) with the style of service (e.g., dinnerhouse, family, QSR).

A third way to categorize food service operations is with the segments utilized by *Restaurants & Institutions* magazine. These segments are the following:

- Burgers
- Pizza
- Sandwiches/bakery
- Mexican
- Coffee/snacks
- Casual dining
- Steak/barbecue
- C-stores
- Seafood
- Italian
- Family dining
- Chicken
- Buffet/cafeteria
- Asian

While *R&I* primarily uses the main food item served (e.g., burgers, pizza, seafood), it also segments by style of cuisine (e.g., Mexican, Italian, Asian).

A fourth classification is presented by Technomic Information Services in its "Technomic Top 500 Chain Restaurant Report." This annual report includes an in-depth industry overview, segment (limited service, quick casual, casual dining, and family style/midscale) performance review and update on emerging chains, leading chain performance, listing of the top 100 restaurant companies, and implications and outlook. Technomic's annual report may be ordered at www.foodpubs.com. Technomic also categorizes the Technomic Power Distributors each year, including the company name and location, sales, sales growth, number of distributor sales representatives (DSRs), and number of accounts.

An additional source of information is *Food Management* magazine's annual listing of the Top 50 Management Companies. This information focuses on the noncommercial food service segment's largest contract management companies, and includes company name and location, Web site, sales volume, number of contracts, major segments served, and a brief profile for each of the top 50.

Yet another listing of food service operations is assembled each year by *Restaurant Business* magazine. This annual report includes casual dining by profiling chain leaders, regional coffee and donut chains, and healthy concepts. It also includes other food service operations sorted by concept.

In addition, *Foodservice Director* magazine presents a performance report for the 150 top business and industry noncommercial food service operations. The report includes the company name and location; whether it is self-operated or contract managed; annual food service sales, including catering; total annual food service purchases; total meal counts segmented by breakfast, lunch, and dinner; whether the business is subsidized by the client and the percentage of subsidy; and the number of categories. *Foodservice Director* publishes a similar annual analysis for self-operated hospitals and long-term care facilities chains.

Why are all these segmentations and annual reports necessary? Depending on the segment of the business in which your food service operation is competing, these annual data give you a point of comparison. Many of the dollar figures reported can easily be converted to percentages, and managers can compare them to figures from their own organizations. Sometimes it is useful to analyze different sources of data to see a more complete picture.

The Process Flow in a Food Service Operation

A food service operation can be thought of as a system of basic operating activities or control points. Each **control point** is a miniature system with its own recognizable structure and function (see Exhibit 2).

The operation's overall success depends upon success in each of these interrelated activities and in controlling the entire process.

A set of **process flow** strategies focuses on each of the ten control points. This approach systematizes the otherwise overwhelming task of managing the food service operation. The program involves maximizing value at each control point and implementing procedures for enhancing that value in the course of daily operations. By thus enhancing value at each control point, managers can successfully build an operation that delivers value for customers. When creating and delivering value focuses on food quality, food cost procedures, food safety, and food service delivery, the end result is satisfaction for guests, staff members, and owners.

Menu Planning

Menu planning is the initial control point in the food service system. Because the menu influences the remaining control points, managers must understand all other control points before developing the menu. For example, the menu

Exhibit 2   Control Points in a Food and Beverage Operation

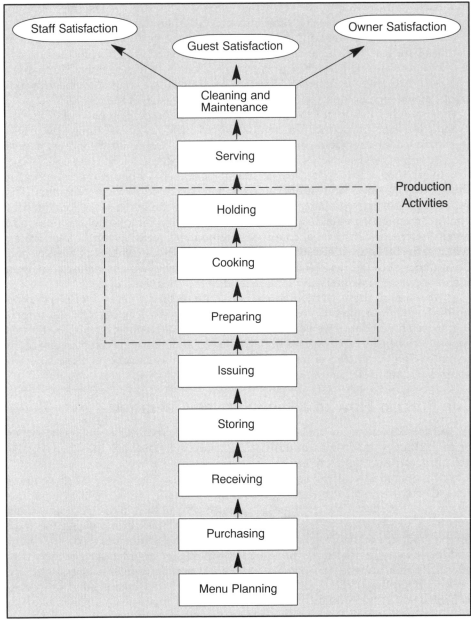

Source: Ronald F. Cichy, *Food Safety: Managing the HACCP Process* (Lansing, Mich.: Educational Institute of the American Hotel & Lodging Association, 2004), p. 5.

affects purchasing, receiving, storing, issuing, preparing, cooking, and service procedures because these procedures vary with the food product in question. The menu also affects and, in some cases, may be affected by the facility's design and layout, equipment requirements, and labor needs. A properly designed food service process flow must begin with the menu.

Purchasing

Purchasing is important for maintaining the value and quality of products, minimizing an operation's investment in inventory, and strengthening an operation's competitive position. Sound purchasing techniques can protect profits, control costs, and reduce risks. A sound purchasing system is essential to the operation's process flow.

Receiving

Receiving is a critical control point because at this point the operation assumes ownership of the products at this point. The receiving function involves checking quality, quantity, and price—all components of value. Proper receiving practices, when combined with skillful purchasing, can maximize the benefits of a carefully planned menu.

Storing

Storing serves to prevent deterioration and theft of valuable food products before the operation uses them. Food products are valuable assets that must be protected from contamination, spoilage, and theft in order to minimize costs and risks and maximize profits and value. Standards for the different types of storage (dry, refrigerated, and frozen) provide this protection.

Issuing

Issuing is the control point at which food products are released from storage. The objective of issuing controls is to ensure that products are only released to the production department with proper authorization. A poorly designed issuing system can undermine a food service operation's process flow, increase risks, jeopardize profits, and subsequently reduce value.

Preparing

Preparing is the series of activities performed on food products before cooking. Cleaning and peeling vegetables, trimming meat, and assembling raw ingredients are examples of preparation activities. Food is exposed to food safety hazards during preparation, which makes food safety standards important at this control point. Quality and cost control standards are likewise important here. These three sets of standards help deliver the planned value for customers.

Cooking

Cooking is the control point at which heat is applied to food in order to change its color, odor, texture, taste, appearance, and nutritional value. Food products are further exposed to food safety hazards during cooking, so this control point must be carefully monitored. Food quality, and therefore the customer's perception of value, is affected during cooking.

Holding

Holding is a critical control point, particularly in food service operations that prepare products well in advance of service. Menu items may be held hot or cold. Holding times should be as short as possible to maintain product quality and reduce food safety hazards. Holding temperatures must also be monitored carefully. When products are held too long, value is reduced.

Serving

Serving involves physically transferring finished menu items from the production department to guests. This control point should be designed to deliver quality products to guests quickly and efficiently. Serving standards should focus on protecting food safety, food quality, and value for the guest.

Cleaning and Maintenance

Cleaning and maintenance is the final control point; it is also one of the most important. Cleanliness is intimately related to every other basic operating activity. Many of the standards at other control points are standards of cleanliness and relate to food safety and maintenance. Other standards impact the cost of food products and the quality as determined by customers.

These ten control points are the foundation of any food service operation. A comprehensive food service process flow must address each point. Specific standards and operating procedures will vary among individual operations. However, ongoing evaluation at each of the control points will help ensure that the process flow in a food service operation maximizes value for customers as customers perceive it in the operation's food quality, food cost control, and food safety.

Resources at Each Control Point

Each of the ten control points in a food service operation's process flow has four resources to consider: people, inventory, equipment, and facilities.

People are perhaps the most important resource, since the people in the food service operation ultimately are responsible for delivering value to the customers. These people include the operation's internal customers—the staff members who create and deliver the products and services that add value for external customers. If the food service operation has a full-time purchasing agent, that person is responsible for ensuring that the right quality and quantity of products are available for sale to external customers at the right price. A part-time purchasing agent, or a department head in some food service operations, also has the same responsibilities. In either case, these buyers have a responsibility to work with the team in the food service operation to enhance value in the customer's experience.

Inventory is a necessary element of adding value because this inventory is transformed into products that draw the external customers to the food service operation to buy them. If the necessary quantity and quality of inventory are not available when the external customers are in the food service operation, their expectations will not be exceeded and are likely to not even be met. As a result of this inadequate inventory, external customers may not ever return to the food service operation.

Inventory is controlled by using a variety of purchasing tools, including standard purchase specifications, food sample data sheets, purchase orders, and increasingly, technology, to enhance value.

Equipment includes the large variety of utensils and other items needed in a food service operation. Fundamentally, this equipment must meet the standards of the operation as well as governmental agencies whose mission is to ensure food safety and reduce other risks (e.g., electrical or gas-related hazards). In many cases, equipment that is selected for a food service operation must have a relatively long useful life. This, again, maximizes value for the food service operation, as well as the operation's customers.

Facilities are a large part of the first impressions formed by both internal customers and external customers. These resources "house" the food and beverage service experience for both customer groups. Shabby or unkempt facilities often make both customer groups feel as if the operation's owners and managers really do not care. When facilities are well maintained and send the message that "you are welcome here and we care," internal customers are more likely to be motivated to create and deliver the products and services that the external customers find valuable. And this value translates to customer loyalty, word-of-mouth advertising, and repeat business.

Menu Planning and the Purchasing Function

Menu planning is the start of the food service process flow. In many respects, the menu is the mission statement for a food service operation. It defines the operation's concept and communicates that concept to guests. The menu attempts to provide what guests expect from their overall hospitality experience. It also serves as a plan for the entire food service system. The success of menu planning determines the success of the other control points and the overall value delivered to customers.

Generally, **dynamic menus** are preferable to static menus. However, menu variability depends on the seasonal availability of raw ingredients, the number and kinds of courses offered, the potential for using leftovers and local ingredients, the operation's image, and the demands of its target markets. In many respects, the menu is never complete; menu planning is an ongoing process. The process is continuous because guests' perceptions of value are ever increasing.

A food service operation's staff members are important to the success of its menu. Before management begins menu planning, the skill levels of production and service staff must be assessed. It may be helpful to consider the production staff and service staff separately, although their functions are closely related in practice. The production staff produces menu items within the confines of the kitchen. In planning the operation's menu, the objective is to avoid overloading any one person or work station. A well-planned menu features items that the operation's kitchen staff can consistently produce while maintaining the operation's quality, cost, and food safety standards. All of these elements contribute to the perceived value by guests.

Management should be realistic in determining what can be accomplished with the existing staff. For example, consider a kitchen in a metropolitan hotel where several menu items are prepared from scratch. If all meats are received in the wholesale-cut form (which is less expensive than the retail- or portion-cut form), the staff has to do the retail butchering. If the production staff is not properly trained in butchering wholesale cuts of meat into retail cuts, a lot of time and money will be wasted, and unnecessary food safety hazards will abound. Rather than saving the operation money, this poorly conceived arrangement increases the food cost, adds to the labor cost, and destroys the value delivered by the food service system. Such problems can be avoided by planning the menu with personnel limitations in mind.

Distributors must also be considered when planning a menu. Although distributors are not, strictly speaking, under the manager's control, they can contribute to the success of the business. Particularly at the menu planning control point, their input and suggestions can help make the business more profitable while enhancing the guests' satisfaction. For example, distributors can offer preparation and merchandising suggestions for various menu items. Excellent food service operations view their distributors as partners and use their distributors as sources of market trend information, new promotion ideas, and informal competitive analyses.

Inventory is the total supply of items an operation has in stock. The menu helps managers plan for the finished food products prepared from the items in inventory. Guests' orders deplete the inventory on hand. The operation must periodically replenish inventory if it is to continue offering the items guests are buying. It is important to keep detailed records on the relative popularity of every menu item. This information is useful at the purchasing control point, the next step of the food service process flow.

The menu directly affects the food service operation's purchasing, receiving, and storage requirements. The size of storage areas needed for raw ingredients and finished menu items depends on the menu. One of the primary advantages of a limited menu is that it reduces storage area requirements. In the past, food service managers attempted to diversify their menus, offering a wide variety of items. Since most items were made on site, the number and variety of raw ingredients needed increased significantly with each new item.

Today, the focus is often on rationalization of menu items: the creation of a simplified, balanced menu for the sake of operational efficiency and guest satisfaction. Although this strategy frequently results in a limited menu, the operation can offer several menu items that use the same raw ingredients. The objective of this cross-utilization is to prepare and serve as many menu items as possible with a limited number of raw ingredients. Planning the menu to ensure a balance of menu selections in each category helps streamline the purchasing, receiving, and storing functions.

The decision of whether or not to diversify the menu is driven to a great extent by guest requirements. Guests who dine out frequently are looking for diversity in menu choices. Some food service operators reason that, due to increased competition, they must diversify to build guest loyalty and repeat business, expand business into new meal periods, and draw on a wider guest base. However, while a constantly changing menu offers variety, it can cause confusion in the operation and result in lowered quality standards and value delivered. Alternatives to extensive diversification include highlighting items on the existing menu and adding a few daily specials.

Proponents of **menu rationalization** say that a food service operation should discover what it does best and continually refine it. Menu diversification requires additional staff training and additional time for taking orders and answering guest questions. Perhaps the best strategy is to create a balanced menu by choosing items from a limited inventory-in other words, create a rational, consolidated menu that maximizes cross-utilization.

The proliferation of high-quality convenience foods has made it easier for food service operations to offer new items without buying additional raw ingredients or elaborate equipment. High-quality convenience products can be purchased in semi- or fully-prepared forms. These products reduce in-house labor requirements. Of course, convenience food products usually have a higher AP (as purchased) price than the raw ingredients from which they are made.

It is always best to base initial menu plans on the needs and expectations of the target markets, translated into the customers' requirements. Several other factors may influence the selection of menu items as well. Among these factors are recommended storage conditions; staff member skill levels; product availability and seasonality; the stability of quality and price levels; and the operation's ability to purchase, prepare, and serve the menu item safely while delivering the levels of quality that customers expect.

Any food service operation must make a large investment in equipment before it can open for business. The amount and type of production and service equipment an operation owns determines what items it can produce and place on the menu. It is imperative to select equipment based on capacity, skill levels of staff members, energy and maintenance costs, and initial purchase price. Equipment should be constructed according to nationally recognized food safety standards and/or be listed by accredited testing and listing organizations. But above all, it is critical that equipment be easy to clean, sanitize, and use.

Adding a new menu item may require purchasing new production equipment. Such purchases should not be made without an analysis of the flow of products and people through the work area. This analysis helps management anticipate where cross-traffic may create hazards. Many operations use equipment on wheels or casters, which can be moved easily when necessary. In addition to allowing for adjustments to the product and staff traffic patterns, this mobility facilitates cleaning. Before a new menu item is added, the proper equipment should be available. For example, if the proposed menu change involves adding a soup bar to the dining room, the kitchen must have adequate steam-table, steam-jacketed kettle, or range equipment to reach and maintain safe product temperatures and quality during preparing and cooking.

A change in menu may also have implications for the operation's service equipment. Again, the implications for quality, food safety, and value must be considered beforehand. In the case of the soup bar, for example, the dining room should be equipped with suitable hot-holding equipment before these new items are added to the menu.

A dramatically modified menu can have a devastating effect on the system if proper equipment is not available. Consider what might happen if the owner of a bar that serves a wide selection of drinks and cold snack foods decides to add pizza to the snack food menu. She realizes that equipment to produce and hold the product is necessary; however, she fails to realize the significance of the serving containers. She chooses reusable dishes, thinking that these will be less expensive in the long run than disposable containers. Making a hasty decision on cost alone, the owner neglects to consider the fact that if the pizza is served on a reusable tray, proper provisions must be made for washing, sanitizing, and storing the trays. It is not acceptable to wash the pizza trays in the bar's glass-washing equipment. In the end, she realizes that the addition of this new food item is an expensive endeavor.

The addition of banquet service to a traditional food service operation must also be carefully considered in light of the additional constraints banquets place on menu planning and equipment. For example, if a hotel is planning to serve a banquet for 800, all of the food items cannot be dished for all 800 guests immediately prior to service. Therefore, extra hot-holding and cold storage equipment is essential. The hotel must also limit its banquet menu to allow for the extra handling and holding times involved and protect the product quality.

Because conditions are ever changing, a food service operation's menu must also change. Menu changes are influenced by both external and internal factors.

External factors include guest requirements, economic factors, the competition, supply levels, and industry trends. Guest requirements are perhaps the most important factor to consider in changing a menu. Management should first decide which potential markets it wants to attract with a modified menu. The proposed menu change should then be evaluated in light of its potential impact on the current markets.

Economic factors include the cost of ingredients and the potential profitability of new menu items. The competition's menu offerings can also influence menu decisions. For example, a hotel food service operation located next door to a restaurant offering the "best Chinese food in town" might elect not to serve Chinese cuisine. Supply levels affect the price and the quality and quantity of the proposed menu items. Supply levels are highly variable for some seasonal raw ingredients such as fresh fruits and vegetables. Industry trends are general observations about how the industry is responding to new guest requirements. At present, the overall trend is to put in place strategies to satisfy a more sophisticated, value-conscious guest.

Internal factors that may result in a proposed menu change are an operation's meal pattern, concept and theme, operational system, and menu mix. The typical meal pattern is breakfast, lunch, and dinner. Management must decide if existing meal periods should be continued or altered. The target markets' expectations and requirements directly influence this decision. Any menu change must also be compatible with the operation's concept and theme; a restaurant that is known as the best steakhouse in the city may do itself a disservice by offering fewer steak selections in order to add fresh fish and shellfish to the menu. On the other hand, this change may appeal to a larger more diverse customer base. An operation's image may also rule out certain foods that do not blend with its theme and décor.

Menu changes can be affected by the operation's operational system. For example, a menu change may raise both food and labor costs to unacceptable levels. The production and service staff members may lack the necessary skills to produce and present the new menu item. If extensive new equipment is crucial to the successful production and service of a new item, the change may be too costly. Many operations deal with this factor by designing flexible kitchens with multipurpose equipment. For example, a combination convection oven/steamer can bake, roast, and steam. Tilt skillets can be used for baking, braising, frying, griddling, or steaming.

An operation's existing menu has a certain overall combination or mix of items. This menu mix will be affected by any change in individual items. All of these factors should be evaluated before menu changes are finalized.

Due to rising consumer awareness, truth-in-menu regulations are an increasingly important menu planning consideration around the globe. Truth-in-menu regulations require accurate descriptions of raw ingredients and finished menu items. Purchasing staff help the operation meet these regulations. For example, the correct quality or grade of food products must be stated; care must be exercised when grades are printed on the menu. It is also important that items billed as "fresh" have not been frozen, canned, or preserved in any way. A product's point of origin must also be represented accurately; for example, "fresh Lake Superior whitefish" should indeed be fresh whitefish from Lake Superior. A sample list of common points of origin is presented in Exhibit 3.

The size, weight, and portion advertised on the menu must also be accurate. A bowl of soup should contain more than a cup of soup. Descriptions like "extra tall" drinks or "extra large" salads can open the door to possible guest complaints. "All you can eat" implies that the guest is entitled to exactly that: as much as he or she can eat. For meat items, it is a generally accepted practice to list the precooked weight.

The preparation technique must be accurately described. If there are additional charges for extras (such as substitutions or coffee refills), such charges must be clearly stated on the menu. Any pictures of food products should be accurate. Dietary or nutritional claims, if used, must be precise. "Low calorie," for example, is vague because it implies that the product is lower in calories but does not specify what the product is being compared to. Servers' descriptions should also accurately portray the menu selections.

Some chains (for example, KFC and McDonald's) have developed descriptive brochures and pamphlets that provide nutritional information on their products. This information is available upon request; however, most participating chains report little guest interest. While such brochures may be useful and interesting to only a relatively small number of guests, the information should be available to those who request it. Some people use this information to avoid food allergens; others simply like to know exactly what they are eating.

Exhibit 3   Typical Representations of Point of Origin

Dairy Products	Scrod, Boston
Danish Bleu Cheese	Shrimp
Domestic Cheese	Bay Shrimp
Imported Swiss Cheese	Gulf Shrimp
Roquefort Cheese	Trout
Wisconsin Cheese	Colorado Brook Trout

Dairy Products
Danish Bleu Cheese
Domestic Cheese
Imported Swiss Cheese
Roquefort Cheese
Wisconsin Cheese

Fish and Shellfish
Cod, Icelandic (North Atlantic)
Crab
   Alaskan King Crab
   Florida Stone Crab
   North Atlantic Crab
   Snow Crab
Frog Legs
   Domestic Frog Legs
   Imported Frog Legs
   Louisiana Frog Legs
Lobster
   Australian Lobster
   Brazilian Lobster
   Maine Lobster
   South African Lobster
Oysters
   Blue Point Oysters
   Chesapeake Bay Oysters
   Olympia Oysters
Salmon
   Nova Scotia Salmon
   Puget Sound Sockeye Salmon
   Salmon Lox
Scallops
   Bay Scallops
   Sea Scallops

Scrod, Boston
Shrimp
   Bay Shrimp
   Gulf Shrimp
Trout
   Colorado Brook Trout
   Idaho Brook Trout
Whitefish, Lake Superior

Meats
Beef, Colorado
Ham
   Country Ham
   Danish Ham
   Imported Ham
   Smithfield Ham
   Virginia Style Ham
Pork, Iowa

Poultry
Long Island Duckling
Maryland Milk-Fed Chicken

Vegetables and Fruits
Orange Juice, Florida
Pineapples
   Hawaiian Pineapples
   Mexican Pineapples
Potatoes
   Idaho Potatoes
   Maine Potatoes

Source: Ronald F. Cichy, *Food Safety: Managing the HACCP Process* (Lansing, Mich.: Educational Institute of the American Hotel & Lodging Association, 2004), p. 74.

Characteristics of the Purchasing Control Point

We have already established that once menu planning is complete, purchasing is the next step in the food service process flow. The menu determines what ingredients must be purchased and in what amounts. One of the major objectives of purchasing is to obtain the right quality and quantity of items at the right price from the right distributor. The goals are to maintain quality, strengthen the operation's competitive position, minimize investment in inventory, and add value.

Purchasing is an important control point for cost and quality controls. Many food service operations spend 30 to 50 percent of their total sales revenue on product purchasing. Reducing purchasing costs can translate directly to the operation's bottom line. Failing to properly control food costs can have a more devastating effect than overspending in most other cost categories. It is not surprising, then, that many operators' primary concern is food cost. Rising food costs often force management to reexamine the operation's purchasing needs.

A **potential cost analysis** (see Exhibit 4) is a breakdown of each menu item served at each meal period. The menu item is tracked for each day of a month. In addition to each menu item, the analysis shows that item's cost, the total cost (number of menu items × cost per item), the selling price for each menu item, the total sales for each menu item (number of items sold × sales price for each), and the food cost percentage for each menu item. At the bottom of the form, the total food cost (as a dollar value and a percentage) as well as the total food sales are shown. Exhibit 5 gives an example of how an operation might compare its potential cost analysis to the actual costs it incurred.

In addition to the menu, several other factors dictate purchasing needs. The forecasted sales volume is an estimate of how much business a food service operation will have on a given day. This information, along with the operation's standard recipes, can be used to calculate the amounts of ingredients needed. Certain external factors also affect purchasing needs. The size and frequency of orders, for example, are affected by how much lead time the distributor requires before a delivery can be made. The operation's distance from the distributor may also affect quantities purchased. For example, a steakhouse located high in the mountains or in a rural area would probably receive less frequent deliveries than a steakhouse in a downtown metropolitan area. More frequent deliveries usually mean smaller orders, which results in less money tied up in inventory.

Of course, the quantities of food ordered and the money invested in inventory are not the only purchasing concerns. Quality and food safety standards must also be considered at this control point. A low-quality or unsafe product is never a bargain, no matter how inexpensive it is. It can unnecessarily increase the food service operation's risks. Value-added activities in purchasing affect the ultimate value delivered to external customers.

The factors affecting purchasing needs are directly related to the functions of the purchasing control point. These purchasing functions are:

- Establishing and maintaining an adequate supply of food and non-food products.

- Minimizing the operation's investment in inventory.

- Maintaining the operation's quality, food safety, and cost standards while reducing risks.

- Maintaining the operation's competitive position.

- Buying the product, not the deal.

- Enhancing the value experienced by the operation's customers.

Customer Requirements

When considering the fundamental reason for creating a food service operation, two basic questions surface:

Exhibit 4 Sample Potential Cost Analysis

Potential Cost Analysis

COVERS

BREAKFAST	M	T	W	T	F	S	S	M	T	W	T	F	S	S	M	T	W	T	F	S	S	M	T	W	T	F	S	S	M	T	W	TTL	Item Cost	Total Cost	Sell Price	Total Sales	Food Cost %
DATE	1	2	3	4	5	6	7	8	9	10	11	12	13	14	15	16	17	18	19	20	21	22	23	24	25	26	27	28	29	30	31						
Total Covers from POS	121	140	137	125	116	87	222																									950					
Breakfast Buffet	47	76	68	67	48	34	88																									428	$ 3.20	$ 1,369.60	$ 12.95	$ 5,542.60	24.7%
Continental Buffet	27	32	22	20	18	12	0																									131	$ 1.57	$ 205.67	$ 7.95	$ 1,041.45	19.7%
																																0	$ -	$ -	$ -	$ -	#DIV/0!
Three Egg Omelet	15	22	12	8	24	10	4																									95	$ 3.70	$ 351.50	$ 7.95	$ 755.25	46.5%
Fruit Yogurt Nut Bread	1	3	14	6	3	2	0																									29	$ 1.80	$ 52.20	$ 6.25	$ 181.25	28.8%
Egg White Omelet	4	8	6	6	7	10	0																									41	$ 2.11	$ 86.51	$ 7.95	$ 325.95	26.5%
American Breakfast	22	32	18	26	17	11	4																									130	$ 1.88	$ 244.40	$ 7.25	$ 942.50	25.9%
Blueberry Pancakes	4	12	18	10	9	28	32																									113	$ 1.12	$ 126.56	$ 6.95	$ 785.35	16.1%
French Toast	6	17	22	21	14	33	24																									137	$ 1.27	$ 173.99	$ 6.95	$ 952.15	18.3%
Waffles	5	8	16	17	20	40	0																									106	$ 1.54	$ 163.24	$ 7.25	$ 768.50	21.2%
																																0	$ -	$ -	$ -	$ -	#DIV/0!
Chilled Grapefruit Half	1	5	4	3	8	2	1																									24	$ 0.45	$ 10.80	$ 3.25	$ 78.00	13.8%
Seasonal Sliced Melon	2	2	6	7	4	12	5																									38	$ 0.67	$ 25.46	$ 3.25	$ 123.50	20.6%
Asst. Cold Cereal	14	8	16	14	14	3	0																									69	$ 0.77	$ 53.13	$ 3.25	$ 224.25	23.7%
Asst. Cold Cereal / fruit	10	12	10	8	5	19	0																									64	$ 0.85	$ 54.40	$ 4.25	$ 272.00	20.0%
Granola / Fruit	3	5	4	4	2	5	2																									25	$ 0.97	$ 24.25	$ 4.25	$ 106.25	22.8%
Cran-Raisin Oatmeal	2	9	16	18	9	2	2																									57	$ 0.47	$ 26.79	$ 4.25	$ 242.25	11.1%
Bakery Basket	12	14	10	9	8	14	12																									79	$ 1.08	$ 85.32	$ 3.25	$ 256.75	33.2%
																																0	$ -	$ -	$ -	$ -	#DIV/0!
English Muffin	8	4	5	9	18	2	2																									48	$ 0.28	$ 13.44	$ 2.50	$ 120.00	11.2%
Toast	15	18	19	14	14	9	4																									93	$ 0.24	$ 22.32	$ 2.60	$ 232.50	9.6%
Bagel	6	10	12	5	6	0	0																									39	$ 0.45	$ 17.55	$ 2.50	$ 97.50	18.0%
Bagel w/ cream cheese	3	14	5	16	2	3	9																									52	$ 0.64	$ 33.28	$ 2.95	$ 153.40	21.7%
Sausage	1	0	0	9	5	0	0																									15	$ 0.47	$ 7.05	$ 2.50	$ 37.50	18.8%
Bacon	0	2	6	3	0	9	2																									22	$ 0.33	$ 7.26	$ 2.60	$ 66.00	13.2%
Ham	0	5	4	0	2	1	1																									13	$ 0.70	$ 9.10	$ 2.75	$ 35.75	25.5%
																																0	$ -	$ -	$ -	$ -	#DIV/0!
Orange Juice	18	24	33	44	38	42	0																									199	$ 0.37	$ 73.63	$ 2.95	$ 587.05	12.5%
Grapefruit Juice	3	5	18	15	9	14	3																									67	$ 0.39	$ 26.13	$ 2.95	$ 197.65	13.2%
Apple Juice	1	0	5	2	0	3	2																									13	$ 0.24	$ 3.12	$ 2.95	$ 38.35	8.1%
Cranberry Juice	6	4	5	4	3	9	12																									43	$ 0.26	$ 11.18	$ 2.95	$ 126.85	8.8%
V-8 Juice	0	0	2	1	3	3	0																									9	$ 0.30	$ 2.70	$ 2.95	$ 26.55	10.2%
Tomato Juice	0	0	0	0	0	0	0																									0	$ 0.29	$ -	$ 2.95	$ -	#DIV/0!
Reg. Coffee	42	44	52	38	32	18	54																									280	$ 0.11	$ 30.80	$ 1.95	$ 546.00	5.6%
Decaf. Coffee	12	15	11	8	9	16	64																									135	$ 0.15	$ 20.25	$ 1.95	$ 263.25	7.7%
Hot Tea	3	5	6	5	4	3	3																									29	$ 0.18	$ 5.22	$ 1.95	$ 56.55	9.2%
2% Milk	2	0	5	14	11	3	21																									56	$ 0.20	$ 11.20	$ 1.95	$ 109.20	10.3%
Skim Milk	1	2	2	1	3	0	0																									9	$ 0.23	$ 2.07	$ 1.95	$ 17.55	11.8%
																																0	$ -	$ -	$ -	$ -	#DIV/0!
																																0	$ -	$ -	$ -	$ -	#DIV/0!
																																0	$ -	$ -	$ -	$ -	#DIV/0!
																																0	$ -	$ -	$ -	$ -	#DIV/0!
																																0	$ -	$ -	$ -	$ -	#DIV/0!
																																0	$ -	$ -	$ -	$ -	#DIV/0!
																																0	$ -	$ -	$ -	$ -	#DIV/0!
																																0	$ -	$ -	$ -	$ -	#DIV/0!
																																0	$ -	$ -	$ -	$ -	#DIV/0!
PDR Parties																																0					
Totals																																0		$ 3,360.12		$ 16,298.66	21.9%

Cost Potential 21.9%

Exhibit 5   Sample Actual vs. Potential Cost Comparison

Actual vs. Potential Comparison Worksheet   Date: Jul-03

MTD						Revenue	YTD					
Liquor	Beer	Wine	Non	Allow.	Ttl.		Liquor	Beer	Wine	Non	Allow.	Ttl.
156	381	500	1,303		2,340	Room Service	972	2,157	4,960	5,219		13,308
568	446	713	670	(383)	2,014	3 Meal Restaurant	5,889	5,470	9,428	6,448	(1,513)	25,722
5,968	5,937	2,892	665		15,462	Lounge/Bar	51,366	61,745	27,376	4,429		144,916
0	75	51	865		991	Banquets	5,295	4,085	6,411	26,762		42,553
342	359	542	5,048		6,291	Catering	32,203	24,302	17,855	60,354		134,714
0	0	0	0		0	Allow.	0	0	0	0		0
7,034	7,198	4,698	8,551	(383)	27,098	Totals	95,725	97,759	66,030	103,212	(1,513)	361,213

MTD	%	Potential	COSTS	YTD	%	Potential
1,304	18.5%	18.0%	Liquor	15,113	15.8%	18.0%
2,185	30.4%	20.0%	Beer	23,488	24.0%	20.0%
1,579	33.6%	29.0%	Wine	22,493	34.1%	29.0%
746	8.7%	18.0%	Non	22,619	21.9%	18.0%
(192)	50.1%		Allow.	(2,450)	161.9%	
5,622	20.7%		Totals	81,263	22.5%	

- Who are the customers?
- What are their requirements?

These two questions and their answers are perplexing for some food service operators because they base the products and services offered in their food service operations *not* on what customers require, but on what they (the operators) *think* customers will like. This is a dangerous strategy because it may lead to false conclusions about what customers require. These false conclusions will result in a menu that is planned *not* with customer requirements at the forefront, but with other driving forces, such as the operator's need to simply minimize costs and maximize profits.

When asking, "Who are our customers?" there is a wealth of general demographic data available in general publications and in food service–specific publications, such as *Nation's Restaurant News, Restaurant Business, Restaurants & Institutions, Food Management, Food Service Distributor,* and others. These demographic descriptors include food service customers categorized by age, household income, gender, education level, frequency of dining out in a food service operation, and other demographic factors. While these general data may be somewhat useful, what is really important to understand is who the customers of a specific food service operation are.

Recall that it is the value *as perceived by external customers* that is critical to identify and act upon. How to obtain this critical input and ways to make sense with the information received are what sometimes puzzle food service operators.

There are several ways to obtain answers to the "What are their requirements?" question, including:

- Contact by guest-service staff or management.
- Comment cards.
- Focus groups.

- Secret shoppers.

- Shopping the competition.

- Surveys.

Contact by guest service staff or management takes place countless times each day in a food service operation. However, these individuals have to be trained to ask the right questions to gain customer requirement data that is usable. Thus, questions about specific menu items, the level of service delivered, or the quality experienced are better than simply asking "How was everything?" Once the customer responds to the specific question, it is critical to listen carefully and then record the comment so it can be utilized to improve value as perceived by the customer.

Comment cards may be useful in identifying customer requirements provided that the right questions are asked. Comment cards must be easy to fill out and give the customer the opportunity to respond to an open-ended question. Questions about the appearance, taste, temperature, texture, and timeliness of food are helpful if the customer is given a response range (from "always" to "most of the time" to "sometimes" to "seldom/hardly ever," for example).

As with verbal feedback, written comments must be summarized and analyzed so patterns and trends are identified for improvement. If a customer complains on a comment card and leaves his or her name/address, it is important for someone from the food service operation to contact that customer to inform him or her how the complaint was resolved and to thank the guest for this valuable feedback. Complaints help food service operators see the operation as it is from the customer's perspective of value, and as such, are valuable sources of essential feedback.

Focus groups are usually assembled with current and potential customers. They provide the opportunity to expand the first question—"Who are our customers?"—to include, "Who are our potential customers?" Focus groups must be facilitated by an individual who helps keep the conversations on track and well "focused," so the feedback is meaningful. In-depth discussions about the customers' perceptions of value and quality, opportunities for process improvements, products and services presently offered, and products and services that customers would like offered are all valuable focus group discussion topics. Sometimes product samplings are part of a focus group. Product samplings are often utilized to obtain feedback about potential menu items before they are added to the menu. Focus group members who are sampling products are asked about the product's appearance, flavor, possible selling price, and overall appeal.

Secret shoppers pose as customers and experience the entire service process, including products, and then file a detailed report. The goal of using a secret shopper is to see the food service operation as the customer sees it. The secret shopper is not known to the internal customers or management of the operations in the case of a chain restaurant. Once again, the goal is to experience the operation's products and services as an external customer would do so, and this anonymity is essential.

Shopping the competition is not necessarily designed to determine what a particular food service operation's customers require, but what competitors are offering to appeal to those who may or may not currently be that operation's customers. Often shopping the competition will be done by managers and staff members who want to experience what others are doing to add value to the food service experience.

Sometimes shopping the competition is called benchmarking, which, simply stated, is learning from another operation with the goal of raising levels of product and service quality leading to customers' heightened perceptions of value. Benchmarking another operation helps our operation adapt, modify, and apply process flow improvements. In some cases, looking outside the operation for these improvements will stimulate improvements within an operation.

Surveys are more formal ways of identifying customer requirements. Surveys are often linked to a specific function (e.g., a banquet) or event (e.g., a special theme night). Surveys usually include specific questions about food and beverage quality (appearance, flavor, temperature, and other quality factors important to the customer), service quality (timeliness, levels of service, and other factors important to the customer), what pleased the customer overall, what the customer would have liked to have experienced differently overall, and problems that occurred during the experience. Surveys are categorized based on responses so internal customers and management can identify areas for process improvement.

The overall goal of identifying areas for improvement in a food service operation's process flow is not to simply fix the blame for the problem. By fixing the problem only for this time, managers have handled the resolution of a symptom, not the root cause of the problem. By fixing the blame, managers answer the question "Who is responsible for the problem?" Rather, the goal is to identify and answer "Why did the problem occur?" and make changes in the process so the problem does not occur again. This is the basis for continuous improvement of the food service process flow.

Forecasting

Forecasting is an attempt to predict the future as accurately as possible. In purchasing, it is often helpful to forecast the prices of such products as center-of-the-plate items (meat, for example). A price forecast is a plan that depends on gathering data, examining past history, assessing current and expected events, and converting. Buyers need both short-term and long-term plans.

For example, consider the purchasing of meat by a buyer for a steakhouse. Short-term planning should extend for several ordering cycles. If inventories are replenished weekly, one month is considered short term. The purpose is to predict events so that price increases are avoided. An example of this involves planning around holidays. Several predictable things happen during holiday seasons:

- Processing plants take the day off, so the week has one less day for meat production.

- More people dine out, so larger quantities will be consumed than during regular periods.

- Distributors do not work on the holiday, but the workload for preceding days is heavier. Because of this, distributors are more likely to run out of products.

Other items covered in a short-term plan are seasonal business and promotions. Strikes of unionized workers at any point in the distribution chain also require special attention and, if possible, their duration should be estimated. Predicting these events permits the purchaser to maintain an orderly flow of product delivery.

Long-term planning enables the food service operation to generate financial budgets and to undertake market forecasting. Price forecasting is the result of a series of calculations and assumptions directed toward managing future events.

Today, meat price forecasting begins with the United States Department of Agriculture (USDA). The USDA maintains historical data on price and production levels, consumption and spending habits, and other factors of interest to buyers. It also publishes data estimating the number of animals available on a specified date, the number marketed since the last report, and the age or market condition of animals in inventory. Figures for daily slaughter rates and farmers' intended herd replenishment are also available. These figures are relatively accurate and used by economists to generate price forecasts.

The USDA also publishes general price information that can be helpful in forecasting prices. Independent companies use these figures to develop forecasts, which are offered to subscribers for a fee. Most of the major economic planning companies have agricultural departments which issue price forecasts. Trading companies issue advice to encourage trading on futures exchanges.

If the USDA predicts either more or fewer animals than anticipated, price swings can be dramatic. A significant world event, such as a trade embargo, the threat of war, or political upheaval, can also influence prices. Meat buyers should follow the Chicago Board of Trade (CBOT) contracts for the feed grain complex and the Chicago Mercantile Exchange (CME) contracts for feeder cattle, slaughter cattle, hogs, and pork bellies. As already noted, a great many factors influence the accuracy of price forecasting. Still, the wise purchaser understands and uses price information in an effort to determine the appropriate time to buy.

Although prices cannot be forecasted for specific days, given relevant information, judgments can be made that cover specific periods of time. Three important sources of information for forecasting prices are:

- Historical records of the food service operation.

- Judgments of distributors.

- Judgments of independent forecasting firms.

Buyers should always start with historical data from their own operations. What happened during a specific time frame in past years? What were the prices of competing products such as ground beef or pork loin? After answering these questions, the buyer looks to outside sources for information; distributors considered first. What do they think will occur? Generally, more than one distributor is contacted and a consensus of their opinions is formed. There are a number of paid price forecasting services available.

Forecasting is an ongoing process and some schedule should be established to update information. The schedule should fit the operation's needs, but forecasting should take place at least quarterly; many organizations update monthly. Processors, of course constantly update forecasts since their accuracy usually means the difference between profit and loss.

Common Purchasing Mistakes

One of the most common mistakes in purchasing is not carefully identifying the requirements of customers. When this is not done, as described earlier, the danger is that the wrong products will be purchased and offered for sale to customers. When this mistake is made, one of two outcomes usually occurs: (1) the customer does not order the product from the menu, or the product ends up staying in inventory or being used for some other purpose; or (2) customers order the product from the menu and their requirements are not met. These customers may or may not choose to return to the food service operation.

Two other common mistakes are related. The first is to compare what is actually used (and should be reordered) with what should be used based on the operation's standard recipes. What should be used predicts what should be purchased. But, what was actually used takes into account product waste and spoilage and theft. If waste, spoilage, and theft are taking place in the food service operation, this indicates that another part of the process flow must be fixed at its root cause if these problems are to be decreased or eliminated.

The second mistake is to compare usage cost with purchase cost for a product. The cost to purchase a product, say whole chickens, is called the "as purchased (AP)" cost. This is the price paid to the distributor, in the case of chickens on a per pound basis. This price is *not* the price for an edible portion of boneless chicken breast served on the menu. The "edible portion (EP)" cost per pound of boneless, skinless chicken breasts is much higher because there is less weight left after a bone-in breast from a chicken has its bone and skin removed. This EP cost per pound is much higher and is used to set the selling price. If the AP cost is used to set the selling price, the food cost percentage will be much higher on that chicken entrée item because the wrong price was used.

Customer Lifestyle Changes

The lifestyles of customers directly impact what food service operations purchase and offer on their menus. Consumer research attempts to identify lifestyle changes that can translate into changes in food service operations. Today, consumers dine out at full-service restaurants more than once each week on average. In general, men tend to dine out more frequently than women.

As household incomes have risen and as the consumer population has continued to age, dining out has also increased. Those with a household income of $75,000 or more and those 50 years of age or older tend to dine out more frequently than those with lower household incomes who are younger.

More than one-third of restaurant guests say they notice brand-name products on the menu; roughly the same percentage notices brand-name condiments on the tables of restaurants. The same is true with recognizable brands in beverages. It appears that brand recognition improves the opinion of a food service operation by its guests.

The most popular ethnic foods in food service operations are Chinese, Mexican, and Italian. In addition, food service operations that specialize in steaks are also popular among consumers. When asked what the important factors are for repeat visits to a full-service restaurant, consumers in general responded with the following (in order of priority):

Factor	Rank
Cleanliness	1
High food quality	2
Use of fresh food	3
Comfortable/relaxed atmosphere	4
Prompt service	5
Good value for the money	6
Wide menu variety	7
Convenient location	8
No lines or waiting	9
A place to connect/socialize	10

From this list of important factors, one could perhaps conclude that at least five are directly related to the operation's purchasing effectiveness: cleanliness (i.e., the purchase and use of correct cleaning and sanitizing chemicals), high food quality, use of fresh food, good value for the money, and wide menu variety. While these general trends are helpful, what really matters is how the customers of a specific operation would rank these factors. The ranking for customers of a specific operation point out customer requirements.

Other trends have been identified when it comes to dining out in food service operations. In no particularly ranked order, these trends include:

- Dining that encourages participation in sports (e.g., bowling).

- Entertainment to attract a wider variety of guests (e.g., video games, streetball, Harley Davidson motorcycle simulators, restaurants with a Star Trek theme, simulated rain forests, and food service operations with DJs).

- Food service operations that feature unique beverage options (e.g., a large variety of flavored martinis, including bubblegum, green apple, and watermelon; a bourbon and red wine drink known as the Badhattan; Irish margaritas made with Jameson Irish whiskey instead of tequila; or a Nantucket Bloody Mary garnished with olives stuffed with roasted tomatoes).

- Comfort foods on the menu (e.g., soups, roasts, meatloaf, chicken pot pie, mashed potatoes, macaroni and cheese, stuffed cabbage, pasta sauces, stuffed peppers).

- Foods guests may not prepare at home, but that allow them to ingest mega calories in a food service operation (e.g., 1,400-calorie burgers, 700-calorie hand-scooped ice cream shakes, fried chicken, enormous omelet sandwiches, triple-cheese stuffed pizzas, French toast stuffed with sweetened cream cheese).

- Farm-to-table organic foods, as consumers become increasingly aware of the origin of their food (e.g., organic beef and poultry, organic eggs) and prefer foods without synthetic chemicals.

- Increasing use of HealthyDiningFinder.com, sponsored by the National Restaurant Association and the California-based Healthy Dining program. (This Web site allows consumers to find restaurants that offer nutritious options, based on the type of cuisine, price range, and zip code.)

- Food prepared to go. (When consumers do not want to dine out, they may prefer to stop at a food service operation to pick up food that is ready to eat at home.)

- Food on demand in hotel food service (i.e., guests want what they want when they want it). Examples include special cooking methods and ingredients, featured local ingredients, specific dietary requests, and foods without certain allergens.

The Role of Internal Customers in the Purchasing Process

Internal customers are staff members who directly represent the food service operation to external customers. Internal customers who are in guest-contact positions (e.g., dining room servers, hosts, bus persons) have the most direct contact with customers of any food service staff member. As such, these guest-contact internal customers have opportunities to continuously monitor guest expectations.

Define Specification Needs

Internal customers can greatly assist in the ongoing definition of purchase specification needs for a food service operation. By listening to guests, they can discover what guests prefer and do not like. Guests may tell these servers about a similar dining experience that they had elsewhere and what they enjoyed about it, including certain menu choices. When this "market intelligence" is shared by these internal customers with those responsible for menu planning and purchasing, a rich form of market information with the focus of customer requirements is available. For example, a guest may request a vodka martini made from Ciroc vodka, produced from French grapes. If this vodka choice is not available in the food service operation and if enough guests request this specific brand of vodka, it should be purchased and made available for sale. To do otherwise is to *not* meet the customers' requirements.

Define Volume Requirements

Internal customers can also assist with the definition of volume requirements. If a sufficient number of guests are requesting Ciroc vodka in the example used earlier, it may justify the purchase and sale of this upscale vodka in the food service operation.

While it is extremely difficult to add a menu item if it is only occasionally requested by customers, the addition is justified if sufficient potential volume exists. So too, if the popularity of another menu item (fresh oysters on the half shell, for example) is diminishing, the reduced volume may justify removing the item from the menu.

Teamwork

Internal customers create and deliver the products and services for guests that add value, as perceived by the guests, by working as a team. The team includes all those in guest-contact as well as in support positions without guest contact. The team includes the menu planners and those responsible for purchasing food and beverage products. The team also includes those who receive, store, and issue the food and beverage products. Internal customers who purchase, receive, store, and issue may have little or no contact with the customers, yet their actions and decisions affect the value and satisfaction customers receive. When products are produced, cooked, and held, still other team members such as cooks and chefs are involved in producing what the guests ultimately consume.

Once ready for service, the products are served to guests and value is added by servers who help transform the products into a memorable dining experience. So food and beverage servers are part of this team that adds value. Also included are hosts, cashiers, bus persons, and any other internal customer who has an impact, either directly or indirectly, on customer satisfaction. Of course, managers and other support staff (e.g., bookkeepers, accountants, and maintenance staff) also are part of the team.

It is the team of internal customers that makes the food service experience. By working together toward a common goal (i.e., delivering value to customers), aligning themselves with the values and vision of the food service operation, and then collaborating to deliver the desired results, the team ends up adding value for guests.

Essentials of Food Safety

The food safety program in a food service operation builds on the food service process flow described earlier. It is a program designed to reduce overall food safety risks by identifying the risks at each control point in a food service operation.

HACCP Process

The food safety program of choice is a modified version of the **Hazard Analysis and Critical Control Point** (HACCP—pronounced "HAH-sep") approach developed jointly by the Pillsbury Company, the United States Army's Natick Laboratories, and the National Aeronautics and Space Administration in 1974.

HACCP is a systematic approach to identifying, evaluating, and controlling food safety hazards. Food safety hazards are biological, chemical, or physical agents that are reasonably likely to cause injury or illness in the absence of their control. HACCP systems are designed to prevent the occurrence of potential food safety hazards. The food safety risk management program presented here incorporates HACCP and also includes controls for maintaining food quality and managing food costs, thereby improving the customers' perceptions of value.

Hazard analysis serves as the basis for establishing critical control points. Critical control points (CCPs) are those activities or procedures in a specific food system where loss of control may result in an unacceptable health risk. Critical limits establish appropriate standards that must be met at each CCP. The final step in HACCP is to monitor and verify that potential hazards are controlled. All of this information is documented in the HACCP plan—a written document that delineates the formal procedures for following HACCP principles.

The food safety program presented here is a HACCP–based approach that focuses on the ten control points common to most food service operations. Standards and procedures for each control point are presented as they relate to the four resources under a manager's control: inventory, people, equipment, and facilities. A resource evaluation is necessary for each of the ten control points. The result is a systematic approach to managing risks.

Because the hospitality industry is labor-intensive—that is, it relies on large staffs—people are an important resource. It is management's responsibility to train staff members in proper food safety practices. Failing to control this important resource undermines the food safety program and jeopardizes the operation's bottom line.

Inventory is an essential management resource because it is converted into revenue and, ultimately, into profits. Inventory in a food service operation normally consists of food products, beverages, and non-food items such as linens and cleaning chemicals. Inventory control is a vital link in an operation's cost and quality control systems, as well as delivering the expected value to customers. Inventory items are assets that must be protected from spoilage, contamination, pilferage, and waste.

The food service operation's equipment represents a substantial investment. Equipment selection is important to a food safety program, as is the proper cleaning and maintenance of each piece of equipment. A food service operation's facilities also represent a sizable investment, and their design and layout have a great impact on the success of a food safety program.

A formalized program ensures a continuous effort toward better food safety. It guarantees that important points are not overlooked or forgotten in the course of daily operations and personnel changes. Naturally, a comprehensive program costs money. However, it provides an immediate payback to the food service operation by:

- Meeting guest expectations, upon which the operation's success (and everyone's job) depends.

- Protecting guest and staff health, thereby reducing staff member absences.

- Reducing the operation's liability for accidents, injuries, or deaths.

- Increasing the useful life of the operation's facilities and equipment.

- Increasing the effectiveness and reducing the cost of cleaning procedures with the proper use of chemicals.

- Reducing the risks associated with the storage and application of toxic chemicals by standardizing products and procedures.

- Simplifying supervision with the use of checklists.

- Eliminating product waste and simplifying work methods through the use of written cleaning procedures.

- Establishing management objectives which can be used to measure the progress of the food service operation toward reducing risks.

- Providing an acceptable return on investment for the owners of the food service operation.

- Reducing the risks of operating a food service operation.

As this list of benefits indicates, a comprehensive food safety program does not cost as much as it pays. However, the return on this investment depends on how well management communicates the food safety standards and how well everyone performs to uphold these standards. Management must make food safety part of daily operations and make all staff members aware of its importance.

The HACCP system is prevention-based. It is designed to prevent potential food safety problems. Risks are reduced by, first, assessing the risks of a product or food production process, and, second, determining the steps that must be taken to control these risks.

The HACCP system identifies and monitors specific foodborne hazards. The hazard analysis establishes critical control points, which identify those points in the process that must be controlled to ensure food safety. In addition, critical limits are established that document the appropriate parameters that must be met at each CCP. CCPs are monitored and verified in subsequent steps to ensure that risks are controlled. All of this information is specified in the HACCP plan.

HACCP plans must include process flow diagrams, product formulations, training plans, a corrective action plan, and a verification plan. These HACCP plans enable food managers and staff members to assess whether the food service operation has a system of controls that will sufficiently ensure safety of the products. The plan must include enough detail to facilitate staff members' and management's understanding of the operation and the intended controls.

When used properly, HACCP is an important food safety tool. The key to success is staff member training. For each of the food safety steps they affect, staff members must know which control points are critical and what the critical limits are at these points. Management must routinely follow up to verify that all staff members are controlling the process by complying with the critical limits.

HACCP is a system of preventive controls that effectively and efficiently ensures that food products are safe in a food service operation. It emphasizes the food service operator's role in continuous improvement: rather than relying only on periodic facility inspections by regulatory agencies to point out deficiencies, food service operations should engage in ongoing problem solving and prevention. HACCP clearly identifies the food service operation as the final entity responsible for ensuring the safety of the food it sells. It requires the food service operation to analyze its preparation methods in a rational, scientific manner to identify CCPs, and holds it responsible for maintaining records that document adherence to the critical limits related to these CCPs. This results in continuous self-inspection.

A food service operation's use of HACCP requires development of a plan to prepare safe food. The plan must be shared with the regulatory agency, which must have access to CCP monitoring records and other data necessary to verify that the HACCP plan is working. With conventional inspection techniques, a regulatory agency can only determine conditions that exist during the time of the inspection. However, both current and past conditions can be determined when a HACCP approach is used. Therefore, the regulatory agency can more effectively ensure that processes are under control. The HACCP approach to ensuring food safety is preventative, while traditional inspection is reactive.

In the hazard analysis step, management must answer a series of questions for each control point in the food service process flow diagram. The questions are listed in Exhibit 6. Once these questions are answered, preventive measures (which may be physical or chemical) can be taken to control hazards. For example, inspecting purchased food products carefully during receiving is a physical preventive measure.

Recall that a **critical control point** is a step or procedure at which control can be applied and a food safety hazard prevented, eliminated, or reduced to acceptable levels. Some CCPs are cooking, chilling, product formulation (recipe) control, prevention of cross-contamination, and certain aspects of environmental and staff member hygiene. While there may be many control points in a food service process, few may be critical control points.

Monitoring includes a planned sequence of measurements or observations taken to ascertain whether a CCP is under control. Monitoring procedures establish an accurate record for future verification. Monitoring procedures should: (1) track the food service system's operation so that a trend toward a loss of control can be identified and corrective action taken to bring the process back into control before a deviation occurs; (2) indicate when a loss of control and a deviation have actually occurred, and corrective action must be taken; and (3) provide written documentation for use in verification of the HACCP plan.

Although some say that practice makes perfect, perfection is rarely achieved. A corrective action plan determines the disposition of any food produced while a deviation is occurring, corrects the cause of the deviation and ensures that the CCP is under control, and maintains records of corrective action. Specific corrective action plans are required for each CCP. Corrective action procedures should be well documented in the HACCP plan. When a deviation occurs and is corrected, more frequent monitoring may be temporarily required to ensure that it has indeed been corrected.

The first phase of the verification process involves the scientific or technical verification that critical limits at CCPs are satisfactory. This can be complex and may require outside expert help. The second phase of verification ensures that the HACCP plan is functioning effectively. This involves frequent reviews of the HACCP plan, verification that the plan is correctly followed, review of CCP records, and determination that appropriate risk-management decisions and product dispositions are made when production deviations occur. The third phase comprises documented periodic revalidations, independent of audits. The revalidations are performed by the HACCP team. The fourth phase is verification by the regulatory authority.

Exhibit 6   Questions For Hazard Analysis

1. **Ingredients**
   - Does the food contain any sensitive ingredients that are likely to present microbiological hazards (e.g., *Salmonella, Staphylococcus aureus*), chemical hazards (e.g., aflatoxin, antibiotic, or pesticide residues), or physical hazards (stones, glass, bone, metal)?

2. **Intrinsic factors of food**

   Physical characteristics and composition (e.g., pH, type of acids, fermentable carbohydrate, a_w, preservatives) of the food during and after the process can cause or prevent a hazard.
   - Which intrinsic factors of the food must be controlled to ensure food safety?
   - Does the food allow survival or multiplication of pathogens and/or toxin formation before or during the process?
   - Will the food allow survival or multiplication of pathogens and/or toxin formation during subsequent control points, including storage or consumer possession?
   - Are there similar products in the marketplace? What has been the safety record for these products?

3. **Procedures used for the process**
   - Does the procedure or process include a controllable step that destroys pathogens or their toxins? Consider both vegetative cells and spores.
   - Is the product subject to recontamination between production (e.g., cooking) and packaging?

4. **Microbial content of the food**
   - Is the food commercially sterile (i.e., low acid, canned food)?
   - Is it likely that the food will contain viable spore-forming or nonspore-forming pathogens?
   - What is the normal microbial content of the food stored under proper conditions?
   - Does the microbial population change during the time the food is stored before consumption?
   - Does that change in microbial population alter the safety of the food?

5. **Facility design**
   - Does the layout of the facility provide an adequate separation of raw materials from ready-to-eat foods?
   - Is positive air pressure maintained in product packaging areas? Is this essential for product safety?
   - Is the traffic pattern for people and moving equipment a potentially significant source of contamination?

6. **Equipment design**
   - Will the equipment provide the time/temperature control that is necessary for safe food?
   - Is the equipment properly sized for the volume of food that will be prepared?
   - Can the equipment be sufficiently controlled so that the variation in performance will be within the tolerances required to produce a safe food?
   - Is the equipment reliable or is it prone to frequent breakdowns?
   - Is the equipment designed so that it can be cleaned and sanitized?
   - Is there a chance for product contamination with hazardous substances, e.g., glass?
   - What product safety devices such as time/temperature integrators are used to enhance consumer safety?

Exhibit 6 *(continued)*

---

7. Packaging

- Does the method of packaging affect the multiplication of microbial pathogens and/or the formation of toxins?
- Is the packaging material resistant to damage, thereby preventing the entrance of microbial contamination?
- Is the package clearly labeled "Keep Refrigerated" if this is required for safety?
- Does the package include instructions for the safe handling and preparation of the food by the consumer?
- Are tamper-evident packaging features used?
- Is each package legibly and accurately coded to indicate production lot?
- Does each package contain the proper label?

8. Sanitation

- Can the sanitation practices that are employed adversely affect the safety of the food that is being produced?
- Can the facility be cleaned and sanitized to permit the safe handling of food?
- Is it possible to provide sanitary conditions consistently and adequately to ensure safe foods?

9. Staff member health, hygiene, and education

- Can staff member health or personal hygiene practices adversely affect the safety of the food being produced?
- Does the staff understand the food production process and the factors it must control to ensure safe foods?
- Will the staff inform management of a problem that could negatively affect food safety?

10. Conditions of storage between packaging and the consumer

- What is the likelihood that the food will be improperly stored at the wrong temperature?
- Would storage at improper temperatures lead to a microbiologically unsafe food?

11. Intended use

- Will the food be heated by the consumer?
- Will there likely be leftovers?

12. Intended consumer

- Is the food intended for the general public, i.e., a population that does not have an increased risk of becoming ill?
- Is the food intended for consumption by a population with increased susceptibility to illness (e.g., infants, the elderly, the infirm, and immunocompromised individuals)?

Source: Ronald F. Cichy, *Food Safety: Managing the HACCP Process* (Lansing, Mich.: Educational Institute of the American Hotel & Lodging Association, 2004), p. 17.

The preparation and maintenance of the written HACCP plan is the responsibility of the food service operation's managers. The plan must detail hazards, identify CCPs and critical limits, specify CCP monitoring and recordkeeping procedures, and outline the implementation strategy.

The food service operations with the highest risks are targeted for inspection by regulatory authorities, based on the type of food served, the process flow the foods require, the volume of food produced and served, the population served, and the operation's previous compliance history. All of these variables can affect the probability of a foodborne illness outbreak in a food service operation.

The HACCP inspection views a food service operation and its control points as a total process by identifying CCPs in an attempt to prevent food safety hazards. Regulatory agencies may take individual program, personnel, operation, and jurisdiction differences into account when establishing procedures for assigning food service operations and preparing for and conducting inspections.

The menu and the food product flow are the places to start the review for the HACCP inspection. A complete process flow diagram should be reviewed by the regulatory authorities, even though only a portion of the steps will take place during the inspection. The focus during the inspection must be, first and foremost, the food.

The sources of food, storage practices, and process flow steps all should be noted. Risk assessment data guide the allocation of time and focus during the inspection. Complex, higher-risk food processes that involve multiple ingredients, potentially hazardous foods, long holding times, foods to be cooled, and reheating steps should be given a high priority. Foods that have been implicated in foodborne illness should receive high priority, too. Other high risk indicators are foods prepared in large volumes and those requiring manual assembly and manipulation during preparation or portioning.

Conclusion

Purchasing can be risky if menu planning is haphazard and the objectives of purchasing are not clearly understood. The risks can be reduced if the purchaser is armed with knowledge about the food service operation's:

*   Quality, food safety, and cost standards.

*   Food production methods.

*   Purchasing procedures.

*   Distributors.

Knowledge of quality, food safety, and cost control standards is most important. Jeopardizing the operation's food safety risk management program in order to save a few dollars on the purchase price can be a very costly mistake. Similarly, to compromise the food service operation's quality standards is to risk losing guests. The buyer must strike a balance between these types of control, all of which determine the value the guest receives, the overall satisfaction with the guest experience, and the success of the food service operation.

The buyer must know purchasing procedures to operate efficiently. A planned, organized system—complete with written product specifications, purchase orders, and product evaluation forms—increases the buyer's control. By carefully reviewing issuing records, the buyer can help establish par stocks (minimum quantities) for each product the operation should have on hand. This helps eliminate costly stockouts. An operation cannot negotiate either price or quality, or substantially affect value in positive ways, when it always buys at the last minute.

Knowledge of distributors and competitors completes the purchasing success formula. Distributors can be a valuable source of market formation. They can assist the operation in solving yield, food safety, quality, and cost problems. Successful food service operations are also not afraid to develop reciprocal supply loan relationships with competitors; such relationships are usually beneficial.

Endnotes

1. Readers interested in a more detailed description of the HACCP process should consult Ronald F. Cichy, *Food Safety: Managing the HACCP Process* (Lansing, Mich.: Educational Institute of the American Hotel & Lodging Association), 2004.

Key Terms

bars, taverns, and lounges—Operations that offer alcoholic beverages, but typically have limited or no food services.

business/industry organizations—Organizations in which food service options range from vended services in manufacturing plants to gourmet dining facilities in the executive dining rooms of large banks, insurance companies, and other businesses.

caterers—Operations that provide service for large or small banquet functions and may provide service on or off site.

chain restaurants—Food service operations that are part of a multi-unit organization.

cleaning and maintenance—The final control point in the food service process flow. It is intimately related to every other basic operating activity.

comment cards—A way to identify customer requirements that involves giving customers an opportunity to respond to an open-ended question.

commercial food service operations—Operations that seek to maximize profits through the sale of food and beverages.

control point—One of a food service operation's basic operating activites. Each control point is a miniature system with its own recognizable structure and function.

cooking—The control point at which heat is applied to food in order to change its color, odor, texture, taste, appearance, and nutritional value.

critical control point—A step or procedure at which control can be applied and a food safety hazard prevented, eliminated, or reduced to acceptable levels.

dynamic menus—Menus that may vary with seasonal availability of raw ingredients, the number and kinds of courses offered, the potential to use leftovers and local ingredients, the operation's image, and the demands of its target markets.

economic factors—Ingredient costs and potential profitability of new menu items.

educational institutions—Part of the noncommercial food service segment that includes public and private elementary and secondary schools, and post-secondary institutions.

equipment—A food service resource that includes the large variety of utensils and other items needed in an operation.

external factors—Factors outside the food service operation that influence menu changes, including guest requirements, economic factors, the competition, supply levels, and industry trends.

facilities—A food service operation resource that houses the food and beverage experience for both internal and external customers.

family-service operations—Operations that offer comfort foods in a relaxed setting, typically without the availability of alcoholic beverages.

focus group—A group of potential customers assembled to discuss their perceptions of value and quality, opportunities for process improvements, products and services, and other relevant topics.

forecasting—Attempting to predict the future by gathering data, examining past history, assessing current and expected events, and converting.

franchisee—The owner of a specific outlet in a food service franchise.

franchises—A special category of chain operations in which a franchisee pays fees to a franchisor in exchange for the right to use the name, building design, and business methods of the franchisor.

franchisor—The party that owns the name, building design, and business methods in a franchise agreement.

freestanding eating and drinking places—Commercial food service operations that include independent operations, chain operations, and franchises.

Hazard Analysis and Critical Control Point (HACCP) system—A program to establish and monitor food safety controls for people, products, equipment, and inventory.

hazard analysis—The process used to establish critical control points in a HACCP system.

healthcare facilities—An important part of the noncommercial food service segment. Operations may be privately owned or managed by government agencies.

holding—The control point at which menu items are held at hot or cold temperatures.

independent operation—A food service operation that is owned by an owner or owners who have one or more operations that have no chain relationship.

internal customers—Staff members who directly represent the food service operation to external customers.

internal factors—Factors directly related to the food service operation that influence menu changes, including the operation's meal pattern, concept and theme, operational system, and menu mix.

inventory—A food service resource that centers around the items required to produce the products that a food service operation sells.

issuing—The control point at which food products are released from storage.

leisure and recreation facilities—Part of the noncommercial food service segment that includes theme parks, national and state parks, sports arenas and stadiums, race tracks, drive-in movie theaters, bowling centers, summer camps, and hunting lodges.

lodging food service operations—Operations found in lodging properties that may include coffee shops, fine dining, family restaurants, or specialty restaurants.

managed services operations—Noncommercial food service operations that are run by private management companies.

menu planning—The initial control point in a food service system.

menu rationalization—Creation of a simplified, balanced menu for the sake of operational efficiency and guest satisfaction.

noncommercial food service operations—Operations that exist in organizations for which providing food and beverage service is not the primary mission. These operations often seek to minimize expenses while focusing on providing nutritious meals.

on-site food service operations—Noncommercial food service operations located within institutions such as businesses, hospitals, or schools.

people—A food service operation's most important resource. An operation's people are ultimately responsible for delivering value to customers.

potential cost analysis—A cost breakdown of each menu item served at each meal period.

preparing—The control point that includes the series of activities performed on food products before cooking.

private clubs—Part of the noncommercial food service segment that includes country (golf) clubs, city clubs, athletic clubs, and military, tennis, and yacht clubs.

process flow—The series of basic operating activities or control points involved in running a food service operation.

public cafeterias—Operations that offer a wide variety of menu items, but limited table service.

purchasing—The control point that is important for maintaining the value and quality of products, minimizing the investment in inventory, and strengthening an operation's competitive position.

quick-service restaurants—Operations that offer fast counter service with a limited variety of menu options.

receiving—The control point at which an operation assumes ownership of the products it has purchased.

secret shoppers—Individuals who pose as customers and experience the entire service process, including products, and file a detailed report.

serving—The control point at which finished menu items are physically transferred from the production department to guests.

shopping the competition—A way to identify customer requirements by finding out what competitors offer to appeal to customers.

storing—The control point at which an operation strives to prevent deterioration and theft of food products before their use.

surveys—A more formal way to identify customer requirements. Surveys usually include specific questions about food and beverage quality, service quality, what pleased the customer overall, what the customer would have liked to experience differently overall, and problems that occurred during the experience.

 Review Questions ————————————————————————————

1. What are the food service segments?

2. How can the different structures of food service organizations be described?

3. What are the essential elements in the food service process flow (from menu planning to cleaning and maintenance)?

4. What are the unique characteristics of the purchasing control point?

5. What are customer requirements as they relate to lifestyle changes and healthier fare?

6. How do internal customers create and deliver value through purchasing?

7. How can information on customer requirements be obtained?

8. What are the internal and external factors that may affect a menu change?

9. How does forecasting help the food service operator predict the future?

10. What are some common purchasing mistakes and how can they be avoided?

11. What is HACCP, and how is it related to ensuring food safety during purchasing?

 References ————————————————————————————————

Anonymous. "Return Performance Report for 150 Top B&I Units." *Foodservice Director* (May 15, 2005).

Anonymous. "Performance Report for Top Self-Op Hospitals." *Foodservice Director* (June 15, 2005).

Anonymous. "Performance Report for Top Contracted Hospitals." *Foodservice Director* (June 15, 2005).

Anonymous. "Performance Report for 75 Long-Term Care Chains." *Foodservice Director* (July 15, 2005).

Anonymous. "2005 Full Service Restaurant Consumer Research Study." *Restaurant Hospitality* (July 2005).

Brumback, Nancy. "Heyday's Over: American Casual Dining Trends Segment Report." *Restaurant Business* (September 15, 2005).

Cichy, Ronald F. *Food Safety: Managing the HACCP Process.* Lansing, Mich.: Educational Institute of the American Hotel & Lodging Association, 2004.

Colchamiro, Jeff. "Food on Demand." *Lodging* (May 2006).

"Food Management's 2005 Top 50 Management Companies." *Food Management* 40, no. 10. (September 2005): 42–50.

Halperin, Mark. "Chefs' Survey Summary: Fingers to the Wind, Hands in the Dough, Chefs Offer Takes on Trends Worth Watching in Years Ahead." Center for Culinary Development.

Horovitz, Bruce. "Restaurant Sales Climb with Bad-For-You Food." *USA Today* (May 12, 2005).

Keates, Nancy. "Strange Brews." *The Wall Street Journal* (July 8, 2005): 1.

Kim, Katharine and Chrissy Shott. "Industry Outlook Remains Positive Despite Moderate Decline in Restaurant Performance Index." National Restaurant Association. May 31, 2006. Available on-line at www.restaurant.org/press room/print/index.cfm?ID=1272.

Krummert, Bob. "A Lucky Strike For Full Service." *Restaurant Hospitality* (April 2005).

Marshall, Erika and Annika Stennson. "New Restaurant Nutrition Web Site 'HealthyDiningFinder.com' Provides Opportunities for Restaurants to Grow Guest Base." National Restaurant Association. February 6, 2006.

"Nation's Restaurant News Top 100 Report." *Nation's Restaurant News* (June 27, 2005).

Ninemeier, Jack D. *Planning and Control for Food and Beverage Operations,* 6th Ed. Lansing, Mich.: Educational Institute of the American Hotel & Lodging Association, 2004.

Purcell, Denise. "Comfort Foods: Soothing the Soul, Filling the Cash Register." *Specialty Food* (July 2005).

Ramseyer, Rick. "Sans Sprouts: Healthy Concepts Segment Report." *Restaurant Business* (August 15, 2005).

"Restaurant Industry 2005 Fact Sheet." Chicago: National Restaurant Association, 2005.

"Restaurant Industry Food-and-Drink Sales Projected through 2004 Report." *National Restaurant Association Executive Summary.* Washington, D.C.: National Restaurant Association, 2004.

"Restaurants & Institutions Top 400 Report." *Restaurants & Institutions* (July 1, 2005).

Riell, Howard. "Menu Trends." *The Consultant.* Foodservice Consultants Society International. Bonus Issue 2004.

Technomic Top 500 Chain Restaurant Report 2006. Chicago: Technomic Information Services, 2006.

Technomic 2004 Power Distributors. Chicago: Technomic Information Services, 2004.

Wahlgren, Eric. "That's Entertainment." *Business Week Online* (June 2, 2005).

Internet Sites

For more information, visit the following Internet sites. Remember that Internet address can change without notice. If the site is no longer there, you can use a search engine to look for additional sites.

American Culinary Federation
www.acfchefs.org

American Dietetics Association
www.eatright.org

Food Service Director
www.fsdmag.com

Nation's Restaurant News
www.nrn.com

National Association of College &
  University Food Services
www.nacufs.org

National Restaurant Association
www.restaurant.org

National Restaurant Association
  SmartBrief
www.smartbrief.com/nra

Restaurant Business
www.restaurantbiz.com

Restaurants & Institutions
www.rimag.com

Chapter 3 Outline

Competencies

3

Purchasing Systems and Personnel

PURCHASING MAKES A DIRECT CONTRIBUTION to the quality created and delivered throughout the entire food service operation. After the menu is set, purchasing is the next control point that permits the people of the operation to ultimately meet the requirements of the operation's customers, guests, or members.

There are a number of skills, knowledge, and behaviors required if purchasing staff members are to be effective. Ethical guidelines are required as beacons for behaviors and guideposts for actions. In order to build an effective purchasing system, the market, the distributor's role, and internal market research must be understood. For example, group purchasing can help the operation maximize value.

Both management and leadership are required in the purchasing system. Purchase specifications help achieve control of purchasing systems and clearly communicate requirements to distributors. Pricing, cost controls, payment policies and ordering procedures must be understood by the food service operator. Security in a food service operation is more important today than in the past and will be even more essential in the future.

How Purchasing Contributes to Managing for Quality

Quality is simply doing the right thing right. Doing the right thing is effectiveness. Doing things right is efficiency. Quality, then, has elements of both effectiveness and efficiency. But how do we know what "things" to choose? With the many possible areas for focus, how is it possible to select those that will really make a difference in managing for quality?

Managing for Quality

The answer lies in a clear identification of customers and their requirements. We have already established that there are two broad categories of customers: internal and external. **Internal customers** are the operation's staff members. They include managers and line-level staff. **External customers** are those who bring their time and money to the operation to purchase the products and services that the operation offers for sale. External customers are called guests at lodging properties, members at private clubs, and patients in healthcare facilities. Other customers include distributors, who may act as partners in the food service operation's

Exhibit 1   Managing for Quality in a Food Service Operation

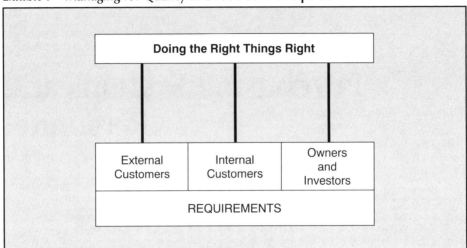

continuous improvement process. Continuous improvement (CI) means doing whatever you are doing a little better each time.

Managers must also consider financial requirements tied to the owners and investors in the operation. Without their investment of time and funds, the food service operation would not exist or be able to meet the requirements of internal and external customers.

A model of managing for quality is presented in Exhibit 1. Note that the requirements of internal customers, external customers and owners/investors form the foundation of the model. Internal customers are at the center, the core, of the model. If internal customers are selected, oriented, and trained to create and deliver the products and services that external customers and other internal customers require, requirements of owners and investors are most likely to be met. Together, these groups support the focus on managing for quality (i.e., doing the right things right).

Where does purchasing fit into this model? Purchasing is a strategic set of processes and related tactics that are designed to ensure that products, supplies, and services at least meet the requirements. Once the requirements are clearly understood, purchasing personnel can set out to fulfill needs, wants, and expectations by obtaining the required products, services, and supplies. If there is a difference between what is produced and what is required, purchasing staff can also help identify what the difference costs and what actions can be taken to reduce or eliminate or reduce the difference. This will move toward meeting the requirements.

The Purchasing Process

The **purchasing process** can be viewed as a series of related activities as illustrated in Exhibit 2. The process in Exhibit 2 is a way to view every step required for purchasing in a sequence starting at the beginning. The process illustrated in

Exhibit 2   The Purchasing Process

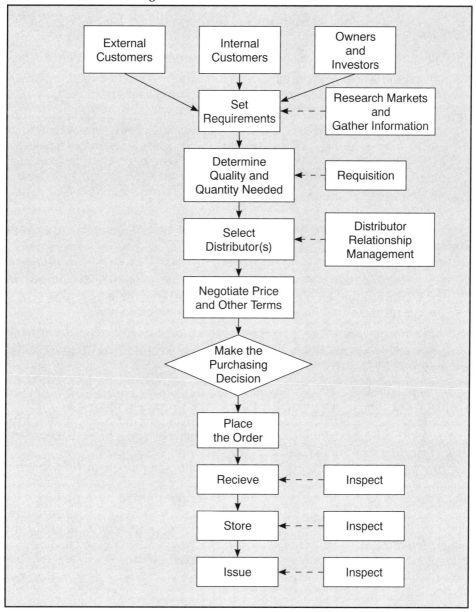

Exhibit 2 is the order in which all the steps would take place if everything went according to plan. By using this process flow as a template, deviations from the plan can be identified and action can be taken to correct the process and put it back on course.

Notice that the purchasing cycle involves the following activities:

1. The chef in the food department and the bartender (or bar manager) in the beverage department complete an issue requisition when items are needed.

2. The storeroom responds by issuing required products to the user department.

3. When products in inventory reach a predetermined reorder point, the storeroom forwards a purchase requisition to the purchasing department.

4. The purchasing department orders required products from the proper distributor, perhaps using a purchase order or a purchase record. Increasingly, food service operators place orders with distributors using e-commerce (business-to-business) technology. Purchasing personnel send or transmit the purchase order or purchase record information to the receiving and accounting departments. (Purchase orders, purchase records, and e-purchasing procedures are discussed later in this chapter.)

5. The distributor delivers the products to the receiving department along with a delivery invoice.

6. The receiving clerk places products in the storeroom and forwards the delivery invoice, perhaps with other documents, to the accounting department. In some properties, these documents, are reviewed by the food and beverage management staff before being routed to accounting personnel.

7. After further processing of necessary documents, accounting department personnel send payment to the distributor and file copies of the purchasing/receiving forms for accounting and control purposes.

This purchasing cycle is repeated every time products are ordered. You can see that purchasing is more than "picking up the phone and placing an order." It is a complex cycle of activities requiring special planning and control procedures that create an audit trail (a series of records, documents, and reports that trace the flow of resources through a food service operation).

The purchasing process begins with input about requirements from internal customers, external customers, distributors, and owners/investors. These requirements encompass the needs, wants, and expectations of the three groups, with the added expertise of the distributor, and should be met, if not exceeded. Sometimes input from external customers takes precedence in setting requirements (when determining which grade of steaks customers are willing to purchase, for example). Sometimes input from internal customers governs setting the requirements, such as choosing dining-room uniforms based on both comfort and ease of laundering. Sometimes the distributor provides valuable information about customer preferences and trends in the market. In still other cases, requirements are determined by owners (the amount to spend on a new oven for the kitchen, for example). Usually, there is a balance among the three groups and the distributor in setting requirements. When requirements are being set, purchasing staff can assist by researching markets, investigating new products, reporting changing market conditions, and gathering other information so that decision makers can make the right choices.

The next step in the process is to determine the quality and quantity needed for each product, service, and supply. Quality is determined by the precise definitions developed for the requirements. Quantity is determined by assessing the amounts of products and supplies in inventory and comparing these to the forecasted usage levels. Quality for services is best approached by deciding which level of services best meet requirements. Quality and quantity requirements are best presented in a purchase specification. One of the tools that is useful for determining quantity is a requisition from a staff member indicating the need to order additional inventory.

Once the quality and quantity needed are determined, the next step in the process is to select a distributor or distributors. These sources for products, services, and supplies delivered to the food service operation are selected based on quality, service, value, and price. It is critical to practice distributor relationship management in the spirit of a partnership that is beneficial to both organizations.

Negotiating price and other terms is the next step in the process after the distributor has been selected. Paying the lowest price is the goal, provided the product fulfills the quality, quantity, service, and value requirements detailed in the purchase specification. Other terms to be negotiated may include delivery times, payment terms, and value-added services (such as promotional materials for a new menu item).

The next step is indicated as a diamond rather than a rectangle because it represents a decision. Making the purchasing decision requires careful analysis of all available information. When the decision is made, an order is placed with the distributor detailing all that is required. This is also the step at which an agreement on payment terms should be reached. Sometimes an order is placed electronically, sometimes it is placed via facsimile machine, and sometimes it is placed face-to-face with the distributor's sales representative.

When the order is fulfilled in the distributor's warehouse and loaded on the distributor's truck, it is transported to the food service operation. Even though transportation is not pictured on the purchasing process flow diagram, it is a critical control point for the distributor at which products should be carefully handled from the standpoint of food safety and food security. Of course, this also applies to beverage products.

One of three necessary inspections takes place when products and supplies are delivered to a food service operation's receiving area. In the receiving, storing, and issuing steps, the assessment is in terms of quality and quantity *as specified*. During receiving, the agreed upon price is also checked. Once products and supplies are received at the food service operation, ownership is transferred from the distributor to the operator. Any problems that may be present in the products or supplies are now owned by the operator, so a detailed inspection makes good business sense. Soon after products and supplies are received, they must be properly stored.

During storing, products should be monitored regularly to determine that quality is being maintained at acceptable levels. Storage areas are frequently locked to guard against losses in quantity due to theft, and to reduce or eliminate food security risks.

An overarching part of the purchasing process is the maintenance of necessary records. The HACCP process has a set of recordkeeping requirements. These make good business sense because they reduce risks. Other records, including orders placed with each distributor, stockouts, and adherence to specifications, may be also useful. The recordkeeping process has been made more manageable through the use of computer technology in food service operations.

The idea behind presenting purchasing as a process is so that those responsible for purchasing in a food service operation can understand the importance of managing the overall process, rather than individual products. It is essential that requirements are clearly defined so that specifications can be accurately written. Then it becomes a matter of using the specifications to communicate the initial requirements so that the final requirements will be met for the customer, guest, or member. It is impossible to obtain the desired quality in a product unless the required quality was first specified. While it is always possible to take an acceptable product and make it worse due to careless handling, it is never possible to take an unacceptable product and make it better and acceptable to the customer.

Role of Department Managers. In the past, mid-size and large hotels had specific departments to identify manufacturers and distributors, create product specifications, and purchase food and beverage products, supplies, and services. Today and in the future, department managers will be required to perform many of these activities as operations contain costs, downsize, and require managers to multi-task.

What can be done to contribute to the effectiveness and efficiency of the purchasing process as these changes take place? Some managers are creating partnerships with distributors. In many cases, these relationships are at the department level with the executive chef creating a partnership with one set of distributors and the director of housekeeping developing a partnership with another group of distributors who better help meet the housekeeping department's needs and expectations. This department-by-department purchasing process helps strengthen relationships, control budgets, and may help in emergencies when products are needed on short notice.

In hotels that are clustered by brand in one geographical area, there is value to working together in the purchasing process. In some cases, these hotels participate in group purchasing. Working together in the cluster helps department managers stay in tune with new ideas and trends, purchase together regional products at a cost savings due to volume, improve quality for the same cost, and maximize efficiency. Clusters of freestanding and on-site food services could also benefit from group purchasing.

Preparation. Preparation is a key in managing the purchasing process, just as in any activity in a food service operation that is of strategic importance. Think about it this way: if you are meeting face-to-face with a distributor's sales representative, that individual is prepared with market and industry facts and trends, information about the products and supplies available, options for the purchasing of services, and the ability to provide value-added services. In order for the person responsible for purchasing to add value to the process, that individual must be similarly prepared.

If a new product or service is being added to the food service operation, a timeline for implementation and rollout is part of the preparation. Carefully defining requirements is also part of the preparation. Consider the array of internal customers that may need to provide input prior to purchasing software. Included will be the users of the software, internal customers in accounting or bookkeeping, general management, and others possibly affected by the purchase. Having their input before the salesperson arrives is part of the preparation.

Preparation also includes a checklist of the questions to be answered by the distributor's sales representative. Additional preparation involves concerns about cost savings, the proposed budget for the software, and the possible need to add hardware to accommodate the software purchase.

Scripted Demos. As an additional way to make the purchasing process more efficient and effective, **scripted demos** have been utilized for focusing and controlling distributor presentations. While the example presented is for a technology system, it can apply to other services, products, and supplies during the purchasing process.

The product purchased must meet the requirements of the operation and its customers, fit within budgets, generate cost savings, and provide years of reliable service to the food service operation. These are the four starting assumptions for scripted demos. Once these are understood and determined, then the purchasing process includes the following steps:

- Focus on system capabilities that apply directly to current and future transactions.

- Control the details of the purchasing process.

- Direct distributor presentations so that competing distributors' systems process identical data.

- Involve many people in the definition of system requirements.

Focusing on the system capabilities helps to ensure that the system will be selected to fit the operation, rather than having to change the operation to fit the system. The details include a written purchase specification, as well as a timeline. The timeline assists management in maintaining food service operations while testing the responsiveness of the system.

Processing identical data for competing systems is essential so processing technique differences can be compared. Rather than highlighting technological features, require distributors to focus on data processing capabilities involving many kinds of data. This should result in better selection and acceptance of a new system.

While scripted demos can readily be applied to technology, they also apply to the comparison of two different distributors who are competing to supply the operation with any number of food and beverage products, as well as services. The same four process steps could be altered to fit the specifics of each situation. They assist the people responsible for purchasing in making objective decisions.

Determining Value in the Purchasing Process. Value in the purchasing process can be described generally in terms of the quality, service, and price requirements, or by utilizing specific elements of each. For example, a distributor is more valuable to a food service operator if the distributor's sales representatives understand the growing sophistication of the operator's customers. Both quality and service are enhanced for the operator and the operator's customers when the distributor's representatives suggest innovative and appropriate menu items.

In terms of price, many food service operators have moved away from prices simply quoted based on volume and even simple cost-plus pricing contracts. Today's more knowledgeable food service operator should know to inquire about the distributor's landed costs and net costs, as well as marketing and promotion programs available from manufacturers. Landed costs include the cost of the product plus related costs, such as transportation, port charges/import fees, inspection fees, and foreign exchange conversion (if applicable). Net costs are the final costs to a distributor, including all rebates and allowances from the manufacturer.

Both operators and distributors are concerned with operational efficiencies and potential cost savings. Distributors are constantly monitoring and trying to find ways to reduce warehousing and logistics (including transportation) costs and the cost of their products and services. Operators are searching for ways to save labor, reduce food costs, achieve better portion control, apply new technology, and squeeze a bigger bottom line out of the budget.

Consolidation has also affected value as fewer larger corporate distributors dominate the market. There are fewer choices of regional and local distributors who are strong and independent. As consolidation has progressed in distribution, there has been a focus on increasing order and drop sizes, becoming a "prime distributor" for major food service accounts, and offering segment-specific (e.g., products used in quick-service restaurants) products and services.

Skills, Knowledge, and Behaviors Required in Purchasing Personnel

Large operations may still have a separate staff dedicated to the purchasing process. Increasingly, however, even in medium-sized and larger food service operations, department managers are doing the work that was once done by purchasing staff. In an entrepreneurial operation, the owner is usually involved in all purchasing decisions, depending on the operation's size and purchasing volume. The skills, knowledge, and behaviors presented in this section, then, do not just apply to purchasing personnel, but they are necessary in anyone who has a substantial role to play in the purchasing process.

Recruitment and Selection

Recruitment is designed to develop a pool of qualified candidates. Purchasing personnel function in several roles. The focus of some of their roles has become more strategic and less transactional, particularly in larger food service operations and in chains. Ideally, the operation wants to recruit a candidate who has expertise in food service operations as well as food service purchasing, has a global awareness of purchasing, has the ability to work well with other departments and organizations, understands business processes and systems, knows how technology can help the purchasing process become more efficient and effective, and can learn quickly and adapt to inevitable changes.

Selection is designed to choose the best candidate from the pool that has been recruited. Selection of purchasing personnel is frequently based upon educational background, process expertise, an understanding of the business, global awareness, understanding of technology, communication skills, analytical and math skills, and the ability to learn quickly. When the individual is carefully and thoughtfully selected, it helps avoid unnecessary turnover.

Educational Background. Some food service organizations look for purchasing personnel with at least some formal training in food service purchasing or business management. For a smaller operation, perhaps a single course in food service purchasing would be sufficient. Other operations will require an associate's or two-year degree, a bachelor's or four-year degree, or perhaps even a master's degree, depending on the complexity of the position requirements.

It is always desirable for staff to continue their education and professional development beyond the classroom. An ideal way to do so is through a trade association such as the American Hotel & Lodging Educational Institute. This nonprofit educational foundation has a variety of independent learning and group study courses, as well as professional certifications. The Institute's Web site has many resources for food service professionals (see Exhibit 3).

Health screening tests, contacts with previous employers, and background checks by outside agencies may be required. Some food service operators require background checks to verify education and experience before selecting individuals. Some background checks cover the applicant's credit record, driving record, and police record. Other organizations sometimes require personality assessments in an attempt to determine how well the applicant "fits" with the overall culture of the organization and, specifically, with the purchasing department. Others believe attitude is a more important selection criterion than experience, since skills and knowledge can be learned in a training program, while it is difficult, if not impossible, to change a person's attitude or beliefs.

Process Expertise. It has already been established that purchasing must be viewed as a process, in a systemized fashion. By seeing purchasing as a process, it is possible to improve the efficiency and effectiveness of the process steps and the overall process.

Components of the process can be viewed as opportunities to add value to the operation. Informed contract negotiations will add value to the purchasing process, as will enhanced customer satisfaction through quality and service. Closer and more cooperative relationships with distributors in the form of distributor relationship management (DRM) is a necessary part of process expertise. New product design/selection can also enhance the process by reducing costs and improving quality and time to market to meet customers' requirements.

An additional part of process expertise is the ability to specify and then monitor HACCP as part of the overall food safety requirement. HACCP requires that food sources and distributors have a food safety process in place and are inspected and certified for compliance. More information about food safety appears later in this chapter.

Exhibit 3   Food Service Educational Resources

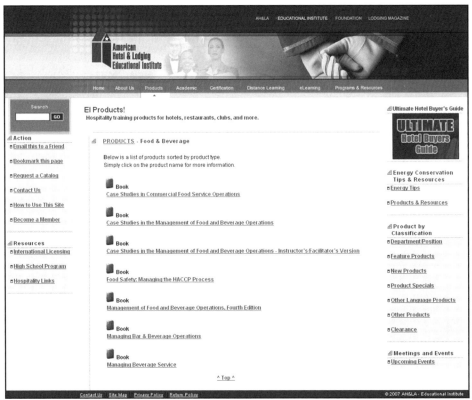

Source: www.ei-ahla.org/product_display2.asp?type=food.

A third example of process expertise is understanding the **logistics** of purchasing, particularly from the distributor's perspective. Logistics considers such issues as whether a food service operation is able to live with two drops (deliveries) per week or if it requires four drops. The size of the drops (larger drops are easier to make), physical condition and readiness of the food service operation's receiving area (cluttered and inaccessible vs. clean, organized, and easily accessible). Understanding process logistics from the distributor's point of view may result in the ability to obtain lower prices for purchases.

Understand the Business. Understanding the business of purchasing broadly includes developing a purchasing strategy, planning early and agreeing on requirements, recognizing purchasing contracts, understanding the food service distribution channel, regularly monitoring performance, and continuously improving. While negotiating the best prices in contracts and other purchasing agreements is essential, understanding the business also leads to the ability to coordinate the many details of the purchasing process with receiving, production, food safety, other operations, and technology personnel. Coordination with distributors is also important, so purchasing personnel must understand distribution from the distributor's perspective, including manufacturing, warehousing, logistics, transportation, and ways that each member in the food service distribution channel adds value.

Understanding the business includes knowing and being realistic about what can be expected when it comes to long-term pricing and supply guarantees (for produce and beef, for example) as commodity markets fluctuate. Perhaps the best that purchasing personnel can do in such markets is to be realistic and negotiate a fair cost-plus contract and honor the agreement when prices go down (a buyer's market) and when prices rise (a seller's market).

Purchasing personnel must also be realistic when contracts are being negotiated. Those who understand the business know that the lowest prices for daily drops at multiple locations are not possible unless the volume is sufficient to justify these extra costs for the distributor. When negotiating with manufacturers to obtain the lowest price, one could not realistically expect to also receive extensive merchandising and promotional support with that lowest price. When custom bid prices are received from manufacturers, it is not realistic to also expect rebates, group purchasing deals, and promotional discounts.

Global Awareness. The role of importers has become more prominent with purchasing personnel today as food service menus feature more international products in an attempt to be more competitive. With improved transportation and logistics, food and beverage products and supplies are readily available from around the world. It is critical that purchasing personnel understand the role that these global manufacturers, distributors, and importers play in the purchasing process. Purchasing personnel must understand how each of these members of the global food service distribution channel adds value and makes money so the transactions that occur end up being profitable for all involved. There is at least one other important part of global awareness, and that is the trend toward outsourcing the manufacturing of products and providing of services to other countries that can provide the products and services at a lower cost per unit. In some operations, this global outsourcing has resulted in virtual teams from around the world that maximize the design of the purchasing process for added value.

Information Technology. The opportunity to create virtual teams from around the globe linking individuals, groups, and departments, as well as distributors and operators, has been facilitated by advances in information technology (IT) systems. IT also helps distributors more rapidly complete the required information for bids and requests for proposals (RFPs). When tight time schedules compress the real time available to gather such bids and RFPs, on-line, Web-based technology can provide more rapid response, particularly from individuals who travel frequently and do not have much administrative support to develop traditional written bids or RFPs. IT is also increasingly being used to manage the details of product specifications, product data, and ordering. More IT applications here are certain to develop.

Communication Skills. One of the primary communication tools in the purchasing process is the purchase specification. This communication tool is designed to get away from treating all products as commodities. That is to say, if a specific manufacturer's brand of a product is specified but not available, it is best to avoid simply including the statement "or equivalent." While this statement may be required in some bid situations, it is always best to communicate exactly, in writing, what "or equivalent" means.

It is also a good idea when writing specifications to be as detailed as possible to ensure that the operation receives the product that customers require. In the case of United States Department of Agriculture (USDA) specifications for meat products, important considerations might be the amount of added water permitted, animals fed without the use of added antibiotics, and the use of binders and thickeners and other additions. Purchasing personnel are responsible for communicating, both in writing and verbally, requirements in the form of right products, supplies, and services; right quantities; right times; and right prices. All of this adds up to value for the food service operator.

Analytical and Math Abilities. Purchasing personnel are required to have basic math skills, including the ability to add and subtract, multiply and divide, and calculate percentages. These personnel are sometimes required to verify counts or calculate the cost per unit given the case price and the number of products (count) in the case. The use of a calculator and computer spreadsheet software is also required for purchasing personnel.

In some cases, purchasing personnel are required to conduct a total-cost evaluation that goes beyond simply calculating the cost of products. This calculation may include all or several of the elements of value in the channel and may also require analysis of cost-benefit and/or cash flow. Thinking analytically is a requirement for purchasing personnel.

Learn Quickly. Conditions in the food service distribution channel frequently change rapidly. To deal with these rapid changes and need for flexibility and adaptability, some larger chains have developed a "hard core/soft core" purchasing organization. The "hard core" is a centralized, small team of purchasing personnel who monitor the purchasing process, keep track of purchasing information systems, define and evaluate purchasing strategy, develop and build strategic relationship with members in the channel, and coordinate purchasing training and management development programs. The "hard core" is strategically focused and moves from project to project, transferring its strategic expertise.

The "soft core," on the other hand, is in specific departments and is responsible for operational purchasing, given the operational expertise and responsibilities of the "soft core." The "soft core" are specialists in their areas of responsibility and interact with the "hard core" when specific purchasing requirements are being developed, as well as in continuous improvement efforts at the departmental level. While a small food service entrepreneur probably will not be able to afford the infrastructure of a "hard core" and "soft core," it may be useful to think of what purchasing processes take place in light of the strategic vs. operational focus.

The skills, knowledge, and behaviors identified in effective purchasing personnel are necessary if the purchasing process is to add value for the food service operator. It is this blend of skills, knowledge, and behaviors that sets apart one food service operation from another and gives it a competitive advantage.

Exhibit 4   Activities of the Purchasing System

MANAGEMENT	LEADERSHIP
Develop, communicate, and enforce policies and procedures.	Develop and communicate values and philosophy.
Design, communicate, and implement procedures and tasks.	Manage systems and processes.
Organize and direct operations.	Monitor stakeholder requirements (expectations, needs, wants).
Control and measure results.	Support and develop people.
Foster consistency and stability.	Engage in continuous improvement.
Do things right.	Do the right things.

Source: Adapted from Ronald F. Cichy and Philip J. Hickey, Jr,. *Managing Food and Beverage Service,* 3d ed. (Lansing, Mich.: Educational Institute of the American Hotel & Lodging Association, 2005).

Management and Leadership Activities in Purchasing

Management is different than leadership, yet both sets of activities in the form of knowledge, skills, and behavior are essential in the purchasing system. The two sets of activities are contrasted in Exhibit 4.

Management activities include developing, communicating, and enforcing policies and procedures. These policies and procedures help ensure that the products, supplies, and services purchased meet the requirements of customers. Leadership activities are developing and communicating the values and philosophy within the operation's culture. Here the values and philosophy address ethics, quality, service, price, and value from the operator's perspective, keeping customer requirements in mind.

Management activities design, communicate, and implement procedures and tasks. An essential procedure is the use of purchase specifications that clearly communicate requirements. A task would be carefully checking deliveries during receiving to determine that they conform to the specifications. Leadership entails managing systems and processes. Examples of processes include purchasing and HACCP. When problems occur, the idea is not to fix blame on a person, but rather, to fix the process so the problem does not happen again.

Management is responsible for organizing and directing operations. Organization includes both human resources and inventory/facilities resources. Directing operations help the food service operation maximize efficiency. Leadership focuses on monitoring the needs, wants, and expectations of stakeholders. When leaders are knowledgeable of the requirements of internal customers, external customers, and owners/investors, they can meet needs, satisfy wants, and exceed expectations.

Managers control and measure results. This measurement is necessary because the metrics are going to tell the story of the results achieved. Each of the stakeholder groups, and individual stakeholders within a group, may have conflicting desired results; however, the outcomes must be balanced. Leaders support and develop people realizing that the purchasing system will only be as good as the managers, leaders, and staff members who are directly responsible for these activities. To support and develop these internal customers likewise supports and develops the purchasing system.

Managers foster consistency and stability. It is the responsibility of managers in the purchasing system to do their part to ensure predictability and reliability by minimizing variation in regard to quality, service, price, and value. Leaders engage in continuous improvement. Continuous improvement is based on assessment and a constant striving to find ways to do what we do better. There are a number of tools (e.g., flow charts, and cause and effect diagrams) to help manage for quality and assist with continuous improvement.

Managers do things right; they are efficient. Leaders do the right things; they are effective. A purchasing system requires both management and leadership activities to work.

Market Research

Market research is required if purchasing professionals are to stay current about preferences of customers, movements and changes in the market, and developments affecting distribution partners. Several sources for this research exist with professional trade associations, including trade publications, academic journals, distributors in the food service distribution channel with specific expertise, and Internet sites.

Market

Market research is designed to investigate the fundamental structure of the market. Recall that the food service distribution channel is made up of various types of primary and secondary members. Perhaps one food service operation is affected only by the three primary members—source, manufacturer, distributor—of the channel. If the operation has a prime distributor program, perhaps the interaction is only with the prime distributor and one or two other secondary distributors who specialize in certain products (e.g., produce). The channel may be structured to include some or all of the secondary members in more complex, larger food service operations. In any case, it is critical to understand the structure of the market and the role that each member plays.

Market research also includes an analysis of competitors as well as who controls the market. In larger cities, there are likely to be more distributors competing for the purchasing business of a food service operation than in a remote, rural area. Part of market research includes financial aspects, such as market size/volume, and growth rate, as well as key market ratios. Trade magazines such as *Institutional Distributor* are excellent sources for this information. The third component of market research is market trends. These trends not only identify channel members' trends, but also should include research into government regulations that are pending, and technology changes and their implications. A state trade association that is tied to the national trade association is a good source of information on trends in government regulation. Some national trade associations also have specialized committees (e.g., AH&LA's Food and Beverage Committee) that monitor certain aspects of the market.

Distributor

Some market research is available from local, regional, and national distributors. Sometimes the research data are somewhat biased to present a particular distributor in the best competitive light. A more balanced view can be obtained by contacting multiple distributors.

Distributor research is designed to reveal each distributor's capabilities so the food service operation can determine that distributor's capacity for meeting requirements as specified. Capabilities that will be of interest are the distributor's operations, product offerings, service offerings, and investments in cutting-edge technology. In addition, it may be helpful to investigate a distributor's position in the channel in terms of corporate strategies, market standing, and pricing structures. A third area for distributor research is the financial elements of the distributor's business. These might include various financial ratios, as well as product cost build-up. Product cost build-up is useful, but it may be too difficult and time consuming to determine. Essentially, it is a calculation of what a product should cost the distributor, based on the components that make up the total product cost, including the distributor's operating costs and structures.

Publicly-held companies are much easier to obtain distributor research from than privately-held companies. However, operators may be surprised by how much information a distributor in search of their purchasing business is willing to share.

Internal

It has been suggested that the most important research of the three categories is the internal research. We have already described this research as determining the requirements of internal customers and external customers based on their needs, wants, and expectations. This research also includes quantities required and an estimate of overall purchasing volume. It starts with how the food service operation uses the product or service that is to be purchased.

The objective of this research in all three categories is to not only better define requirements, but understand the impact that the various elements—markets, distributors, and internal customers—have on the process of purchasing. Through this understanding, a strategic perspective can be obtained, and strategic decisions will help the organization be more competitive.

Ethics of Food Service Operators

Perhaps the greatest challenge in defining **ethics** in purchasing is that many people, both on the seller's side and the buyer's side, may not even be aware of what is expected. While purchasing professionals may be held to a higher standard of ethical conduct than others in business and industry, it is the responsibility of a food service operator to provide guidelines for ethical behavior. Sometimes, ethical conflicts arise in decisions that impact quality or profitability. Unfortunately, sometimes people who receive bonuses in food service operations do not receive such incentives for ethical behavior. Too often, ethical behavior not only goes unrewarded, it is also not a part of the decision-making process.

Tie Ethics to the Operation's Culture

Ethical behavior has always been the foundation of acceptable business practices. Managers often know intuitively what is right based on individual moral values, and have acted in ways to do what is right. These actions sometimes were based on personal guidelines, including "when in doubt, don't do it," and "if it feels like it is unethical, it probably is." While it is impossible to create a written rule for every ethical contingency, it is possible to communicate what the ethical standards, guidelines, and expectations in the operation are, and give examples of ethical dilemmas and then try to help staff members work through the sometimes complex scenarios.

Some food service operators have tied ethics to the organization's culture, philosophy, and core values. For example, one operation may simply state that it is not acceptable to choose one distributor over another based on political preferences. Another may state that we do not allow the personality of a distributor's sales representative or driver to enter into purchasing decisions. A third may focus on the need to always reinforce and strengthen the operation's image and reputation.

Regarding an organization's philosophy of ethical behavior, it is a good idea to detail the following in writing:

- The operation is committed to fairness, consistency, quality, and ethical behavior.

- The people in the operation will adhere to all policies and procedures.

- The operation will seek maximum value for the time and resources spent in purchasing.

- The operation will promote fair and honest relationships with distributors.

The philosophy should be translated into a written policy statement for the operation that describes in clear and unambiguous language the foundation for ethical behavior.

An operation's core values also enter into ethical discussions. Those organizations that value honesty and trust and communicate these values in writing will have the necessary stimulus for acting honestly with trust in relationships. Other core values related to ethics include integrity, credibility, and accountability. Guidelines exist and may be obtained from trade associations (e.g., the Educational Institute's *Ethics in the Hospitality and Tourism Industry*).

Once these philosophies and core values are developed, they should be shared with everyone in the food service operation, as well as with current and prospective distributors and other business partners (e.g., clients in health care, alliance partners). This will help ensure uniformity in ethical behavior. Regardless of whether the relationships are domestic or international, ethics apply worldwide.

It is the culture, philosophy, and core values of the operation that guide the development of rules or guidelines, and codes of ethics. These principles include treating internal customers, external customers, members of the food service distribution channel, and owners/investors with dignity, fairness, and honesty; doing no intentional harm to others; knowing, understanding, and following these principles at all times; and doing what you promise (being dependable) and following through on all commitments (being responsible).

Examples

Perhaps one of the best ways to bring a focus to ethical issues is to discuss examples. While some examples appear to be black and white (i.e., clear) regarding ethical choices, while others are gray in color (i.e., less clear and certain). Consider the following:

1. You are asked by one distributor's sales representative to produce copies of price quotes from another distributor before the choice of which distributor to purchase from has been made.

2. You are sent a case of wine as a holiday gift from one of your distributors.

3. You are offered a cash rebate for the purchase of a certain product at a food show.

4. You and your family are invited to a NASCAR race as the guests of a distributor in the distributor's private suite.

5. You decide to purchase products from your sister-in-law's company even though the prices are slightly higher than another distributor's.

6. You obtain proprietary information (e.g., financial statements) from one distributor and share it with a competing distributor.

7. You form a close, personal relationship with an outsource provider of temporary banquet servers.

8. You use an on-line reverse auction to solicit bids from distributors but know in advance to whom you want to award the bid.

9. Two cases of lettuce arrive in unusable condition and you ask the distributor's sales representative for a credit for the two cases.

10. A case of burgers has passed its expiration date and the distributor will not give you credit for a return. You cook and serve the burgers in the staff cafeteria.

11. You ask a distributor's representative for his case price for lettuce. When he quotes it, you tell him a competitor distributor's case price and say, "If you beat that price, you have my business."

12. You decide to purchase products and services from a distributor because your boss "strongly recommends" that you do so.

Each of these scenarios could provide the bases for a discussion about ethics in the food service operation. Consider each briefly:

1. One of the reasons operators never share distributor pricing information with other distributors is, given that distributors know competitors' costs for material, labor, and overhead, the difference is profit. This is not ethical because the information provided by the operator gives one distributor an unfair advantage over another.

2. Each operation needs a policy about gifts. The fundamental question is: Is it a gift or a bribe? If you give individual bottles from the case to staff members as appreciation recognition, is it ethical? Normally the only acceptable gifts are those that have "small intrinsic value," or are "infrequent and minimal."

3. Some operations encourage their staff to attend food shows, but they are not allowed to purchase while there because cash from rebates may end up in staff members' pockets instead of benefiting the operation. Is there a difference in a publicly-held food service operation compared to an independent single unit food service operation?

4. This is another example of why operations should have a policy regarding gifts.

5. This is clearly unethical.

6. Again, operators should not share information about one distributor with another distributor.

7. It depends what is meant by the close *personal* relationship and how it affects your objectivity and fairness in the purchasing process.

8. E-commerce has expanded with on-line reverse auctions, an area that has potential for abuse. Distributors are online and are bidding directly against competitors in real-time. If the decision has been made on which distributor will be selected prior to the reverse auction, it may force another distributor to bid lower than it normally would bid, or the customer could enter his own bid to encourage lower bids. The customer could also phone a preferred distributor after the reverse auction is finished and ask that distributor to bid even lower to win the business. All of these practices are unethical.

9. This is an acceptable business practice.

10. This is unethical, but it demonstrates the pressure sometimes faced when weighing quality, food cost percentages, and ethical issues.

11. Again, sharing pricing information between distributors is unethical.

12. What would you do? Should you simply follow your boss's orders? Should you look for the distributor that provides the greatest value for the operation?

Consequences of Unethical Behavior

Managing ethics in a food service operation requires an ongoing set of strategies that are process-oriented and involve conversations with a number of individuals.

The process part includes codes of ethics, incorporation of ethical statements into the operation's philosophy and core values, authorization forms, and policies and procedures. The conversations must center around ethical dilemmas and scenarios and how to develop the preferred behavior in the food service operation. It is important for those involved to feel that the process and behaviors are fair and just. Once the process is developed, it must be communicated and followed.

Top management must set an example by communicating, supporting, and protecting ethical behaviors. Ethics relate to personal decisions; however, the decisions must be made within the operation's ethical guidelines and policies. Fundamentally, people are expected to decide, act, and then accept responsibility for their actions.

One has only to consider the latest televised corporate scandals to realize the dire consequences and ramifications of not acting ethically. Executives in all size organizations and in a variety of industries are being held to uphold the public trust in all actions, create transparency in all contracts and business dealings, avoid preferential treatment or the appearance of preferential treatment, and provide maximum value for customers (internal and external), as well as answer to all investors. Once a reputation is lost, it can take forever to rebuild. Sometimes rebuilding the reputation for the individual or the organization is impossible. The stakes are high and the consequences are severe for not acting ethically. Food service operators and everyone in a food service operation must commit to ethical behavior.

Components of Group Purchasing

Group purchasing organizations (GPOs) are characterized by a common organization that coordinates purchasing for a number of individual food service operations. The goal of GPOs is to achieve an efficient and effective purchasing system, resulting in lower prices for products and services and supplies with consistent, or perhaps improved, quality.

Advantages of GPOs include standardized quality, reduced prices, reduced time with distributor's representatives (which allows more time for other activities that boost purchasing value), and enhanced competitive advantage, particularly for small entrepreneurs. Disadvantages that can occur include a loss of autonomy in purchasing decisions for the individual operator, some limitation of quality choices due to fewer product and service options, a slow, committee-based decision process, and a reduction in loyalty from distributors not included in the organization.

Prime Distributors

Recall that a **prime distributor** is a distributor who has the majority or all of an operation's purchasing business. These so-called prime distributors can offer reduced prices to operators because of the wide variety of products, supplies, and services that they have available for sale, and the other related advantages. Related advantages usually include time (reduced due to the elimination of selection from a wider variety of distributors, fewer orders to process, and less time to receive products and supplies from multiple distributors), building trust in the relationship with the prime distributor (rather than spreading this out over several distributors), and purchasing leverage for the operation. Often GPO distribution contracts require members to purchase at least 85 percent of their volume from the prime distributor.

Buying Groups and GPOs

The advantages and disadvantages of GPOs were already presented. An additional advantage in healthcare is the possibility of remaining self-operated and independent by joining a GPO, rather than becoming a contracted food service operation. In healthcare organizations, GPO contracts can cover all supplies (from pens to syringes to paper napkins), equipment (from CAT scanners to ranges), and even capital goods (e.g., carpeting), as well as food and beverage products.

How do GPOs make money? First, the GPO charges "administration fees" (that can be as much as 3 percent of volume) to distributors for participating in the program. After the group covers its overhead, the remainder of the fees is returned to GPO members. Second, GPOs negotiate marketing allowances or rebates from manufacturers on a per case basis, as an incentive to build volume. Then rebates are returned to GPO members, again based on volume. Third, GPOs make money through deviated pricing, that is off-invoice credit by a distributor at the time of invoicing. The distributor then bills back these amounts to the manufacturer.

In some cases, it is difficult to separate a GPO from its distributors. In some cases, a close partnership between a GPO and one particular distributor has resulted in a sole-source relationship, which is controversial to the distributors not included. GPOs are more aggressive in their marketing to prospective members than in the past, particularly as they promote more sophisticated data management—a hallmark of GPOs. What has emerged are more sophisticated e-commerce and e-exchange Web sites for most major GPOs.

From a manufacturer's perspective, an advantage to a GPO is the ability to set-up agreements, programs, promotions, and terms with one group rather than each individual member of the group. This saves time and money. For single-product-line manufacturers, GPOs help protect market share through building loyalty and growing volume. Manufacturers can also use buying groups to efficiently distribute marketing and promotional materials (i.e., announcements, catalogs, flyers). Additional savings for manufacturers occur when they attend GPO conferences and meet with representatives of distributors all in one location.

GPOs usually try to avoid sole-carrier contracts with a single manufacturer. Sometimes when a custom product is being purchased, only one source is available for that product.

One of the ways that smaller independent distributors are staying competitive is by joining buying groups. While many manufacturers spend the majority of their time with larger distributors, a buying group helps smaller distributors band together to create a national identity that gets the attention of manufacturers. This helps independent distributors in the group obtain better pricing from manufacturers (their distributors), remain independent, and maintain some competitive advantage over larger distributors. Since manufacturers would rather deal with a larger entity for the reasons noted earlier, membership in alliances and groups allows smaller distributors access to manufacturers. Related marketing and promotional tools are available from the manufacturer to members of the alliance that are normally not available for lower volume individual distributors. Membership in the alliances also results in the availability of manufacturer-sponsored training and educational development to enhance product knowledge and the application of those products in a food service operation.

Some buying groups have moved to give members of the GPO a choice when it comes to distributors, particularly at the national level. In these GPOs, members must commit to purchase at least 85 percent of their volume through the regional distributor.

Sometimes GPOs require members to pass all purchases through a central office that pays manufacturers with a single check. This helps the GPO guarantee payment and enforce the GPO membership requirements, giving the GPO additional leverage with manufacturers based on the facts and data collected.

Affiliated members are not full members of a GPO, but they agree to purchase from the approved prime distributor. They usually obtain prices similar to, if not exactly the same as, regular members of the GPO, without paying the fees required for full membership. If the advantage in pricing is the same for full members and affiliated members of a GPO, some might question the ethics and legality of the arrangement. The obvious advantage to both full members and affiliated members is that purchasing volume drives prices. More volume means lower prices for all—full and affiliated members alike. Affiliated members may not have the same types of additional services available to them as full members. The trend toward affiliated membership is likely to continue in the future, and it may be particularly appealing to small entrepreneurial food service operators.

In the future, members of GPOs are likely to demand more customized programs, tailored to their unique market segment niche (e.g., casual dining featuring fresh seafood) or geographical area (e.g., East Coast vs. West Coast). Members will also continue to push GPOs to increase ideas for the member food service operators to build sales, such as branding opportunities, marketing ideas, promotion tools and materials, and strategies to increase food service revenues from all customer sources.

Co-Ops

A trend in purchasing today, particularly for smaller, independent food service operators, is outsourcing of purchasing functions to organizations called **co-ops**. While GPOs generally refer to for-profit organizations (e.g., freestanding food service operations, food service operations in hotels), co-ops usually refer to the noncommercial, on-site, and not-for-profit segment categories.

Outsourcing purchasing functions is a way to obtain buying clout due to enhanced purchasing volumes. While preserving independence in for-profit food service operations and self-operation in on-site food service operations, co-ops help trim costs, enhance technology applications (e.g., software and Web-site ordering) for smaller operators, and make it easier to track price changes.

Some independents would argue that their dedication to quality in their products and services is greater than the chains. Joining a co-op focused on similar quality values permits the independent to compete and provide a higher level of quality at a lower cost per unit. One example is wine purchasing, for which co-op pricing can be lower than simply purchasing directly from a distributor.

Co-ops help lower volume. Food service operators improve their profit margins and reduce time spent on purchasing and the management of the purchasing process. The merged volume from smaller operations is more attractive to manufacturers.

Procurement Services Companies

There are specialized procurement services companies for both hotel and restaurant food service operations. They have one strategy in common: to purchase the best available products, supplies, and services at the lowest possible costs to the operators.

Avendra, LLC. Avendra, LLC (see Exhibit 5) was founded by ClubCorp, Fairmont Hotels and Resorts, Hyatt Hotels Corp., Marriott International, and Six Continents Hotels. Today, nearly 200 hospitality companies representing over 4,000 lodging properties purchase through Avendra's negotiated contracts. Avendra was started by these five lodging companies after they realized that they all purchased basically the same products, supplies, and services to capitalize on economies of scale through larger purchasing volumes. The result is a reduction in purchasing costs at the property level.

Avendra is responsible for managing the relationships among manufacturers, distributors, and purchasers. This includes financial audits, negotiating competitive prices for hotels, performing quality assurance audits, and managing variables in the distribution channel. The goal is to save at least 10 percent on annual purchasing costs.

Other hotel companies are pursuing a different approach to the purchasing process. Carlson Hospitality Worldwide has created Provisions to provide lodging and food and beverage purchasing services to about 1,000 hotels. Provisions negotiates competitive pricing on food and beverage products, supplies, and FF&E (furniture, fixtures, and equipment). Carlson created Provisions because the company believes it has a better understanding of its own unique brands and the brands' requirements. Provisions also believes it can respond more rapidly to changes with reduced overhead costs.

As a third option for hotel purchasing, Starwood Hotels & Resorts Worldwide believes that the lowest costs and highest efficiency is achieved when purchasing is coordinated internally. Starwood has multiple brands (e.g., Sheraton, Westin, W) with many proprietary products (e.g., The Heavenly Bed). Starwood has employed electronic purchasing for about one-fifth of its purchasing through manufacturers' Web sites.

Instill Corporation. Instill Corporation (see Exhibit 6) assists freestanding restaurants and other food service operations as a supply chain solution provider. Currently, Instill serves quick-service, full-service, and food service management operations with purchase data, hidden cost savings, suggestions to optimize the

Exhibit 5 Avendra Procurement Solutions

Source: www.avendra.com.

purchasing process, and quality management that is based on brand protection, risk management, and operational excellence.

Operations that choose to work with Instill can choose from a module list of services and solutions. For example, in the procurement category, operators can choose purchasing, order guide manager, receiving, unit inventory, or integration categories. Much of what is available through Instill is Web based.

Automatic Merchandising Buying Groups. At least two buying groups that service the vending or automatic merchandising industry are important to discuss. These buying groups help members save money through rebates on group purchases made under contractual agreements.

Better Vending Association, Inc. (BVA) is a co-op of independent vending and coffee service operators that began in 1970. Each member accesses earnings from BVA–approved distributors based on rebate dollars. BVA states that, since 1970, the co-op has earned over 70 million in rebates from its extensive list of distributors.

Exhibit 6   Instill Corporation

Source: www.instill.com.

Vendors Purchasing Council, Inc. (VPC) is another co-op that maintains a database to track reports for each member showing rebates earned quarterly. This large buying group, like BVA, offers incentives to members from manufacturers due to the collective buying strength of VPC members. VPC advertises that it represents over 350 members with collective sales in excess of $1.8 billion and purchases of over $700 million annually.

Both BVA and VPC consist of a network of independent operators.

Ethical Considerations

Much of the ethics discussion already presented applies to GPOs. There are some additional ethical issues that are specific to GPOs, as follows:

- GPOs should clearly state in writing that they act first and foremost as representatives of their member organizations.

- GPO staff are not permitted to own equity in any participating manufacturer or distributor.

- Participating manufacturers or distributors are not permitted to own equity in a GPO.

- No GPO is permitted to have an equity interest in a participating manufacturer or distributor unless it benefits GPO members.

- When the GPO conducts a technology audit, the assessment should be confidential, fair, timely, and unbiased.

- GPOs will have a written manufacturer and distributor grievance procedure.

- GPO contracts should be for three years or less, unless longer-term contracts are in the best interest of members.

- Administrative fees for GPO contracts should not exceed 3 percent.[1]

The Basics of Purchase Specifications

Quality Requirements

Quality in the purchasing function refers to the suitability of a product for its intended use. The more suitable a product, the higher (better) its quality. For example, a super colossal olive may represent the right quality product for garnish or salad purposes. It may not, however, represent the proper quality if it is chopped and used as a salad bar topping.

Decisions about quality requirements are first made when the goals of the business are established and subsequent marketing plans are developed. At that time, the spirit and intent of the food and beverage operation's quality standards are determined. Later, **standard purchase specifications** are documented in detail to indicate the requirements for products suitable for every intended purpose. These specifications provide detailed descriptions of the quality, size, and weight desired for particular items.

The relationship between quality and price is referred to as value. Just as the guest considers value when deciding what to order in the restaurant or lounge, food and beverage managers must also consider value when choosing products to purchase by carefully evaluating each product's quality (suitability for intended use) in relation to its cost.

The format for purchase specifications illustrated in Exhibit 7 indicates specific quality requirements. Notice that the specifications not only describe the desired product, but also specify how the product will be used. In addition, this form tells the distributor about the operation's procedures for ensuring that the delivered item does, in fact, meet the required quality specifications. Standard purchase specifications must:

- Accurately describe minimum quality requirements.

- Clearly and simply indicate the food and beverage operation's needs.

- Realistically define needs, yet not limit the number of acceptable distributors.

Exhibit 7   Purchase Specification Format

(Name of food and beverage operation)

1. Product name: _____

2. Product used for:

   > Clearly indicate product use (such as olive garnish for beverage and hamburger patty to be grilled for sandwich).

3. Product general description:

   > Provide general quality information about desired product. For example, "iceberg lettuce; heads to be green, firm without spoilage, excessive dirt, or damage. No more than 10 outer leaves; packed 24 heads per case."

4. Detailed description:

   > Purchaser should state other factors that help to clearly identify desired product. Examples of specific factors, which vary by product being described, may include:
   >
   > - Geographic origin
   > - Variety
   > - Type
   > - Style
   > - Grade
   > - Product size
   > - Portion size
   > - Brand name
   > - Density
   > - Medium of pack
   > - Specific gravity
   > - Container size
   > - Edible yield, trim

5. Product test procedures:

   > Test procedures occur at time product is received and as or after product is prepared or used. For example, products to be at a refrigerated temperature upon delivery can be tested with a thermometer. Portion-cut meat patties can be randomly weighed. Lettuce packed 24 heads per case can be counted.

6. Special instructions and requirements:

   > Any additional information needed to clearly indicate quality expectations can be included here. Examples include bidding procedures, if applicable, labeling and packaging requirements, and special delivery and service requirements.

Source: Jack D. Ninemeier, *Planning and Control for Food and Beverage Operations,* 6th ed. (Lansing, Mich.: Educational Institute of the American Hotel & Lodging Association, 2004), p. 190.

Generally, specifications should be developed for most products purchased. However, there is a need to be practical in following this principle. Developing detailed specifications for products such as salt and other seasonings or bar swizzle sticks may not be justified. Instead, managers involved with the purchasing function should first develop specifications for expensive, high-volume items and then formalize quality requirements for other products as time permits. In some operations, 75 percent of all product dollars buys only 25 percent of all products. These few significant items require purchase specifications.

When items, such as liquor or ketchup, are purchased by brand, the brand itself becomes the specification. However, it is still necessary to specify container size and special instructions.

Quality concerns are important when purchasing alcoholic beverages as well as when purchasing foods. However, liquor, wines, and beers are generally purchased by brand name and, as noted above, the brand then becomes the specification. Many food and beverage operations feature a range of quality and, therefore, a range of prices for the alcoholic beverages being served. Liquor may be available in a house brand—also called pour brand, well brand, or speed rail brand (named after the shelf typically located close to the bartender for quick access)—and a call brand. Other properties offer very high quality brands referred to as premium brands. Many beverage consumers prefer a specific brand, and the manager must make a marketing decision to determine which call and premium brands to offer. In addition, many guests judge the overall quality of the restaurant in part by the quality of house brands available. For example, a high-check-average restaurant will not likely offer a low quality house brand. In fact, some food and beverage operations offer only call or premium brands as a statement about the quality of all products offered by the property.

Wine is also purchased with similar concerns in mind. Many properties offer a house brand and numerous better known and higher quality wines on their list. House brands may be available by the glass or carafe (sometimes in different sizes). Today, a wide number of microbreweries produce beers that are very popular with many guests. Food and beverage managers may offer several brands at different prices. The history of the label, the guest's experience with the brand, and the amount of advertising run by beverage manufacturers and distributors all influence the perceived quality and popularity of alcoholic beverages offered by the food service operation.

Developing Purchase Specifications

Purchase specifications are developed through the efforts of several departments, staff, and other individuals. Consider three groups in particular: food and beverage personnel, purchasing staff, and distributors.

The food and beverage department must make the final decisions regarding purchase specifications for the products the operation uses. The responsibility of menu planning rests with this department; specifically, with the food service manager. Since the menu determines required items as well as intended use, specifications need only be developed for those menu items.

This department may suggest distributors. Staff members have a wealth of information from trade journals, trade shows, and contacts in other operations. Their feedback can suggest distributors who can then provide appropriate information for developing specifications.

Specifications for Small Food Service Operations

Are purchase specifications practical for small operations in which the manager must perform a wide variety of tasks in addition to purchasing? Yes. With slight modifications to the development process, they can be just as helpful for the small operator as they are for large organizations.

Many of the techniques suggested throughout this chapter are relevant to the small operation. For example, it is possible to write brief statements to describe the most important quality factors. Soliciting help from distributors can also be time-efficient and beneficial. Likewise, giving priority to the relatively few "A" items in an operation will help ensure that attention is given to the most important products being purchased. As this is done, time is made available for managing the many other concerns that confront operators of small food service organizations.

Food and beverage personnel also evaluate and test items received under tentative purchase specifications. The expertise of the food service staff is invaluable in measuring the adequacy of specifications, from the perspective of both operations and guest satisfaction.

The responsibility of the purchasing staff is to obtain information and provide assistance—not to make the final decisions. For example, purchasers question distributors, study applicable product data, conduct make-or-buy analyses, and research topics suggested by the food service manager.

Purchasing staff arrange for sample/trial orders. Through use of tentative specifications, they obtain sample products for analysis and selection by food and beverage personnel. Purchasers can evaluate initial shipments of these samples and check to see that incoming products meet specifications. Exhibit 8 provides a data sheet that may be used to evaluate food samples.

Purchasers also provide advice about specifications. Their experience in developing specifications, working with eligible distributors, and evaluating product samples is of invaluable assistance to line managers.

Distributors are not directly responsible for developing specifications. They do, however, provide information and assist the food service operation in this process. In general, distributors may:

- Inform operators about available products.

- Offer advice on activities and attitudes of other operations toward various products.

- Counsel buyers regarding new products about to be introduced. Distributor representatives often learn about new products before operators and purchasers do.

- Review and critique proposed specifications. Distributors may evaluate whether a product defined by the specification is useful. Whenever practical, specifications should apply to products offered from more than one suppler.

Exhibit 8   Food Sample Data Sheet

1. Product: _____

2. Brand Name: _____

3. Presented By: _____   Date: _____

4. Varieties Available: _____

5. Shelf Life: (Frozen) _____   (Thawed, Refrigerated, Dry) _____

6. Preparation and Sanitation Considerations: _____

   _____

   _____

   _____

7. Menu Suggestions: _____

8. Merchandising Aids Available (Poster, Table Tents, etc.): _____

9. Case Size (Number of Portions): _____

10. Portion Size: _____

11. Distributed By: _____

12. Minimum Order: _____

13. Any Additional Ordering Information: _____

    _____

14. Lead Time: _____

15. Approximate Price Per Serving: _____

NOTE: Were the following information sheets received with products?

    a. Nutritional and Ingredient Analysis: Yes _____   No _____

    b. Specification Sheet: Yes _____   No _____

Source: Ronald F. Cichy, *Food Safety: Managing the HACCP Process* (Lansing, Mich.: Educational Institute of the American Hotel & Lodging Association, 2004), p. 79.

Specifications for Current Products. When a product is in current use, the food service manager and purchaser are probably both familiar with it and are able to judge its suitability. They recognize the required characteristics and are able to identify which products meet minimum quality standards. Exhibit 9 shows the basic steps required to develop specifications for current products.

After the specification is developed, purchasers should submit copies to eligible distributors, indicating that price quotations should be based on the quality descriptions defined by the specification. Contracts should state remedies available to the operator upon receiving substandard products or performance.

Exhibit 9   Developing a Specification for a Current Product

Step 1   Select a sample judged to be of proper quality.

Step 2   Ask the distributor providing the product to describe it (size, grade, etc.).

Step 3   Write a specification using information described in this chapter.

Step 4   Ask other eligible distributors to critique and improve the tentative specification.

- Does it describe the correct quality?

- Is it available from several sources?

Step 5   Modify the written description as necessary.

Step 6   *Use* the specification.

Specifications for New Products. Exhibit 10 outlines the process that can be used to establish specifications for new products. Many governmental and trade references can also provide assistance. Based upon this information, several distributors should be able to provide samples that may accommodate the purchaser's needs.

Specifications in Cooperative Purchasing Systems. The use of centralized (pool, group, or cooperative) purchasing systems is increasing in many segments of the hospitality industry. By combining orders from many operations, buyers can take advantage of volume purchase discounts. Such a system, however, should be established and operated under the guidance of legal counsel to ensure that federal and state antitrust laws are not violated.

Participating purchasers must agree on minimum quality requirements for items to be purchased. Frequently, developing specifications acceptable to all concerned parties is one of the most time-consuming aspects of implementing a centralized purchasing system. In fact, if standardized specifications cannot be agreed upon, it is difficult to continue with the planning necessary to develop a centralized system.

A committee approach is frequently used in developing specifications. Wide differences in specifications must generally be minimized in order to take advantage of volume discounts. This usually entails some compromise on specifications by individual members of the buying cooperative.

Participation in centralized purchasing typically is not an either/or decision. It is possible to purchase some items through the cooperative system and purchase others on an independent basis, though cost advantages to centralized purchasing are decreased when this mixed approach is used.

Specifications for Specific Products. We have indicated some general factors to consider in developing specifications. Exhibit 11 reviews specific concerns addressed in the development of purchase specifications for various products

Exhibit 10   Developing a Specification for a New Product

Step 1	Give a verbal description of product needs to reputable distributors and stress the product's use.
Step 2	Analyze samples that are provided.
Step 3	Select a product of correct quality.
Step 4	Ask the distributor providing the product to describe it.
Step 5	Write a specification using information described in this chapter.
Step 6	Ask other distributors to critique and improve the specification.
Step 7	Modify the specification as necessary.
Step 8	*Use* the specification.

required by food service operations. As a specification is developed, this information might best be used by considering whether each factor is both necessary and important. If so, the purchaser should incorporate information addressing that concern in the specification.

Comprehensive Recall Process. Recalls are actions taken by businesses to remove a product from the market. The process for a comprehensive recall must be known in advance and included in the purchase specification. Recalls may be initiated by the business, by the Food and Drug Administration's (FDA) request, or by FDA order under statutory authority.

Recalls fit into one of three classes as follows:

- Class I recalls due to a situation in which there is a reasonable probability that the use of or exposure to a violating product will cause serious health emergencies or death.

- Class II recalls due to a situation in which use of or exposure to a violating product may cause temporary or medically reversible adverse health consequences or where the probability of serious adverse health consequences is remote.

- Class III recalls due to a situation in which use of or exposure to a violating product is not likely to cause adverse health consequences.

The FDA coordinates product recalls. Current recalls may be reviewed at the FDA's Web site (www.fda.gov/opacom/7alerts.html). Examples of Class I recalls include kettles that leached lead into food, packages labeled fruit and nut chocolate base that actually contained peanut chocolate base with peanuts as an ingredient, and smoked salmon contaminated with the *Listeria monocytogenes* pathogen. Examples of Class II recalls include holiday cookies with undeclared food colors and an undeclared allergen (wheat), and produce with a pesticide residue. An

Exhibit 11   Purchase Specification Factors for Specific Products

Meat

- Inspection (mandatory)
- Grading (if desired)
- IMPS numbers
- Weight/thickness limitations
- Fat limitations
- Aging of product (when needed)
- State of refrigeration
- Miscellaneous (packaging, etc.)

Seafood

- Type (finfish or shellfish)
- Market form (finfish—whole, eviscerated, etc.; shellfish—alive, whole, shucked, etc.)
- Condition (describe flesh, eyes, skin, gills, etc.)
- Grade (if desired and available)
- Inspection (if available)
- Place of origin (if necessary)
- State of refrigeration
- Miscellaneous (count, sizing, packaging)

Poultry

- Type (chicken, turkey, duck, goose)
- Class (broiler, hen)

- Grading (if desired)
- Inspection (mandatory)
- Style (whole, breasts, breasts w/ribs, etc.)
- Size (weight limitations)
- State of refrigeration
- Miscellaneous (packaging, etc.)

Fresh Fruits and Vegetables

- Grade (if desired)
- Variety
- Size
- Type of container
- Weight per container
- Count per container
- Growing area

Processed Fruits and Vegetables

- Grade (if desired)
- Variety
- Drained weight or count per case
- Weight per case
- Packing medium
- Can/package size
- Variety and/or style
- Growing area (only if necessary)

example of a Class III recall is a package that contained chocolate chunk cookies, but was labeled as espresso mocha cookies.

Providing early alerts about applicable recalls related to products purchased from a distributor is a valued service. With this information, the food service operator can take action more quickly with the recalled products in inventory before they actually harm a customer.

Other Purchasing Tools. Several other management tools help control the purchasing process, one of which is the **food sample data sheet** (Exhibit 9). This sheet helps standardize the evaluation of a product. It can be used to record purchasing, storing, preparing, and serving information about products that the operation is sampling and considering for purchase. The food sample data sheet makes product selection more objective.

Purchasing the Proper Quantities

Purchasing the proper quantities of items is just as important as developing correct quality specifications. Typical problems that can arise when too much of a product is ordered are:

- Cash flow problems resulting from excessive money tied up in inventory.

- Increased storage costs for interest, insurance, and sometimes rented storage space.

- Deterioration of quality or damaged products.

- Increased potential for theft and pilferage.

Purchasing insufficient quantities also has potential disadvantages—dissatisfied guests not able to order what they want because of stockouts, emergency and rush orders that are frequently expensive and time-consuming, and lost volume-purchase discounts.

To avoid these problems, food and beverage managers must periodically assess a number of factors—such as those that follow—that affect the purchase of proper quantities.

- *Popularity of menu items.* As unit sales of menu items increase, additional quantities of ingredients are obviously needed.

- *Product cost concerns.* Higher product costs may result in increased selling prices, which, in turn, may result in decreased sales levels. In this case, the need for continued purchase of the product should be evaluated. Also, management may make judgments about future prices and buy more if prices are expected to increase or buy less if prices are expected to decrease. This is called **speculative purchasing** and should be done only by management, based on information provided by the purchaser.

- *Available storage space.* Available space may limit quantities purchased. Storage space in dry, frozen, and refrigerated areas may not be adequate to accommodate quantity purchases.

- *Safety levels.* Safety level refers to a minimum quantity of product that should always be available in inventory to help ensure that stockouts do not occur. Maintaining a safety level of products in inventory may require buying a quantity above that actually needed to allow for delivery delays, increased usage, or other unexpected developments.

- *Distributor constraints.* Distributors may specify minimum dollar or poundage requirements for delivery. Also, some distributors may refuse to break cases, bags, or other packing containers to meet overly specific order quantities (or if they do break cases, there is likely to be a significant increase in per-unit price). Therefore, the standard commercial packaging units influence quantities purchased.

Perishable Products

Perishable items such as fresh produce, bakery, and dairy products should be used as soon as possible after receipt. These types of products are normally purchased several times weekly according to the following formula:

$$\text{Quantity Needed} \ - \ \text{Quantity Available} \ = \ \begin{array}{c}\text{Quantity to Purchase for}\\\text{Immediate Use}\end{array}$$

Sample procedures for purchasing perishable products are as follows:

1. Determine normal usage rates. For a normal two-day purchasing period, for example, assess the specific number of cases of selected produce items, pounds of fresh meat, fresh poultry fryers, and other perishable products the property typically uses.

2. Assess the amount of each item currently in inventory.

3. Calculate the quantity to purchase by subtracting the quantity available (step 2) from the quantity needed (step 1).

4. Adjust routine quantities as necessary for special functions, holidays, or other non-routine events.

When purchasing items for immediate use, some operations that use manual purchasing systems use a form such as the one illustrated in Exhibit 12. When reviewing the perishable product quotation/call sheet, note that the perishable items needed are listed in column 1 and the quantity of each item needed for the time covered by the order is in column 2. The inventory amount noted in column 3 is determined by an actual physical count of the quantity on hand. The amount to order (column 4) is determined by subtracting the amount on hand (column 3) from the amount needed (column 2). In the first example, only 3½ cases of spinach are needed (6 cases – 2½ cases = 3½ cases), but 4 cases should be purchased if distributors will not break cases or if the increased broken case price is judged excessive.

The prices quoted by eligible distributors are listed in columns 5, 6, and 7. Each distributor has copies of the food and beverage operation's quality specifications on which to base the price for each item. The buyer can either select the distributor with the lowest total price for everything required or use several distributors, depending on who has the lowest price item by item. However, minimum delivery requirements may limit this purchasing option. Also, the in-house processing cost for each order (usually not assessed but frequently expensive) should be considered. E-commerce, which is discussed later in this chapter, can reduce the paperwork required to collect the necessary information. In addition, large operations may subscribe to electronic newspapers that provide real-time price information.

Nonperishable Products

To determine the quantity of nonperishable products to purchase, it is often practical to use a minimum/maximum system of inventory management. This system is based on a concept discussed earlier: only a few of all items purchased represent

Exhibit 12 Perishable Product Quotation/Call Sheet (Manual System)

Item	Amount			Supplier		
	Needed	On Hand	Order	A & B Co.	Green Produce	Local Supplier
1	2	3	4	5	6	7
Spinach	6 cs	$2^{1}/_{2}$ cs	4 cs	22^{00}/cs = $88.00	14^{85}/cs = $59.40	21^{70}/cs = $86.80
Ice Lettuce	8 cs	1 cs	7 cs	17^{00}/cs = $119.00	16^{75}/cs = $117.25	18^{10}/cs = $126.70
Carrots	3-20#	20#	2-20#	14^{70}/bag = $29.40	13^{90}/bag = $27.80	13^{80}/bag = $27.60
Tomatoes	2 lugs	$^{1}/_{2}$ lug	2 lugs	18^{60}/lug = $37.20	18^{00}/lug = $36.00	18^{10}/lug = $36.20
			Totals	$861.40	$799.25	$842.15

Source: Jack D. Ninemeier, *Planning and Control for Food and Beverage Operations,* 6th ed. (Lansing, Mich.: Educational Institute of the American Hotel & Lodging Association, 2004), p. 193.

high-cost or high-frequency-of-use items. Minimum/maximum ordering systems give first attention to these high-priority items and help managers determine when products must be purchased and how much of each product to order.

For each purchase item, the minimum/maximum ordering system assesses the minimum quantity below which inventory levels should not fall and the maximum quantity above which inventory levels should not rise. The minimum inventory level is the safety level—the number of purchase units that must always remain in inventory. The maximum inventory level is the greatest number of purchase units permitted in storage. The maximum inventory level of purchase units permitted in storage is the usage rate plus the minimum (safety) level.

The most important factor for determining when more purchase units must be ordered is, of course, the rate at which they are used by the operation. The usage rate is the number of purchase units used per order period. Purchase units are counted in terms of the number of shipping containers of normal size for each product. For example, if ten cases (six #10 cans in each) of crushed tomatoes are normally used between deliveries, the usage rate for crushed tomatoes is ten cases.

In addition to usage rates, managers must determine a lead-time quantity for each purchase item. The lead-time quantity is the number of purchase units withdrawn from inventory between the time an order is placed and when it is delivered. Again, purchase units are counted in terms of normal size shipping containers. For example, if two cases of crushed tomatoes are used between ordering and receiving, the lead-time quantity is two cases. This lead-time quantity is separate from the safety (minimum) level of purchase units kept in inventory. The safety level must allow for such things as late deliveries and greater than normal usage.

The **order point** is the number of purchase units in stock when an order is placed. The order point is reached when the number of purchase units in inventory equals the lead-time quantity plus the safety level:

$$\begin{array}{ccc} \text{Purchase Units at} \\ \text{Order Point} \end{array} = \begin{array}{c} \text{Purchase Units in} \\ \text{Lead Time} \end{array} + \begin{array}{c} \text{Purchase Units in} \\ \text{Safety Level} \end{array}$$

If products are ordered at the order point, the quantity in inventory will be reduced to the safety (minimum) level by the time products are received. When the order arrives, the inventory level for the product will again be brought back to the maximum level. Examples of the minimum/maximum order inventory system are found in Exhibit 13.

The Purchase Order System

To this point, we have discussed control procedures that apply before the actual purchasing task. Before the purchasing process begins, the food and beverage operation should have established minimum quality standards and provided them to potential distributors, calculated quantities of products to be purchased, determined order points for each purchase item, and considered eligible distributors. It is important that control procedures be built into the actual purchasing process as well. For this purpose, large food and beverage operations use a purchase order system.

With a **purchase order system**, a purchase order is sent (by mail, fax, or electronically) to the distributor awarded the order. Information about the order is retained in the purchasing department and is also circulated internally among the receiving and accounting departments. The purchase order formally identifies the product, quantity, unit cost, and total cost agreed upon by the distributor and purchaser have agreed to. In addition, the purchase order may include guarantees, warranties, payment requirements, inspection rights, "hold harmless" provisions, and other legal and contractual concerns.

A purchase order, such as the example shown in Exhibit 14 for a manual purchasing system, is the food and beverage operation's record of the specifics of all incoming shipments.

The operation must pay the agreed-to price for no less than the agreed-to quality for the amount ordered. Higher-than-necessary food and beverage costs are frequently traced to communication and coordination problems among the several departments or personnel involved in purchasing. When properly used, the purchase order minimizes these problems.

Rather than using a purchase order system, smaller food and beverage operations may simply summarize purchase order information by using an in-house purchase record form, such as that shown in Exhibit 15. The **purchase record** performs the same functions as the purchase order, except that it is not given to distributors. It provides the food and beverage operation with a detailed record of all incoming shipments. Affected personnel and departments must know all the specifics about incoming food and beverage products. Without a written record,

Exhibit 13   Minimum/Maximum Order System

Example 1. Assume:
  Purchase unit = case (6 #10 cans)
  Usage rate = 2 cases per day
  Order period = monthly (30 days)
  Monthly usage rate = 2 cases/day × 30 days = 60 cases
  Lead time = 4 days
  Lead-time usage rate = 4 days at 2 cases/day = 8 cases
  Safety level = 4 days at 2 cases/day = 8 cases
  Order point = lead time + safety level
    16 cases = 8 cases + 8 cases
  Maximum level = usage rate + safety level
    68 cases = 60 cases + 8 cases
  When ordering at the order point, the quantity to order is the monthly usage rate.
This is shown by the following calculation:

Order point	16 cases
Monthly usage rate	60 cases
Total cases available	76
Lead-time usage rate	− 8
Maximum level	68 cases

So the maximum level is maintained.

Example 2. When placing an order before the order point is reached, such as when putting together an order for numerous products from a supplier, first determine the number of cases in storage, then subtract the order point from the amount in storage.

Amount in storage	25 cases
Order point	− 16 cases
Excess over order point	9 cases

The amount to order is the usage rate minus the number of cases in excess of the order point:
  51 cases = 60 cases − 9 cases

The decision to order 51 cases can be proved:

Cases ordered	51
Amount available	25
Total	76
Lead-time usage rate	− 8
Maximum level	68

Again, the maximum inventory level is maintained.

Source: Jack D. Ninemeier, *Planning and Control for Food and Beverage Operations*, 6th ed. (Lansing, Mich.: Educational Institute of the American Hotel & Lodging Association, 2004), p. 196.

busy management staff may forget the details. Properly used, the purchase record helps to control food and beverage costs.

110 *Chapter 3*

Exhibit 14   Purchase Order

Purchase Order Number: _____	Order Date: _____	
	Payment Terms: _____	
To: _____ (supplier)	From/ Ship to: _____ (name of food service operation)	
_____ _____ (address)	_____ _____ (address)	
Please Ship:	Delivery Date: _____	

Quantity Ordered	Description	✓	Units Shipped	Unit Cost	Total Cost

Total Cost _____

Important: This Purchase Order expressly limits acceptance to the terms and conditions stated above, noted on the reverse side hereof, and any additional terms and conditions affixed hereto or otherwise referenced. Any additional terms and conditions proposed by seller are objected to and rejected.

_____
Authorized Signature

Source: Ronald F. Cichy, *Food Safety: Managing the HACCP Process* (Lansing, Mich.: Educational Institute of the American Hotel & Lodging Association, 2004), p. 80.

Basics of Pricing and Cost Controls

When purchasing products and services, operators usually have several pricing options available. However, each option carries with it certain requirements and limitations. A great deal depends on the willingness of distributors to enter into

Exhibit 15   In-House Purchase Record (Manual System)

Date Ordered: _____							
Delivery Date: _____			Supplier: _____				
Item Description	**Unit**	**Price**	**No. of Units**	**Total Cost**	**Invoice No.**	**Comments**	

Source: Jack D. Ninemeier, *Planning and Control for Food and Beverage Operations,* 6th ed. (Lansing, Mich.: Educational Institute of the American Hotel & Lodging Association, 2004), p. 15.

these purchasing arrangements. Similarly, a purchaser may be limited to specific options by the nature and volume of the business.

As a food service operation grows, it often experiences cost advantages simply as a result of its size. Distribution charges may be lower due to consolidation of orders or distributors may offer discounts based on greater purchase volume. These benefits, related to the operation's larger size, are termed economies of scale.

Ways to Specify Costs and Components of Cost

Ride the Market. The phrase "ride the market" simply means waiting until the products are needed, then taking bids or negotiating with a single distributor to fulfill purchase needs.

This method is common among operations with a "maintenance" purchasing philosophy. In effect, these operations are permitting their cost decisions to be made by others in the market. Generally, these buyers receive prices at the top of the market's range. They have inadequate information to make the judgments and take the risks that lead to lower costs.

Cost-Plus. Using cost-plus, a contract is developed to price goods at a specified rate over the distributor's cost. To be successful, various aspects of costs are specified to be either included or excluded. The task then involves measuring and managing the distributor's costs.

This measurement is best done through use of independent price sources. Base cost may also be determined by reviewing actual invoices of the distributor. The purpose of cost-plus is to establish a lower level of pricing than would be achieved through maintenance buying.

Buy-and-Inventory. When a continuing supply of product is required, a fixed quantity can be bought and stored in inventory. These buys may be made to guarantee supply of a critical item or to avoid anticipated price increases. In either case, all costs of storage, handling, inventory, and potential loss of value (through damage or obsolescence) must be calculated. An estimate of the product's future cost is necessary to calculate the economic consequences of the transaction.

Long-Term Contract. Long-term contracts may be based on fixed or accelerating prices. To be cost-effective, however, prices should be forecasted by the purchaser well in advance of entering into such agreements. While similar in many respects to buy-and-inventory, long-term contracts make the distributor responsible for the physical management of products. In most cases, payment is made by the buyer upon receipt of the merchandise. Many of these contracts have clauses that authorize price accelerations to offset storage and carrying costs.

Hedging. For certain products, hedging (also called forward contracting) can be accomplished through the futures markets. Because these contracts are "on margin" or leveraged (that is, using credit to enhance speculative capacity), investment and carrying costs are less. However, the buyer is at risk for the total contract amount.

This option will only be utilized by operations with relatively large volumes and sophisticated purchasing systems. Information is readily available regarding future price levels and is of major importance to even small operators. Such information reflects the market's estimate of future price levels and provides a negotiating tool for all buyers.

The bottom line is that the food service operator needs to define the cost or the distributer may end up defining the operator's costs. For example, manufacturers sometimes give allowances (rebates) to distributors. The operator will end up paying for these rebates back to the distributor if the operator does not carefully define costs.

When the distributor has to move products form one location to another, then logistics costs can also be charged to the operator. The operator wants to be certain that the invoice cost vs. the time cost with unauthorized added costs. Other costs that might be added, if not specified, are marketing costs, spoilage cost for perishable products, label allowances when buying private labels, the distributor has to add the cost of putting its own label on a product, and freight costs.

One additional consideration relative to cost is the difference between margin of sale and mark-up of cost. They are not the same. If the mark-up on a cost in a cost-plus contract is 10 percent, the margin on sale for that same product would be 11 percent—in other words, 1 percent higher. Most distributors operate on a margin on sales basis. However, when comparing costs between two different distributors, it is important to clarify the basis for the costs.

Food Cost and Food Cost Percentage

The basic actual monthly cost of sales for food and beverages is calculated as follows:

Exhibit 16   Information for Basic Cost of Sales Calculation

Required Information	Cost of Sales: Food	Cost of Sales: Beverage
Beginning Inventory	Physical Inventory Forms (last month)	Physical Inventory Forms (last month)
+ Purchases	Daily Receiving Report*	Daily Receiving Report*
− Ending Inventory	Physical Inventory Forms (end of current month)	Physical Inventory Forms (end of current month)
*The source document for these purchases is the delivery invoice. Larger operations with formal accounting procedures may post information from the delivery invoices to a "purchase journal" after payment. This source, representing invoices for products received *and* paid for during the month plus delivery invoices representing products received but *not* paid during the month, may also be totaled to determine the value of purchases for the month. (Note: the value of credit memos, if any, which represent items on delivery invoices that are rejected/returned, must be deducted from the value of purchases.)		

Source: Jack D. Ninemeier, *Planning and Control for Food and Beverage Operations,* 6th ed. (Lansing, Mich.: Educational Institute of the American Hotel & Lodging Association, 2004), p. 308.

$$\text{Cost of Sales} \;=\; \text{Beginning Inventory} \;+\; \text{Purchases} \;-\; \text{Ending Inventory}$$

For example, assume:

	Food	Beverage
Beginning Inventory	$124,500	$36,800
Purchases	+ 85,000	+ 29,500
Ending Inventory	− 112,250	− 27,500
Cost of Sales	$ 97,250	$38,800

Exhibit 16 illustrates the sources of information for calculating the basic cost of sales. As you review these sources, note that the value of product inventory is calculated only once monthly. The value of ending inventory on the last day of one fiscal period (such as July 31) is the same as the value of beginning inventory on the first day of the next fiscal period (August 1).

Where manual accounting systems are used, the value of food and beverage purchases for the month can be obtained from the sum of the daily receiving reports for the period. Delivery invoices may be attached to these documents. If all the daily receiving reports are completed correctly, they will separate all food and beverage purchases, thus reducing the time needed to make these calculations. If a daily receiving report is not used, the value of purchases will be represented by the sum of delivery invoices, adjusted as necessary by applicable request-for-credit memos. In this case, however, it will be necessary to separate invoice items into food and beverage categories before making purchase calculations.

The use of integrated purchasing, receiving, and accounts payable software eases the tasks of manual "paper shuffling" and routing. Managers can still pay based on individual delivery invoices or from statements that summarize one or more invoices. As part of the payment process, items can be sorted into food and beverage categories, tallies for the period can be aggregated, and the total purchase cost of food and beverage products can be easily and accurately calculated on a timely basis.

Values of ending inventories for food and beverage items can be taken directly from the physical inventory system. It is important to be consistent in:

- The method used to calculate the cost of inventory items (some inventory valuation methods are discussed in the next section).

- Decisions such as how to treat the value of food supplies in workstations and the value of opened bottles behind the bar.

- Whether items in broken (open) cases, in miscellaneous storage areas, or in process are to be considered "in storage" and under inventory control, or whether they are considered issued and are to be included as part of the costs incurred during the period for which costs are being calculated.

Calculating Inventory Value

The value of inventory is a critical element in calculating the cost of sales. It is also important to use a consistent method to calculate inventory. There are four generally accepted methods for calculating inventory:[2]

- *First in, first out (FIFO).* The FIFO approach assigns the first, or earliest, product costs to *issues*—in other words, it values issues in the order in which the costs were incurred. As a consequence, the products in storage are valued at the most recent product costs.

- *Last in, first out (LIFO).* The LIFO approach assigns the last, or most recent, product costs to *issues*. As a consequence, the products in storage are valued based on the costs of the inventory most recently purchased. This leads to an inventory cost that more accurately reflects current replacement costs.

- *Actual cost.* The value of stored products is the total value represented by the individual costs of the units in storage when the inventory is taken.

- *Weighted average.* The quantity of products purchased at different unit costs is considered by weighing the prices to be averaged based on the quantity of products in storage at each price when the inventory is taken.

Adjustments to Basic Cost of Sales

One reason to calculate the cost of sales is to determine, with reasonable accuracy, the product cost incurred in generating revenues. However, to make the information more meaningful and useful, some adjustments to the basic cost of sales may be helpful. This is because the unadjusted basic cost of sales will include costs not directly related to generating revenue. For example, in operations where meals are provided free of charge or at a reduced charge to staff members, the food cost (and food cost percentage) will be overstated if the cost of sales is not adjusted to compensate for these meals. These food expenses were incurred to feed staff members,

Exhibit 17   Adjustments to Basic Cost of Sales

Cost of Sales: Food	Charge to:	Cost of Sales: Beverage	Charge to:
Value of Beginning Inventory + Purchases − Value of Ending Inventory		Value of Beginning Inventory + Purchases − Value of Ending Inventory	
Unadjusted Cost of Sales: Food		Unadjusted Cost of Sales: Beverage	
+ Transfers to Kitchen	Food Cost	− Transfers to Kitchen	Food Cost
− Transfers from Kitchen	Bev. Cost	+ Transfers from Kitchen	Bev. Cost
− Employees' Meal Cost	Labor Cost		
− Value of Complimentary Meals	Promotion Expense	− Value of Complimentary Drinks	Promotion Expense
Net Cost of Sales: Food		Net Cost of Sales: Beverage	

Source: Jack D. Ninemeier, *Planning and Control for Food and Beverage Operations,* 6th ed. (Lansing, Mich.: Educational Institute of the American Hotel & Lodging Association, 2004), p. 313.

not to generate revenue. The cost of meals to staff members is properly considered a labor or benefits cost rather than a food cost.

Some food service managers use the unadjusted cost of sales as their monthly food and beverage costs because they believe that the increased degree of accuracy does not warrant the increased amount of time it takes to make adjustments. However, even food and beverage operations with relatively small annual revenue levels (less than $500,000) may note a significant difference in product costs when adjustments are made to yield a more accurate picture of the cost of generating revenues.

When adjustments are made to the basic cost of sales, the amount deducted must be charged to some other expense category. Managers who want a more accurate identification of the costs of food and beverage products that generated revenue may make any or all of the adjustments listed in Exhibit 17. If any of these adjustments are made to the actual cost of sales, they also must be reflected in how standard food costs are calculated for comparisons to be meaningful. Note, however, that computerized systems generating ideal (theoretical) costs based on number of items sold times recipe costs already exclude irrelevant costs; typically, no adjustments need be made. Once calculated, the actual monthly cost of food or beverages, should be compared with standard costs, budgeted performance expectations, and, if useful, past financial statements.

Introduction to Yield

The term yield means the net weight or volume of a food item after it has been processed and made ready for sale to the guest. The difference between the raw or **as purchased (AP) weight** and the prepared or **edible portion (EP) weight** is termed a production loss. For example, if 25 pounds (AP weight) of pork tenderloin are purchased and, after trimming and roasting, 22.5 pounds remain, there is a production loss of 2.5 pounds (25 pounds AP weight minus 22.5 pounds EP weight).

In general, there are three steps in the production process. The first is preparation, which includes such activities as meat trimming and vegetable cleaning. The second step is cooking. Holding, the third step, includes the portioning of those products that have not been pre-portioned. A "loss" can occur in any of these steps.

A **standard yield** results when an item is produced according to established standard production procedures outlined in the standard recipe. It serves as a base against which to compare actual yields. For example, if the standard purchase specifications are adhered to, and a meat item is properly trimmed, cooked, and portioned, the actual yield should closely approximate the standard yield.

Determining Standard Yield. Standard yields are determined by conducting a yield test. Ideally, everything that does not have a 100-percent yield should be tested. Examples of items with 100-percent yield (100-percent edible portion) are some portion-controlled products such as meats and those convenience foods that only need to be plated. However, from a practical standpoint, yield tests are typically performed only on high-cost items or on lower-cost products used in large quantities.

The yield from a product depends on several factors, including the grade, original weight, and preparation and cooking methods. Therefore, it is helpful for a food and beverage purchaser to compare the yields for similar products from different distributors. It may be possible to substitute a raw product with a lower cost per unit that provides a yield similar to that of a higher cost product, without compromising the operation's quality standards.

An example of the results of a yield test (sometimes called a butcher test when done for meat) is shown in Exhibit 18. In this example, eight oven-prepared beef rib sections, averaging 20 pounds, 4 ounces each, were cooked and trimmed, and the bones were removed according to an operation's standard recipe and standard preparation and cooking procedures. (Note that eight rib sections were used in this example to provide a more accurate basis for the yield calculations.) By weighing the meat at each step, the loss due to cooking and trimming can be assessed.

Since the AP weight is already known (162 pounds), the meat must next be weighed when it is removed from the oven after cooking. By subtracting the cooled weight from the original weight, you can determine the loss in cooking—in this example, an average of 3 pounds, 14 ounces per rib section. Next, the fat cap and bones must be removed and the remaining meat weighed. This is the edible portion or servable weight—in this example, an average of 11 pounds, 3 ounces per rib section. Subtracting the edible portion (servable) weight from the cooked weight indicates that the loss in carving and bones averaged 5 pounds, 3 ounces.

Cost per Servable Pound. Once the edible (servable) portion weight is determined, a **cost per servable pound** can be determined. To find the cost per servable pound, first establish the yield percentage. The **yield percentage** (sometimes called **yield factor**) is the ratio of servable weight to original weight. It is calculated by dividing the servable weight by the original weight (normally both weights are expressed in ounces; there are 16 ounce in one pound) and multiplying the quotient by 100 to convert the decimal to a percentage. For example:

$$\frac{\text{Servable Weight}}{\text{Original Weight}} \times 100 = \text{Ratio of Servable Weight to Original Weight}$$

$$\frac{(11\ \text{lb} \times 16\ \text{oz per lb}) + 3\ \text{oz}}{(20\ \text{lb} \times 16\ \text{oz per lb}) + 4\ \text{oz}} = \frac{179\ \text{oz}}{324\ \text{oz}} \times 100 = 55.25\% \text{ (rounded)}$$

Exhibit 18   Summary of Yield Test Results

#109

Item: *Oven Prepared Beef Rib*   Grade: *USDA Choice*
Pieces: *8*   Total Weight: *162 lb*   Average Weight: *20 lb, 4 oz*
Average Item Cost: *$120.49 at $5.95/lb*
Supplier: *Various*

Summary of Yield Test Results

Cooking and Portioning Details	Weight	% of Original Weight	Cost Per Servable Lb	Cost Factor
Edible Portion (EP) Weight	11 lb 3 oz	55.25%	$10.77	1.81
Loss due to fat trim & bones	5 lb 3 oz	25.62		
Loss due to cooking	3 lb 14 oz	19.13		
As Purchased (AP) Weight	20 lb 4 oz	100.00%		

Other Data:
   Cooked at 300°F for 4 hrs, 45 min

Source: Jack D. Ninemeier, *Planning and Control for Food and Beverage Operations,* 6th ed. (Lansing, Mich.: Educational Institute of the American Hotel & Lodging Association, 2004), p. 68.

This means that 55.25 percent of the purchase weight of the beef ribs will be available for service to guests.

The cost per servable pound is found by dividing the AP price by the yield percentage. For example:

$$\frac{\text{AP Price}}{\text{Yield Percentage}} \quad = \quad \text{Cost per Servable Pound}$$

$$\frac{\$5.95}{0.5525} \quad = \quad \$10.77 \text{ (rounded)}$$

In other words, if beef ribs cost $5.95 per pound, $10.77 will be required to produce one pound of product that can be plated and served to guests.

The cost per servable pound is the information needed to calculate standard portion costs.

One can make a similar calculation to determine that total AP quantity needed once the yield percentage is known. Assume that fifty 8-ounce edible portions of beef ribs in the above example are required for a banquet and that there is a 55.25 percent yield. What quantity of beef ribs will be needed to yield the 25 pounds (50 portions at 8 ounces per portion) that are requested?

$$\frac{\text{Quantity Needed} \times \text{Edible Portion}}{\text{Yield Percentage}} \quad = \quad \text{Quantity to Purchase/Prepare}$$

$$\frac{50 \text{ portions} \times 8 \text{ oz/portion}}{.5525} = 724 \text{ oz (rounded)}$$

The cook will have to prepare approximately 45.25 pounds (724 ounces divided by 16 ounces per pound) to yield the 25 servable pounds that are needed for the banquet.

The Cost Factor. The **cost factor** is a constant value that may be used to convert new AP prices into a revised cost per servable pound when purchase prices change. The cost factor assumes that the standard purchase specifications, standard recipe, and standard yield remain the same. The cost factor is obtained by dividing the cost per servable pound, calculated as part of the yield test, by the original AP cost per pound. For example:

$$\frac{\text{Cost per Servable Pound}}{\text{AP Price per Pound}} = \text{Cost Factor}$$

$$\frac{\$10.77}{\$5.95} = 1.81$$

Any time the AP cost changes from the amount used to calculate the original cost per servable pound in the yield test, a new cost per servable pound can be computed by multiplying the cost factor by the new AP price. For example, if the AP price for the beef ribs increased to $6.29 per pound, the new cost per servable pound would be:

New AP Price	×	Cost Factor	=	New Cost per Servable Pound
$6.29	×	1.81	=	$11.38

One final note: it is critical that all established standards remain the same. Proper use of the cost factor is dependent on the operation adhering to the same standard purchase specifications and following the preparation and cooking methods exactly as used in the yield test.

The pack size in a case affects the yield. For example, a 30-pound case of frozen vegetables will yield more ounces and more portions than six 5-pound containers of those same vegetables or twelve 2-pound containers of the same vegetables in a case. Since pack sizes may change, sometimes with availability or with a particular manufacturer, the portion cost is critical. The portion cost is the amount that an operator pays for a specific portion size of that product. Another yield consideration is the score of canned products, say peach halves. A 98-score can of peach halves will yield more than a 91-score can of peach halves, even though the can size may be identical. In that case, it is always important to count that product in the can.

The Ordering Process

Ordering is the next step in the purchasing process after the purchasing decision has been made. Ordering is usually prompted by an indication from a department or area of the food service operation that a product or supply is needed. In larger operations, ordering is stimulated by a purchase requisition from the person responsible for the storeroom. In larger food service operations, the process of ordering is formalized with use of a purchase order. In smaller independent operations, a simple purchase record may work just fine. In either case, the purchasing needs are communicated to the distributor during ordering.

Electronic Ordering

There is an economic advantage to utilizing electronic methods of placing orders if those who use the Internet see it as adding value through better and faster information, reduced prices, and enhanced services. However, some food service operators, admittedly more traditional in their views, prefer face-to-face conversation with the distributor's sales representative. To them, the value is in the personal relationship with the sales representative and the one-on-one interactions. Still other food service operators prefer to place their orders via facsimile, perhaps after being sent a reminder list of frequently ordered products, supplies, and services by the distributor's sales representative.

One of the most frequent sources of economic value via the Internet is the investigation of food service equipment and supplies. The categories include kitchen equipment, paper and disposable products, and tabletop supplies. As a whole, the common characteristics of these three product categories is that they are nonperishable and purchased less frequently than food and beverage products. Those using the Internet for these purchases cite economic value in the global reach and immediacy. With an Internet connection, a food service operator can almost order any product available from anywhere in the world in just a short amount of time.

E-Sourcing. Even though we sometimes think of electronic transactions as cold and not relationship oriented, they can be quite people-oriented since they frequently require several e-mail communications and they may be supplemented by telephone conversations. Some food service operators prefer **e-sourcing** to face-to-face discussions with sales representatives.

One of the keys to having e-sourcing work is to design the systems so that they fit the needs of the customers. Trying to get customers to conform to a system that is simply designed with the manufacturer or distributor in mind simply does not work. For example, when a customer contacts a manufacturer or distributor on-line, that individual should be asked what the preferred method is to contact the customer—by e-mail, telephone, or facsimile. A specific customer service representative at the manufacturer or distributor should be charged with being the point of contact for that customer. If, for example, an order was placed for a customer with a manufacturer and the shipment is being sent after the agreed-upon date from the factory, the IT system should notify the appropriate customer service representative at the distributor who is responsible for contacting the customer by the customer's preferred means of communication.

Because some purchasers do not take a long-term relationship-focused approach to e-sourcing, there exists some ill will when e-sourcing is used merely to pit one distributor against another. When the only goal of e-sourcing is obtaining the lowest possible prices on products, supplies, or services, everyone involved perceives it as a negative. Distributors may feel forced to participate in on-line negotiations and do so reluctantly. While they suffer domestic profit losses in some cases, the distributors do not want to risk losing business opportunities in the future. When purchasers make decisions on price only, and treat what is being purchased only as a commodity, they tend to ignore delivery, quality, reliability, service, and other value-added elements such as information. Consequently, distributors often feel undervalued in this imbalanced purchasing process.

To avoid these traps, it is suggested that purchasers prioritize delivery, quality, reliability, service, and price, after the requirements are determined. Then the purchase specifications can be developed, and bids can be sought and evaluated based on the prioritized list. Clear specifications communicate the purchaser's requirements and expectations. From the manufacturer's or distributor's point of view, clearly written and complete purchase specifications help the organization decide that either this is a promising business opportunity or it is a bidding situation that simply is not in the best interest of the manufacturer or distributor.

Unlimited access to worldwide distributors and manufacturers is an advantage to e-sourcing. But it is also a disadvantage since those who do not meet the criteria as specified by the purchaser must be evaluated as well and eliminated. And this elimination has to happen before negotiations begin or else the highly qualified will be competing with the unqualified manufacturers and distributors. If this step in the process does not take place, a purchaser runs the risk of choosing a distributor who may offer the lowest bid, but also offers inferior quality and late deliveries. In addition to price, competing bidders must be evaluated on factors important to the purchaser, which may include:

- Applicable certification.

- Delivery options.

- Immediately available inventory options.

- Locations.

- Overall business practice integrity.

- References.

- Revenue.

- Tangible assurances of experience, quality, and reliability.

- Track record for meeting deadlines.

- Value-added services.

- Years in business.

There are benefits to both purchasers as well as distributors and manufacturers with e-sourcing. For the distributors and manufacturers, new business opportunities, ability to protect margins by taking part in bidding activity in real time, access to competitive market data as input to future bidding and pricing decisions, and reduced paperwork and time to respond to requests for proposals are potential benefits. For purchasers, benefits may include substantial cost savings, access to distributors and manufacturers from around the world, ability to secure higher quality products and supplies and services, streamline the negotiation process (RFP) through bid analysis, and reduced costs and time for administrative activities.

There are two basic options for e-sourcing, which typically is defined as on-line purchasing negotiations:

- *On-line forward auctions*—one seller and many purchasers who compete against each other. The auction is real time and is designed to stimulate demand by the buyers and increase the price. Manufacturers and distributors sometimes use forward auctions to sell excess capital equipment and materials, outdated capital equipment and materials, and/or services being liquidated.

- *On-line reverse auctions*—one purchaser and many sellers who compete against each other. The auction is in real time and is designed to capture the purchaser's business and decrease the price. Purchasers start the process by distributing purchase specifications for products, supplies, and/or services.

E-Purchasing. The purchasing of products, supplies, and services on-line is called e-purchasing. Just like in face-to-face or facsimile purchasing, e-purchasing begins with an analysis of requirements, and is followed by detailing in writing what those are in the form of a purchase specification. The process of determining whether or not e-purchasing is to the advantage of the food service operation begins with a needs analysis. The needs analysis examines what the operation is attempting to achieve with e-purchasing, how the cost associated with e-purchasing will be covered, the importance of having an e-purchasing process that only includes the operation versus one that may include others in a GPO, support for e-purchasing from top management and operational-level managers, effect on current distribution, and how existing accounting, control, communication, and technology systems can support e-purchasing.

Following the needs analysis, it is important to conduct a market evaluation either formally by issuing a request for information (RFI) or informally by having conversations with sales representatives. Once the needs and market are understood, a request for proposal (RFP) can be issued for the software to drive e-purchasing. Scripted demos can be applied here and help make the evaluation of the proposals more objective. Evaluation of the proposals is the next step with the goal of developing a short list of those who can meet the requirements. The last step is negotiation and beginning the relationship.

More food service operations are using the Internet to comparison shop and order products, supplies, and services electronically. Advantages often cited include reduced costs, reduced time and associated boosts in productivity, and enhanced information. The information available ranges from product-usage reports and order listings and inventory levels to pricing and order quantities, and service levels.

The ordering and delivery processes for e-purchasing typically start with the food service operation logging on the day before the desired delivery with a user name and protected password. The operator then reviews an on-line order

Exhibit 19   E-Purchasing with Gordon Food Services

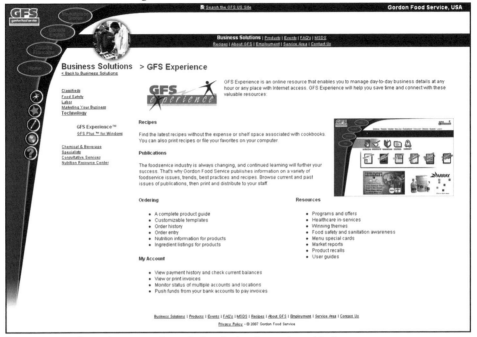

Source: www. gfs.com/content_us/bussolutions/tech_gfsexperience.html.

guide and selects quantities and prices. Order guides are usually customized to that particular operation and follow the set-up of the storage area for ease of use and efficiency. Exhibit 19 contains information on e-purchasing from Gordon Food Services.

While e-purchasing orders can be placed from any computer, the process does often require the purchase of hardware and software so the system can be accessed, particularly if the transactions are data-heavy and high-volume. Usually, when a requested product or supply is out-of-stock, a substitute with pricing is automatically offered. The e-purchasing system has applicability for small independent operations to larger chain food service operations. When a food service operation (e.g., a contract on-site operation) changes managers abruptly, one advantage to an e-purchasing system is that all the data and records on ordering are still available to quickly be used by the new manager of the operation. In that sense, an e-purchasing system helps the operation efficiently and effectively manage through such a crisis as abrupt management turnover. These records are also helpful if the food service operator decides to change to a different manufacturer or distributor.

GPOs have embraced e-purchasing to maintain purchasing programs, control negotiation, ensure distributor compliance, manage program data, and provide product-tracking and data-analysis services to members. Answers to questions such as "What is my drop size?", "What is my compliance?", "Am I getting the

Exhibit 20 E-Purchasing with ChoiceBuys

Source: http://apps.choicecentral.com/choicebuys.

price I contracted for?", "Are the products being purchased the ones I specified?", and "How accurate is my forecasting?" can all be readily and, in most cases, rapidly answered.

The hotel segment is also active in e-purchasing. Choice Hotels International has an electronic portal called ChoiceBuys (see Exhibit 20). The e-purchasing system reduces costs for operators while benefiting franchisees, distributors/manufacturers, and franchisors. Sunstone Hotel Investors, LLC has created BuyEfficient, a wholly-owned subsidiary to channel rebates or incentives from manufacturers and distributors back to the lodging properties.

Bar Codes and Radio Frequency Identification Tags. Bar codes are an electronic tool that has been used in the retail grocery industry for years. Scanning these bar codes on retail products gives the individual responsible for staffing the checkout line the ability to process orders quickly with fewer errors. So, too, products and supplies have been bar coded for use in the food service distribution channel. This permits scanning of product information when products enter inventory at the distributor's warehouse, when they are selected and placed on the delivery truck, and when they arrive at the receiving area of the food service operation.

Radio frequency identification (RFID) tags are similiar to bar codes; however, radio frequency scanners are used to read the information. This takes the place of traditional bar code scanners. The advantage is that products can be added to inventory when they arrive on the loading dock. The tags combined with scanners can also generate invoices quickly, and this information can be used to maintain records of stock levels and inventory. Future advances of this technology could include communication among manufacturers, distributors, and food service operations, the generation of electronic purchase orders, and placing of special orders directly with the manufacturer.

Security Considerations of Food Service Operations ————

Food service managers must be prepared for security threats. Only intensive preparation can help ensure that they will handle emergencies in a professional manner with minimal threat to both staff members and guests. In this section we will outline security issues that food service operations might experience.

Terrorism

There is a real concern in the United States and elsewhere that terrorists might be seeking ways to contaminate the food supply using biological or chemical agents. **Bioterrorism** takes place when harmful biological substances are intentionally used by terrorists to injure or terrorize others. Sometimes these substances are introduced into food. Bioterrorism agents include anthrax and ricin. Anthrax is a serious disease caused by *Bacillus anthracis*, a bacterium that forms spores. Anthrax was used as an agent of bioterrorism in 2001 when it was deliberately spread through the U.S. postal system via contaminated letters. Ricin is a toxin found in the seeds of the castor bean plant; this toxic protein is so deadly that just one milligram can kill an adult. Chemicals that can contaminate food include pesticides, mycotoxins, heavy metals, and other acutely toxic chemicals such as cyanide. These harmful substances and many others can be introduced into food anywhere along the food chain between farm and table by terrorists. Imported food could be tainted with biological or chemical agents before it even enters the United States, or toxins might be introduced at a domestic food-processing plant.

There has already been one terrorist attack in the United States involving food. In 1984, members of a religious commune in rural Oregon tried to influence a local election by poisoning the salad bars of several restaurants with *Salmonella* bacteria to sicken voters. The group hoped to take over county government by preventing local citizens from voting. Although no one died, 751 people became ill.

Food Safety and Defense

Food safety and defense fall under the jurisdiction of several centers and offices within the FDA, including the Center for Food Safety and Applied Nutrition and the National Center for Toxicological Research. The FDA is responsible for the safety of about 80 percent of the U.S. food supply. The exceptions are meat, poultry, and processed egg products, which are under the jurisdiction of the USDA. FDA oversight includes the safe production, processing, storage, and holding of domestic and imported food. If a terrorist-related incident involving the deliberate contamination of food occurred in the United States, the FDA would work closely with federal, state, and local authorities to identify the problem, investigate, and get the contaminated food products off the market quickly.

Theft and Economic Security

In small food service operations, where owners/managers may purchase and receive the products themselves, control procedures are less concerned with theft than with obtaining the best value. In larger operations, where other personnel take on purchasing tasks, security becomes an increasingly important concern. The control process must guard against several types of theft that are possible during the purchasing process.

Kickbacks. In several common types of kickbacks, the buyer for the food and beverage operation works in collusion with someone from the distributor's company. The kickback can be money or gifts. Either way, the owner of the operation is the loser. In one kickback scheme, products are purchased at prices that are higher than those posted. The two thieves then split the difference between the real and inflated prices. To best control this type of theft, the owner/manager can routinely review invoices and ask such questions as, "Why are so many products purchased from the same distributor?" The manager can also periodically review the selection of distributors and solicit price quotations randomly to ensure that prices paid are the best—or at least competitive—for the quality and quantity of products being purchased.

In another kickback scheme, the delivery invoice is padded by adding items that were not received, or it is increased by adding unreasonable charges for handling or some other service. This scheme works well when the same staff member does the receiving and the purchasing. Therefore, a system that separates the purchasing and receiving tasks could prevent this type of theft.

In large food service operations, purchasing may be the responsibility of a staff purchasing department. Receiving and storing activities may be performed by persons in the accounting department, Under this system, products do not come under the control of production staff until they are issued. This system helps reduce the possibility that one person, working alone, can implement a kickback scheme.

Fictitious Companies. Purchasing personnel can steal by setting up a nonexistent company that submits invoices for products never received. Managers can periodically review invoice payment distributions by examining the names of payees on company checks. Unless the manager is familiar with the distributor, checks should never be sent to companies with only post office box addresses.

Reprocessing. Distributors may try to send an invoice to the food and beverage operation for processing a second time. To avoid this type of theft, operations need an internal system to verify which invoices have not been paid and to cancel invoices when they are paid.

Delivery Invoice Errors. Intentional arithmetic errors, short weight or counts, wrong quality, and similar "mistakes" can cost the operation money. Management or office personnel must check all arithmetic on invoices and statements—even when they are computer-generated—and follow proper receiving practices to catch these mistakes. Whether they are innocent mistakes or fraud, the bottom line is the same: the food service operation loses money.

Credit Memo Problems. When products are not delivered or when deliveries are short of the quantities ordered, a request-for-credit memo should be issued to reduce the original delivery invoice by the value of the items not delivered. The distributor should then issue a credit memo to adjust the account. Managers and receiving staff should never accept a "we'll deliver it later and not charge you" comment from the truck driver. A request-for-credit memo should be written and attached to the delivery invoice. The manager should also alert the operation's accounting department to ensure that the distributor properly processes the credit to the buyer's account. Normally, credit memo forms in multiple parts are provided by the delivery person. It is helpful for the property to also have blank copies of a generic form available in case the delivery person does not have copies.

Quality Substitutions. Quality substitutions occur when a price is quoted for the proper quality item but a lower quality item is delivered. Proper receiving practices can help prevent paying more for a lower quality product. Brand or label substitutions are also possible if receiving personnel are not familiar with products ordered. If alert staff do recognize product problems, the distributor can exchange the products for those of proper quality. This problem occurs more frequently than some purchasers may suspect and requires close attention to both purchasing and receiving duties.

Purchaser Theft. Purchasers might practice a variety of other thefts: purchasing for their own use, reciprocal purchasing for their own benefit, or purchasing products wholesale with the intention of reselling them to selected staff members or to others. Using an effectively designed purchasing system can help reduce these types of potential problems.

Other Security Considerations

After the terrorist attacks of September 11, 2001, the FDA conducted food supply vulnerability assessments and later issued guidelines on security measures that the food industry could take to minimize terrorism risks. A critical component of controlling threats from deliberate food contamination is the ability to rapidly test large numbers of samples of potentially contaminated foods for a variety of biological, chemical, and radiological agents. The FDA has worked closely with Centers for Disease Control and Prevention and the USDA to establish the Food Emergency Response Network (FERN)—a national network of laboratories ready to respond to a food security emergency.

Under the authority of the Public Health Security and Bioterrorism Preparedness and Response Act of 2002, signed by President George W. Bush in June 2002, the FDA developed the following new regulations that address provisions of the law:

- *Registration of food facilities.* This regulation, which became effective in December 2003, requires owners and operators of foreign or domestic food facilities that manufacture or process, pack, or hold food for human or animal consumption in the United States to submit information to the agency about the facility and emergency contacts.

- *Prior notification of imported food shipments.* This regulation, which also became effective in December 2003, requires the FDA to receive prior notice of imported food shipments before the food arrives at a U.S. port. The FDA expects to receive about 25,000 notifications about incoming shipments every day.

- *Establishment and maintenance of records.* Manufacturers, processors, packers, importers, and others are required to keep records that identify the source from which they receive food and where they send it.

- *Administrative detention.* The FDA now has the authority to detain any food for up to 30 days if there is credible evidence that the food poses a serious threat to humans or animals.

For more information about food safety, you can call the FDA's toll-free consumer information line at 1-88-SAFEFOOD, or visit www.foodsafety.gov. Typing "terrorism and food" in an Internet search engine can lead you to the latest government articles and other information relating to this topic.

Endnotes

1. Adapted from Curt Werner, "Facing Tough Questions on Ethics, GPOs Seek Ways to Respond," *Healthcare Purchasing News* 26, no. 12 (December 2002), p. 14.

2. Readers seeking a more in-depth exploration of inventory systems should see Jack D. Ninemeier, *Planning and Control for Food and Beverage Operations,* 6th ed. (Lansing, Mich.: Educational Institute of the American Hotel & Lodging Association, 2004), pp. 228–237.

Key Terms

as purchased (AP) weight—The raw weight of a meat product.

bioterrorism—Attacks in which harmful biological substances are intentionally used to injure or terrorize others.

co-op—A volume purchasing organization that is usually found in the noncommercial, on-site, and not-for-profit food service segments.

cost factor—A constant value that may be used to convert new AP prices into a revised cost per servable pound when purchase prices change.

cost per servable pound—Information needed to calculate standard portion costs, determined by dividing the as purchased (AP) price by the yield percentage as a decimal.

edible portion (EP) weight—The weight of a meat product after trimming and cooking.

e-sourcing—Use of electronic communication methods in purchasing.

ethics—The study of moral principles.

external customers—Those who bring their time and money to the operation to purchase the products and services it offers for sale.

food sample data sheet—A purchasing control document that helps standardize the evaluation of a product an operation is considering for purchase and makes product selection more objective.

group purchasing organization—A common organization that coordinates purchasing for a number of individual food service operations.

internal customers—An operation's staff members.

logistics—Purchasing considerations such as the number of deliveries an operation requires per week, delivery size, and the condition of an operation's receiving area.

market research—An investigation of data about the fundamental structure of the market.

order point—The number of purchase units in stock when an order is placed.

prime distributor—A distributor that has all or the majority of an operation's purchasing business.

purchase order system—A system in which a written document formally identifies the product, quantity, unit cost, and total cost that both the distributor and purchaser have agreed to.

purchase record—A document similiar to a purchase order that is not given to a distributor.

purchasing process—The series related activities that takes place when food service operation buys products or services for use in meeting its customers' requirements.

quality—Doing the right things right.

recall—An action taken by a business to remove a product from the market.

scripted demo—A way to make the purchasing process more efficient and effective by focusing and controlling distributor presentations.

speculative purchasing—Buying more if prices are expected to increase and buying less if prices are expected to decrease. This should be practiced only by management.

standard purchase specification—A guideline for distributors that provides detailed descriptions of the quality, size, and weight desired for particular items.

standard yield—The amount of product that results when it is produced according to standard procedures outlined in a standard recipe.

value—An element of the purchasing process that can be described in terms of the food service operation's quality, service, and price requirements.

yield factor—See yield percentage.

yield percentage—The ratio of servable weight to original weight, calculated by dividing the servable weight by the original weight and multiplying by 100.

 Review Questions ——————————————————

1. How does purchasing contribute to managing for quality in a food service operation?

2. What are the steps in the purchasing process?

3. What are the methods to determine value in the purchasing process?

4. What are the skills, knowledge, and behaviors required in effective purchasing personnel?

5. Why are ethics important and what is the role of ethics in purchasing?

6. In terms of market research, what are the essential considerations in defining the market, distribution, and internal aspects?

7. What are the components of group purchasing?

8. How are management and leadership activities related to purchasing?

9. What are the basic elements of a food purchase specification?

10. How are the basics of pricing and cost controls, including payment policies, related to purchasing?

11. What are the considerations in the ordering process, including e-purchasing?

12. How are security considerations in food service operations addressed during purchasing?

 References ——————————————————

"Choosing Your Food Service Provider For Your Restaurant." *Allfoodbusiness.com.* Available on-line at www.allfoodbusiness.com/Choosing_A_Foodservice.php.

Anonymous. "An Alternate GPO Model." *Food Management* 40, no. 1 (January 2005): p. 32.

Anonymous. "Making Choice a Core Value." *Food Management* 40, no. 1 (January 2005): p. 26.

Anonymous. "Purchase Power." *Hospitality* (June 2003): p. 25.

Atkinson, William. "New Buying Tools Present Different Ethical Challenges." *Purchasing* 132, no. 4 (March 6, 2003), p. 27.

Barrat, Christopher and Heather Wood. "Should You Accept Christmas Gifts?" *Supply Management* 6, no. 14 (December 13, 2001): p. 28.

Brooks, Andrew and Steven Forth. "The Right Person." *Purchasing B2B* 44, no. 10 (December 2002): p. 16.

Carbonara, Joseph M. "Innovating a Successful Future." *Foodservice Equipment & Supplies* 58, no. 4 (April 2005): p. 13.

Day, Alan. "The Knowing-Dealing Gap." *Supply Management* 9, no. 16 (August 5, 2004): p. 17.

Dlaboha, Ihor. "A Partnership at All Levels." *ID Sales Pro* 39, no. 7 (July/August 2003): p. 17.

Ellingson, Rick. "Life After FEDA." *Foodservice Equipment & Supplies* 58, no. 6 (June 2005): p. 50.

Hollar, Marilyn B. "Risk Management Ethics." *Rough Notes* 147, no. 8 (August 2004): p. 90.

Hume, Scott. "Good Buys Are Hard to Do." *Restaurants & Institutions* 115, no. 2 (February 1, 2005): p. 55.

Kasavana, Michael. "Scripted Demos: Directing Vendor Product Presentations." *Hospitality Upgrade* (2001).

Killeen, Sean. "Foodservice Operators Pooling Their Purchases or Dealing with Prime Vendors Can Net Significant Savings. Are You Engaging in These Efforts?" *Foodservice Director* 14, no. 4 (April 15, 2001): p. 20.

Lawn, John. "Common Mistakes that Purchasing Managers Make." *Food Management* 38, no. 2 (February 2003): p. 6.

Lawn, John. "Seven More Mistakes Purchasing Managers Make." *Food Management* 38, no. 3 (March 2003): p. 8.

Lawn, John. "The GPOs: Where Do They Go from Here?" *Food Management* 40, no. 1 (January 2005): pp. 22–34, 64.

Lawn, John. "What Operators and Distributors Have in Common." *Food Management* 36, no. 11 (November 2001): p. 6.

Levin, Mike. "Right Today Wrong Tomorrow." *Summit* 7, no. 2 (March 2004): p. 19.

Murray, J. Gordon. "New Roles for Purchasing: Researchers, Detectives, Teachers, Doctors and Architects." *The International Journal of Public Sector Management* 15, no. 4/5 (2002): p. 307.

Murray, Pat. "A Dual Viewpoint on Service." *Foodservice Equipment & Supplies* 56, no. 10 (October 2003): p. 29.

O'Brien, Liam. "3663 Named Outsourcing Leader." *Supply Management* 9, no. 11 (May 27, 2004): p. 11.

Prentkowski, Dave. "More Than A Catalog Cut-Sheet." *Foodservice Equipment & Supplies* 57, no. 2 (February 2004): p. 23.

Riell, Howard. "Q: What Do You Do if Clients Are Not Happy with Items You Sold Them?" *Foodservice Equipment & Supplies* 58, no. 1 (January 2005): p. 39.

Stem, Harry. "Buying Groups: A Perspective." *Foodservice Equipment & Supplies* 56, no. 5 (May 2003): p. 31.

Trent, Robert J. "The Use of Organizational Design Features in Purchasing and Supply Management." *The Journal of Supply Chain Management: A Global Review of Purchasing and Supply* (August 2004).

Vurva, Richard. "Hey, Look Me Over." *Progressive Distributor.* Available on-line at www.progressivedistributor.com/progressive/archives/Marketing/alliances.htm.

Watkins, Ed. "Shopping Spree." *Lodging Hospitality* 60, no. 3 (March 1, 2004): p. 46.

Williams, Jay and Tom Schrack. "Buying Groups—What Good Do They Do?" *Foodservice Equipment & Supplies* 56, no. 5 (May 2003): pp. 66–68.

Internet Sites

For more information, visit the following Internet sites. Remember, that Internet addresses can change without notice. If the site is no longer there, you can use a search engine to look for additional sites.

Avendra LLC
www.avendra.com

Better Vending Association
www.bettervending.com

Ethics in Business
www.foodreference.com/html/
artethics.html

FDA Recalls, Market Withdrawals,
  and Safety Alerts
www.fda.gov/opacom/7alerts.html

Instill Corporation
www.instill.com

Process Mapping and Flow Charting
www.isixsigma.com/
tt/process_mapping

Reverse Auctions
www.nu.com/business/frictionless/
reverse_auction_primer.pdf

Chapter 4 Outline

Competencies

4

The Distributor

FOOD SERVICE OPERATORS WHO SUCCEED GENERALLY IDENTIFY their distributors as partners and commit to working with these partners. These partners collaborate with the operator by aligning with the food service operation's values, vision, mission, and strategic goals. The distributor and the operator work together to share the operation's values, help move it closer to its vision, purposefully realize its mission, and achieve its strategic goals.

Characteristics of Distributor Partners

Partners live on a two-way street. That is, a partnership is not one-sided. Rather, each partner should find the relationship mutually beneficial. In the case of a partnership between a food service operator and a distributor, the distributor becomes another "arm," or resource, of the operation.

The Role of Consultant

The role of the **distributor sales representative (DSR)** has evolved in the relationship. The DSR used to be an order taker with a focus on selling the operator as much as possible during any sales call visit. Today's progressive DSR is a consultant who provides product samples, menu ideas, and information about changing market conditions. Of course, a sale is still part of the relationship, but it is not the primary reason for the relationship. A good example of a relationship is a prime distributor that provides most of the products purchased by the food service operation. The prime distributor adds value to the relationship since the sales volume is relatively high, often representing the majority of products purchased by that operation. So it is in the best interest of a prime distributor to nurture and build a relationship with the operator.

The consulting relationship goes beyond products and menu suggestions. Some DSRs make suggestions about tableware and table-top appearance. Others are capable of making suggestions for improved kitchen layout and more efficient food service equipment. Still others help the food service operator by providing software analysis of menu item popularity and profitability based on contribution margins (sales price minus the cost of a food item). Other DSRs can provide consulting advice on key personnel (e.g., chefs) recruitment or point-of-sale systems.

Prime Distributors

A **prime distributor** or prime vendor is one who provides the majority of products purchased by a food service operator. The prime distributor is the main source of food and beverage as well as other products (e.g., cleaning and sanitizing chemicals) purchased by the food service operation. In its role as the principal source of products purchased, a prime distributor is a key partner and must take a leading role in the operator-distributor partnership.

Prime distributors are the first source of products and services because they provide the greatest value to the food service operator, its owners, and its customers. This value is embedded in the prime distributor's ability to meet the food service operation's requirements for deliveries, pricing, product selection, quality, and additional services. These result in significant cost and time savings for the operator, which can then be passed on to the customers to further enhance the value that they perceive.

Prime distributor relationships often require a contract between the distributor and the operator. The contract gives the operator improved cost control in the prices paid for key menu items. The contract gives the prime distributor a higher percentage of the operator's total volume of purchases. To be effective and worthwhile, the contract must be mutually beneficial to the operator and the distributor.

When purchasing products and services, food service operators usually have several options available. However, each option carries with it certain requirements and limitations. Much depends on the willingness of distributors and operators to enter into these purchasing arrangements. Similarly, a purchaser may be limited to specific options by the nature and volume of the food service operation.

As a food service operation grows, it often experiences cost advantages simply as a result of its size. Distribution charges may be lower due to consolidation of orders. Distributors may offer discounts based on greater purchase volume. These benefits relating to the food service operation's larger size are termed economies of scale. Common purchasing options include riding the market, cost-plus pricing, cost-percentage pricing, market pricing, buy-and-inventory pricing, long-term contracts and hedging.

DSR Training and Expertise

One of the many ways to evaluate a distributor is by assessing the expertise and training of its DSRs. When there is a constant turnover of DSRs at a particular distributor, there is likely a problem with the ways that these internal customers (i.e., the DSRs) are treated by the distributor. This red flag may point to a credibility problem with that distributor. Of course it is difficult, if not impossible, to build a long-term, mutually beneficial partnership with a distributor when DSRs are constantly leaving and new DSRs are taking their place.

One strategy to reduce DSR turnover is training. Investing in DSRs' professional development pays dividends in their retention. From the food service operator's perspective, this training to build expertise goes far beyond a simple understanding of the products, services, operating philosophies, and policies of the distributor.

Well-trained DSR partners have an in-depth understanding of the culture and philosophies of the food service operators that they serve. They understand the strategic goals, vision, values, and mission of each particular operator. They also have expertise about the food service operation's focus on fresh products, product costs that can affect the prices charged to the operation's customers, quality and ways that the operation manages for quality, as well as the service delivery systems in place in that unique food service operation. Well-trained DSRs know, fundamentally, that their food service operations depend on them for service that meets or exceeds their expectations, just as the operation's customers expect the same service excellence.

Know the Food Service Operation. A distributor partner takes the time necessary to get to know the food service operation. This knowledge certainly includes the functions of purchasing and procurement relative to the buying process, the profitability focus in commercial operations or cost-control emphasis in noncommercial operations, an emphasis on obtaining the best value based on price and quality standards, and communications. But the knowledge goes beyond purchasing to include the functions listed in Exhibit 1.

The DSR must know the operation's product and service specifications because they communicate the requirements of the operation and its customers —both internal and external. Internal customers include, for example, production personnel, service staff, and other staff members responsible for delivering value to external customers. External customers are those who pay (with their money as well as an investment of time) for the products and services created and delivered.

Beyond purchasing policies, procedures, and specifications, DSRs must be knowledgeable of the food service operation's inventory/warehouse management systems, ways to enhance relationships with the DSR's distributor, contracts, human resources management, and general management, as listed in Exhibit 1. While the focus of Exhibit 1 is commercial food service operations, many of these same functions apply in noncommercial food service operations. Knowledge is power and the more knowledge that a DSR has about the functions of each unique food service operation, the more likely that DSR will be to create powerful, long-lasting relationships with operators.

Recall that the food service operation begins with the process flow. When a DSR understands that process flow in general and how it relates to each specific food service operation, the DSR is better able to add value to the process, both for the operator and the operator's customers.

In addition to understanding the general food service process flow, an individual operator will want the DSR to know the unique features of that particular operation. For example, perhaps the operation's menu is planned seasonally, with changes based on the availability of fresh, seasonal ingredients. This operator, then, would want the DSR to suggest ingredients and menu items for possible inclusion in the new seasonal menu as it is being planned. Consider a small food service operator with insufficient storage space in the operation. This operator will want the DSR to be able to offer more frequent deliveries, based on the operation's sales volume. Next consider an operator who is planning a major capital investment to upgrade the kitchen. This operator would expect someone at the distributor to have the knowledge to be able to help with a new kitchen layout and the specifications for purchasing new kitchen equipment.

Exhibit 1   Typical Functions in Commercial Food Service Operations

I. Purchasing/Procurement
   1. Issue purchase orders for needed products and services.
   2. Recognize the importance of the buying process and its impact on the operation and distributors.
   3. Coordinate the procurement and distribution of food items with production operations.
   4. Contribute to the operation's profits by effective purchasing policies and procedures.
   5. Obtain the best value at the lowest price consistent with established quality standards and delivery schedules.
   6. Maintain files of distributors' stock lists, catalogs, price sheets, and discounts.
   7. Forecast market conditions, availability of materials, and economic conditions.
   8. Keep informed of current laws, rules, and regulations affecting purchasing.
   9. Monitor purchase orders to determine if deliveries are correct.
   10. Check purchase orders for clarity and completeness.
   11. Handle communications concerning overshipment, shortages, price changes, and related matters.
   12. Determine the cost of deliveries and the best method of transportation.

II. Specifications
   1. Develop specifications for products and services in cooperation with personnel responsible for production.
   2. Audit packaging specifications.
   3. Authorize rejection of materials that fail to meet specifications.
   4. Promote standardization of materials and services through specifications.
   5. Maintain file of current specifications.

III. Inventory/Warehouse Management
   1. Conduct periodic physical counts of stocks to verify records.
   2. Minimize losses from pilferage, spoilage, or obsolescence.
   3. Minimize operating costs for storage of food and supplies.
   4. Determine necessary stock levels to provide adequate food and supplies and to minimize capital investment.
   5. Inspect storage areas.
   6. Monitor records of inventory, materials on order, and potential demands for food and supplies.
   7. Monitor maintenance and repair of storage facilities.

IV. Distributor Relationships
   1. Select distributors.
   2. Negotiate reasonable terms with distributors.
   3. Act as liaison between distributors and other departments in the operation.
   4. Compare distributors' product quality, services, dependability, and costs.
   5. Create goodwill for the operation through effective trade relations.
   6. Solve problems with distributors.
   7. Establish a system for distributor rating and selection.
   8. Work with distributor sales representatives to identify new products, materials, and processes.
   9. Oversee distribution of bids and receipt of quotations.
   10. Investigate distributors' facilities.
   11. Interview salespersons.

V. Contracts
   1. Negotiate contracts for food, supplies, and services.

Exhibit 1 *(continued)*

2. Determine whether open market or contract purchasing is preferable for various products and services.
3. Coordinate review of contracts by legal counsel and/or other appropriate personnel.

VI. Human Resources Management
1. Develop job descriptions for purchasing and storeroom personnel.
2. Aid in training purchasing and storeroom personnel.
3. Manage purchasing and storeroom personnel.
4. Promote good relations between purchasing and other personnel in the organization.
5. Select qualified personnel for purchasing and storage functions.
6. Train buyers to follow established purchasing procedures.
7. Determine staffing needs for purchasing and storage functions.
8. Supervise clerical activities involved in purchasing

VII. General Management
1. Monitor flow of products through the food service system, from purchasing to production to service.
2. Serve on policy-making team of the operation.
3. Participate in "make-or-buy" decisions.
4. Maintain current knowledge of changing markets by reviewing trade literature, attending trade shows, and other means, such as the Internet.
5. Establish priorities for meeting objectives.
6. Develop policies and procedures to guide performance and to reduce duplication of effort.
7. Support a program of data processing.
8. Meet with personnel in the operation to discuss problems with products, deliveries, or services, and ways to fix the problems.
9. Develop a budget for operation within the scope of responsibility.
10. Review financial statements to monitor expenditures in operational areas.
11. Coordinate efforts with those who are responsible for managing for quality.
12. Promote energy conservation in operations within the scope of responsibility.
13. Contribute effectively to improving the value that the operation creates and delivers for its customers.

Adapted from Kimberly A. Loecker, Marian C. Spears, and Allene G. Vaden, "Purchasing Managers in Commercial Foodservice Organizations: Clarifying the Role," *Professional* (Spring 1983), pp. 9–16.

In addition to the specifics of the operation and the control points in the process flow, operators would expect distributors to know that negotiation of product prices is in the best interest of both the operator and the distributor. Negotiation begins by taking the viewpoint that while the focus is on creating a distributor-operator relationship, both players in the relationship have their own best interests in mind. The goal of each is to make money for their organization; these profits help the organizations survive and thrive.

Part of the negotiation strategy is to always ask the DSR for item prices before placing the order. This helps the DSR know that the operator cares about costs and profitability. Negotiation is not designed to bully the distributor into agreeing to a price so low that the distributor does not make a profit. Rather, the goal is to have both understand the costs associated with purchasing and be able to reach a compromise so that the transaction is mutually beneficial.

Second, the DSR must know that the operator does not intend to purchase *all* products from that one distributor. While there are exceptions and the purchasing relationships that are of highest strategic importance are those that involve the highest volumes of products purchased, it may be wise for the operation to have two sources for purchasing any particular product and regularly request bids from both distributors. This can help the operator with product availability at the lowest possible prices and will help the DSR understand that the maximizing of value, based on both quality and price, is essential.

Third, the DSR must know that the operator understands the distributor's costs. Take, for example, delivery costs. The DSR must know and explain to the operator that when a distributor can change from three deliveries each week with a value of $1,200 each to two deliveries each week with a $1,800 value (note: in both cases, the total purchases from that particular distributor for the week is $3,600, either 3 × $1,200 or 2 × $1,800), the costs are lowered for the distributor. This is because the truck must be loaded, stopped, and unloaded three times in the first case, but only twice in the second case. Whenever a distributor can reduce the costs of distribution to a particular operator, this may result in reduced prices paid by that operator for purchases from the distributor.

Finally, the DSR must understand that the operator will check all deliveries during the receiving control point. Products sold by count will be counted; products sold by weight will be weighed; the total order as placed will be verified as the total order received, including receiving checks for quality as specified.

Menu Analysis, Design, Evaluation, and Ideas

The menu is the blueprint or mission statement for a food service operation. As a mission statement, the menu describes the purpose of the operation or why the operation exists. While the menu's purpose is to communicate the many products and services offered for sale to external customers, the operation's larger purpose is to add a distinctive source of value for its external customers. As a blueprint, the menu lays out a plan to create a foundation on which to build the external customer's memorable service. These experiences begin with the menu and are enhanced by the products and services purchased.

Frequent **menu analysis** is essential since the final menu is never written. Rather, the process of menu development is ongoing and evolutionary. This is where distributors come in as a valuable source of menu ideas based on the needs of the food service operation and its customers. Operators expect DSRs to listen to their needs and understand their customers' requirements. Then, based on their knowledge of local market requirements and availability of products, DSRs would make suggestions to the operators for menu additions, changes, or deletions. Menu analysis should go beyond each menu item's popularity and profitability.

DSRs can greatly enhance menu analysis by offering information about how to understand each menu item's role in adding overall value, and what customer preferences are and how they are changing, along with what competitors of the food service operation are doing to address these preferences. This value is added by distributors since DSRs see the food service market as a bigger picture due to the number of operators with which they do business. Their information can greatly enhance the operation's menu analysis by suggesting appropriate products that could be added to the menu.

Operators appreciate the value added when a DSR is familiar with the operation and its menu before making suggestions. When a DSR has invested the time necessary to dine at a food service operation and study the menu, the suggestions from that DSR are more meaningful to the operator. When a DSR suggests a food product not currently being purchased by the operator, the best approach is to show multiple uses for that product so it can be cross-utilized and the menu can be rationalized. This cross-utilization and menu rationalization is particularly beneficial when there is limited storage space at the food service operation.

Menu design is a service offered by full-service distributors. Sometimes, the menu will be physically designed with an appealing layout. In other cases, the actual printing of the menu can be handled by a distributor. Both types of design services add value for the relationship.

Menu evaluation is somewhat related to menu analysis. Menu evaluation sometimes is driven by the operation's food cost percentage, although this is not always the best place to start. Rather, it is better to evaluate each menu item's popularity with customers, as well as profitability as defined by its contribution margin. The **contribution margin** for a menu item is the sales price for that menu item minus its food cost as follows:

$$\text{Contribution margin in \$} = \text{Sales Price in \$} - \text{Food Cost in \$}$$

It is called contribution margin because it is the dollar amount that menu item contributes to cover all nonfood costs in the food service operation as well as contribute to the operation's profit requirements. Some distributors have software programs available for use by their food service operation customers that calculate popularity and profitability.

Menu ideas from the DSR can supplement the menu changes under consideration by the food service operator. One set of ideas may be for ways to improve the quality of menu items. This may take the form of alternative products or preparation methods. Another set of ideas may be related to commodity (e.g., oils, grains) pricing and forecasted trends from experts at the distributor from manufacturers that the distributor represents. Other operators like when DSRs give their ideas on operational improvements, specifically how the operation's staff members can better use the distributor's products or obtain additional cost savings by being more operationally efficient. Other ideas are useful when the distributor's experts come into the food service operation and work with production staff on new menu concepts. The ideas and products must fit the operation's needs, based on customer requirements.

Ideas for Staff Training and Retention

Staff training is an ongoing process in a food service operation. Staff training is a retention strategy because an investment in staff training leads to staff development and a feeling that the operator cares about the staff.

Staff training is a service provided by leading distributors who are in sync with their operators' training needs. This training may take the form of recipe development or production-technique training for kitchen staff. It may include how to properly use, clean, and maintain food service equipment for production staff, as well as those responsible for the cleaning and maintenance control point.

Staff training has critical implications for food service equipment purchasing. Fundamentally, it is important that equipment used in a food service operation be inspected and tested by the appropriate organization (e.g., Underwriters Laboratories for electrically-powered equipment, American Gas Association for gas-powered equipment), as well as be evaluated by the National Sanitation Foundation. Distributors of food service equipment can also help train those who are specifying such purchases to provide details about all interior and exterior surfaces; classifications (i.e., equipment make, model, and size); specifications of additional guarantees from the manufacturer such as extended warrantees; pricing that includes the equipment as well as any necessary delivery and assembly and installation, required start-up operations and adjustments to the equipment; required mechanical details (e.g., amps, drain size, gas connection size, phase, volts, and water connection size); and when the equipment will be delivered to the operation. This training will also help the operation minimize or avoid costly delays and errors.

HACCP

In terms of the distributor, the goal of applying Hazard Analysis and Critical Control Point (HACCP) principles ultimately is to help safe products be delivered to the operation's customers by making certain that products are purchased from an approved source. But how does a food service operator decide whether a distributor is an approved source?

Approved distributors generally meet or exceed the following food safety criteria:

- Approved distributors have a HACCP program that works. Minimally, the distributors are expected to follow the same HACCP procedures as those being followed in the food service operation. In addition, distributors who sell fresh products should have a Good Agricultural Practices Plan.

- Approved distributors have clean and well-maintained plant and warehouse facilities, inspected regularly by appropriate federal (e.g., Food and Drug Administration, United States Department of Agriculture, other agencies) and/or state regulatory agencies. Visit the distributor's facilities.

- Approved distributors purchase the products that they sell from approved suppliers and manufacturers. Ask to see the records of those who supply your distributors. Ask regulatory agencies about the food safety records of the distributors. Ask competitors about their experiences with that distributor's food safety practices.

- Approved distributors take pride in the condition of their delivery trucks, both inside and outside. When products are being delivered, check the delivery vehicles for cleanliness and physical appearance, to determine if products are being delivered at the proper refrigerated and frozen storage temperatures, and to ascertain if raw products are shipped in the delivery vehicle separated from fresh produce and processed food products.

- Approved distributors deliver products at times that the food service operator specifies (i.e., *not* during a busy lunch period or when no one is there to receive the products), so that the products may be received properly and their quality determined, as specified by the operation's receiving control point standards.

- Approved distributors deliver products that are of the specified quality and quantity. There is an absence of such unacceptable products as products in broken shipping containers, dented cans, leaky packaging, and/or unsafe packaging.

- Approved distributors have staff members who have been trained in HACCP and utilize these tools to help ensure product safety.

Regional, National, and International Expertise

Regional, national and international expertise on the part of distributor staff is important in at least two situations. The first reason is that distributors with regional expertise can provide the food service operator with detailed information about the availability of locally grown regional food products. Perhaps the operation's customers require additions to the menu of organic food items grown on local farms. A knowledgeable DSR with regional expertise can assist the food service operation by providing organic products from the region to purchase.

National expertise may be important to a food service operator who is trying to capitalize on national food trends. If a DSR is in tune with these national trends, he or she can assist the operation with menu changes. A second reason for national expertise on the part of the DSR relates to chain restaurants with national coverage. Given the similarity of menu offerings across the nation in these chains, the organization may prefer to do business with prime distributors who have the ability to meet the chains products and services requirements nationwide. This would be true for a food service franchisor who sells franchises across the nation, as well as for a chain of food service operations that are owned and operated by a corporation across the nation.

Increasingly, international expertise is essential for distributors. This expertise is necessary for several reasons. First, with the proliferation of food service operations that feature cuisines from other countries, authentic food ingredients may only be available from that country, requiring knowledge of international commerce and import regulations on the part of the distributor. Second, several U.S.–based food service chains are expanding their operations to other countries. Here, again, a knowledgeable distributor network in those countries is critical if the chain is to maintain its consistent food product and service standards. And, third, food service operations from other countries are increasingly looking to extend their number of food service operations into the United States. International expertise of distributors makes this expansion possible and adds value for the operators seeking to expand.

Exhibit 2   Building a Team of Distributors

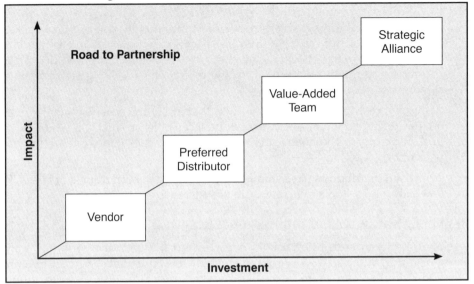

Integrated

Integrated food service operations view their distributors as strategic partners in the strategic vision, mission, values, and goals. An integrated approach to purchasing results in a strategic alliance as illustrated in Exhibit 2.

On the *y* (vertical) axis impact is indicated. As the impact of the integrated relationship increases, you move up the *y* axis. The *x* (horizontal) axis indicates investment, as the investment increases, you move to the right of this axis.

Begin by locating the lowest impact, lowest investment distributor in Exhibit 2. This is the **vendor**, one who simply provides products or services based on price alone. A vendor is not a strategic integrated partner because the vendor has relatively low impact and there has been a relatively low investment in the relationship.

The attributes of a vendor include providing products at a specified price and specified levels of quality and consistency. These vendors are expected to ship products to the operator as scheduled. The vendor is also expected to deliver on all commitments. Some operators expect vendors to be aware of environmental and social justice issues and act accordingly. Operators also expect vendors to be open to discussions about further purchasing opportunities.

Next is the **preferred distributor.** The preferred distributor has a higher impact than the vendor, as well as a greater investment on the part of the distributor and the operator. The attributes of a preferred distributor include all of those of the vendor plus operating as a point source and providing quality assurance inspections. These preferred distributors participate in forward contracting on supply and pricing of products. Preferred distributors also help with cost-saving projects and add value through logistics management. Preferred distributors are excellent sources of market intelligence and leads on opportunity buys. Preferred distributors also add value by providing innovative new ideas.

Moving up, **value-added teams** show a still greater impact and investment. Perhaps these value-added items consist of representatives from both the distributor and the operator. They are classified as "value-added" because they have the greatest impact and investment of the three options discussed thus far. Value-added teams provide all the previous value-added attributes, plus they understand and contribute to the food service operation's strategy. These teams assist with new product and resource development. Some operators also select value-added team members based on the team member's ability to contribute to the development of a more diverse, specifically minority, set of approved distributors.

At the top in terms of both impact and investment is the **strategic alliance** between the operator and the distributor. This is the most integrated of the four because the greatest investment has been made, resulting in the greatest impact. Strategic alliance distributors are fully integrated into the values, vision, mission, and strategic goals of the food service operation. These strategic partners work in sync with the operator to help make the vision a reality for the operator's customers.

A strategic alliance includes all of the previous attributes plus several other strategic initiatives. There is strategic alignment in the long-range strategy resulting from sharing information and collaborating on initiatives. There is a vertical integration of resource investment. There are also long-term programs in this relationship, including contracting/contract farming and potential cross-investment. As a result, there is integrated product development by all partners in the strategic alliance relationship.

Distributors as Resources

We started our discussion by stating that the ultimate goal in the partnership with a distributor is to create a unique resource; that is, another "arm" of the food service operation. Distributors and operators work together in a mutually beneficial relationship fueled by a cooperative, collaborative partnership. This is the case as the distributor moves up from vendor status to a strategic alliance.

The Process to Select Distributor Partners

Selection of a distributor partner must be more than simply a chance occurrence. Selection must be made based on a set of criteria that are critically important to the food service operation and its customers. Perhaps it would be best to begin the process of distributor selection by asking some of the following questions of prospective distributors:

- Based on the current list of products that I am ordering, what items do you have in stock for delivery?

- For the items that you do not distribute, what is your recommendation for a source of supply?

- How does your distributor business take care of special orders?

- Based on my average **drop size** (i.e., the average dollar amount of each delivery), can you deliver to fit my schedule (e.g., at times other than busy lunch periods and when receiving staff members are not available to properly receive the order)?

- If you cannot meet my preferred delivery schedule, is it possible to pay an additional drop charge to obtain the schedule that I prefer?

- Can we agree on a period of time (e.g., day of the week and hours of the day) in which my deliveries can occur?

- Are you able to provide a recipe costing service?

- What expertise does your distributor business provide to enhance service (e.g., menu suggestions, menu design, menu analysis, layout and design)?

- What is your relationship with manufacturers and brokers, and will I have access to their expertise?

- What is the compensation mix (i.e., salary and bonus based on volume sold) for your DSRs?

- Can you provide training tools for my production and service staff and ideas to improve the retention of my internal customers?

- Is your key staff trained in the HACCP process? How will you help my operation comply with food safety requirements?

By asking and answering these questions, the stage will be set to begin the selection of distributors. But first, the food service operator must define the characteristics of an acceptable distributor.

A food service operation requires distributors that meet product quality and price concerns while providing dependable service. The operator should build long-term relationships with those distributors who consistently furnish useful information, meet quality standards, and offer the best prices. As the routine activities of ordering, expediting, invoice processing, and payment take place, the food service operation needs to have distributors who participate in a "partnership," rather than foster an adversarial (win-lose) relationship.

Definition of an Acceptable Distributor

An acceptable distributor is one with whom the operator can build a long-term relationship. Characteristics of acceptable distributors include the following:

- The distributor must have the capability and commitment to perform well.

- The distributor must provide timely information regarding price changes and maintain a competitive price level.

- The distributor must understand the market served by the food service operation and must have ideas about how to best meet this market's needs, including special services.

- The distributor must be able to consistently provide the proper quality and quantity of products and services.

- The distributor must inform the operator of new or improved products and services that may be applicable to their operations.

- The distributor must have an ongoing interest in improving products and services provided to the operation.

- The distributor must be professional. It should be easy to follow up on problems, resolve difficulties that arise, and negotiate any concerns.

- The distributor's facilities must meet or exceed accepted levels of food safety.

- The distributor must be financially capable of growing with both the industry and its customers.

- The distributor must be ethical, honest, and fair.

The interests of both operators and distributors are served when a cooperative, working relationship exists. If either party tries to take advantage of the other by engaging in an "I win, you lose" strategy, then problems will be created.

How does one develop a list of potential distributors? While one-stop shopping has its benefits, most operators will be required to deal with more than one distributor, most of which are specialized. The objective is to have as few distributors as possible, yet still obtain the desired levels of quality, service, and price, all of which lead to value.

The first step in the process is to identify the product and service categories that are required. These might include:

- Laundry service.

- External maintenance (lawn and garden service).

- Linen.

- Meat and seafood and poultry.

- Produce and processed fruits and vegetables.

- Dairy products.

- Bakery products.

- Paper goods.

- Cleaning and maintenance supplies.

- Engineering supplies.

- Office supplies.

- China, glass, silverware, and smallware.

- Computer/technology products and services.

- Cleaning and maintenance services.

- Furniture, fixtures, and equipment.

While some consolidation of categories is probable, most moderately sized food service operations will have many separate distributors. After identifying the product and service categories and determining possible consolidations, the next step is to determine some sequence of review of distributors. For new operations about to open, review and selection must be complete to coincide with opening. For existing operations, the schedule will reflect a potential cost savings, some deficiency with the current distributor, or a new requirement.

The number of potential distributors is, in part, a function of the demographics in the area in which the operation is located. Many distributors may be found in urban areas where sales potential is high. On the other hand, some rural locations may have only one distributor for some product classes. The task is to locate these potential distributors promptly, then decide if they can be deemed "eligible."

Experienced food service operators typically are aware of distributors who carry the products and services required, but they may not be aware of the best sources of products and services. The best sources of products and services are determined by a number of criteria.

Visit the Facilities. The place to start is to arrange a visit to the distributor's facilities. When selecting which distributors' facilities to visit, first select those are located close to the food service operation. A distributor located relatively close to the operation will more likely offer the operator more favorable delivery times, transportation costs, and reduced unexpected delays of deliveries.

Once at the facility, it is important to assess the general appearance of the distributor's physical facilities. Evaluate the cleaning and maintenance of the facilities as well as the overall appearance. Ask to walk through the process flow for products beginning with products ordered and received by the distributor, through storage of products, through in-house processing of products by the distributor, through receipt of orders from the food service operators, to picking orders and loading delivery trucks, to the return of trucks that have made deliveries. Product handling and time-temperature control are important for food safety, and operators should assess these processes at the distributor's facilities.

Also assess the distributor's staff during the visit by looking for staff product handling procedures. In addition, the general appearance (i.e., uniforms) of the distributor's staff is important to evaluate. During the visit the operator can also assess that distributor's ability to provide technical support (based on product knowledge) and assist the operator with other services (i.e., menu planning).

Time with Principals. The **principals** of the distributor are the owners or senior managers. By meeting with them during the visit to the distributor, the operator can begin to assess their competence and commitment, past experience, and communication. It is also a good idea to ask the principals about the position and reputation, financial strength, and management skills of others in the distributor's organization. The financial condition of a potential distributor is important because once it is selected to provide products and services for the food service operation, the operator wants to be reasonably certain that the distributor remains in business. Most operators expect this time with principals to go beyond just this initial meeting. Loyalty of both the operator and distributor is enhanced when the time with principals extends throughout the length of the relationship.

Recipe Costing. One of the value-added services that a distributor can make available to the operator is **recipe costing.** Knowledge of recipe costing begins with the distributor taking the attitude that the distributor intends to be the operator's "best expert." The expertise extends beyond simple product knowledge.

Most recipe costing today is done with the help of computer software. The place to begin is the selection of the recipe to be produced. Many recipe management software programs contain a standard recipe file, an ingredient file, and a menu item file.

The standard recipe file lists the ingredients and quantities needed for that recipe, the cost of each ingredient (usually in pounds), the item cost of each ingredient, and the total cost of producing the menu item using that standard recipe. Increasingly, standard recipe files are expected to contain nutrition information.

The ingredient file contains the purchase unit, cost per purchase unit, and the cost per recipe unit for each ingredient. The menu item file contains the list of recipes to be served for all meal periods and the number (both projected/forecasted and actual) of menu items. Often included in the menu item file is the selling price of the menu item, recipe code number, and sales totals by each menu item.

One quickly realizes how daunting a task it would be to prepare all this information without the aid of a computer and recipe software. Distributors who can provide this service are valuable partners.

Access to Brokers and Manufacturers. A **broker** is an intermediary in the food service distribution chain. The broker represents the manufacturer or processor as an independent contractor. Brokers do not take title to the products, but rather encourage distributors to purchase products from the processor or manufacturer to sell to the operator.

A **manufacturer** or **processor**, on the other hand, converts raw materials (e.g., grains) to products directly usable by the operator (e.g., breads, pasta, batter mixes, frozen doughs). While brokers add time and place value by getting the right products to the right places at the right times, manufacturers and processors add form value by transforming raw materials (e.g., steers and heifers) into a form used by the food service operator (e.g., steaks, ground beef).

Why would an operator like access to brokers and manufacturers? One reason is that as manufacturers are developing new products and processes that may improve quality and reduce costs, the operator's requirements must be made known. Access provides this communication link, communicating requirements to the manufacturer and broker will stimulate the development of product lines that complement existing products and fill a need.

When the manufacturer and broker clearly understand the operator's requirements and expectations, there can be a better fit with the products that are manufactured. Some manufacturers and brokers offer rebates for products purchased during promotions. Sometimes the rebates are based on volume purchases. Knowledge of the rebates from the source (e.g., manufacturer) will effectively help the operator reduce the per unit costs of products purchased under such rebate programs.

Manufacturers and brokers can also help add value through training programs for the operator's staff members. Usually when food service equipment is purchased, a representative of the manufacturer visits the operation to ensure that installation is proper and that the staff knows how to use the equipment, as well as clean and maintain the equipment to prolong its useful life and, therefore, maximize the return on investment in that equipment by the operator.

In-Stock Ratios. If a distributor does not have a product in stock when an operator orders it, the product cannot be delivered. This is why many operators make it a practice to purchase from more than one distributor. If one distributor is out of an item, other approved distributors may have the item available.

Rather than focusing on **in-stock ratios** for *all* items, it is better to concentrate on critical items only. Critical items are those that the food service operation features (e.g., cod for the Friday-night fish fry) or is famous for (e.g., N.Y. strip steaks at a steakhouse), or otherwise represents a large portion of the operation's sales (e.g., pasta at an Italian restaurant). Minimizing stock-outs is important if a distributor is to be an acceptable source of reliable supply, particularly for critical items.

An in-stock ratio is simply the number of times a particular product is delivered as specified divided by the total number of times the product has been ordered. It appears mathematically as follows:

$$\text{In-Stock Ratio} = \frac{\text{Number of times the product is delivered as specified}}{\text{Number of times the product was ordered}}$$

Consider baby back ribs ordered by a food service operation whose signature entrée is barbecued ribs. In a three-month period, when the ribs were ordered from distributor D, the in-stock ratio was:

$$\text{In-Stock Ratio} = \frac{18}{24} = .75$$

This means that three out of four times when ribs were ordered from distributor D, they were in stock and delivered as specified. If distributor R can deliver them 22 of the 24 times ordered, the in-stock ratio jumps to .92. Based on the in-stock ratio only, distributor R would be preferred.

On-Time Delivery. On-time deliveries are impossible to assess when an operator is considering a distributor without having a record of the organization's on-time history. However, this information may be obtained by asking the distributor for customer references and then phoning the customers to ask how the distributor has performed, including on-time deliveries. While the distributor's customer is on the telephone, the operator can also inquire about whether there have been any problems experienced with that distributor and how the distributor resolved the problems.

Competitors are not the enemy; rather, they can be a source of critical information about distributors if competitors are willing to share information about distributors, including their track record of on-time deliveries. Then both operators can learn from each other's experiences. In addition to on-time deliveries, a related issue is substitute products offered when the distributor is out of the original product specified. Some operators also track a related metric—how complete the deliveries are based on what was originally ordered.

When checking distributor references with competitors, the food service operator might also inquire about the distributor's ability to provide customer service, the performance of people on the distributor's team—drivers, DSRs, and support staff—and the experience of the distributor's team members. Given the tendency of people to select only references who will give a positive endorsement, sometimes operators ask distributors to provide a few former customers who the operator can contact. This may give a more balanced view of the reference check for the distributor. It is not acceptable to ask competitors to reveal what they pay for a particular product from a distributor, although questions about communications, customer service, value-added services, and problem-solving are all legitimate.

Damage and Spoilage. Because of their direct impact on quality and value, food service operators usually regularly track the amount of damage and/or spoilage in products delivered by each distributor. Damaged goods are not usable and may have been contaminated. When a product is damaged and unusable, and it is needed in the food service operation, alternative sources for that product have to be quickly identified and engaged.

Both product damage and spoilage occur due to careless, yet usually avoidable, errors on the part of the distributor's staff members. Damaged products may have been scratched, dented, smashed, or broken in the distributor's warehouse, during picking (i.e., assembling) and loading on the delivery vehicle, in the delivery vehicle if it is not loaded properly, or as the product is being delivered. In any case, they are not acceptable and should be removed from the invoice. Spoiled products may simply have remained in the distributor's storage area too long, may have not been stored at the correct temperature, or both. If damaged and spoiled products continue to be delivered, it is time to find a different distributor.

Error Ratios. Error ratios are similar to in-stock ratios in that they divide one number by another. The difference, however, is that the operator wants a higher in-stock ratio (indicated by a larger number) and a lower error ratio (as reported by a smaller number). Error ratios help assess the accuracy of a distributor.

Once again, there may be several sources of errors. If the operator orders products electronically, the wrong product code may have been entered by the operator. If the correct product was ordered, an error may have occurred when someone was picking the order at the distributor before it was placed on the delivery vehicle. Or the wrong product may have been taken off the delivery vehicle and delivered to the operation's receiving area. In the case of in-stock ratios, on-time deliveries, damage and spoilage, error ratios, and integrity of the cold chain, the operator sees the dramatic impact that a well-organized receiving control point has on minimizing these problems before they become the operator's responsibility after they have been received.

Integrity of the Cold Chain. The **cold chain** refers to maintaining products at acceptable refrigerated and frozen temperatures throughout receipt at the distributor's warehouse, while in storage at the warehouse, during transportation on the delivery vehicle, and during receiving. The goal is to minimize the time that refrigerated and frozen food products, especially potentially hazardous food products, are exposed to the temperature danger zone. The **temperature danger zone** (TDZ) is 41° F (5° C) to 140° F (60° C).

Potentially hazardous foods should not be held within this range of temperatures. A potentially hazardous food is a food that requires temperature control because it is in a form capable of supporting the rapid and progressive growth of infectious or toxigenic microorganisms. This may include the growth and toxin production of *Clostridium botulinum* or, in raw shell eggs, the growth of *Salmonella enteritidis*. Potentially hazardous foods include an animal food (a food of animal origin) that is raw or heat-treated, a food of plant origin that is heat-treated or consists of raw seed sprouts, cut melons, and garlic and oil mixtures. Potentially hazardous food does *not* include:

- An air-cooled hard-boiled egg with shell intact.

- A food with a water activity value (i.e., amount of available water) of 0.85 or less.

- A food with a pH level (i.e., level of acidity or alkalinity) of 4.6 or below when measured at 75° F (24° C).

- A food, in an unopened, hermetically sealed container (i.e., a can), that is commercially processed to achieve and maintain commercial sterility under conditions of unrefrigerated storage and distribution.

Examples of potentially hazardous foods include animal products such as fish, meat, and poultry. Also included are some plant products, such as refried beans, cooked rice, seed sprouts (germinated soybeans, mung beans, alfalfa sprouts), processed garlic in oil, and tofu and other moist soy protein products. In some jurisdictions, potentially hazardous foods do not include clean, whole, uncracked, odor-free shell eggs. Other jurisdictions include such eggs as potentially hazardous foods. Check state and local food codes for the specifics in your particular area.

Time and temperature requirements are interrelated. Fluctuating temperatures are hazardous to food products because they can favor food spoilage or the proliferation of illness-causing microbes. The temperature at which raw ingredients are stored influences later bacterial activity; thus storage in the delivery vehicles, as well as products in the delivery vehicle, must be kept to a minimum.

Food distribution should protect the integrity of the cold chain throughout handling, storage, and transportation by the distributor. Frequent temperature checks should verify that products are not in the TDZ.

Response to Requests for Emergency Deliveries. Despite a food service operator's best efforts to accurately forecast product volume requirements, sometimes an operation simply exhausts its inventory before the next scheduled delivery. A very important role played by the purchasing department is the provision of necessary items at the right time. The concept of continuous supply is critical to customer satisfaction. From the perspective of food production and service staff, purchasing personnel are at fault when required products are not available. Purchasing staff must follow up on orders to help ensure that distributors meet contractual requirements regarding such concerns as quality, quantity, and delivery dates. Effective purchasing is required to provide a continuous source of supply. Unavailability of a menu item due to stockouts (depleted inventory) produces dissatisfied guests and may discourage repeat business.

Some distributors have retail or wholesale store outlets, so operators who find themselves short on inventory can simply go to that distributor's outlet to purchase the inventory needed. For example, Gordon Food Service is a distributor headquartered in Grand Rapids, Michigan, with a number of Marketplace stores conveniently located in the Midwest.

Sometimes, a temporary inventory shortage can be covered by an operation's competitor. For example, if the operation has developed a relationship with a competitor where helping each other out in times of inventory emergencies is the norm, then the competitor will be willing to "bail out" the operation in times of need and will expect the same when the competitor is short of inventory.

Another option is to contact the operation's DSR with a plea to deliver inventory that is in short supply in the operation. A DSR who is willing to provide this service even on a busy holiday weekend, for example, will be seen by the food service operator as adding tremendous value in the form of service beyond what is usually offered or expected. This strengthens the relationship.

Response to Catastrophic Situations. Usually, one cannot accurately predict catastrophes such as hurricanes, tornadoes, floods, fires, or snowstorms. It is a good idea to have a conversation with the DSR before such a catastrophe hits a food service operation or its surrounding area.

Consider a mountain resort at which all the guestrooms are full, but guests cannot leave because of a snowstorm. The resort's DSR may help the operation contact other accounts in the area who have available inventory. This, again, is an advantage to creating a relationship with certain competitors before the operation tries to call on them in times of need. In other situations, a distributor may or may not be able to assist with continuity of supply. Circumstances vary, but it is critical to have the conversation before the catastrophic situation takes place.

Integrated. An integrated distributor is one that can provide the very best products and services based on the needs of the operation's customers. The ability to develop an integrated approach to purchasing depends on a professional relationship with distributors. Both the buyer and seller must be able to relate to each other's interests in order to develop a mutual commitment for overall success and for pleasing customers. The distributor who is honest, fair, and reasonable in dealings with the food service operator will have a competitive edge over others without these traits.

Being a distributor is more than just taking an order and delivering it. Operators expect distributors to know their expectations. Some distributors emphasize that their DSRs do not focus only on sales, but that they are marketing associates (MAs) who are willing to spend time with operators on menu analysis, inventory controls, and ordering systems that make the operator's life easier. Other integrated distributors have the capability to provide financial advice, menu design ideas, and assistance with developing promotions and marketing plans.

An integrated distributor is not one that simply focuses on the sales transaction. Rather, an integrated distributor helps develop win-win relationships when negotiating prices for products and services. These favorable financial terms help both the operator and distributor be profitable. Sometimes the selection of a distributor involves trade-offs. An operator cannot expect a number of additional services if he or she is only willing to purchase at the lowest price. The operator must carefully assess the distributor's prices in relation to the quality of products needed by, and the level of service given to, the operation. This is value, that is, the relationship between price and quality.

Integrated distributors have shared beliefs about ethics. Both the distributor and operator must value the ethical treatment of each other and the customers. Ethics requires being honest and fair in the ongoing relationship with each other.

Integrated distributors share this vision and these values with all in the organization. For example, the appearance, attitudes, and courtesy of the distributor's delivery personnel contribute to the impressions formed by the food service operation's internal customers.

Integrated distributors provide a supply of continually updated information. It is important in the fast-changing and increasingly competitive world for operators to keep up with new technology. Purchasing personnel are in constant contact with distributors who, in turn, are in contact with manufacturers, other distributors, and many food service operations. Purchasers can be a valuable source of information about new products and services. Purchasing staff should collect new ideas and information from distributors to pass on to user departments. This, too, is part of being integrated.

Prime versus Secondary Distributors

Traditionally, distributors have specialized in specific product lines such as meat, fresh produce, canned goods and groceries, and specialty items. While this still remains somewhat the norm, today many distributors have broadened their product lines to carry a vast range of products. In fact, some distributors carry or can obtain almost any product, supply item, or piece of equipment needed by a food service operation. Some food service operators order all products from only one distributor, which is sometimes referred to as one-stop shopping.

Should purchasers consider use of a one-stop shopping service if available? One-stop shopping obviously eliminates the potentially time-consuming process of selecting a multitude of individual distributors. Another advantage is reduced time necessary to negotiate with distributors, process orders and receive incoming goods. Also, dealing with one distributor tends to build the distributor's trust in the operation and provides purchasing leverage for the operation.

Possible disadvantages of one-stop shopping include:

- *Higher prices.* Distributors selling popular products at competitive prices typically sell other items at a higher markup. When all products are purchased from one distributor, prices paid for some items will likely be higher than those available elsewhere. (On the other hand, one-stop shopping may reflect volume efficiencies conferred by consolidated shipments from a single source, resulting in lower prices.)

- *Lack of specialized information.* With an increased number of product lines comes a decreased likelihood that a sales representative can be an "expert" in each of the many items being offered.

- *Decreased variety within a product line.* Typical one-stop distributors offer relatively few varieties of each item and, in many cases, may offer only one.

When a prime distributor is utilized, operators usually select **secondary distributors** to supplement what they purchase from the prime distributor. A prime distributor is often selected because consolidating as many purchases as possible with one distributor usually leads to the best prices paid for products, enhanced services (sometimes known as leverage), and better terms (e.g., payments for invoices, deliveries). In addition, the prime distributor reduces the number of deliveries from multiple distributors and the associated time and costs of the deliveries.

On the other hand, a secondary distributor or set of distributors may be to the advantage of the food service operator in a number of ways. One advantage is that a secondary distributor may offer unique, specialty products such as bakery products, dairy products, fresh produce, or meat and seafood products. Sometimes the secondary distributor offers better prices or improved quality or both for these products.

A secondary distributor may be seen as a back-up to the prime distributor, particularly if the prime distributor is out of stock on a product ordered by the food service operator. Even though the prime distributor may offer a substitute, the substitute may not be satisfactory to the operation. So in selecting a secondary distributor, it is critical to evaluate the distributor's product listing and ability to deliver smaller drops on shorter notice.

A secondary distributor is often used as a "fill-in" specialist where this distributor is the backup, but still receives enough of the total order to make it profitable and to be able to justify the relationship. In some cases, the specialist is selected because of the ability to offer a full line of frozen food products in addition to other products purchased by the operation. This will help keep prices competitive, or at least provide another source of price comparisons, for the food service operator.

Some specialty secondary distributors offer a wide assortment of disposable and paper products for the operator. Because these products usually take up relatively huge amounts of storage space for the distributor and for the operator, the operator must carefully evaluate the price per unit of buying large quantities of these items against the cost of storage.

Secondary distributors sometimes offer a cash-and-carry or will-call service so that when an operator depletes inventory, the operation can send someone to the distributor to buy it, load it in the vehicle, and drive it to the operation. These will-call and cash-and-carry services usually require that credit has been authorized in advance.

In any case, it is important to treat the secondary distributor as the prime distributor is treated. This will yield a more productive relationship for all.

Purchasers should not be afraid to purchase from other than their established distributors. After all, new distributors are going into business daily just as new food service operations open with great frequency. Many professional purchasers initiate trial or sample orders with a new distributor to help in evaluating their interest in a continuing relationship.

In order to reduce the possibility of "surprises" during initial orders, detailed agreements should be made between the buyer and seller about products, quality, quantity, time of delivery, services, and related requirements. In other words, the purchaser should practice the same basic principles of purchasing management that are needed each time an order is placed.

References should be requested of the new distributor and then contacted. Purchasers should be aware that distributors may offer large discounts and provide exceptional service as their business is developing. What sets preferred distributors apart, however, is a long-term and ongoing concern for price, quality, and consistency of service. This is the formula for value.

Food Defense and Security Considerations for Distributors —

Food defense and security considerations have become increasingly important in today's distribution system. Security must be addressed in purchase specifications, include both physical and personnel aspects, cover intentional contamination, and address the real threat of bioterrorism.

Written Specifications

By addressing security in product specifications, the food service operator alerts distributors that security of products is a vital concern. Some chain operators begin addressing security when they issue a **request for proposal (RFP)** from a distributor. The chain buyer may ask, for example, for a description of the distributor's security procedures from when the products are received at the distribution facility through storage in the facility, loading of delivery vehicles, and delivery of products including transportation from the distributor to the operator. When these become part of the written specifications, all parties are reminded of the critical need for distributors to protect the security of products and the integrity of the distribution system.

Physical Facilities

Protection of the physical products is very important because they can easily be violated and the security breached. A number of principles must be followed by the distributor; many of these same principles apply to security of products in a food service operation.

After the distributor identifies the items that are to be tightly controlled and which locations are to be considered storage areas, security procedures can be designed to ensure that those items are secured in those locations until they are selected to fill an order on a delivery vehicle.

Only authorized staff members should be permitted in storerooms. In addition to management, authorized staff may include receiving and storage personnel. Smaller distributors can keep storage areas locked and involve management directly in receiving and issuing activities. When a manager is present to unlock the storeroom door, theft is less likely. This procedure is more easily implemented if removal of products from storage is done only at specified times.

The storage areas, included refrigerators, freezers, and beverage storage areas should be completely lockable. Depending on available equipment, one section of refrigerated or frozen storage might be used to secure expensive items. Or a lockable shelving unit (or cage) can be used. In this way, expensive refrigerated products, such as fresh meats and seafood, or beverages being held refrigerated can be secured. At the same time, personnel still have access to produce, dairy, and similar products that are less likely to be stolen.

Refrigerated and frozen storage units should be lockable with reasonably strong lock clasps and door hinges. Storeroom walls should extend to the ceiling, and there should be no way to enter through the ceiling from another room. If there are windows, they should at least be made secure and unopenable. The point is to design, within practical limits, storage areas that are difficult for unauthorized personnel to enter without being detected.

The goal is to reduce opportunities for pilferage. The answers to common-sense questions such as "How would I steal from my storage areas if I were a dishonest staff member?" may point to security loopholes in storage areas.

Only those distributor's staff members who need keys should have them. Manual locks or combinations should be changed routinely, as well as each time a staff member with access to keys leaves the distributor's employment. An excellent policy is that all keys remain at the distributor at all times, securely locked in the manager's office when not in use. Some distributors may feel key control procedures are unnecessary. However, a significant number of products representing substantial dollar outlays can be lost because of inadequate key control. The potential for such losses should convince distributors to emphasize this aspect of the physical product control system.

Modern locking systems eliminate the need for traditional keys. Pins correlating with a "combination code" can be depressed by authorized personnel who have memorized the code. When these individuals no longer need access to lockable areas, combinations can be quickly (and inexpensively) changed. Other systems may use plastic cards, similar to credit cards, with coded information designed to operate locks. These systems are in common use. Either of these or related systems may yield information about the identity of persons entering lockable areas, time of entry, and length of time that the individual was in the area. Moreover, they make the process of changing the locks fast and easy, so busy distributors are more likely to do so. Increasingly, these and related systems provide more specific control information to help ensure that only persons authorized to enter storage areas do gain access to these locations.

Today, the physical facilities of the distributor must be protected. A chain link fence around the distributor's facilities, including delivery vehicles not in use, can add to security, but the fence must be locked and its security monitored. Similarly, delivery vehicles must be secured by locks when the delivery person leaves the vehicle to deliver products. While the security fence can be inspected when the food service operator visits the distributor's facilities, the security of vehicles can be checked by the operator in the receiving control point during deliveries. Both procedures can be written into purchase specifications.

Personnel Concerns

Generally, the reason that products suffer from security breaches in a distributor's operation is because a distributor's employee neglected to follow security procedures and policies. While these people can be trained to limit access, lock storage areas, and control keys, it is essential that these security concerns become second nature to each staff member in the distributor's facility, as well as to all supervisors and managers.

Constant reinforcement of initial security training is important because it emphasizes the importance of the security procedures and serves as a constant reminder that security is a top priority. Checklists and management follow-up can help ensure that personnel follow defined security procedures.

Contamination Hazards

Recall that food safety hazards in a HACCP system may be biological, chemical, or physical hazards that are reasonably likely to cause illness or injury in the absence of control. Some of the potential biological hazards are listed in Exhibit 3. These biological hazards are bacterial, viral, and parasitic organisms, and they are grouped in Exhibit 3 on the basis of risk severity.

Chemical hazards may be naturally occurring or may be introduced during food processing. Sometimes this food processing takes place in the distributor's facilities, such as the processing of heads of romaine into cut greens for Caesar salad or the unintentional addition of industrial chemicals during food processing. Note that Exhibit 4, which lists chemical hazards and examples, also includes poisonous or toxic chemicals intentionally added. This intentional contamination is known as sabotage.

Why would someone want to sabotage the food supply before the products reach the distributor's facility, during storage prior to delivery by the distributor, or during transportation in a delivery vehicle on its way to a food service operation? Perhaps the saboteur wants to "get back at" the distributor for a feeling of being treated wrongly or unjustly. Or perhaps the one who adds intentional contamination is attempting to make a statement of discontent by hurting others who will be affected by consuming the contaminated food products. A third reason why intentional contamination may take place is that the saboteur is looking for attention or recognition by doing something that affects others in a negative way.

The third possible category of food contamination is physical hazards (see Exhibit 5). Again, physical hazards may intentionally be added to food products by a disgruntled staff member. Or, perhaps more likely, this category of hazards may be accidentally added to food products as is the case when the wrong container is used (e.g., glass that breaks rather than metal scoops) or personal effects (e.g., jewelry) are worn that have no place in food processing areas.

Bioterrorism

Bioterrorism takes place when harmful biological substances are intentionally used to injure or terrorize others. Sometimes these substances are introduced into food. These biological substances can be added to food at any point in the food distribution channel from the source to manufacturing to delivery to the food service operation. There is a real concern in the United States and elsewhere that terrorists might be seeking ways to contaminate the food supply using biological or

Exhibit 3   Hazardous Microorganisms and Parasites Grouped By Severity of Risk

Severe Hazards

Clostridium botulinum types A, B, E, and F
Shigella dysenteriae
Salmonella typhi; paratyphi A, B
Hepatitis A and E
Brucella abortis; B. suis
Vibrio cholerae 01
Vibrio vulnificus
Taenia solium
Trichinella spiralis

Moderate Hazards: Potentially Extensive Spread

Listeria monocytogenes
Salmonella spp.
Shigella spp.
Enterovirulent *Escherichia coli* (EEC)
Streptococcus pyogenes
Rotavirus
Norwalk virus group
Entamoeba histolytica
Diphyllobothrium latum
Ascaris lumbricoides
Cryptosporidium parvum

Moderate Hazards: Limited Spread

Bacillus cereus
Campylobacter jejuni
Clostridium perfringens
Staphylococcus aureus
Vibrio cholerae, non-01
Vibrio parahaemolyticus
Yersinia enterocolitica
Giardia lamblia
Taenia saginata

Source: Ronald F. Cichy, *Food Safety: Managing the HACCP Process* (Lansing, Mich.: Educational Institute of the American Hotel & Lodging Association, 2004), p. 14.

chemical agents. Many of the terrorism-related concerns that apply to food service operations also apply to distributors.

Food Safety and HACCP Essentials for Distributors —————

One of the most impactful actions that food service operators can take is to write quality requirements into bids and purchase specifications. One of those quality requirements should be that distributors comply with HACCP, and that manufacturers and sources from whom the distributors purchase must be inspected and certified as complying to HACCP.

Exhibit 4 Types of Chemical Hazards and Examples

Naturally Occurring Chemicals
Mycotoxins (e.g., aflatoxin) from mold
Scombrotoxin (histamine) from protein decomposition
Ciguatoxin from marine dinoflagellates
Toxic mushroom species
Shellfish toxins (from marine dinoflagellates)
Paralytic shellfish poisoning (PSP)
Diarrhetic shellfish poisoning (DSP)
Neurotoxic shellfish poisoning (NSP)
Amnesic shellfish poisoning (ASP)
Plant toxins
Pyrrolizidine alkaloids
Phytohemagglutinin

Added Chemicals
Agricultural chemicals: pesticides, fungicides, fertilizers, insecticides,
    antibiotics, and growth hormones
Polychlorinated biphenyls (PCBs)
Industrial chemicals
Prohibited substances (21 CFR 189)
    Direct
    Indirect
Toxic elements and compounds: lead, zinc, arsenic, mercury, and cyanide
Food additives:
    Direct—allowable limits under GMPs
        Preservatives (nitrite and sulfiting agents)
        Flavor enhancers (monosodium glutamate)
        Nutritional additives (niacin)
        Color additives
    Secondary direct and indirect
        Chemicals used in establishments (e.g., lubricants, cleaners,
        sanitizers, cleaning compounds, coatings, and paints)
Poisonous or toxic chemicals intentionally added (sabotage)

Source: Ronald F. Cichy, *Food Safety: Managing the HACCP Process* (Lansing, Mich.: Educational Institute of the American Hotel & Lodging Association, 2004), p. 15.

Reputation

Fundamentally, distributors must be licensed, reliable, and reputable. This helps ensure that the distributor's products meet both federal and local/state standards for food safety. A distributor's food safety reputation can be checked with local and state regulatory agencies. Phone the agencies and inquire about whether a particular food distributor has had identified problems with food safety or health code violations.

In addition, the reputation of the distributor can be checked with other food service operators. The reputation of the distributor is also, in part, observable first-hand through a visit to the distributor's place of business. Food service operators should attempt to answer the following questions about a distributor's reputation:

Exhibit 5   Physical Hazards

Material	Injury Potential	Sources
Glass fixtures	Cuts, bleeding; may require surgery to find or remove	Bottles, jars, lights, utensils, gauge covers
Wood	Cuts, infection, choking; may require surgery to remove	Fields, pallets, boxes, buildings
Stones, metal fragments	Choking, broken teeth, cuts, infection; may require surgery to remove	Fields, buildings, machinery, wire, staff members
Insulation	Choking; long-term if asbestos	Building materials
Bone	Choking, trauma	Fields, improper plant processing
Plastic	Choking, cuts, infection; may require surgery to remove	Fields, plant packaging materials, pallets, staff members
Personal effects	Choking, cuts, broken teeth; may require surgery to remove	Staff members

Source: Ronald F. Cichy, *Food Safety: Managing the HACCP Process* (Lansing, Mich.: Educational Institute of the American Hotel & Lodging Association, 2004), p. 16.

- Does the distributor's delivery staff cooperate with the operator's staff to conduct a detailed inspection during receiving at the food service operation?

- Does the distributor's delivery staff permit the operator's staff to inspect the delivery vehicles during receiving?

- Does the distributor have clean delivery vehicles that maintain correct product temperatures?

- Does the distributor use appropriate, durable, leak-proof, protective packaging for food products?

- Does the distributor train and retrain the distributor's staff in acceptable food safety practices? Answers to these questions can indicate the distributor's reputation for maintaining food safety standards.

Checklists

Checklists are relatively easy ways to determine whether a distributor follows acceptable procedures for food safety. If the distributor has a HACCP plan in place, it is easier to verify compliance during inspections. Just as in a food service operation, the preparation and maintenance of the written HACCP plan is the responsibility of the distributor's managers. The plan must detail hazards, identify critical control points (CCPs), critical limits, specify CCP monitoring and recordkeeping procedures, and outline the implementation strategy.

Recordkeeping makes the system work. The level of sophistication of recordkeeping depends on the complexity of the distributor. The simplest effective recordkeeping system is the best.

The approved HACCP plan and associated records must be on file at the distributor. The plan should include:

- A list of the HACCP team and assigned responsibilities.

- A description of each food product and its intended use.

- A flow diagram indicating CCPs.

- Hazards associated with each CCP and preventative measures.

- Critical limits.

- Monitoring systems.

- Corrective action plans for deviations from critical limits.

- Recordkeeping procedures.

- Procedures for verification of the HACCP system.

Other information in the HACCP plan can be tabulated using the format shown in Exhibit 6. Some examples of records obtained during the operation of the HACCP plan are described in Exhibit 7.

Inspection

The HACCP inspection views a distributor and its operation as a total process by identifying CCPs in an attempt to prevent food safety hazards. Regulatory agencies may take individual program, personnel, distributor, and jurisdiction differences into account when establishing procedures for assigning distributors and preparing for and conducting inspections.

The food product flow is the place to start the review for the HACCP inspection. Full food-flow diagrams should be reviewed by the regulatory authorities even though only a portion of the steps will take place during the inspection. The focus during the inspection must be, first and foremost, the food.

The sources of food, storage practices, and process flow steps all should be noted. Risk assessment data guide the allocation of time and focus during the inspection. Complex, higher-risk food processes that involve multiple ingredients, potentially hazardous foods, and long storage times should be given a high priority. Foods that have been implicated in foodborne illness should receive high priority, too. Other high risk indicators are foods stored in large volumes and those requiring manual assembly and manipulation during processing at the distributor.

Accurate measurements during inspections are essential. Accuracy of measurements depends on at least two variables: calibration of the equipment and procedures followed by the person taking the measurements. Critical limits to be measured include temperature, pH, water activity, and food additive concentrations. In some cases, they also may include warewashing process, wash/rinse/heat sanitization, sanitizer concentrations, pressure and time measurements, light distribution, and insect and rodent infestations.

Temperature. Food product internal temperatures should be taken in the geometric center of the product. Ambient temperature (i.e., the temperature of a storage area) monitoring devices should be used to indicate where further investigation is

Exhibit 6 HACCP Information Reporting Form

Process Step	CCP	Chemical/ Physical/ Biological Hazards	Critical Limit	Monitoring Procedures/ Frequency/ Person(s) Responsible	Corrective Action(s)/ Person(s) Responsible	HACCP Records	Verification Procedures/ Person(s) Responsible

Source: Ronald F. Cichy, *Food Safety: Managing the HACCP Process* (Lansing, Mich.: Educational Institute of the American Hotel & Lodging Association, 2004), p. 22.

warranted. Temperatures monitored between packages of food, such as milk cartons or packages of meat, can also indicate the need for further examination. However, the temperature of a potentially hazardous food itself, rather than the temperature between packages, is usually necessary for regulatory citations. The three dimensions of bacterial load, temperature, and time must be considered when inspecting the process.

Modern thermometers that measure temperature electronically, rather than bimetal types that rely on thermal expansion of two different metals, are recommended by regulatory authorities. Such modern thermometers yield faster responses and provide greater overall accuracy. Before internal food temperatures are taken, the probe must be cleaned and sanitized. Boiling water, alcohol swabs, or sanitizers can destroy pathogens on the probe. When a series of temperatures is taken, it is important that the probe be thoroughly cleaned and sanitized between uses to prevent cross-contamination.

pH measurements. The pH measurement is the acidity or alkalinity of a food product and is important in determining if a food is potentially hazardous. The closer the food approaches the critical limit of 4.6, the more precise the measurement should be.

Water activity measurements. **Water activity** (a_w) is another factor used to determine if a food is considered potentially hazardous. It is the amount of available water in a food. Frozen and dried foods have less available water. The a_w is measured with a laboratory or field a_w meter.

Exhibit 7   Types of HACCP–Plan Records

1. **Ingredients**
   - Supplier certification documenting compliance with establishment's specifications.
   - Establishment audit records verifying distributor compliance.
   - Storage temperature record for temperature-sensitive ingredients.
   - Storage time records of limited shelf-life ingredients.

2. **Processing**
   - Records from all monitored CCPs.
   - Records verifying the continued adequacy of the food processing procedures.

3. **Packaging**
   - Records indicating compliance with specifications of packaging materials.
   - Records indicating compliance with sealing specifications.

4. **Finished product**
   - Sufficient data and records to establish the efficacy of barriers in maintaining product safety.
   - Sufficient data and records establishing the safe shelf life of the product, if age of product can affect safety.
   - Documentation of the adequacy of the HACCP procedures from an authority with knowledge of the hazards involved and necessary controls.

5. **Storage and distribution**
   - Temperature records.
   - Records showing no product shipped after shelf-life date on temperature-sensitive products.

6. **Deviation and corrective action**
   - Validation records and modification to the HACCP plan indicating approved revisions and changes in ingredients, formulations, preparation, packaging, and distribution control, as needed.

7. **Staff member training**
   - Records indicating that food staff members responsible for implementing the HACCP plan understand the hazards, controls, and procedures.

Source: Ronald F. Cichy, *Food Safety: Managing the HACCP Process* (Lansing, Mich.: Educational Institute of the American Hotel & Lodging Association, 2004), p. 23.

Food additive concentrations. Samples of food are sometimes collected and sent to a laboratory for analysis.

Warewashing process evaluation. Because proper cleaning and sanitizing of food-contact surfaces are important safeguards of public health, the washing, rinsing, and sanitizing processes must be verified for distributors who also process food products to ensure that they meet regulatory provisions.

Mechanical warewashers are required to have data plates that indicate acceptable parameters for temperatures and cycle times for particular machines.

Wash/rinse/heat sanitization measurement. Devices used for measuring food product temperature can also be used for determining the critical limits of washing, rinsing, and sanitization. Three-compartment sinks and many mechanical warewashers have water vats that can be checked with a probe thermometer and compared to the installed thermometer readings.

Insect and rodent infestation. Physical evidence of insect and rodent infestation can take the form of dead vermin, droppings, nesting, gnawings, and grease marks on the walls. A bright flashlight, a magnifying lens, and an ultraviolet light to detect rodent urine stains can reveal infestations.

Recall Processes and Procedures

Recall processes and procedures must be in place in case a product recall is necessary. A distributor's response to a recall will likely depend on whether it is Class I, Class II, or Class III. Recall procedures are necessary in the event that a food product has to be quickly removed from distribution.

Indemnity Insurance

Because of the increased incidences and costs of litigation, manufacturers usually carry indemnity insurance. Since food contamination can be the source of lawsuits based on both negligence and strict liability, this insurance is necessary. In the case where there is no indemnity insurance, the operator may have to sign a waiver of liability. If a distributor obtains products from another distributor, the operator may have to sign a waiver of liability.

Essentials of Ethics from the Distributor's Perspective

Ethics is the study of moral principles concerning what is right based on an individual's deeply held values. Ethical discussions focus on the "right thing to do," and often refer to moral obligations, a person's duty to behave or act a certain way, or behaviors/actions that are fair.

Concerns about ethics have become more prominent in business. The leaders of these organizations failed themselves, their internal and external customers, their shareholders (if publicly held), or owners (if privately held) because of their ethical improprieties. In all of these cases, the message became clear quickly: we expect our business leaders to behave and act in an ethical way by doing what is right. Ethical behavior is tied to both the economic responsibilities and legal responsibilities of business leaders. Economic responsibilities are those that require a business to make a profit or generate a surplus (in nonprofit organizations). Legal responsibilities include expectations that the organization's leaders will comply with the laws governing the business.

Policies, Assessment, and Improvement

Ethical responsibilities relate to society's expectations that there are certain norms of behavior that may not be written into law but are required for the organization to operate properly.

Policies related to ethical behavior are needed in organizations because individuals may not always understand what is ethical without such policies. Some say that ethical behavior is simply acting according to the values and rules a person was taught as a child. One problem with this view is that it depends on who taught an individual his or her values. It is better to examine for yourself what you believe.

Policies related to ethics in purchasing should address the following:

- Operators should select equipment, products, and services based on intended use. It is important for the operator to give to distributors clearly written specifications that detail the use of the item being purchased. It is equally important for the distributors to match the item being sold to those requirements.

- Clearly state the health and safety requirements for the distributor to meet. The distributor must do everything possible to meet those requirements.

- The operator must specify the requirements for product testing, inspection, and/or certification in the specification. The distributor is obligated to meet these requirements.

- The operator must be able to rely on the distributor's representatives for correctly presented product information and other requirements. The distributor must provide these to the operator.

- Operators who use bids must do so in an equitable way so that the integrity of the bidding process is preserved. The distributor must be able to deliver on the bids and products/services included. There can be no "backroom deals," which represent unfair purchasing practices based on awarding bids to inappropriate distributors.

- Policies must clearly set an ethical direction for both the operator and distributor during the purchasing control point. These policies may include collaboration between the two businesses, the expectations of training and education, and/or the supervision of the purchasing process by both the operator and distributor.

- Base ethical policies on a commitment to establishing trust in the relationship between the operator and distributor. Reinforce this with actions and only do business with those organizations that work to build and maintain this trust.

Assessment of ethics requires the operator and distributor to regularly measure, audit, and monitor the overall purchasing process. Obviously, it is in the operation's best interest to monitor the ethical behaviors and adherence to ethics policies on the part of distributors. There must be a fair approach to assessment that is known to all parties. The approach may utilize an independent third party to verify compliance with ethical norms.

For example, a policy may clearly state that the operator purchase from approved distributors, not directly from manufacturers or manufacturers' representatives. If a manufacturer's representative tries to sell a product directly to the operator, this policy should be strictly followed.

In the case of public, not-for-profit institutions, the purchasing practices are often subject to independent, third-party (e.g. governmental agency) audits. With chain food service organizations, often this audit is done by the chain's corporate representatives (e.g., those responsible for quality assurance standards). Both types of organizations acknowledge that these assessments are important if the public's trust and confidence are to be preserved, as well as making good business strategy sense.

Benefits

There are numerous benefits to acting in ethical ways during the purchasing control point. One advantage is that during turbulent times, ethical policies help quell the storm and help both the operator and distributor lead through times of change.

Ethics policies also help promote teamwork and a partnership between the operator and distributor. Ethical values and standards of conduct are aligned throughout the organization's internal customers and leaders, as well as the organization's distributor. Another benefit is that clearly stated ethics policies help those in the organization and its distributors develop and grow. By facing reality as it exists, it is possible to take actions to move the organization forward.

Ethical policies also help ensure that other policies and procedures in the organization are legal. This is related not just to the purchasing control point, but also to other control points in the organization as well as to human resources functions such as recruitment and selection. It is much better to spend extra time and other resources on ensuring ethical and legal behavior now than it is to pay the consequences of illegal actions later.

Ethical values and policies also help develop and promote an organization's unique position and image in the competitive marketplace. A positive position and image can build the confidence of internal customers and external customers that the organization will do the right things by acting ethically and responsibly. Ethical policies also work to build the credibility and legitimacy of leaders, boost the organization's ethical culture, enhance trust in business relationships with operators and distributors, and support continuous improvement. A clearly defined program addressing ethics is initially costly to develop and implement, but there are many more benefits than expenses.

Culture of Ethics

A culture of ethics is built on a foundation of ethical values and ethics policies. Each individual in the organization contributes to the culture by his or her actions, behaviors, and decisions. Employees should answer two key questions:

- Is this the best action, behavior, or decision for the organization in which I work?

- Is this the right action, behavior, or decision for everyone involved?

When a staff member practices self-enrichment at the organization's expense, it usually violates ethical standards of behavior. This practice almost inevitably turns out to be harmful to the greater good and may even harm others. For example, if a person responsible for purchasing pilfers from the operation, the behavior is unethical. It will not withstand an honest ethical examination or assessment.

In the same way, an organization that requires staff members to act unethically destroys the ethical culture and ignores the ethical values. Sometimes the individual has to stand up to the organization to do the right things. Even if this puts the individual at odds with others in the organization, the only way to preserve the culture of ethics is to act ethically.

Leaders in distributors and food service organizations must set the example. These leaders have a responsibility to model the way and act ethically at all times. By promoting a culture of ethics and acting with integrity, these leaders can convey the critical importance of acting ethically.

The Distributor's Role in Helping Operations Become More Effective

In the spirit of a partnership between the operator and distributor, the operator increasingly relies on the distributor to help the food service operation become more effective. Recall that being effective means doing the right things, and, as such, it is tied directly to ethical behavior. There are a number of ways that a distributor can assist the operator in becoming more effective.

Value-Added Services

A distributor who helps an operator become more effective adds tremendous value to the partnership. The partnership must be based on collaboration. Collaboration implies working together so that both partners benefit. **Value-added services** are usually made available by distributors in response to requests from operators. The process of collaboration begins with the partners listening to each other.

Once the information is obtained, the distributor decides if the value-added service can realistically be offered. Value-added products or services can broaden the product line offered by that distributor, and often new products can be bundled with existing products. Without value-added products and services, the purchase of existing products may simply be viewed by the operator as buying commodities, that is, done on price alone. In an era where economic conditions justify closely monitoring costs of products and services, value-added products and services can build operator loyalty to a distributor.

Value-added services in the simplest sense involve a transformation of a distributor from being a simple "order-taker" to one who can recommend the most effective products and services available to the operator. When a distributor takes the time to learn about the operation's customers' requirements, and then suggest the most appropriate products and services to meet those requirements, value is added.

Another value-added service is assistance with calculating costs. When product costs are collaboratively quantified and measured, the true value addition from that distributor can be determined and then compared to costs from another distributor.

Distributors add value when they participate in buying alliances, since the cost of individual products and services generally is reduced for the operator.

Other distributors add value when they assist in lowering the total costs of purchasing to the operator, as well as managing problems of products or services performance, if they occur.

Accounts Receivable

Accounts receivable by a distributor are funds that must be paid by the food service operator for products and services purchased from that distributor. One way that distributors can assist operators is by lengthening the time period that operators have to pay invoices and/or reducing the interest operators must pay. Of course, the distributor must take a close look at his or her cash flow to determine if any of this is possible or realistic.

Some distributors offer operators summary billing services that prepare a summary of products purchased by category. Others furnish managed inventory (MI) in which the distributor takes responsibility for ordering, receiving, and stocking inventory. While this reduces the time spent by the operator, the trade off may be a possible loss of control during the receiving control point.

Distributors also can assist with a price/cost analysis that provides operators with specific price breaks from each distributor. Coupled with the most favorable payment policies, these analyses can help operators become more profitable.

Delivery Times/Frequency

Deliveries by distributors are critical to having the right products/services available for sale by the operator at the right times. When a delivery arrives at a food service operation, it enters the receiving control point. During receiving, a selected and trained representative of the operator must be available to properly check the quality and quantity of what is being delivered. This is crucial because ownership is being transferred from the distributor to the operator during receiving.

The time that receiving takes place affects how thoroughly receiving personnel can check product quality and quantity. If receiving takes place at a small food service operation with no full-time receiver during a busy lunch rush, proper receiving principles are likely to be violated. Say that the receiving is done by the head cook. The head cook is busy preparing lunch meals for guests in the dining room. To be effective, the operator should work with the distributor to schedule a mutually agreeable receiving time.

Delivery frequency is in part dictated by the volume of products purchased. In general, a higher volume will dictate more frequent deliveries. Sometimes a secondary distributor can help provide additional opportunities for more frequent deliveries, particularly if that distributor is a specialty distributor (e.g., fresh produce).

The trend today with many distributors is to consolidate deliveries; that is, to deliver less frequently. This is due to rising personnel and operating (e.g., gasoline or diesel fuel) costs on the part of the distributor.

Also related to deliveries is the ability of the distributor to provide the best labeling and packaging of products delivered. By providing operator-friendly labeling and packaging, the distributor reduces the time required by the operator to recognize a delivery and move it to storage.

Operators usually discover if a distributor is out of stock on products ordered at the time of delivery. Sometimes this is too late for the operator to find an alternative source of the needed product or products. Distributors should instead let operators know what is missing from an order in advance of delivery so adequate time exists for the operator to find a suitable alternative.

Average Order Size

Average order size refers to the amount of products ordered and delivered at one time. The distributor's objective is to increase average order size, because larger "drops" of products delivered less frequently are more profitable for the distributor.

When a distributor considers the cost to load a delivery vehicle, fuel to move it from the distributor's facility to the food service operation, the delivery driver's salary and benefits, and the cost to unload the drop, larger orders usually are more profitable.

This must, however, be balanced with the operator's needs. Perhaps the operator does not have sufficient storage space for such refrigerated products as fresh fish or dry storage space for such bulky items as paper and disposable products. This operator would prefer smaller drops delivered more frequently.

One solution for distributors is to increase drop sizes by adding products that operators are requesting. By capturing a larger percentage of the operator's total purchases, average order size will increase. Another way for distributors to build average order size is to assist operators with new menu items and/or with promoting existing menu items to build the volume of products needed to fulfill this growing demand.

One solution for operators is to select more than one qualified distributor, or to utilize a prime distributor and several secondary distributors. Secondary distributors are often more than willing to build their business by delivering to the operator more frequently in smaller drops.

Proprietary Items

Proprietary items are products or services unique to a specific distributor. Perhaps one distributor has the exclusive rights to sell a product for a specific manufacturer in a certain geographic region. Or perhaps that distributor has developed its own private brand of a product (e.g., food base, soup, salad dressing) that is offered under its private label. That is also an example of a proprietary brand.

With the growing interest in locally grown food, some distributors have created alliances with local farmers that are exclusive to that particular distributor. Some operators specify these locally grown food products because of enhanced nutritional values, better flavors, support for the local economy, environment concerns, fresher products, and because their external customers are demanding such products.

A fresh produce distributor may have the exclusive right to sell produce from one specific local farm or set of farms. With the growing number of consumers wanting to know the sources of the foods that they eat and the popularity of organic farms, these proprietary brands may offer a distributive marketing advantage for the operator with external customers.

Salesperson versus Electronic Ordering

Some operators prefer not to order electronically and instead want the DSR to personally visit to take orders. As you might imagine, this can be a more expensive way for distributors to do business and the operator may have to pay more for this service. Perhaps a compromise is to blend face-to-face ordering with the DSR with sometimes ordering electronically.

Other operators believe they are more effective if they can simply place orders via phone, fax, or Internet. It all depends on the operator's ordering requirements and the distributor's ability to meet those requirements.

Electronic ordering may be more efficient for some operators because it cuts down on the amount of time required. It can also enhance the accuracy of the order. Distributors should more effectively be able to pick orders in the warehouse and load them on the delivery vehicle when orders are placed electronically. Some distributors utilized radio frequency (RF) technology and bar codes to more accurately assemble orders. The RF scanners also help provide the operator details of orders including quantities of products ordered and frequency of these orders.

These electronic ordering systems can help operators become more effective by providing details about product availability, product prices and specifications, purchase order status, and the tracking of delivery shipments. With fewer chances for human errors, the technology-based systems save time and enhance accuracy of information provided to the operator.

More and more distributors are offering on-line ordering, inventory management software and electronic order entry to operators. This helps operators save time and money, therefore helping them become more efficient and effective.

 Key Terms

accounts receivable—Funds that must be paid by the food service operator for products and services purchased from a distributor.

average order size—The average amount of products ordered and delivered at one time.

broker—An intermediary in the food service distribution chain that represents the manufacturer or processor as an independent contractor.

cold chain—The steps at which refrigerated and frozen products must be maintained at proper temperatures. This includes receipt at the distributor's warehouse, storage at the warehouse, transportation on the delivery vehicle, and at receiving.

contribution margin—The sales price for a menu item minus its food cost.

distributor sales representative (DSR)—A consultant who represents a distributor and provides product samples, menu ideas, and information about changing market conditions.

drop size—The dollar amount of a delivery to a food service operation.

error ratio—A figure that helps assess a distributor's accuracy. An operator wants a low error ratio.

in-stock ratio—The number of times a particular product is delivered as specified divided by the total number of times the product has been ordered.

manufacturer—A member of the food service distribution channel that converts raw materials into products that can be used by a food service operation.

menu analysis—An evaluation of an operation's menu as part of an ongoing and evolutionary development process.

on-time delivery—Information on this metric can be obtained by asking distributors for customer references.

potentially hazardous food—A food that requires temperature control because it is in a form capable of supporting the rapid and progressive growth of infectious or toxigenic microorganisms.

preferred distributor—A distributor with more impact than a vendor that also functions as a point source and provides quality assurance inspections.

prime distributor—A distributor that provides the majority of products purchased by a food service operator.

principals—The owners or senior managers of an organization.

processor—See manufacturer.

proprietary items—Products or services unique to a specific distributor.

recipe costing—Using a standard recipe file, an ingredient file, and a menu item file to determine a menu item's cost.

request for proposal—A written document that formally requests a relevant pool of product/service distributors to send in written proposals or bids for the specific products/services needed.

secondary distributor—A distributor used to supplement the items an operation purchases from a primary distributor.

strategic alliance—A relationship in which a distributor is fully integrated into the values, vision, mission, and strategic goals of the food service operation.

temperature danger zone—A range of temperatures from 41° F (5° C) to 140° F (60° C) at which potentially hazardous foods should not be held.

value-added services—Services that involve a transformation of a distributor from being a simple order taker to being able to recommend the most effective products and services available to an operator.

value-added team—A team of representatives from both a distributor and an operator that work together to contribute to the development of the food service operator's strategy.

vendor—A company that provides products or services based simply on price alone.

water activity—The amount of available water in a food.

Review Questions

1. What are the key characteristics of a distributor partner?

2. How is a distributor partner selected? What criteria might be utilized to make the selection?

3. What are the food defense and security considerations of distributors?

4. How are the principles of food safety and HACCP essentials applied to distributors?

5. What are the essentials of ethics from the distributor's perspective?

6. What roles does a distributor play in helping food service operations become more effective?

 References

10 Benefits of Managing Ethics in the Workplace. Carlsbad, Calif.: CRM Learning, 2005.

Anonymous. "A View from the NRA." *Foodservice Equipment & Supplies* 57, no. 12 (December 2004): p. 19.

Anonymous. "Buyers: Keep It Simple When Tracking Savings." *Purchasing* 133, no. 1 (January 2004): pp. 46–47.

Anonymous. "How Purchasing at H-P Builds Ethics in Supply Chain." *Supplier Selection and Management Report* 4, no. 12 (December 2004): pp. 6–7.

Bensky, Gary. "Specifications Key to Getting What you Want in Foodservice Industry." *Nation's Restaurant News* (June 2004): p. 26.

Buck, Vicky. "Don't Shop Til You Drop." *Michigan Restaurateur* (September/October 2004): pp. 28–33.

Cebi, Ferhan and Demet Bayraktar. "An Integrated Approach for Supplies Selection." *Logistics Information Management* 16, no. 6 (2003): p. 395.

Cichy, Ronald F. *Food Safety: Managing the HACCP Process.* Lansing, Mich.: Educational Institute of the American Hotel & Lodging Association, 2004.

Cole, Sharon R. "Distributors Move Beyond Paper." *Business Forms, Labels & Systems* 40, no. 2 (February 2002): pp. 32–36.

Cox, David, John Harris, and Jeff Suber. "Make a Wish." *Nation's Restaurant News* 6, no. 1 (April 2002): p. 16.

Cox, John. "Vendor Vetting." *Network World* 22, no. 18 (May 9, 2005): p. 51.

Desiderio, Lori. "Consultative Selling: Don't Let Your Customer Cherry Pick." *ID New York* 38, no. 4 (April 2002): p. 47.

Effective Purchasing Procedures for Equipment in the Food & Drink Industries. Health & Safety Executive (HSE). Available on-line at www.hsebooks.co.uk.

Emanuelli, Paul. "Eye of the Storm." *Purchasing B2B* 46, no. 8 (October 2004): pp. 18–23.

Ford, William. "Choosing Partners for Profit." *Foodservice Equipment & Supplies* 56, no. 1 (January 2003): p. 62.

Forrest, Wayne. "Buyers and Suppliers Team Up for Greater Savings." *Purchasing* 134, no. 4 (March 2005): pp. 17–20.

Hahn, Eric. "How Prime Vendor Contracts Work." *Restaurant Voice*, 2006. Available on-line at www.restaurantvoice.com/Better-Operations/prime_vendor_contracts.html.

Hernandez, Jorge. "Check It In—If It Checks Out." *Progressive Grocer* 81, no. 13 (September 2002): p. 56.

Hume, Scott. "Good Buys are Hard to Do." *Restaurants & Institutions* 115, no. 2 (February 2005): p. 55.

Jacoby, David. "Focus on the Right Suppliers." *Purchasing* 134, no. 3 (February 17, 2005): p. 64).

Lawn, John. "A Primary Case for a Secondary Supplier." *Food Management* 38, no. 1 (January 2003): p. 6.

Lawn, John. "Seven More Mistakes Purchasing Managers Make." *Food Management* 38, no. 3 (March 2003): p. 8.

Lieberman, Karen and Bruce Nissen. *Ethics in the Hospitality and Tourism Industry.* Lansing, Mich.: Educational Institute of the American Hotel & Lodging Association, 2005.

Ninemeier, Jack D. *Planning and Control for Food and Beverage Operations,* 6th Ed. Lansing, Mich.: Educational Institute of the American Hotel & Lodging Association, 2004.

Riell, Howard. "Distribution Logistics: Making Best Practices Better." *Foodservice Equipment & Supplies* 56, no. 5 (May 2003): pp. 60–63.

Robbins, Stuart. "Strategy Divided by Four." *Supply Management* 10, no. 6 (March 2005): p. 117.

Rowe, Megan. "To Market, To Market." *Restaurant Hospitality* 88, no. 10 (October 2004): pp. 41–45.

Schechter, Mitchell. "Low Price Losers." *Food Service Equipment & Supplies* (November 2003): p. 11.

"Selecting Suppliers." National Restaurant Association Educational Foundation's International Food Safety Council, 2002. Available on-line at www.nraef.org/nfsem/2002/images/pdfs/Week1_Activity.pdf.

"Why Eat Locally and Sustainably Grown Food?" Madison, Wisc.: REAP Food Growers, 2005. Available on-line at www.reapfoodgroup.org/WhyBuyLocal.htm.

Internet Sites

For more information, visit the following Internet sites. Remember, that Internet addresses can change without notice. If the site is no longer there, you can use a search engine to look for additional sites.

Commercial Food Equipment Service
 Association
www.cfesa.com

Electric Foodservice Council
www.foodservicecouncil.org

Foodservice Consultants Society
 International
www.fcsi.org

International Foodservice Manufacturers Association
www.ifmaworld.com

Recipe ShowCase
www.recipeshowcase.com

Chapter 5 Outline

Buyer-Distributor Relationships
    Reasons an Operator Buys from a
       Distributor
    Alliances
    Communication
    Commonalities in the Distributor and
       the Buyer
    Trust and Honesty
    Performance
    Mutually Beneficial Relationships
    Long-Term Net Financial Outcome
    Distributor Relationship Management
    Emotional Intelligence Skills
    Balanced Scorecard
Ethics
    Fairness
    Objectivity
    Integrity
    Benefits
    Examples
    Code of Ethics
    Policies and Standards
Essentials of the Negotiation Process
    Dynamics of the Process
    Steps in the Process
    Preparation before Negotiations
    Empowerment to Make a Commitment
    Negotiation Essentials
    Lessons in Negotiation

Competencies

1. Explain the intricacies of buyer-distributor relationships. (pp. 175–197)

2. Detail the ethical requirements and issues in buyer-distributor relationships. (pp. 197–201)

3. Describe the essential elements of the negotiation process between buyers and distributors. (pp. 201–214)

5

Buyer-Distributor
Relationships

THIS CHAPTER PRESENTS THE ESSENTIAL ELEMENTS of relationships between food service buyers and distributors. Often, the reason a buyer purchases from one distributor instead of another is because of the relationship developed with the selected distributor over time.

It is usually not just the relationship with the buyer and the distributor sales representative (DSR) that cements the loyalty between the two. Rather, the relationships extend on to the interactions between the food production staff, receiving staff, storeroom staff, and the distributor's delivery personnel. Of course, the relationship is also based on the services and products the distributor provides.

Buyer-Distributor Relationships

It has been said that people buy from people, not from organizations. It stands to reason, then, that the relationships are developed between people in one organization and people in another organization; that is, people in the food service operation and people in the distributor's organization. But what are the key elements of or reasons why an operator buys from the distributor?

Reasons an Operator Buys from a Distributor

The food service business is a relationship business that is based on people. Unlike other aspects of retail business (e.g., clothing retail stores, electronics retail stores), the relationships with people are essential in food service. The relationships may be top-to-top, in which a distributor's senior executives develop relationships with senior executives at a food service operation, and simply evaluate programs based on quarterly reviews of the results. Or the relationship may be established between an owner-operator of an independent food service operation and a relatively small local distributor.

These relationships may involve interactions that occur face-to-face, via the telephone, or electronically using **e-purchasing** tools. A face-to-face relationship is the traditional way that food service operators and distributors have done business. Before electronic purchasing methods existed, the DSR who came through the operator's back door and took the time to develop the relationship got the order. While this relationship was also based on performance (e.g., a beer delivery person putting the beer in the right coolers for the operator), it had service as its foundation. An operator may purchase from a distributor that the operator does not "like," based on the way the distributor performs or services the operation.

Telephone relationships are different from face-to-face interactions. Some operators prefer telephone dealings with distributors because they take less time and can be more efficient. Perhaps the way to view telephone relationships, where the operator places the order on the telephone instead of face-to-face, is as a complement to face-to-face relationships.

When the Internet was introduced as a means to strengthen relationships between food service buyers and distributors, some were skeptical that e-purchasing could actually replace face-to-face or telephone ordering. Businesses certainly are becoming increasingly dependent on electronic media and the Internet. Longer term, it will be necessary to pinpoint the exact effects that e-purchasing has on the price of products and the services that the operator expects. In theory, the prices of products bought through e-purchasing should be lower since the same costs (e.g., labor in the distributor's operation) are lower. These same products should, again in theory, arrive at the operation's back door with fewer mistakes and errors.

The use of e-purchasing can help reduce product inventory costs as well as help both the distributor and operator manage their critical processes (e.g., inventory control, receiving) more effectively and efficiently. This may add enough value for operators that the loss of face-to-face relationships is outweighed by the savings. This is particularly true for those operators interested in participating in on-line reverse auctions in terms of preparing effective requests for proposals (RFPs), qualifying distributors, development of unique specifications, and varying geographic locations for individual restaurants in a nationwide chain).

As important as e-procurement applications have become and will become in the future, they may never become more important than other factors on which a relationship is evaluated. These other factors include strategic alliances (whether they are long-term and positive), communication (whether it is face-to-face, based on honesty, helpful in solving problems, and based on some sense of shared values and vision), trust (being trustworthy and trusting others, being straightforward and clear, being honest), performance (solving problems, communication, listening skills), mutual benefit (shared values and vision, both organizations "profit" from the relationship), and emotional intelligence capabilities (skills such as adaptability, cooperation, conflict management, empathy, and openness).

Alliances

In the broadest sense, a co-op or buying group is an **alliance** that facilitates relationships between buyers and sellers. Operators become members of buying groups by paying a monthly fee, as well as an initiation fee in some cases.

These alliances deliver the best prices to their members because there is strength in numbers (often referred to as economies of scale) when purchasing certain food products. The per-unit product cost is reduced because the volume of products purchased far exceeds the purchase volume of any single operator. Usually members of buying groups and co-ops receive allowances for the volume of products purchased.

Group purchasing organizations (GPOs) may also offer improved services to members. For example, if a number of healthcare organizations become members of a GPO, part of the services provided may include enhanced inventory management tools, assessment tools for patient and resident satisfaction at the members' operations, and/or housekeeping programs. In the case of self-operated colleges and universities that become part of a GPO, perhaps the highest value-added service that the buying group can provide is objective ways to measure how buying power is being maximized. This metric is often of keen interest to the administration of the member colleges and universities. So, too, independent restaurateurs can take advantage of services offered by GPOs, including menu analysis software, ideas for marketing and promoting products purchased, and a connection to regional and national food service trends.

Alliances with distributors may be particularly advantageous when there is a downturn in the economy. When a distributor is connected to both manufacturers and manufacturers' representatives, and can connect these two vital product/service providers to the operator, products and services can be delivered to the operator in a timely manner with fewer errors, and most likely at a lower cost. So really, then, alliances exist across the food service distribution channel from sources to manufacturers to the manufacturers' representatives to brokers to distributors and to operators. Sometimes these alliances result in additional added services such as training of the operator's staff members in the case of equipment purchases, time invested in demonstrations by the manufacturers' representatives or brokers as to how new products can be utilized and priced at a profit for the operator's customers, and support services with promotions and marketing in the forms of table tents, promotional displays, and menu copy.

Communication

Relationships between a distributor and an operator are based on honest and timely communication. Recall that the most critical communication skill is **listening**—listening to needs and expectations, translating these into requirements, then working diligently to meet or exceed the requirements. Communication in various forms adds value to the operator-distributor relationship.

Communication must be open and honest. By "leveling" with each other in terms of stating requirements, and what each party can do to meet those requirements, a distributor and operator strengthen their relationship. Honest communication is accurate and includes any changes in needs and expectations. Open communication is frequent in that it communicates changes to requirements in a timely manner.

Operators prefer distributors who communicate clearly, directly, and frequently. Perhaps this makes the case for face-to-face over electronic communication. The relationship developed by an operator with a specific DSR is an intense stimulus for distributors to minimize turnover in DSRs. When turnover is minimized, that DSR has been able to get to know the unique needs and expectations of a particular food service operator. This helps develop shared values and vision, both of which take time to emerge through the interactions of both partners committed to the relationship. It also contributes to the problem-solving abilities of the DSR, as the DSR gets to know the operator over time.

Relationships do not simply happen; they require work from all parties involved. Communication based on honesty creates trust that strengthens relationships. When distributors and operators invest time and effort in these communication-based relationships, they become more valuable. Perhaps this is one of the reasons why e-purchasing is preferred with some operators. With the use of the Internet and e-mail to communicate clearly, information sharing is enhanced.

There is another element of communication that must be addressed in the purchasing function: negotiations and conflict resolution. Even though purchasing systems and processes are initially constructed and refined to eliminate recurring problems, problems inevitably surface due to variation in the actions of the people involved. The negotiations process is inherent with problems since both the distributor and operator are attempting to negotiate the best position and terms for their respective organizations. Sometimes what is in the best interest of the distributor is not in the best interest of the operator, and vice versa.

What is expected from the standpoint of communication is that both parties work on joint problem solving and that there is some give and take, as well as compromise. Issues that are sources of conflict must be resolved at the source; otherwise these same conflicts are likely to surface again in the future. Confrontation and coercion do not work in open communication; rather, an understanding of each other's position and where the other person is "coming from" is preferred. When each party communicates cooperatively and exchanges needed information, the best solutions to problems can be discovered and implemented. When communication enhances development of relationships, the alliance between distributor and operator results in a unique competitive advantage.

Commonalities in the Distributor and the Buyer

Distributors and buyers should share common values, visions, and missions. Recall that values represent how people in an organization will behave and will act. As such, **values** are a statement of acceptable ways to interact with others, including distributors. Examples of these values include honesty, fairness, timeliness, openness, sharing of information, and mutual benefit.

Vision is built on the foundation of values. Vision answers the question: What do I want to create in my organization? Vision often is a picture of the ideal future, with the full understanding that perfection is rarely achieved. But if we begin with less than the ideal vision, mediocrity may result.

Mission answers the question: Why do we exist as an organization? Most organizations exist to add some distinctively unique source of value for their customers, both internal and external. Value may be apparent when the operator offers a wide variety of appealing menu items, or when the distributor makes software available to help the operator have better information that results in improved efficiency.

When the distributor and operator share values, vision, and mission, there is tremendous resulting enhanced power due to synergy. Synergy can be described by the idea that the whole is greater than the sum of its parts. That is, synergy means that the relationship between the operator and distributor makes the results more powerful than either organization can achieve on its own.

For example, a family-owned distributor may be able to relate well to a family-owned operator because of commonalities in ownership and operating philosophies, including values, vision, and mission. These commonalities often lead to anticipatory services provided by the distributor, since the distributor can think ahead and make suggestions and provide ideas for the operator. This greatly helps the operator in decision making.

Identifying commonalities between the distributor and operator can help both work together more effectively. One example is responding to the increased sophistication of food service customers. To the extent that both understand this continuous demographic change, both can work together to become more successful in satisfying changing customer requirements.

Another commonality is the shift away from traditional **bracket pricing** (simply based on the volumes of products purchased) and elementary **cost-plus pricing** (based on the distributor's cost plus a reasonable markup) to inquiries by operators about ways to save additional costs in purchasing products. Operators may inquire about a distributor's added costs and net costs for products. Operators may also want to know what promotional or growth programs manufacturers are offering distributors because they may be passed along as cost savings for the operator. This commonality lies in sharing information from the distributor to the operator so each can make better decisions.

The struggle to enhance profitability and/or contain costs is another commonality. When both parties feel a loss of control due to competitive pricing, they can work together to come up with a mutually agreeable solution that addresses each other's profit objectives. In on-site food service, an added pressure is that subsidies for food service clients have diminished.

A commonality shared by both distributors and operators is the desire to make each of their organizations more efficient in terms of operating systems. Distributors are constantly evaluating their warehousing and logistics (movement of products) costs, the actual vs. desired profitability of each food service operator customer, and the cost that it requires to make a sale to a particular operator. Operators are also striving to become more efficient through reduced labor costs, often by purchasing products with built-in labor (e.g., prepared entrées, prewashed and bagged salad ingredients). These help operators achieve increased control over labor costs as well as product costs, food costs, portion control, and profitability.

Another commonality is **consolidation** due to mergers and acquisitions for both distributors and operators. While distribution is largely controlled by a few large corporate distributors, the smaller, independent regional or local distributors are diminishing in number. In on-site food service, there are fewer regional and local contract providers as national management companies have acquired these through mergers.

Operators are focusing on building customer loyalty and retention in an effort to build check averages and increase frequency of visits. These same operators are concentrating on upselling to add sales through cross-merchandising and convenience retailing (e.g., foods prepared to go). Distributors at the same time are focused on improving the average order size and drop sizes by encouraging operators to engage the distributor as a "prime distributor." In many cases, this requires the distributor to add a wider variety of segment-specific products to its line and to offer specialized services required by each food service segment.

Trust and Honesty

Trust and honesty are the foundations of the operator-distributor relationship. In the past, too many relationships operated on principles of coercion and a lack of fairness and integrity resulting in toxic, unsavory outcomes. Today, the key to building operator's loyalty is to do so based on honesty and trust.

One of the most essential ingredients to an effective relationship between the distributor and operator is trust. Trust strengthens the relationship if it is characterized by timely and open communication, listening to accurately identify the other party's needs and expectations, translating these needs and expectations into requirements, working diligently to meet or exceed the requirements, working collaboratively to solve problems when they occur and to anticipate and resolve problems before they take place, and being proactive and timely.

Trust and honesty take place when information is shared. If an operator shares vital information with a distributor, the distributor is better positioned to help the operator achieve strategic goals. These goals are realized when the distributor acts as a consultant to the operator in providing products and services that help achieve the goals.

Trust is built based on sharing the truth and being dependable. Dependability in the distributor-operator relationship means that the two parties can rely on each other to keep promises. The dependability is based on integrity and a respect for the expertise of each. Trust is also based on shared values that lead to collaboration in working toward vision and mission. Trust does not mean that both parties in the relationship always agree. However, disagreements are handled with respect and empathy for both points of view.

Performance

Performance is simply delivering on what was promised. The evaluation of performance must be objective, not subjective, and based on criteria known in advance by all parties in the relationship.

Those with purchasing responsibilities are very busy indeed. Much effort is required to properly perform the wide range of responsibilities that are integral to the purchasing function. Perhaps the most challenging task facing those with purchasing responsibilities is that of evaluating the purchasing system.

How well is the purchasing system working? How can it be improved? How should priorities for improvements be established? These and related questions can only be answered through the process of performance evaluation. Operators should not conduct evaluations only when they find time or when they get around to it. Rather, **purchasing system evaluation** activities must be part of an ongoing process, conducted according to basic management principles.

The Need for Evaluation. The evaluation of a purchasing system has two primary objectives: (1) to measure the extent to which current purchasing goals are being met, and (2) to improve the system in order to more effectively achieve future purchasing goals and enhance performance. These objectives can best be attained by means of a critical analysis that measures, monitors, and improves the purchasing system's productivity.

Evaluation of the purchasing process helps provide the information and financial control essential for effective management. Food service operations typically work within small profit margins. If an operation is to succeed, it is essential to minimize purchasing costs, which constitute a significant percentage of the operation's total income. At the same time, the operation must maintain its required quality levels. How much the operation spends for purchases is relatively easy to measure (the income statement recaps this information for each fiscal period). However, it may be more difficult to discover whether each purchase dollar represents a necessary and reasonable cost, and yields enhanced value for the food service operation.

In addition to contributing to cost-effectiveness, an evaluation of the purchasing system can lead to other benefits. An evaluation may reveal ways to improve the overall effectiveness of the purchasing process. While change for the sake of change should be discouraged, purposeful change is desirable. Analysis of current purchasing procedures may generate new ideas regarding work practices which can aid operators, purchasing staff, and the operation as a whole. Since guests will be affected by actions of the purchasing department, evaluation of the purchaser's performance becomes even more essential.

A food service operation comprises a number of closely related sub-systems. Many departments depend heavily on the purchasing function. They should, therefore, provide feedback on issues such as product yields, quality, delivery times, and shortages.

Changes in the purchasing system may produce spin-off effects leading to changes in other departments. For example, procedural improvements for conducting make-or-buy analyses may suggest that food products with built-in labor should be purchased. Several changes may then occur with the production department: fewer personnel hours may be involved in the food production tasks and more time may be available to accomplish other activities.

Evaluation Principles. We have noted that an operator needs to assign a high priority to the process used to evaluate performance. We have also indicated reasons why objective evaluation is vital to proper purchasing. It is useful to review a number of basic principles that are directly related to this performance evaluation.

To be most effective, evaluation of performance must be done in an objective manner, on a timely basis, and with input from purchasing staff and others outside the department. Exhibit 1 outlines the basic performance evaluation process and shows how the management functions relate to one another. In the context of purchasing, for example, measurable goals must be developed. Based upon these goals, purchasing tasks must be organized, coordinated, and communicated to ensure that resources allocated to the purchasing function are used efficiently.

Purchasing staff must be hired, trained, supervised, and evaluated. In food service operations, purchasing tasks may be spread among various personnel or handled by a single person. In this situation, specific tasks should be included in position descriptions for those designated staff members.

Exhibit 1   The Performance Evaluation Loop

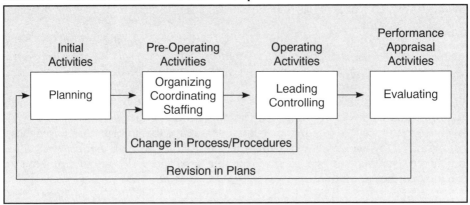

Purchasing activities must also be controlled. Expected performance must be compared with actual performance, and corrective action taken as necessary. Evaluation is part of this control process.

Purchasing Performance Evaluation. Who should be responsible for the evaluation of the purchasing system performance? Typically, the evaluation is conducted by department managers, who additionally may be responsible for preparing position descriptions, creating financial controls, setting dollar purchase limits, and qualifying distributors. Exhibit 2 lists questions to consider when conducting a performance evaluation of a purchasing system.

Top-level management will be concerned about aspects of purchasing related to quality and economics. How much money is being spent? How can expenses be reduced without sacrificing quality? Top-level management, however, is seldom involved in the actual performance evaluation process. Its role generally is to establish policies identifying what the organization expects from the purchasing function (e.g., to purchase required goods and services at the lowest possible price consistent with quality and service standards established by the operations department).

Managers often review the effectiveness of the purchasing system by studying income statements. However, purchasing practices may not be the cause of higher (or lower) purchasing costs. For example, market prices may have changed unexpectedly. Sometimes, excessive purchasing costs may be traced to problems in other control points of the food service system, such as receiving, storing, issuing, production, or service—all of which are typically beyond the control of purchasing staff. These examples illustrate the need to establish definable and measurable goals for the purchasing control point. The purchasing department can be given direct responsibility for these goals and allowed control over areas that may affect the department's ability to achieve them.

Purchasing departments should participate in the performance evaluation process. They should know, for example, whether policies, plans, budgets, and other financial goals are followed consistently. They should also be made aware of

Exhibit 2   Performance Evaluation Questions

The purchaser is most concerned with ensuring that the basic purchasing goals are met. Much of the performance evaluation process focuses on these goals. However, there is typically a wide range of other performance factors in the purchasing management system that lend themselves to objective evaluation. Consider the following questions:

- Is the purchasing department properly organized?
- Are all purchasing positions cost effective?
- Is there a coordinated flow of communication between purchasing and other departments?
- Are purchasing policies reasonable from the perspective of both operation and distributor personnel?
- Do reports and records circulated among departments provide adequate and timely information?
- Is the importance of effective purchasing recognized throughout the operation?
- Are all purchasing procedures written and consistently followed?
- Are purchasing activities centralized within the food service operation?
- Are all purchasing staff selected, trained, and qualified for the work they do?
- What procedures are used to select the "best" distributors?
- Does the purchasing department function in a staff (advisory) role rather than a line (management) role?

situations that may create purchasing problems that do not turn up on the financial statements. For instance, the purchaser should examine relationships with distributors, and encourage feedback from the production staff.

A basic management rule states that persons responsible for a task cannot be solely responsible for evaluating its completion. This certainly applies to the purchasing staff. However, input from the purchasing staff should be solicited as the performance evaluation process develops. Staff members are knowledgeable about the purchasing system and may have suggestions for its improvement.

Operating personnel should also be involved in performance evaluation. They may suggest ways to improve equipment, products, services, and the purchasing system itself. This type of feedback enhances the communication process. For example, a manager may find that a specific product is undesirable in quality. An evaluation may reveal, however, that the purchasing department is using an outdated specification. Management may have changed the specific need for an item without notifying the purchasing department of the updated quality requirements. Communication between management and purchasing staff may uncover problems like this as the performance evaluation process unfolds.

When an operation undertakes an internal performance evaluation, several advantages are apparent. An internal evaluation saves time and expenses associated with hiring an external organization for performance evaluation. Internal evaluation can also be an effective tool to help resolve subtle problems that may go unnoticed in the course of day-to-day operations. Also, operational goals are more likely to be achieved when all concerned individuals become familiar with the operation's systems and procedures, which make actual results measurable.

There are also some potential disadvantages to an internal evaluation process. The evaluation process may receive too low a priority within the operation, or may be ignored altogether. Also, current staff may lack the expertise and broad-based experience required to define or resolve performance problems. Concerns about discipline or job loss, reduced level of self-esteem, or fraudulent work practices may discourage purchasing staff from objectively evaluating current performance.

These disadvantages may be countered by supplementing an internal performance evaluation with the use of outside consultants who can offer a fresh and objective evaluation of purchasing performance. Consultants are sometimes employed to analyze and resolve problems that may include the purchasing system. For instance, when consultants are hired to investigate excessive operating costs, the purchasing system may also be scrutinized. The consultants' findings may then be integrated within the internal evaluation report.

The Evaluation Process. The process of performance evaluation in purchasing resembles an internal control audit and addresses such questions as: Do proper policies and procedures exist? Are they accurately used in purchasing transactions? What level of performance is achieved as measured against pre-established standards?

Evaluating purchasing performance involves three basic steps. The first step identifies the goals of purchasing. These goals should reflect the operation's established philosophies and be clearly written and communicated to all purchasing personnel. The second step assesses performance by comparing the actual results of purchasing activities against the goals set forth in step one. The final step in the evaluation process improves the purchasing system by implementing the necessary corrective actions to resolve any performance deficiencies revealed in step two.

Basic purchasing goals involve concerns about product, quality, price, quantity, distributors, and timing. Purchasing goals must be reasonable and within the control of purchasing department staff members. Once general goals pertaining to each of these broad areas have been identified, they may be further defined in terms of specific actions that will help to achieve them. This can best be done by keeping a simple question in mind: "What do we want to accomplish and how will we measure whether we are successful?" Each food service operation must establish goals and action plans appropriate for its own particular situation. The following set of goals and action plans is offered only as an illustration of the kind of specificity and measurability that is necessary in the first step of the performance evaluation process.

If the goal is to purchase the right products, action plans may include the following:

1. Items will be rejected and price adjustments will be made no more than five times this year because of quality problems.

2. Instances where items accepted from a distributor are found to be inferior in quality will not occur more than once this year.

3. Distributors will be asked to provide suggestions about quality requirements at least twice this year.

If the goal is to purchase at the right price, action plans may include the following:

1. Total cost of purchased goods will increase or decrease in direct proportion to sales. Since the ratio of sales revenue to gross purchasing cost was four to one last year, this year the ratio should also be four to one.

2. Per-unit costs of expensive and large-volume products will increase or decrease in direct proportion to the Consumer Price Index (CPI).

If the goal is to purchase in the right quantities, action plans may include the following:

1. There will be no more than ten stockouts for all items this year.

2. Items in inventory will be controlled so that the maximum limit is not exceeded more than ten times during the year.

3. No more than a specified value of perishable items will need to be discarded annually.

If the goal is to purchase from the right distributor, action plans may include the following:

1. Samples and prices will be obtained this year for all major products with the goal of identifying eligible distributors.

2. There will be no more than ten complaints of any kind against any distributor within the coming year.

3. There will be no cases of back-door selling by a distributor. (Back-door selling occurs when the salesperson bypasses the designated purchaser in order to persuade another staff member to exert influence on the purchasing decision.)

If the goal is to purchase at the right time, action plans may include the following:

1. There will be no more than ten rush orders this year.

2. A distributor will not deliver later than an agreed-upon date more than eight times this year.

3. Distributors will never deliver more than one week early.

A wide range of additional goals and action plans can also be established. For example, action plans may call for a specific number of make-or-buy analyses, purchase-specification evaluations, and equipment purchase studies to be developed during a specific fiscal period. Personnel in the purchasing department may be required to attend professional development seminars and other training activities. Budgetary goals, development of policy handbooks, and computerization all lend themselves to quantification and objective measurement.

How does one determine whether performance leads to goals actually being achieved? Obviously, procedures for assessment must be determined when goals are first established. This is the reason for extending goals to include specific, measurable purchasing actions. Comparing actual performance to expected performance (outlined in the goal-setting action plan) is the central element in the evaluation activity.

How often should the comparison process take place? The answer to this question depends upon the goals. If goals relate to performance covering a period of six or twelve months, evaluation must take place at the end of that period. Some formal performance evaluation of the purchasing process is in order as preparation for the evaluation of purchasing staff begins.

If the comparison suggests that goals have not been attained, it will be necessary to implement a decision-making process to discover the reason(s) for failure and to plan corrective action strategies to improve performance.

Some variance between expected and actual performance is permitted before corrective action must be taken. If the plan is to develop 20 purchase specifications during a particular period, a questioning process to uncover problems may only be necessary if less than 18 are actually developed. A variance of 10 percent, for example, may be acceptable to certain food service operations in this instance. Regardless of the variance limit, purchasing problems become of greater concern as the frequency of occurrence increases.

The goal-setting and action plan method of assessing performance may be supplemented by a variety of other techniques. For example, requests for price quotation sheets and actual delivery invoices can be used to determine current prices and can be compared with similar documents from previous periods. These assessments can review both per unit costs and charges for total volumes of purchases (if volumes were similar to quantities purchased during previous periods).

Various inventory tools can be used to help evaluate purchasing procedures related to quantity. Perpetual inventory forms can assist the operator in keeping a running account of stock levels of critical items. Other forms can be used to calculate quantities and values of stock on hand during calculations of physical inventory. Another useful metric is to measure average rates of inventory turnover.

Choice of distributors is another goal worth assessing. Rating sheets that evaluate distributors, credit memos indicating a poor delivery record, and relevant correspondence between accounting and the distributor can help in evaluating whether the right distributor has been used.

Logs are in-house records related to operational activities. Critical incident logs can be maintained to record delivery and/or storage problems that relate to purchasing performance. Work logs can be used to indicate stockouts and times when maximum inventory levels were overridden.

Assume that the assessment of performance indicates a problem: the incidence of stockouts is unacceptable, with approximately 25 percent more stockouts than planned. A traditional decision-making approach might be used to resolve the problem. This begins with problem definition and expands to consideration and analysis of alternatives. It concludes with testing of possible solutions and implementation of revised procedures.

Corrective action is then required to solve the problem. After procedures to reduce problems have been undertaken, it becomes necessary to evaluate how well they work. The purpose of this evaluation is twofold: (1) to ensure that the problem (excessive variance between planned and actual goal attainment) is solved, and (2) to make certain that no other problems are created.

During this evaluation, it is necessary to observe the extent to which the problem is reduced. Input from top-level managers, purchasing staff, and production department staff may prove valuable. Suggestions about further improvements can be solicited from this group. Time will be needed to gather enough objective information to evaluate the appropriateness of the corrective action.

The list of supplemental factors to evaluate can become extensive. However, the point to remember is that the most important concerns must be addressed first in an evaluation program. Over time, other elements can be considered, as the process of improvement is continuous.

Exhibit 3 shows a sample form used to note factors worth considering as performance evaluation activities are undertaken. While a unique list needs to be developed for each operation, the form does suggest a practical process for evaluation. After selecting each activity to be considered, the evaluator can indicate (by marking either "Yes" or "No") whether improvements are needed. Specific comments can indicate examples of problems and propose corrective action strategies that might be helpful.

Ideally, the purchasing evaluation guide should be completed by personnel in several departments. Over time, it should be possible to track performance improvements and eliminate the repetition of similar performance problems. If several activities require improvements, problems of the highest priority should be selected for immediate attention; other activities can be addressed after the more critical problems are resolved. Once problems have been identified, a time frame for solving them should be established. This element of timing is an integral part of purchasing performance improvement.

As a supplement to internal performance evaluation, it may be beneficial to request that distributors evaluate an operation's purchasing practices. The list of questions must be framed differently and some responses may be discarded, but excellent suggestions are often received. Experienced distributors know that it is always less costly for them to retain customers than to obtain new ones, so they may be willing to help in the evaluation process.

Focus on Distributor Performance. Procedures to evaluate whether products are being purchased from the right source were noted earlier. However, since the distributor is such an integral element in the success or failure of the purchasing department, much attention should be focused on evaluating distributor performance.

Food service operators are obviously concerned with operating costs. Distributors should be able to deliver products of the quality specified when they are needed and at the lowest possible cost.

Exhibit 3   Purchasing Evaluation Guide

Date _____

Completed by staff member in:
- ☐ Purchasing Dept.
- ☐ Food/Bev. Dept.
- ☐ Management
- ☐ Accounting Dept.

Instructions: For each of the following activities consider whether improvements can be made that will make purchasing more effective. Specific ideas/suggestions will be very helpful.

Activity	Yes	No	Comments
1. Organization of purchasing dept.			
2. Relations with user dept.			
3. Purchasing controls.			
4. Receiving controls.			
5. Storage controls.			
6. Make/buy analysis.			
7. Writing purchase specifications.			
8. Locating/working with suppliers.			
9. Personnel cooperation.			
10. Employee training.			
11. Document processing for payment.			
12. Policies.			
13. Standard operating procedures.			
14. "Paperwork."			
15. Product quality determination.			
16. Product quantity determination.			
17. Expediting/follow-up.			
18. Delivery timing.			
19. Other activities (list).			

Source: Jack D. Ninemeier, *Purchasing, Receiving, and Storage: A Systems Manual for Restaurants, Hotels, and Clubs* (New York: Van Nostrand Reinhold Company, 1983), p. 315.

Situations sometimes arise when a low-cost distributor does not perform satisfactorily in terms of service or quality. Most operators do not want to eliminate a potentially cost-effective distributor, so steps should be taken to determine whether distributor performance can be improved. Such steps may include the following:

- The purchaser should meet with the distributor to establish and discuss the basic performance problems.

- The distributor should be asked to determine the nature and cause of performance problems. Often, the problem relates to the hospitality operation itself (its ordering systems, for example).

- The purchaser should visit the distributor's facility to assess its capacity and cleanliness. The purchaser should check for adequate inventory levels, food safety in storage areas, proper storeroom temperatures, and well-trained and efficient personnel.

If at all possible, it is better to help a current distributor improve below-standard performance rather than replace the distributor with one that may have higher prices. However, if poor performance continues, obviously the distributor must be eliminated from eligibility.

More often, the operator already has a number of distributors who provide satisfactory quality and service. In this case, the operator concentrates on finding ways to reduce costs. To be successful, the operator must seek competitive prices or find some other means to measure the distributor's price performance.

Mutually Beneficial Relationships

Mutually beneficial relationships benefit all parties that are committed to making the outcomes the best that they can be under the circumstances. Rather than searching for ways to place the blame on others- manufacturers, manufacturers' representatives, brokers, distributors, distributor sales representatives (DSRs)— mutually beneficial relationships require all to take ownership and responsibility to fix problems because the solutions benefit all in the relationship.

In the past, distributors and operators entered relationships for self gain. The goal was simply to make more money for the distributor organization by selling more products, or the goal was only to increase profits in a commercial food service operation or control costs in an on-site food service operation. These relationships did not work because they were too one-sided. It was win-lose; if someone won, the other person in the relationship lost. Today's relationships must be based on mutual gain and result in a win-win outcome for the parties involved.

Long-Term Net Financial Outcome

Every organization in food service has a desired **long-term net financial outcome**. With commercial food service operations, the financial outcome is usually generation of sufficient earnings to be able to invest back into the operation as well as make a profit. With on-site and managed services food service operations, reinvesting in the operation is essential, but their organizations are not motivated by profits. Rather, the focus is on containing costs to maximize the amount available to reinvest.

Most operations look at their financial outcomes each month or each quarter to help pinpoint areas for improvement. It is equally important to consider the longer term, say financial outcomes annually or over a period of years. While it may be possible that a loss occurs due to an investment in the short-term (e.g., technology), it is important to look at the effects of that needed investment over the long run and consider the net financial outcomes. The net financial outcome is the revenues or cost savings generated over some defined period, usually longer than one year, compared to the required expenses of the improvement over that same period.

Distributor Relationship Management

Distributor relationship management (DRM) is the concept of customer relationship management as applied to an operation's distributors. Operations that focus on distributor relationship management view distributors as customers. Just as with internal customers (staff members) and external customers (those who pay for the operation's products and services), operations that practice DRM engage and listen to their distributors as they make clear decisions to guide the operation. When listening to distributors, try to identify their needs and expectations so they can be translated into requirements. Then try to decide how to help the distributor meet or exceed the identified requirements.

It is important to realize that one of the commitments of DRM is to regularly discuss what the operation's distributors require over time, since their requirements change and evolve. The answers to this perpetual inquiry provide direction on what needs to be done and how all parties in the relationship can help contribute.

When an operation gives feedback to a distributor, that distributor will also be encouraged to provide meaningful feedback to the operator. This two-way communication will strengthen the relationship. A distributor provides more than products and services; a value-added distributor provides information that helps the operator meet or exceed the expectations of external and internal customers. When applying the concept of distributor relationship management, the distributor is treated as a strategic ally and partner.

Distributor relationship management includes regular briefings and assessments, the outcomes of which are shared with the distributor. This information identifies possible areas for improvement in the food service system. Other information flows from/to the distributors from/to the operator across all the areas in which the two organizations interface. This regular information exchange strengthens the partnership. Ideas for putting a DRM program in practice are presented in Exhibit 4.

Emotional Intelligence Skills

Emotional intelligence (EI) is a set of skills and competencies that are extremely important in purchasing. EI is an understanding of how individuals perceive, utilize, and manage their emotions and others' emotions. EI combines intrapersonal (awareness of self and feelings) with interpersonal (awareness of others and empathy) understanding. If a staff member responsible for purchasing can identify, understand, and manage his or her own emotions, then he or she can also help influence the emotions of others (e.g., distributors and staff members).

In a study of private club managers, three EI factors or dimensions were identified: IN, OUT, and RELATIONSHIPS. Our study categorizes the skills and competencies of emotional intelligence into three different factors: IN (combining awareness of self and self-leadership), OUT (combining awareness of others and empathy), and RELATIONSHIPS. The IN factor had eight different competencies, the OUT factor had seven different competencies, and the RELATIONSHIPS factor had five different competencies. The top three competencies for each of the factors are presented in Exhibit 5.

The top three competencies of the IN factor represent the intrapersonal dimensions of emotional intelligence. Since leadership is first, foremost, and always an inner quest, we begin the examination of emotional intelligence by focusing on the

Exhibit 4   Ideas for Putting a DRM Program into Practice

1. Begin with an assessment of how key distributors perform relative to the require-ments in the contract.
2. Prioritize which distributors to include in the DRM program.
3. Clearly articulate the objectives of the program in writing to all involved parties, and link the objectives to the operation's strategic goals.
    a. Working with selected distributors to increase value received
    b. Innovation
    c. Developing strategies for new markets
4. Understand what each distributor requires from the relationship. If necessary, modify the operation's requirements to achieve mutual benefit.
5. Invest resources, including programs, systems, metrics, teams with members from both the operation and distributor, detailed cost analysis, and others.
6. Make fact-based decisions by using the right metrics (e.g., spending patterns with each supplier), enhanced by the right software and sources of information.
7. Involve all who can bring value to the DRM process, including internal customers.
8. Determine responsibilities for each part of the DRM process based on who can best add value at that step. Those responsible for day-to-day operations may not be best suited for the development of long-term strategies.
9. Be creative and use tools to enhance creativity, such as brainstorming, cross-functional teams, teams made up of distributor and operator representatives, and joint meetings.
10. Utilize contingency planning since all relationships do not last forever. Develop alternative strategies with different distributors.

Source: Adapted from Peter Smith, "More Than a Beautiful Friendship," *Supply Management* (February 3, 2005).

capabilities within the leader. These capabilities may be broadly categorized as awareness of self and self-leadership.

The number-one ranked IN competency is the leader's ability to use feelings to positively influence his or her own behavior. This self-awareness is absolutely essential since it results in self-leadership. In purchasing, positive influencing of self-behavior is critical since the leader operates in an environment of experiences created and delivered for customers. The leader's actions must project positive and optimistic possibilities. The second IN competency links self-awareness with self-leadership in service of self-development. This capability is desired since it leads to self-improvement and continuous improvement, two highly desirable charac-teristics in purchasing. The third IN competency is the ability to use emotions in the thinking process. Relevant decisions often combine cognitive (thinking) with non-cognitive (feelings) aspects to more fully arrive at a decision that takes into account all affected.

The three OUT competencies are examined next. They combine the aware-ness of others with empathy, the ability to view the world from the perspectives of others. The top-ranked OUT competency is the ability to read the feelings of

Exhibit 5   Emotional Intelligence Competencies

Factor	Competency	Ranking
IN	I am able to use awareness of my feelings to positively influence my behavior.	1
	I am open to my feelings, and I am able to adjust them in myself to promote personal understanding and development.	2
	I am able to use my feelings in my thinking process.	3
OUT	I can read the feelings of other people.	1
	I am able to perceive feelings in others.	2
	I am sensitive to other people's emotions.	3
RELATIONSHIPS	I can easily build and participate in mutually satisfying relationships characterized by openness and affection.	1
	I am able to express and use feelings to communicate emotions with others.	2
	I am able to clearly communicate in relationships with others.	3

others. This is a logical extension of the IN skill to be aware of the leader's own emotions. Said another way, it is virtually impossible to be aware of the feelings of others without first being aware of your own emotions. The perception of feelings of others is ranked as the number-two OUT competency.

Some would say that perception is reality and we tend to agree. Perceiving others' feelings is critical to a leader's ability to respond appropriately to those feelings, particularly during negotiations in the purchasing process. Different feelings require different responses and it may be thought of as adapting one's leadership styles to the situation, as defined by the feelings of others. Just imagine how valuable this can be as a purchasing staff member adapts to a distributor's needs one moment and a staff member's needs the next.

Sensitivity to the emotions of other people is the third-ranked OUT competency. This sensitivity begins with an awareness of feelings in others and is then built on an ability to see the world from the perspective of the other person. This is empathy, a most valuable skill in the purchasing process. It is important to see the customers from the operator's and staff members' perspectives, including their inner, often hidden, motivators.

The third factor is RELATIONSHIPS—the bonds between people. The first competency is the building of mutually satisfying relationships characterized by openness and affection. The openness refers to a trusting relationship built on honesty. Trusting relationships are one of the foundations of effective leadership. Affection indicates a feeling more than "like," but characterized by "love." If purchasing staff members say they "love" a particular distributor, then they are expressing much more loyalty than if they simply say "like."

The second ranked RELATIONSHIPS item refers to communication of feelings, another foundation of effective leadership. This communication helps reinforce trust in the relationships. Expression of these emotions is part of the third-ranked competency, clear communication in relationships. This communication with staff members and distributors leads to understanding that transcends barriers and promotes further development of the relationships that are so vital to successful food service operations, in general, and purchasing, in particular.

These emotional intelligence competencies are skills that purchasers can begin to or continue to practice. They should be viewed as competencies to practice and skills to build, rather than principles. They complement the essentials of leadership in purchasing. In effect, each day in an operation is an opportunity to practice and improve emotional intelligence skills in service of becoming a more effective purchasing leader.

Balanced Scorecard

Traditional measuring devices in food service operations include profit and loss statements, balance sheets, and cash flow statements. For example, a balance sheet consists of tangible assets such as money, inventory, equipment, facilities, and others. A food service operation also has intangible assets, including brand equity, customer relationship management, customer loyalty, goodwill, and projected future earnings, among others.

Accounting systems generally do not report the value of customer relationship management with any of the three customer groups in a food service operation: internal customers, external customers, and distributors. Yet investment in customer/distributor relationship management is clearly one that requires time, effort, and other resources, including money.

A **balanced scorecard** is designed to indicate capital owned by the operator other than just financial capital. The traditional categories included in a balanced scorecard are the following:

- Customer Satisfaction

- Financial

- Human Resources

- Organizational Effectiveness

- Marketing/Growth

A balanced scorecard is constructed based on the values, vision, and mission of the food service operation. Once these are defined, strategic goals can be developed to describe in detail how the values, vision, and mission will become a reality. A strategic goal can be thought of as a plan of action, based on the behaviors described in the values, to move the organization toward its vision, with its mission as the guide or beacon. Each strategic goal needs an identification of the following:

- Who is primarily responsible for implementing the goal and who will assist in the implementation?

- What is the time frame for implementation of the strategic goal?

- How will progress toward achieving the strategic goal be measured; in other words, what are the metrics?

A food service operation's strategic goals must be tied to the allocation of resources such as time, money, people, inventory, equipment, and facilities. Overall, strategic goals define the focus and priorities of the operation.

The measurement of strategic goals is essential if progress is to be objectively assessed. A balanced scorecard as presented in Exhibit 6 is a tool for measuring progress toward strategic goals.

The balanced scorecard has five categories. Within each category, the desired results are indicated for the current planning period—usually the current fiscal or calendar year. The to-date performance indicates the year-to-date progress toward meeting the result. The fourth column indicates last year's performance in the result area. The column to the right of it specifies the metric to be used to measure the outcome or result. And the sixth column shows how often the metric will be used to assess the progress.

In the **customer satisfaction** category, both the operator's overall satisfaction with the distributor, as well as the distributor's overall satisfaction with the operation, are assessed. The assessment may be in the form of a written survey containing some or all of the quality indicators presented in Exhibit 7. The quality indicators selected for the desired results must be based on the requirements of the distributor and the operator. Assessment could take other forms such as focus groups, or evaluation by independent third parties (e.g., consultants or mystery shoppers). Customer satisfaction may include metrics that assess the needs, expectations, requirements, and suggested areas/actions for improvement during feedback.

Financial results usually are tied to sales/revenues, costs, and/or profitability. Another area for financial assessment is staff productivity. A distributor's delivery-driver productivity is increased when the drop size to a particular operator increases. An operation's staff productivity increases when products with built-in labor are purchased.

Human resources metrics measure the distributor's satisfaction with the operator's human resources (e.g., purchasing staff, receiving and storing staff, accounting/payables staff, management, ownership) and the operator's satisfaction with the distributor's staff (owners, managers, DSRs, delivery personnel, billing staff). Human resources could also evaluate expectations of these various staff members, recruitment assistance with staff (e.g., the distributor may be able to recommend a qualified applicant for a vacant culinary position at the operation), assistance with training (e.g., when the DSR arranges for a manufacturers' representative to train dishwashers on how to properly use the dish machine and associated chemicals), and turnover rates in DSRs. Recall that DSR turnover can negatively affect the distributor-operator relationship.

Organizational effectiveness is assessed in relation to the purchasing control point from both the operator's and distributor's points of view. Recall that each control point has a process or series of steps that are completed. The identification of the process and activities/functions at each step of the process is the place to start. Once identified, specific areas for improvement can be targeted and the improvements implemented and then evaluated. Other areas of organizational effectiveness include the staffing requirements for both the operator and distributor. Technology is another area to evaluate for organizational effectiveness assessments.

Exhibit 6   Balanced Scorecard Elements

Desired Results	Planned Performance for the Year	To-Date Performance for this Year	Last Year's Performance	Metric(s)	How Often Metric(s) Used
1. Customer Satisfaction • Operator's overall satisfaction with the distributor • Distributor's overall satisfaction with operator					
2. Financial • Increase in profitability • Reduction in costs					
3. Human Resources • Operator's satisfaction with distributor's staff members • Distributor's satisfaction with operator's staff members					
4. Organizational Effectiveness • Operator's effectiveness at the purchasing control point • Distributor's contributions to the effectiveness of the purchasing control point					
5. Marketing/Growth • Increased sales for the operator as a result of the distributor relationship • Increased sales for the distributor as a result of the operator relationship					

Exhibit 7   Measuring Distributor Performance

1. **Customer Services**

   ___ Number of complaints or adjustments in dollars and units relative to product volume distributed

   ___ Number of emergency orders

   ___ Order backing and average time to ship ("turnaround time")

   ___ Distributor staff error rates

   ___ Number of back orders

   ___ Percentage of invoices filled, by line item and dollar

   ___ Percentage of units shipped relative to goals and previous year's volume

   ___ Number of units delivered per order compared to goals of the previous year

   ___ Percentage of products returned versus previous year

2. **Inventory Control**

   ___ Total inventory dollars and line items

   ___ Inventory turnover (total and by product class)

   ___ Stockouts as a percentage of daily issue costs

   ___ Number of items in inventory compared to previous year

   ___ Physical inventory frequency and magnitude of adjustments

   ___ Type of system used (manual or computerized) and its accuracy

3. **Distributor Staff Productivity**

   (Each function is to be measured, including receiving, warehousing, loading, transportation, clerical, and maintenance).

   ___ Cases per labor hour

   ___ Weight or volume per labor hour

   ___ Cases per truck

   ___ Cases per delivery

   ___ Dollars per order (drop size) and delivery

   ___ Time required for delivery

   ___ Trucks loaded per labor hour

4. **Cost Effectiveness**

   ___ Inbound freight cost by unit

   ___ Outbound freight cost by unit

   ___ Vehicle cost per mile

   ___ Costs per case for all warehousing functions

   ___ Sales per labor hour and/or staff member

   ___ Cost percentage to sales compared to previous year

   ___ Sales per vehicle mile

5. **Facility Utilization**

   ___ Storage locations used, expressed as a percent of locations available

   ___ Inventory value per square or cubic foot compared to previous year's value

   ___ Cost per square foot to maintain inventory compared to previous year

Scheduling is also included in organizational effectiveness. For example, when are deliveries scheduled to arrive at the operator's back door? When do deliveries actually arrive? Control procedures are a part of organizational effectiveness. These include receiving controls during delivery and inventory controls of products in storage. Organizational effectiveness also includes the identification of areas for improvement in each activity related to purchasing.

Marketing/growth may be tied to increased sales for both the distributor and operator. When a distributor helps an operator carefully and accurately identify customer needs and expectations and translate them into requirements, both should end up selling more products. In addition to who the customer is and what the customer requires, a third consideration under marketing/growth is pricing of products and services. They must be priced competitively so the operator can make a profit, as well as fairly so the distributor can make a profit. Another area under marketing/growth is promotions and advertising. Merchandising materials furnished to the operator from the distributor or manufacturer help market products and boost sales. Menu design to boost food sales is another example of this type of service. New product introduction is included in the marketing/growth category of balanced scorecard results.

Ethics

Ethics can be defined as a set of principles concerning rightful conduct. In the context of purchasing, two questions need to be asked and answered with regard to ethical decision making:

- Is this the best decision for the organization for which I work?

- Is this the right decision for everyone involved?

Fairness

When it comes to business ethics, **fairness** is evident when the people involved see that a decision benefits both parties. If a distributor tries to "buy" the business of the operator and under-the-table cash rebates are part of the incentive to do business with that distributor, that is unethical. If, on the other hand, a small gift is given to the operator (a pen, for example) in appreciation for doing business, that is ethical. Fairness must be understood by both parties to benefit both parties.

When the operator and distributor both embrace and value fairness, loyalty is built between the two organizations. Fairness obviously relates to product and service pricing and payment terms; however, it is also related to ways that the distributor provides information so the operator can make the right decisions.

An ethical relationship with distributors is critical for several reasons. First, fairness is in the long-range best interest of the food service operation in dealing with all of its customers, including distributors. Second, since staff members performing purchasing functions represent their employer, they must be consistent in their interactions with distributors. Third, the operation can suffer if the purchaser places personal interests before those of the operation.

Ethical standards established at the time of purchasing can permeate the operation and benefit every department. These policies can help ensure that maximum value is received for purchasing dollars expended, improving the operation's competitive edge and value delivered to its customers.

The purchaser's relationship with distributors and other customers should always reinforce and strengthen the operation's image and reputation. Commitment to fairness, consistency, and quality should be the common goals. Toward these ends, the purchaser should:

- Adhere to all of the operation's policies and procedures in order to maximize goals and objectives.

- Seek optimal value for purchasing dollars spent.

- Comply with applicable laws.

- Ensure that the operation enjoys a reputation for fair and honest dealings with distributors.

Operators also have obligations to distributors. Nurturing an ethical relationship between purchaser and distributor strengthens the reputation of the operation, clarifies policies and procedures, and encourages consistent performance from other staff members.

Operators must recognize that distributors should be treated with courtesy, professionalism, and emotional intelligence skills. Under no circumstances should operators divulge the distributor's price or trade secrets. Distributors should be able to trust that the operator has a history of honoring commitments and avoiding legal loopholes.

Objectivity

Objectivity is important in relationships because it helps to ensure fairness. When one makes objective decisions, they are based on facts, not feelings. Objective decision-makers are trusted by others because they are in a relationship for the long run. Rather than making subjective decisions to complete the transaction as a one-time sale, objective partners show in their actions their commitment to building a long-term relationship.

Objectivity is a part of ethical behavior. Objectivity results when policies and procedures are consistently applied today and in the future. This consistency leads people to know what is expected and what behavior is acceptable.

Objectivity leads to confidence in the distributor-operator relationship because all parties know that their long-term interests are being served. Each relies on the other to be objective as the relationship progresses.

Objectivity starts with a mutual commitment to a strategic alliance that optimizes expertise and ethics throughout. This is sometimes a challenge given the changes that have occurred in the industry, specifically, reduced purchasing staff sizes, increased emphasis on strategic goals (particularly relative to costs and value), the emergence of supply chain management as an integrated competitive business strategy, a paradigm shift from basic tactical or operational purchasing to the more strategic elements of distributor-operator relationships, and the growth of the Internet to facilitate e-purchasing.

One of the advantages of Internet-based e-purchasing is that it can make the purchasing process more objective by providing more information to the operator, but ethics requires that this information be safeguarded. One area of concern is reverse auctions in which distributors bid against competitors on-line and in real time. For example, an operator could decide in advance that a certain distributor will get the order, but schedule a reverse auction in order to coerce that distributor into offering prices lower than it normally would. An operator could also phone a distributor after a reverse auction is completed and say that the order will be placed with that distributor if the price can be lowered even more, or the operator could enter his or her own bid in the reverse auction to encourage distributors who are participating to lower their prices to obtain the business.

This ethical concern with reverse auctions includes objectivity, but also extends to confidentiality. Some reverse auctions show the names of the distributors who are bidding as well as their prices. A hallmark of ethical, objective purchasing is that the operator must not share prices of one distributor with other distributors since distributors generally have an idea of what their competitors' costs are for products, labor, and overhead. The remainder can be calculated as profit.

On the other hand, since distributors know the rules in advance of an on-line reverse auction, and presumably assess the risks before participating, reverse auctions can make distributors more "honest," and can help the process become more objective. When operations use reverse auctions, they must decide in advance what objective criteria will be used, inform the distributors of all those criteria, and use them as described.

Integrity

Integrity embraces elements of honesty and fairness. As large as the food service industry is around the globe, it is quite small when it comes to the reputation of an individual distributor or operator. It has been said that your reputation precedes you, meaning that the choices you have made in the past and are making today will add or detract from your reputation. Word of these choices will move through the network of distributors and other operators in the industry.

Integrity requires a balance between the requirements of the operator and the requirements of the distributor. This is sometimes called the "ethical tightrope," because one slip could mean a loss of integrity, personally and as an organization, and quite possibly forever. Integrity is also affected by the responsibility of both the distributor and operator to maintain and strengthen the distributor-operator relationship. Sometimes this can be pressured or stressed as financial pressures arise in either partner. Once integrity is compromised, it may never be rebuilt in the eyes of those who suffered due to the loss of integrity.

Benefits

The costs of maintaining ethical standards in purchasing may seem high at first glance, but not acting ethically is even more costly. Sometimes inappropriate actions can result in legal consequences leading to lawsuits that can have a devastating impact on the reputations of the individuals involved, as well as their organizations. This can also result in lost customers, lost revenues, and fines or penalties.

It takes far more effort to win back a lost customer than it does to behave ethically to keep that customer. Ethical behavior has the advantage of the retention of partners in the strategic alliances.

Examples

A few examples of ethical slips in behavior may point out the possible devastating consequences. DSRs have perhaps the most exposure to ethical pressures of the food service distribution channel members. Usually these DSRs work in relatively unsupervised roles moment-to-moment. They are required to meet sales goals that may increase each period. They are the primary sources of the distributor's revenue increases, since it is through their efforts that the sales transaction is completed. Sometimes, short-term sales goals are more important to their distributor organizations than long-term strategic partnerships. Even though DSRs play a major role in the development of long-term distributor-operator relationships, sometimes the pressures in the short-run lead them to take a plunge off the ethical tightrope.

What if a DSR offers to buy lunch for an operator's purchasing staff? Is this ethical? Perhaps so, if the policy is that if the distributor pays for one lunch, the operator pays for the next. Or what if the person responsible for purchasing is invited as the guest of the distributor to enjoy a NASCAR race in the distributor's private suite at the race track? It is important for the purchasing professional to at least let someone else in the organization—the operator, owner, general manager—know that the invitation has been extended.

Close relationships with prime distributors may cause ethical dilemmas. Acceptance of gifts from these prime distributors may cast the individual or the operator in an unfavorable light with other distributors, the operator's customers, or, if publicly owned, the operation's shareholders. Perhaps the purchasing professional who was responsible for all product purchases at a Big Ten university said it best when he commented about accepting gifts offered by distributors. He said: "I never accept any gift unless I feel comfortable going to the university president's office and telling the president what I have accepted." Would he accept a pen from a distributor? Likely, yes. Would he accept a lunch invitation from the distributor? Perhaps if he could reciprocate and pay for the next lunch. Would he accept an invitation to watch a NASCAR race in the distributor's private suite? Likely not.

While the trend has been to create closer, mutually beneficial relationships between distributors and operators, one must be cautious to not lose objectivity and integrity when making decisions. Sometimes personal relationships that develop beyond business relationships can pose a problem. When a DSR repeatedly offers center-court basketball tickets to the purchasing manager of one of the distributor's major accounts and the manager accepts, it becomes increasingly difficult for that purchasing manager to objectively say "no" to the distributor when objectivity is required.

Code of Ethics

A **code of ethics** expresses in writing acceptable conduct. To be effective, the code of ethics must be adopted and acted upon by all distributors as well as the operator, including all the staff members who could be affected by the code. A sample code of ethics is presented in Exhibit 8.

The code of ethics in Exhibit 8 applies to all distributors, internal customers, and the operator. The purpose of a code is to strengthen the relationship based on the partners in the relationship embracing a common set of acceptable behaviors. This helps the operation add value and continuously improve, and do so in ethical ways.

One element of the code is to protect proprietary information that is shared in the relationship. Value is added by sharing this confidential information, which cannot be disclosed to other distributors. Frequently, the parties in the distributor-operator relationship are asked to sign a non-disclosure agreement to protect the essential proprietary information from being shared with others who are not part of the strategic partnership.

A code of ethics builds on the food service operation's written values, vision, and mission, which are tied to the operation's standards and policies.

Policies and Standards

Policies and standards must be expressed in writing and shared with all individuals who are responsible for living up to them. Distributors must be sent the policies and standards and be informed that they will be uniformly applied. Training in adherence to policies and standards must be part of each staff member's on-going development, beginning with orientation. Some food service operators have a 1-800-number hotline available to internal customers to anonymously report behavior that they believe to be unethical or otherwise inappropriate.

Policies and standards promote awareness, understanding, and implementation of acceptable behaviors. Policies and standards should minimize the risk of acting unethically and possibly illegally. Operations have a responsibility to detail explicitly these standards and orient, train, and retrain people to follow them. Policies and standards are designed to promote ethical behaviors that improve the quality of the distributor-operator relationship, enhance satisfaction of both, and yield results based on fairness, objectivity, and integrity.

Essentials of the Negotiation Process ——————

Entire courses are delivered on the topic of effective negotiations. **Negotiation** is a necessary component of the distributor-operator relationship. In this section, we present an overview of the negotiation process.

Negotiation is a dynamic, not static, process. The steps in the process must be followed, but it is first essential to prepare for negotiations. The seven lessons of negotiations can help operators and distributors become more effective at the process. It is critical that those participating in the negotiations process be empowered to make a commitment; information is power when used with fair and objective criteria.

Exhibit 8   Sample Code of Ethics/Conduct

Our food service operation does business by upholding the strictest ethical standards in our business dealings with distributors, internal customers, and external customers. It is our firm expectation that all distributors, internal customers, and external customers accept, promote, and explore these same standards of conduct.

All internal customers are bound by a code of ethics/conduct that prohibits them from:

1.   Accepting gifts, bribes, personal incentives, and rewards.
2.   Engaging in undisclosed business transactions where a possible or actual conflict of interest exists.
3.   Falsely representing the operation or themselves in business relationships.
4.   Not giving the same opportunities to all qualified distributors.
5.   Making commitments without the required written documentation and prior approvals.
6.   Failing to report questionable behavior of others.
7.   Sharing proprietary, confidential information about the operation, its internal customers, and its distributors.
8.   Discriminating on any basis other than overall value to the operation.

All internal customers will adhere to the following acceptable ethical behaviors:

1.   First and foremost, give consideration to the policies, standards, and objectives of the food service operation.
2.   Obtain maximum value for each purchasing expenditure.
3.   Conduct dealings with potential and current distributors in good faith without intentional misrepresentation.
4.   Be honest in all dealings with distributors, both verbal and written.
5.   Attempt by making every possible effort to resolve conflicts through equitable and mutually agreeable settlements with distributors.
6.   Adhere to ethical and legal purchasing practices.

All internal customers, potential or current distributors are expected to uphold these standards of ethics/conduct. Failure to do so will result in exclusion or elimination from the food service operation's staff or approved distributor pool.

Source: Adapted from "Suppliers of the Neil Jones Food Companies," undated, and "IUPUI Code of Ethics," undated.

Dynamics of the Process

The overall purchasing strategy must be tied to strategic goals. Strategic goals are dynamic and change to meet the changing requirements of food service customers and owners. Purchasing strategies must be linked to the operation's strategic goals, just as the goals are linked to values, vision, and mission. In purchasing, for example, a strategic goal of minimizing costs can easily be linked to the operation's broader strategic goal of maximizing value for its customers.

Part of the dynamic nature of the purchasing negotiation process is to reach a compromise, rather than coerce or "beat up" distributors to get only what the operation requires. The best way to strengthen the distributor-operator relationship is to view it as a long-term partnership that requires periodic negotiation. Another element of a dynamic negotiation process is to determine sources of products or services. In some cases it may make sense to purchase from a single source who provides the best prices for products based on volume purchased. In other cases, it makes more sense to choose a local, smaller, secondary distributor. This may change because market conditions are dynamic. Ethics may enter into a decision to obtain products from one distributor over another.

Another element of dynamic negotiations is the closeness of the relationship with the distributor. This, again, changes over time and is somewhat dependent on the strategic importance of the products purchased. Signature items, such as baby back ribs for a food service operation specializing in ribs, are strategically important and the choice of distributors may be based on which one(s) can provide the best value based on the negotiated price tied to the standard purchase specifications. It all comes down to where the most added value can take place in a relationship with a distributor.

An additional part of the dynamic negotiation process is the methods and timing with which purchased products are delivered to the food service operation. Some distributors will store inventory and deliver it just in time as the operator needs it. Others will require delivery of all purchased products at one time.

Dynamic negotiations also include a consideration of who has the power in the negotiation process. Power can shift from distributor to operator when supply is readily available, and back to the distributor when needed products are scarce. Volume purchasing gives the operator leverage, meaning that the higher the volume purchased from a specific distributor, the more leverage the operator has to influence the terms and conditions being negotiated.

One dynamic element in purchasing today is the shift from a focus on individual product prices to a focus on total cost of purchases. The dynamic nature of the operator-distributor relationship is more apparent with a shift to a total-cost focus. In any case, a dynamic negotiation process requires good communication and decision-making skills. Communication affects the ability of both the operator and distributor to influence and persuade, resolve conflicts, and solve problems during the negotiation process.

The dynamic purchasing negotiation process requires being aware of and taking steps to avoid potential pitfalls, including:

- Unrealistic expectations of long-term pricing and supply guarantees. Some products (e.g., fresh produce, meats) are dynamically influenced by falling and rising prices in commodity markets. It is essential to negotiate a fair price that is based on auditable cost-plus arrangements.

- Unrealistic projections of volume to be purchased. Leverage in the dynamic purchasing process comes from being able to accurately project actual volumes of products to be purchased. Both operators and distributors must be realistically accurate in terms of product volumes.

- Unrealistic demands regarding delivery frequency or drop sizes. Here again, honesty is the best policy. If an operation wants daily deliveries with relatively small drop sizes at multiple locations, it will have less negotiating clout with the distributor.

- Unrealistic timelines for distributors to complete and submit requests for proposals (RFPs) and bids on products to be purchased. RFPs must be both general and specific since they make a formal request to an acceptable group of distributors to provide proposals or bids to deliver the specified products and/or services. Even though time deadlines are sometimes short, operators should give adequate time for distributors to prepare meaningful and accurate proposals and bids.

Steps in the Process

Negotiation is the use of persuasion and information to influence behavior. As the purchaser and distributor enter into a transaction, whether placing an order or securing a price quotation, they negotiate an understanding. The negotiation process enables the purchaser and distributor, through give and take, to reach a mutually beneficial agreement. Successful negotiators develop clear goals, understand the facts, and use timing to their advantage.

Preparing for negotiations must include an identification of why the operator is making the purchase and what value the operator seeks from the purchase. Those operators who negotiate the purchase of products or services strictly on price are not expecting many, if any, value-added services to accompany the negotiations or the products or services purchased. Negotiation based on price is simply a matter of identifying the lowest prices provided based on the specifications of the product/service. Little distributor-operator interaction results when products and services are purchased based only on price. On the other hand, when additional services are desired, the negotiation process changes to one based on value-added services. Operators who seek these value-added services must be willing to pay higher prices, because the services come at a cost to the distributor, manufacturer, or both.

In either case, the negotiation process begins with an identification of the products and services needed and expected. These are translated into an identification of the products and services required. Recall that these requirements are based on the needs and expectations of the operation's customers.

Once requirements are articulated, the potential alternatives can be identified and evaluated. This evaluation is based on the specifications developed in response to the requirements. Then the decision is made, and the negotiations begin for that specific product or service. As a result of the negotiations, a distributor or multiple distributors who can furnish the alternatives are selected. The terms of the purchase are finalized, often in writing, and the products/services are purchased. Exhibit 9 shows the role of negotiation in the purchasing process flow. Notice that the process is continuous, ending with evaluation, which feeds back into the start of the process.

Preparation before Negotiation

An effective negotiation plan requires preparation and evaluation. By collecting preliminary data at this time, a skilled negotiator assesses the needs, strengths, and weaknesses of both parties. This information should provide answers to crucial questions, enabling the purchaser to make intelligent buying decisions. These questions basically fall into three categories:

1. User-related

   a. What does the purchaser need, expect, and require?
   b. How much time can be invested in fact-finding, planning, and negotiation activities?
   c. How quickly is the product/service needed (what are the deadlines)?

2. Distributor-related

   a. What does the seller need and how urgent is this need?
   b. How quickly can the product/service be delivered?
   c. What has been the seller's product delivery and service performance history?
   d. Have changes within the distributor's company affected performance?

3. Negotiation-related

   a. What are the limits to the concessions that can be made?
   b. Who has the authority to make concessions? What are the limitations of authority?
   c. What has been the distributor's negotiating method in the past (collaborative or competitive)?

These and similar questions are considered in order to focus the negotiation and determine the approach most likely to produce satisfactory results. Solid preparation of the type just outlined leads the way to a formalized negotiation plan.

The Negotiation Plan. The **negotiation plan** identifies the resources of the food service operation (e.g., personnel and inventory), the buyer's negotiation method, and the resources at the distributor's disposal (e.g., personnel, inventory, and equipment). The purchaser will hold the advantage during negotiations if he or she can organize this information into a plan of action, but the purchaser must have the appropriate authority to implement this plan.

In negotiations, authority is a source of power. The amount of power that one is perceived to have greatly influences the negotiation process. The purchaser's power is derived from several sources, including the following:

- Position or status within the operation

- Distributor's perception of purchaser's authority

- Knowledge of the food service industry and the food service operation

- Awareness of the competition

- Commitment to meeting obligations

Exhibit 9   Negotiation in the Purchasing Process Flow

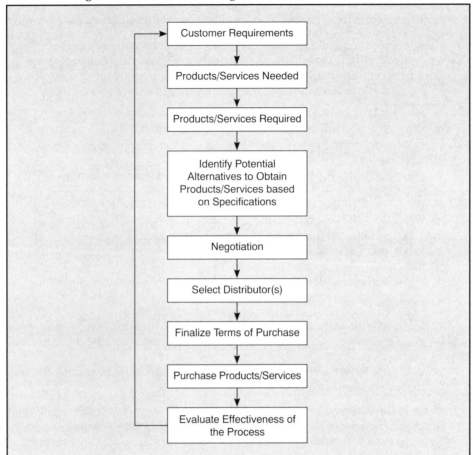

- Willingness to establish long-term relationships
- Reputation for fairness and promptness in paying bills
- Economic factors (for instance, purchase volume)

The purchaser's authority depends on management's commitment to the purchaser and how well the purchaser adheres to the operation's goals and objectives. The purchaser is more effective during negotiations if this power is used strategically.

With this power and a collection of pertinent facts and figures, the purchaser, as negotiator, develops the "game plan." The planning process determines who will do the negotiation. In some cases, a team approach is preferred; one person conducts the actual negotiations while a backup team provides information (facts, options).

The purchaser usually begins the negotiation process and, in doing so, establishes the style or method. There are two methods: collaborative and competitive.

Collaborative negotiations are based upon two assumptions: that compromise is preferable to conflict and that a give-and-take exchange is better than no settlement at all. This method addresses the needs of both parties and facilitates a commitment to that end.

Competitive negotiations can be inflexible, rigid sessions, beginning with tough and usually unreasonable demands. Conflict continues unresolved throughout the entire process, creating an imbalance between negotiators as they grudgingly grant concessions and ignore deadlines.

The risk in using the competitive method is an abrupt break in communications, causing one or both parties to terminate negotiations altogether. However, competitive negotiations can be productive in some situations. For example, this negotiation style works well when there are several sources of supply or when the supply of a product is relatively abundant.

Negotiations can also be classified as "win-win" or "win-lose" according to their outcome. A win-win outcome results in the mutual satisfaction of both parties, who come out of the process feeling they have gained something. It in no way implies that the buyer is easy, pliable, or weak.

In a win-lose outcome, one party gains a sense of satisfaction while the other party feels frustrated. When negotiations break down into this situation, the purchaser may initially win the advantage, but may eventually receive unsatisfactory performance from the distributor. Impatience and insecurity contribute to the win-lose situation.

Techniques for Negotiating. The negotiation plan prepares the foundation for the next phase of the process—the strategy. Through the use of location, timing, negotiation method, communication (telephone or face-to-face or electronic), and authority, the purchaser gains the advantage.

The purchaser should choose the location for negotiations. The site chosen, in this case, may be the food service operation. However, it may be to the purchaser's advantage to visit the distributor's facilities in order to obtain additional information, meet other members of that organization, and evaluate quality, storage, shipping, and food safety processes.

The purchaser should realize the importance of timing. For instance, the purchaser's initial advantage of placing the order diminishes as the deadline approaches. The original goals and objectives of management need to be firmly fixed in the negotiator's mind, along with an awareness of the distributor's own set of needs (differences in deadlines, prices, and volume). These pre-established goals should be attained before the final session. Conflict should only occur on minor points during the final stages.

The purchaser's negotiation method or style should be flexible. Beginning with a collaborative approach, the purchaser may then switch to a more competitive strategy (such as providing fewer options as the distributor invests more time). At this point, the purchaser could list potential benefits to the distributor as a result of conducting business with the food service operation. Termination of the negotiation process is less likely to occur as the distributor invests more time and expectation levels are raised.

Communication is a central factor in formulating strategy. The purchaser should evaluate the suitability of negotiations conducted over the telephone, on-line, or in person. Pros and cons can be found in either approach depending on the situation.

For example, the telephone and on-line forfeit visual feedback and preparation. Whenever transactions occur in these ways, the purchaser should submit to the distributor a written summary (memorandum) of all the issues discussed and the resulting agreements made. The distributor is less likely to retract or take issue with the transaction later.

Face-to-face communication also carries disadvantages. There is no way to return a call when it is more convenient and when more time is needed to assemble necessary information. The distributor expects immediate feedback. While face-to-face communication generally reduces the risk of misinterpretation, it can create problems since the communication is spoken rather than written.

Listening skills are the cornerstone of effective communication. Knowing how to listen (letting the distributor provide the bulk of information) and when to speak judiciously can significantly influence a negotiation's outcome. Listening also improves the level of feedback to the distributor's proposals.

Productive communication and interaction can be marred, however, by personality conflicts and ego differences. By identifying problems in the early stages of negotiation, more compatible personality types can be substituted, decreasing the threat of a "win-lose" outcome.

Dealing with persons with proper authority can work to the purchaser's advantage during negotiations. The decision-maker within the distributor's organization, not the intermediate representative, holds the power. Lost time and misunderstandings can be avoided if the purchaser deals directly with the appropriate person.

Sometimes, the purchaser may suggest to the distributor that a third party be brought into the process, because the purchaser lacks the appropriate authority to negotiate. To avoid the inclusion of a third party, the distributor may concede additional demands. (Note that in this case, the purchaser is switching from a collaborative to competitive method.) The purchaser should observe the distributor's reaction to this strategy and be prepared to seek alternative solutions.

Topics of Negotiation. A buyer desires to give up as little as possible during the negotiation and hopes to gain as much value as possible from the distributor. In the process, concessions are inevitably made by both parties. Some suggestions for managing concessions during negotiations are as follows:

- Attempt to have the other side make the first concession. Do not accept the first offer made on a significant point.

- Set negotiating goals very high. Do not give up something without receiving something in return.

- Avoid responding to a high demand with a counteroffer. (First, request that the demand be reduced.)

- Be aware of the economic and strategic consequences of concessions, which may also significantly affect your abilities and aspirations.

- Ensure that each concession received brings you closer to your negotiating goal.

- Recognize that all concessions should be tentative until you decide to make them final.

Base price is, of course, a major topic for negotiation. The best negotiating approach is typically to agree upon a base price and then negotiate adjustments to the base price for concessions made by the buyer.

However, other topics contribute to the pricing as well. For instance, the purchaser may save by taking advantage of rebate agreements and discounts for volume purchases. However, legal counsel should be consulted on these procedures. Payment terms can also be devised to reduce purchase costs if the purchaser pays cash or agrees to a short billing period.

Specific clauses can be used to limit rising prices. Some restrictive clauses limit price increases to a maximum percentage or specify dates by which increases must be scheduled. Escalator or de-escalator clauses adjust costs by using price indicators, including private/government indexes and the expenses of raw material and labor.

Closing Negotiations. When negotiations are closed (that is, when goals have been met and conflicts resolved) all relevant information discussed thus far should be contractually agreed upon—sometimes orally, but preferably in writing. Written contracts specify the precise commitments and responsibilities of both purchaser and distributor. Some purchasers write the contract on their own letterhead.

In all negotiations, the purchaser should strive to make the transaction profitable. The purchaser should learn to predict, not expect, and combine those predictions with experience to gain a sense of the probable. Finally, the purchaser has to know when to conclude negotiations and move on to other concerns. Understanding human nature helps accomplish this closure of the negotiation process.

Empowerment to Make a Commitment

When representatives of the distributor and operator are empowered to make a commitment, these individuals believe they are making a significant contribution to the negotiations process, as well as adding value during purchasing. **Empowerment** requires training and information. Individuals participating in negotiations must be trained to do so effectively, based on the direction of the organization, having the tools to fulfill responsibilities, and being authorized to make a commitment for the organization. This is true whether the organization is a food service operation or a distributor.

Empowerment comes from having the right information. This starts with the values, vision, mission, and strategic goals of the organization. They must be made known and people must understand how they can contribute to them during the negotiation process. Decisions must be made without fear of failure. When failure occurs or mistakes are made, the people in the organization move on, learn from the mistakes, and try diligently to not make the same mistakes again.

Creativity is a component of empowerment. Finding creative solutions during negotiations is the hallmark of successful compromise. If people understand the desired results, they will make the right decisions if they are empowered to do so.

Empowerment is strengthened when people have the right information, have the authority to make a commitment, and work together to achieve desired results. Necessary information during purchasing negotiations includes total product costs, relevant financial information about the operation and the distributor, volume to be purchased, desired services to accompany the products, frequency and size of deliveries, payment terms, and what the products will be used for in the operation.

The authority to make a commitment begins with a full understanding of the clearly defined areas of responsibility. These define in which boundaries the decisions can be made, and which decisions are outside the boundaries and, therefore, are off-limits. This is why teams of people frequently participate in negotiations. Individual team members have complimentary skill sets and areas of responsibility to make decisions which empower the team even more. All team members must understand the organization's goals as they relate to the negotiation process. These goals give the team the framework within which it is empowered to operate.

In negotiations, working together to achieve desired results begins with an understanding of each person's role in the process. Food service operations staff have a role that is different from, but complimentary to, financial staff. The team members must also understand the operational systems in both the distributor's organization and the operator's organization. The systems and their component processes govern what is negotiated.

Negotiation Essentials

Information is a source of power, so power in negotiation is with those who are listening and learning, not with those doing all of the talking. Asking questions to obtain relevant information leads to power for negotiation. Open-ended questions are preferred to those with a simple "yes" or "no" answer.

Sometimes power is based on adding information from another source. For example, before a commitment is made during negotiation, is it necessary to obtain legal clearance? If this necessary information is not obtained in advance of making the agreement, what happens if the legal experts say "no?" The most successful negotiators identify, in advance, what the other parties in the negotiations require. Then they use those requirements to accurately identify the products or services that meet those requirements.

Maximizing **leverage** must be done in an ethical way. Consider an independent food service operator who inquires about the price of a specified product from DSR #1 and obtains that price. If DSR #2 from a different distributor asks what DSR #1's price quote is, it is unethical to give that information to DSR #2. There is a fine line in negotiation and, if the line is crossed, the integrity of the operator can be compromised forever.

Leverage also relates to how critically the products/services are needed by the operator and how essential it is for the DSR to sell those products and services. If an agreement is not reached during negotiations, what is the Plan B for the operator and for the distributor? Is the product/service easily obtained from another distributor (for the operator) or can the product/service easily be sold to another operator (for the distributor)? Generally, the more a person needs something, the weaker is that person's leverage power in negotiations. So too, the less a person needs something, the stronger the person's leverage power in negotiations. Understanding leverage is a critical element of negotiations.

The criteria used in negotiations must be fair to all parties involved. When standards, specifications, and goals are objective, the process usually leads to compromise and a signed agreement. Fair, objective criteria go beyond the price of products/services. These criteria also include specifications, profitability, marketing conditions, and defined efficiency/benefits gained from purchasing the products/services.

The offer-concession strategy in the negotiation process begins with an understanding of each party's requirements. Recall that negotiations are not designed to be win-lose. Rather, each person in the process must feel as if it was a good deal—a win-win situation. This is the case when negotiated prices start high and then can be reduced because of discounts for increased volume purchased.

Negotiation is a challenging process and it is not possible to control all of its elements. Sometimes controlling the agenda is used as a strategy, but it is important to not rush too quickly to quoting prices without first having a detailed understanding of the requirements of all parties in the negotiations. Sometimes, it takes a second or third meeting to understand requirements completely before attempting to come to a final agreement.

Conflict resolution is an essential part of the negotiations process. Starting from the basis that the goal is a long-term, mutually beneficial relationship between the operator and the distributor, the time taken to resolve conflicts will pay dividends for the strength of the relationship in the future.

Conflict resolution includes finding commonalities on which all parties can agree. When one party states a concern, the other party should repeat it back so it is apparent that it is clearly understood by both. Patience is important since this deliberate approach helps keep the process moving. Sometimes discussions must be mediated so an agreement can be reached.

The overall goal of negotiations is to arrive at a win-win agreement. This begins with planning desired outcomes before entering the room, yet being flexible enough to compromise when necessary. The essentials also include an identification of each person's requirements. Some of this work, again, can be done in advance, but a clarification of the accuracy of your pre-negotiation assessments is important early in the meeting. The strategy here is to find ways that a mutually beneficial common ground can be found. Input from all parties seated at the table is essential.

One technique is to begin with the identification of an issue that everyone can embrace and agree on. If all parties cannot agree, a compromise must be worked out. Usually in negotiation the compromises are give-and-take, that is, if one gives in on one issue, it is often expected that the other will give in on the next issue under discussion. With minor issues, this may not be a problem. Major issues, linked to essential requirements, usually require more discussion until agreement is reached.

Once the issues are addressed and resolved, the next essential step is to make an offer. In the case of price, frequently the distributor will offer a higher price and the operator will ask for a lower price. Here is where an understanding of BATNA comes into play. When there are more options and choices, it is easier to negotiate a favorable agreement. But you must know the limits beyond which you will not agree.

Once the offer is made, it may be necessary to introduce a concession or compromise—in other words, to give in on a particular point being negotiated. It is usually expected that if one party offers a concession and it is accepted, the other party will offer the next concession. For example, if a distributor asks an operator to extend the deadline for delivery of a new range for the kitchen and it is accepted, then the operator may also ask the distributor for more relaxed payment terms for the equipment.

The final step is to reach agreement on the details and terms of the purchase. This is closing the negotiation process, and the details and terms are put into writing.

Lessons in Negotiation

In 2004, nine purchasing professionals were assembled from small and large organizations. Collectively, this group brought more than 150 years of experience to the discussions about how non-textbook knowledge makes a difference in purchasing. Their seven lessons included the following:

1. Turn off the computer and engage in conversation. Face-to-face conversation is a critical skill, although some purchasers and distributors rely on e-mail almost exclusively. With the increasing number of e-mail messages each day, a preferred way to communicate may be face-to-face or on the telephone. Messages sent via e-mail are one-way communication. Two-way communication methods, such as telephone or face-to-face conversations, enhance relationships because key issues can be addressed and problems can be solved.

2. Learn how to manage long-term relationships with distributors. Long-term relationships go beyond simply obtaining the best price. Sometimes the best price has hidden risks that become hidden costs (e.g., exposure to risks such as food safety). The lowest cost from a distributor who is difficult to deal with does not add as much value as negotiating and obtaining the best cost from a distributor with whom you want to have a long-term relationship. Effectively, this results in a change from a commodity purchase to a value-added purchase. Value-added purchases result in relationships where the operator and distributor work together.

3. Obtain information through networking. Purchasing staff are increasingly being challenged to access and sort through growing amounts of information, a task that is impossible alone. With people in a network, this daunting responsibility is easier to fulfill. While no one person can know everything, one person can know who to ask for needed information. Finding the right person to assist in each situation is key to identifying the details relevant to a specific decision. Distributors are a valuable source of information about such data as food product market trends or consumer trends.

4. Take the time to assess requirements. When assessing needs and expectations, carefully listen so they can be translated into requirements. One way a distributor adds value is in assisting the operator in formulating these requirements in a creative way, realizing that some requirements are constantly changing and evolving. Constantly challenge the process by asking "Why are we doing _____ this way?" and "Is there a better way to achieve our goals?" This applies to all areas of negotiations, cost savings, and value enhancement. When an operation develops a new market or when customer requirements change, as they often do, there will be alterations and adjustments. Help from the network is essential. Listening is, once again, a critical and essential skill.

5. Stay current. Purchasing professionals stay up on trends and understand the food service industry, as well as issues facing their distributors. By identifying trends early, particularly as they relate to global sources of supply, you can take advantage of opportunities earlier than competitors. Those responsible for purchasing must learn new ways to help their organizations continuously improve.

6. Teamwork helps bridge differences. With the variety of requirements, and sometimes conflicting needs and expectations, working together in a team helps address everyone's requirements. Effective teamwork leads to thinking both strategically and tactically. Teamwork maximizes the collective knowledge of the operation, if the team includes both internal customers and distributors. Teamwork also contributes to long-term relationships and mutual benefit. Teamwork during negotiations reduces conflict and leads to resolution of differences. Teamwork helps identify the interests of all parties, can indicate why some are resistant to change, and show how individuals can assist in the operation's strategic and tactical goals.

7. Be passionate. In any profession, passion is an essential ingredient if people are to enjoy what they are achieving. Some elements of the purchasing process are stressful, such as negotiations, enforcing delivery and other deadlines, ensuring that policies and procedures are being followed, resolving conflicts over contracts, and other day-to-day challenges. It is important to try each day to enjoy the people that you work with and the work that you do to add value for the operation.[1]

An article that appeared in *Distributor Selection & Management Report,* entitled "Distributor Negotiation Tactics: What They Don't Teach in School," outlined still more lessons in negotiation.

1. Be prepared before negotiating. Preparation often begins months or weeks before negotiations take place. These preparations include studying the distributor(s) with whom you will be negotiating, including their financial condition, ability to deliver what is being negotiated, capabilities to provide value-added services, assessments from the distributor's current customers regarding performance, turnover of staff especially DSRs, record of safety and delivery schedules, challenges with warrantees, and other issues that might impact the overall relationship. Be prepared with a **best alternative to a negotiation agreement** (BATNA). That is, what will you do as Plan B if the negotiations do not result in an agreement to all the terms you desire? What are the acceptable alternatives?

2. Analyze product costs. A detailed analysis of total product costs includes all the components of the cost of each product, including the profit for the distributor. The components of total product costs include the base product cost plus the costs associated with storing the inventory, duties and fees, insurance, packaging, payment terms, profit for the distributor, transportation, and any other costs related to the product. Product costs are, in part, determined by whether there is excessive demand (a seller's market) or an overabundance of the product (a buyer's market). A product at the start of its life cycle is likely to be more expensive than a product at the end of its life cycle. In addition, sometimes global economic forces have an impact on product cost.

3. Continue to ask questions of the distributors. The point of asking questions and carefully listening to the answers is to more fully understand the processes and procedures necessary to produce a product and make it available for sale. Being a "know it all" does not serve the operation well if this attitude is based on trying to impress another party in the negotiation process, rather than admitting that further explanation is necessary. The questioning approach, on the other hand, will yield useful understanding of the distributor's processes (e.g., how engineering specifications are met for equipment or how chemical analysis relates to processed food products), financial health, human resources issues, capacity to produce what the operation wants to purchase, market conditions, and other relevant information. Information is power, and it takes careful listening to gain this power after asking the right questions.

4. Take into account the distribution channel. The distribution channel includes all business entities from the source to the distributor. When the members of the channel are asked to find ways to work together to achieve economies of scale, synergy is achieved. When strengths of all the players are strategically combined, the channel provides added value to the operator.

5. Negotiate from your plan while still considering the people. When the negotiation plan is thought through in advance and followed, control of the content lies with the operator. The operator should prepare the contract or letter/memo of agreement to summarize the agreement. Detailed note-taking during negotiations sessions provides the basis for the agreement. While the plan and agreement are essential, realize that people make the decisions. Ideas from all involved with negotiations give each person "ownership" of the completed agreement.[2]

Endnotes

1. Jacob Stoller, "What the Experts Don't Teach," *Purchasing B2B* 46, no. 7 (September 2004), pp. 19–23.

2. "Supplier Negotiation Tactics: What They Don't Teach in School," *Supplier Selection & Management Report* 3, no. 3 (March 2003), p. 3.

 **Key Terms**

alliance—A purchasing organization that facilitates relationships between buyers and sellers.

balanced scorecard—A way for an operation to indicate capital other than financial capital.

best alternative to a negotiation agreement—An organization's Plan B if the negotiation process does not end in an agreement to all the terms it desires.

bracket pricing—Pricing based simply on the volume of products purchased.

code of ethics—A written expression of acceptable conduct.

collaborative negotiation—A negotiation method that addresses the needs of both parties and facilitates a commitment to that end.

competitive negotiation—Inflexible, rigid negotiation sessions that begin with tough and usually unreasonable demands.

consolidation—Mergers and acquisitions that result in fewer small, independent distributors and more large corporate distributors.

cost-plus pricing—Pricing based on the distributor's cost plus a reasonable markup.

customer satisfaction—The balanced scorecard category that indicates the operator's overall satisfaction with the distributor, as well as the distributor's overall satisfaction with the operation.

distributor relationship management—The concept of customer relationship management as applied to an operation's distributors.

emotional intelligence—An understanding of how individuals perceive, utilize, and manage their emotions and others' emotions.

empowerment—Occurs when representatives from an operation and a distributor have the ability to make a commitment. It requires training and information.

e-purchasing—Purchasing using electronic tools such as e-mail and on-line ordering.

ethics—A set of principles concerning rightful conduct.

fairness—An aspect of business ethics that is evident when the people involved see that a decision benefits both parties.

financial results—The balanced scorecard item that is usually tied to sales/revenues, costs, and/or profitability.

group purchasing organizations—A common organization that coordinates purchasing for a number of individual food service operations.

human resources—The balanced scorecard item that measures the distributor's satisfaction with the operator's human resources and the operator's satisfaction with the distributor's staff.

integrity—An aspect of ethics that embraces elements of honesty and fairness.

leverage—Power in negotiation that relates to how badly an operation needs products or services and how badly a distributor needs to sell them.

listening—The most important element in communication between a distributor and an operator.

long-term net financial outcome—Generating of sufficient earnings to be able to invest back into the operation as well as make a profit (for commercial operations) or containing costs to maximize the amount available to reinvest (for noncommercial operations).

marketing/growth—The balanced scorecard item that considers who the customer is, what the customer requires, and the pricing of products and services.

mission—The way an operation answers the question, "Why do we exist as an organization?"

negotiation plan—A document that identifies the resources of the food service operation (e.g., personnel and inventory), the buyer's negotiation method, and the resources at the distributor's disposal (e.g., personnel, inventory, and equipment).

negotiation—The use of persuasion and information to influence behavior. It should enable the purchaser and distributor, through give and take, to reach a mutually beneficial agreement.

organizational effectiveness—The balanced scorecard item that involves assessment of the steps at the purchasing control point.

performance—How well a distributor delivers on what it promised.

policies and standards—Ethics tools that promote awareness, understanding, and implementation of acceptable behaviors. They should be expressed in writing and shared with anyone who is expected to live up to them.

purchasing system evaluation—An ongoing process conducted according to basic management principles that answers questions about how well the purchasing system is working and how it can be improved.

values—A statement of acceptable ways to interact with others, including distributors.

vision—A picture of an operation's ideal future that answers the question, "What do I want to create in my organization?"

 # Review Questions ⎯⎯⎯⎯⎯⎯⎯⎯⎯⎯⎯⎯⎯⎯⎯⎯⎯⎯⎯⎯⎯⎯⎯⎯

1. What are the reasons that a buyer purchases from a distributor?

2. How does an alliance work? What are some examples of alliances?

3. What are some examples of commonalities between a distributor and a buyer?

4. What must be evaluated in a purchasing system?

5. What is the evaluation process for purchasing system performance?

6. What are the components of distributor relationship management?

7. How is emotional intelligence defined, and what are the IN, OUT, and RELATIONSHIPS factors?

8. What is a balanced scorecard, and what categories does it include?

9. What are the ethics considerations in the buyer-distributor relationship?

10. What are the essential elements in a code of ethics?

11. What are the elements of the negotiation process?

12. How is a negotiation plan developed, and what is included?

13. What is a BATNA, and how is it used?

 References ——————————————————————————

Anonymous. "An Alternate GPO Model." *Food Management* 40, no. 1 (January 2005): p. 32.

Anonymous. "Critical Knowledge & Skills Purchasing Pros Now Have to Have." *Supplier Selection & Management Report* 4, no. 10 (October 2004): pp. 4–6.

Anonymous. "Facilitating Buyer and Seller Partnerships." *Food Management* 40, no. 1 (January 2005): p. 34.

Anonymous. "Supplier Negotiation Tactics: What they Don't Teach in School." *Supplier Selection & Management Report* 3, no. 3 (March 2003): p. 3.

Arminas, David. "Purchasers Walking 'Ethical Tightrope'." *Supply Management* 7, no. 4 (February 2002): p. 7.

Atkinson, William. "New Buying Tools Present Different Ethical Challenges." *Purchasing* 132, no. 4 (March 2003): p. 27.

Britt, Phillip. "Good Ethics Equals Good Business." *Customer Relationship Management* 9, no. 4 (April 2005): p. 14.

Brownell, Judi, and Dennis Reynolds. "Strengthening the Purchaser-Supplier Partnership: Factors that Make a Difference." *Purchaser-Supplier Partnerships Executive Summary* (Ithaca, N.Y.: The Center for Hospitality Research at Cornell University), pp. 3–28.

Buzalka, Mike. "You Can Always Get What You Want." *Food Management* 35, no. 9: pp. 42–47.

Cichy, Ronald F., Jae Min Cha, and Bonnie Knutson. "The Five Essentials of Private Club Leadership." *FIU Hospitality Review* 22, no. 2 (Fall 2004): pp. 46–58.

Cichy, Ronald F. and James B. Singerling. "Private Club Leadership Essentials." *Club Management* 83, no. 4 (August 2004): 126–130.

Cichy, Ronald F., et. al. "The Emotional Intelligence of Private Club Leaders." *Club Management* 84, no. 4: pp. 38–41.

Clawser, Tom. "Distribution's Culture Clashes." *Industrial Distribution* 94, no. 5 (May 2005): p. 72.

Claycomb, Cindy and Gary L. Frankwick. "A Contingency Perspective of Communication, Conflict Resolution and Buyer Search Effort in Buyer-Supplier Relationships." *The Journal of Supply Chain Management: A Global Review of Purchasing and Supply* (February 2004): p. 30.

Cleary, Patrick and Darryl Legault. "The Negotiation Handbook." *Purchasing B2B* (May 2002).

Doshi, Belinda. "The Price is Right." *Supply Management* 9, no. 20 (October 2004): p. 34.

Fuller, Neil. "Smooth Talk." *Supply Management* 9, no. 5 (March 4, 2004): p. 33.

George, J. "Emotions and Leadership: The Role of Emotional Intelligence." *Human Relations* 53 (2000): pp. 1027–1055.

Gummesson, Evert. "Return on Relationships (ROR): The Value of Relationship Marketing and CRM in Business-to-Business Contexts." *The Journal of Business & Industrial Marketing* 19, no. 2 (2004): p. 136.

Gupta, Umang. "Who is a Customer?" *Issues in Ethics* 12, no. 1 (Spring 2001).

Gustafson, Norma. "Relationships Keep Us Strong when Times are Hard." *Foodservice Equipment & Supplies* 54, no. 10 (October 2001): p. 76.

King, John H. Jr. and Ronald F. Cichy. *Managing for Quality in the Hospitality Industry.* (Upper Saddle River, N.J.: Pearson Prentice Hall), 2006.

Latz, Marty. "The Golden Rules of Negotiation for Sales Professionals." *Agency Sales* 34, no. 12 (December 2004): pp. 50–53.

Law, K., C. Wong, and L. Song. "The Construct and Criterion Validity of Emotional Intelligence and its Potential Utility for Management Studies." *Journal of Applied Psychology* 89, no. 3 (2004): pp. 483–496.

Lawn, John. "Common Mistakes That Purchasing Managers Make." *Food Management* 38, no. 2 (February 2003): p. 6.

Lawn, John. "What Operators and Distributors Have In Common." *Food Management* 36, no. 11 (November 2001): p. 6.

Lieberman, Karen, and Bruce Nissen. *Ethics in the Hospitality and Tourism Industry.* (Lansing, Mich.: Educational Institute of the American Hotel & Lodging Association), 2005.

McNeill, Jack. "How Two 'Fs' Can Make An 'A+'." *Foodservice Equipment & Supplies* 57, no. 1 (January 2004): p. 29.

Murray, John Jr. "When You Get What You Bargained For—But Don't." *Purchasing* 132, no. 4 (March 6, 2004): p. 26.

Pinkney, Ina. "It's All about Relationships." *Foodservice Equipment & Supplies* 55, no. 7 (July 2002): p. 25.

Robbins, Stuart. "Strategy Divided by Four." *Supply Management* 10, no. 6 (March 17, 2005): p. 17.

Roman, Sergio, and Salvadore Ruiz. "Relationship Outcomes of Perceived Ethical Sales Behavior: The Customer's Perspective." *Journal of Business Research* 58, no. 4 (April 2005): p. 439.

Salovey, P. and D. Mayer. "Emotional Intelligence." *Imagination, Cognition, and Personality* 9, no. 3 (1990): pp. 185–211.

Smith, Peter. "More Than a Beautiful Friendship." *Supply Management* 10, no. 3 (February 2005): p. 22.

Stoller, Jacob. "What the Experts Don't Teach." *Purchasing B2B* 46, no. 7 (September 2004): pp. 19–23.

Yama, Elliott. "Buying Hardball, Playing Price." *Business Horizons*. (September/October 2004): pp. 62–66.

Internet Sites

For more information, visit the following Internet sites. Remember that Internet addresses can change without notice. If the site is no longer there, you can use a search engine to look for additional sites.

Buyer Interactive
www.buyerinteractive.com

Emotional Intelligence and Leadership: Validating a new EI Scale
www.cmaa.org/conf/
2006ProcManual/6040.ppt

Emotional Intelligence and Private Club Leadership
www.cmaa.org/conf/
2007ProcManual/7054.pdf

Negotiations
http://web.info.com/infocom.us2/
search/web/negotiations

Purchasing.com
www.purchasing.com

Chapter 6 Outline

Components of the Audit Trail
    Document Flow Prior to Purchasing
    Purchasing Documents
    Post-Receiving Activities
    The Importance of Collaboration
Quality, Cost, and Food Safety Requirements at the Receiving Control Point
    Receiving Personnel
    Receiving Procedures
    Request-for-Credit Memos
    Marking Products
    Economic Security Concerns in Receiving
    Computerized Receiving Systems
Quality, Cost, and Food Safety Requirements at the Storing Control Point
    Storage Personnel
    Inventory Control Policy
    Defining Storage Areas
    Economic Security Concerns in Storage Areas
    Maintaining Quality during Storage
Procedures Necessary for Effective Inventory Controls
    Inventory Turnover
    Inventory Recordkeeping Systems
    Technology and the Inventory Counting Process
Integrating Ordering, Receiving, Invoice Payment, and Inventory Procedures

Competencies

1. Identify the components of the audit trail. (pp. 221–232)

2. Identify the quality, cost, and food safety requirements at the receiving control point. (pp. 232–240)

3. Identify the quality, cost, and food safety requirements at the storing control point. (pp. 240–244)

4. Describe the procedures necessary for effective inventory controls. (pp. 244–253)

6

Receiving, Storing, and Inventory Controls

Pʀɪᴏʀ ᴛᴏ ᴅɪsᴄᴜssɪɴɢ ᴛʜᴇ ᴜɴɪQᴜᴇ ᴄᴏɴᴛʀᴏʟ ᴀᴄᴛɪᴠɪᴛɪᴇs in the receiving and storing control points, along with the associated inventory controls, let us examine the audit trail. The **audit trail** is an organized and systematic flow of documents through the food service distribution system. These documents and an analysis of their flow are used to determine if the system is working properly and, if not, which actions can be taken to correct the problems at the source.

Components of the Audit Trail

How exactly do purchasing and accounting functions relate to each other? The most obvious connection is the payment of the distributor's invoices by the accounting department. Accurate records of products received and support documentation must be generated and maintained in order to control this function.

Source documents are original points of entry for financial information into the accounting system and include such forms as purchase requisitions, purchase orders, purchase records, receiving reports, invoices, and disbursement (payment) vouchers. Exhibit 1 illustrates the movement of source documents within the food service operation and between the operation and its distributors. We will use Exhibit 1 as a guide to review source document flow in the entire purchasing process.

Document Flow Prior to Purchasing

Documentation is required at each stage in the purchasing process. The accounting department must process this paperwork at the time bills are paid. However, before bills are paid, products must be purchased and received. Storage and issuing practices influence consumption and, therefore, purchase requirements.

Requisitions. The **requisition** is used to communicate information from the requesting department (for instance, the kitchen or dining room) to applicable storeroom personnel. This form identifies the type and quantity of product to be removed from inventory. Exhibit 2 illustrates a requisition form. This example includes printed names of required products to simplify the requisition process.

Based upon the authorized requisition, products are then transferred (issued) from storage to the requesting user department. The term "user" refers to the line operating department requiring the products to be issued.

221

Exhibit 1   The Purchasing Cycle: An Audit Trail

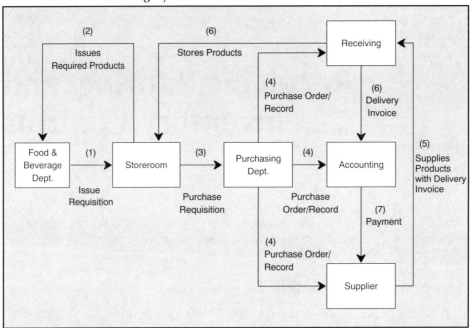

Source: Jack D. Ninemeier, *Planning and Control for Food and Beverage Operations,* 6th ed. (Lansing, Mich.: Educational Institute of the American Hotel & Lodging Association, 2004), p. 186.

Small food service operations may choose not to use requisitions. For instance, staff members may simply remove products directly from storage. This practice may be a practical way of reducing paperwork, but it is a poor method of controlling inventory. This method lacks the written audit trail that is so vital to controlling the flow of assets. Some managers of small food service operations compromise by locking up expensive and theft-prone products and keeping a running balance of the quantity on hand. All other products are withdrawn as needed.

Storeroom Accounting Controls. Food in storage represents a substantial investment to a typical food service operation, which expends approximately 30 to 50 percent of all income dollars on food purchases. Inventory controls are clearly important if one considers storage areas as bank vaults and products within these areas as assets to be protected.

Management of storage activities by accounting personnel rather than the user department is one example of inventory control. Through separation of duties and responsibilities, the accounting department discourages theft and pilferage by being closely involved with storage activities.

One important accounting control tool is the perpetual inventory system. As products enter storage, the quantity is recorded on the perpetual inventory record to show an increase in inventory. As products are removed by using the requisition form, the quantity depleted is also recorded. This running balance enables the

Exhibit 2   Requisition Form

OUTLET: MAIN KITCHEN

GNAC CORPORATION FOOD REQUISITION   № 07131

Time Ordered.............   Date.............   Time Delivered.............

Quan.	ITEM	Quan. Ord.	Quan. Iss.	Unit Cost	Ext. Cost.	√	Quan.	ITEM	Quan. Ord.	Quan. Iss.	Unit Cost	Ext. Cost.	√
	101 Hash Brown							Elbow Macaroni					
	L.I. Duck							Noodles					
	Diced Chicken							Spaghetti					
	Bay Scallops							Vermicelli					
	Breaded Scallops							Rigatoni					
	Cod Cheeks							Barley Pearl					
	Sea Legs							Kidney Beans					
	IQF Flounder							Navy Beans					
	Plain Omelette							Lentils					
	Cuisine D. Romanoff							Green Split Peas					
	Cheese Blintz							Rice					
	Chicken Cordon Bleu							Honey					
	Crepe Nancy							Molasses					
	Pieces Chicken - 4 Pcs.							Worcestershire - Gal.					
	Stuffed Pepper							Open Pit BBQ					
	Stuffed Cabbage							Teriyaki Sauce					
	Lasagna							Mustard					
	Stuffed Shells							White Vinegar					
	Chicken and Dumplings							White Milk					
	Ravioli							Sweet Butter					
	Frozen Scrambled Eggs							Butter Blens					
	Bay Shrimps							Aromat					
								Caraway Ground					
								Celery Salt					
	Tomato Catsup							Salt					
	Tomato Paste							Garlic Powder					
	Tomato Puree							Marjoram Leaves					
	Chili Sauce							Onion Salt					
	Diced Tomato							Oregano Whole					
	All Purpose Tomato							Paprika Hungarian					
	White Whole Potatoes, small							Black Pepper					
	Instant Potatoes							White Pepper					
	Corned Beef Hash							Cornstarch					
	Chopped Clams							Flour					
	Clam Juice							Lemon Juice					
	Sliced Mushroom							Great Garlic Jars					
	Chicken Base							Half & Half - Qts					
	Beef Base							Baked Potatoes (Wrapped)					
	Double Beef Consomme							Brown Sugar					
	Minors Ham Base							Pineapple Juice					
	Minors Clam Base							Cabbage					
	Lobster Base												
	Cottonseed Oil												
	Fry Max												
	Vegetable Spray												

WHITE: Food & Beverage Control   CANARY: Storeroom   ORDERED BY.....................   RECEIVED BY.....................   ISSUED BY.....................

Source: Golden Nugget.

controller (a member of the accounting department), through physical observation and count, to match how much product *is* available to how much product *should be* available. Differences between these figures give a measure of the effectiveness of inventory control methods.

Controls of this type assist the purchasing control point in at least three ways:

- As theft/pilferage is curtailed, quantities of product required in inventory are reduced and, as a result, the total dollar amount committed to inventory is decreased.

- Since a perpetual inventory system logs item quantity, such records provide usage rates and other input useful in making purchase decisions.

- A perpetual inventory system reduces stockouts caused by inaccurate recordkeeping.

Loss prevention not only represents a real savings to the operation, but also contributes to the maintenance of inventory levels. While perpetual inventory recordkeeping may not be necessary for every item, it is advised for the relatively few products that represent the largest portion of food costs, that is, the most expensive inventory.

Purchase Requisitions. Another accounting tool, the **purchase requisition**, is illustrated in Exhibit 3. Storeroom personnel send this form to the purchasing department when product quantity levels reach a preestablished minimum level. Purchase requisitions indicate what products are required, when to order them, and how much of each item is needed to maintain par levels.

Some operations route this form directly to the user department instead of to the purchasing department. A manager who is familiar with usage levels (volume of purchases) and product requirements can confirm that purchase requisitions are appropriate. Sometimes an order guide is used (see Exhibit 4).

Purchasing Documents

Requests for products eventually reach the purchasing department. Provided these documents are authorized and legitimate, the specific function of purchasing begins at this point.

When receiving a purchase requisition from the storeroom, the purchasing department is made aware that additional quantities of the specified products must be purchased. The purchasing professional develops and circulates purchase specifications to all eligible distributors. When purchase requisitions are received from the storeroom, the purchasing task is simplified; the minimum quality of product required is defined in the purchase specifications and several eligible distributors of the products are already identified.

Purchasing staff can use many different methods to solicit prices. Telephone calls, Internet sites, or visits from distributor sales representatives (DSRs) can provide this information. Some large-volume operations use a special purchase order form to solicit requests for price quotations (see Exhibit 5). The distributor who is awarded the purchase then receives a confirming order on the original purchase

Exhibit 3   Purchase Requisition

		PURCHASE REQUISITION		GNOC CORP. **12914**	

Suggested VENDOR(S) and Ordering Information _____

Date Submitted _____
Date Required _____
Dept. of Orig. _____
Requested by _____
Dept. Head _____

QUANTITY	DISTRIBUTION DEPT.	A/C	PLEASE ORDER ITEM(S) LISTED BELOW	EST. UNIT PRICE	EST. TOTAL

JUSTIFICATION: All variations in excess of Budget must be noted below:

FOR PURCHASING USE ONLY	
P.O. #	
SHIP VIA	
DELIVER TO	
F.O.B.	
ORDERED BY	

PRICE/COST INFO REQ. BY DEPT. OF ORIGINATION? ☐ Yes ☐ No

ACCOUNTING

Source: Golden Nugget.

order. Some food service operations tie prices to market indicators and simply order from the approved distributor, assuring the operation that the price will be at a predetermined level above the current market price.

Purchase Order. After selecting the distributor, the purchaser issues a **purchase order** (especially in the case of a large food service operation) or makes an oral or unwritten agreement with the distributor. Documentation is submitted to the receiving department, which needs details regarding products, quantities, and prices for each incoming order. This documentation may be a copy of the purchase order, if one is issued, or an in-house record of the purchase agreement.

A copy of the purchase order is also sent to the accounting department so that a later audit can be performed as part of invoice processing. In large food service operations, an additional copy of the purchase order might be forwarded to the storeroom, confirming the receipt of the purchase requisition, indicating the order

Exhibit 4 Sample Order Guide

ITEM	MON	TUE	WED	THUR	FRI	SAT	SUN
Kiwi							
Cantaloupe							
Honeydew							
Watermelon							
Pineapple							
Cubed Honeydew							
Cubed Cantaloupe							
Cubed Pineapple							
Red Grapes							
Strawberries							
Raspberries							
Parsley							
Tarragon							
Thyme							
Watercress							
Shallots							
Garlic							
Orange Juice							
Grapefruit Juice							
Mushroom - Medium							
Jalapenos							
Ginger							
Spanish Onion							
Red Onion							
Green Onion							
Red Peppers							
Green Peppers							
Tomato - 6x6							
Plum Tomatoes							
Celery							
Carrots							
Baking Potato - 40/80 Count							
Red Bliss Potato - Size B							
Cucumber							
Yellow Squash							
Green Squash							
Broccoli							
Cauliflower							
Leaf Lettuce							
Iceberg Lettuce							
Romaine							
Radicchio							
TKO Mesculan							
Green Cabbage							
Red Cabbage							
Spinach Cello							
Belgian Endive							
Leeks							
Avocado							
Granny Smith Apples - 91 Count							
Red Apples - 88 Count							
Oranges - 80 Count							
Bananas							
Lemons - 140 Count							
Limes - 48 Count							
Grapefruit							
Eggplant							
Yams							
Asparagus							
Cranberries							
White Sweet Potatoes							
Portabellos							
Shitakii Mushrooms							

Exhibit 5 Sample Request for Price Quotation

Purchase Order No.:
Order Date: 04/29/2005

5900880093085

59008800093085

Purchased From: 001105674GL	DELIVERY ADDRESS:					PO Type: Domestic
						Buyer:

				Delivery Date	Payment Terms
Incoterms				04/29/2005	Net 30 Days
PRE Prepaid					

Line No.	Product Code	Order Qty	Order Unit	Description	Price Per Unit $	Net Value $	Qty Received	Pack Size	Stge Loc/ Lot No.
010	1191	1011	GP	CRAB, OPILIO CLUSTERS Brand: Master Cases/Case Weight					

INSP BY	SHIPPING DATA	SHIPPING DATA
	B/L #:	LC #:
	B/L Date:	Shipment:
	Total Kgs:	Feeder Vessel Ship:
	Ctr Number:	Mother Vessel Ship:
	Seal Number:	

GPUJFW1 04/29/2005 15:21:09

of additional products, and noting the quantity of incoming products and date of delivery.

Purchase Record. As an alternative to issuing a purchase order, a small-volume food service operation may instead use an in-house **purchase record**. This saves time for managers who may be too busy to handle the necessary paperwork. The distributor is not provided with a copy, since orders have been placed by informal means (phone, Internet, or personal visit). Receiving personnel should be furnished with a copy of the purchase record so that they can be prepared to properly receive the products when delivered and thus avoid last-minute surprises. Staff members with receiving responsibility need to check incoming products against the purchase record, which indicates products ordered, quantity, and price. Of course, product quality must also be carefully checked during receiving.

Post-Receiving Activities

The purchase order or purchase record is compared with the delivery invoice (see Exhibit 6) and other receiving documents routed from the receiving department with their own copy of the purchasing documents. Management will be interested in determining:

- Whether any discrepancies exist between qualities, quantities, and prices agreed upon at time of purchase and those actually received.

- Whether any products are backordered or out of stock.

- Whether any problems require invoice adjustments. (Credit memos will be discussed later in this chapter.)

- Whether any other issues are raised to indicate possible areas for improvement.

As you can see, the role of the purchasing department extends far beyond the actual purchase of products and services. Purchasing goals involving price, quality, quantity, distributor, and time are more consistently met by screening source documents as they move throughout the various departments. This provides the necessary audit trail and system of checks and balances for accounting.

Billing Process. Even before distributors' invoices are ready for processing, the accounting department plays a role in the procurement process. It has, for example, received a copy of the purchase order or purchase record. Its first active task in the billing process, however, occurs when the **delivery invoice** and (if applicable) the receiving records are routed from the purchasing department.

An initial step in the bill-paying process occurs as the invoice extensions are checked (ideally, for the second time). **Invoice extensions** are the product of the quantity of each item ordered times the purchase price per unit. The importance of this verification cannot be overstated. The invoice is used as the basis for establishing amounts owed to the distributor and, therefore, serves as the basic input to various expense categories on the food service operation's income statement.

There are two basic ways to process distributor invoices for payment: by invoice or by statement. When bills are paid by statement, the purchaser reaches

Exhibit 6   Sample Delivery Invoice

Delivery Invoice

**ABC Club, Restaurant, Institution,
and Hotel Distributor**

Route: _____

Invoice No.: _____

Customer No.: _____

Stop: _____

Sold To: XYZ Hotel   **Ship To:**   XYZ Hotel
              Street Address   Street Address
              City/State/Zip   City/State/Zip

Salesperson	Terms	Customer P.O.	Our Order #	Order Date	Invoice Date

Ordered	Shipped	Item Description	Pack	Weight (lb.)	Unit Price	Amount
6/15	x	L.O. Bacon 18/22	15#	90.00	2.0700LB	186.30
2/6	x	Link Sausage 8/1	6#	12.00	1.5300LB	18.36
1/12	x	Sausage Patties 1.5 oz	12#	12.00	2.3900LB	28.68
1cs	x	Crepe Cheese Blintz 3 oz	24#	1.00	77.860CS	77.86
2 bxs	x	Franks in a Blanket	100PC	2.00	34.500BX	69.00
2/10	x	AB Franks 4/1	10#	10.00	1.8200LB	18.20

Total Items:	Total Boxes:		Total Weight:	Total Due: $398.40

Received On Account: Date:

_____   _____
          Delivered By   Received By

Before signing this receipt, be sure all items are accounted for and are in satisfactory condition. ABC will not be responsible for any shortages or damages after the delivery driver leaves. Service Charge: 1.5 Percent Per Month on Unpaid Balance—18 Percent Annual Rate.

Source: Jack D. Ninemeier, *Planning and Control for Food and Beverage Operations*, 6th ed. (Lansing, Mich.: Educational Institute of the American Hotel & Lodging Association, 2004), p. 207.

an agreement with the distributor that a statement covering all applicable delivery invoices will be sent to the operation on a regular schedule. Invoices that have been filed by distributor are retrieved when the statement is received. Applicable invoices are matched with invoice number, date, amount owed, and other information noted on the statement. The total of all invoices is verified to confirm that the amount requested on the statement is correct. One check is then written to cover all invoices. The invoices should be attached to the statement and information about payment date, check number, and check amount should be recorded. Rubber stamps can be used to quickly and consistently indicate needed information.

When bills are paid by invoice, the same basic information should be recorded on each invoice. The difference is that no statement is sent from the distributor or, at least, a statement is not used as the basis for payment. After extensions are confirmed, invoices are filed by payment date. For example, if an invoice must be paid by the 20th of the month, it may be filed for processing on the 15th of the month. This will allow time for that activity and for mailing the distributor's payment.

In either case, the source documents (statement with attached invoices or invoices alone) should be filed by distributor name after payment. Some operations attach copies of the receiving record and/or purchase order (purchase record) for a complete documentation of the transaction.

Credit Memos. Problems that may arise at the time of receiving include delivery of incorrect quantities and delivery of products that are of the wrong quality or brand. In some operations, these problems are handled simply by making a notation on the delivery invoice before it is signed. While this is often the practice, such notations may go unnoticed or may give rise to questions. Even worse is the common situation in which a verbal agreement is made with the delivery person: "Just sign the invoice this time and we'll bring the products on the next delivery without putting them on the invoice."

The best solution to these problems involves using a credit memo system. A **credit memo** is prepared by distributor personnel and does just what its name implies: it provides a written record of adjustments made to the invoice. This form helps accounting personnel limit payments to those products that were actually received and accepted. Exhibit 7 provides an example of a credit memo.

Distributors provide credit memos for their delivery drivers' use, but they are sometimes forgotten or simply lacking. When credit memos are not immediately available, the food service operation should use a simple form requesting that the distributor issue a credit memo. The request for a credit memo is sent to the accounting and purchasing departments as well as the distributor. The distributor then issues a credit memo or simply credits the food service operation's account.

A proper procedure for processing credit memos may include the following steps:

1. A problem is noted and brought to the delivery driver's attention when products are received. The driver agrees that there is a difference between the incoming shipment and the order included on the original delivery invoice.

2. Applicable information is recorded on the credit memo, including the number of the delivery invoice.

3. The driver signs the credit memo after all required information is noted.

4. The receiving staff member signs the delivery invoice and notes the credit memo number on the delivery invoice.

5. The receiving staff member retains a copy of the credit memo (generally the original). This should be attached to the applicable invoice.

Exhibit 7   Sample Credit Memo

GRACE Restaurant Services	**CUSTOMER ADJUSTMENT MEMO** **69558**

☐ CREDIT   ☐ ADD-ON
☐ DRIVER PICK UP   ☐ WILL CALL
☐ SHORTAGE DEL.   ☐ SHIPPED BY
☐ CREDIT BILLING ADJUSTMENT _____
☐ DEBIT BILLING ADJUSTMENT

SHOP NUMBER   NAME

ADDRESS

CITY   STATE   ZIP   OPENING ORDER ☐

CONTACT   DATE   INVOICE NUMBER

NOT FOR ADD-ON USE

ORIGINAL INVOICE NO.	ORDER DATE	SHIP DATE	ITEM DESCRIPTION	ITEM NUMBER	QUAN-TITY	SELL UNIT PRICE	EXTENDED AMOUNT	ADJ. CODE
			Void					

EXPLANATION:_____

ORIGINATED BY

APPROVED BY

ALL TRANSACTIONS SUBJECT TO FUTURE BILLING PROCESS

CUSTOMER ACKNOWLEDGMENT

CUSTOMER

Source: Grace Restaurant Services, Inc.

6. The delivery invoice with attached credit memo and, as applicable, the purchase order (purchase record) and receiving report is routed through the purchasing department to the accounting department. A purchasing staff member should verify any concerns or problems regarding the credit memo with the receiving staff member or appropriate departmental representative. Frequent notation of credit memo problems provides useful input to the ongoing distributor evaluation process.

7. As soon as the credit memo and invoice are received by accounting, an arithmetic check of all extensions is undertaken.

8. Some operations will call the distributor to confirm that the distributor's copy of the credit memo was received and is being processed.

Before a check is signed, the amount of the original invoice should be reduced by the amount recorded on the credit memo, either on the invoice itself (if this is used for as the basis for payment) or on the statement provided by the distributor.

The entire amount of the invoice is stated and the amount of the credit memo is noted separately. Information about the invoice and credit memo should be noted on the check.

Credit memos should be treated exactly like money, because that is really what they represent. If, for example, credit memos are lost or improperly processed, the food service operator stands to lose the deductions and costs will be higher than they should be. The staff member with receiving responsibility has a most significant role to play in managing quality and costs. The credit memo can be an effective tool to help an operation get value for the money it spends as products and services are received.

Processing Checks. Except when petty cash expenses are involved, payments should always be made by check. For auditing purposes, funds to pay bills should never be taken out of daily income before bank deposits are made. Unless the owner or manager performs both activities, invoice/statement processing and check signing should be done by two different people. For similar reasons, persons who process income records, handle funds, or prepare deposits should not be involved in check-writing procedures.

The invoice/statement with supporting records—purchase order (or purchase record), invoice, and receiving reports—should be given, along with the check, to management to sign. Many operations require more than one signature on large checks. A specific person or distributor organization should be designated on the check, rather than "cash" or "bearer." Top-level management should routinely examine the list of checks written to keep current with new distributors and transactions. Lists of payees should be circulated to the purchasing staff to prevent checks from being written for fraudulent purposes (for example, payment to fictitious companies).

The Importance of Collaboration

Collaborators are those who join forces and pool resources and talents to act as a team. Collaborators work in partnership and cooperate with each other for the good of the organization. Teamwork and communication between purchasing, receiving, storing, and accounting department staff have been represented throughout this chapter. Sometimes large operations have staff accounting specialists with responsibility for each of the activities discussed. By contrast, smaller operations may not have a full-time accountant, and the manager/owner may perform many of the tasks with external assistance from a professional accountant. Other operations may use a bookkeeper for invoice processing, check writing, and other duties. Regardless of the organizational plan, however, the experts in purchasing, receiving, and storing must work closely with the experts in accounting to design systems to control the operation's products and funds.

Quality, Cost, and Food Safety Requirements at the Receiving Control Point

The planning and control that goes into the purchasing process is wasted if no one ensures that products delivered meet the operation's standard purchase specifications. In too many operations, the person who signs the invoice is the person who happens to be closest to the back door when a delivery is made. Great care must be taken to ensure an effective receiving process. Receiving is an important part of the product cost control system. Many managers, unfortunately, have learned an important lesson the hard way: it is very likely that they will *pay* for the quality of product you order; however, it is not certain that they will *receive* the quality ordered (and paid for) unless an effective receiving system is in use. Except as noted, controls related to receiving discussed in this section are applicable to both food and beverage products.

Receiving Personnel

Effective receiving requires knowledgeable receiving personnel. Staff must be selected and trained to receive properly. They must know product quality standards and be able to recognize them when products are delivered. They must also understand all receiving procedures and know how to complete internal receiving records.

The number of persons who receive products varies among food service operations. In a relatively small operation, the manager or the assistant manager may be in charge of receiving. In a larger operation, full- or part-time staff typically handle the receiving function, and the person in charge of receiving may be called a receiving or storeroom staff member or steward. This individual usually reports to the food controller in the accounting department, the assistant manager, or the food and beverage manager.

Regardless of how many individuals are assigned to the receiving function, the general requirements are the same. Naturally, good health and personal cleanliness are essential for the receiver, as well as for all other staff members in the food service operation. To protect the health of guests and staff members alike, strict food safety standards should be part of every aspect of food handling.

Receiving personnel should be able to use all required equipment, facilities, and forms. Increasingly, computerized receiving systems require someone who is able to work with highly technical equipment and systems. Because of the volume of written information to be processed, receiving staff must be able to read and write well. Among other things, they must be able to check the actual products delivered against the written purchase specifications, written purchase orders, and the invoice itself.

Many incoming products will be in heavy cases and a large volume of products will likely be lifted and moved on each shift. A receiving person must be able to perform these physical tasks.

Receiving personnel must be committed to protecting the interests of the operation. While food production experience is invaluable, this does not imply that any kitchen worker in the operation is qualified to perform the receiving function. Only selected and trained staff members should be permitted to receive food and beverage products.

Properly trained receivers know what to do when there is a problem with product deliveries. In this respect, the receiving function is just as important as the purchasing function; as soon as the receiver signs the invoice, the merchandise legally becomes the food service operation's responsibility and is no longer the responsibility of the distributor.

Finally, receiving personnel need cooperation from other departments in the food service operation. They must coordinate purchase requisitions from the departments with the distributors' delivery schedules. Ideally, receiving should take place during slow periods in the operation's daily business cycle. By scheduling deliveries at these times, the receiver's undivided attention can be given to the receiving duties. The operation's delivery hours should be posted on the back door, and the receiver should always be available when deliveries are expected. A distributor's ability to accommodate an operation's delivery hours should be a major consideration in the distributor selection process.

The receiving area should be near the delivery door. Delivery personnel should be allowed only in restricted back-of-the-house areas and should not be permitted in food production or storage areas, access corridors, or other off-limits areas. Since proper receiving requires that most products be weighed or counted, accurate, conveniently located scales are necessary, along with other equipment, such as calculators, marking pens, rulers, files, thermometers, transportation equipment, and perhaps a computer.

Receiving Procedures

Control procedures adopted by food service operations are designed to further strengthen control over products.

Check Incoming Products Against Purchase Orders or Purchase Records. Obviously, the operation does not want to accept products it did not order, receive partial or no deliveries of required products, receive products of unacceptable quality, or pay a price higher than that agreed upon. These problems can be prevented by comparing incoming products against an in-house record of the purchase agreement, as expressed on a purchase order or purchase record.

Check Incoming Products Against Standard Purchase Specifications. Knowledgeable and skilled receiving personnel are needed for this procedure to ensure that deliveries meet specifications. They should not allow themselves to be rushed by delivery persons. Sometimes distributors will agree to deliver products at their risk, allowing the operator to sign and send invoices after inspecting deliveries. Cooperation in receiving is important when assessing distributors. Whether receiving 96-count (to the case) lemons, chilled poultry, or fresh seafood, receiving staff must know how to confirm that the correct product is, in fact, being delivered and that the food service operation is getting what it pays for (i.e., value).

Check Incoming Products Against Delivery Invoices. The distributor provides the delivery invoice, which becomes the basis for subsequent payment claims. A definite policy must be developed, implemented, and enforced for the measuring, weighing, or counting of incoming products to ensure that the proper quantity of product is delivered and billed. In most cases, it is not practical to weigh every item or count every case of product being delivered. It is helpful, however, to routinely weigh/count selected cases on a random basis. Distributor or delivery staff

Exhibit 8 Daily Receiving Report

Date: 8/1/00													Page 1 of 2
				No. of	Purchase		**Distribution**						Transfer
	Invoice		Purchase	Purchase	Unit	Total	Food		Beverages				to
Distributor	No.	Item	Unit	Units	Price	Cost	Directs	Stores	Liquor	Beer	Wine	Soda	Storage
1	2	3	4	5	6	7	8	9	10	11	12	13	14
AJAX	10111	Gr. Beef	10#	6	$ 28.50	$171.00		$171.00					Bill
ABC Liquor	6281	B. Scotch	cs (750)	2	$ 71.80	$143.60			$143.60				Bill
		XYZ Chablis	cs (750)	1	$ 95.00	$ 95.00					$ 95.00		Bill
B/E Produce	70666	Lettuce	cs	2	$ 21.00	$ 42.00	$ 42.00						
					Totals		$351.00	$475.00	$683.50	—	$275.00		

Source: Jack D. Ninemeier, *Planning and Control for Food and Beverage Operations,* 6th ed. (Lansing, Mich.: Educational Institute of the American Hotel & Lodging Association, 2004), p. 208.

members are less likely to short-weigh a count if they expect random inspections. Likewise, price information on the invoice should be verified by reviewing the purchase order or purchase record. Any discrepancies should be handled by a request-for-credit memo.

Accept Incoming Products. Acceptance of deliveries is normally completed when the receiving person signs the delivery invoice (see Exhibit 7). At this point, ownership of the products is transferred to the food service operation, and the products become the operation's responsibility.

Move Accepted Products to Storage Immediately. Security to minimize staff member theft is a concern here. Likewise, the quality of products needing low-temperature storage will deteriorate if they are left at room temperatures, which are frequently very warm in back-of-the-house production areas. Use a stock rotation process; incoming products should be placed behind or beneath products already in inventory.

Complete Necessary Receiving Documents. A typical receiving document is a daily receiving report such as the sample shown in Exhibit 8.

The **daily receiving report** is used to:

- Separate beverage costs—liquor, beer, wine, soda, etc.—from food costs. This information is needed for income statements that isolate revenue and costs of goods sold categories for these products.

• Determine the value of directs if daily food costs are assessed.

• Transfer responsibility for product control from receiving to storeroom personnel (in large operations with different receiving and storeroom personnel).

In examining the daily receiving report, note that information about all incoming products received during the shift can be recorded on one form (with additional pages as needed). Columns 1 to 3 list the distributor's name, invoice number, and products received respectively.

Columns 4 to 7 indicate—for each item—the purchase unit (size of the shipping container—ground beef in 10-pound bags, for example); number of purchase units (six 10-pound bags of ground beef); cost per unit (a 10-pound bag of ground beef costs $28.50, or $2.85 per pound); and total cost of the product being delivered (six 10-pound bags of ground beef at $28.50 equals $171.00). In columns 8 to 13—the distribution columns—the total cost of column 7 of each item is carried over by category. Food products are classified as directs or stores. ("Directs" are charged to food costs on the day of receipt; "stores" enter storage records, such as perpetual inventory forms, and are charged to food costs when issued.) Each beverage item is classified as liquor, beer, wine, or soda. For example, columns in the sample forms note bar scotch and house chablis wine.

Column 14—Transfer to Storage—is used in larger operations with separate receiving and storage staff to indicate that all products received actually enter storeroom areas.

Request-for-Credit Memos

Each time a delivery invoice is modified at the time of receiving, a **request-for-credit memo**, such as that shown in Exhibit 9, becomes necessary. If deliveries do not include the full quantity specified on the delivery invoice, are refused because of quality problems, or are rejected for any other reason, this is noted on the request-for-credit memo. The receiver should never agree to accept delivery free during the *next* delivery of products shorted on the current delivery, but appearing on the invoice. The following procedures should be used to process a request-for-credit memo:

1. Note problems with products on the invoice.

2. Complete the request-for-credit memo, have the delivery person sign it, and return a copy to the distributor, along with the delivery invoice.

3. Attach the operation's copy of the memo to its copy of the delivery invoice. Note the correct amount of the invoice on the face of the invoice.

4. Advise the distributor that the original invoice has been amended by a request-for-credit memo.

5. If short or refused products are subsequently delivered, a separate invoice should accompany the products. The new invoice is processed in the usual manner.

Exhibit 9   Request-for-Credit Memo

Request-for-Credit Memo

(prepare in duplicate)   Number: _____

From: _____   To: _____
_____   (supplier)
_____   _____
_____   _____
                                                         _____

Credit should be given on the following:

Invoice Number: _____   Invoice Date: _____

Product	Unit	Number	Price/Unit	Total Price

Reason: _____   Total: _____

_____   _____
(delivery person)   (authorizing signature)

Source: Jack D. Ninemeier, *Planning and Control for Food and Beverage Operations*, 6th ed. (Lansing, Mich.: Educational Institute of the American Hotel & Lodging Association, 2004), p. 209.

6. Do not file any invoices affected by credit memos. Instead, hold them in a separate file until all issues, such as a distributor's confirmation of a credit, are resolved.

Marking Products

Marking and tagging puts invoice information directly on products. For example, marking case goods or bottles of liquor with the delivery date makes it easier to judge whether stock rotation plans are effective. Also, when valuing inventory, cost data can be taken directly from the cases or bottles if this information is transferred from delivery invoices to storage containers. This eliminates the time needed to search for the information on the daily receiving report, delivery invoice, or in the computerized database. Recording the unit price on products makes it more likely that the operation's staff members will think about them as alternative forms of cash. Therefore, they may be more careful in handling and portioning products, and controlling waste.

Economic Security Concerns in Receiving

Examples of distributor theft possibilities during receiving include the following:

- The distributor may deliver poorer quality products than those ordered, such as inexpensive domestic wines instead of the proper higher quality wines or 30-percent fat content ground beef instead of 20-percent. The operation then pays the price for the higher quality product it did not receive.

- Short-weight or short-count products may be delivered, and the food service operation pays for more products than it receives.

- Thawed products may be represented as fresh, while the operation pays the higher price for fresh.

- Ice may be ground into ground meat products, fillers such as soy products or non-fat dry milk extenders may be added, and meat may be sold with excess fat trim.

- Weight of ice and packaging may be included in the product weight on which price is based.

- **"Slacked out"** seafood—frozen fish that has been thawed and packed in ice—may be sold as fresh.

- Expensive steaks and inexpensive meat may be combined in one container and when the entire container is weighed, the operation may be billed for more expensive steaks than are actually in the container.

- An empty liquor bottle may be included in a case of 12 bottles.

These are just a few of the many ways that distributors can steal from the operation by overcharging for amount and quality. To help guard against theft at receiving, some basic principles should be followed:

1. Have different people receive and purchase, unless the owner/manager performs both duties.

2. Properly select and train receiving staff members. Receiving is too important to leave to whomever happens to be handy.

3. To the extent possible, schedule product deliveries at slow times so that receiving personnel, who may have other duties, have time to receive correctly.

4. Have deliveries made to a specified area of the operation, and make sure that accurately calibrated receiving scales and other equipment are available and used.

5. After receipt, immediately move products to storage. Chances for staff member theft increase the longer products remain unattended.

6. Do not permit DSRs or delivery/route persons access to back-of-the-house production or storage areas. To the extent possible, the receiving area should be close to an outside exit and visible to management personnel.

Exhibit 10 Purchase Alert Report

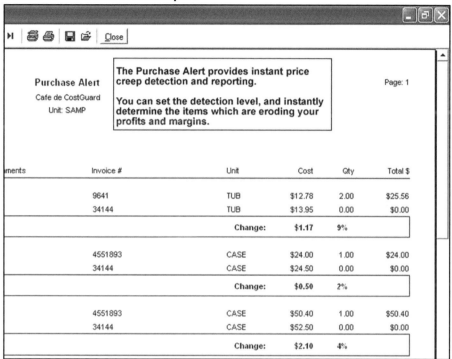

Source: Jack D. Ninemeier, *Planning and Control for Food and Beverage Operations,* 6th ed. (Lansing, Mich.: Educational Institute of the American Hotel & Lodging Association, 2004), p. 211. (Courtesy of CostGuard Foodservice Software, Bronxville, New York)

7. Lock the outside door. Install an audio signal so delivery persons can ring when they arrive. With this practice, receiving personnel have delivery persons in sight during their entire visit.

Computerized Receiving Systems

Computer technology is assisting some food service operations with the receiving control point. Packing cases containing food and beverage products often have universal product code or bar code information attached. Such data indicates product code (name), purchase/delivery date, product price, and, perhaps, other information. An optical scanner is used to read this information and, at the same time, update perpetual inventory levels and develop daily receiving and other reports desired by the operation. This process allows for rapid generation of important control information with minimal chances of error.

Some automated product receiving systems provide managers with information that is difficult and time-consuming to generate manually. Price increases, for example, are easy to detect and track electronically. Exhibit 10 illustrates part of a "Purchase Alert" report that notes different costs for the same product on different delivery invoices. Managers can specify the "detection level" on such alerts. They can determine, for example, which products increased in price by 2 percent or more during the past month.

At operations with multiple outlets, products on a single delivery invoice may be received centrally and transported to separate outlets with associated product costs transferred (assigned) automatically to those outlets. This eliminates the paperwork often required in manual systems to record all products in central inventory and to then issue products to each separate outlet.

Automated systems require the same basic procedures to verify incoming products as their manual-system counterparts. Incoming products are checked by receiving personnel against a hard or electronic copy of the original purchase order. At least one of the several systems available has a feature that addresses food-safety concerns: if there are products for which temperatures should be recorded at time of receipt, a window opens on the screen to facilitate this entry.

Quality, Cost, and Food Safety Requirements at the Storing Control Point

Storage Personnel

It is important to move food and beverage products into storage areas as soon as they are received. In addition, delivery personnel should have only limited access to back-of-the-house areas. This means that staff from the food service operation—not the delivery persons—should be responsible for this transfer from the receiving to the storage area. If deliveries are left unattended in receiving areas, refrigerated and frozen products can easily deteriorate in quality, and dishonest people may have opportunities to steal. As soon as received products are moved to and placed in storage areas, their quality and security can be better ensured by the control procedures built into the operation's storage system. The principles of effective storage systems for both food and beverage products focus on the following three primary concerns:

- Keeping products secure from theft
- Retaining product quality
- Providing information necessary for the financial accounting system

Inventory Control Policy

When designing storage systems, every control procedure must be cost effective. It is generally not practical for managers to attempt to regulate all food and beverage products under a strict system of tight controls. Some operations, for example, may not be able to justify a perpetual inventory system for any but the most expensive products. (Perpetual inventory systems are discussed later in this chapter.) As a result, many food service operations, especially smaller ones, maintain tight control over meats, seafood, liquor, and wine, but not as much control over less expensive and less theft-prone products such as produce and dairy products. Others may expand the list of products needing special controls because of specific

Exhibit 11   The A-B-C-D Classification Scheme for Food Items in Inventory

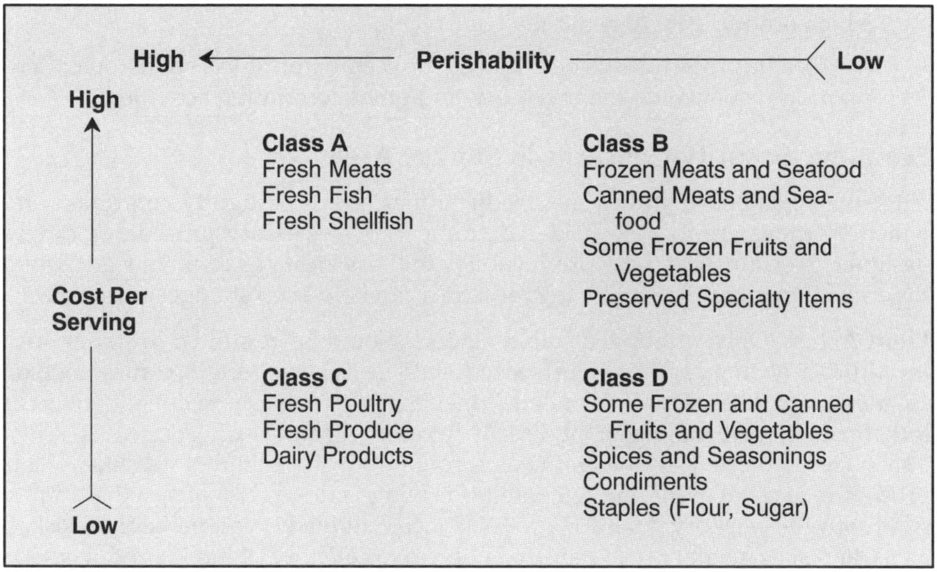

High ←——————— Perishability ——————⟨ Low

High

↑

**Cost Per
Serving**

Class A
Fresh Meats
Fresh Fish
Fresh Shellfish

Class B
Frozen Meats and Seafood
Canned Meats and Sea-
food
Some Frozen Fruits and
Vegetables
Preserved Specialty Items

Class C
Fresh Poultry
Fresh Produce
Dairy Products

Class D
Some Frozen and Canned
Fruits and Vegetables
Spices and Seasonings
Condiments
Staples (Flour, Sugar)

↓

Low

Source: Ronald F. Cichy, *Food Safety: Managing the HACCP Process* (Lansing, Mich.: Educational Institute of the American Hotel & Lodging Association, 2004), p. 107.

concerns. The point is that each food service operation is different, and managers must develop basic control procedures that account for their operations' unique requirements.

One approach that has been useful is based on an **ABCD inventory classification system** that categorizes products according to their perishability and cost per serving. Category A products include those products that are high in both perishability and cost per serving, while category B products are relatively high in cost but low in perishability. Exhibit 11 presents the ABCD approach, indicating the categories and showing examples of inventory products in each category.

One advantage of using this system is the ability to regulate the products needing the tightest control—usually those in categories A and B. Storage procedures and controls for these products should be designed and implemented first. Then, as time permits and practices require, other products in lower priority categories can be brought under tighter control.

Defining Storage Areas

When products are "in storage," they have been entered into inventory records and should be under tight storage control. Each food service operation must define its storage areas. For example, central storerooms and walk-in refrigerators and freezers are obviously storage areas. However, are products still in storage when they are in workstation storage areas such as reach-in refrigerators, pantry shelves, broken-case storage areas, and behind the bar? Managers must designate:

- Which locations are considered storage areas.

- Which products are to be tightly controlled.

- The specific procedures to be followed for keeping products secure, maintaining proper quality, taking inventory, and other accounting activities.

Economic Security Concerns in Storage Areas

After management identifies the products that are to be tightly controlled and which locations are to be considered storage areas, security procedures can be designed to ensure that those products stay in those locations until they are issued to production areas. The following measures can help keep storage areas secure.

Limit Access. Only authorized staff members should be permitted in storerooms. In addition to management, authorized staff in larger operations may include receiving and storage staff members. Smaller operations can keep storage areas locked and involve management directly in receiving and issuing activities. When a manager is present to unlock the storeroom door, staff theft is less likely. This procedure is more easily implemented if issuing is done only at specified times. Alternatively, category A and B products (see Exhibit 11) can be kept in locked areas, and staff members can have freer access to category C and D products.

Lock Storage Areas. The storeroom, freezer, and beverage storage areas should be locked. Depending on available equipment, one section of a walk-in or reach-in refrigerator might be used to secure expensive refrigerated products. Or a lockable shelving unit (or cage) can be used in the walk-in refrigerator. In this way, expensive refrigerated products, such as fresh meats and seafood, or wines being chilled for service, can be secured. At the same time, staff members still have access to produce, dairy, and similar products that are less likely to be stolen.

Refrigerator/freezer units should be lockable with reasonably strong lock clasps and door hinges. Storeroom walls should extend to the ceiling, and there should be no way to enter through the ceiling from another room. If there are windows, they should at least be made secure and unopenable. The point is to design, within practical limits, storage areas that are difficult for unauthorized staff to enter without being detected.

Some operations have a secure precious room. A precious room is a locked storage area within a locked storage area. For example, liquor and expensive buffet chafing dishes might be kept locked in an area within a locked storeroom.

The goal of all of these procedures is to reduce opportunities for pilferage. The answers to such commonsense questions as, "How would I steal from my storage areas if I were a dishonest person?" may point to security loopholes in storage areas.

Minimize Behind-the-Bar Storage. The quantity of alcoholic beverage products kept behind the bar should be minimal since storage space is limited and this area is less secure than the central storage area. Liquor should be locked behind the bar when the bar is closed. Lockable cabinets, roll-down screens, or similar devices can keep beverages out of the reach of cleaning and other staff when the bar is closed.

Control Storeroom Keys. Only staff members who need keys should have them. Manual locks or combinations should be changed routinely and each time a staff member with access to keys leaves the food service operation's employment. An excellent policy is that all keys remain at the food service operation at all times, securely locked in the manager's office when not in use. Some food and beverage managers may feel key control procedures are unnecessary. However, a significant number of products representing substantial dollar outlays can be lost because of inadequate key control. The potential for such losses should convince managers to emphasize this aspect of the operation's control system.

Current locking systems eliminate the need for traditional keys, and a combination code can be entered by authorized staff who have memorized the code. When these individuals no longer need access to lockable areas, combinations can be quickly (and inexpensively) changed. Other systems may use plastic cards, similar to credit cards, with coded information designed to operate locks. Either of these or related systems may yield information about the identity of the persons entering lockable areas, time of entry, and length of time that the individual was in the area. Moreover, they make the process of changing the locks fast and easy, so busy managers are more likely to do so.

Increasingly, these and related systems provide more specific control information to help ensure that only persons authorized to enter storage areas do, in fact, gain access to these locations.

Maintaining Quality during Storage

Improper storage practices can reduce the quality of products in storage. In fact, most food products—including frozen foods—experience a loss in quality if stored too long. While this is especially true for foods, it also applies to some wines and most beers. It is important that control procedures designed to minimize the loss of quality of products in storage be strictly followed. Food costs increase as products judged unfit for use are discarded and replaced. If, because of pressure to keep food costs down, lower quality products are served to guests, those guests may perceive a serious reduction in value.

Rotate Products. Implement the **first-in, first-out (FIFO) inventory rotation method**. The products held in inventory the longest should be the first to be issued to production areas. When newly received products enter storage areas, they should be placed under or behind products already in storage. Marking the date of receipt on every item makes it possible to compare dates of products used in production with those of products in storage areas. Those products in production should have been received at an earlier date than those remaining in storage. This method helps management ensure that stock rotation practices are followed.

Properly Control the Environment. Maintain proper temperature, humidity, and ventilation. Use accurate thermometers and check them routinely. Unless otherwise indicated, proper temperatures are:

- 50° to 70° F (10° to 21° C) for dry storage.
- 40° F (4° C) or lower for refrigerated storage.
- 0° F (–18° C) or lower for frozen storage.

Require management's permission to discard spoiled products. This allows management to judge the effectiveness of their managing for quality procedures and assess the costs of failing to follow the proper storage procedures.

Implement Effective Food Safety Practices. Establish and follow regular cleaning schedules for all storage facilities (as opposed to cleaning only when time becomes available). This applies not only to storerooms and storage spaces, but also to walk-in and reach-in refrigerators and storage equipment. Facilities and equipment should be made of nonporous, easily cleaned materials. Shelving units should be louvered or slotted to permit air circulation. They should not be covered with aluminum foil or any other material that impedes airflow. (Sometimes production staff members cover shelving to reduce the need to clean it. This is an example of misguided decision-making: food safety concerns are more important than cost-reduction tactics.) Lower shelves, drainage racks, and similar storage equipment should be at least two inches from walls and at least six inches above the floor to permit mop and broom cleaning and to discourage rodent and insect infestation and nesting.

In following proper practices, it is important to use professional pest-control services. In light of harmful chemicals and poisons on the market, probably very few food service managers are qualified to plan and manage rodent and insect control programs. It is too dangerous for a well-intentioned but untrained person to spray and spread chemicals in food receiving, storing, production, and service areas.

Store Properly. Store products properly—in their original packaging and away from walls to allow for air circulation, for example. Store products that absorb odors, such as flour, away from products that give off odors, such as onions. Store opened products in clean, labeled, covered containers designed for food storage, rather than using empty glass jars (which can break) or empty #10 cans (which cannot be properly cleaned).

Generally, products should be stored in quantities that can be used within a reasonable time period. There are exceptions to this rule, such as investments in wines and volume purchases made as hedges against price increases. However, these decisions should be made by top management, not by purchasing staff. Beverage products are generally stored for less than one month. Food products classified as stores are usually used within an even shorter time period. Perishable products are purchased two or more times weekly.

Procedures Necessary for Effective Inventory Controls ——

Inventory control procedures play an important role in the economic security concerns of the control system. There are several other reasons for designing and implementing effective inventory recordkeeping systems:

- Financial accounting systems need inventory values to generate monthly statements. The value of products in inventory is considered part of the operation's current assets (for the balance sheet) and is also used to assess costs (for the income statement).

- Daily control procedures may require knowing the quantity of products currently available. For example, a food service manager may wish to keep a perpetual inventory record of selected expensive products to allow frequent and quick assessment of any differences between the quantity that should be in storage and how much is actually there.

- Inventory records help managers determine not only when to order new products, but also how much of each product to order.

Inventory Turnover

One important function of keeping accurate inventory records is to allow managers to assess how much money is being invested in nonproductive inventory. The value of goods in inventory is typically calculated on a monthly basis to provide information—such as cost of sales—for financial accounting systems. Nonproductive inventory refers to products in storage that are not issued to production areas during the time period (usually monthly) covered by financial records. To determine how much money is tied up in non-productive inventory, managers measure the inventory turnover rate. The inventory turnover rate shows the number of times in a given period that inventory is converted or turned into revenue. In financial terms, it measures the rate at which inventory is turned into food or beverage costs required to generate food or beverage revenue.

$$\text{Inventory Turnover Rate} \ = \ \frac{\text{Cost of Food in Dollars}}{(\text{Beginning Inventory} + \text{Ending Inventory}) \div 2}$$

Inventory turnover rates can be determined for food or beverage products in storage. The inventory turnover is calculated by dividing the cost of food (or beverages) used by the average food (or beverage) inventory (in dollars). The average inventory value is determined by adding the value of inventory at the beginning of the time period in question (usually a month) to the value of inventory at the end of that period and then dividing the sum by two.

Inventory Recordkeeping Systems

There are two basic kinds of recordkeeping systems for products in storage: physical inventory and perpetual inventory. A physical inventory system involves actual observation and counting of stored products on a periodic basis. A perpetual inventory system involves keeping a running balance of the quantity of stored products by recording all newly purchased products as they enter storage areas and all quantities issued from storage to production areas.

Physical Inventory System. A **physical inventory system** is used to periodically assess the value of food and beverage products in inventory. This is done at least monthly to develop information needed for the balance sheet and income statement. Inventory value is counted as a current asset, and inventory values, both at the beginning and end of the financial period, are a factor in assessing food and beverage costs (cost of sales).

Before a physical inventory of stored products can be taken, the food service manager must make several decisions about the design of the physical inventory system by answering such questions as:

1. Which products should be considered when making an inventory count? This decision is partially related to the question of which areas are to be considered storage areas under the control of the inventory system. For example, does inventory include products in broken-case and workstation storage areas? What about products in process, such as frozen poultry thawing in the refrigerator? What products are stores and included in inventory, and what products are directs and excluded from inventory?

2. How should monetary value be assigned to products in inventory? One method is to calculate the actual cost of stored products at the time inventory is recorded. Another method is to use the average costs of stored products over several inventory counts. Others include the **last-in, first-out (LIFO) inventory valuation system** and the **first-in, first-out (FIFO) inventory valuation system.** Under the LIFO system, the costs of the products most recently added to inventory (last in) are the costs assigned when products are issued (first out). This leads to cost of sales figures that more accurately reflect current replacement costs. In times of inflation, it also tends to create a smaller total inventory value. That is, since the most recent (and usually most expensive) costs are the first to be "issued," the remaining inventory is made up of the earlier (and usually lower) costs. Conversely, under the FIFO system, the oldest (and usually lowest) costs are "issued" first, leaving the more recent (and usually higher) costs remaining in inventory. This creates a higher total inventory value and a lower cost of sales. (Note, however, that seasonal price variations—for example, those that occur with fresh fruit—will sometimes cause recent purchases to cost less than earlier purchases.) Typically, an accountant helps determine the best inventory valuation system for the food service operation. This is because inventory values affect food costs that affect profitability and, therefore, tax obligations. (Do not confuse the FIFO and LIFO inventory valuation methods with the FIFO inventory rotation method. Inventory valuation deals with assigning costs; inventory rotation deals with the actual products removed from storage and issued. You should always issue the oldest products in the storage room first; the value that you assign to those products can vary based on the valuation method used.)

3. How should costs of such products as opened containers of spices in production areas and opened bottles of liquor at the bar be handled? Often, the cost of such opened, unused products is assumed to average out. In other words, their value is thought to remain approximately the same from month to month. So, once an estimated cost is established, it can be used monthly.

4. What are the procedures to be used in counting the products in inventory? Persons involved in managing storage areas should not take inventory counts alone. Perhaps the food inventory can be taken by the food manager (not the chef), while the beverage manager (not the bar manager) takes the beverage

Exhibit 12   Physical Inventory Form

Physical Inventory							
Type of Product: _____				Month _____		Month _____	
Product	**Unit**	**Amount in Storage**	**Purchase Price**	**Total Price**	**Amount in Storage**	**Purchase Price**	**Total Price**
Col. 1	Col. 2	Col. 3	Col. 4	Col. 5	Col. 6	Col. 7	Col. 8
Applesauce	6 #10	4 $\frac{1}{3}$	$15.85	$68.63			
Green Beans	6 #10	3 $\frac{5}{6}$	18.95	72.58			
Flour	25# bag	3	4.85	14.55			
Rice	50# bag	1	12.50	12.50			
				Total	$486.55		

Source: Ronald F. Cichy, *Food Safety: Managing the HACCP Process* (Lansing, Mich.: Educational Institute of the American Hotel & Lodging Association, 2004), p. 108.

inventory. In both situations, a representative from the accounting office can assist in conducting the physical inventory.

As stored products are observed and counted in a manual inventory system, a physical inventory form (Exhibit 12) can be used to record inventory information. When reviewing the form, note:

1. Products (column 1) can be listed in the same order as they are found in the storage area (or on the perpetual inventory form). Listing products in this sequence makes the task of locating products on the form easier when taking the inventory count. It also reduces the likelihood that products will be missed when inventory is taken.

2. The storage unit (column 2) is the basis on which products are purchased and costs are assessed. For example, in the inventory shown in Exhibit 12, applesauce is purchased and stored in cases containing six #10 cans each, while flour comes in 25-pound bags.

3. The amount in storage (column 3) is determined by actually counting the products in storage. With one technique, one person counts while a second person records the quantities on the inventory form. In another, two people can make independent counts and compare results before entering information on the inventory form.

4. Purchase price (column 4) is the cost per storage unit (column 2) of the product. Price information is easier to record if products are marked with their unit prices at the time they are received and stored.

5. Total price (column 5) is the total cost of the amount of each product in inventory. It is calculated by multiplying the number of stored products (column 3) by the purchase price per storage unit (column 4).

6. Columns 6 through 8 are used to repeat the above inventory valuation procedures for a second month.

7. The total food and beverage costs (recorded at the bottom of column 5) calculated by the physical inventory are used by accounting personnel to develop financial statements. They can also be used by food service managers to calculate inventory turnover rates.

8. A physical inventory indicates only how much of each product is in inventory and the actual value of all stored products. Two limitations of a physical inventory system are that it does not indicate how much of each product should be available and what the value of products in inventory should be. A perpetual inventory system compensates for these shortcomings.

Perpetual Inventory System. A **perpetual inventory system** keeps a running balance of the quantity of food and beverage products in inventory. It operates like a bank checking account. When more food or beverages are put in the storage area (the bank), the balance is increased. As products are removed (issued), the balance decreases. At any time, then, the amount of products that should be currently available is known.

Large operations with specialized storage and accounting personnel may use a perpetual inventory system for all, or almost all, products in storage. Small food and beverage operations may find it more practical to use perpetual inventory control only for expensive products and those purchased in large quantities.

A sample perpetual inventory form (which can be used with a manual system) is shown in Exhibit 13. Note the following when studying the form:

1. Information about each product under perpetual inventory control is recorded on a separate form/inventory card.

2. Each time a product enters inventory (column 2) or is removed from inventory (column 3), the balance in inventory (column 4) is adjusted.

3. Columns are repeated on the right so the form can be used for a longer time period.

4. The form does not have information about product cost. With this system, control is based on the number of units, not their cost. Costs can be assessed when taking physical inventories and recording on the form in Exhibit 12.

A physical count is still necessary with a perpetual inventory system to verify the accuracy of the inventory balances. When using a perpetual inventory system, someone other than the staff members who maintain the perpetual inventory records should perform the physical inventory used for verification.

Exhibit 13   Perpetual Inventory Form

Perpetual Inventory

Product Name: *P.D.Q. Shrimp*   Purchase Unit Size: *5 lb bag*

Date	In Carried Forward	Out 15	Balance	Date	In Carried Forward	Out	Balance
Col. 1	Col. 2	Col. 3	Col. 4	Col. 1	Col. 2	Col. 3	Col. 4
5/16		3	12				
5/17		3	9				
5/18	6		15				
5/19		2	13				

Source: Ronald F. Cichy, *Food Safety: Managing the HACCP Process* (Lansing, Mich.: Educational Institute of the American Hotel & Lodging Association, 2004), p. 107.

When the physical count of a product differs from the quantity indicated on the perpetual record, a control problem may exist, and management must determine the reason for the variance. Perhaps products are not being recorded at the time of receipt or issue, or perhaps theft is occurring. The purpose of control procedures is to take a systematic view when such problems surface. Management's task is to discover the cause of a problem and fix it at its root cause.

Technology and the Inventory Counting Process

Technology can also assist in the inventory valuation process through optical scanning. **Universal product code (UPC) information** on product packages can be scanned to quickly and accurately assess the quantity of unopened product packages in inventory. Scanning results can provide helpful information for verifying perpetual inventories and for determining cost-of-goods-sold data when actual food and beverage costs are calculated.

The use of **bar code technology** has been relatively slow to catch on in food service operations. In fact, bar code applications were available in the commercial marketplace for many years before systems were developed and adapted for use in the food service industry. Hand-held wireless bar code scanning equipment allows fast and accurate counting of products in inventory. Bar code information labels can be provided by distributors on incoming containers or they can be printed in-house for products lacking the distributor's labels. Information regarding quantity, unit cost, and total cost of products in inventory can be quickly assessed and transferred to inventory records. It is possible for multi-unit operators to receive inventory information on a by-unit basis by Internet connection. Chains and other food service operations with multiple outlets/kitchens/storerooms can optically scan specific inventories; information can then be summarized for all outlets.

Even though bar code technology has numerous advantages over the handwritten entry of inventory data, it is still not fully automatic; the products to be counted must still be manually scanned. Another technology, **radio frequency identification** (RFID), may be used more frequently in the future to fully automate inventory recordkeeping. RFID technology uses transponder tags to wirelessly transmit electronic product codes (EPCs) to other devices using radio frequency waves. The tags are attached to shipping containers and identify the contents. EPC "readers" communicate with the tag through the use of radio frequencies.

A key difference between RFID and bar code technology is that RFID eliminates the need for the line-of-sight reading on which bar coding depends. Moreover, RFID scanning can be done at greater distances (up to 90 feet, as opposed to just a few inches with a bar code reader).

RFID readers can be placed in storage shelves or racks, and each time an item is removed from the shelf and whenever the level of product inventory falls below a predetermined point, a notice is sent to the automated inventory tracking system. The system also detects products stored at an incorrect location.

As recommended earlier, physical inventory counts are typically taken monthly. Some food service operations with limited menus, such as quick-service restaurants, may take physical counts more often (even daily) when there are unusual variances between ideal and actual costs. The physical inventory tells how much (number of products and dollar value) of each item is on hand. However, how much should be available, based on actual sales during the period?

Automated systems can tally the total number of all menu products sold during the period under analysis and "extend" the quantities of ingredients specified in standard recipes for that quantity of sales. For example, assume a restaurant offers two products containing ground beef: hamburger on a bun and meatloaf platter. Assume also that 375 hamburgers and 125 meatloaf platters were sold during the time period of analysis. If the standard recipes for hamburgers and meatloaf require 4 ounces and 6 ounces of ground beef, respectively, 140.6 pounds of ground beef should have been used to produce these two products in the quantities sold (375 hamburgers × 4 oz = 1,500 oz; 125 meatloaf platters × 6 oz = 750 oz; 1,500 oz + 750 oz = 2,250 oz; 2,250 ÷ 16 oz /lb = 140.6 lbs). Similarly, a system can track and extend all ingredients from the sales of all other products. A report indicating the ideal inventory usage can be generated (see Exhibit 14).

By contrast, Exhibit 15 shows an actual inventory usage report that indicates the actual quantity of inventory products that has been used (as noted in the exhibit, usage is based on the quantity in inventory at the beginning of the period, plus purchases, plus or minus adjustments, and minus ending inventory quantities). Any difference between ideal and actual usage represents a potential control problem (why and where are excess products being used?) and represents lost profits to the food service operation.

Managers can use automated inventory management systems to learn where inventory shrinkage is occurring. They can review control procedures to determine

Exhibit 14   Ideal Inventory Usage Report

Ideal Inventory Usage Report						
Date: 8/21/2002	This details how much inventory you SHOULD have used. This					Page: 1
Time: 4:10 PM	includes any Sales Mix depletions and Requisitions.					
From 1/1/2002 to 12/31/2002						
Details: Yes						Total Sales: $2651.65

	Item		Ideal Usage		% of	Food
Item Name	Unit	$	Unit	$	Group	Cost %
DAIRY						
Cheese\Swiss	LB	2.96	6.1	18.00	2.7	0.7
Ice Cream/Sherbert	TUB	12.78	1.7	21.36	3.2	0.8
Oleo Blend Margarine	LB	1.08	2.4	2.57	0.4	0.1
Whipped Topping	5 GAL	38.95	0.3	9.98	1.5	0.4
** Total for DAIRY			10.4	51.90	7.7	2.0
GROCERY						
Almonds, Diced	CASE	92.58	0.0	2.47	0.4	0.1
BBQ Sauce - Bull's Eye	CASE	49.97	0.3	12.49	1.9	0.5
Bread-Burger Bun 4 1/2 s.s	PACKAG	1.39	8.0	11.12	1.7	0.4
Bread-Rye Bread	LOAF	2.30	5.6	12.95	1.9	0.5
Bread-White Bread 5x5	LOAF	1.91	16.5	31.43	4.7	1.2
Chocolate Syrup	CASE	42.09	0.1	2.66	0.4	0.1
French Fries	CASE	18.67	4.7	87.90	13.1	3.3
Ketchup-Heinz	CASE	27.98	2.0	56.46	8.4	2.1
Liquid Fry Shortening	CASE	15.40	0.9	13.98	2.1	0.5
Maraschino Cherries	CASE	50.40	0.4	21.52	3.2	0.8
Mayonnaise\Bulk	BOX	16.58	0.1	1.79	0.3	0.1
Onions - Sliced	LB	1.18	4.8	5.61	0.8	0.2
Ortega Peppers	CASE	30.21	0.5	14.72	2.2	0.6
Pickle Spears	TUB	29.40	0.6	16.96	2.5	0.6

Source: Jack D. Ninemeier, *Planning and Control for Food and Beverage Operations,* 6th ed. (Lansing, Mich.: Educational Institute of the American Hotel & Lodging Association, 2004), p. 236. (Courtesy of Cost-Guard Foodservice Software, Bronxville, New York)

where, if at all, corrective actions can be implemented. As this occurs, they can reduce variances between actual and ideal inventories and, in the process, better control costs, thus adding value.

Integrating Ordering, Receiving, Invoice Payment, and Inventory Procedures

Integration of ordering, receiving, invoice payment, and inventory procedures is sometimes referred to as a centralized accounting approach. The process begins by creating inventory, listing pack sizes and units, based on the menus and national purchasing agreements in chains.

Next inventory is divided into segments, which are used for bid sheets, as well as purchasing guides. The segments include:

- Chemicals.

- Dairy products.

Exhibit 15   Actual Inventory Usage Report

Date: 8/21/2002
Time: 3:30 PM
From 1/1/2002 to 12/01/2002 (# of days: 365)
Sort by: Group
Details: Yes

Actual Inventory Usage Report
Your Company Name Here
Unit: SALVP

Page: 1

Total Sales: $26,511.85

Item Name	Item Unit	$	Opening Unit	$	Purchases/Builds Unit	$	Adjustments Unit	$	Closing Unit	$	Last Counted	Usage Unit	$	% of Gross	Food Cost %
DAIRY															
Cheese/Swiss	LB	2.96	12.0	35.52	0.0	0.00	0.0	0.00	5.0	14.80	01/21	7.0	20.72	2.1	0.8
Ice Cream/Sherbet	TUB	12.78	3.0	41.85	2.0	25.56	0.0	0.00	0.0	0.00	01/21	5.0	67.41	6.9	2.5
Oleo Blend Margarine	LB	1.08	45.0	48.60	25.0	27.00	0.0	0.00	0.0	0.00	01/21	70.0	75.60	7.7	2.9
Whipped Topping	5 GAL	38.95	3.0	116.85	3.0	116.85	0.0	0.00	0.0	0.00	01/21	6.0	233.70	23.9	8.8
** Total for DAIRY			63.0	242.82	30.0	189.41	0.0	0.00	5.0	14.80		89.0	397.43	40.7	15.0
GROCERY															
Almonds, Diced	CASE	92.59	0.5	46.29	1.0	92.59	0.0	0.00	1.0	115.72	01/21	0.3	23.15	2.4	0.9
BBQ Sauce - Bull's Eye	CASE	49.97									1/21	0.5	24.98	2.6	0.9
Bread-Burger Bun 4 1/2 s.s	PACKAGE	1.39									1/21	18.0	25.02	2.6	0.9
Bread-Rye Bread	LOAF	2.30									1/21	7.0	16.10	1.6	0.6
Bread-White Bread 5x5	LOAF	1.91									1/21	7.0	13.37	1.4	0.5
Chocolate Syrup	CASE	42.09									1/21	0.2	7.02	0.7	0.3
French Fries	CASE	18.67									1/21	7.0	128.69	13.0	4.8
Ketchup-Heinz	CASE	27.99									1/21	1.6	41.91	4.3	1.6
Liquid Fry Shortening	CASE	15.40									1/21	1.8	27.72	2.8	1.0
Maraschino Cherries	CASE	30.40									1/21	0.1	7.17	0.7	0.3
Mayonnaise/Bulk	BOX	18.59									1/21	1.1	19.11	2.0	0.7
Ortega Peppers	CASE	30.21									1/21	0.5	15.55	1.6	0.6
Pickle Spears	TUB	29.40									1/21	-5.5	-161.70	-16.5	-6.1
Pineapple Topping	CASE	35.55	0.8	29.63	1.0	35.55	0.0	0.00	1.5	53.32	01/21	0.3	11.85	1.2	0.4
Strawberry Topping	CASE	42.95	0.8	30.72	1.0	42.95	0.0	0.00	0.8	35.79	01/21	1.0	40.89	4.2	1.5
** Total for GROCERY			108.9	709.74	94.0	767.89	0.0	0.00	180.1	1,289.51		40.8	208.92	24.4	9.0
MEAT															
Breaded Chicken	CASE	32.50	3.0	97.50	2.0	65.00	0.0	0.00	0.2	6.50	01/21	4.8	156.00	16.0	5.9
Ham	LB	1.66	26.0	43.16	25.0	41.50	0.0	0.00	52.0	86.32	01/21	-1.0	-1.66	-0.2	-0.1
Roast Pork	LB	3.11	17.0	52.87	25.0	77.75	0.0	0.00	58.0	180.38	01/21	-16.0	-49.76	-5.1	-1.9
** Total for MEAT			46.0	190.53	52.0	184.25	0.0	0.00	110.2	273.20		-12.2	104.58	10.7	3.9
PRODUCE															

> **Actual Inventory Usage Report**
>
> This report provides your ACTUAL cost of goods for any period of time. It's calculated by taking opening inventory + purchases +/– adjustments – closing inventory.
>
> These are many sorting options; in this case, we sorted by group.
>
> Note: we included the entire report on this screen, so it looks very small.

Source: Jack D. Ninemeier, *Planning and Control for Food and Beverage Operations,* 6th ed. (Lansing, Mich.: Educational Institute of the American Hotel & Lodging Association, 2004), p. 237. (Courtesy of Cost-Guard Foodservice Software, Bronxville, New York)

- Dry goods.
- Meats.
- Paper products.
- Poultry products.
- Produce products.
- Seafood.

On a designated day, inventory is assessed compared to par levels. This information is combined with forecasted business levels and the order is placed.

Once food is delivered, the operation should do a detailed receiving check. The invoice is stamped with a purchase stamp, recorded on the receiving log, and then forwarded for approval. The invoice must ultimately be approved for payment by the general manager of the food service operation.

Another method to integrate these processes is the checkbook accounting method. Checkbook accounting follows the idea that "if you want to spend it, you have to have the money." The checkbook is completed with the following:

- Distributors' names
- Invoice number (completed when the actual invoice is received)

- Date received (completed when received)
- Total amount you want to spend
- Balance remaining in the account

The checkbook accounting method may be ideal for smaller operations with fewer staff members.

Endnotes

1. Much of this chapter was adapted from Ronald F. Cichy, *Food Safety: Managing the HACCP Process* (Lansing, Mich.: Educational Institute of the American Hotel & Lodging Association, 2005) and Jack D. Ninemeier, *Planning and Control for Food and Beverage Operations,* 6th ed. (Lansing, Mich.: Educational Institute of the American Hotel & Lodging Association, 2004).

Key Terms

ABCD inventory classification system—A technique for grouping inventory items on a relative basis according to perishability and cost per serving, with Class A items being high in both perishability and cost per serving; Class B items being relatively high in cost, but low in perishability; Class C items being relatively low in cost per serving, but relatively high in perishability; and Class D items having both the lowest perishability and the lowest cost per serving.

audit trail—A series of records, documents, and reports that traces the flow of resources through an operation.

bar code technology—Use of hand-held wireless bar-code scanning equipment to allow fast and accurate counting of products in inventory.

credit memo—A form issued by a distributor to adjust a food service operation's account. It is issued in response to a request-for-credit memo when products are spoiled, do not meet the operation's specifications, or are delivered in wrong quantities.

daily receiving report—A record of everything a food service operation receives; shows what was received, the date of delivery, the name of the distributor, the quanity, the price, and any other relevant comments.

delivery invoice—A distributor's statement detailing all the products being delivered to a food service operation.

first-in, first-out (FIFO) inventory rotation method—Products held in inventory the longest are the first to be issued to production areas; when newly received products enter storage areas, they are placed under or behind products already in storage.

first-in, first-out (FIFO) inventory valuation system—The earliest inventory costs incurred are assigned when products are issued.

invoice extensions—The product of an item's price and the quantity received.

last-in, first-out (LIFO) inventory valuation system—The most recent inventory costs incurred are assigned when products are issued.

perpetual inventory system—A running balance of the quantity of stored products kept by recording all newly purchased items as they enter storage areas and all quantities issued from storage to production areas.

physical inventory system—The practice of physically counting stored products on a periodic basis.

purchase order—A form that contains the details of an order placed with a distributor and helps maintain purchasing control. This form is completed by the operation's buyer and sent to the distributor.

purchase record—A piece of documentation that provides a small food and beverage operation with an in-house, detailed record of the specifics of all incoming shipments. It performs the same functions as a purchase order.

purchase requisition—A document that indicates what products are required, when to order them, and how much of each item is needed to maintain par levels.

radio frequency identification—Technology that uses transponder tags to wirelessly transmit electronic product codes (EPCs) to other devices using radio frequency waves.

request-for-credit memo—A form issued by a food service operation to initiate processing of a credit memo when products are spoiled, do not meet the operation's specifications, or are delivered in wrong quantities.

requisition—A form for requesting inventory; an internal communication tool that shows which department needs which items. Required before products can be issued.

slacked out—Items that have been thawed out and packed in ice, but are sold as fresh.

universal product code (UPC) information—Information on product packages that can be scanned to quickly and accurately assess the quantity of unopened product packages in inventory.

⟨?⟩ Review Questions

1. What are the main components of the audit trail and how are they used?

2. How is a purchase requisition utilized in the control process?

3. Why is a purchase order used to provide documentation?

4. What is the typical billing process in a food service operation?

5. What is the function of a credit memo?

6. What are the requirements for selecting and training receiving staff members?

7. How are receiving procedures utilized to maintain control?

8. What are the security concerns during receiving?

9. How are storing procedures utilized to maintain control?

10. How is the first-in, first-out (FIFO) inventory rotation method used?

11. What is the formula used to calculate inventory turnover and why is it important?

12. How do the physical inventory system and the perpetual inventory system differ?

References

Cichy, Ronald F. *Food Safety: Managing the HACCP Process*. Lansing, Mich.: Educational Institute of the American Hotel & Lodging Association, 2005.

Lauer, Elizabeth. "Inventory Control: How Much Is Your Menu Costing?" *Hospitality Upgrade* (March 24, 2000).

Ninemeier, Jack D. *Management of Food and Beverage Operations,* 4th Ed. Lansing, Mich.: Educational Institute of the American Hotel & Lodging Association, 2005.

Ninemeier, Jack D. *Planning and Control for Food and Beverage Operations*, 6th Ed. Lansing, Mich.: Educational Institute of the American Hotel & Lodging Association, 2004.

Internet Sites

For more information, visit the following Internet sites. Remember that Internet addresses can change without notice. If the site is no longer there, you can use a search engine to look for additional sites.

eRestaurant Services
www.erestaurantservices.com

Food Connex Integrated Management Solutions
www.foodconnex.com

Food Safety Resource Center
www.foodservice.com/food_safety

Foodservice Report
www.foodservicereport.com

Receiving and Storing Food in the Restaurant
www.allfoodbusiness.com/Safe_Food_Storage.php

What is LIFO and FIFO?
www.wisegeek.com/what-is-lifo-and-fifo.htm

Chapter 7 Outline

Food Safety and Nutrition
    Labeling
    Nutrition
Law of Agency
Sales Law
Antitrust Laws
    Major Antitrust Statutes
Purchasing Contracts
    Request for Information and Request
       for Proposal Components
    Contract Elements
    Warranties
    Remedies for Contract Breach
    Conflicts of Interest
    Group Purchasing Contracts
    Cancellation Clauses

Competencies

1. Explain the federal, state, and local food laws applicable to purchasing. (pp. 257–266)

2. Identify the requirements of purchasing contracts. (pp. 267–274)

7

Legal Issues in Purchasing

LEGAL REQUIREMENTS IMPACT FOOD SERVICE OPERATORS and distributors just as ethical requirements do. Those responsible for purchasing in food service operations need not become legal experts; however, it is useful to have some general knowledge of the law in order to recognize and avoid some of the legal problems that operators may encounter.

Laws vary from state to state, and sometimes within states and local jurisdictions. Therefore, it is difficult to generalize applicable laws for all locations and operations. It is always extremely important to obtain applicable information and counsel from a licensed attorney as specific legal problems are encountered.

Food Safety and Nutrition

It is essential to view a food service operation as a system of interrelated activities that can positively or negatively affect food safety for internal customers and external customers, as well as the financial well being of owners and investors in the operation.

While a food service operation is viewed as a system of control points starting with menu planning and followed by purchasing, receiving, and storing, the distributor also plays a vital role in food safety. It is critical to view the entire food distribution chain—from the source, to the manufacturer, to the distributor, to the operator—when ensuring food safety. Often, state and local laws pertaining to food safety govern acceptable practices and policies.

Labeling

Food labeling is more important than it has been in the past because customers are more sophisticated and aware of food ingredients. These customers are more likely to check labels for the presence of trans fats, high fructose corn syrup, sodium, calories, and other information. While it is unlikely that a particular customer will ask to see what label came with which food product, it is essential for the personnel responsible for food purchasing to be able to understand what is contained on a food product's label and inform production and service staff so they can pass accurate information on to customers.

How to Read a Label. The best source of information about reading a label is the food product's manufacturer. Most manufacturers have readily available food product labels that detail nutritional information (i.e., vitamins and minerals, carbohydrates, proteins, fats, and other ingredients contained in their food products).

The distributor can assist by providing additional information, connecting the operator with the manufacturer's representative, and/or connecting the operator with the manufacturer directly. These same resources can be used to train those responsible for purchasing in the food service operation to intelligently read and interpret label information.

Food Allergens. The United States Food and Drug Administration (FDA) is also aware of the increased interest in potential **food allergens** in products. Allergy sufferers must avoid certain foods (e.g., peanuts, wheat) that could result in an allergic reaction. The FDA is pushing for foods with possible allergens to be labeled so that they are easily understood by all consumers. Non-technical, easily understood terms are essential for those suffering from food allergies.

Other steps being taken are the addition of the statement "may contain…" on food products that may have possible allergens added during processing. For example, the statement "may contain wheat" may be added to food products that could have been inadvertently in contact with wheat during processing. Some manufacturers are voluntarily putting these advisory statements on their food product labels. Some ingredients are currently not covered by food labeling laws (e.g., colors, flavors, spices), while progressive manufacturers are adding these to food product labels.

Country of Origin. U.S. legislators have pushed to add **country of origin labeling** for meat products sold in the United States. The voluntary labeling will highlight meat products that originated in the United States. In general, the labeling is widely supported by U.S. livestock producers. Other groups are pushing for voluntary country of origin labeling for fresh produce and seafood products as well.

Organic Food. The term "organic" may have different meanings, depending on context. Today's usage of the term "organic" usually means the food product was produced or grown naturally, free from pesticides, growth hormones, and other chemicals that some customers believe to be harmful or do not want in the foods they consume.

Organic foods include plants and animals that are grown and processed on organic farms. What differentiates organic farms is that they do not use chemicals, such as herbicides or pesticides, or antibiotics, hormones, and unnatural fertilizers. Crop rotation, cultivation practices, and natural pest control and cycles are critically important to organic farmers. When processed foods are identified as organic, it means they have no (or a very limited amount of) artificial ingredients and preservatives. There are an estimated 10,000 certified organic farms across the United States, and organic farming is one of the fastest-growing segments of agriculture.

Organic products tend to be more expensive than other similar foods since they are only a small part (estimated to represent only about 1 percent of total sales) of the U.S. food industry. Nevertheless, organic products are growing in popularity in some food service segments (i.e., college and university food service).

Perhaps a new federal labeling law for organic foods will encourage more manufacturers to develop these food products and make them more readily available. The labeling change would help differentiate organic product choices and, therefore, provide a marketing advantage to these products. More customers are demanding more organic products because they perceive these products to be fresher and natural, premium healthy choices, and a safer alternative to mainstream food products due to recent food safety problems. The more affluent older customers and those who live a physically fit lifestyle, as well as those on college and university campuses, seem to be obsessed with consuming more organic foods.

Prior to the federal law, most organic foods were certified by state and private agencies. The labeling law may make organic food products more readily available through main-line distributors. In the meantime, some food service operators have initiated "farm-to-fork" programs that link operators with local farmers who produce and grow organic products. These farmers are typically small businesses who welcome a predictable and dependable market for their food products.

Nutrition

Food service customers are increasingly making lifestyle choices and changes that contribute to healthier living. Food service operators are selling less alcohol today than a decade ago. More guests are choosing smaller portion sizes and demanding foods that are low in fat, sodium, cholesterol, and sugar than in years past. Vegetarian menu items are appealing to a growing number of those who consume meals away from home. Nutrition and health issues are not fads, but trends that are expected to grow in importance with the aging of the population.

Nutrition Basics. An understanding of the fundamentals of nutrition is a foundation for exceeding guests' expectations. Food consists of nutrients as its building blocks. The kinds and qualities of nutrients, along with their order and arrangement, determine the characteristics of a food product.

Much of the nutrient content of the raw materials used in food service kitchens is determined by the genetic makeup of the plant or animal. Nutrient quality is also influenced by the kind of fertilizer or feed used. Once the food is harvested, however, its nutrient profile changes. Some changes are out of an operation's control; others can, to some extent, be managed. For example, the food service operation controls:

- How foods are received and how rapidly they are stored.

- Storage conditions, including light, temperature, time, and relative humidity.

- Handling conditions—whether the product is thawed, frozen, or canned.

- How the food is prepared, cooked, held, and served.

The operation's objective should be to avoid losing more nutrients than necessary. The six nutrient classes are:

- Proteins.

- Carbohydrates.

- Lipids (fats and oils).

- Vitamins.

- Minerals.

- Water.

The three nutrients that provide energy to the human body are proteins, carbohydrates, and lipids. Weight for weight, proteins and carbohydrates have equal energy values (4 kilocalories per gram), while lipids have over twice as much energy (9 kilocalories per gram).

Proteins are large molecules that consist of amino acids linked together chemically. Proteins play several critical roles. They function as enzymes to speed up the rate of chemical reactions in the body, are used for transportation and storage of other components of the body, help produce antibodies that recognize and control foreign substances such as viruses and bacteria, generate and transmit nerve impulses in the body, and can be used as a source of energy. The recommended daily intake of protein varies based on a person's age and activity level. Important sources of protein include meat, poultry, fish, seafood, milk and milk products, legumes (e.g., dried beans and peas), soybeans, and nuts. The quantity and quality of protein found in each of these foods will vary, based on the amounts and kinds of amino acids present in the foods.

Carbohydrates are classified into three broad categories: monosaccharides, disaccharides, and polysaccharides. Both monosaccharides and disaccharides are known as sugars.

Monosaccharides are the simplest of the three carbohydrates and include glucose, fructose, and galactose. Glucose is the primary source of energy within the human body. It is found in some fruits and vegetables (e.g., grapes, young peas, and carrots). Fructose, the sweetest of all sugars, is present with glucose in many fruits; it also is found in honey and corn, and is used as a sweetener in many processed foods. Galactose is normally only found linked to glucose.

When two monosaccharides bond together, they form a disaccharide. Disaccharides include sucrose, lactose, and maltose. Sucrose is common sugar, and it also gives fruits their characteristic sweet taste. Lactose is the only carbohydrate found in milk. Maltose is produced in malted grains and is important in the production of alcoholic beverages.

Polysaccharides are the most complex carbohydrates. They include starches, cellulose, glycogen, pectin, agar, and alginate. These carbohydrates are useful in cooking, can improve the "mouth feel" of certain foods, and help the digestive process. A healthy diet emphasizes complex carbohydrates in foods that are high in fiber (e.g., vegetables, fruits, and whole grains), rather than sugary foods.

Fats and oils are collectively known as **lipids**, and are made up of fatty acids and glycerol. Although we group them together, there are differences between fats and oils. Fats are usually found in animal products, while oils are usually extracted from vegetable sources. Fats are solid at room temperature and contain a large amount of saturated fatty acids. Oils, on the other hand, are liquid at room temperature and contain more unsaturated fatty acids.

Fats or oils and water generally do not mix. However, when a substance known as an emulsifying agent is added, the mixture stabilizes and does not separate, because an emulsion is created. Milk and ice cream are examples of fat-in-water emulsions, butter is an example of a water-in-fat emulsion, and margarine is a water-in-oil emulsion. Some other important food emulsions include mayonnaise, hollandaise sauce, cream soups, and some salad dressings. Some of these foods contain egg yolks, which are natural emulsifiers.

Nearly all meats contain fat. Food service personnel can reduce the amount by trimming away all of the visible fat, but the resulting meat may be far from fat free. There can remain a considerable amount of fat within the tissue of the meat, a characteristic known as "marbling." The one common food of animal origin that can be made virtually fat free is milk; skim milk has less than 1.6 percent fat, allowing it to qualify for "fat-free" labeling.

There are a number of sources of fat in the diet. The fat content of meat can vary from animal to animal and from one part of the animal to another. Some fish, particularly salmon and trout, are relatively high in fat compared to other fish. Butter can contain as much as 80 percent fat, while margarine may have just as much oil. Unless they are specially produced, milk and milk products—including yogurt, sour cream, and cheese—contain fat. Fat typically plays an important role in the preparation of pastries and breads.

Most foods of plant origin, such as grains, fruits, and vegetables, are low in fat when harvested. (One notable exception is the avocado, which contains a high percentage of fat.) For example, only one-thousandth of the weight of a potato is fat. But when a potato is prepared by frying or by adding sour cream, butter, margarine, and/or cheese, the fat content can easily be one hundred times the original. Potatoes are not high-fat foods, but extra ingredients can add considerable calories and fat.

The average adult American is in little danger of consuming too little fat. In fact, the situation is just the opposite. One estimate states that adult Americans consume, on average, 40 percent of their total energy needs in the form of fats and oils.

Vitamins are required by the body to maintain health. These essential nutrients are found in foods in very small amounts, but their importance is great. Vitamins help speed the release of energy from proteins, carbohydrates, and lipids. (By themselves, vitamins cannot be used by the body for energy.)

The vitamin content of food changes as it is harvested, processed, shipped, stored, prepared, cooked, and held for service. For example, when wheat is refined into flour, many of the B vitamins present in the original bran are lost. In addition, heat, light, and oxygen can have devastating effects on the vitamin content of food. Water-soluble vitamins are lost when food is soaked or cooked in excessive amounts of water for long periods of time.

Minerals are inorganic and critically important to human nutrition. For nutrition purposes, minerals are chemical elements other than carbon, oxygen, hydrogen, and nitrogen. Minerals are lost from food when they dissolve in the water used to soak or cook food products. However, they are generally much more stable than vitamins when exposed to heat, light, or oxygen. Minerals important to the human body include calcium, iron, sodium, chlorine, potassium, phosphorus, iodine, and magnesium.

Water is essential to life, and all living organisms contain it. It is the vehicle in which chemical reactions take place. It also transports nutrients to cells and carries waste products away from cells and out of the body.

Water is available from three sources: liquids, solid foods, and internally through oxidation. (Oxidation forms water inside cells as a byproduct of chemical reactions.) Soda, beer, and fruit juices contain a high percentage of water. Fruits and vegetables are largely water; melons are as much as 94 percent water, while cabbage contains roughly 90 percent water.

Dietary Guidelines and Labeling Laws. A healthy diet can be sustained by following these **dietary guidelines**:

- Eat a variety of foods.

- Choose foods low in fat and cholesterol.

- Include foods with adequate starch and fiber.

- Limit high-sugar foods.

- Avoid foods high in sodium.

- Limit processed and refined foods.

- Consume alcoholic beverages in moderation.

For more than a decade, labeling laws focused on the fat content of foods. The FDA is shifting the focus to reporting and emphasizing calories on food labels, since consuming excessive calories contributes to obesity. Under review is a shift in the "Nutrition Facts" information on product labels to spotlight calories in the food as a Percent Daily Value.

Debate continues to escalate over which foods are "good" for you and which foods are "bad." Whether the subject is fat, calories, antioxidants, vegetarian or vegan diets, or various ethnic cuisines, mountains of conflicting data usually do little more than confuse the public. When in doubt regarding the soundness of nutrition advice, it may be best to consult a registered dietitian.

Law of Agency

Sometimes, especially in smaller food service operations, the owner is the purchaser. As the size of the operation increases, someone else usually assumes the purchasing responsibilities, thus representing the owner. Frequently, in larger operations, an owner hires a manager who then employs a purchaser. According to the **law of agency,** however, the buyer may be acting on behalf of the owner—not the manager. In the role of agent, the purchaser may have the power to obligate the operation within the limits of the discretion that has been delegated.

The law generally recognizes that a purchaser may act as agent for the food service operation and has the authority to legally obligate it. This is the case when the purchaser is formally told to represent the operation and/or has been permitted to act as if performance is on the operation's behalf.

By contrast, a sales representative, whose job it is to generate business, may in fact not be able to establish prices and make "binding" agreements beyond broad parameters established by the distributor. An important principle of negotiation requires that one negotiate with a person in appropriate authority. Therefore, the purchaser must typically negotiate with the sales manager, not with a sales representative.

In serving as an agent for the owner, a purchaser may often perform the following duties:

- Represent the best interest of the operation.

- Keep secret information confidential.

- Follow instructions that are within the law.

- Keep within the limits of expressed or implied authority.

- Act ethically.

A purchaser may obligate the operation by his or her decisions and commitments. In other instances, it may be the purchasers themselves who are liable; this is the case, for example, when a purchaser (1) contracts without the proper authority to do so, (2) agrees to be personally responsible, (3) receives money that is due to the operation, and (4) receives money that is due to the distributor.

Sales Law

Sales law is addressed in the Uniform Commercial Code. One specific area of sales law that buyers should understand is transportation and title. The place of delivery and method of shipment should be specified in the contract. (Contract law will be discussed later in this chapter.) In the absence of an agreement otherwise, the place of delivery generally is the seller's place of business. Selection of the transportation mode and selection of carrier influence when title passes and are, therefore, extremely important.

"FOB" (free on board) and **"CIF" (cash, insurance, freight)** are terms that indicate when title passes and when responsibility is assumed for the shipment. For example, "FOB Shipping Point" means that the buyer assumes title when the seller puts goods in the hands of a carrier. "FOB Destination" means that the buyer assumes title when the goods are delivered to the buyer's specified delivery point in the specified condition.

These occurrences can be altered by specific contract agreements. For example, the buyer can agree to an FOB shipping point price, but specify in the contract that it is the seller's responsibility to have the goods delivered at a specified time and in a specified condition. If this is a condition of the contract, the seller is responsible to file any necessary claims against the carrier.

The law of agency has an impact upon transportation responsibility. Assume that the goods are contracted FOB destination and that the buyer reserves the right to select the carrier. If the buyer then asks the seller to "ship the best way," the buyer has asked the seller to act as his or her agent. Under certain conditions, title then can pass FOB the seller's dock. The best solution is to have the terms spelled out in the contract and to perform under those terms.

CIF means that the buyer assumes title when the goods reach the buyer's dock. This is the common procedure for import/export shipments. Where these shipments require customs clearance or FDA inspection, the buyer normally takes title upon the completion of those procedures. Depending on the contract, the buyer can specify that the goods clear dock procedures and be placed into a bonded warehouse where title will pass.

The preceding factors affect title considerations. This is important since responsibility for theft, damage, loss, and spoilage usually rests with the party who has title at the time that loss occurs.

Antitrust Laws

No food service operator can afford to be unaware of federal and state **antitrust laws.** Their reach is too broad, their enforcement is too strict, and their penalties are too severe to be ignored. Moreover, a food service operator can violate the antitrust laws and be subject to their penalties without meaning to do so.[1]

The general aim of antitrust laws is simple: the regulation of business conduct to preserve competition and to prevent economic coercion. Antitrust laws are primarily concerned with limiting collusive conduct between competitors ("horizontal" agreements) and with regulating certain forms of activity between businesses that do not compete but are in a vertical relationship (a food service operator and its customers or distributors, for example).

Antitrust laws are based upon the simple assumption that vigorous but fair competition results in the most efficient allocation of economic resources and the best terms of sale to consumers.

Major Antitrust Statutes

Three major statutes comprise the bulk of federal antitrust laws: the **Sherman Act** of 1890, the **Clayton Act** of 1914 and its amendments, and the **Federal Trade Commission Act** of 1914. The statutory framework of the antitrust laws is broad. In addition, many states have enacted their own antitrust laws governing activities conducted exclusively within the state and not in "interstate or foreign commerce." ("Interstate commerce" refers to business activity that moves between two or more states.) Some state statutes, in fact, expand the scope of prohibited activity beyond that of the federal antitrust laws on conduct occurring within the state. Furthermore, each state has its own case law interpreting its own antitrust statutes.

Sherman Act. Section 1 of the Sherman Act is the cornerstone of our antitrust laws. It states in pertinent part:

> Every contract, combination in the form of trust or otherwise, or conspiracy, in restraint of trade or commerce among the several States, or with foreign nations, is declared to be illegal.

According to the United States Supreme Court, this broad statutory mandate prohibits every contract, combination, or conspiracy that constitutes an *unreasonable* restraint of trade. The courts have interpreted the word "contract" broadly to mean any form of understanding. A duly executed, written agreement is not required. A wink, a nod, or even silence in response to statements by others may be enough for a jury to infer that an agreement in violation of antitrust laws has been reached.

In determining what restraints of trade are unreasonable, the courts apply two general rules: the **per se rule** and the **rule of reason.** Some types of restraints are deemed to be inherently anticompetitive and are automatically presumed to be unreasonable. Such restraints are called per se violations of antitrust laws and are absolutely forbidden regardless of alleged justifications for, or the competitive benefits from, a particular activity. The term per se is derived from the Latin meaning "by itself" and denotes that proof of the alleged conduct alone proves the violation—no defense of the reasonableness or propriety of the conduct under the circumstances will be considered by the courts in determining whether a violation of law has occurred. Among the business practices that the courts have held to be per se violations of Section 1 of the Sherman Act are:

1. Horizontal or vertical agreements fixing or tampering with prices (for example, two or more food service operators agreeing on the prices they will charge their customers).

2. Horizontal agreements allocating geographic areas, customers, or products or services (for example, two food service operators agreeing as to which conventions each operator will bid upon while the other refrains from bidding).

3. Horizontal or vertical agreements boycotting third parties (for example, the members of a food service association agreeing that they will establish unreasonable terms for any future memberships to block some of their competitors from joining and thereby prevent them from gaining the competitive benefits of association membership services).

4. In certain circumstances, conditioning the purchase of one product or service on the purchase of another product or service (for example, a food service operator telling a customer that he or she cannot rent the grand meeting room unless he or she uses the operator's florist to decorate it).

If a particular activity is not classified as illegal per se, then the second standard, a so-called rule of reason standard, is applied to determine whether the activity violates Section 1 of the Sherman Act. Under this standard, proof that the party engaged in a particular activity is not itself proof of an antitrust violation. Rather, the court examines the various facts and circumstances surrounding the party's actions and decides whether the party intended to restrain trade unreasonably or whether, regardless of its intent, the conduct had the effect of unreasonably restraining trade.

An agreement not to compete following the sale of a business is an example of the types of business arrangements commonly judged by the rule of reason standard. However, any agreement with a competitor or customer that affects the production, distribution, or sale of a product or service and is not governed by the per se standard is potentially subject to examination under the rule of reason standard.

In summary, agreements with competitors to fix or tamper with prices or other terms of sale, or to allocate territories or customers, or to refuse to deal with specific parties are unlawful. Other agreements among two or more food service operators that affect the furnishing or sale of a service may be found unlawful, depending on the circumstances. Therefore, before any action is taken to enter into or to implement such agreements, a plan should first be submitted for analysis by legal counsel.

Clayton Act. The Clayton Act has been amended several times. These amendments include the Robinson-Patman Act of 1936 and the Celler-Kefauver Amendment of 1950. The Clayton Act more precisely describes certain types of prohibited business activity than does the Sherman Act. However, it is still necessary to examine the case law to determine whether certain conduct falls within the Clayton Act's statutory proscriptions.

Federal Trade Commission Act. Section 5 of the Federal Trade Commission Act empowers the Federal Trade Commission (FTC) to attack anticompetitive practices that violate the Sherman and Clayton Acts and to attack practices that, while not Sherman or Clayton Act violations, nonetheless constitute unfair methods of competition. Under Section 5, the FTC also has a consumer protection mandate from the U.S. Congress. Under this mandate, the FTC has attacked misrepresentations in advertising and other sales or marketing practices that it judged to be deceptive to the consumer.

Relationships with Distributors. Food service operators and their purchasing staffs should not collectively determine whether or not they will deal with certain distributors or customers. Following are several types of agreements that a food service operator, even though it acts individually and not after consultation with a competitor, should *not* enter into with its distributors or customers. A food service operator generally has the right to select its distributors or customers. However, such decisions should never be based on the willingness of the distributor or customer to enter into certain arrangements. For example:

- A food service operator should not restrict a distributor's right to determine individually the prices of its products to others.

- A food service operator should not require a distributor or customer to deal exclusively with it generally or within a certain geographic area unless the arrangement has been submitted for prior review by legal counsel and has met with counsel's approval after a full analysis of the circumstances.

The **Robinson-Patman Act** is of primary concern to purchasers. This Act makes it unlawful to sell the same products to competing customers at different prices if their requirements are essentially the same. Likewise, a purchaser may not induce a lower price than that offered to like buyers. While the buyer is not expected to know the competitor's prices (that raises other legal issues) if he or she knowingly induces and accepts a lower price, the purchaser is equally at risk with the seller.

Advertising allowances and brokerage are particularly scrutinized under antitrust law since they have been frequently abused. It is unlawful to use either as a basis for price discrimination. Advertising allowances must be offered proportionally to equal buyers.

Purchasing Contracts

A contract is a binding agreement between two or more persons that specifies the obligations of each individual. A contract consists of an offer by one person and acceptance by another. Generally, a bid is an offer that is made before the acceptance that creates the contract.

Request for Information and Request for Proposal Components

Today, many food service operators issue **requests for information** (RFIs) before issuing **requests for proposals** (RFPs) to distributors. While an RFP is a written document that formally requests a relevant pool of distributors to send in written proposals or bids for the specific products/services needed, an RFI is a written request for information. The RFI precedes the RFP; however, there is no obligation to send an RFP to an unqualified distributor who has replied to an RFI. Elements of an RFI include:

- A description of the food service operation in as much detail as is necessary for the distributors to understand the nature of the operation and its customers.

- A detailed description of the operation's product/service requirements.

The RFI is sent to a larger number of selected distributors than the RFP. Those that respond favorably with a desire to participate in the process are sent a more detailed RFP. An RFP contains the following:

- Introduction

- Proposal instructions, requirements, details

- Request for the distributor's background or experience

- Exhibits

- Appendix

The overall goal in sending RFPs to distributors is to clearly state the requirements for the intended purchase of products/services, and then have the distributor tell the operator what these products/services will cost. An RFP is not a contract and usually contains a statement that the requirements may be amended if conditions change at the operation.

The RFP is used to clearly communicate which products/services are required, encourage competition among selected distributors, and result in a proposal submitted to the operator that is of high quality and can be assessed objectively. This is more probable if a pool of highly qualified distributors is selected to receive the RFPs. Fewer higher quality proposals returned are preferred to a larger number of lower quality or inappropriate responses.

Deciding who receives an RFP is a matter of choice. A good strategy is to ask competitors who they would recommend for certain products/services. Local, state and national trade associations (e.g., AH&LA) frequently can be sources of possible RFP recipients; many distributors are allied members of the associations.

RFPs must contain information that is both specific (i.e., the requirements of the products/services) and general (i.e., flexibility when possible). RFPs must be

Exhibit 1   Suggestions for Enhancing RFP Effectiveness

For the RFP Document	For the Distributor
Be complete and detailed.	Be concise.
Include open-ended questions.	Be honest in claims made.
Prioritize what is in the RFP.	Be precise based on requirements.
Look ahead regarding requirements.	Provide useful samples.

Weigh each of the responses on a scale from fully compliant to non-compliant.

written clearly with the operation's goals in mind. Sometimes an RFP suggests that bidders attach an addendum to their proposals if they would like to propose an alternative solution to what was requested in the RFP.

The RFP introduction requires specific answers to how, when, and where questions. The introduction must also include the name and location of the food service operation, required products and services, dates and timelines, the reason(s) that the RFP is being issued, the operation's strategic and tactical goals, and the operation's values, vision, mission, history, philosophy, and culture. The next section is the proposal instructions, details, and requirements. This section details the instructions for completing the proposal, including the contact person and address at the food service operation, and the format to follow. Details include the evaluation criteria that will be used to select the distributor and the schedule that will be followed. Requirements include all the necessary information. The scope of the work (if it is a service, for example, a renovation of the kitchen), as well as the due date for submitting the proposal, must also be included in the RFP.

The distributor's experience and background are used to qualify the bidders, even though a preliminary check of expertise and track record may have already taken place prior to the RFP. Part of the qualification is a review of the distributor's financial statements, and the profile of principals in the distributor organization, as well as references from other operators. Professional distributor organizations usually are very willing to share this information.

Exhibits may include details about the operation's sales histories, menu, menu pricing, a list of current food service equipment, and other pertinent information. The appendixes usually contain additional details of what is required such as staff resources and financial guidelines. Additional suggestions to improve the effectiveness of RFPs are presented in Exhibit 1.

After all proposals are submitted following the deadline date, they are evaluated fairly based on a uniform set of criteria. It is also very useful to review those proposals that were not accepted and explain the reasons why unsuccessful bidders were rejected. This may also give the food service operator ideas for refining the RFI and RFP process in the spirit of continuous improvement.

Contract Elements

As was stated earlier, a **contract** is a binding agreement. It is critical to make certain the language is accurate and says what is meant before signing the contract.

It is prudent to ask an attorney experienced in contract law to review all contracts before signing.

Generally, a contract is an offer by one person and acceptance by another. Bids are offers that are made before acceptance, which creates the contract. In food service purchasing, a bid is usually an informal, sometimes oral, and often short-term offer. Once a seller agrees to sell products or services at a certain price and after the buyer accepts the offer, the seller can be held to the contract regardless of changes in market conditions. Buyers have responsibility to fulfill their obligations, including timely payment.

In any contract, consideration must be present. Consideration, in most contracts, consists of payment by the purchaser for the products and services that are delivered by the seller. However, consideration may be in the form of a promise to deliver or make payment on a delivery.

Generally, an offer may be withdrawn before it is accepted by another party. However, after acceptance, the contract becomes binding. The acceptance has to conform to the terms of the offer. For example, if the seller phones a buyer and offers a specified meat product (USDA Choice #168 inside rounds at $8.00 per pound, for example) and the buyer responds with an order for 400 pounds, the contract is in force.

However, if in the preceding example the buyer asks the seller to lower the price to $6.50 per pound, no agreement or contract has been made. This is a counteroffer, which would require acceptance by the seller. An offer must be accepted within a reasonable time if no deadline is specified. Usually, the length of time is determined by the commercial practice prevalent in trading that specific commodity or commodity group.

A contract is invalid if it is illegal or somehow induced by misrepresentation or fraud. A contract is also invalid if a mistake was made and one party had prior knowledge of the error and did not inform the other party.

A contract contains the essential elements of an agreement, which usually includes the parties to the agreement, price, specifications, quantity, required delivery date, payment terms, delivery method, and any other material and essential details. A written contract is often easier to enforce than an oral agreement. Moreover, the Uniform Commercial Code Section 2-201 generally provides that a contract for the sale of goods for a price of $5,000 or more is only enforceable if it is in writing. Oral contracts, however, are commonplace within the food service industry. Operators must be familiar with the commercial practices surrounding the classes of merchandise. Again, the operator should review state laws and the customary practice prevailing for that class of commodities. Excerpts from a sample food service purchasing contract are presented in the chapter appendix.

The operator must make certain that the products and services received are the same as what was requested. Close inspection of all incoming orders is always a crucial step in the receiving control point.

Warranties

When an operator purchases food products under a contract, an **express warranty** accompanies the products indicating that they will conform to the specifications in the contract. This may include any factual description of what the operator agreed to purchase, model year, performance specifications, and physical size. The delivered products must match this description in the contract.

Unless the contract states that they are excluded, an operator who buys a product is also entitled to **implied warranties.** Implied warranties assure the operator that the product is fit for the ordering purposes of such a product. When a seller is aware of an operator's specific needs, and the operator relies on the distributor to use his judgment and skill in recommending a product, the implied warranty also is in place.

There are two basic kinds of warranties: express warranties and implied warranties. Express warranties are oral or written representations, which become part of the basis for the sale, made by the seller to the buyer relating to the goods. Implied warranties are those imposed by law on the sale unless the seller negates or limits them to the extent permitted by the law (e.g., the UCC). Generally speaking, if the seller is a merchant with respect to the kind of goods being sold, a warranty that the goods shall be merchantable is implied in a contract for sale. No particular language or action is necessary to evidence those implied warranties that arise in a sale pursuant to law.

The Uniform Commercial Code sets forth in Article 2 the law of warranties as applied to transactions for the sale of "goods." The code defines goods as:

> All things (including specially manufactured goods) that are movable at the time of identification to the contract for sale other than the money in which the price is to be paid, investment securities (Article 8) and things in action. "Goods" also includes the unborn young of animals and growing crops and other identified things attached to realty as described in the section on goods to be severed from realty (Section 2-107).

Express Warranties. The Code describes the requirements of express warranties as follows:

> (1) Express warranties by the seller are created as follows:
>   (a) Any affirmation of fact or promise made by the seller to the buyer which relates to the goods and becomes part of the basis of the bargain creates an express warranty that the goods shall conform to the affirmation or promise.
>   (b) Any description of the goods which is made part of the basis of the bargain creates an express warranty that the goods shall conform to the description.
>   (c) Any sample or model that is made part of the basis of the bargain creates an express warranty that the whole of the goods shall conform to the sample or model.
> It is not necessary to the creation of an express warranty that the seller use formal words such as "warrant" or "guarantee" or that he have a specific intention to make a warranty, but an affirmation merely of the value of the goods or a statement purporting to be merely the seller's opinion or commendation of the goods does not create a warranty.

The whole purpose of the law of warranties is to determine what the seller has in essence agreed to sell. As Official Comment No. 3 to Section 2-313 of the Code states:

No specific intention to make a warranty is necessary if any of these factors is made part of the basis of the bargain. In actual practice, affirmations of fact made by the seller about the goods during a bargain are regarded as part of the description of those goods; hence no particular reliance on such statements need be shown in order to weave them into the fabric of the agreement. Rather, any fact which is to take such affirmations, once made, out of the agreement requires clear affirmation proof. The issue normally is one of fact.

Implied Warranties. As mentioned earlier, implied warranties are those that are automatically imposed by law unless the seller *expressly* negates or limits them to the extent permitted under the Uniform Commercial Code, as adopted and perhaps modified by each state (except Louisiana). There are two basic kinds of implied warranties under the Code: that the goods are merchantable and that they are fit for a particular purpose.

    Implied warranty of merchantability. Section 2-314 of the Code states (in part):

(1)   Unless excluded or modified (Section 2-316), a warranty that the goods shall be merchantable is implied in a contract for their sale if the seller is a merchant with respect to goods of that kind. Under this section, the serving for value of food or drink to be consumed either on the premises or elsewhere is a sale.

(2)   Goods to be merchantable must be at least such as

    (a)   pass without objection in the trade under the contract description; and

    (b)   in the case of fungible goods, are of fair average quality within the description; and

    (c)   are fit for the ordinary purposes for which goods of that description are used; and

    (d)   run, within the variations permitted by the agreement, of even kind, quality and quantity within each unit and among all units involved; and

    (e)   are adequately contained, packaged, and labeled as the agreement may require; and

    (f)   conform to the promises or affirmations of fact made on the container or label if any.

Official Comment No. 13 to Section 2-314 states:

In an action based on breach of warranty, it is of course necessary to show not only the existence of the warranty but the fact that the warranty was broken and that the breach of the warranty was the proximate cause of the loss sustained. In such an action an affirmative showing by the seller that the loss resulted from some action or event following his own delivery of the goods can operate as a defense. Equally, evidence indicating that the seller exercised care in the manufacture, processing or selection of the goods is relevant to the issue of whether the warranty was in fact broken. Action by the buyer following an examination of the goods which ought to have indicated the defect complained of can be shown as matter bearing on whether the breach itself was the cause of the injury.

Implied warranty of fitness for a particular purpose. Another type of implied warranty that may benefit food service operations is the implied warranty of fitness for a particular purpose. Section 2-315 states the rule with respect to this implied warranty.

> Where the seller at the time of contracting has reason to know any particular propose for which the goods are required and that the buyer is relying on the seller's skill or judgment to select or furnish suitable goods, there is unless excluded or modified under the next section an implied warranty that the goods shall be fit for such purpose.

Seller's disclaimers of express and implied warranties. In many contracts the seller attempts to disclaim the existence of any express or implied warranties with respect to the goods sold. Section 2-316 of the Code deals with disclaimers of both kinds of warranties. The general purpose of Section 2-316 is explained by Official Comment No. 1 as follows:

> (1) This section is designed principally to deal with those frequent clauses in sales contracts which seek to exclude "all warranties, express or implied." It seeks to protect a buyer from unexpected and unbargained language of disclaimer by denying effect to such language when inconsistent with language of express warranty and permitting the exclusion of implied warranties only by conspicuous language or other circumstances which protect the buyer from surprise.
> (2) The seller is protected under this Article against false allegations of oral warranties by its provisions on parol and extrinsic evidence and against unauthorized representations by the customary "lack of authority" clauses.

As Section 2-316(2) makes clear, there must be rather specific language to disclaim the implied warranties of fitness for a particular purpose and of merchantability. Subsection 3 points out, however, that certain language, such as expressions that the goods are purchased "as is" or "with all faults," will negate any implied warranties. However, one state's Supreme Court has held that while an "as is" clause may negate implied warranties, express warranties made by the seller continue to provide a remedy if the sold item or goods did not live up to the express warranty.

As Section 2-316 states:

> Unlike the implied warranty of merchantability, implied warranties of fitness for a particular purpose may be excluded by general language, but only if it is in writing and conspicuous.

Official Comment No. 8 to Section 2-316 reads, in part:

> Application of the doctrine of "caveat emptor" in all cases where the buyer examines the goods regardless of statements made by the seller is, however, rejected by this Article. Thus, if the offer of examination is accompanied by words as to their merchantability or specific attributes and the buyer indicates clearly that he is relying on those words rather than on his examination, they give rise to an "express" warranty. In such cases the question is one of fact as to whether a warranty of merchantability

has been expressly incorporated in the agreement. Disclaimer of such an express warranty is governed by subsection (1) of the present section.

    The particular buyer's skill and the normal method of examining goods in the circumstances determine what defects are excluded by the examination. A failure to notice defects which are obvious cannot excuse the buyer. However, an examination under circumstances which do not permit chemical or other testing of the goods would not exclude defects which could be ascertained only by such testing. Nor can latent defects be excluded by a simple examination. A professional buyer examining a product in his field will be held to have assumed the risk as to all defects which a professional in the field ought to observe, while a nonprofessional buyer will be held to have assumed the risk only for such defects as a layman might be expected to observe.

Questions about whether or not a food service operator as buyer has a warranty should be referred to a lawyer. Often there are remedies under the law of warranties if the buyer is willing to pursue his or her rights and if the pursuit is worth the projected legal expense under the circumstances.

Remedies for Contract Breach

What should a purchaser do if a distributor fails to abide by a binding contract? From the buyer's perspective, this usually occurs if the product fails to meet specifications or when the price differs from what was agreed upon in the contract.

    Disputes about whether products are "in" or "out" of specification start with the terms of the contract. Interpretation of a written contract will usually rest only on what is in that contract. Oral deletions or oral addenda may not be considered to modify a written contract; whenever possible, purchasers should commit agreement terms to writing.

    Standard remedies for contract breach are (1) to require specific performance, (2) to revise the agreement and seek restitution, or (3) to obtain damages. Damages are usually assessed on the basis of actual loss incurred, and much effort goes into establishing the dollar amount that represents compensatory damages.

Conflicts of Interest

High standards of professionalism are required of purchasers as they interact with suppliers. Conflicts of interest often result in personal and financial gains at the expense of the food service operation and, ultimately, its customers.

    To maintain an honest reputation, purchasers should avoid personal use of the food service operation's property, personal purchases for non-business purposes, and any financial interest in a distributor's company. The food service operation should formulate specific policies regarding solicitations for charitable or political donations, travel and related expenses incurred in visiting a distributor's location, and personal concessions from distributors.

    Sometimes, individuals responsible for purchasing are prone to the temptation of accepting gifts, loans, and cash in return for favors bestowed upon a distributor's organization. While some operations place upper limits as to the value of gifts that can be accepted, the best policy is to reject any gift, no matter how small its value. A professional purchaser considers the operation's interest, not personal benefit.

Group Purchasing Contracts

Recall that a group purchasing organization (GPO) has increased purchasing power because it aggregates product purchases, resulting in more leverage and better economies of scale. This results in better pricing for the GPO's members. Usually the contract with the distributor requires that the operators purchase some majority (e.g., 80 percent) of all purchases from that distributor. This requires, in many cases, all or most of the members of the GPO to standardize the products they purchase. When most or all of a GPO's members make a commitment to purchase a standardized set of products from specific manufacturers, a corresponding reduction in per unit cost of the products that is passed on to the GPO members.

Large chains may be able to operate as GPOs if all franchisees agree to purchase all or part of the same products from a particular manufacturer or nationwide distributor. A sample national agreement is presented in Exhibit 2. Note that the agreement contains the manufacturer's as well as the distributor's contact information, the specified products' details, special procedures and special instructions, and the participation requirements.

Cancellation Clauses

One final essential element of a contract is the cancellation clause. A **cancellation clause** is frequently included in a contract because it permits the food service operation to get out of a contract. Usually the cancellation clause is based on poor performance by the distributor and requires a 60-day notice from the operator.

Consider the case of an on-site contract food service organization that operates food services in business and industry and healthcare segments. A cancellation clause is a form of an "insurance policy" in the event that the organization merges with another contract food service organization or is acquired by a larger food service organization. The cancellation clause can save the merged or acquired organization a great deal of money, since it is likely that it will be required to use the purchasing services provided by the distributors of the other organization.

Endnotes

1. The section on warranties and antitrust law is adapted from Jack P. Jefferies and Banks Brown, *Understanding Hospitality Law,* 4th ed. (Lansing, Mich.: Educational Institute of the American Hotel & Lodging Association), 2001.

Key Terms

antitrust laws—Laws that regulate business conduct to preserve competition and to prevent economic coercion.

cancellation clause—A contract clause that allows a food service operator to end its agreement with a distributor.

Exhibit 2   Sample National Agreement

Issue Date	
Agreement Number	

Manufacturer	Name	Contact	Phone	Fax

Distributor	Name	Contact	Phone	Fax

Specified Products	Item	Pack Size	SUPC#	MFG#	Price to Food Service Operations

Procedures & Special Instructions _____

National Pricing   Delivered to Food Service Operations   ☒ YES   ☐ NO

Effective Dates _____

Participation Requirements   ☒ Hotels   ☒ Company-Owned Food Service Operations
☒ Franchised Food Service Operations

Food Service Operation Contact: _____ , Vice President Food and Beverage

Phone: _____   Fax: _____

E-mail: _____

carbohydrate—A nutrient that comes in the form of monosaccharides, disaccharides, and polysaccharides.

cash, insurance, freight (CIF)—A shipping term that means the buyer assumes title when the goods reach the buyer's dock.

Clayton Act—An antitrust statute that more precisely describes certain types of prohibited business activity than does the Sherman Act.

contract—A binding agreement that consists of an offer by one party and acceptance by another.

country of origin labeling—A voluntary labeling system that will highlight meat products produced in the United States.

dietary guidelines—Suggested steps for maintaining a healthy diet.

express warranty—Oral or written representations related to the goods, which become part of the basis for the sale, made by the seller to the buyer.

Federal Trade Commission Act—A statute that empowers the Federal Trade Commission to enforce antitrust statutes.

food allergen—An ingredient (such as peanuts or wheat) that may cause an allergic reaction in some consumers.

food labeling—Indicating a food product's ingredients, nutritional content, potential allergens, country of origin, and other factors on the product's packaging.

free on board (FOB)—A term that indicates when title passes and when responsibility is assumed for a shipment.

implied warranty—A warranty that assures the operator that the product is fit for its ordering purposes. It is imposed by law unless the seller negates or limits it.

law of agency—The law that recognizes that a purchaser may act as agent for the food service operation and has the authority to legally obligate it.

lipid—The collective name for the fats and oils found in food products.

mineral—An inorganic substance that is critically important to human nutrition.

organic food—Food produced without the use of herbicides, pesticides, antibiotics, hormones, and unnatural fertilizers.

per se rule—A rule with which a competitive restraint is deemed to be inherently anticompetitive and is automatically presumed to be unreasonable.

protein—A nutrient that comes in the form of molecules that contain amino acids. Sources of protein include meat, poultry, fish, seafood, milk and milk products, legumes, soybeans, and nuts.

request for information—A document that precedes an RFP to solicit information from an initial pool of potential distributors.

request for proposal—A written document that formally requests a relevant pool of distributors to send in written proposals or bids for the specific products/services needed.

Robinson-Patman Act—A statute that makes it unlawful to sell the same products to competing customers at different prices if their requirements are essentially the same.

rule of reason—Proof that a party engaged in a particular activity is not in itself proof that the party committed an antitrust violation.

sales law—The legal aspects of purchasing that are addressed in the Uniform Commercial code, including transportation and title.

Sherman Act—A U.S. law that prohibits every contract, combination, or conspiracy that constitutes an unreasonable restraint of trade.

vitamin—An essential nutrient that the body cannot use by itself. Vitamins help speed the release of energy from protein, carbohydrates, and lipids.

 # Review Questions

1. Why is food labeling important, and what should be included?

2. How do food allergens impact food service operators?

3. What are organic foods, and why are they important in food service operations?

4. What are the six nutrient classes, and how are the various nutrients used by the human body?

5. What is the law of agency, and how does it apply to food service operations?

6. How do federal and state antitrust laws affect food service operators and their relationships with distributors?

7. What are RFIs and RFPs?

8. What are the elements of a purchasing contract?

9. What is the difference between an express warranty and an implied warranty?

10. What are some potential conflicts of interest in purchasing, and how can they be avoided?

 # References

Anonymous. "Manufacturers Pressured to Respond to Food Allergies." *Food Management* 36, no. 10 (October 2001): pp. 13–14.

Anonymous. "Organic Has its Own Label—So Now What?" *Food Management* 37, no. 11 (November 2002): 12–13.

Anonymous. "USA: Meat Industry Bodies Support Origin Labeling Move." *Just-Food.com* (May 5, 2005).

Fortin, Neal D. "Fats in the Fast Lane." *Food Product* (March 2005).

Ramsay, John. "Trading Rights." *Supply Management* 8, no. 13 (June 2003): p. 19.

Steele, Jeremy W. "Going Organic: Farmers See Growth in More 'Natural' Crops." *Lansing State Journal* (July 10, 2006): p. 1.

Internet Sites

For more information, visit the following Internet sites. Remember that Internet addresses can change without notice. If the site is no longer there, you can use a search engine to look for additional sites.

The New Food Label
www.fda.gov/opacom/background
ers/foodlabel/newlabel.html

Food Labeling Fact Sheets
www.fsis.usda.gov/fact_sheets/
food_labeling_fact_sheets/index.asp

Common Food Allergens
www.foodallergy.org/allergens/
index.html

Nutrients in Foods
www.umass.edu/nibble/infolist.html

Dietary Guidelines for Americans
www.health.gov/dietaryguidelines

Chapter Appendix

TO BE ADVISED CORPORATION
Direct Buy General Terms and Conditions
(Food, Packaging, Supplies)

The party executing these General Terms and Conditions, _____, a _____ _____ company having a place of business at _____ (the "Supplier") has been approved or may be approved in the future to be approved by To Be Advised Corporation, d/b/a _____ ("TO BE ADVISED CORPORATION") to produce, manufacture and/or sell certain items to TO BE ADVISED CORPORATION, Inc. for its Company owned and operated in the United States of America and Canada, (collectively, the "Company" and agrees that these terms and conditions, dated _____, 20XX ("Effective Date") shall apply for the Term specified below.

1. **Term.** This agreement shall be effective on the Effective Date set forth above and shall continue for the period that the Supplier remains a TO BE ADVISED CORPORATION Approved Supplier ("Term"). Upon expiration, TO BE ADVISED CORPORATION shall have the right to renew this Agreement for additional twelve (12) month periods upon thirty (30) days written notice to Supplier.

    TO BE ADVISED CORPORATION may terminate this Agreement without cause, at any time, in whole or in part, upon thirty (30) days prior written notice to Supplier. TO BE ADVISED CORPORATION may also terminate this agreement at any time and without cause if Supplier is no longer an Approved Supplier to TO BE ADVISED CORPORATION. Termination of this Agreement for any reason shall be without prejudice to any rights which shall have accrued to the benefit of either party prior to such termination. The provisions of Sections 7(c), 8(a)–(e), 13, 14, 15, 16, 17, 18 and 19 hereof shall survive the termination of this Agreement. Termination of this Agreement shall not relieve either party from obligations which are expressly indicated to survive termination of this Agreement and shall not terminate TO BE ADVISED CORPORATION's obligation to pay all undisputed invoices for products which have been shipped prior to termination....

6. **Sale and Pricing**

    (a) **Approved Products.** Supplier shall sell to the TO BE ADVISED CORPORATION only those products that have been approved by TO BE ADVISED CORPORATION as reflected in Attachment A form, as same may be revised from time to time by TO BE ADVISED CORPORATION or in Purchase Orders submitted to Supplier from time to time by TO BE ADVISED CORPORATION (collectively, the "Approved Products").

    (b) **No Set Quantities.** Supplier acknowledges there is no assurance that any particular quantity of Approved Products will be purchased by TO BE ADVISED CORPORATION. TO BE ADVISED CORPORATION shall not have any liability to Supplier if the actual volumes of Approved Products that Supplier sells to the Company are for any reason (including without limitation the discontinuation of any Approved Product) less than any volume estimate previously provided by TO BE ADVISED CORPORATION to Supplier.

(c) **Most Favorable Price.** Supplier represents, warrants and agrees that the prices, net of all discounts, for the Approved Products are not, and shall not at any time be, greater than those prices then currently being charged to any other customer for substantially similar items purchased in substantially similar quantities. If Supplier reduces its prices for such items to any other customer while these general terms shall be in effect, then Supplier shall correspondingly reduce the prices to TO BE ADVISED CORPORATION for the Approved Products and so advise TO BE ADVISED CORPORATION. Upon request, Supplier shall provide certification of compliance with this provision.

(d) **Invoicing and Payment Terms.** Supplier shall submit invoices for Approved Products after shipment of said Approved Products and upon completion of any services provided by Supplier. All invoices shall be submitted to the address specified in the Purchase Order or the Written Price Contract issued by TO BE ADVISED CORPORATION. Company agrees to pay all undisputed invoiced amounts net thirty (30) days after Company's acceptance of the Approved Products delivered by Supplier unless otherwise specified in the Purchase Order or Written Price Contract issued by Company.

(e) **Pricing.** Pricing, including any discounts, for the Approved Products shall be agreed upon by the parties and captured in TO BE ADVISED CORPORATION's Pricenet system or in Written Price Contracts or Purchase Orders issued by TO BE ADVISED CORPORATION. These prices shall also be reflected on any purchase orders issued by TO BE ADVISED CORPORATION. The price to be paid by TO BE ADVISED CORPORATION, shall include all taxes, tariffs, customs, charges, and duties (collectively "Impositions"). Any Impositions which Supplier may be required to pay or collect, under any existing or future law, upon or with respect to the sale, measured by the receipts from the sale thereof, shall be paid by Supplier. Should Supplier claim that it is exempt from any Impositions, then Supplier shall furnish TO BE ADVISED CORPORATION with an exemption certificate which has been issued by an appropriate governmental authority. Supplier hereby agrees to indemnify and hold TO BE ADVISED CORPORATION harmless for any and all Impositions and penalties or fines assessed against TO BE ADVISED CORPORATION or Supplier, whether or not due to Supplier's claimed exemption from such Imposition. TO BE ADVISED CORPORATION shall not be responsible for any additional charges of any kind, including, but not limited to charges for boxing, packing, drayage, cartage, or other extras.

7. **Shipping, Transportation and Packing**

(a) **Shipping.** Supplier shall, at its expense, ship the Approved Product F.O.B. destination for purchases within the United States and DDP (as defined by the Incoterms) for international purchases, to the destination(s) specified by TO BE ADVISED CORPORATION in accordance with the shipping instructions set forth in Attachment B, as applicable. The delivery schedule shall be as set forth by TO BE ADVISED CORPORATION in the Purchase Order and time for such deliveries shall be of the essence. Failure to deliver the Approved Products by the required delivery date(s) shall be deemed a breach of the Agreement and TO BE ADVISED CORPORATION shall have all rights and remedies available to it at law or equity, including the right to reject the delivery. If Supplier has knowledge that anything may prevent or threatens to prevent timely performance of the Services under these General Terms and Conditions, Supplier shall immediately notify TO BE ADVISED CORPORATION's representative thereof and include all relevant information concerning the delay or potential delay.

Supplier shall give reasonable prior notice of the date and time the Approved Products will be ready for delivery to the operator of the storage facility designated by TO BE ADVISED CORPORATION as the Destination Point. TO BE ADVISED CORPORATION agrees to furnish or to have the storage facility furnish the facilities and labor to unload the Approved Products from the trucks at the Destination Point.

(b) **Excess Products.** Except for customary quantity variations recognized by trade practice, Approved Products in excess of those specified in a Purchase Order will not be accepted by TO BE ADVISED CORPORATION and such Approved Products will be held at Supplier's risk. TO BE ADVISED CORPORATION may, and at Supplier's direction shall, return such Approved Products at Supplier's risk and expense, and all transportation charges shall be paid by Supplier.

(c) **Risk of Loss.** Risk of Loss of the Approved Products shall pass from Seller only upon delivery of Approved Products at the Destination Point. Notwithstanding the foregoing, identification of the Approved Products under Section 2-501 of the UCC will occur on the date of the Purchase Order. This section will survive termination of the Agreement.

(d) **Transportation and Packing.** All Approved Products shall be suitably packed or otherwise prepared for shipment to protect the same fully during transportation. Shipments shall be made as specified without charge for boxing, carting or storage unless otherwise specified. All Approved Product shall be forwarded in accordance with TO BE ADVISED CORPORATION's instructions, by the route and method of transportation taking the lowest transportation rate.

8. **Certain Representations, Warranties and Agreements of Supplier.** Supplier represents and warrants TO BE ADVISED CORPORATION, and agrees with TO BE ADVISED CORPORATION as follows:

(a) **Specifications.** All Approved Products shall be manufactured, produced, transported, stored, and shipped by Supplier in accordance with all quality assurance and other requirements of TO BE ADVISED CORPORATION (collectively, the "TO BE ADVISED CORPORATION Specifications" and the policies from time to time communicated by TO BE ADVISED CORPORATION to Supplier (collectively, the TO BE ADVISED CORPORATION Policies").

(b) **Product Information.** Any and all "Product Information and Nutritional Data Sheet," "Supplier Profile" or similar information request forms provided to TO BE ADVISED CORPORATION by Supplier have been and will be completed by Supplier accurately and to the best of Supplier's knowledge.

(c) **Food Products.** All food products, including food articles, food ingredients and food packaging comprising any Approved Products, or any part there of, sold to TO BE ADVISED CORPORATION, and the manufacturing, or pricing of such products shall: (i) be in full compliance with all applicable federal, state, and local laws, rules and regulations (collectively, the "Laws"), including without limitation the Federal Food, Drug and Cosmetic Act ("FDCA"), as amended from time to time, and the rules and regulations promulgated from time to time by the United States Department of Agriculture ("USDA"); (ii) be manufactured, produced, transported, stored, shipped and delivered in accordance with all Laws, including without limitation the "Good Manufacturing Practices" under the FDCA or comparable regulations of the USDA, the TO BE ADVISED CORPORATION Specifications and the TO BE ADVISED CORPORATION Policies; (iii) not be adulterated or misbranded within the meaning of the FDCA or USDA or any other Law; (iv) not be a food product which may not, under applicable Laws, be introduced into interstate commerce; and (v) not be a food product adulterated or misbranded under any applicable Law.

(d) **General Warranties**. The Approved Products shall be merchantable and fit for their intended purpose, and shall meet or exceed the TO BE ADVISED CORPORATION Specifications in all respects.

Chapter 8 Outline

Competencies

1. Describe how meat and meat products are produced, supplied, and priced. (pp. 285–286)

2. Explain the inspection and grading processes for meat. (pp. 286–287)

3. Explain the system through which meat is purchased. (pp. 287–288)

4. List the sources of available information to assist in purchasing decisions for meat products. (pp. 288–293)

5. Identify the major cuts of beef, pork, veal, and lamb, and describe the primary characteristics of each. (pp. 288–296)

6. Explain the requirements, content, and importance of specifications for meat. (pp. 296–301)

7. Describe management considerations related to purchasing meat products. (pp. 301–302)

8

Meat Products

Meat products typically represent a major portion of most food service operations' food costs. Because of this, it is very important that meat product purchasing decisions be carefully considered.

Most food service operations purchase some type of meat products. Meat products can be cut from the animal, as in beef, veal, pork and lamb, or processed, as in bacon, sausage, and cold cuts.

Meat Production and Processing

Beef cattle production is primarily based in the lower Midwest and southern sections of the United States. Pork production is based in the upper-Midwestern United States. Veal is primarily produced in areas known for dairy production, including Minnesota, Wisconsin, Illinois, New York, Texas, and California. Lamb production is centered in the western United States, although a large amount is imported from Australia and New Zealand. Meat processing is centered near the areas of production.

Factors Affecting Meat Supplies

The supply and production of meat are cyclical. If too many animals are brought to market and too much meat is produced, the oversupply lowers the price. This lower price produces less revenue for ranchers who, in turn, reduce the number of animals brought to market the following season. This reduced supply tends to increase prices. The increased prices create more supply, and the cycle continues.

Other factors can influence supply. Milk cows sometimes are brought to market due to low milk prices, which increases meat supplies. Disease and potential for disease can reduce the supply of meat. Natural disasters and severe weather can reduce supplies. Transportation problems can affect the ability to get animals to market. Furthermore, high demand for a certain specific meat product can affect the supply of certain types or cuts of meat. Large food service chains can potentially buy up all the available product for special promotions, thereby affecting the supply to the rest of the industry. For example, a large barbecue restaurant chain may decide to offer a rib promotion and purchase large quantities of the available rib inventory for a particular time period, thereby creating a shortage of ribs. Some restaurant chains actually secure their inventory by raising their own livestock for their meat products.

Exhibit 1   Sample USDA Wholesomeness Inspection Stamps

Sample Stamp	Use
38 U.S. INSP'D&P'S'D	Carcass (Hanging Meat)
U.S. INSPECTED AND PASSED BY DEPARTMENT OF AGRICULTURE EST. 38	Prepackaged/Processed Meat Products

Factors Affecting Meat Costs and Pricing

The meat processing industry is controlled mostly by such large national organizations as Cargill, Tyson, and Smithfield.[1] The price of grain used as feed largely determines the cost of raising the animal and producing the meat. Because production and processing facilities are located in less populated areas, transportation represents a large percentage of the cost of meat products. Meat prices are determined primarily by supply levels. Supply levels can be influenced by the size of herds, weather conditions, and grain supplies.

Meat Inspection and Grading

Quality grading of meat applies to beef, veal, and lamb products. Pork products are primarily graded for yield with some consideration of quality. Meat animals, carcasses and products must pass inspection for sanitation and healthiness, which is referred to as wholesomeness. Once a meat product has passed inspection for wholesomeness, it becomes available for quality inspection. Sample USDA wholesomeness inspection stamps are shown in Exhibit 1. Meat quality inspection is a service provided by the federal government, but it must be paid for by the processor. Grading is based on the amount of **marbling** (fat in the muscle tissue), the condition of the meat, the appearance and amount of fat, and the appearance of the bones. Quality grading is a marketing issue—not a requirement. Products that are not graded are often sold under private labels or sold under the label of "**no-roll**," which means no stamp has been rolled onto the product.

Beef products are graded primarily with two designations—USDA Prime and USDA Choice. Officially, there are six other lesser-quality designations, but for practical purposes in food service, Prime and Choice are the only quality

Exhibit 2   USDA Classification and Grading Schedule for Carcass Meats

Animal	Grade Designations*
Beef	
Quality grades	
• steer, heifer, cow**	prime, choice, good, standard, commercial, utility, cutter, and canner
• bull and stag	choice, good, commercial, utility, cutter, and canner
Yield grades (cutability)	1, 2, 3, 4, 5
Calf	prime, choice, good, standard, utility, cull
Veal	prime, choice, good, standard, utility, cull
Lamb, Yearling Mutton, and Mutton	
Quality grades for lamb and yearling mutton	prime, choice, good, utility, cull
Quality grades for mutton	choice, good, utility, cull
Yield grades (cutability)	1, 2, 3, 4, 5
Pork Carcasses	
Quality grades	
• barrows and gilts	U.S. No. 1, 2, 3, 4, utility
• sows	U.S. No. 1, 2, 3, medium, cull

*In descending order
**Cows are not eligible for prime grade.

designations considered. It is also important to understand that the Choice category includes products in a range of quality levels. Food service buyers, for the most part, only purchase USDA Prime products and USDA Choice products in the top half of the category. Exhibit 2 gives the USDA classification and grading schedule for beef and other carcass meats.

Yield grades range from USDA 1 through USDA 5. Yield grades of 1 contain more useable meat than grade 5. Yield is determined by the amount and placement of bone and fat in the carcass or meat product. USDA yield grade stamps are shown in Exhibit 3.

Meat Purchasing Systems

How a buyer purchases meat for an establishment will be determined primarily by the size of the business and how it is organized. In a large company-owned chain, the meat purchasing decision may be made by a purchasing manager at the regional or corporate level. In a franchise or chain, buyers may be encouraged to purchase meat and meat products from a primary distributor. Independent operators, of course, will have the most choices as to how and from whom meat will be purchased. In any case, it is important to work with suppliers and distributors that are well known and trusted. Meat buyers should visit the distributor's facilities to observe how the meat is handled, stored, and transported, paying special attention to food safety practices. Shipping practices should also be investigated, including how the meat products will be shipped and when deliveries will be scheduled.

Exhibit 3   USDA Yield Grade Stamps

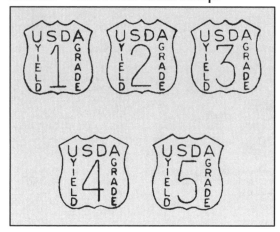

Most buyers will likely purchase meat on a weekly—even daily—basis unless they work for a large company with economies of scale or have a large storage facility. The most common purchasing method is to ask distributors for price bids based on the operation's meat specifications. Exhibit 4 shows a guide to meat prices from Urner Barry Publications.

Market Forms of Meat

Food service organizations generally purchase fresh meat cut to the buyer's specifications or frozen meat in standard cuts and quantities.

Wholesale

Meat purchased at the wholesale level consists primarily of fresh products in the whole or partial carcass stage. Food service operations with butchering facilities and trained personnel will often buy large sections of meat products and fabricate the cuts to their own specifications.

Retail

Most meat purchased for restaurants is processed into retail-level condition. Retail cuts of meat can be fresh or frozen and can be based on specific buyer specifications or based on standard cuts popular in the market. Typically, these retail cuts will be sealed in plastic and boxed using standard weights and sizes.

Beef Cuts and Characteristics

A beef carcass is separated for fabrication into several **primal cuts.** Additional cuts, shown in Exhibit 5, are fabricated from these primal cuts.

- *Chuck.* The least expensive of the primal cuts, it is sometimes used for roast beef and stew meat. The weight range is from 80 to 94 pounds.

Exhibit 4 Urner Barry's *HRI Buyer's Guide*

URNER BARRY PUBLICATIONS, INC.

HRI Buyers' Guide

A current guide to commodity prices paid to wholesalers and purveyors by hotels, restaurants and institutions.

Beef

BOXED BEEF CUTS

IMPS	FL	Description	Wts	Prime	Choice	Select
109A	1	Rib, Rst Rdy	Dn	-	515-525	510-520
109A	1	Rib, Rst Rdy	Up	-	515-525	510-520
112A	3	Lip-On, Bnls	Dn	-	**730-740 -**	**635-645 +**
112A	3	Lip-On, Bnls	Up	1000-1010	**730-740 -**	**635-645 +**
114	1	Shoulder Clod		-	**205-210 +**	**195-200 +**
116C	1	Chuck Roll		-	**210-215 +**	**205-210 +**
120	1	Brisket, D-O		-	**165-170 +**	**160-165 +**
123A	3	Shrt Plate, Shrt Rib		-	**365-375 +**	**335-340 +**
124	4	Rib, Back Rib (Fz)		-	**70-75 -**	**70-75 -**
136		Ground Beef 75%		-	**155-160 -**	-
136		Ground Beef 80%		-	170-175	-
1136		GB Patties 75%		-	170-175	-
1136		GB Patties 80%		-	180-185	-
1136A		GB, TVP		-	-	-
1136A		GB Patties, TVP		-	-	-
160	1	Round, Part Bnls		-	180-190	180-190
161	1	Round, Bnls		-	**195-205 +**	190-200
167	1	Knuckle		-	**205-215 +**	**205-215 +**
167A	4	Knuckle, Pld		-	**215-225 +**	**215-225 +**
168	1	Inside Round, Untr		-	**220-230 +**	**215-225 +**
170	1	Gooseneck Rnd		-	**185-195 +**	**180-190 +**
171B	3	Outside Round		-	**190-200 +**	**185-195 +**
171C	3	Eye of Round		-	230-240	230-240
174	1	Short Loin, 2x3		**990-1000 +**	**580-590 +**	**480-490 -**
175	3	Strip, B-I, 1x1		-	-	-
180	1	Strip, Bnls, 2x3	Dn	-	605-615	500-510
180	1	Strip, Bnls, 2x3	Up	-	605-615	500-510
180	1	Strip, Bnls, 1x1		-	**720-730 -**	600-610
184	1	Top Butt, Bnls	Dn	-	**355-365 -**	**305-315 -**
184	1	Top Butt, Bnls	Up	-	**355-365 -**	**305-315 -**
185B	1	Ball-Tip	Dn	-	300-310	295-305
185B	1	Ball-Tip	Up	-	350-360	350-360
189A	4	Tenderloin, PSMO	Dn	-	1195-1205	1015-1025
189A	4	Tenderloin, PSMO	Up	-	1275-1285	1095-1105
191A	4	Tenderloin Butt		-	**1135-1145 +**	**955-965 -**
193	4	Flank Steak		-	**620-630 +**	**530-540 -**
121D	4	Inside Skirt		-	**395-405 -**	**395-405 -**
121C	4	Outside Skirt		-	**400-410 +**	**400-410 +**

Beef Situation

Contrary to our previous HRI report where declines in wholesale beef prices spurred HRI pricing lower, the past week saw many items gain in value. Packers have been able to achieve increases in the wholesale pricing of most end cuts and some loin items. Demand for Mother's Day features helped push prices upward. Ground beef held steady for the most part, as demand and supplies remained well balanced.

Bruce Longo
Urner Barry Publications, Inc.
732-240-5330 ext 263
blongo@urnerbarry.com

BOXED BEEF PORTION CUTS

IMPS	FL	Item	Wts	Prime	Choice
1100		Cube Steak		-	370-380
1112A	3	Lip-On, Bnls	Dn	-	-
1112A	3	Lip-On, Bnls	Up	-	1070-1080
1173		Porterhouse Steak		-	1060-1070
1174		T-Bone Steak		-	945-955
1180		Strip Loin Steak, Bnls		-	1100-1110
1184		Top Butt Steak, Bnls		-	-
1184A		Top Butt Steak, Semi-Cntr-Cut, Bnls		-	820-830
1184B		Top Butt Steak, Cntr-Cut, Bnls		-	860-870
1189A		Tenderloin Steak, Side On, Defatted		-	1620-1630
1190		Tenderloin Steak, Side Off, Defatted		-	1910-1920
1190A		Tenderloin Steak, Side Off, Skined		-	1970-1980

BEEF VARIETY & PROCESSED MEATS

IMPS	Item	
601	Brisket, Bnls, D-O, Corned	210-220
625	Beef Brisket, Corned, Ckd	340-350
604	Inside Round, Corned	290-300
623	Inside Round, Ckd	410-420
608	Outside Round, Corned	280-290
624	Outside Round, Corned, Ckd	370-380
701	Beef Liver	-
702	Beef Liver, Sliced (Frzn)	-
703	Beef Liver, Portion Cut (Frzn)	-
721	Oxtails	480-490

"Urner Barry's HRI Buyer's Guide"

Editor: Michael W. O'Shaughnessy
Market Reporters: Randy Pesciotta, Russell Whitman, Joseph Muldowney, Bill Smith, Bruce Longo, Janice Brown and Mary Ann Zicarelli

Published one time weekly in a variety of media
by Urner Barry Publications, Inc.
P.O. Box 389, Toms River, NJ 08754-0389

Copyright© 2006

Urner Barry Publications, Inc. ISSN 0270-4161
Phone 732-240-5330 • Fax 732-341-0891 • Web site www.urnerbarry.com

URNER BARRY'S HRI Buyer's Guide is available by mail for $289 per year. Back issues $4 ea. This report is also available via fax, email and through Urner Barry's flagship service Comtell Online.

The UB Products that are identified in the Services and Products Order Form are offered to you conditioned on your acceptance without modification of the terms, conditions, and notices contained herein. Please read the End-User License Agreement (the "Agreement), a copy of which is available at www.urnerbarry.com and which has been received by the contact named on the Services and Products Order Form, before utilizing this Urner Barry product. Your use of a particular UB Product(s) may also be subject to additional terms set forth in the Agreement. Your use of the UB Product(s) constitutes your acceptance of all of the terms, conditions, and notices set forth in the Agreement. Urner Barry reserves the right to amend, remove, or add to these terms, conditions and notices at any time without notice. Accordingly please continue to review the Agreement whenever accessing or using the UB Product(s). If at any time you do not accept the Agreement along with the terms and conditions outlined in the Services and Products Order Form, you may not use this or any UB Product.

The information, commentary and price quotations contained herein are intended solely for the internal, confidential and exclusive use of Urner Barry subscribers. All subscribers expressly agree that they will not sell, communicate or give any of said information, commentary or price quotations to any other person, firm or corporation, including any governmental agent or agencies whatsoever and any news distributing or communications company or service. The use of quotations for contractual or other purposes is beyond the control of Urner Barry, which in no case assumes any responsibility for such use. The quotations given herein represent, to the best of the reporters knowledge, prevailing wholesale values in the specified grades of each commodity, based on sales to stores or warehouses from receivers and wholesale distributors, and on indications of willingness and ability to buy. They represent in the judgment of the publishers an accurate picture of current business, but they are not official in any sense of the word. The publishers disclaim and do not assume responsibility for any damages, alleged or otherwise, that may result or claim to have resulted from any use made by any person or any reliance by any person upon any of the statements of quotations appearing at any time herein.

Symbol Explanation: cwt - hundredweight; b - bid; ax - asked; n - nominal; r - reinstated quote; LTL - less than trucklot; TL - trucklot; FOB - Freight On Board.

Prices reflect Urner Barry quotations, based on the FOB Midwest River area for fresh, standard product for spot delivery unless otherwise stated. **Bold Type** indicates change from previous close.

FAT LIMITATIONS (FL) DESCRIPTION

Maximum Average Fat Thickness		Maximum Fat at any point
1.	¾" (19mm)	1"
2.	¼" (6mm)	½"
3.	⅛" (3mm)	¼"
4.	Practically free (75% surface lean exposed)	⅛"
5.	Peeled/Denuded	⅛"
6.	Peeled/Denuded, surface membrane removed	⅛"

Source: *Urner Barry's HRI Buyers' Guide* (Toms River, N.J.: Urner Barry Publications, Inc., 2007).

Exhibit 5   Beef Food Service Cuts

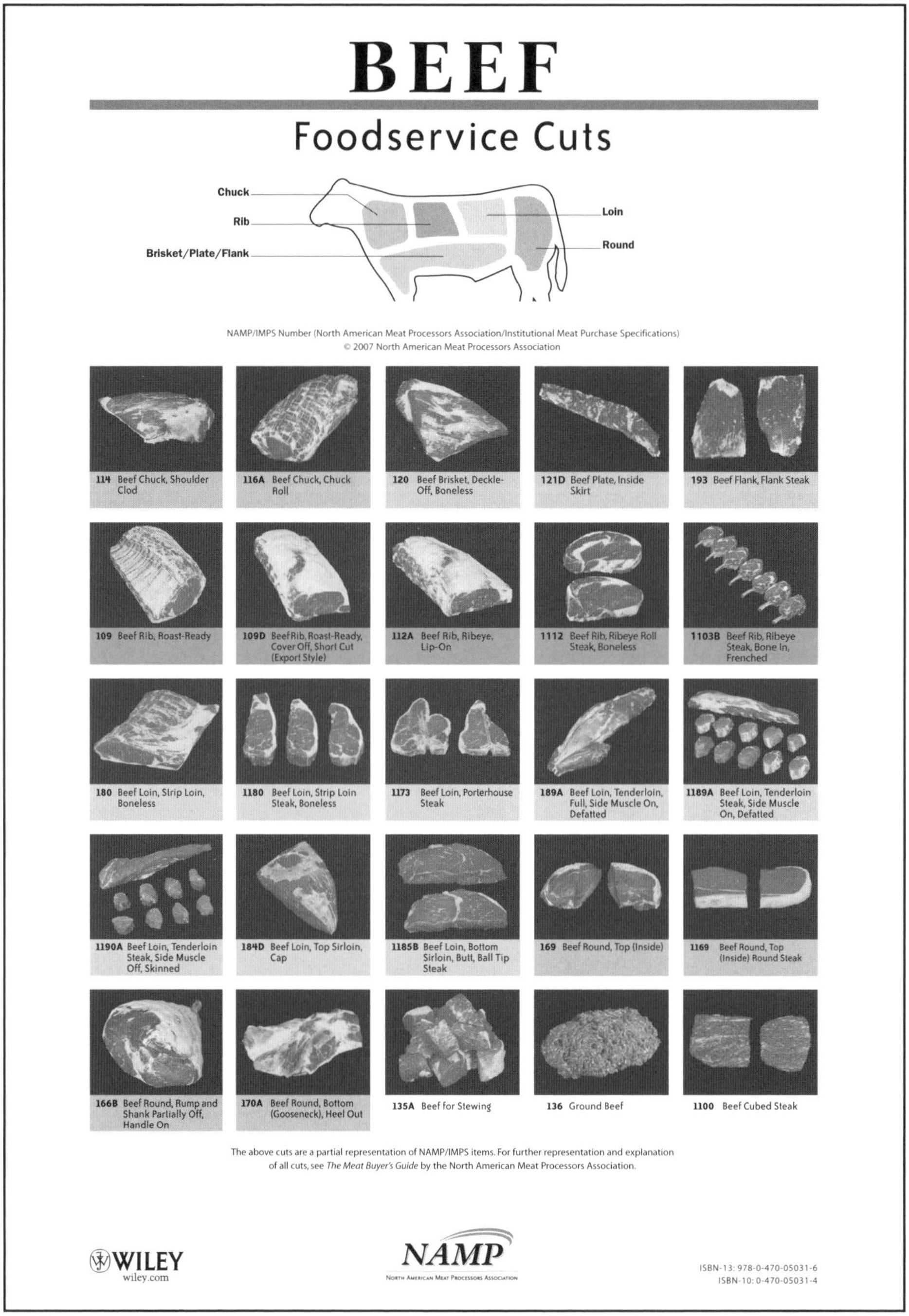

Source: North American Meat Processors Association, *Beef Foodservice Poster, Revised.* © 2007, NAMP. Reprinted with permission of John Wiley & Sons, Inc.

- *Rib.* This is the second most valuable per pound of the primal cuts. Rib eye steaks, rib roasts and short ribs come from this area. The weight range is from 28 to 35 pounds.

- *Loin.* The loin is the most expensive per pound of the primal cuts. The best-known steaks, like New York Strip, T-bone, and Porterhouse, as well as the tenderloin used for fillets, come from the loin area.

- *Round.* The round is relatively low in cost, but has good flavor and high yield. Top round and bottom round steaks and roasts, as well as the steamship round (popular for use for carving) comes from this primal cut.

- *Brisket.* The brisket is usually cooked slowly over low heat, as with a smoked brisket or corned beef brisket.

- *Plate.* This primal cut is used for short ribs and ground beef.

- *Flank.* This primal cut contains a flat oval muscle that is covered in a thick membrane or silverskin. Flank steak is popular for use in Southwestern cooking and items such as fajitas.

Exhibits 6 and 7 are examples of on-line resources that food service operators can use to learn about meat cuts.

Pork Cuts and Characteristics

Fresh pork products include pork roast, pork chops, ribs, pulled pork, and sausage. Cured pork products, including bacon, ham, Canadian bacon, and sausage, are the most popular. Like beef, pork can also be identified by its primal cuts.

- *Shoulder butt.* Products from this primal cut include blade steaks, blade roasts, ground pork, and sausage.

- *Picnic shoulder.* Picnic hams and roasts come from this primal area.

- *Loin.* Most popular pork products come from the loin primal cut area. This area contains the pork tenderloin, rib chops, loin chops, rib roast, sirloin chops, and sirloin roasts.

- *Side.* Spare ribs and bacon come from the side primal cut area.

- *Leg.* Ham and ham roasts come from the leg primal cut area, which is also referred to as the pork belly.

Exhibit 8 illustrates basic pork cuts.

Processed Pork Products. Processed pork products can be cured or fresh and are very popular because of their versatility as ingredients. The most popular processed pork products are bacon, Canadian bacon, ham and sausage.

Bacon. Bacon is available in slabs or sliced. It is produced by brining and smoking meat from the pork belly. Sliced bacon can be purchased in different thicknesses. Thin-sliced bacon contains 28–32 slices per pound. Thick-sliced bacon contains 10–14 slices per pound. Bacon is purchased by the number of slices per pound. Canadian bacon is brined and smoked meat from the boneless pork loin section. Canadian bacon can be purchased either whole or sliced.

Exhibit 6   On-Line Beef Cut Resource

Source: www.beeffoodservice.com/cuts/info.aspx?code=57.

Ham. Ham comes from the hind leg section of the hog. Hams can be cured or uncured, fresh or smoked, bone-in or boneless, and whole or formed. Cured hams are produced by injection with or immersion in a salt solution. This process gives ham its characteristic flavor and color. However, it also tends to dry the ham, so water is often added back in. Such products should be labeled "water added." If a ham is to be smoked, this is done after the curing process. Smoking, like curing, is done to lend a particular flavor and color to the ham. Whole hams can be purchased with the bone in or removed. Boneless ham is often desirable because the yield is easier to quantify. Formed hams are produced by separating the whole ham into its basic muscles, trimming the fat, curing, and then stuffing the muscles into a casing. Formed hams are popular for slicing due to the uniformity of the meat and the lack of large amounts of fat. The quality of a formed ham can be determined by its lower percentage of added fat and water. Most all boneless formed hams are fully cooked and ready to eat.

Sausage. Sausage is produced by taking fresh ground pork meat and adding spices, seasonings, fat, and fillers to give a particular characteristic. The mixture can then be stuffed into a casing to form it for cooking purposes. For example, Cajun spices, coarse black pepper, and garlic are added to ground pork to produce a popular spicy sausage called andouille. There are three main types of sausages: fresh, smoked or cooked, and dried or hard. Fresh sausage includes products like

Exhibit 7   On-Line Food Service Resources

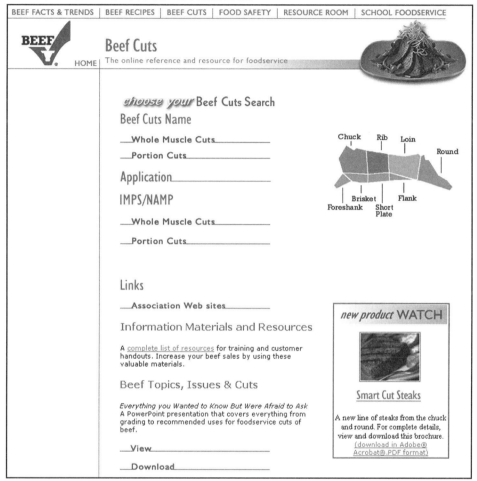

Source: www.beeffoodservice.com/cuts/default.aspx.

ground sausage, breakfast sausage, Italian sausage, and bratwurst. Smoked and cooked sausages have been prepared from raw ingredients, then treated with preservative chemicals such as nitrates. The smoking and cooking is done to give the sausage a particular characteristic. Examples of smoked and cooked sausage include hot dogs, bologna, kielbasa, and knockwurst. Dried or hard sausages are produced from cured pork then dried under carefully controlled conditions using bacterial fermentation to create a distinct flavor for the finished product. Examples of dried or hard sausages include pepperoni and salami.

Veal Cuts and Characteristics

Veal cuts are similar to beef primal cuts. The big difference between beef and veal is the tenderness of veal. Veal comes from young beef animals raised on special

Exhibit 8   Pork Cuts

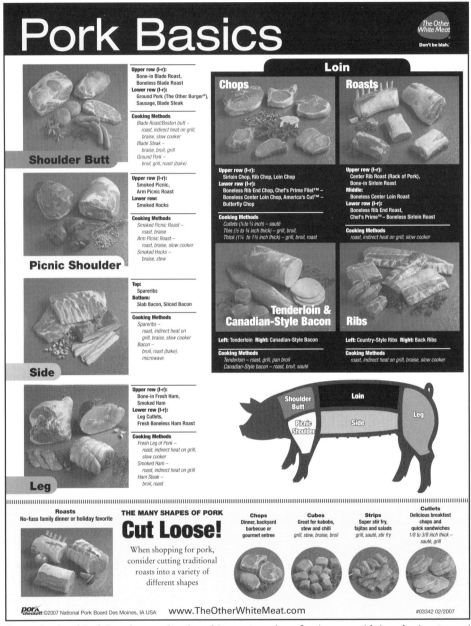

Source: National Pork Board, www.theotherwhitemeat.com/aspx/beginners_guide/purchasingstorage/purchasingPorkPrint.htm.

diets. The primal cuts include the shoulder, rack, loin, leg, and shank or breast. Exhibit 9 shows basic veal cuts.

Exhibit 9   Veal Food Service Cuts

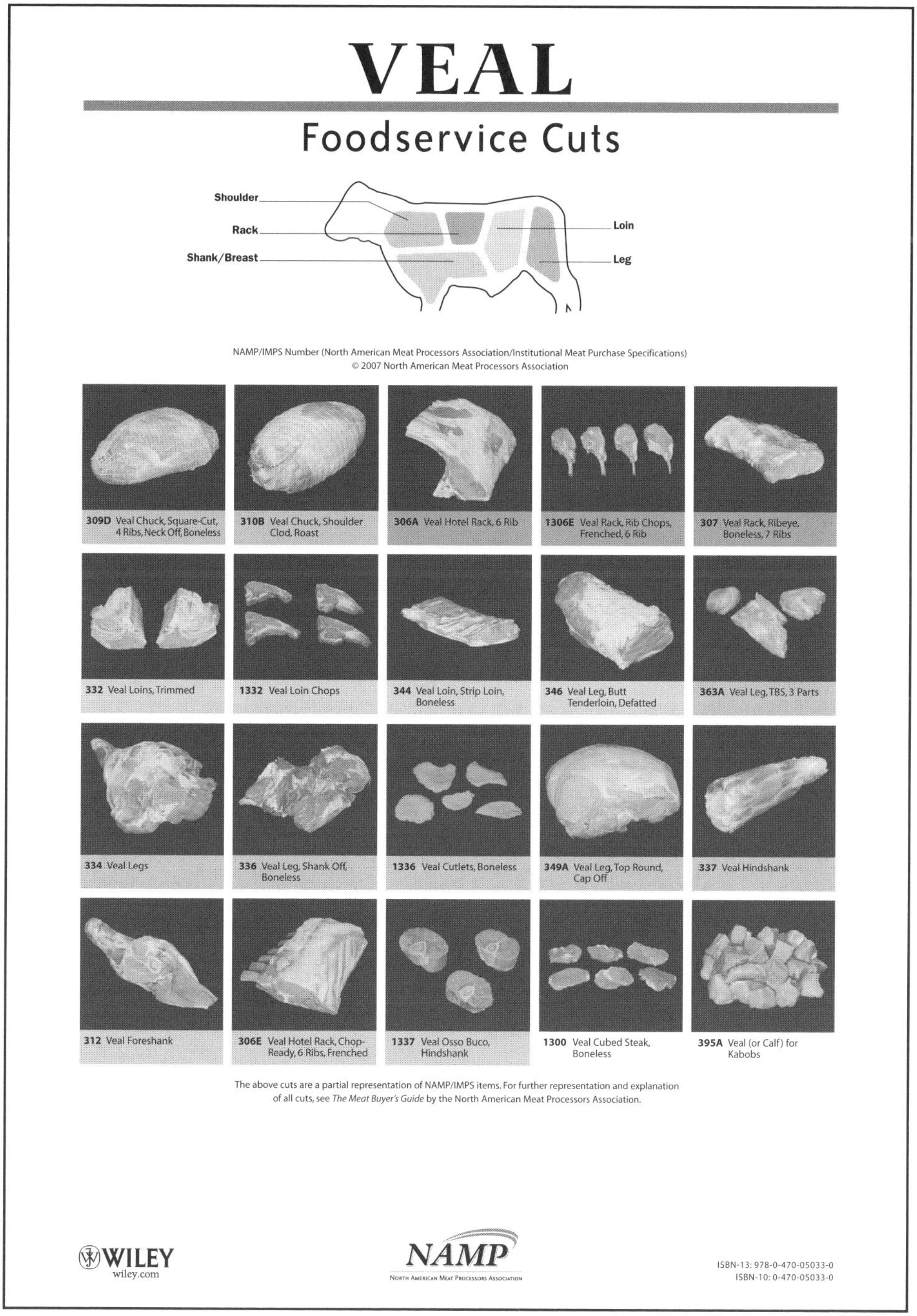

VEAL
Foodservice Cuts

Shoulder
Rack
Shank/Breast
Loin
Leg

NAMP/IMPS Number (North American Meat Processors Association/Institutional Meat Purchase Specifications)
© 2007 North American Meat Processors Association

309D Veal Chuck, Square-Cut, 4 Ribs, Neck Off, Boneless

310B Veal Chuck, Shoulder Clod, Roast

306A Veal Hotel Rack, 6 Rib

1306E Veal Rack, Rib Chops, Frenched, 6 Rib

307 Veal Rack, Ribeye, Boneless, 7 Ribs

332 Veal Loins, Trimmed

1332 Veal Loin Chops

344 Veal Loin, Strip Loin, Boneless

346 Veal Leg, Butt Tenderloin, Defatted

363A Veal Leg, TBS, 3 Parts

334 Veal Legs

336 Veal Leg, Shank Off, Boneless

1336 Veal Cutlets, Boneless

349A Veal Leg, Top Round, Cap Off

337 Veal Hindshank

312 Veal Foreshank

306E Veal Hotel Rack, Chop-Ready, 6 Ribs, Frenched

1337 Veal Osso Buco, Hindshank

1300 Veal Cubed Steak, Boneless

395A Veal (or Calf) for Kabobs

The above cuts are a partial representation of NAMP/IMPS items. For further representation and explanation of all cuts, see *The Meat Buyer's Guide* by the North American Meat Processors Association.

WILEY
wiley.com

NAMP
North American Meat Processors Association

ISBN-13: 978-0-470-05033-0
ISBN-10: 0-470-05033-0

Source: North American Meat Processors Association *Beef Foodservice Poster, Revised.* © 2007, NAMP. Reprinted with permission of John Wiley & Sons, Inc.

Lamb Cuts and Characteristics

Lamb meat comes from an animal less than 14 months of age. The meat from animals 14 months and older is referred to as **mutton**. The primal cuts of lamb are the shank/breast, shoulder, rack, loin, sirloin, and leg. The demand for lamb is low compared with other meat products. Because of this, national production volume is small, making access to lamb carcass and primal cuts limited. Most lamb is sold according to a buyer specification or based on standard specifications. Common lamb cuts are shown in Exhibit 10.

Institutional Meat Purchase Specifications ——————

The North American Meat Processors Association (NAMP), National Live Stock and Meat Board, USDA Agricultural Marketing Service Livestock Division, and food service purchasing managers, through a cooperative effort, have established standard meat specifications referred to as **Institutional Meat Purchase Specifications** (IMPS).

Standards

The *Meat Buyer's Guide*, published by NAMP, includes these specification numbers as well as a description and picture of each meat cut. These IMPS numbers allow buyers to order specific meat cuts without having to prepare their own specifications. The IMPS number is constructed with the first digit of the number referring to the type of product and the remaining digits referring to a specific cut and trim. Using the IMPS number when ordering assures buyers that they will get the exact cut of meat they desire. For example beef products begin with #100 to designate a whole beef carcass. #100A designates a whole beef carcass, trimmed. Subsequent numbers designate the different side, forequarters, and primal cuts. Portion-cut products have four-digit designations. For example, boneless strip loin steaks are designated by #1180 and the center cut would be designated by #1180A. The #1 added to the beginning of the IMPS number indicates portioned items. Beef items begin with #100, lamb with #200, veal with #300, pork with #400, and further processed and byproduct items #500–#800. Exhibits 11–14 contain IMPS numbers for various meat products.

Writing Specifications

If IMPS numbers or NAMP specifications are not used, then meat buyers must indicate the exact cut of meat they desire with muscles that should be included, location of the cut within the carcass or primal cut, and exact dimensions of the cut. It is important that buyers use the terminology related to the NAMP specifications so the processor will understand the written specifications.

Meat Products and Food Safety ——————

Federal meat inspection ensures that meat is processed in a wholesome manner and that it is safe when it leaves the processor. It is up to the food service operator to

Exhibit 10   Lamb Cuts

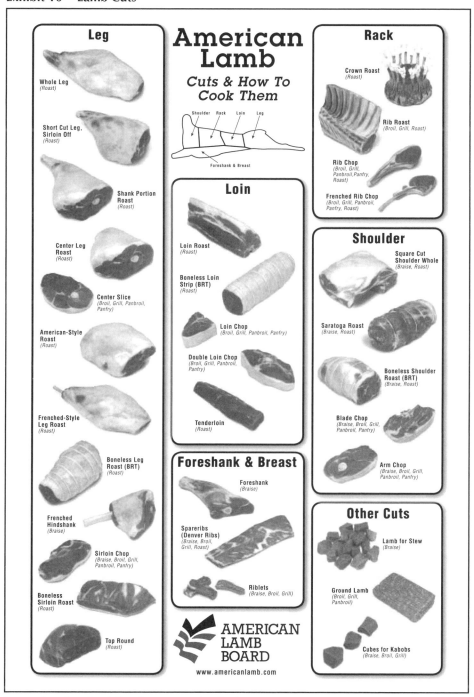

Source: American Lamb Board, www.americanlamb.com.

Exhibit 11   Partial List of IMPS Numbers for Beef Products

Item No.	Product	Item No.	Product
100	Carcass	159	Round, Primal, Boneless
101	Side	161	Round, Shank Off, Boneless
102	Forequarter	163	Round, Shank Off, 3-Way, Boneless
102A	Forequarter, Boneless	164	Round, Rump and Shank Off
103	Rib, Primal	165	Round, Rump and Shank Off, Boneless
107	Rib, Oven-Prepared	165A	Round, Rump and Shank Off, Bone-less, Special
109	Rib, Roast-Ready		
109A	Rib, Roast-Ready, Special	167	Round, Knuckle
109B	Rib, Blade Meat	168	Round, Top (Inside), Untrimmed
111	Rib, Spencer Roll	170	Round, Bottom (Gooseneck)
112	Rib, Ribeye Roll	170A	Round, Bottom (Gooseneck), Heel Out
112A	Rib, Ribeye Roll, Lip-On	171	Round, Bottom (Gooseneck), Untrimmed
113	Chuck, Square Cut		
114	Chuck, Shoulder Clod	171A	Round, Bottom (Gooseneck), Untrimmed, Heel Out
114A	Chuck, Shoulder Clod Roast		
115	Chuck, Square-Cut, Boneless	171B	Round, Outside Round
116	Chuck, Square-Cut, Clod Out, Bone-less	171C	Round, Eye of Round
		172	Loin, Full Loin, Trimmed
116A	Chuck, Chuck Roll	173	Loin, Short Loin
117	Foreshank	174	Loin, Short Loin, Short Cut
118	Brisket	175	Loin, Strip Loin
119	Brisket, Deckle On, Boneless	181	Loin, Sirloin
120	Brisket, Deckle Off, Boneless	182	Loin, Sirloin Butt, Boneless
121	Plate, Short Plate	183	Loin, Sirloin Butt, Boneless, Trimmed
121A	Plate, Short Plate, Boneless	184	Loin, Top Sirloin Butt, Boneless
122	Plate, Full	185	Loin, Bottom Sirloin Butt, Boneless
122A	Plate, Full, Boneless	185A	Loin, Bottom Sirloin Butt, Flap, Bone-less
123A	Short Plate, Short Ribs, Trimmed		
123B	Rib, Short Ribs, Trimmed	185B	Loin, Bottom Sirloin Butt, Ball Tip, Boneless
125	Chuck, Armbone		
126	Chuck, Armbone, Clod Out, Boneless	185C	Loin, Bottom Sirloin Butt, Tri-Tip, Boneless
127	Chuck, Cross-Cut		
128	Chuck, Cross-Cut, Boneless	185D	Loin, Bottom Sirloin Butt, Tri-Tip, Boneless, Defatted
132	Triangle		
133	Triangle, Boneless	186	Loin, Bottom Sirloin Butt, Boneless, Trimmed
134	Beef Bones		
135	Diced Beef	189	Loin, Tenderloin, Full
135A	Beef for Stewing	189A	Loin, Tenderloin, Full, Side Muscle On, Defatted
136	Ground Beef		
136A	Ground Beef and Vegetable Protein Product	190	Loin, Tenderloin, Full, Side Muscled Off, Skinned
137	Ground Beef, Special	191	Loin, Tenderloin, Butt
155	Hindquarter	192	Loin, Tenderloin, Short
155A	Hindquarter, Boneless	193	Flank, Flank Steak
158	Round, Primal		

Source: www.ams.usda.gov/LSG/imps/imps100.pdf.

keep the meat safe once the product is received through storage and service. Food safety standards must be maintained at all levels of storage, preparation, cooking, and service. Fresh meat should be stored at temperatures between 35–40° F (2–4° C).

Exhibit 12   Partial List of IMPS Numbers for Pork Products

Item No.	Product	Item No.	Product
400	Carcass	516	Pork Shoulder (Cured and Smoked)
400A	Whole Roasting Pig	517	Pork Shoulder, Skinned (Cured)
401	Leg (Fresh Ham)	518	Pork Shoulder, Skinned (Cured and Smoked)
401A	Leg (Fresh Ham), Short Shank		
402	Leg (Fresh Ham), Skinned	525	Pork Shoulder Picnic (Cured)
402A	Leg (Fresh Ham), Skinned, Short Shank	526	Pork Shoulder Picnic (Cured and Smoked)
402B	Leg (Fresh Ham), Boneless	527	Pork Shoulder Picnic (Cured and Smoked), Boneless, Tied
403	Shoulder		
404	Shoulder, Skinned	530	Pork Shoulder Butt, Cellar Trimmed, Boneless (Cured and Smoked)
405	Shoulder, Picnic		
406	Shoulder, Boston Butt	535	Belly, Skin-On (Cured)
407	Shoulder Butt, Cellar Trimmed, Boneless	536	Bacon, Slab (Cured and Smoked), Skin-On, Formed
408	Belly	537	Belly, Slab (Cured and Smoked), Skinless, Formed
409	Belly, Skinless		
410	Loin	539	Bacon, Sliced (Cured and Smoked), Skinless
411	Loin, Bladeless		
412	Loin, Center Cut, 8 Ribs	541	Bacon, Sliced (Cured and Smoked), Ends and Pieces
413	Loin, Boneless		
413A	Loin, Roast, Boneless	545	Pork Loin (Cured and Smoked)
414	Loin, Canadian Back	546	Pork Loin, Bladeless (Cured and Smoked)
415	Tenderloin		
416	Spareribs	550	Canadian Style Bacon (Cured and Smoked), Unsliced
416A	Spareribs, St. Louis Style		
417	Shoulder Hocks	555	Jowl Butts, Cellar Trim (Cured)
418	Trimmings	556	Jowl Squares (Cured and Smoked)
419	Jowl	558	Spareribs, Fully-Cooked
420	Pig's Feet, Front	559	Spareribs (Cured and Smoked)
421	Neck Bones	560	Hocks, Ham (Cured and Smoked)
422	Loin, Back Ribs	561	Hocks, Shoulder (Cured and Smoked)
423	Loin, Country-Style Ribs	562	Clear Fatback (Cured)
500	Ham, Short Shank (Cured)	563	Feet, Front (Cured)
501	Ham, Short Shank (Cured and Smoked)	1400	Steak Cubed
		1406	Boston Butt Steaks
502	Ham, Short Shank, Skinned (Cured)	1407	Shoulder Butt Steaks, Boneless
503	Ham, Short Shank, Skinned (Cured and Smoked), Fully-Cooked	1410	Loin Chops
		1410A	Loin, Rib Chops
504	Ham, Skinless, Partially Boned (Cured and Smoked)	1410B	Loin, End Chops
		1411	Loin Chops, Bladeless
505	Ham, Boneless (Cured and Smoked), Fully-Cooked	1412	Loin Chops, Center Cut
505A	Ham, Boneless, Tied (Cured and Smoked), Fully-Cooked	1412A	Loin Chops, Center Cut, Chine Bone Off
508	Ham, Boiled, Boneless (Cured), Fully-Cooked	1412B	Loin Chops, Center Cut, Boneless
		1413	Loin Chops, Boneless
509	Ham, Boneless (Cured and Smoked), Fully-Cooked, Special	1495	Coarse Chopped Pork
		1496	Ground Pork Patties
515	Pork Shoulder (Cured)	1496A	Ground Pork and Vegetable Protein Product Patties

Sources: www.ams.usda.gov/LSG/imps/imps400.pdf and www.ams.usda.gov/LSG/imps/imps500.pdf.

Exhibit 13 Partial List of IMPS Numbers for Veal Products

Item No.	Product	Item No.	Product
300	Carcass	330A	Hindquarter, 2 Ribs
303	Side	331	Loins
304	Foresaddle, 11 Ribs	332	Loins, Trimmed
304A	Forequarter, 11 Ribs	334	Legs
306	Hotel Rack, 7 Ribs	335	Leg, Boneless, Roast Ready, Tied
308	Chucks, 4 Ribs	336	Leg, Shank Off, Boneless, Roast
308A	Chucks, 5 Ribs		Ready, Tied
309	Chucks, Square-Cut, 4 Ribs	337	Hindshank
309A	Chucks, Square-Cut, 5 Ribs	338	Trimmings
309B	Chuck, Square-Cut, 4 Ribs, Boneless	339	Trimmings, Special
309C	Chuck, Square-Cut, 5 Ribs, Boneless	341	Back, 9 Ribs, Trimmed
309D	Chuck, Square-Cut, 4 Ribs, Neck Off,	342	Back, Strip, Boneless
	Boneless, Tied	1300	Cubed Steak
310	Chuck, Outside Shoulder, Boneless	1301	Cubed Steak, Special
310A	Chuck, Shoulder Clod	1302	Veal Slices
310B	Chuck, Shoulder Clod, Roast	1306	Rack, Rib Chops, 7 Rib
311	Chuck, Blade Portion, Neck Off,	1309A	Chuck, Shoulder Blade Chops
	Boneless	1332	Loin Chops
311A	Chuck, Inside Roll, Boneless	1336	Cutlets
311B	Chuck, Chuck Eye Roll, Boneless	1396	Ground Veal Patties
312	Foreshank	1396A	Ground Veal and Vegetable Protein
313	Breast		Product Patties
330	Hindsaddle, 2 Ribs		

Source: www.ams.usda.gov/LSG/imps/imps300.pdf.

Exhibit 14 Partial List of IMPS Numbers for Lamb Products

Item No.	Product	Item No.	Product
200	Carcass	233B	Leg, Shank Off
202	Foresaddle	233C	Leg, Trotter Off, Partially Boneless
203	Bracelet	233D	Leg, Shank Off, Partially Boneless
204	Rack	233E	Leg, Steamship, 3/4, Aitch, Removed
206	Shoulders	234	Leg, Boneless, Tied
207	Shoulders, Square-Cut	234A	Leg, Shank Off, Boneless, Tied
208	Shoulder, Square-Cut, Boneless,	235	Back
	Tied	236	Back, Trimmed
209A	Ribs, Breast Bones Off	238	Trimmings
209B	Shoulder, Ribs	1204B	Rib Chops
210	Foreshank	1204C	Rib Chops, Frenched
230	Hindsaddle	1207	Shoulder Chops
231	Loins	1232A	Loin Chops
232	Loins, Trimmed	1296	Ground Lamb Patties
233	Legs	1296A	Ground Lamb and Vegetable Protein
233A	Leg, Trotter Off		Product Patties

Source: www.ams.usda.gov/LSG/imps/imps200.pdf.

Cooked and processed cooked meats should be physically located above fresh meat products in storage. Frozen meat products should be maintained at a temperature of –10° F (–23° C) or lower.

Diseases like *bovine spongiform encephalopathy* (BSE), which is commonly known as mad cow disease, and hoof-and-mouth disease should not be a problem if meat has undergone federal or state inspection. An outbreak of disease can, however, affect the supply and demand of meat and must be considered when purchasing implicated products.

Management Considerations

Purchasing meat products is based for the most part on consideration of quantity, quality, and types of cuts. Studying consumer trends, utilizing distributor recommendations and referring to standard specifications can help managers make responsible decisions.

Meat on the Menu

Meat items are usually the highest cost items on a menu and, therefore, the selection of meat products on the menu can make a big difference in the profitability and the popularity of a restaurant or food service operation. Alternative meat cuts developed by meat processors, such as tri-tip and flatiron steaks, can be added to a menu as popular cost-effective alternatives. Cost-effective meat items can be featured on menus. The selection of meat items for a menu should take into consideration the full utilization of the product, whether it be as a byproduct or as a leftover item.

Meat Alternatives

Meat is not right for every menu or occasion. Many alternatives exist for meat products. Seafood and poultry items often substitute well into many meat recipes. Some food service operators have had success with game meats, such as bison, buffalo, ostrich, and venison. Meat substitutes such as tofu, vegetables, and grain patties can be offered as vegetarian alternatives.

AP versus EP

As purchased (AP) versus edible portion (EP) is a matter of AP prices and condition versus the EP cost after cleaning, trimming, and fabricating. Meats for food service are often purchased in portion-controlled, plastic-encased, boxed cases. This ensures that the price paid for each portion provides the fullest edible portion. AP price and EP cost can become a problem with meats that must be cut and/or portioned to order. Sliced prime rib must be weighed to ensure the proper portion is being served or costs will get out of control. Sandwich meat must be portioned correctly by weight with an accurate scale or the cost per sandwich will be adversely affected. The move toward the use of pre-portioned and portion-controlled meat products can result in a higher AP price, but when labor cost, staff expertise, and EP cost is considered, it can result in a true savings. Consider two examples.

Butchering cost and yield. Assume 8 pounds of pork tenderloin is purchased at a price of $4.25 per pound. The AP cost would be 8 lb × $4.25/lb = $34.00. The product has no bone, but quite a bit of fat and will need to be trimmed. After trimming, we have 2 pounds, 8 ounces (2.5 pounds) of fat, and 12 ounces (.75 pounds) of useable meat has been trimmed off. This leaves us with 4.75 pounds of useable meat (8 lb − 2.5 lb − .75 lb = 4.75 lb). Let's say the fat is worth $0.10 per pound and the trimmed meat is worth $2.49 per pound.

Fat cost:	2.5 × $.10	=	$.25
Trimmed useable meat cost:	.75 × $2.49	=	$1.87
EP cost:	$34.00 − $.25 − $1.87	=	$31.88

When the total EP cost is divided by the amount of useable meat left, the useable pork tenderloin ends up costing the operation $6.71 per pound ($31.88 ÷ 4.75 = $6.71).

Cooking loss. Assume a 12-pound boneless ham roast is purchased at a price of $1.69 per pound. The total AP cost is $20.28 (12 lb × $1.69/lb = $20.28). After cooking, the ham weighs 10 pounds, 4 ounces (10.25 pounds), which makes the EP cost $1.98 per pound ($20.28 ÷ 10.25 lb = $1.98/lb).

Endnotes

1. "Top 200 Annual Industry Report," *Meat Processing* (June 2006), pp. 28–63.

Key Terms

bovine spongiform encephalopathy (**BSE**)—A major food safety concern for meat products. Also known as mad cow disease.

hoof-and-mouth disease—A highly contagious livestock disease that poses a food safety concern for meat products.

Institutional Meat Purchase Specifications (IMPS)—Standard numbers used to identify specific cuts of meat.

marbling—Fat in the muscle tissue of meat.

mutton—Lamb meat from animals older than 14 months of age.

no-roll—A product that has not been graded and has had no stamp rolled on it.

primal cut—The main cut of meat from which retail cuts are fabricated.

Review Questions

1. How does the production and supply of meat affect its pricing?

2. How is meat inspected?

3. How is meat graded?

4. What is the difference between inspection and grading of meat products?

5. What agencies are involved in meat inspection?

6. What agencies are involved in meat grading?

7. What are some of the different distribution channels through which meat is purchased?

8. What are the major cuts of beef, pork, veal, and lamb, and what are the primary characteristics of each?

9. What are the major types of processed meat products?

10. What are the requirements and content of specifications for meat and meat products?

11. What are some of the sources of information available to assist in purchasing decisions for meats and meat products?

Internet Sites

For more information, visit the following Internet sites. Remember that Internet addresses can change without notice. If the site is no longer there, you can use a search engine to look for additional sites.

American Lamb Board
www.americanlambboard.org/

American Veal Association
www.vealfarm.com/index.asp

Beef for Food Service Professionals
www.beeffoodservice.com/

Federal Meat Inspection Act
www.fsis.usda.gov/Regulations_&_
Policies/Federal_Meat_Inspection_
Act/index.asp

Food Market
www.foodmarket.com

Institutional Meat Purchase
 Specifications
www.ams.usda.gov/lsg/stand/imps.htm

North American Meat Processors
 Association
www.namp.com

Pork Checkoff
www.theotherwhitemeat.com/

Pork Food Service
www.porkfoodservice.com/

Urner Barry *Yellow Sheet*
www.yellowsheet.com

Chapter 9 Outline

Fish and Shellfish Harvesting
Factors Affecting Fish and Shellfish Supplies
Factors Affecting Fish and Shellfish Costs
   and Pricing
Fish and Shellfish Inspection
Fish and Shellfish Grading
Fish and Shellfish Purchasing Systems
   Market Forms of Fish
   Market Forms of Shellfish
   Major Fish Categories
   Major Shellfish Categories
   Fish and Shellfish Specifications
Management Considerations
   Food Safety Issues
   Overharvesting
   Featuring Underutilized Species
   Raw Fish Usage

Competencies

1. Describe how fish and shellfish are harvested, supplied, and priced, and explain the factors that influence fish and shellfish population. (pp. 305–307)

2. Explain the inspection and grading process for fish and shellfish. (pp. 307–308)

3. Describe the distribution channels through which fish and shellfish are purchased. (pp. 308–311)

4. List available sources of information to assist in seafood purchasing decisions. (pp. 310–311)

5. Understand the differences in quality and use among fresh, frozen, and processed fish and shellfish. (pp. 311–312)

6. Identify the major categories of fish and shellfish and the primary characteristics of each. (pp. 313–315)

7. Explain the requirements, content, and importance of specifications for fish and shellfish. (pp. 315–319)

8. Describe management considerations related to purchasing seafood products. (p. 320)

9
Seafood

PURCHASING FRESH FISH AND SHELLFISH is probably the most challenging buying process a purchasing manager will encounter. Processed fish products are much easier to buy and, for the most part, are standardized. However, the purchase of fresh fish is very much dependent upon the availability of the product and a distributor to provide the product. In large cities, fish and shellfish can be purchased fresh at the local market. For the vast majority of operators, however, fresh fish and shellfish must be purchased through a distributor. The availability of any one item is dependent upon the supply available to the distributor. A steady supply of one type of fresh fish is, therefore, often a problem. Menus must often be revised daily based upon supply and price considerations. Pricing and supply information can be found in *Urner Barry's Seafood Price-Current* (see Exhibit 1).

Fish and Shellfish Harvesting

Fish inhabit all of the oceans and most of the lakes, rivers, and streams of the world. Most fish species are shelf dwellers—that is, they live in areas close to coastal areas where continental shelves exist. The fish also **spawn**, or lay their eggs, in the same areas. Fresh fish purchased for food service operations in the United States are, for the most part, caught and **harvested** in U.S. waters by U.S. fishermen. Most imported fish and shellfish products must be frozen or canned due to their perishability.

A popular trend has been the practice of **aquaculture**—that is, raising fish and shellfish under controlled conditions in controlled environments. Fish farms may utilize controlled ponds to raise and harvest a wide variety of fish and shellfish. Most fish farming is done with freshwater species, but saltwater aquaculture has been increasing. The most popular types of fish and shellfish raised through aquaculture include trout, salmon, tilapia, crawfish, shrimp, scallops, oysters, mussels, and clams. Raising shellfish through aquaculture techniques has been most valuable because conditions that lead to contamination, such as bacterial growth, can be controlled. Fish farming is beneficial because it reduces the risk of contamination in supply and ensures consistent quality.

Fish and shellfish purchasers must be aware of where the fish they are purchasing is harvested. There are waters in the United States where fish and shellfish should be avoided. Problems such as sewage contamination, lead or heavy metal contamination, and viral or bacterial contamination can make fish and shellfish harvested from those areas dangerous for human consumption. There are also areas of water where the harvesting of certain species of fish has been banned due to overfishing of the area and/or species.

Exhibit 1 Urner Barry's Seafood Price-Current

URNER BARRY'S Seafood PRICE CURRENT
ESTABLISHED 1858

"Urner Barry's Seafood Price-Current"
Editor: Paul B. Brown, Jr.
Market Reporters: James Kenny,
Janice Brown, MaryAnn Zicarelli, Angel Rubio
Published Tuesday and Thursday in a variety of media
by Urner Barry Publications, Inc.
P.O. Box 389 Toms River, NJ 08754-0389
Copyright 2007
Urner Barry Publications, Inc. ISSN 0270-417X
Phone 732-240-5330 • Fax 732-341-0891 • www.urnerbarry.com

SHRIMP COMPLEX (Ex-Warehouse, East or West Coast, LTL)

Shell-On, Headless

Count per lb.	Wild, Gulf of Mexico, Domestic, Brown	Wild, Gulf of Mexico, Domestic, White	Cooked, Southeast Asian, Tail-On, Black Tiger	Cooked, Asian, Tail-On, White	Farm Raised, Southeast Asian, P&D, Tail-On, Black Tiger	Farm Raised, Asian, Raw P&D, Tail-On, White	Wild, Mexican, No. 1, White*	Wild, Mexican, No. 1, Brown*	Wild, Central American, No. 1, Brown*	Wild, Central & South American, White	Farm Raised, Central American, White	Farm Raised, Asian, White
<10	10.55-10.65	10.55-10.65							11.25-11.50	11.25-11.50		
<12	9.00-9.10	9.25-9.35		8.75-8.85			9.50-9.60	9.25-9.35	9.25-9.35	9.25-9.50		
<15	6.60-6.70	6.30-6.40					6.60-6.70	6.00-6.25	6.00-6.25	6.00-6.25		
16-20	5.15-5.25 +	5.25-5.35 +	8.20-8.40	7.20-7.30			5.40-5.50	5.05-5.15	5.00-5.25	5.00-5.25	4.85-4.95	
21-25	4.75-4.85 +	5.25-5.35 +	6.60-6.80	6.00-6.10		5.50-5.60	4.90-5.00	4.75-4.85			3.95-4.05	4.20-4.30
26-30	4.35-4.45 +	4.55-4.65 +	5.95-6.15		4.60-4.70	4.65-4.75					3.80-3.90	3.60-3.70
31-35	3.60-3.70	3.75-3.85									3.20-3.30	3.05-3.15
36-40	3.15-3.25	3.40-3.50	5.00-5.20								2.80-2.90	2.80-2.90
41-50	2.95-3.05	3.25-3.35	4.00-4.20	4.04-4.10							2.45-2.55 +	2.40-2.50 +
51-60	2.75-2.85	3.10-3.20	3.60-3.70	3.50-3.60							2.30-2.40	2.25-2.35
61-70	2.70-2.80		3.30-3.40	3.30-3.40	*FOB WC	*FOB WC			*FOB WC		2.15-2.25	2.15-2.25
71-80											2.00-2.10	2.05-2.15
81-90	-	-										

Head-On** (Count per kg, $ per lb.)

Count per kg.	Farm Raised, Central & South American, White, Head-On*	Farm Raised, India, Black Tiger	Farm Raised, Bangladesh, Black Tiger	Farm Raised, Southeast Asian, Black Tiger	Farm Raised, Asian, Easy Peel, White	Farm Raised, Asian, Easy Peel, Black Tiger
<10						
<12		9.90-10.00	9.90-10.00	9.95-10.05		
<15		6.70-6.80	6.55-6.65	6.90-7.00	7.00-7.10	
16-20		5.70-5.80	5.60-5.70	6.00-6.10	5.85-5.95	
21-25		5.35-5.45	5.25-5.35	5.55-5.65	5.20-5.30	
26-30	20-30	4.40-4.50		4.80-4.90	3.55-3.65	4.65-4.75
31-40	30-40 3.05-3.15	3.70-3.80	3.40-3.50	3.90-4.00	2.90-3.00	
41-50	40-50 2.40-2.50				2.55-2.65	
51-60	50-60 2.10-2.20				2.50-2.60	
61-70	60-70 2.00-2.10					
71-90	70-80 1.85-1.95					
91-110	80-100 1.75-1.85					
111-130	100-120 1.65-1.75					
131-150						

Count per lb.	Farm Raised, Asian, Easy Peel, Freshwater
2-4	
4-6	10.40-10.60
6-8	9.10-9.30
8-12	6.60-6.80
13-15	5.70-5.90
16-20	4.60-4.80

**Count per kg, $ per lb.

Peeled, Headless, Finished Count

Count per lb.	Cooked, Southeast Asian, Tail-On, Black Tiger	Cooked, Asian, Tail-On, White	Farm Raised, Southeast Asian, Raw Asian, P&D, Tail-On, Black Tiger	Farm Raised, Asian, Raw, P&D, Tail-Off, White	Farm Raised, Asian, Raw, P&D, Tail-Off, White
<10					
<12					
<15					
16-20	8.75-8.85				
21-25	7.20-7.30	5.95-6.15	5.50-5.60	6.00-6.20	
26-30	6.00-6.10	5.25-5.35	5.00-5.20	4.60-4.70	5.15-5.25
31-40	4.00-4.10		4.00-4.20	3.65-3.75	4.10-4.20
41-50	3.95-4.05	3.50-3.60	3.60-3.70	3.40-3.50	3.80-3.90
51-60	3.55-3.65	3.30-3.40	3.30-3.40	3.20-3.30	
61-70	3.35-3.45	3.15-3.25		3.10-3.20	
71-90	3.15-3.25	3.00-3.10		3.00-3.10	
91-110	3.00-3.10				

Count per lb.	Wild, Gulf of Mexico, Domestic, PUD	Wild, Central & South American, PUD	Asian, PUD	Wild, Central & South American, PTO
36-40	3.30-3.40			
41-50	3.15-3.25			
51-60	3.00-3.10			
61-70	2.90-3.00			
71-90	2.85-2.95			
91-110	2.70-2.80 +	2.65-2.75		
111-130	2.45-2.55	2.45-2.55		
131-150	2.20-2.30	2.35-2.45		
151-200	1.75-1.85	2.15-2.25		
201-300	1.50-1.60	1.65-1.75		
301-500		1.20-1.30		

Shrimp Situation

White Shrimp: 41-50 count shell-on headless white shrimp are full steady to firm and wanted. 51-60 count Latin white shrimp are steady to full steady. 36-40 count Asian white shrimp adjusted slightly lower with some lower offerings noted. The balance of the market is steady.

Black Tiger Shrimp: 26-30 count and smaller shell-on headless shrimp are barely steady as white shrimp readily replace that product. Larger count shrimp are steady and in limited supplies. New season offerings are increasing but have not yet increased available inventory.

Shrimp Imports: March shrimp imports are down almost 10% leaving year-to-date imports up only slightly. Of all the major shrimp suppliers only China and Malaysia reflected higher imports in March versus a year ago.

Gulf Domestic Shrimp: The lackluster fishing effort thus far has not allowed packers to replenish inventories of HLSO shrimp in any significant way. Holes are not being filled and supplies of remaining sizes declining. As a result, the market for HLSO shrimp ranges full steady to firm. PUD's were subject to slight adjustments, though mostly unchanged.

Source: *Urner Barry's Seafood Price-Current* (Toms River, N.J.: Urner Barry Publications, Inc., 2007).

Factors Affecting Fish and Shellfish Supplies ──────────

Many factors can affect the supply of fresh fish. Most of the factors are related to weather or acts of nature. Rough weather and high seas can keep fishermen from going out. Changes in water temperature can affect the life, size, and availability of fish. Drought conditions can affect the supply of freshwater fish due to reduced water levels in rivers and lakes. Since many types of fish are harvested and imported frozen into the United States, a disruption in the transportation system can affect the supply of fish.

Fresh fish and shellfish are often shipped the same day or overnight to cities and locations in non-coastal areas of the United States. The fish are often shipped by air, so any disruption in airfreight can affect the availability of supplies.

Factors Affecting Fish and Shellfish Costs and Pricing ──────

With the exception of aquaculture, fish and shellfish are among the few food items that generally are captured or harvested from the wild with little control over the development of the product. Most other protein products, like beef, pork, lamb, and poultry, as well as most vegetable products, are raised and harvested under controlled conditions. Fish and shellfish are truly subject to the forces of nature. This lack of control causes the cost and price of fish and shellfish to fluctuate on a daily basis based on the availability of and demand for the product. No other food source is quite so price sensitive. Processed and frozen fish and shellfish can be controlled and price points decided upon, which allows pricing contracts to be an acceptable consideration. It is not unusual to see price contracts for such common items as frozen shrimp. However, the price for fresh red snapper or Maine lobster may vary weekly, or even daily, based on the availability of the products. Another significant issue for fresh fish and shellfish is the aforementioned problem of shipping. Since fresh fish items are often shipped by airfreight due to their perishability, their costs must also account for shipping. Shipping can add 10 percent or more to the cost of the product and with rising fuel costs, the expectation is that the cost of shipping will only continue to increase.

The best way for buyers to ensure they are paying a fair price for seafood is to work with reputable distributors. Because quality is such a major consideration with seafood, good relationships with a few key distributors is important. Occasionally, a block buy of seafood will become available to a distributor. If a trusted distributor offers a good price, it might be worth offering the item as a special. Be wary—if the price sounds too good to be true, it often is. Good buys are often available for frozen or processed seafood products. Good prices for large quantities of frozen shrimp become possible during the height of the harvesting season and should be considered if storage is available.

Fish and Shellfish Inspection ─────────────────

The federal government provides an official program for the inspection and grading of seafood and fish products through the National Marine Fisheries Service (a department of the National Oceanic and Atmospheric Administration and the

United States Department of Commerce [USDC]). However, unlike other protein products, fish and shellfish are not subject to mandatory federal inspection. The inspection of fish and fish products is conducted by the United States Food and Drug Administration (FDA) at food production and processing plants through its Hazard Analysis and Critical Control Point (HACCP) program. The FDA periodically inspects processing plants for conformity to HACCP principles. Additionally, federal and state agencies cooperate in the inspection of beds where clams, oysters, and mussels are raised and harvested. If seafood products are given a USDC grade, they can be determined to have been inspected for wholesomeness. Additionally, seafood can be inspected and graded only in U.S. processing plants. Imported seafood products are subject to FDA inspection in the United States, and are also usually subject to inspection in their country of origin. Seafood products that are processed and packaged in the United States can be inspected voluntarily by the USDC and given the **Packed Under Federal Inspection** (PUFI) seal of approval. This indicates that the product has been inspected and determined to be clean, safe, and wholesome. The PUFI seal may be a good way to ensure that seafood products are safe, but the inspection is only feasible for processed products. There is no clear inspection program for truly fresh seafood; therefore, the relationship with the distributor is very important.

Fish and Shellfish Grading

The USDC primarily grades processed fish and shellfish products, such as pre-cooked, breaded, and some frozen products. Grading is based on the fish product's appearance, size, uniformity, color, number of defects, odor, flavor, and texture. The federal grades for fish products are:

- *Grade A.* These products have the best quality, are uniform in appearance, and are free of defects.

- *Grade B.* These are good quality products that are suitable for food service sale. Grade B fish products have more blemishes and defects than Grade A items.

- *Grade C.* These products are wholesome and safe for use, but their appearance makes them unsuitable for service where appearance is important. Grade C products are usually only used in finished products, such as casseroles, soups and stews where appearance is not an issue.

For all practical purposes, the Grade A stamp is the only designation used for selection. The lower grades are normally sold to processors who process the fish item into other convenience foods. Exhibit 2 shows federal inspection and grading stamps for fresh seafood products.

Fish and Shellfish Purchasing Systems

Fish and shellfish, because they are generally harvested from the wild, create unique situations for purchasing. In a typical scenario, the fish is caught by fishermen who may perform a small amount of processing on the boat, depending on the type of fish. The fish product is then sent to a processor for bulk processing,

Exhibit 2   Federal Inspection and Grading Stamps

which could include packing and freezing the product. This processor is likely located off the shore of the United States. The processor located in the United States would then receive the product and perform some further processing and packaging. The product is then sent to the distributor (in the case of fresh seafood, this might be the next step after the fisherman), who would provide the product to the food service establishment. The end user (the food service establishment) would purchase the product from the distributor.

This purchasing process is different in the case of fresh fish and shellfish. It is important for a buyer to deal with a reliable, consistent, reputable distributor. This distributor can be local or located near the fishing areas such as the East Coast, Gulf Coast, or the Pacific Coast of the United States.

If the distributor is local, the buyer will make purchase decisions based on availability and the supplier will take care of the details. If the buyer desires to purchase directly from the source supplier, the buyer will likely need to contact that source supplier and negotiate the price of the fish and the cost of transportation. In general, if a food service facility is located in an area that will require source supplier shipments to be sent via air, it might be best to investigate the availability of a local distributor. In any case, because of the variability of fish and shellfish, it is important to deal with trusted distributors because of the expertise they can add to the relationship.

Reference materials can be valuable sources of information. *Seafood Business* magazine (www.seafoodbusiness.com) is a monthly publication with current information and a yearly buyers' guide. It also publishes the *Seafood Handbook* (see Exhibit 3), which is a comprehensive reference detailing the sourcing, cooking, nutrition, product forms, and seasonal availability for more than 100 seafood

Exhibit 3   Seafood Handbook

Contents

Seafood HANDBOOK

The comprehensive guide
to sourcing, buying and preparation

Source: *Seafood Handbook* (Portland, Maine: Seafood Business, 2005).

species. Urner Barry's *Seafood Price-Current* newsletter is published twice weekly with current seafood prices for the major seafood types and markets. The Seafood Selection Guide is available on-line from the National Marine Fisheries Service at http://seafood.nmfs.noaa.gov/consumer3.htm. The Web site www.seafood.com also contains a wealth of information for seafood buyers.

An additional concern when purchasing fish and shellfish is the minimum order requirement instituted by some distributors. If not dealt with properly, minimum order requirements, particularly for fresh seafood, may make the cost of an item prohibitive.

Market Forms of Fish

Fresh. Fresh fish should meet certain standards to be accepted. The product should be packaged in an airtight container if chill packed and properly drained if ice packed. The eyes should be clear, round, and bright. The fish should spring back when touched. The gills should be pink or red and clean. The fish should also be slime-free and the odor should be fresh and mild with no fishy or ammonia-like scent.

Frozen. Frozen fish products should be packaged to prevent **freezer burn** (dehydration and discoloration due to moisture loss). The product should never be thawed and refrozen. The odor and texture of the fish when thawed should be similar to a freshly caught item. Imported fish is often frozen into blocks for shipment to the United States for further processing.

Individually quick frozen (IQF). **Individually quick frozen** (IQF) means that each fish piece has been frozen individually and then packaged. Typically, ready-to-use fish items, such as shrimp and crab legs, are best purchased in IQF form.

Block frozen. Block frozen means the fish product has been frozen into a solid block with the pieces together. These blocks usually weigh five pounds or more. Commodity fish products such as cod, raw shrimp, and scallops are often block frozen.

Glazed. **Glazed** fish products are given a protective coating of ice to protect them from dehydration. The glaze should be rinsed off to check for quality and weight.

Breaded. Breaded fish products, such as fish fillets, clams and shrimp are specified as the amount of breading as a percentage of the finished total product weight. Most breaded fish products are also packed IQF.

Soaked or dipped. Some fish products are soaked or dipped in an alkaline phosphate solution during processing. This is done to help the fish product retain its natural moisture. This practice is allowed by the FDA. Some buyers believe the dipping gives the product a meaty texture or chemical flavor. Be aware of this practice when purchasing fish products.

Exhibit 4 lists characteristics of the many varieties of fish.

Market Forms of Shellfish

Fresh. Fresh shellfish should be purchased live and should be moving to be considered fresh. Fresh shellfish and mollusks should be shipped with a covering

Exhibit 4   Fish Characteristics

White meat, very light, delicate flavor

Cod, Pacific sand dab, cusk, haddock, lake whitefish, southern flounder, Dover sole, Rex sole, summer flounder, yellowtail flounder, Pacific halibut.

White meat, light to moderate flavor

Snook, whiting, sea trout, butterfish, red snapper, catfish, American plaice, lingcod, winter flounder, mahi mahi, cobia, wolf fish, English sole, sauger.

Light meat, very light, delicate flavor

Shovelnose sturgeon, smelt, pollack, ocean perch (Pacific), walleye, brook trout, white sea bass, grouper, bluegill, white crappie, rainbow trout, tautog.

Light meat, light to moderate flavor

Atlantic salmon, pink salmon, lake sturgeon, monkfish, sculpin, ocean perch (Atlantic), scup, northern pike, rockfish, Eastern pollack, carp, swordfish, blackdrum, Greenland turbot, spot, sheepshead, Buffalo fish, croaker, chum salmon, pompano, striped bass, sand shark, perch, lake trout, mullet, coho salmon, eel.

Light meat, more pronounced flavor

Atlantic mackerel, king mackerel, Spanish mackerel, redeye mullet, blue runner.

Darker meat, light to moderate flavor

Black sea bass, ocean trout, chinook salmon, red (sockeye) salmon, bluefish.

---

of moist paper or seaweed and have been maintained at a temperature of 40–45° F (5–7° C). Mollusk shells should be tightly closed or should close tightly when tapped on. All shellfish should be properly documented and tagged as appropriate. Tags for fresh shellfish must be kept on record for 90 days after the shellfish has all been sold.

Frozen. Frozen shellfish and mollusks are usually either IQF or block frozen. Shellfish that has been processed out of the shell is most often sold in IQF form. Examples include peeled shrimp and crab legs. Some mollusks, such as oysters and clams, are shelled and block frozen. Shrimp with the shell intact is most often block frozen. In any case, the frozen product should be packaged to prevent air infiltration and be frozen with no sign of thawing and refreezing.

Breaded. As with fish, several shellfish products are sold pre-breaded. The most popular examples are breaded shrimp and breaded clams. As with breaded fish, specifications should state the acceptable amount of breading as a percentage of the total weight of the product.

Soaked or dipped. As with fish products, several shellfish products—in particular shrimp and scallops—are treated with alkaline phosphate solution to help the product retain moisture. Care should be taken when purchasing these products to make sure the soaking or dipping has not added extra weight to the product, driving up the cost.

Canned. Canned shellfish is usually in pieces and packed in water.

Exhibit 5 lists several terms useful when purchasing shellfish products.

Exhibit 5   Fish/Shellfish Terminology

Round:	The fish as it comes from the water. The head may be on or off.
Drawn:	The fish is completely eviscerated.
Steaked:	Portioning by slicing steaks at right angles to the backbone, against the grain. Halibut, salmon, and swordfish are offered in this form. As with any portioning of this type, watch the end cuts.
Fillets:	Portioning by cutting parallel to the backbone. Specify size and packaging, such as layer pak, snap pak, and cello wrap.
Sticks:	Generally prebreaded, formed portions of any available fish variety. May be made from solid or minced flesh.
Count:	Either count per pound (as in shrimp 16/20) or size for each unit. In the case of lobster tails, "4/6" means each tail is within the 4- to 6-ounce size range.
Butterflied:	An item that has been separated against the natural seams. Shrimp is butterflied when it is partially split. Fillets may be butterflied to give better plate coverage.
Headless Shrimp:	The same as "shell-on." The head has been removed and discarded, leaving the tail. These are green (raw) shrimp.

Major Fish Categories

Fish can be categorized primarily as either saltwater (marine) or freshwater varieties. Beyond that, fish is further categorized as either flatfish or roundfish. Flatfish have their eyes on either side of the body, while roundfish have their eyes next to each other on top of the head. Fish can also be categorized as fat fish or lean fish, depending upon the amount of oil it contains. Because there are more than 200 varieties of fish sold worldwide, buyers should know exactly what type of fish they want when ordering from a distributor. Care should be taken with names because some species or variety names are used for marketing purposes and may not accurately reflect the exact species of the fish. A good example of this problem is snapper. Red snapper is a highly prized fish from the Gulf Coast region of the United States. However, red snapper has recently been overfished and catch limits have been implemented. This has, unfortunately, led to unscrupulous suppliers labeling other species, such as grouper, as snapper.

The most popular species of fish include:

- Saltwater (marine) species
  - Codfishes
    - Cod
    - Haddock
    - Pollack

- Flatfish
  - Flounder
  - Halibut
  - Sole
  - Turbot
- Mackerel
  - Jack
  - King
  - Pacific
- Mahi Mahi
- Monkfish
- Ocean Perch
- Orange Roughy
- Salmon
  - Chinook
  - Coho
  - Pink
  - Sockeye
  - Steelhead
- Swordfish
- Tuna
  - Ahi
  - Bluefin
  - Yellowfin
- Freshwater species
  - Catfish
  - Perch
  - Pike
    - Northern
  - Trout
    - Lake
    - Rainbow
    - Speckled
  - Tilapia
  - Walleye
  - Whitefish

Major Shellfish Categories

The shellfish category includes organisms that live in the ocean and have a visible shell. The shellfish category includes two subcategories: mollusks and crustaceans.

Mollusks include oysters, clams, scallops, squid, and snails. **Crustaceans** include shrimp, lobster, crab, and crayfish (crawfish).

Major shellfish categories include:

- Shrimp (varieties refer to the color before cooking)
  - Brown
  - White
  - Pink
- Lobster
  - American
  - Maine
  - Spiny (Rock)
- Crab
  - Blue
  - Dungeness
  - King
  - Snow
- Clams
  - Cherrystone
  - Littlenecks
  - Chowder
- Oysters
  - Eastern
  - Olympia
  - Pacific
- Scallops
  - Bay
  - Sea
- Crayfish (Crawfish)
- Mussels
- Squid

Exhibit 6 lists characteristics of popular fish and shellfish varieties.

Fish and Shellfish Specifications

Fish and shellfish specifications must be written to detail all the information needed to ensure that the buyer receives what he or she desires from the distributor.

The specification should include the exact name of the product, product size, grade, brand name, product yield, the size of the package or container, type of packaging, the product form, the point of origin and handling instructions. Exhibits 7–10 are sample specifications for various seafood items.

Exhibit 6   Popular Fish and Shellfish

Species/Variety	Pack Size	Season	Countries of Origin	Comments
Shellfish				
Clams *East Coast* Littlenecks Cherrystone Steamers Ipswich Surf (Skimmer) Razor *West Coast* Littlenecks Cherrystone Butter Pismo Surf Razor	Sold by bushel or bag. Counts vary by geographical area. Also sold shucked.	Year-round depending on weather.	Both U.S. coasts.	Only New England (or soft shell) are true clams. All hard shell also known as quahogs. Large sizes used for chowder. Littlenecks and cherrystones are both small quahogs.
Crabs & Crabmeat King Blue Snow Stone Dungeness	Live crabs sold by count in each market area. Cooked frozen meat from king and snow available, also legs and claws. Blue crabmeat usually sold fresh or pasteurized.	Warm months in producing areas. King and snow harvest is fall through spring.	King—Alaska through Aleutians Blue—Chesapeake to Gulf Snow—Alaska through Aleutians Stone—Gulf of Mexico Dungeness—Oregon and Washington	King crabmeat best for freezing. Most live crabs utilized near catch area. Blue crab caught as hard and soft shell. Leg or lump meat desired over body.
Lobsters • True or American	Sold live by the pound: • Jumbo = over 3 lb • Large = 1 1/2 to 2 1/2 lb • Quarters = 1 1/4 to 1 1/2 lb • Chicken = 3/4 to 1 lb	Year-round with some restrictions.	N.E. coastline of North America. Approximately 30% come from Canada.	North American lobster normally has two large claws. Culls are lobsters with one claw or a deformed/broken claw.
• Spiny Lobster	Varies with country of origin. • Brazil = 10-lb boxes • Australia = 20-lb & 25-lb boxes • U.S. = 20-lb boxes	Usually Nov. through March for New Zealand & Australia. Year-round in some areas of Gulf and Caribbean.	Brazil, New Zealand, Australia, U.S., Central America.	Also known as rock lobster and crayfish. It is best to specify size (oz) per tail and count per carton.
Oysters	Sold by the count in cartons. Medium = 200 per ctn. Also sold shucked by the gallon.	Year-round with best quality in fall and winter.	Practically worldwide.	Oysters from colder water are considered superior.
• Eastern or Atlantic (Bluepoint, Long Island, Chincoteague, etc.)	• X-Large = 160 per gal Large or X-Selects = 160/200 per gal Medium or Selects = 200/300 per gal Standards = 300/400 per gal		New England, Middle and South Atlantic, Gulf of Mexico.	
• Pacific (Westcott Bay, Olympia, European)	• Large = under 65 per gal Medium = 65/96 per gal Small = 97/144 per gal X-Small = over 144 per gal		Pacific Coast, Japan, Korea.	

Exhibit 6 *(continued)*

Species/Variety	Pack Size	Season	Countries of Origin	Comments
Prawns	Same as shrimp, shell-on under 7 count/5-lb box, under 10 count/5-lb box, under 12 count/5-lb box, under 15 count/5-lb box	Caught during shrimping season.	Practically worldwide.	May be called scampi or Spanish reds. Larger sizes of shrimp.
Scallops Bay Sea Callico	Cut to the following counts per lb: Jumbo = 10/15; Large = 18/22; also counts of 30/40, 50/70, 70/90, 80/100, etc.	Year-round in some producing areas. For North Atlantic, generally from July through Dec.	N.E. North America, Nova Scotia, New England, England, Argentina, Australia, Iceland.	Packed differently by various countries of origin. Available individually quick frozen (IQF), block frozen, breaded. Bay scallops considered superior to sea variety.
Shrimp White Pink Brown	Sold shell-on (green), peeled and deveined (P&D), breaded and cooked. Sizing under 15 per lb, 16/20, 21/25, 26/30, 31/40, 41/50, etc. Generally packed in 5-lb boxes.	Year-round in some producing areas. For North America, generally July through Dec.	Gulf, Central & South America, Persian Gulf, China Sea.	Generally uniform count identification worldwide. Certain countries of origin may be less particular on sizing. White, pink, and brown shrimp considered desirable, in that order. P&D counts relate to shell-on counts. 16/20 P&D shrimp are from 21/25 shell-on shrimp.

Fish

Species/Variety	Pack Size	Season	Countries of Origin	Comments
Canned Fish • Salmon	Generally 1-lb cans.	Aug. to Nov.	Northwestern U.S., North America.	For varieties see frozen section.
• Tuna	Generally 60-oz cans.	Year-round.	Japan, Taiwan, U.S., South Atlantic, Puerto Rico, South Pacific, San Diego.	Primarily albacore, yellowfin, skipjack varieties. Albacore is labeled white meat; other varieties light meat. Bluefin popular for raw oriental products.
Cod	Whole, fillets, blocks, or portions; cello wrap, layer pack, and IQF; skin-on or skinless.	Year-round, primarily July to Dec., age 6 to 9 yrs. when caught.	Canada, Iceland, Scotland, Norway, Japan, both U.S. coasts, England, Denmark.	A mild, white moist fish —good for breading. Size variations from some packers. Freezes well. Scrod is a form of cod weighing 1 1/2 lb or less.
Flounder Southern Winter Summer Yellowtail	Whole or fillets; cello wrap, layer pack, and IQF; skin-on or skinless.	July to Dec., with some year-round fishing.	Canada, Iceland, England, Scotland, both U.S. coasts, Denmark.	A flatfish normally sold whole or as fillets. Low in fat. Often confused with sole. Usually sized within a 2-oz tolerance.
Haddock	Whole, fillets, or portions; cello wrap, layer pack, and IQF; skin-on or skinless.	Year-round, primarily July to Dec.	Canada, Iceland, Scotland, Norway, New England, both U.S. coasts, Denmark.	A member of the cod family. Flesh is whiter. The catch is much less than cod. Commands a price premium over cod.
Halibut	Whole, fillets, or portioned (steaks). Whole halibut, under 10 lb—chickens; also 10/20 lb, 20/40 lb, 40/60 lb, 60/80 lb.	July, Aug., Sept. Catch controlled by Joint Commission of Fishing Nations.	U.S. (North Pacific and Alaska), Japan, Russia.	Moist, white flesh, mild flavor, good for broiling or baking.

(continued)

Exhibit 6 *(continued)*

Species/Variety	Pack Size	Season	Countries of Origin	Comments
Mackerel Jack (Atlantic) Spanish King Pacific	Whole or fillets—sizing of fillets usually within 2-oz tolerance, i.e., 4/6 oz, 6/8 oz, etc.	• Jack—July to Oct. • Spanish & King—Dec. to March. • Pacific—July to Oct.	• Jack—North Atlantic (U.S.) • Spanish—Gulf ports (U.S.) and Mexico • King—South Atlantic, Gulf, Pacific Coast • Pacific—North Pacific	King usually exported to Caribbean nations. Spanish and king are flavorful fish, high in fat.
Perch, Ocean ("Redfish" or "Rosefish")	Skinless or skin-on; generally filleted; cello wrap, layer pack, and IQF. Fillets portioned as follows: 12/16 per lb, 4/6 per lb, 8/12 per lb, 2/4 per lb, 6/9 per lb.	July to Dec., with some year-round fishing	Canada, Iceland, Norway, Germany, Japan, both U.S. coasts.	Sizing is generally much less precise on this item than on haddock, cod, and flounder.
Pollack	Whole or fillets; cello wrap, layer pack, and IQF; skin-on or skinless; 11-18 lb at age of 6 yrs. 20″ to 30″ length.	Year-round, primarily July to Dec.	Canada, Iceland, Scotland, Norway, Japan, North Atlantic (U.S.) and Alaska.	Considered a member of the cod family. The flesh, however, is darker and less desirable. Has more fat and sells for less than cod.
Rainbow Trout	4, 6, 8, 10, 12 oz fillets. Available breaded also.	Year-round, freshwater.	U.S. (Idaho), Japan, Denmark.	"Farmed" fish. Expensive, Japanese somewhat less expensive.
Red Snapper Mangrove Yellowtail Vermillion	Generally filleted 6/8, 8/10, 10/12, 12/14, 14/16; can be bought whole head on, dressed 3/4, 4/6, 6/8, 8/10 lb each.	Year-round.	Gulf, Taiwan, Ecuador, Mexico, Brazil.	Gulf has only true snapper w/red tinge. Far East tends to be gray and less flavorful.
Salmon Chinook or King Pink or humpback Silver or coho Red or sockeye Chum, dog, or fall	15/25 lb each, round 5/7 lb each, round 7/12 lb each, round 5/16 lb each, round 8/14 lb each, round Whole, steaked, or canned.	Aug. to Nov.	N.W. Pacific, Oregon to Bering Sea. Some North Atlantic, Nova Scotia.	Chinook—bright salmon color Pink—light pink, canning variety Silver—reddish orange Red—reddish-dark, strong flavor Chum—light to pinkish red, strongest flavor, migratory fish
Sea Trout	Generally filleted 4/5, 5/6, 6/8, 8/10; IQF and cello pack.	Year-round.	Eastern seaboard of U.S., some Gulf, Central, and South American ports.	Fish run 1 to 4 lb round. Supply medium.
Sole Winter Lemon Dover English	Skin-on or skinless, generally filleted, all configurations from 1 oz to 10 oz each; IQF and cello pack; also dressed, whole head on.	July to Dec., with some year-round fishing.	North Atlantic predominantly, also Canada, Iceland, Scotland, Germany, Holland, Norway.	Member of flounder family. Price will vary dramatically with varieties.
Turbot, Greenland	Sized fillets and dressed with head on.	July to Nov.	Greenland, Norway, Iceland, Newfoundland.	Also known as blue halibut, gray halibut, or mock halibut, now Greenland turbot. Denmark turbot is different.
Whiting (or Silver Hake)	Generally sold skin-on. H&G (headed and gutted), whole is in 8/16 oz range. Available filleted in 4/8 oz range.	Year-round.	Maine, Canada, South Africa, Argentina, Brazil.	Inexpensive fish.

Exhibit 7   Sample Specification for Green Headless Shrimp

Item:	16/20 green (raw) headless shrimp.
Grade:	U.S. Grade A, or must meet USDC "Packed Under Federal Inspection" requirements.
Packaging:	5-pound frozen boxes; 10 boxes to each 50-pound master carton. Label to identify product and packer, net and gross weights, count per pound, and date packed.
General Requirements:	Must not exceed bacterial levels allowable under FDA standards; either white or pink species; must be packed in accordance with good commercial practice.
Specific Requirements:	To average 18 shrimp per pound and have less than 1% broken pieces. Product to be from current year's production and have a minimum of 5% glaze.
Handling:	Receiving temperature to be no higher than 0°F (-18°C).

Exhibit 8   Sample Specification for Breaded Shrimp

Item:	16/20 breaded shrimp, 40% breading.
Grade:	U.S. Grade A, or must meet USDC "Packed Under Federal Inspection" requirements.
Packaging:	3-pound boxes; 8 boxes to each master carton of 24 pounds. Label to identify product and packer, count per pound, and date packed.
General Requirements:	Must not exceed bacterial levels allowable under FDA standards; either white or pink species; must be layer-packed in accordance with good commercial practice.
Specific Requirements:	From 21/25 green (raw) headless shrimp, machine-breaded, butterfly type, tail off, oriental-type breading from ABC Breading Company. To average 23 count per pound with no broken pieces. Product to be from current year's production.
Handling:	Receiving temperature to be no higher than 0°F (-18°C).

Exhibit 9   Sample Specification for Block-Frozen Sea Scallops

Item:	30/40 block-frozen sea scallops, Canadian or domestic.
Grade:	U.S. Grade A, or must meet USDC "Packed Under Federal Inspection" requirements.
Packaging:	5-pound boxes; 10 boxes to each 50-pound master carton. Label to identify product and packer, count per pound, and date packed.
General Requirements:	Must not exceed bacterial levels allowable under FDA standards; must be packed in accordance with good commercial practice.
Specific Requirements:	To average 35 pieces per pound, uniformly cut. Product to be from current year's production.
Handling:	Receiving temperature to be no higher than 0°F (-18°C).

Exhibit 10   Sample Specification for Frozen Cod Fillets

Item:	Frozen cod fillets, skinless and boneless, 6-8 ounces each.
Grade:	U.S. Grade A, or must meet USDC "Packed Under Federal Inspection" requirements.
Packaging:	Snap or layer pack; 10-pound box; 4 boxes to each 40-pound master carton. Label to identify product and packer, count per pound, and date packed.
General Requirements:	Must not exceed bacterial levels allowable under FDA standards; must be packed in accordance with good commercial practice.
Specific Requirements:	From Canadian or domestic sources. Product to be from current season's production.
Handling:	Receiving temperature to be no higher than 0°F (-18°C).

Management Considerations

Food Safety Issues

Fish and shellfish can, because of the waters they swim in, be contaminated by many different toxins, parasites, bacteria and viruses. These contaminants can be transferred to humans when the fish or shellfish are eaten. Certain fish are susceptible to toxin contamination because of their environment, size, and makeup. Mercury contamination in tuna is one example of this. Shellfish are particularly susceptible to bacterial and viral contamination if the water where the beds are located are contaminated by sewage. Fish can also be infected with parasites that can be transmitted to humans. Purchasing from a reputable distributor, using standard purchase specifications, and closely inspecting shipments upon receipt are the best methods for preventing food safety problems with seafood.

Overharvesting

Some fish and shellfish species, due to their popularity or the decline of their environment, have become endangered. If its breeding area has been contaminated or compromised in some manner, a species may not be able to reproduce in sufficient quantities to sustain itself. Additionally, the popularity in restaurants of some seafood species has created overharvesting conditions in which fishing fleets literally catch all of the fish available and do not leave enough breeding stock available to sustain the species. Examples of seafood species that have been subject to overharvesting include swordfish, red snapper, scallops, certain types of oysters, salmon, monkfish, and sea bass.

Featuring Underutilized Species

The top five species of fish—tuna, shrimp, haddock, cod, and flounder—account for about 60 percent of the volume of fish served in the United States. Many **underutilized species** of seafood are not utilized more often because of marketing. Many of the underutilized species are unknown to the general public—whitefish, redhake, and skate, for example—while others have unfortunate names like dogfish, carp, and fluke. Efforts are underway by the National Marine Fisheries Service to identify and market underutilized seafood species. Buyers of seafood should stay aware of these efforts.

Raw Fish Usage

The use of raw fish for popular menu items, like **sushi, seviche, and sashimi** is increasing. Seafood served raw must be of the highest quality and must be handled with the utmost care to ensure it will be safe for consumption. The biggest concern with raw fish service is the presence of parasites. Freezing and cooking can kill parasites, but marinating and smoking will not.

🔑 Key Terms

aquaculture—Raising fish and shellfish under controlled conditions in controlled environments.

crustaceans—A category of shellfish that includes shrimp, lobster, crab, and crayfish (crawfish).

freezer burn—Dehydration and discoloration of frozen products due to moisture loss

glazed—Fish products that are given a protective coating of ice to protect them from dehydration.

harvesting—Capturing fish and shellfish from their natural habitats or from captivity.

individually quick frozen—A form of packaging in which each fish piece is frozen individually and then packaged.

mollusks—A category of shellfish that includes oysters, clams, scallops, squid, and snails.

Packed Under Federal Inspection—A seal of approval that indicates that the product has been inspected and determined to be clean, safe, and wholesome.

spawning—Fish laying their eggs.

sushi, seviche, sashimi—Popular menu items that use raw fish.

underutilized species—Seafood species that are not often used in food service operations.

 # Review Questions

1. How do the ways fish and shellfish are harvested affect the supplies and prices?

2. What is the inspection process for fish and shellfish?

3. What is the grading process for fish and shellfish?

4. What are some of the distribution channels through which fish and shellfish are purchased?

5. What are the differences in quality and use among fresh, frozen, and processed fish and shellfish?

6. What are the major categories of fish, and what are the primary characteristics of each?

7. What are the major categories of shellfish, and what are the primary characteristics of each?

8. What are the requirements and content of specifications for fish and shellfish?

9. What are the factors influencing fish and shellfish population and availability? How does this affect purchasing decisions?

10. What are some of the sources of information available to assist in purchasing decisions?

Internet Sites

For more information, visit the following Internet sites. Remember that Internet addresses can change without notice. If the site is no longer there, you can use a search engine to look for additional sites.

National Marine Fisheries Services
www.nmfs.noaa.gov

Seafood Business Magazine
www.seafoodbusiness.com

Seafood.com
www.seafood.com

Seafood Handbook
www.seafoodhandbook.com

Urner Barry Publications
www.urnerbarry.com

USDC Seafood Inspection Program
http://seafood.nmfs.noaa.gov

Chapter 10 Outline

Poultry Production and Processing
Factors Affecting Poultry Supplies
Factors Affecting Poultry Costs and Pricing
Poultry Inspection
Poultry Grading
Poultry Purchasing Systems
Poultry Cuts and Characteristics
    Chicken
    Turkey
    Other Poultry
Poultry Market Forms
NAMP *Meat Buyer's Guide* Numbers
    Standards
Poultry Purchase Specifications
Poultry Food Safety Issues
Management Considerations
    Free-Range and Organic Products
    Turkey as a Low-Fat Alternative

Competencies

1. Describe how poultry and poultry products are produced, supplied and priced. (pp. 325–326)

2. List available sources of information to assist in poultry purchasing decisions. (p. 326)

3. Explain the inspection and grading process for poultry. (pp. 326–328)

4. Understand the system through which poultry is purchased. (p. 328)

5. Know and identify the major cuts of poultry and the primary characteristics of each. (pp. 328–332)

6. Explain the requirements, content and importance of specifications for poultry. (pp. 332–333)

7. Explain the food safety issues specific to poultry. (p. 333)

8. Describe management considerations related to purchasing poultry products. (pp. 333–335)

10

Poultry

Poultry Production and Processing

Birds that have been **domesticated** and raised for their meat are referred to as poultry. Poultry includes chickens, ducks, geese, and turkeys. Non-domesticated birds used in food service are referred to as game birds. Examples of game birds include wild ducks and geese, pheasants, and quail.

Chicken, because of its lower fat and cholesterol content than red meat, has been increasing in popularity with health-conscious consumers. This popularity has made chicken the fastest growing protein product in the United States. Chicken's short production cycle allows processors to effectively react to the demands of the market. Chickens can be raised to maturity in five to six weeks. Chickens are also economical to raise due to their low feed-to-weight ratio, meaning that it takes less feed to raise chickens for the amount of protein they produce as compared, for example, to beef.

Chicken production has been integrated in large production facilities. These chicken production facilities have their own hatcheries, feed mills, and processing plants all on one side. The mature chicken can be processed into various marketable forms or shipped to other processors who prepare the final product.

For the most part, poultry—specifically chicken—is considered a commodity and is readily available in various forms (e.g. whole, in pieces, fresh, frozen) at similar quality levels in all areas of the United States.

Factors Affecting Poultry Supplies

Since poultry generally is a commodity, supply is usually not a problem. At issue on occasion is the availability of poultry items in the form needed. A notable situation occurred several years ago when the two quick-service giants, McDonald's and Burger King, both decided to introduce new chicken items on their menus. The demand for chicken increased dramatically, which reduced the overall supply to the other food service companies and drove up the price. It took several months for the market to recover. The factory production standards used in poultry processing usually ensure a steady supply of products.

Factors Affecting Poultry Costs and Pricing

The same issues that apply to the availability of poultry products also apply to costs and pricing. Because poultry is a commodity, the price is closely tied to the demand for the product. The factory processing and short birth-to-maturity cycle keep the prices and costs more predictable in the poultry industry than in other protein animals.

Costs and pricing can fluctuate for some specialty items that are only raised in certain areas of the country. For instance, organic free-range chickens raised in California will command more of a premium in New York, not only because they are a specialty item, but also due to transportation costs. Processed poultry items, such as cooked and rolled breast meat, diced meat, and pulled meat, also may have some variances in cost due to the uniqueness of the product and its availability in different markets. Food service operators who purchase large quantities of chicken or other poultry products should consider entering into long-term contracts or a buyer-distributor relationship that will allow the food service operator to hedge against large price increases. Poultry market prices can be found in the *Poultry Market News Report*, available through the United States Department of Agriculture's (USDA) Agricultural Marketing Service, and in the Urner Barry *Price-Current* (see Exhibit 1).

Poultry Inspection

The Poultry Products Inspection Act, passed in 1957, regulates poultry sold through interstate commerce. The Wholesome Poultry Products Act, passed in 1968, requires that state inspection standards be at least equal to federal standards. Product inspection is mandatory for all poultry processors, whether the product is raw, frozen, canned, or otherwise processed. The cost of inspection is paid by the processor so it is included in the overall cost of the poultry product. Federal or state inspectors inspect raw poultry from the beginning to the end of the slaughtering process. The **wholesomeness** of the product is verified from the bird's arrival at the plant to the end product. Depending on the type of processing performed, plants may also be inspected for proper cooking, temperatures, ingredient percentages, finished product, weight, storage temperatures, and the overall sanitation of the production line and packaging. Inspected and approved products receive the USDA stamp for wholesomeness (see Exhibit 2).

Poultry Grading

The Agricultural Marketing Service (AMS), a department of the USDA, performs federal poultry grading. Federal grading is an option that must be paid for by the producer, but many states require federal grading. Most specifications call for a grade designation, and almost all poultry is graded (see Exhibit 2).

Poultry is graded with three possible designations:

- *Grade A.* Grade A birds are full, fleshed, well finished, and attractive in appearance. This is the top quality designation.

- *Grade B.* Grade B birds usually have some minor appearance or dressing concerns, such as torn skin. The bird is less attractive, but is still free of broken bones.

Exhibit 1 *Urner Barry's Price-Current*

URNER BARRY'S Price-Current

URNER BARRY — ESTABLISHED 1858

URNER BARRY MARKET INDICES & USDA GRAIN QUOTATIONS

	05/11/07	05/12/06
Urner Barry Egg Index	.617	.264
Urner Barry Chicken Index	.801	.457
Urner Barry Turkey (Tom) Index	.899	.729
Urner Barry Turkey (Hen) Index	.364	.711
Yellow Sheet Beef Index	1.623	1.406
Yellow Sheet Pork Cutout	74.933	69.082
Urner Barry HLSO Farm-Raised White Shrimp Index	--	--
Urner Barry HLSO Black Tiger Shrimp Index	--	--
Urner Barry Fresh Farmed Salmon Index	--	--
USDA Kansas City No.2 Yellow Corn	3.49	2.28
USDA Omaha Corn, US 2 Yellow	3.46	2.19
USDA Kansas City Hard Red Wheat	4.77	4.81
USDA Minneapolis Dark Northern Spring Wheat	5.34	4.74
USDA Chicago Soft Red Winter Wheat	4.53	3.62
USDA Crude Decatur Oil	33.39	26.09
USDA Central Illinois 48% Soybean Meal Truck	196.80	184.80

CME CHEESE, $/lb.

Cash Trading Prices, Closing Prices	TL
Barrels	1.6625
40# Blocks	1.7000

USDA - CCC PURCHASES OF DAIRY PRODUCTS, lbs.

(000 omitted)	This Week	Last Year	Since 10/01/06	Same Period Last Year
CHEESE				
20-Apr	0	0	0	0
27-Apr	0	0	0	0
4-May	0	0	0	0
11-May	0	198	0	0
NONFAT DRY MILK				
20-Apr	0	0	0	9,867
27-Apr	0	0	0	20,432
4-May	0	0	0	27,253
11-May	0	0	0	33,249

Symbol Explanation:
ax - Asked; **b** - Bid; **n** - Nominal; "**–**" - Unquoted; **bstd** - Basted; **LTL** - Less Than Trucklot; **TL** - Trucklot; **FOB** - Freight On Board; **RTC** - Ready To Cook; **WOG** - Without Giblets; **r** - Reinstated Quote.

Prices reflect Urner Barry quotations, based on the fresh, delivered warehouse prices for standard product delivering within 1-7 days unless otherwise stated. **Bold Face Type** indicates change from previous day's close.

USDA CHEESE, $/lb.

NORTHEAST WHOLESALE CHEESE

	LTL*
Cheddar 10# Prints	1.7400-2.2600
Cheddar Single Daisies	1.6975-2.1825
Cheddar 40# Block	1.7950-2.0700
Process 5# Loaf	1.8075-2.0475
Process 5# Sliced	1.8225-2.1325
Muenster	1.8150-2.0125
Grade A Swiss Cuts 10-14#	2.5500-2.6500

Updated: *May 09, 2007*

MIDWEST WHOLESALE CHEESE

	LTI*
Process American 5# Loaf	1.8800-2.0275
Brick And/Or Muenster 5#	1.9800-2.2225
Cheddar 40# Block	1.8500-2.2650
Monterey Jack 10#	1.9800-2.2650
Blue 5#	2.5325-2.6800
Mozzarella 5 - 6# (Low Moisture, Part Skim)	1.8500-2.3650
Grade A Swiss Cuts 6-9#	2.3050-2.9700

Updated: *May 09, 2007*

FOREIGN TYPE CHEESE

	Imported - LTI*	Domestic - LTI*
Roquefort	2.6400-4.5900	2.0600-3.5475
Blue	3.6900-6.0900	2.5625-2.8225
Gorgonzola	--	3.4675-3.8875
Parmesan (Italy)	--	--
Romano (Italy)	2.1000-3.6900	--
Provolone (Italy)	3.4400-6.0900	2.1025-2.2600
Romano (Cows Milk)	--	3.2500-3.3925
Sardo Romano (Argentine)	2.8500-3.2900	--
Reggianito (Argentine)	2.6900-3.2900	--
Jarlsberg-(Brand)	2.9500-4.2300	--
Swiss Cuts Switzerland	--	2.5500-2.6500
Swiss Cuts Finnish	--	--
Swiss Cuts Austrian	2.5900-3.4500	--
Edam	--	--
2 Pound	--	--
4 Pound	--	--
Gouda, Large	--	--
Gouda, Baby (5/Dozen)	--	--
10 Ounce	27.8000-31.7000	--

Updated: *May 09, 2007*
*1,000-5,000 lb. Mixed Lots

"Urner Barry's Price-Current"

Editor: Michael W. O'Shaughnessy
Associate Editors: Richard A. Brown,
Randy Pesciotta and Russell W. Whitman
Market Reporter: Greg Deppeler

Published 5 times weekly in a variety of media
by Urner Barry Publications, Inc.
P.O. Box 389, Toms River, NJ 08754-0389

Copyright© 2007

Urner Barry Publications, Inc. • ISSN 0273-9992
Phone: 732-240-5330 • Fax: 732-341-0891
Web site: www.urnerbarry.com • E-mail: mail@urnerbarry.com

URNER BARRY'S PRICE-CURRENT is available via fax, e-mail and through Urner Barry's flagship service *Comtell Online*. PDF back issues are available for $5 each.

The UB Products that are identified in the Services and Products Order Form are offered to you conditioned on your acceptance without modification of the terms, conditions, and notices contained herein. Please read the End-User License Agreement (the "Agreement"), a copy of which is available at www.urnerbarry.com and which has been received by the contact named on the Services and Products Order Form, before utilizing this Urner Barry product. Your use of a particular UB Product(s) may also be subject to additional terms set forth in the Agreement. Your use of the UB Product(s) constitutes your acceptance of all of the terms, conditions, and notices set forth in the Agreement. Urner Barry reserves the right to amend, remove, or add to these terms, conditions and notices at any time without notice. Accordingly please continue to review the Agreement whenever accessing or using the UB Product(s). If at any time you do not accept the Agreement along with the terms and conditions outlined in the Services and Products Order Form, you may not use this or any UB Product.

The information, commentary and price quotations contained herein are intended solely for the internal, confidential and exclusive use of Urner Barry subscribers. All subscribers expressly agree that they will not sell, communicate or give any of said information, commentary or price quotations to any other person, firm or corporation, including any governmental agent or agencies whatsoever and any news distributing or communications company or service. The use of quotations for contractual or other purposes is beyond the control of Urner Barry, which in no case assumes any responsibility for such use. The quotations given herein represent, to the best of the reporters knowledge, prevailing wholesale values in the specified grades of each commodity, based on sales to stores or warehouses from receivers and wholesale distributors, and on indications of willingness and ability to buy. They represent in the judgment of the publishers an accurate picture of current business, but they are not official in any sense of the word. The publishers disclaim and do not assume responsibility for any damages, alleged or otherwise, that may result or claim to have resulted from any use made by any person or any reliance by any person upon any of the statements of quotations appearing at any time herein.

Source: *Urner Barry's Price-Current* (Toms River, N.J.: Urner Barry Publications, Inc., 2007).

Exhibit 2   USDA Inspection Stamp and Grade A Shield

- *Grade C.* Grade C birds are less attractive in appearance than Grade B birds and may have parts missing.

Standards of quality include the amount of fat, the amount of flesh, the appearance of the flesh, color, the uniformity of the bird, and the presence of pin feathers, discoloration and bruising, missing parts, broken or disjointed bones, or any other processing defects. In practice, few poultry products below grade A are sold to food service operations. Grades B and C poultry are usually processed into other products, such as nuggets, patties, and luncheon meats. Exhibit 3 outlines the characteristics of Grade A poultry products.

Poultry Purchasing Systems

Depending upon the type, quality, and standards desired, poultry buyers should be able to purchase almost any product they need. Special requests, particularly for fresh birds, may be more difficult to fulfill in some smaller markets. Major food service distributors carry many types of poultry products. Local distributors will usually carry a sufficient selection of products for most buyers and may be the best source for fresh poultry products. Occasionally, special requests can be fulfilled by local farms, particularly for organic poultry products. However, local farms should only be used if the product is subject to continuous inspection for wholesomeness.

Poultry Cuts and Characteristics

Poultry is grouped into different classes or categories primarily based on the maturity, and sometimes the sex, of the bird. Younger birds are smaller and more tender. More mature birds have relatively tougher meat and are larger in size.

Exhibit 3   Grade A Poultry Characteristics

Buy Quality Poultry with Confidence

These emblems signify that the poultry has been examined and certified to the quality indicated by a U.S. Department of Agriculture grader.

Grade A is the highest grade available.

Grade A whole carcasses and parts:

- are fully fleshed and meaty.
- have normal conformation and shape.
- are free of disjointed or broken bones.
- are free of pinfeathers.
- are free of exposed flesh and discolorations.

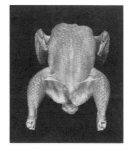

Grade A boneless-skinless poultry products:

- are free of bone, cartilage, tendons, bruises, blood clots, and other discolorations.

Boneless-skinless products shown: (L) Whole breast, breast halves, and tenderloins; (R) Thigh and drum.

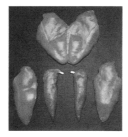

  United States Department of Agriculture   May 1996
Agricultural Marketing Service   AMS-626
Poultry Division

Source: www.ams.usda.gov

Younger birds are usually sold whole or in pieces. More mature birds have their meat processed into other products, such as soups and casseroles.

Chicken

Broilers or fryers. These are young chickens of either sex that usually are 9 to 13 weeks of age and 1½ to 3½ pounds. They are available fresh or frozen in the whole form, halved, quartered, or cut up into 8 or 9 pieces.

Roasters. Roasters are young chickens of either sex that usually are 12 to 20 weeks of age, are between 4 and 7 pounds, and have more fat than broilers. Roasters are usually available fresh or frozen in the whole form.

Capons. Capons are castrated male chickens, usually under 8 months of age. Capons weigh between 6 and 9 pounds, are large-breasted, and have more fat than broilers or roasters. Capons are usually available fresh or frozen in the whole form.

Hens, fowls, and stew chickens. These are female chickens of more than 10 months of age. They weigh between 4 and 7 pounds. These chickens are usually retired egg layers and their meat is used in processed poultry products.

Rock Cornish or Cornish game hens. These are young chickens bred from Cornish game hens or cross-bred with another breed of chicken. They are usually 5 to 6 weeks of age, weigh less than 2 pounds, and are available fresh or frozen in the whole state, halved, quartered, or in pieces.

Exhibit 4 shows some of the chicken cuts used in food service operations.

Turkey

Fryer-roasters. These are young turkeys of either sex, usually under 16 weeks of age, weighing between 4 and 8 pounds.

Young hens. Young hens include female turkeys from 5 to 7 months of age, weighing 8 to 14 pounds.

Young toms. These are male turkeys from 5 to 7 months of age, weighing over 12 pounds.

Yearling hens. These are female turkeys under 15 months of age, weighing from 20 to 30 pounds.

Yearling toms. Yearling toms are male turkeys under 15 months of age, weighing form 20 to 30 pounds.

Other Poultry

Ducklings. Ducklings include young ducks of either sex, between 8 and 16 weeks of age, weighing less than 7 pounds. Available frozen or fresh in the whole form or split into halves.

Ducks. Ducks are birds of either sex, over 16 weeks of age, weighing 6 to 8 pounds. Available frozen or fresh in the whole form or split into halves.

Geese. Young geese may be of either sex, usually 8 to 16 weeks of age, weighing 6 to 14 pounds. Available frozen or fresh, usually in the whole form.

Poultry Market Forms

Most poultry, particularly chicken, is available in a variety of market forms. The birds may be whole and eviscerated (entrails and organs removed), halved,

Exhibit 4   Chicken Food Service Cuts

CHICKEN

Foodservice Cuts

NAMP Number (North American Meat Processors Association)
© 2007 North American Meat Processors Association

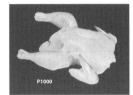

Broiler

Capon, Broiler, Cornish, Poussin

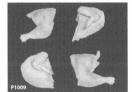

Broiler, Quartered

Eight-Piece Broiler

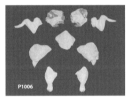

Nine-Piece Broiler

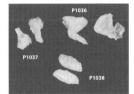

Wings

Thighs

Boneless Breasts

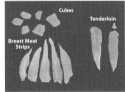

Breast Meat

Portion-Controlled Breast Meat

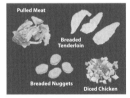

Value-Added Chicken

The above cuts are a partial representation of NAMP items. For further representation and explanation
of all cuts, see *The Meat Buyer's Guide* by the North American Meat Processors Association.

WILEY
wiley.com

NAMP
NORTH AMERICAN MEAT PROCESSORS ASSOCIATION

ISBN-13: 978-0-470-05035-4
ISBN-10: 0-470-05035-7

Source: North American Meat Processors Association, *Chicken Foodservice Poster, Revised.* © 2007, NAMP.
Reprinted with permission of John Wiley & Sons, Inc.

quartered, or cut into 8 to 9 pieces. Products can be boned, breaded, minced, cut into diced pieces, rolled, or precooked. If not purchased whole, poultry is usually cut and portioned. Portioned pieces can then be sold in bone-in or boneless forms. For practical purposes of transportation and storage, most portioned pieces of poultry are packaged individually quick frozen (IQF). Poultry purchased fresh from local distributors may be ice packed. Poultry may also be sold vacuum packed and refrigerated in the fresh state. Buyers should be aware that even though they may be purchasing poultry by portion size, the product will be sold by the case with an overall weight. Always specify the required portion size and number of portions desired when comparing case prices.

NAMP *Meat Buyer's Guide* Numbers

The North American Meat Processors Association (NAMP), National Live Stock and Meat Board, USDA Agricultural Marketing Service Livestock Division, and food service purchasing managers, through a cooperative effort, have established standard specifications for poultry items, referred to as NAMP numbers.

Standards

The *Meat Buyer's Guide*, published by NAMP, includes these specification numbers as well as a description and picture of each cut of poultry. These NAMP numbers allow buyers to order specific poultry cuts without having to prepare their own specifications. The NAMP number is constructed with the first digit of the number referring to the type of product and the remaining digits referring to a specific cut and trim. Using the NAMP number when ordering assures buyers that they will get the exact cut of poultry they desire. For example, poultry products begin with the #P designation. #P1000 designates a whole chicken broiler, and subsequent numbers designate the different cuts and pieces. For example, chicken broiler breast quarters are designated by #P1010 and the breast quarter without the wing would be designated by #P1011. The second digit refers to the poultry class, with #P10 referring to a broiler or fryer, #P11 to a roaster, #P12 to a capon, #P13 to a fowl, #P14 to a poussin (a young chicken under 8 weeks of age) and #P15 to a rock Cornish game hen. Chicken items begin with #P1000, turkey with #P2000, duck with #P3000, and goose with #P4000. Specialty and game bird products like guinea, quail, and pheasant are designated with #5000–#7000.

Poultry Purchase Specifications

Even though as a commodity poultry products are usually of fairly uniform quality, it is still a good idea to prepare a complete specification that contains the exact details of an operation's requirements. This is particularly important if a buyer has special product requirements.

Poultry purchase specifications should include the following elements:

* *Exact name of the product.* This is important because the federal government has standards of identity for most poultry products.

- *U.S. grade.* Grade A is most commonly required.

- *Brand name.* For many buyers, the brand is important because of the value added or because it is specified on the menu.

- *Product size.* Be sure to specify the portion size, if applicable.

- *Container/package size.* Specify the total amount of product in the case as well as the overall weight.

- *Packaging type.* Specify whether the product should be sealed in plastic or ice packed, for example.

- *Specific requirements.* Special instructions, such as skin or skinless, the acceptable time period between receiving and processing, and seasoning requirements.

- *Handling procedures.* Refrigeration or freezing requirements.

Exhibits 5–8 show sample specifications for various poultry products.

Poultry Food Safety Issues

Safety is a prominent poultry-product quality issue. Food safety risks associated with poultry include pathogenic bacteria, such as *Salmonella, Campylobacter jejuni, Clostridium perfringens, Listeria monocytogenes*, and *Staphylococcus aureus*, all of which are recognized causes of foodborne illnesses. There is also concern about avian influenza (bird flu) being transmitted into the domesticated bird population. In addition to these pathogens, which are typically carried from live poultry into processing, other chemical (i.e., drug and pesticide residues) and physical (i.e., bone fragments, foreign objects) hazards may exist in poultry products. Consequently, a significant portion (10–20 percent) of reported foodborne illness is attributed to poultry products. In addition to these recognized hazards, new concerns related to antibiotic-resistant bacteria, more virulent bacterial strains, and foodborne toxins continue to a concern. The poultry industry has been developing more effective sampling, detection, and identification methods, but the best strategies continue to be buying only from reputable distributors and enforcing safe food handling practices in the food service operation.

Management Considerations

Free-Range and Organic Products

Free range is a method of farming in which the animals are permitted to roam freely instead of being cooped or contained in any manner. The idea is to allow the animals as much freedom as possible to live out their lives in a reasonably natural way. The USDA requires that chickens raised for their meat have access to the outdoors in order to receive the free-range certification.

Organic poultry products come from animals that are given no antibiotics or growth hormones. Farmers must not use feed that contains most conventional pesticides, fertilizers made with synthetic ingredients or sewage sludge, bioengineering techniques, or ionizing radiation. Before a product can be labeled "organic," a

Exhibit 5   Sample Specification for Fresh Whole Broilers

Item:	Fresh whole broilers, weighing 2.75 pounds each, plus or minus 2 ounces
Grade:	USDA Grade A
Packaging:	Packed two birds per vacuum-sealed, CO_2-flushed bag; ten bags to each master carton; USDA data and production date to be displayed on exterior of carton
General Requirements:	Without necks or giblets
Specific Requirements:	Birds to be received within three days of processing
Handling:	Receiving temperature (internal product) not to exceed 34° F (1° C)

Exhibit 6   Sample Specification for Fresh Cut-Up Broilers

Item:	Fresh cut-up broilers, weighing 2.75 pounds each, plus or minus 2 ounces
Grade:	Plant Grade A
Packaging:	Packed two birds per vacuum-sealed, CO_2-flushed bag; ten bags to each master carton; USDA data and production date to be displayed on exterior of carton
General Requirements:	Without necks or giblets; eight-cut with keel bone split; separated at natural joints by using knives (no saw)
Specific Requirements:	Birds to be received within three days of processing
Handling:	Receiving temperature not to exceed 34° F (1° C)

Exhibit 7   Sample Specification for Fresh Turkey Breasts/Thigh Roasts

Item:	Fresh, raw, boned, and tied breast/thigh roasts made from young tom turkeys; each roast to weigh 8 pounds, plus or minus 8 ounces
Grade:	USDA Grade A
Packaging:	One roast per vacuum-sealed, CO_2 flushed package; five roasts to each master carton; USDA data and production date to be displayed on exterior of carton
General Requirements:	Composed of 60% breast, 40% thigh meat; all solid pieces to be used only from these two parts
Specific Requirements:	No skin, fillers, binders, or seasoning

Exhibit 8   Sample Specification for Frozen, Oven-Roasted Turkey Breasts

Item:	Fresh, oven-roasted turkey breasts from young tom turkeys; finished weight of 9 pounds, plus or minus 8 ounces
Grade:	USDA Grade A
Packaging:	Each roast individually vacuum-sealed; frozen at minus 40° F (4° C) or lower; four roasts to each master carton; USDA data and production date to be displayed on exterior of carton
General Requirements:	Natural shape; hand formed; no more than three solid pieces to each roast; breast meat only
Specific Requirements:	Skin-on; no broth or fillers

government-approved certifier must inspect the farm where the animals are raised to make sure the farmer is following all the rules necessary to meet USDA organic standards. Not all free-range poultry is organic because the only requirement is space for the animal to roam. However, organic poultry, by definition of the USDA, must be raised as a free-range animal. Is free-range and organic poultry better in flavor than conventionally raised poultry? That, of course, is a business question that must be addressed in terms of an operation's customers and their expectations and preferences. Most experts agree that free-range organic poultry does taste different than conventionally raised poultry, but the food service operator will need to determine the quality difference through testing. Free-range and organic poultry do demand a premium price in the market due to the additional costs involved in raising the animals and the smaller supply of products available.

Turkey as a Low-Fat Alternative

As consumers have become increasingly concerned with health and nutrition, turkey has become a common alternative to beef and other types of meat. According to the National Turkey Federation, consumers eat nearly 17 pounds of turkey per person. Consumption of turkey has grown more than 100 percent in the last 25 years. This trend has been attributed to today's new diet choices and increased popularity in the marketplace. Turkey is the number-four protein choice among most consumers. Using lean turkey can lower the fat content in a meal. Turkey is rich in calcium and protein and low in sodium compared to other meats. It is also significantly lower in calories, cholesterol, and fat than many other meats on the market, and is an excellent source of iron, potassium, phosphorus, zinc, and B vitamins.

The variety of turkey products available to food service buyers includes ground turkey, turkey tenderloin, steaks, boneless breasts, and drumsticks. Some of the popular meals that use turkey as an alternative include lasagna, pizza, spaghetti, and burgers. Operations can substitute ground turkey for ground beef in just about any recipe that usually calls for ground beef. Turkey is also a readily available product with a price lower than or comparable to beef and other red meat products.

Key Terms

domesticated—A term used to describe birds that are raised on farms for the purpose of poultry production.

free-range—A term used to describe poultry that has been raised with room to roam freely instead of being cooped or contained.

organic—A term used to describe poultry products that were raised without antibiotics or growth hormones.

wholesomeness—The safety of a poultry product. It is verified by inspection for proper cooking, temperatures, ingredient percentages, finished product, weight, storage temperatures, and the overall sanitation of the production line and packaging.

Review Questions

1. What is the inspection process for poultry?

2. What is the grading process for poultry?

3. What are the different ways poultry can be purchased?

4. What are the major types of poultry used in the food service industry?

5. What are the major cuts of poultry and the primary characteristics of each?

6. What are the requirements and content of specifications for poultry?

7. What are the important food safety issues specific to poultry?

8. What are some of the sources of information available to assist in making purchasing decisions for poultry?

 Internet Sites

For more information, visit the following Internet sites. Remember that Internet addresses can change without notice. If the site is no longer there, you can use a search engine to look for additional sites.

National Organic Program
www.ams.usda.gov/NOP

Turkey Facts and Trivia
www.eatturkey.com/consumer/stats/
stats.html

Urner Barry Publications
www.urnerbarry.com

USDA Poultry Grading Standards
www.ams.usda.gov/poultry/
standards/index.htm

USDA Poultry Programs
www.ams.usda.gov/poultry

Chapter 11 Outline

Dairy Production and Processing
Factors Affecting Dairy Supplies
Factors Affecting Dairy Costs and Pricing
Dairy Purchase Specifications and Standards
    Milk
    Butter
    Frozen Dairy Products
    Processed Milk Products
    Inspection of Dairy Products
    Grading of Dairy Products
    Dairy Product Food Safety Issues
    Non-Dairy Alternatives
Cheese
Eggs
    Egg Production and Processing
    Factors Affecting Egg Supplies
    Factors Affecting Egg Costs and Pricing
    Inspection of Eggs
    Grading of Eggs
    Egg Purchasing Systems
    Egg Specifications
    Egg Food Safety Issues

Competencies

1. Describe how dairy products are produced, supplied, and priced. (pp. 339–340)

2. List the sources of available information to assist in purchasing decisions for dairy products. (p. 340)

3. Explain the requirements, content, and importance of specifications for dairy products. (pp. 340–344)

4. Explain the inspection and grading processes for dairy products. (pp. 345–346)

5. Identify and explain the variety, designations, and standards for cheeses. (pp. 346–348)

6. Describe how eggs and egg products are produced, supplied and priced. (pp. 348–349)

7. Explain the inspection and grading process for eggs. (pp. 350–351)

8. Explain the requirements, content and importance of specifications for eggs. (pp. 352–353)

9. Describe the food safety issues specific to eggs. (pp. 353–354)

11

Dairy Products and Eggs

PURCHASING DAIRY PRODUCTS CAN BE A CHALLENGE. The wide variety of products available force a buyer to be knowledgeable about a wide range of products, including milk, cream, butter, cheeses, and frozen products. It is also important that buyers understand how milk moves through the supply and distribution system since it is the primary component of the various dairy products. Eggs are an easier commodity to understand since the primary consideration is the type of product needed. As a commodity, eggs are limited in the varieties that need to be considered.

Dairy Production and Processing

Dairy production occurs in almost every U.S. state; however, most of the processing is concentrated in the principal dairy producing states of California, Wisconsin, New York, and Pennsylvania. Historically, milk supply was provided by local producers. However, new processing and refrigeration technology has allowed nationwide distribution of milk products, which has increased supplies and kept costs in check.

All milk sold to food service operations must be pasteurized. Milk is pasteurized through a process called high temperature, short time (HTST) **pasteurization**. In this process, milk is heated to 161° F (72° C) for 15 seconds to destroy disease-causing pathogens. Most milk sold to the public is also homogenized. **Homogenization** is a process that breaks down fat in the milk into fine particles so it remains in suspension and does not separate from the milk fluids.

Factors Affecting Dairy Supplies

Milk is a commodity and is readily available to most markets. Milk shortages are rare; however, the supply of milk does vary slightly with the seasons. Cows produce more milk during the spring and summer. This creates an oversupply problem for the milk producing industry, but price stabilization regulations set up by the United States Department of Agriculture (USDA) and the dairy industry help to keep the milk supply constant to the marketplace. Other dairy products, such as cheese, butter, processed milk products, and frozen dairy products are rarely in shortage. The ready supply of milk used in their production ensures adequate supplies of these dairy products. The exception would be the availability of certain types of cheese due to the special nature of the manufacturing process. Additionally, many cheeses are imported so the supply can be affected by international transportation problems. Dairy products are usually available through the normal distribution channels available to food service operators. The decision to buy from a local distributor versus a national or regional distributor is largely a decision based on the relationship, service, and price provided by the distributor.

Factors Affecting Dairy Costs and Pricing

Federal and state regulations influence the price of milk and, therefore, milk products. Legislation establishes the prices milk producers receive for their milk. These prices are based on market orders and are published monthly in the USDA's *Dairy Market News* publication (see Exhibit 1) for different jurisdictions in the United States. The U.S. government must also purchase any surplus cheese, butter, and dry milk in order to maintain price stability in the market.

The government support establishes price parity for milk producers, but it also encourages producers to overproduce milk so the government will purchase it. So, while this keeps the prices of milk products reasonably stable, it also may be setting the cost of the product higher than need be given the supply and demand. The pricing of other dairy products is based on the cost of milk and, therefore, follows fluctuations in milk prices when they occur. In addition to the aforementioned *Dairy Market News*, the Urner Barry *Dairy & Egg Letter* (see Exhibit 2) is a good source of dairy product price information.

Dairy Purchase Specifications and Standards

The standards established for milk products make purchase specifications fairly straightforward to create. The elements of the specifications are similar to other food products, but the standards are easily defined. Specifications should include the milk product's:

- Exact nature.
- Intended use.
- U.S. grade.
- Brand name, if applicable.
- **Butterfat content** (should coincide with the name of the product).
- Weight or volume.
- Container size, including the number of products in a container if necessary.
- Packaging (carton, plastic bag).
- Yield.
- Form (whole, crumbled, dried).
- Special requirements, such as percentage of ingredients.
- Handling procedures (refrigerated or frozen).

Exhibit 1 *Dairy Market News*

WEEK OF MAY 7 - 11, 2007	DAIRY MARKET NEWS	VOLUME 74, REPORT 19

NATIONAL DAIRY MARKET AT A GLANCE

CHICAGO MERCANTILE EXCHANGE (CME) CASH MARKETS (05/11):
BUTTER: Grade AA closed at $1.4900. The weekly average for Grade AA is $1.4720 (+.0495).
CHEESE: Barrels closed at $1.6525 and 40# blocks at $1.6950. The weekly average for barrels is $1.6240 (+.0235) and blocks, $1.6805 (+.0315).
BUTTER: The CME cash butter price continues to increase. Churning across the country remains seasonally active, although cream supplies have tightened. Class II cream demand is building as ice cream production increases. As has been the case for much of the spring, current butter production is surpassing demand, thus surplus is clearing to inventory. CME butter inventories increased by 3.4 million pounds last week to stand at 129.2 million pounds. Some butter producers and handlers are voicing their concern about butter supplies later in the year. Butter production for March totaled 140.1 million pounds which was 1.1% lower than March 2006. The Western region of the country produced 47% of the total, the Central region produced 43%, with the Atlantic region generating 10% of the monthly total. Butter demand is fair at best, following typical spring/early summer buying patterns.
CHEESE: Cheese prices are erratic with barrels and blocks both lower and higher. Interest in blocks and natural varieties remains fairly strong considering recent declines and the overall higher price level, especially this near the annual peak production period. Process interest is spotty, slower where buyers have reacted to recent weakness and steady where prices are set monthly. Mozzarella offerings remain tight as expensive and limited offerings of NDM impact yields. Some customers have reported getting shorted on mozzarella orders. Cheese production is increasing seasonally though yields are steady to often lower.
FLUID MILK: Milk production across the Southern tier of states is trending steady to lower as warmer weather arrives and starts to affect cow comfort. Milk production in the Northern states is holding steady to increasing as the spring flush finally takes hold. Class I sales are steady in most regions, though handlers anticipate order reductions to start filtering through as spring terms draw to a close at various education institutions. Some retail features are helping boost fluid demand. Interest in condensed skim is mostly stronger, with heavier requests for the week coming from Class II facilities. Some facilities report being unable to fill all requests for spot loads due to lower milk intake. Cream multiples are steady to slightly higher in the West. Availability is decreasing in the West as the heat picks up and fat tests start to decline. Central and Eastern cream availability is steady to higher for the week. Increasing interest is noted from Class II manufacturers as the ice cream production cycle moves forward.
DRY PRODUCTS: Prices for low/medium and high heat nonfat dry milk moved strongly higher. Nonfat dry milk supplies remain short of domestic and international buyer interest, which is continuing to drive prices higher in all regions. Most regions report adequate facility capacity to process milk intakes. Dry buttermilk prices increased and buyer interest seems undeterred by recent price levels. Production levels are steady to somewhat lower as requests for condensed buttermilk are increasing from Class II manufacturers, and fat tests in various regions are beginning to decline. Whey protein concentrate 34% prices moved higher on a firm market. Interest from various industry quarters is steady to variable, with some buyers feeling hesitant to sign onto long term contracts at current prices. Dry whey prices adjusted lower in the Northeast,

the Western mostly average increased slightly, and the Central price range widened. Western whey continues to have the advantage of export interests driving the market and recent price fluctuations are allowing some Central whey to move into that arena. Both buyers and sellers are aware of recent dry whey price increases in Europe and are curious as to whether or not those market forces will again strengthen U.S. dry whey prices in the short term. Lactose prices are generally unchanged and the market is firm. Market participants are trying to determine market trends for the remainder of 2007. Though some end users have reformulated away from lactose, domestic and international interest is apparent in the marketplace and it is questionable whether any recent conversions away from lactose will have sufficient cumulative impact to moderate prices. Dry whole milk prices moved higher on a firm market. Production levels are mostly steady and based on contract commitments, but inquiries to manufacturers on spot load availability are increasing.
MARCH DAIRY PRODUCTS HIGHLIGHTS (NASS): Butter production was 140.1 million pounds in March, 1.1% below March 2006 but 4.4% above February 2007. American type cheese production totaled 338.5 million pounds, 0.7% above March 2006 and 10.8% above February 2007. Total cheese output (excluding cottage cheese) was 836.8 million pounds, 1.9% above March 2006 and 11.8% above February 2007. Nonfat dry milk production, for human food, totaled 117.5 million pounds, 8.8% below March 2006 but 19.8% above February 2007. Dry whey production, for human food, was 94.6 million pounds, 3.0% below March 2006 but 10.5% above February 2007.
FEBURARY 2007 MAILBOX PRICES (AMS & CDFA): In February 2007, mailbox milk prices for selected reporting areas in Federal milk orders averaged $14.92, $.26 more than the previous month. The component tests of producer milk in February 2007 were: butterfat, 3.78%; protein, 3.11%; and other solids, 5.70%. On an individual reporting area basis, mailbox prices increased in all Federal milk order reporting areas except three, and ranged from $17.27 in Florida to $13.19 in New Mexico. In February 2006, the Federal milk order all-area average mailbox price was $13.56, $1.36 lower.
MARCH FLUID MILK SALES (AMS): During March, about 4.8 billion pounds of packaged fluid milk products is estimated to have been sold in the United States. This was 0.1% higher than March 2006. After adjusting for calendar composition, sales in March 2007 were 0.5% lower than March 2006. On an individual product basis, after adjusting for calendar composition, sales of organic whole milk, low fat milk (1%), fat-free (skim) milk, organic fat-reduced milk, and buttermilk increased from March 2006, while sales of whole milk, flavored whole milk, reduced fat (2%) milk, and flavored fat-reduced milk decreased from a year earlier. The timing of the Easter holiday this year likely had no impact on the change in sales from March 2007 compared to March 2006.
MAY MILK SUPPLY AND DEMAND ESTIMATES (WAOB): Milk production is forecast to increase in 2008 reflecting strong milk prices and expected improved availability of hay. Milk cow numbers are likely to be only fractionally below 2007 and milk per cow growth should increase more rapidly than in 2007. Commercial use of fat and skim solids is expected to remain strong, and commercial stocks will likely tighten. Butter prices are forecast to increase in 2008 but cheese prices are forecast to decline slightly. Continued strength in export demand as well as domestic use of nonfat dry milk (NDM) and whey will help support prices with the annual average price of NDM above 2007.

****SPECIALS THIS ISSUE****

INTERNATIONAL DAIRY MARKET NEWS (PAGE 8)
DAIRY FUTURES (PAGE 9)
MARCH DAIRY PRODUCTS HIGHLIGHTS (PAGE 10)
FEBURARY 2007 MAILBOX PRICES (PAGE 11)

MARCH FLUID MILK SALES (PAGE 12)
MAY MILK SUPPLY AND DEMAND ESTIMATES (PAGES 13 - 14)
DAIRY GRAPHS (PAGES 15 - 16)

CHICAGO MERCANTILE EXCHANGE CASH TRADING

PRODUCT	MONDAY MAY 7	TUESDAY MAY 8	WEDNESDAY MAY 9	THURSDAY MAY 10	FRIDAY MAY 11	WEEKLY CHANGE*	WEEKLY AVERAGE#
CHEESE							
BARRELS	$1.6250 (-.0100)	$1.6125 (-.0125)	$1.6000 (-.0125)	$1.6300 (+.0300)	$1.6525 (+.0225)	(+.0175)	$1.6240 (+.0235)
40# BLOCKS	$1.6700 (-.0325)	$1.6700 (N.C.)	$1.6750 (+.0050)	$1.6925 (+.0175)	$1.6950 (+.0025)	(-.0075)	$1.6805 (+.0315)
BUTTER							
GRADE AA	$1.4550 (N.C.)	$1.4650 (+.0100)	$1.4725 (+.0075)	$1.4775 (+.0050)	$1.4900 (+.0125)	(+.0350)	$1.4720 (+.0495)

CHEESE: carload = 40,000-44,000 lbs., BUTTER: carlot = 40,000-43,000 lbs. *Sum of daily changes. # Weekly averages are simple averages of the daily closing prices for the calendar week. Computed by Dairy Market News for informational purposes. This data is available on the Internet at WWW.AMS.USDA.GOV/MARKETNEWS.HTM NOTE: CME NDM on Page 2.

Source: www.ams.usda.gov/marketnews.htm.

Exhibit 2   *Dairy & Egg Letter*

URNER BARRY PUBLICATIONS, INC.

WEEKLY INSIDER'S Dairy & Egg Letter

MARKET GUIDE & FORECASTER - FIRST WITH ALL THE FACTS YOU NEED

Number 19 · **Wednesday, May 9, 2007** · **Volume 34**

NORTHEAST EGGS WHOLESALE PRICE RECORD
(Cents per Dozen)

	2003	2004	2005	2006	2007
Large White	.71	.77	.60	.55	1.05
Large Brown	.87	.91	.63	.61	.98
Medium White	.68	.71	.49	.52	.97
Small White	.52	.57	.45	.44	.74

Data Updated: May 9, 2007

REGIONAL WHOLESALE PRICE RECORD
(Cents per Dozen)

	NE	MW	SE	SC
Large White	1.05-.03	1.01-.03	1.07-.03	1.06-.03
Large Brown	.98	.96	.98	.99
Medium White	.97-.03	.95	.98	.97
Small White	.74	.72	.74	.74

Data Updated: May 9, 2007

WEDNESDAY'S BREAKING STOCK (Cents per Dozen)
General Trading Prices-Nest Run
Dlvrd-Net Weights-Material may or may not be included

Region	42-44 lbs	48-50 lbs	50/up lbs
Eastern Standard	.51-.53	.57-.59	.59-.60
Eastern Certified	--	--	--
Central Standard	.51-.53	.58-.60	.60-.61
Central Certified	--	.60-.62	--

Data Updated: May 9, 2007

MIDWEST FOODS ASSOCIATION
Monday Inventory - Done on a Matched Plant Basis

	Inventory	Change	Members
Apr-30	58,351	-5.4	14
May-07	81,603	+28.8	14

Data Updated: May 9, 2007

USDA LIGHT TYPE FOWL SLAUGHTER
U.S. Fowl Slaughter (Birds in Thousands)

Date	2004	2005	2006	2007
Apr-07	1,234	1,671	1,185	1,117
Apr-14	1,362	1,740	1,018	1,114
Apr-21	1,464	1,687	1,208	1,026
Apr-28	1,424	1,651	1,110	1,156
YTD Total	18,967	20,284	25,725	21,876

Data Updated: May 9, 2007

COMMERCIAL EGG MOVEMENT REPORT
(Pounds in Thousands)
Week Ending - April 28, 2007

	Cases	% Change Last Week	% Change Last Year
North Atlantic	170.7	-1%	-8%
East North Central	623.1	-8%	+7%
West North Central	287.3	-1%	-1%
South Atlantic	181.1	+5%	+0%
South Central	51.5	-7%	-7%
West	175.1	-3%	+1%
TOTAL	1,488.8	-4%	+1%

Data Updated: May 9, 2007

EGG PROCESSING REPORT - USDA
Plants Under Federal Inspection
Comparisons Based on Matched Plants
(Pounds in Millions)

Total Production	Cases Broken	Last Year	Liquid	Last Year	Dried	Last Year
Mar-17	1,242.5	+0.2	48,544	+0.3	2,339	+5.4
Mar-24	1,270.0	+1.2	49,738	+0.6	2,176	-11.4
Mar-31	1,259.5	-0.2	49,371	-0.6	2,493	+0.4
Apr-07	1,254.5	-0.3	49,120	-1.0	2,292	-20.5
Apr-14	1,302.0	-0.1	51,123	+0.3	2,490	-16.3
Apr-21	1,231.7	-9.2	47,295	-11.4	2,340	-24.1
Apr-28	1,204.2	-11.9	47,541	-11.0	2,031	-37.8

In-Line Production	Current Week	Previous Week	Last Year
	48.20%	47.50%	46.90%

Data Updated: May 2, 2007

USDA - CCC
Weekly Support Purchases (Pounds in Thousands)

CHEESE	This Week	Last Year	Since Oct 1st Last Year	Same Period This Year
Apr-13	0	0	0	0
Apr-20	0	0	0	0
Apr-27	0	0	0	0
May-04	0	0	0	0
NONFAT				
Apr-13	0	0	0	0
Apr-20	0	0	0	0
Apr-27	0	0	0	1,307
May-04	0	0	0	9,867

Data Updated: May 9, 2007

MONTHLY PER CAPITA EGG PRODUCTION

	2005	2006	2007
Jan	.712	.717	.819
Feb	.713	.717	.820
Mar	.720	.727	.832
Apr	.708	.723	
May	.700	.704	
Jun	.702	.822	
Jul	.700	.823	
Aug	.702	.822	
Sep	.707	.825	
Oct	.716	.824	
Nov	.725	.834	
Dec	.725	.835	
Average	.711	.781	

AVERAGE ANNUAL QUOTATIONS

	2005	2006	2007
Large	.7134	.7762	1.1231
Medium	.5534	.6294	.9843
Small	.4350	.5014	.8110
Simple Avg.	.5673	.6357	.9728
Weighted Avg.	.6675	.7331	1.0797

Large 75%, Medium 20%, Pullets 5%
Data Updated: April 25, 2007

Urner Barry's
Weekly Insider's Dairy & Egg Letter

Editor: Randy Pesciotta

Published weekly in a variety of media
by Urner Barry Publications, Inc.
P.O. Box 389, Toms River, NJ 08754-0389

Phone 732-240-5330 · Fax 732-341-0891
www.urnerbarry.com

Copyright© 2007
Urner Barry Publications, Inc. ISSN 0270-4153

URNER BARRY'S WEEKLY INSIDER'S DAIRY & EGG LETTER
is available on Foodmarket.com and through Urner Barry's
flagship service Comtell Online.

Bold Type indicates revision. *Italic Type* indicates projection.

URNER BARRY EGG QUOTATIONS

FROZEN -	L.T.L.	Trucklots
30 Lb. Cans, Per Lb.-	3,600 lbs.+	20,000 lbs.+
Whole, No Color	.730-.740+.010	.690+.010
Whites	.710-.730	.660-.680
Yolk Sugar 43% solids	.830-.840	.780-.800
Yolk Salt 43% solids	.780-.800	.740-.770

LIQUID IN POTABLE CONTAINERS		
Whole	.750-.780	.720-.740
Whites	--	--
Sugar Yolk	--	.790-.830
Salt Yolk	.830-.850	.770-.820

EGG SOLIDS	L.T.L. 2,700 lbs. +	Truckloads 20,000 lbs. +
Whole Plain	2.50-2.55+.02	2.40-2.45+.02
Yolk	1.77-1.82+.02	1.67-1.72+.02
Albumen, Spray	5.20-5.30	5.05-5.10
Blend: 65-75% whole egg		
25-35% corn syrup	1.93-1.98	1.88-1.93

LIQUID EGGS	Tanker, Track per lb.	
	Standard	Certified
Whole, Unpasteurized	.530-.550	.550-.570
Custom Pack, Pasteurized	.590-.600	.610-.620
Whites, Unpasteurized	.540-.560	.560-.580
Custom Pack, Pasteurized	.590-.610	.610-.630
Yolk, 43% solids, Unpasteurized	.660-.680+.010	.660-.680+.010
Custom Pack, 43% Pasteurized	.690-.700+.010	.690-.700+.010
Yolk, Salt 43% solids, 10% salt	.660-.680	--

INSTITUTIONAL PACKS - FROZEN
PURE PAK Containers 30-32 lb. Case Wt. Dlvrd, LTL

Whole	.750-.770
Whites	.740-.770
Yolk, Sugar	.850-.870

Data Updated: May 9, 2007

Source: *Dairy & Egg Letter,* (Toms River, N.J.: Urner Barry Publications, Inc., 2007).

Exhibit 3   Typical Specifications for Dairy Products

Specification 1	Fluid milk—Grade A 1 gallon whole milk
Specification 2	• Butter, 92 score (A): 1-lb prints; 30-lb carton • Butter, 92 score (A): 72-count chips; 24-lb carton • Butter, 92 score (A): 90-count reddies; 24-lb carton • Butter, 92 score (A): whipped, 30% overrun; 7-lb tubs
Specification 3	Milk shake mix Weight per gallon = 9 lb

Butterfat	3.5 %
Non-fat dry milk solids	12.0 %
Cane sugar	8.5 %
Stabilizer (not to exceed)	0.35%
Total solids	24.35%

Specification 4	Bulk vanilla ice cream—3-gallon container Weight per gallon = 4.5 lb

Butterfat	12.0%
Non-fat dry milk solids	13.0%
Cane sugar	13.0%
Stabilizer	0.5%
Flavoring	2.0%
Overrun	100.0%

Specification 5	Regular processed American cheese 27% milkfat, 30% non-fat solids, 43% moisture, no aged cheese 160 slices per 5-lb package
Specification 6	Sharp processed American cheese 27% milkfat, 30% non-fat solids, 43% moisture, aged cheddar added for flavor 160 slices per 5-lb box
Specification 7	Regular processed cheese food 23% milkfat, 23% non-fat solids, 44% moisture 160 slices per 5-lb box

Exhibit 3 contains sample specifications for several dairy products.

Milk

Standards and specifications for milk and milk products are based on the percentage of butterfat contained in the product. The fat content varies for different products. The USDA Food Safety and Inspection Service sets the standards for specific products with the terms defined by the standard. For example, whole milk must have a minimum butterfat content of 3.25 percent and half-and-half must have a minimum butterfat content of 10.5 percent (see Exhibit 4).

Butter

Butter is a milk product produced by adding a milk acid and churning the product into butterfat. Butter must have a minimum of 80 percent butterfat. Butter is available in many forms, but the most common forms used in food service are one-pound blocks and whipped butter in seven-pound tubs. Butter chips, or reddies,

Exhibit 4   Minimum Butterfat and Non-Fat Milk Specifications Requirements

		Minimum Butterfat (%)	Minimum Non-Fat Milk Solids (%)
1.	Fluid whole milk	3.25	8.25
2.	Homogenized	3.25	8.25 Fat uniformly distributed
3.	Vitamin "D"	3.25	8.25 Minimum of 400 USP Vitamin "D" units per quart
4.	Skimmed	0.50	7.75
5.	Low fat	0.2 to 2.0	8.25
6.	2%	2.00	10.00 Generally
7.	Buttermilk	0.50	8.25
8.	Evaporated whole milk	7.5	18.00
9.	Evaporated skim milk	0.2	18.00
10.	Sweetened condensed	8.5	19.5 Sugar added
11.	Non-fat dry milk	1.5	In the dry product—5% moisture max.
12.	Whole dry milk	26.0	In the dry product—5% moisture max.
13.	Half & half	10.5	8.25
14.	Table cream	18.0	8.25
15.	Sour cream	18.0	8.25 Culture added 0.2% acidity
16.	Light whipping cream	30.0	8.25
17.	Heavy whipping cream	36.0	8.25
18.	Ice cream	10.0	10.00 Plus sugar, flavor, stabilizers
19.	Frozen custard	10.0	10.0 Plus egg yolks and ice cream ingredients
20.	Fruit sherbet	1.0 to 2.0	2.0 to 5.0 Total milk solids
21.	Milk shakes	3.25	8.25
22.	Butter	80.00	

Source: United States Department of Agriculture, *Federal and State Standards for the Composition of Milk Products.* Agricultural Handbook No. 51. Washington, D.C., January 1, 1980.

are used in portion-control situations. These are convenient forms for single use, often served with the chips wrapped in foil or individually portioned in plastic cups or on paper.

Frozen Dairy Products

The federal government sets minimum standards for frozen dairy products (see Exhibit 5). However, quality standards are not established and it is up to the buyer to test products and specify products that meet the operation's needs. One important consideration is overrun. **Overrun** is the percentage by volume of air incorporated into the product during the mixing process. Specifications for frozen dairy products should state an acceptable level of overrun.

Processed Milk Products

Processed milk products such as sour cream, evaporated milk, sweetened condensed milk, and dry milk have standards set by the government, but quality must be determined by the buyer and specified for the distributor. Products should be tested for quality before decisions are made on specifications. Specifying brand names for such products can sometimes help to ensure product reliability.

Exhibit 5   Minimum Standards for Frozen Dairy Products

Product	Milkfat (%)	Total Milk Solids (%)	Minimum Weight (lb/gal)
Plain ice cream	10	20	4.5
Chocolate or flavored ice cream	8	16	4.5
Frozen custard	10	20	4.5
Milk shake mix	3.25	11.5	
Sherbet—minimum	1	2	6.0
standard	2	4	6.0

Source: United States Department of Agriculture, *Federal and State Standards for the Composition of Milk Products.* Agricultural Handbook No. 51. Washington, D.C., January 1, 1980.

Inspection of Dairy Products

Milk is subject to strict federal, state, and local health regulations, and milk production is subject to regular inspection by various agencies, depending upon location and jurisdiction. The U.S. Public Health Service and the Food and Drug Administration have established the Pasteurized Milk Ordinance, which regulates activities regarding feeding dairy cows, handling milk, pasteurization, and milk storage temperatures.

Grading of Dairy Products

Milk grades are based on the bacterial content of the finished fluid milk and are indicated as follows:

- *Grade A.* This milk is suitable for sale to consumers

- *Manufacturing grade.* This is sometimes referred to as Grade B. Manufacturing grade milk has a bacterial content too high for sale to consumers, but it is still suitable for products that go through further processing, such as cheese, butter, and ice cream.

Other factors to consider in grading are whether the milk is certified or **fortified**. Milk found to have a very low bacteria count can be certified as safe for consumption by infants and the elderly or sick. This is not the same as grading, but it may be a requirement in such food service environments as hospitals, extended care facilities and daycare centers. Additionally, milk may be fortified with vitamins A and D.

Most milk products are not graded because graded milk is used in the production of the product. A few products do have grades established as follows:

- Dry nonfat milk—extra or standard

- Dry whole milk—premium, extra, or standard

- Butter—AA, A, or B

- Cheddar, Colby, Swiss, and Monterey Jack cheeses—AA, A, B, or C

Exhibit 6   Descriptions of Quality Grades for Butter

U.S. Grade AA (93 Score)
.... Delicate, sweet flavor, with fine highly pleasing aroma.
.... Made with high-quality, fresh sweet cream.
.... Smooth texture, with salt completely dissolved.

U.S. Grade A (92 Score)
.... Pleasing flavor, made from fresh cream; fairly smooth texture.

U.S. Grade B (90 Score)
.... May have slightly acid flavor; generally made from sour cream.

Butter bearing USDA Grade Shields must be produced in a sanitary plant approved by the USDA.

Source: United States Department of Agriculture, *Federal and State Standards for the Composition of Milk Products.* Agricultural Handbook No. 51. Washington, D.C., January 1, 1980.

Dry milk is graded according to its color, flavor, bacterial count, odor, scorching (which can happen if the milk is overheated during the drying process), appearance, texture, how well it dissolves, and moisture content. Butter grades are based on the butter's flavor, color, texture, odor, freshness, and body (shape) (see Exhibit 6). Cheese is graded according to its color, appearance, flavor, texture, odor, smoothness of finish, and body. Exhibits 7 and 8 list various government standards for cheese.

Other dairy products may use terms associated with quality that do not necessarily reflect any official government grades. Ice cream may be labeled premium, regular, or competitive. Additional information important to consider would be the "sell by" dates included on many dairy products due to their perishability.

Dairy Product Food Safety Issues

As stated before, milk served to the public must be pasteurized and inspected as safe before it can be sold. Food safety problems encountered with milk usually occur at some point after the processing of the fluid milk. The biggest concern is spoilage due to the perishability of milk. Frozen dairy desserts are subject to pathogen contamination, particularly by *Listeria monocytogenes,* because of its tolerance for lower temperatures. *Listeria* contamination can occur in frozen dairy machines if they are not properly cleaned and sanitized.

Non-Dairy Alternatives

Non-dairy alternative products are often considered for food service operations that serve customers who require special diets. Non-dairy products can be alternatives for customers who need low-fat products or those who cannot tolerate **lactose** (the sugar found in milk). Non-dairy products also are less expensive and less perishable than traditional dairy products.

Cheese

The popularity of cheese contributes to the variety of cheeses available and creative development of new products. The types and varieties of cheese available

Exhibit 7   Moisture and Milkfat Standards for Cheese

Variety	Maximum Moisture (%)	Minimum Milkfat in Solids (%)	Minimum Milkfat in Cheese (%)
Cottage—regular	80	—	4
Cream	55	—	33
Camembert	—	50	25
Limburger	50	50	25
Bleu	46	50	27
Monterey	44	50	28
Muenster	46	50	27
Roquefort	45	50	27.5
Cheddar	39	50	30.5
Colby	40	50	30
Gouda	45	46	25.3
Swiss	41	43	25.4
Parmesan	32	32	21.8
Romano	34	38	25.1
Mozzarella—regular	52/60	45	18
Mozzarella—low moisture, part skim	45/52	30/45	14
Provolone	45	45	24.8
Pasteurized Processed Cheese	43	47	27
Processed Cheese Food	44	—	23
Cold Pack Cheese	42	47	27
Cold Pack Cheese Food	44	—	23

Source: United States Department of Agriculture, *Federal and State Standards for the Composition of Milk Products.* Agricultural Handbook No. 51. Washington, D.C., January 1, 1980.

Exhibit 8   Grading Standards for Cheddar Cheese

AA   Meets federal standards for fat and moisture content. The cheese has a fine, highly pleasing cheddar flavor, a smooth compact texture, uniform color, and attractive appearance. The plant in which the cheese is produced must meet USDA sanitary requirements.

A   Same as AA, but there may be some variation in flavor and texture between packages.

All packages carrying the USDA grading shield must also show the cure category:

Mild	partly cured (usually 2 to 3 months)
Mellow Aged	moderately ripened (4-7 months)
Sharp	fully ripened (8-12 months)

Any product aged over 12 months may be labeled "very sharp."

Source: United States Department of Agriculture, *Federal and State Standards for the Composition of Milk Products.* Agricultural Handbook No. 51. Washington, D.C., January 1, 1980.

can fill an encyclopedia. Processing methods for cheese vary from region to region. Many cheeses have European origins. Regulations in Europe require some types of cheeses to be produced under very special circumstances in very specific regions.

For example, what is generically referred to as bleu cheese, if produced in a specific region, is named after that region. Roquefort is produced in southern France; Stilton is produced in England, and Gorgonzola is produced in Italy. All are varieties of bleu cheese.

Cheese varieties are determined by the raw material (milk), texture, the **ripening** process, and the length of curing. Cheeses can be unripened, mold ripened, or bacteria ripened.

Processed cheese is a blend of fresh and aged cheeses that have been pasteurized and sometimes blended with other ingredients. Processed cheese products can be packaged in block loaves or shredded.

Products that do not match the government's definition for cheese are referred to as cheese food products. Cheese food products have cheese, fat, and more moisture. Their composition may lower costs and may make the products acceptable for use in certain situations.

Eggs

Purchasing eggs is a relatively simple activity. As a commodity, the quality of eggs is standardized. Factors to consider include the type of product, size, and whether to buy processed products.

Egg Production and Processing

Egg production takes place in two different ways. Production plants can be integrated as part of the chicken-farming process, with the egg production performed either on the farm or by local subcontractors. Production can also take place at farms dedicated exclusively to producing eggs. Integrated production facilities provide all types of eggs—fresh, frozen, and processed. Because of the large numbers of chickens and eggs processed, they can produce eggs at a lower price. Egg farmers, on the other hand, provide services that large production farms cannot supply. Egg farms may provide different varieties of eggs and several sizes that are not available in all markets. Egg farms, if based locally, may also provide fresher eggs.

Fresh eggs need to be refrigerated at a temperature below 45° F (7° C) to best preserve them for delivery. As eggs age, they lose moisture, with the white getting thinner and the yolk getting weaker. Old eggs will have a larger air sac at the larger end of the egg than fresher eggs. Eggs layed by hens have a natural coating that must be cleaned off before sale. This exposes the eggs to potential moisture loss, so they are coated with a natural oil to help them retain moisture.

Factors Affecting Egg Supplies

Like chicken, eggs are a commodity and are readily available in most U.S. markets. The supply of eggs is stable because hens lay eggs year-round. Problems only occur when local egg farms or distributors experience supply disruptions due to natural disasters or problems on the farm. For example, severe weather may disrupt transportation and cause supply problems.

Exhibit 9   Egg Sizes

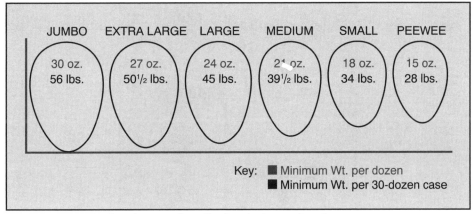

JUMBO	EXTRA LARGE	LARGE	MEDIUM	SMALL	PEEWEE
30 oz. 56 lbs.	27 oz. 50½ lbs.	24 oz. 45 lbs.	2¹ oz. 39½ lbs.	18 oz. 34 lbs.	15 oz. 28 lbs.

Key: ■ Minimum Wt. per dozen
■ Minimum Wt. per 30-dozen case

Source: American Egg Board, www.aeb.org/foodservice/eggproducts.htm.

Exhibit 10   Shell Weight Classes

Weight Class	Minimum Net Weight (oz/doz)	Minimum Net Weight (lb/30 doz)	Minimum Weight for Individual Eggs (oz/doz)
Jumbo	30	56.0	29
Extra Large	27	50.5	26
Large	24	45.0	23
Medium	21	39.5	20
Small	18	34.0	17
Peewee	15	28.0	—

An average lot tolerance of 3.3% in the next lower weight class is permitted as long as no individual case exceeds 5%.

Source: United States Department of Agriculture, *United States Standards, Grades, and Weight Classes for Shell Eggs*, AMS 56, Table I. Available on-line at www.ams.usda.gov/poultry/pdfs/AMS-eggst-2000.pdf.

Factors Affecting Egg Costs and Pricing

As a commodity, eggs are subject to the laws of supply and demand. Because the supply of eggs is relatively constant, their price varies little. Supply disruptions or high demand may increase prices temporarily, but they do not usually vary greatly from month to month. The cost of eggs is more likely to vary depending on the distributor due to the services offered. Large egg distributors will provide eggs at a lower cost, but freshness may not be ideal. Local distributors might provide fresher eggs, but the cost will be higher. The price of eggs will also vary depending on their size. If eggs are used in recipes based on weight, they can be priced by the ounce in order to decide the best value. Exhibits 9 and 10 classify eggs based on size and shell weight.

Exhibit 11   Federal Grade Marks for Eggs

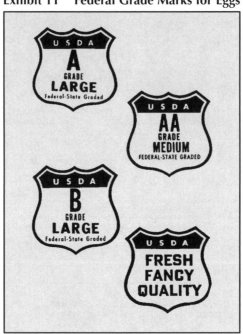

Inspection of Eggs

The Egg Products Inspection Act (1970) provides for the continuous inspection of egg processing. The act also controls the handling and use of eggs that cannot be sold to the public due to damage. Included in this act are the standards for grades and weight classes. Some damaged eggs that have been rejected for appearance problems can be used in processed products. Eggs in which the shell has been compromised must be destroyed. All processed egg products must be tested for *Salmonella* bacteria. Shell eggs and processed egg products can be pasteurized (heated to 130° F (54° C) for 45 minutes) to ensure safety. Many local health codes require that pasteurized eggs and egg products be used in recipes that will not require further cooking.

Grading of Eggs

Egg grading is a voluntary service offered by the USDA Agricultural Marketing Service. It must be paid for by the egg processor. Not all production facilities in all states utilize the federal grading designations, but they may use a state grade designation. Only federally graded eggs and egg products will carry the USDA shield (see Exhibit 11).

Shell eggs can be graded AA (Fresh Fancy), A, and B as follows:

- *Grade AA.* These are top-quality eggs. The egg must be free from defects. Only the freshest eggs receive a Grade AA designation. Once an egg is more than one week old, it becomes Grade A.

Exhibit 12   USDA Standards for Quality of Individual Shell Eggs

Quality Factor	Specifications for Each Quality Factor		
	AA Quality	A Quality	B Quality
Shell	Clean Unbroken, practically normal	Clean Unbroken, practically normal	Clean to slightly stained Unbroken, may be slightly abnormal
Air Cell	1/8 inch or less in depth May show unlimited movement and may be free or bubbly	3/16 inch or less in depth May show unlimited movement and may be free or bubbly	3/8 inch or less in depth May show unlimited movement and may be free or bubbly
White	Clear Firm	Clear May be reasonably firm	Clear May be slightly weak
Yolk	Outline slightly defined Practically free from defects	Outline may be fairly well defined Practically free from defects	Outline may be well defined May be slightly enlarged and flattened May show definite but not serious defects

Source: United States Department of Agriculture, *United States Standards, Grades, and Weight Classes for Shell Eggs,* AMS 56. Available on-line at www.ams.usda.gov/poultry/pdfs/AMS-eggst-2000.pdf.

- *Grade A.* Like Grade AA, the egg must be free from defects. Grade A eggs are usually older than AA eggs with thinner whites and yolks than AA eggs.

- *Grade B.* The shells may show signs of staining. Whites are thin and yolks are easily broken.

Exhibit 12 lists more specific USDA standards for egg quality grading.

When purchasing eggs by the case, all eggs may not be of the same grade quality. Grading tolerances are listed in Exhibit 13. Buyers can outline acceptable tolerances in their product specifications. The greatest advantage of USDA grading is the guarantee that the eggs have also been subject to federal inspection and, therefore, can be deemed safe.

Egg Purchasing Systems

In order to best determine where and from whom they should purchase eggs, buyers need to determine what types of eggs they need and how the eggs will be

Exhibit 13   Grading Tolerances for Eggs in Cases

Quality Required for Lots of Two or More Cases		
USDA Grade	At Origin	At Destination
Grade AA (Fresh Fancy)	87% AA	80% AA
Grade A	87% A or better	82% A or better
Grade B	90% A or better	90% B or better
Quality Required for Individual Cases in a Lot		
USDA Grade	At Origin	At Destination
Grade AA (Fresh Fancy)	77% AA, 13% A or B, 10% Check (max.)	62% AA, 28% A or B, 10% Check (max)
Grade A	77% A (min.), 13% B, 10% Check (max.)	72% A (min.), 10% B, 10% Check (max.)
Grade B	80% B (min.), 20% Check (max.)	80% B (min.), 20% Check (max.)

Source: United States Department of Agriculture, *United States Standards, Grades, and Weight Classes for Shell Eggs,* AMS 56. Available on-line at www.ams.usda.gov/poultry/pdfs/AMS-eggst-2000.pdf.

used. If eggs will only be used in finished products, processed egg products will likely be the best choice. Since standards are not established for most processed egg products, buyers should rely on brand reputation and product convenience. Products should be tested before selection.

For fresh eggs, there are several factors to consider in the purchasing decision. Deciding upon a distributor depends mostly on the services offered and the buyer's requirements for egg freshness. If delivery convenience is highly desired and egg freshness is not a critical issue, then eggs may be best purchased from full-line food service distributors. If the freshest eggs are desired, buyers should look for local distributors who supply eggs from local farms. In any case, buyers should realize that proper handling is the best way to ensure they are receiving the highest quality eggs. Buyers should investigate distributors thoroughly before making a purchasing decision.

Egg Specifications

Eggs can be purchased fresh in the shell, as frozen whole eggs, as yolks only, as whites only, as cooked yolks, or pasteurized in many other forms including dried, liquid and frozen. Processed eggs are sold in cartons and tubes.

For fresh shell eggs, the most important specification beyond the USDA grade is size. Eggs are available in six weight classes: jumbo, extra large, large, medium, small, and peewee. Food service operators typically request large eggs since they are used in most recipes. Whole egg products must, by law, contain at least 24.7 percent egg solids by weight to be called a whole egg product. Buyers should be aware that egg substitutes exist that may provide some versatility in purchasing. Products such as reduced-cholesterol eggs may be specified as a replacement for whole egg products if customers require that type of product.

Exhibit 14   Sample Specifications for Egg Products

Specification #1

Item:	USDA Grade A Large fresh eggs
Packaging:	30-dozen cartons; cartons carry appropriate shield stamps and lot number identifications
Requirements:	90% Grade A or better (no C's or checks) and 97% Large or better (no small eggs); delivered within two days of inspection
Handling:	Cartons identified in USDA standards and carrying appropriate shield stamps and lot number

Specification #2

Item:	Frozen whole eggs
Grade:	Packed under continuous USDA inspection with certificates furnished
Packaging:	30-pound cans
Requirements:	Pasteurized; negative for *Salmonella* bacteria; Color Level Three (Whole eggs and yolks are sold with different color levels, which carry different prices. More color, up to a point, commands a higher price.)

Specification #3

Item:	Frozen yolks—45% solids
Grade:	Packed under continuous USDA inspection with certificates
Packaging:	30-pound cans; yolks packed with a percentage of sugar or salt, ranging from an average of 2% to as high as 12% (the percentage must be indicated)
Requirements:	Pasteurized; negative for *Salmonella* bacteria; Color Level Four

Specification #4

Item:	Table-ready egg blend—30/32% solids
Grade:	Produced within last six months in inspected plant
Packaging:	Packed in eight 4-pound pure pack cartons; shield stamp on exterior carton
Requirements:	All egg solids (no milk, sugar, salt, or other ingredients)

Egg specifications should include:

- The exact name of the item.
- The intended use.
- U. S. grade designation.
- Brand name.
- Size of the product.
- Size of the container.
- Packaging.
- Product form.
- Specific requirements.
- Handling procedures.

Exhibit 14 contains sample specifications for several egg products.

Egg Food Safety Issues

Eggs, because of their fragility, are subject to damage and possible contamination. All fresh eggs are vulnerable to *Salmonella* bacteria transferred to the egg from the hens. For this reason, eggs must be refrigerated and handled as a potentially hazardous food. If a final egg product is not going to be cooked, pasteurized egg products should be considered for purchase. Exhibit 15 lists suggestions for safe

Exhibit 15   Suggestions for Safe Egg Handling

Storage/Recieving

- Store in cooler immediately upon receipt.
- Refrigerate at 45° F (7° C) or below.
- Store away from strong odors.
- Rotate—first in/first out.
- Take out eggs only for immediate use.
- Never stack egg flats near grill or stove.

Handling

- Wash hands with soap and warm water.
- Use clean, uncracked eggs.
- Avoid pooling and combining eggs.
- Use clean, sanitized utensils and equipment.

Preparation

- Cook eggs thoroughly.
- Hold cold egg dishes below 40° F (4° C).
- Hold hot egg dishes above 140° F (60° C).
- Never leave egg dishes at room temperature for more than one hour.

Source: American Egg Board, www.aeb.org.

egg handling. Egg safety and training materials can also be ordered by contacting the American Egg Board at 1460 Renaissance Drive, Park Ridge, IL 60068, or by phone at (847) 296-7043, fax at (847) 296-7007, or e-mail at aeb@aeb.org.

 **Key Terms**

butterfat content—The part of a standard or specification for milk and milk products that helps determine what the product is. For example, whole milk must have a minimum butterfat content of 3.25 percent and half-and-half must have a minimum butterfat content of 10.5 percent.

fortified—Milk with added nutrients, such as vitamin A or vitamin D.

homogenization—A process that breaks down fat in the milk into fine particles so it remains in suspension and does not separate from the milk fluids

lactose—The sugar found in milk and milk products.

overrun—The percentage by volume of air incorporated into a frozen dairy product during the mixing process.

pasteurization—A process in which milk is heated to remove disease-causing pathogens.

ripening—An element that helps determine cheese variety. Cheeses can be unripened, mold ripened, or bacteria ripened.

Review Questions ─────────────────────────────

1. What are the factors that affect how dairy products are produced, supplied, and priced?

2. What are the requirements and content of specifications for dairy products?

3. What are the different varieties, designations, and standards for cheeses?

4. What is the inspection process for dairy products?

5. What is the grading process for dairy products?

6. What are some of the sources of information available to assist in purchasing decisions for dairy products?

7. What are the factors that affect how eggs and egg products are produced, supplied and priced?

8. What is the inspection process for eggs?

9. What is the grading process for eggs?

10. What are the requirements and content of specifications for eggs?

11. What are the food safety issues specific to eggs?

 Internet Sites ─────────────────────────────

For more information, visit the following Internet sites. Remember that Internet addresses can change without notice. If the site is no longer there, you can use a search engine to look for additional sites.

American Egg Board
www.aeb.org

Cheese.com
www.cheese.com/default.asp

Cheese Market News
www.cheesemarketnews.com/
mainframe.html

Dairy Market News
www.ams.usda.gov/Dairy/MNCS/
INTER.HTM

Grade A Pasteurized Milk Ordinance
www.cfsan.fda.gov/~ear/
pmo03toc.html

Land O'Lakes All About Cheese
www.landolakes.com/mealIdeas/
AllAboutCheese.cfm

Urner Barry Publications
www.urnerbarry.com

Chapter 12 Outline

Introduction
Fresh Fruit
    Quality Grades for Fresh Fruit
    Fresh Fruit Varieties
Fresh Vegetables
    Quality Grades for Fresh Vegetables
    Fresh Vegetable Varieties
Fresh Produce Distribution Systems
    Distribution
    Packaging
Costs, Pricing, and Yield of Fresh Produce
Processed Fruits and Vegetables
    Grading, Specifications, and Quality
    Distribution
    Pricing and Yield
Produce Food Safety Issues
Management Considerations
    Farm Fresh
    Sustainability

Competencies

1. Identify the factors important to quality in fruits and vegetables. (pp. 357–360, 368–370)

2. Provide the major categories and varieties of fresh fruits and vegetables. (pp. 357–377)

3. Identify the major growing areas, availability, pricing factors and storage issues for fresh fruits and vegetables. (pp. 357–377)

4. Explain the requirements, content and importance of purchase specifications for fresh produce. (pp. 357–377)

5. Describe the distribution, processing and packaging options for fresh produce. (pp. 377–378)

6. Explain the factors that affect yield for fresh produce, and describe their effect on costs. (p. 378)

7. List available sources of information to assist in produce purchasing decisions. (p. 378)

8. Describe the market forms of processed fruits and vegetables. (pp. 378–379)

9. Explain the requirements, content and importance of purchasing specifications for processed fruits and vegetables. (pp. 379–382)

10. Describe management considerations related to purchasing produce products. (pp. 383–384)

12

Produce

FRUITS AND VEGETABLES ARE GROWN over much of the United States in some form or another; however, five states account for more than 70 percent of the fruit and vegetable production in the United States. California is by far the largest producer of fruits and vegetables, accounting for more than 45 percent of all U.S. production. Florida, Arizona, Georgia, and Texas follow in production, accounting for about 25 percent of the production combined. Mexico supplies a large part of the produce imported into the United States, particularly vegetables.

Fruit and vegetable production is seasonal. In the winter months, cold-weather states depend upon southern and western states for supply. In the summer months, northern and eastern states can produce fruits and vegetables to supply local markets and specialty markets. Certain products, such as asparagus and pumpkins, are only produced once per year and, therefore, their supply and prices are affected by this seasonality. Other crops such as carrots, melons and peppers can be harvested several times per year, especially in warm-weather climates.

It can be difficult for buyers to become proficient in purchasing produce. The fluctuations in quality and quantities available require buyers to stay knowledgeable of market details on a daily basis. The large variety of fresh produce available in the market also makes purchasing a challenge for buyers.

Fresh Fruit

Purchasing fresh fruit requires knowledge of the market due to the variety of fruit available and the high perishability of fruit. Purchase specifications for fresh fruit items are particularly important because of the non-standard nature of the product. Fresh fruit items can vary widely in size, appearance, and quality depending upon the season, growing region, and type of product. The following section provides details that can be used to develop purchase specifications for some of the most popular types of fresh fruit. Exhibit 1 provides U.S. grades, pack sizes, and storage requirements for fresh fruit. Exhibit 2 contains a chart of availability for fresh fruit.

Quality Grades for Fresh Fruit

The United States Department of Agriculture (USDA) has established grade standards for most fresh fruits. The grades are used extensively as a basis for trading among growers, shippers, wholesalers, and retailers. Grade standards are used to a limited extent in sales from retailers to consumers. Use of U.S. grade standards

Exhibit 1   Fresh Fruit—U.S. Grades, Pack Sizes, and Storage Characteristics

Product	U.S. Grades	Pack Sizes	Storage Characteristics
Apples	Extra Fancy, Fancy, #1, and Utility	Loose in cartons weighing 38 to 40 pounds, or tray pack cartons weighing 40 to 45 pounds. Counts range from 48 to 198 per carton.	Soften rapidly in warm temperatures. Store at temperatures around 30°F (-1°C).
Apricots	#1 and #2	Lugs weighing 24 to 26 pounds.	Store at temperatures from 32°F (0°C) to 36°F (2°C).
Avocados	#1, Combo, #2, and #3 (grades for Florida only)	California packs—one-layer flats weighing 12 1/2 pounds with counts of 9 to 35 per flat. California and Florida pack double-layer 25-pound lugs with counts of 18 to 96.	Ripen at room temperature, then refrigerate until use.
Bananas	No U.S. grades	Cartons of 40 pounds in assorted sizes; some markets offer a uniform 150 count per carton in petite size.	Bananas should be purchased at the ripeness stage that will hold until anticipated usage.
Blackberries/ Raspberries	#1 and #2	Normally packed in 12-pint flats with overfilled baskets.	Store at 32°F (0°C) with 90% relative humidity.
Blueberries	#1	Shipped in 12-pint flats with overfilled baskets.	Store at 32°F (0°C) with 90% relative humidity.
Cantaloupes	Fancy, #1, Commercial, and #2	Half crates weighing 38 to 41 pounds; 2/3 crates weighing 53 to 55 pounds; and full crates weighing 75 to 85 pounds. Counts range from 12 to 46 depending on container size.	Store at 40°F (4°C).
Cherries	#1 and Commercial	Normally shipped in 20-pound lugs.	Refrigerate at 34°F (1°C).
Coconuts	No U.S. grades	Usually sold by the dozen.	Refrigerate at 34°F (1°C).
Cranberries	#1	Typically packed in cartons of 24 one-pound units and 25-pound bulk.	Store at 32°F (0°C) with 90% relative humidity.
Grapefruit	Fancy, #1, Combo, #2, and #3	All areas—7/10 bushel cartons weighing between 38 and 42 pounds with counts ranging from 23 to 64.	Store at 50°F (10°C).
Grapes	Fancy, #1 Table Grapes, and #1 Juice Grapes	Weights vary by shipping area. Normally shipped in flats weighing 17 to 20 pounds and lugs weighing 20 to 26 pounds.	Store near 32°F (0°C) with 90% relative humidity.
Honeydews	#1, Commercial, and #2	Bliss cartons (29 to 32 pounds) or 2/3 cartons (5 to 10 melons with total weight of 30 to 34 pounds)	Honeydews may have to be pre-ripened by letting stand in a warm room for several hours (or days).
Lemons	#1, #1 Export, Combo, and #2	Standard cartons described for grapefruit, weighing between 37 and 40 pounds. Standard counts range from 63 to 235 per carton (115, 145, 165, and 200 counts are most popular).	Store at 50°F (10°C).

Exhibit 1 *(continued)*

Product	U.S. Grades	Pack Sizes	Storage Characteristics
Limes	#1 and Combo	Cartons weighing 10, 20, and 40 pounds. Counts range from 72 to 126 for 20-pound cartons (96 and 108 counts are most popular).	Store at 50°F (10°C).
Nectarines	Fancy, Extra #1, #1, and #2	Generally packed in two-layer lugs of 20 pounds. Counts range from 50 to 84.	Refrigerate at 35°F (2°C).
Oranges	Fancy, #1, Combo, and #2	Standard fruit cartons with counts ranging from 48 to 162 (mandarin orange counts generally 176 or 210).	Refrigerate at 35°F (2°C).
Peaches	Fancy, Extra #1, #1, and #2	Boxes weighing 17 to 18 pounds with counts ranging from 40 to 65; Los Angeles Lug (two-layer) weighing 18 to 23 pounds with counts ranging from 50 to 80.	Peaches ripen rapidly at room temperature. Refrigerate at 32°F (0°C).
Pears	Extra #1, #1, Combo, and #2	Cartons weighing 44 to 45 pounds with counts ranging from 80 to 165; 100 count is a popular eating size.	Store at 40°F (1°C).
Pineapples	Fancy, #1, and #2	Cartons weighing 40 pounds with counts of 8-9-10-12-14-16; 1/2 cartons weighing 20 pounds with counts of 4-5-6-7.	Store at room temperature to ripen, then hold at 45°F (7°C).
Plums	#1	Usually packed in 28-pound lugs with counts ranging from 126 to 225.	Refrigerate at 34°F (1°C).
Strawberries	#1, Combo, and #2	Normally packed in 12-pint flats with baskets heaped.	Store at 32°F (0°C) with 90% relative humidity.
Watermelons	Fancy, #1, and #2	Usually sold individually with a minimum weight specification of 20 pounds recommended.	Store at 65°F (18°C).

is voluntary. In most cases, however, some state laws and federal marketing programs require grading and grade labeling of certain fruits.

Most packers grade their fruits, and some mark consumer packages with the grade. If a package carries a grade, the packer is legally obligated to make the contents measure up to official grade requirements. Some shippers, wholesalers, and distributors use USDA or state grading services.

Grade designations are most often seen on packages of pears and apples. Other fruits occasionally carry grade designations, which include the following:

- *U.S. Fancy.* **Fancy** means premium quality. Only a small percentage of fruit is packed in this grade.

- *U.S. No. 1.* No. 1 means good quality and is the most commonly used grade for most fruits.

Exhibit 2   Fresh Fruit Availability

LEGEND: PEAK | AVG | LIGHT | NONE

	JAN	FEB	MAR	APR	MAY	JUN	JULY	AUG	SEP	OCT	NOV	DEC
APPLES												
APRICOTS												
AVOCADOS												
BANANAS												
BLUEBERRIES												
CANTALOUPE												
CHERRIES												
CRANBERRIES												
GRAPEFRUIT												
GRAPES												
HONEYDEW												
KIWIFRUIT												
LEMONS												
LIMES												
MANGOES												
NECTARINES												
ORANGES												
PAPAYA												
PEACHES												
PEARS												
PINEAPPLES												
PLUMS												
RASPBERRIES												
STRAWBERRIES												
TANGERINES												
WATERMELON												

Source: Produce Marketing Association.

- *U.S. No. 2 and U.S. No. 3.* No. 2 is noticeably superior to No. 3, which is the lowest grade practical to pack under normal commercial conditions.

Fresh Fruit Varieties

Apples. The many varieties of apples differ widely in appearance, flesh characteristics, seasonal availability, and suitability for different uses.

For good eating as fresh fruit, the commonly available varieties are: Red Delicious, McIntosh, Granny Smith, Empire, and Golden Delicious. Use tart or slightly acidic varieties, such as Gravenstein, Grimes Golden, Jonathan, and Newtown, to make pies and applesauce.

For baking, the firmer fleshed varieties—Rome Beauty, Northern Spy, Rhode Island Greening, Winesap, and York Imperial—are widely used.

Look for: Firm, crisp, well-colored apples. Flavor varies in apples and depends on the stage of maturity at the time that the fruit is picked. Apples must be mature when picked to have a good flavor, texture, and storing ability. Immature apples lack color and are usually poor in flavor. They may have a shriveled appearance after being held in storage.

Most apples are marketed by grade and consumer packages show the variety, the grade, and the size. U.S. grades for apples are Extra Fancy, Fancy, No. 1, and combinations of these grades. **Utility** is a less desirable grade. Apples from the far western states are usually marketed with state grades, which are similar to U.S. grades.

Avoid: Overly ripe apples (indicated by a yielding to slight pressure on the skin and soft, mealy flesh) and apples affected by freeze (indicated by internal breakdown and bruised areas). Scald on apples (irregularly shaped tan or brown areas) may not seriously affect the taste.

Apricots. Most fresh apricots are marketed in June and July, but a limited supply of imported apricots is available in large cities during December and January. Domestic apricots are grown principally in California, Washington, and Utah.

Apricots develop their flavor and sweetness on the tree, and should be mature but firm when they are picked.

Look for: Apricots that are plump and juicy looking, with a uniform golden-orange color. Ripe apricots will yield to gentle pressure on the skin.

Avoid: Dull-looking, soft, or mushy fruit and very firm, pale yellow, or greenish-yellow fruit. These characteristics indicate overmaturity or immaturity, respectively.

Avocados. Avocados, grown in California and Florida, are available all year. Two general types and a number of varieties of each are grown. Avocados vary greatly in shape, size, and color, depending on type and variety. Most tend to be pear-shaped, but some are almost spherical. Fruits weighing less than $1/2$ pound are most commonly available. Some have rough or leathery textured skin, while others have smooth skin. The skin color of most varieties is some shade of green, but certain varieties turn maroon, brown, or purplish-black as they ripen.

Avocados are of good eating quality when they are properly ripened and have become slightly soft. This **ripening** process normally takes from three to five days at room temperature for firm avocados. Ripening can be slowed by refrigeration. When preparing avocados, immediately place the peeled fruit in lemon juice until ready for use to prevent browning of the flesh.

Look for: Slightly soft avocados that yield to gentle pressure on the skin for immediate use. For use in a few days, buy firm fruits that do not yield to the squeeze test. Leave them at room temperature to ripen. Irregular light-brown markings are sometimes found on the outside skin. These markings generally have no effect on the flesh of the avocado.

Avoid: Avocados with dark sunken spots in irregular patches or cracked or broken surfaces. These are signs of decay.

Bananas. Unlike most other fruits, bananas develop their best eating quality after they are harvested. This allows bananas to be shipped great distances. Almost our entire supply of bananas, available year-round, is imported from Central and South America. Bananas are sensitive to cool temperatures and will be injured at temperatures below 55° F (13° C). For this reason, they should never be kept in the refrigerator. The ideal temperature for ripening bananas is between 60° and 70° F (16–21° C). Higher temperatures cause them to ripen too rapidly.

Look for: Bananas that are firm, bright in appearance, and free from bruises or other injury. The state of ripeness is indicated by skin color. Best eating quality has been reached when the solid yellow color is specked with brown. At this stage, the flesh is mellow and the flavor is fully developed. Bananas with green tips or with practically no yellow color have not developed their full flavor potential.

Avoid: Bruised fruit (indicating rapid deterioration and waste), discolored skins (a sign of decay), or a dull, grayish, aged appearance (showing that the bananas have been exposed to cold and will not ripen properly). Occasionally, the skin may be entirely brown, but the flesh will still be in prime condition.

Blackberries, Raspberries, Boysenberries. Blackberries, raspberries, boysenberries, dewberries, loganberries, and youngberries are similar in general structure. They differ from one another in shape or color, but quality factors are very similar for all.

Look for: A bright, clean appearance and a uniform good color for the species. The individual small cells making up the berry should be plump and tender, but not mushy. Look for berries that are fully ripened with no attached stem caps.

Avoid: Leaky and moldy berries, which can usually be seen through the openings in the ventilated plastic containers. Also look for wet or stained spots on wood or fiber containers as possible signs of poor quality or spoiled berries.

Blueberries. Fresh blueberries are on the market from May through September. Generally, the large berries are cultivated varieties and the smaller berries are wild varieties.

Look for: A dark blue color with a silvery bloom. This silvery bloom is a natural, protective, waxy coating. Buy blueberries that are plump, firm, uniform in size, dry, and free of stems or leaves.

Avoid: Soft, mushy, or leaking berries.

Cantaloupe (Muskmelon). Cantaloupe, generally available from May through September, is produced principally in California, Arizona, and Texas. Some are also imported early in the season.

Look for: Three major signs of full maturity. First, the stem should be gone, leaving a smooth symmetrical, shallow base called a "full slip." If all or part of the stem base remains, or if the stem scar is jagged or torn, the melon is probably not fully mature. Second, the netting or veining should be thick, coarse, and corky, and should stand out in bold relief over some part of the surface. Third, the skin color (ground color) between the netting should have changed from green to yellowish-buff, yellowish-gray, or pale yellow.

A cantaloupe can be mature, but not ripe. A ripe cantaloupe will have a yellowish cast to the rind, have a pleasant cantaloupe aroma, and yield slightly to light thumb pressure on the blossom end of the melon.

Most cantaloupe are quite firm when freshly purchased. While some may be ripe, most have not yet reached their best eating stage. Hold them for two to four days at room temperature to allow completion of ripening. After conditioning the melons, some people like to place them in the refrigerator for a few hours before serving.

Avoid: Overly ripe fruit, as indicated by a pronounced yellow rind color, a softening over the entire rind, and soft, watery, and insipid flesh. Small bruises normally will not hurt the fruit, but large bruised areas should be avoided, since they generally cause soft, water-soaked areas underneath the rind. Mold growth on the cantaloupe (particularly in the stem scar, or if the tissue under the mold is soft and wet) is a sign of decay.

Cherries. Excellent as dessert fruit, most sweet cherries are produced in the western states and are available from May through August. Red tart cherries also called sour or pie cherries and used mainly in cooked desserts, have a softer flesh, lighter red color, and a tart flavor. They generally are shipped to processing plants and are sold frozen or canned.

Look for: A very dark color, which is the most important indication of good flavor and maturity in sweet cherries. Bing, Black Tartarian, Schmidt, Chapman, and Republican varieties should range from deep maroon or mahogany red to black for richest flavor. Lambert cherries should be dark red. Rainier cherries should be straw-colored. Good cherries have bright, glossy, plump-looking surfaces and fresh-looking stems.

Avoid: Overly mature cherries lacking in flavor, indicated by shriveling, dried stems, and a generally dull appearance. Decay is fairly common at times on sweet cherries, but because of their normal dark color, decayed areas are often inconspicuous. Soft, leaking flesh, brown discoloration, and mold growth are indications of decay.

Coconuts. Coconuts come to the United States year-round with peak availability in October, November, and December. Growing areas include Mexico and Central America.

Look for: Good quality coconuts that are heavy for their size. Shake the coconut to hear the milk inside.

Avoid: Coconuts without milk (an indication of spoilage). Also avoid coconuts with wet or moldy "eyes" (the soft spots on top of the shell).

Cranberries. A number of varieties of fresh cranberries are marketed in large volume from September through January. They differ considerably in size and color, but are not identified by variety names.

Look for: Plump, firm berries with a lustrous color. Duller varieties should at least have some red color.

Avoid: Brown or dark, discolored berries and soft, spongy, or leaky berries. These should be sorted out before cooking, because they may produce an off flavor.

Grapefruit. Grapefruit is available all year, with the most abundant supply from January through May. While Florida is the major source of fresh grapefruit, there also is substantial production in Texas, California, and Arizona. Several varieties are marketed, but the principal distinction is between those that are "seedless" (having few or no seeds) and the "seeded" type. Another distinction is color of flesh. Pink- or red-fleshed fruit is most common, but white-fleshed varieties are also available. Grapefruit is picked "tree ripe" and is ready to eat when purchased at the store.

Look for: Firm fruits that are heavy for their size. Thin-skinned fruits have more juice than coarse-skinned ones. If a grapefruit is pointed at the stem end, it is likely to be thick-skinned. Rough, ridged, or wrinkled skin can also be an indication of thick skin, pulpiness, and lack of juice. Grapefruit often have skin defects such as scale, scars, thorn scratches, or discoloration. This usually does not affect how the fruit tastes.

Avoid: Soft, water-soaked areas, dull color, and soft, tender peel that breaks easily with finger pressure. These characteristics are symptoms of decay.

Grapes. Most table grapes available are of the European type, grown principally in California and Arizona. Only small quantities of eastern-grown American-type grapes are sold for table use.

European-type grapes are firm fleshed and generally have high sugar content. Common varieties are Thompson seedless (an early green grape), red seedless (an early red grape), Tokay and Cardinal (early, bright red, seeded grapes), and Emperor (late, deep red, seeded grapes). These all have excellent flavor when well matured.

American-type grapes have softer flesh and are juicier than European types. Concord grapes, which are blue-black when fully mature, have outstanding flavor. Delaware and Catawba are also popular.

Look for: Well-colored, plump grapes that are firmly attached to the stem. White or green grapes are sweetest when the color has a yellowish cast or straw color, with a tinge of amber. Red varieties are better when red predominates on all or most of the berries. Bunches are more likely to hold together if the stems are predominantly green and pliable.

Avoid: Soft or wrinkled grapes, or bunches of grapes with stems that are brown and brittle. These are the effects of freezing or drying. Also avoid grapes with bleached areas around the stem ends (indicating injury and poor quality) and leaking berries (a sign of decay).

Honeydew Melons. The outstanding flavor characteristics of honeydews make them highly prized as a dessert fruit. The melon is large (four to eight pounds), bluntly oval in shape, and generally very smooth with only occasional traces of surface netting. The rind is firm and ranges from creamy white to creamy yellow, depending on the stage of ripeness. The stem does not separate from the fruit, and it must be cut for harvesting.

Honeydews are available to some extent almost all year round, due in part to imports during the winter and spring. Chief sources, however, are California, Arizona, and Texas. The most abundant supply is available from July through October.

Look for: A soft, velvety texture indicating maturity. Slight softening at the blossom end, a faint pleasant fruit aroma, and a yellowish-white to creamy rind color indicate ripeness.

Avoid: Dead-white or greenish-white color and a hard, smooth feel are signs of immaturity. Large, water-soaked, bruised areas are signs of injury. Cuts or punctures through the rind usually lead to decay. Small, superficial, sunken spots do not damage the melon for immediate use, but large decayed spots do.

Lemons. Most of the nation's commercial lemon supply comes from California and Arizona, and is available year-round.

Look for: Lemons with a rich yellow color, reasonably smooth-textured skin with a slight gloss, and those that are firm and heavy. A pale or greenish-yellow color indicates very fresh fruit with slightly higher acidity. Coarse or rough skin texture is a sign of thick skin and not much flesh.

Avoid: Lemons with a darker yellow or dull color, or with hardened or shriveled skin (signs of age), and those with soft spots, mold on the surface, and punctures of the skin (signs of decay).

Limes. Most limes sold are produced in Florida or imported from Mexico, and are marketed when mature. Imported limes are mostly of the smaller "seeded" variety.

Look for: Limes with glossy skin and heavy weight for the size.

Avoid: Limes with hardened or shriveled skin (signs of age), and those with soft spots, mold on the surface, and skin punctures (signs of decay).

Nectarines. This fruit, available from June through September from California, combines characteristics of the peach and the plum.

Look for: Rich color and plumpness, and a slight softening along the "seam" of the nectarine. Most varieties have an orange-yellow background color between the red areas, but some varieties have a greenish background color. Bright-looking fruits that are firm to moderately hard normally will ripen within two or three days at room temperature.

Avoid: Hard, dull fruits or slightly shriveled fruits (which may be immature and of poor eating quality) and soft or overly ripe fruits, or those with cracked or punctured skin or other signs of decay.

Russeting or staining of the skin may affect the appearance but not detract from the internal quality of the nectarine.

Oranges. California, Florida, Texas, and Arizona produce our year-round supply of oranges. Leading varieties from California and Arizona are the Washington navel and the Valencia, both characterized by a rich orange skin color. The navel orange, available from November until early May, has a thicker, somewhat more pebbled skin than the Valencia; the skin is more easily removed by hand, and the segments separate more readily. It is ideally suited for eating as a whole fruit or in segments in salads. The western Valencia orange, available from late April through October, is excellent for juicing or for slicing in salads. Florida and Texas orange crops are marketed from early October until late June. Parson Brown and Hamlin are early varieties, while the pineapple orange—an important, high-quality orange for eating—is available from late November through March. Florida and Texas Valencias are marketed from late March through June. The Florida Temple orange is available from early December until early March. Somewhat like the California navel, it peels easily, separates into segments readily, and has excellent flavor.

Oranges are required by strict state regulations to be mature before being harvested and shipped out of the producing state. Skin color is not a reliable index of quality, and a greenish cast or green spots do not mean that the orange is immature. Fully matured oranges often will turn greenish (called "regreening") late in the marketing season. Some oranges are artificially colored to improve their appearance. This practice has no effect on eating quality, but artificially colored fruits must be labeled **color added**. "Discoloration" is often found on Florida and Texas oranges, but not on California oranges. This is a tan, brown, or blackish mottling or specking over the skin. It has no effect on eating quality and, in fact, often occurs on oranges with thin skin and superior eating quality.

Look for: Firm and heavy oranges with fresh, bright-looking skin that is reasonably smooth for the variety.

Avoid: Lightweight oranges, which are likely to lack flesh content and juice. Very rough skin texture indicates abnormally thick skin and less flesh. Dull, dry skin and spongy texture indicate aging and deteriorated eating quality. Also avoid decay—shown by cuts or skin punctures, soft spots on the surface, and discolored weakened areas of skin around the stem end or button.

Peaches. A great many varieties of peaches are grown, but only an expert can distinguish one from another. These varieties, available May to November, fall into two general categories: freestone (in which the flesh readily separates from the pit) and clingstone (in which the flesh clings tightly to the pit). Freestones are usually preferred for eating fresh or for freezing, while clingstones are used primarily for canning, although they are sometimes sold fresh.

Look for: Peaches that are fairly firm or becoming a trifle soft. The skin color between the red areas (ground color) should be yellow or at least creamy.

Avoid: Very firm or hard peaches with a distinctly green ground color, which are probably immature and won't ripen properly. Also avoid very soft fruits, which are overly ripe. Do not buy peaches with large flattened bruises areas of discolored flesh underneath or peaches with any sign of decay. Decay starts as a pale tan spot that expands in a circle and gradually turns darker in color.

Pears. The most popular variety of pear is the Bartlett, which is produced in great quantities (in California, Washington, and Oregon) both for canning and for sale as a fresh fruit. With the aid of cold storage, Bartlett pears are available from early August through November. Several fall and winter varieties of pears are grown in Washington, Oregon, and California, and shipped to fresh fruit markets. These varieties—Anjou, Bosc, Winter Nellis, and Comice—keep well in cold storage and are available over a long period, from November until May.

Look for: Firm pears of all varieties. The color depends on variety. For Bartletts, look for a pale yellow to rich yellow color; Anjou or Comice—light green to yellowish-green; Bosc—greenish-yellow to brownish-yellow (the brown cast is caused by skin russeting, a characteristic of the Bosc pear); Winter Nellis—medium to light green.

Pears that are hard when you purchase them will probably ripen if kept at room temperature, but it is wise to select pears that have already begun to soften to be reasonably sure that they will ripen satisfactorily.

Avoid: Wilted or shriveled pears with dull-appearing skin and slight weakening of the flesh near the stem, which indicates immaturity. These pears will not ripen. Also avoid spots on the sides or blossom ends of the pear, which means that corky tissue may be underneath.

Pineapples. Pineapples are available all year, but are most abundant from March through June. Hawaii, Puerto Rico, and Mexico are principal suppliers. Present marketing practices, including air shipments, allow pineapples to be harvested as nearly ripe as possible. They are delivered to market near the peak of sweetness, with color ranging from green to orange and yellow. A mature green pineapple will normally turn yellow to orange within a few days at room temperature, but many are already fully colored when they are purchased.

Look for: Bright color, fragrant pineapple aroma, and a very slight separation of the eyes or pips—the berry-like fruitlets patterned in a spiral on the fruit core. At their mature stage, pineapples are usually dark green, firm, plump, and heavy for their size. The larger the fruit, the greater the proportion of edible flesh.

As the popular varieties ripen, the green color turns to orange and yellow. When fully colored, pineapples are golden yellow, orange-yellow, or reddish brown, depending on the variety.

Avoid: Pineapples with sunken or slightly pointed pips, dull yellowish-green color, and dried appearance, all of which are signs of immaturity. Also avoid bruised fruit, shown by discolored or soft spots, which are susceptible to decay. Other signs of decay are traces of mold, unpleasant odor, and eyes that are dark and watery.

Plums and Prunes. Quality characteristics for both are very similar, and the same buying tips apply to both.

A number of varieties of plums are produced in California and are available from June to September. Varieties differ slightly in appearance and flavor, so purchasers should buy and taste one to see if that variety is appealing.

Only a few varieties of prunes are commonly marketed, and they are all very similar. Prunes are purplish-black or bluish-black, with a moderately firm flesh that separates freely from the pit. Most commercial production is in the northwestern states. Fresh prunes are available from August through October.

Look for: Plums and prunes with a good color for the variety, in a fairly firm to slightly soft stage of ripeness.

Avoid: Fruits with skin breaks, punctures, or brownish discoloration. Also avoid immature fruits (relatively hard, poorly colored, very tart, sometimes shriveled) and overmature fruits (excessively soft, possibly leaking or decaying).

Strawberries. The first shipments of strawberries come from southern Florida in January, and then production increases, gradually spreading north and west into many parts of the country before tapering off in the fall. Strawberries are in best supply in May and June.

Look for: Berries with a full red color, a bright luster, firm flesh, and the cap stem still attached. The berries should be dry and clean, and usually medium to small strawberries have better eating quality than large ones.

Avoid: Berries with large uncolored areas or with large seedy areas (poor in flavor and texture), a full shrunken appearance or softness (signs of overripeness or decay), or those with mold, which can spread rapidly from one berry to another.

Note that in most containers of strawberries, a few will likely be less desirable than others. Try to look at some berries lower in the container to be sure that they are reasonably free from defects or decay.

Watermelons. Although watermelons are available to some degree from early May through September, peak supplies come in June, July, and August. Judging the quality of a watermelon is very difficult unless it is cut in half or quartered.

Look for: Firm, juicy flesh with good red color that is free from white streaks; and seeds that are dark brown or black. Seedless watermelons often contain small white, immature seeds, which are normal for this type.

Avoid: Melons with pale-colored flesh, white streaks (or "white heart"), and whitish seeds (indicating immaturity). Dry, mealy flesh or watery, stringy flesh are signs of overmaturity or aging after harvest.

A few appearance factors may be helpful (though not totally reliable) in guiding satisfactory selection of an uncut watermelon. The watermelon surface should be relatively smooth, the rind should have a slight dullness (neither shiny nor dull), the ends of the melon should be filled out and rounded, and the underside or "belly" of the melon should have a creamy color.

Fresh Vegetables

Concerns about nutrition and healthy eating habits have increased the demand for fresh vegetables in food service operations. Purchase specifications for fresh vegetable items are particularly important because of the non-standard nature of the product. Fresh vegetable items can vary widely in size, appearance and quality depending upon the season, growing region, and type of product. The following section provides details for which purchasing specifications can be developed for some of the most popular types of fresh vegetables. Exhibit 3 provides U.S. grades, pack sizes, and storage requirements for these fresh vegetables. Exhibit 4 contains an availability chart for fresh vegetables.

Quality Grades for Fresh Vegetables

The USDA has established grade standards for most fresh vegetables. The standards are used extensively as a basis for trading between growers, shippers, wholesalers, and retailers. Use of U.S. grade standards is voluntary in most cases. However, some state laws and federal marketing programs require official grading and grade labeling of certain vegetables.

Most packers grade their vegetables, and some mark the consumer packages with the grade. If a package carries a grade, the packer is legally obligated to make the contents measure up to the official grade. Some packers, wholesalers, and distributors use official USDA or federal/state grading services. Grade designations are most often seen on packages of potatoes and onions. Other vegetables occasionally carry the grade name. Grade designations include:

- *U.S. No. 1.* No. 1 is the grade that you will most often see. Vegetables of this grade should be tender and fresh-appearing, have good color, and be relatively free from bruises and decay.

Exhibit 3   Fresh Vegetables—U.S. Grades, Pack Sizes, and Storage Characteristics

Product	U.S. Grades	Pack Sizes	Storage Characteristics
Artichokes	#1 and #2	Cartons weighing 20 to 25 pounds with counts ranging from 18 to 60.	Store at 38°F (3°C).
Asparagus	#1 and #2	Bunched (approximately 12 bunches of 2 pounds each per crate) or loose (30 pounds per case).	Packed upright in crates with a moist base to preserve quality.
Beans	Fancy, #1, combo, and #2	Cartons or baskets weighing from 26 to 31 pounds.	May be held for short period between 45°F (7°C) and 50°F (10°C).
Broccoli	Fancy, #1, and #2	Half cartons containing 14 to 18 bunches (each weigh 1 1/2 pounds).	Store at 34°F (1°C).
Brussels Sprouts	#1 and #2	Pint containers (12 per tray, or about 9 pounds); 25-pound cartons.	Store at 34°F (1°C).
Cabbage	#1 and Commercial	Cartons or bags weighing 50 to 60 pounds; Savoy cabbage normally packed in 40-pound cartons.	Store at 34°F (1°C).
Carrots	A, B, #1, and Commercial	Varies, most commonly packed as 48 one-pound units and bulk bags weighing 25 to 50 pounds.	Store at 34°F (1°C).
Celery	Extra, #1, and #2	Cartons or wire bound crates of 60 pounds, with counts of 18, 24, 30, 36, or 48 bunches.	Store at 32°F (0°C).
Corn	Fancy, #1, and #2	Wire bound crates of 50 pounds; counts range from 54 to 66.	May be stored at 32°F (0°C) for a short time period.
Cucumbers	Fancy, Extra #1, #1, #1 Small, #1 Large, and #2	Packed in lugs, West Coast lugs, and cartons.	Store at 45°F (7°C).
Iceberg Lettuce	Fancy, #1 Commercial, and #2	West—varies in weight per case from 35 to 55 pounds; normally 18, 24, or 30 heads per standard western carton.	All varieties of lettuce may be stored at 34°F (1°C).
Leaf Lettuce	Fancy	Varies, but mostly in 24-quart hampers weighing about 10 pounds.	
Boston Lettuce	#1	Varies, best to purchase by the pound.	
Onion	#1, Combo, #2, and Commercial	Usually packed in 50-pound mesh fiber bags.	Should be stored under dry conditions.
Romaine	#1	Western lettuce cartons holding 24 heads and weighing approximately 40 pounds.	Store at 34°F (1°C).
Sweet Peppers	Fancy, #1, and #2	Bushels with various counts; 80 count is a good size for stuffing.	Store between 46°F (7°C) and 48°F (9°C), with relative humidity of 85%.

(continued)

Exhibit 3 *(continued)*

Product	U.S. Grades	Pack Sizes	Storage Characteristics
Potatoes	Extra #1, #1, and #2	Cartons with counts ranging from 60 to 120 per carton.	Store in cool, dry, dark area. Raw potatoes should *not* be refrigerated.
Sweet Potatoes	Extra #1, #1, Commercial, and #2	Normally packed in bushel baskets of approximately 50 pounds.	Store at 50°F (10°C) with low humidity and use promptly.
Tomatoes	#1, Combo, #2, and #3 (field grading standards; grade identification is lost in repacking)	Sold by the box, which may contain 10, 20, 25, or 30 pounds; weight may vary by 10%.	Bring to full color at 55°F (13°C). Store between 40°F (4°C) and 50°F (10°C) until used.

- *U.S. Fancy.* U.S. Fancy vegetables are of more uniform shape and have fewer defects than U.S. No. 1.

- *U.S. No. 2 and No. 3.* U.S. No. 2 and No. 3 have lower quality requirements than Fancy or No. 1, but they are still nutritious. The differences are mainly in appearance, waste, and consumer preference.

Fresh Vegetable Varieties

Artichokes. The globe artichoke is the large, unopened flower bud of a plant belonging to the thistle family. The many leaf-like parts that make up the bud are called "scales." Produced domestically only in California, the peak of the crop comes in April and May.

Look for: Plump, globular artichokes that are heavy in relation to size and compact with thick, green, fresh-looking scales. Size is not important with respect to quality.

Avoid: Artichokes with large areas of brown on the scales and with spreading scales (a sign of age, indicating drying and toughening of the edible portions), grayish-black discoloration (caused by bruises), mold growth on the scales, and worm injury.

Asparagus. California, New Jersey, Washington, and Michigan are the chief sources of domestically grown asparagus.

Look for: Closed, compact tips; smooth, round spears; and a fresh appearance. A rich green color should cover most of the spear. Stalks should be almost as far down as the green extends.

Avoid: Tips that are open and spread out, moldy or decayed tips, or ribbed spears (spears with up-and-down ridges or that are not approximately round). They are all signs of aging, and indicate tough asparagus and poor flavor. Also avoid excessively sandy asparagus, because sand grains can lodge beneath the scales or in the tips of the spears and are difficult to remove in washing.

Beans (Snap). Snap beans, produced commercially in many states, are available throughout the year. Most beans available for food service will be the common

Exhibit 4 Fresh Vegetable Availability

LEGEND: PEAK AVG LIGHT NONE

	JAN	FEB	MAR	APR	MAY	JUN	JULY	AUG	SEP	OCT	NOV	DEC
ARTICHOKES												
ASPARAGUS												
BEANS												
BROCCOLI												
CABBAGE												
CARROTS												
CAULIFLOWER												
CELERY												
CHINESE CABBAGE												
CORN												
CUCUMBERS												
EGGPLANT												
ENDIVE												
ESCAROLE												
GARLIC												
GREENS												
LETTUCE, ICE												
LETTUCE, ROMAINE												
MUSHROOMS												
ONIONS, GREEN												
ONIONS, DRY												
PEAS												
PEPPERS, BELL												
PEPPERS, CHILI												
POTATOES, TABLE												
RADISHES												
SPINACH												
SQUASH												
SWEET POTATOES												
TOMATOES												
TOMATOES, CHERRY												
TURNIPS, RUTABAGAS												

Source: Produce Marketing Association.

green podded varieties, but large green pole beans and yellow wax beans are occasionally available.

Look for: A fresh, bright appearance with good color for the variety. Get young, tender beans with pods in a firm, crisp condition.

Avoid: Wilted or flabby bean pods, serious blemishes, and decay. Thick, tough, fibrous pods indicate overmaturity.

Broccoli. A member of the cabbage family and a close relative of cauliflower, broccoli is available throughout the year.

California is the heaviest producer, although other states also produce large amounts of broccoli.

Look for: A firm, compact cluster of small flower buds, with none opened enough to show the bright-yellow flower. Bud clusters should be dark green, sage green, or even green with a decidedly purplish cast. Stems should not be too thick or too tough.

Avoid: Broccoli with spread bud clusters, enlarged or open buds, yellowish-green color, or a wilted condition, which are all signs of overmaturity. Also avoid broccoli with soft, slippery, water-soaked spots on the bud cluster. These are signs of decay.

Brussels Sprouts. Another close relative of cabbage, Brussels sprouts develop as enlarged buds on a tall stem, with one sprout appearing where each main leaf is attached. The "sprouts" are cut off and, in most cases, are packed in small containers, although some are packed loose in bulk. Although they are often available about 10 months of the year, peak supplies appear from October through December.

Look for: A fresh, bright-green color, tight fitting outer leaves, firm body, and freedom from blemishes.

Avoid: Brussels sprouts that are pale green or yellow in color, have loose leaves, or have soft spots.

Cabbage. Three major varieties of cabbage are available: smooth-leaved green cabbage, crinkly-leaved green Savoy cabbage, and red cabbage. All types are suitable for any use, although the Savoy and red varieties are more in demand for use in slaw and salads.

Cabbage may be sold fresh (called "new" cabbage) or from storage. Cabbage is available throughout the year, since it is grown in many states. California, Florida, and Texas market most new cabbage. Many northern states grow cabbage for late summer and fall shipment or to be held in storage for winter sale.

Look for: Firm or hard heads of cabbage that are heavy for their size. Outer leaves should be a good green or red color (depending on type), reasonably fresh, and free from serious blemishes. The outer leaves (called "wrapper" leaves) fit loosely on the head and are usually discarded, but too many loose wrapper leaves on a head cause extra waste. Some early-crop cabbage may be soft or only fairly firm, but is suitable for immediate use if the leaves are fresh and crisp. Cabbage out of storage is usually trimmed of all outer leaves and lacks green color, but is satisfactory if not wilted or discolored.

Avoid: New cabbage with wilted or decayed outer leaves or with leaves that have turned decidedly yellow. Worm-eaten outer leaves often indicate that the worm injury penetrates into the head.

Storage cabbage with badly discolored, dried, or decayed outer leaves probably is over-aged. Separation of the leaves' stems from the central stem at the base of the head also indicates over-age.

Carrots. Freshly harvested carrots are available year-round. Most are marketed when relatively young, tender, well colored, and mild flavored—an ideal stage for use as raw carrot sticks. Larger carrots are packed separately and used primarily for cooking or shredding. California and Texas market most domestic carrots, but many other states produce large quantities.

Look for: Carrots that are well formed, smooth, well colored, and firm. If tops are attached, they should be fresh and of a good green color.

Avoid: Roots with large green "sunburned" areas at the top (which must be trimmed) and roots that are flabby from wilting or show spots of soft rot.

Cauliflower. Although most abundant from September through January, cauliflower is available during every month of the year. California, New York, and Florida are major sources. The white edible portion is called the curd and the heavy outer leaf covering makes up the jacket leaves. Cauliflower is generally sold with most of the jacket leaves removed, and is wrapped in plastic film.

Look for: White to creamy-white, compact, solid, and clean curds. A slightly granular or "ricey" curd texture will not hurt the eating quality if the surface is compact. Ignore small green leaflets extending through the curd. If jacket leaves are attached, a good green color is a sign of freshness.

Avoid: A spreading of the curd, which is a sign of aging or overmaturity. Also avoid severe wilting or discolored spots on the curd. Smudgy or speckled curds are signs of insect injury, mold growth, or decay, and should be avoided.

Celery. Celery, a popular vegetable for a variety of uses, is available throughout the year. Production is concentrated in California, Florida, Michigan, and New York. Most celery is the "Pascal" type, which includes thick-branched, green varieties.

Look for: Freshness and crispness. The stalk should have a solid, rigid feel and leaflets should be fresh or only slightly wilted. Also look for a glossy surface, stalks of light green or medium green, and mostly green leaflets.

Avoid: Wilted celery and celery with flabby upper branches or leaf stems. Celery can be freshened somewhat by placing the bottom end in water, but badly wilted celery will never become really fresh again.

Celery with pithy, hollow, or discolored centers in the branches also should be avoided. Celery with internal discoloration will show some gray or brown on the inside surface of the larger branches near where they are attached to the base of the stalk.

Also avoid celery with blackheart, a brown or black discoloration of the small center branches; insect injury in the center branches or the insides of outer branches; and long, thick seed stems in place of the usually small, tender heart branches.

Chicory, Endive, Escarole. These vegetables, used mainly in salads, are available practically year-round, but primarily in the winter and spring. Chicory or endive has narrow, notched edges, and crinkly leaves resembling the dandelion leaf. Chicory plants often have "blanched" yellowish leaves in the center, which are preferred by many people. Escarole leaves are much broader and less crinkly than those of chicory. Witloof or Belgian endive is a compact, cigar-shaped plant that is creamy white from blanching. The small shoots are kept from becoming green by being grown in complete darkness.

Look for: Freshness, crispness, tenderness, and a good green color of the outer leaves.

Avoid: Plants with leaves that have brownish or yellowish discoloration or that have insect injury.

Corn. Sweet corn is available practically every month of the year, but is most plentiful from early May until mid-September. Yellow-kernel corn is the most popular, but some white-kernel and mixed-color corn is sold. Sweet corn is produced in a large number of states during the spring and summer, and most mid-winter supplies come from south Florida. For best quality, corn should be refrigerated immediately after being picked. Corn will retain fairly good quality for a number of days if it is kept cold and moist after harvesting.

Look for: Fresh, succulent husks with good green color, silk ends that are free from decay or worm injury, and stem ends (opposite from the silk) that are not too discolored or dried.

Select ears that are well-covered with plump, not-too-mature kernels.

Avoid: Ears with under-developed kernels that lack yellow color (in yellow corn), old ears with very large kernels, and ears with dark yellow or dried kernels with depressed areas on the outer surface. Also avoid ears of corn with yellowed, wilted, or dried husks, or discolored and dried-out stem ends.

Cucumbers. Although cucumbers are produced at various times of the year in many states and imported during the colder months, the supply is most plentiful in the summer months.

Look for: Cucumbers with good green color that are firm over their entire length. They should be well developed, but not too large in diameter.

Avoid: Overgrown cucumbers that are large in diameter, have a dull color, and have turned yellowish. Also avoid cucumbers with withered or shriveled ends, which are signs of toughness and bitter flavor.

Lettuce. Lettuce owes its prominence in our diets to the growing popularity of salad. It is available throughout the year from California, Arizona, Florida, New York, New Jersey, and other states. Four types of lettuce are generally sold: iceberg, butter-head, Romaine, and leaf.

Iceberg lettuce is the major type. Heads are large, round, and solid, with medium green outer leaves and lighter green or pale green inner leaves.

Butter-head lettuce, including the Big Boston and Bibb varieties, has a smaller head than iceberg. This type will have soft, succulent light green leaves in a rosette pattern in the center.

Romaine lettuce plants are tall and cylindrical with crisp, dark-green leaves in a loosely folded head.

Leaf lettuce includes many varieties—none with a compact head. Leaves are broad, tender, succulent, and fairly smooth, and they vary in color according to variety.

Look for: Signs of freshness. For iceberg and Romaine lettuce, the leaves should be crisp. Other lettuce types will have a softer texture, but leaves should not be wilted. Look for a good, bright color—in most varieties, medium to light green. Some varieties have red leaves.

Avoid: Heads of iceberg type that are very hard and that lack green color (signs of overmaturity). Such heads sometimes develop discoloration on the inner leaves and midribs, and may have a less desirable flavor. Also avoid heads with irregular shapes and hard bumps on top, which indicate the presence of overgrown central stems.

Check the lettuce for tip burn, a tan or brown area around the margins of the leaves. Look for tip burn on the edges of the head leaves. Slight discoloration of the outer or wrapper leaves will usually not hurt the quality of the lettuce, but serious discoloration or decay definitely should be avoided.

Mushrooms. Grown in houses, cellars, or caves, mushrooms are available year-round in varying amounts. Most come from Pennsylvania, but many are produced in California, New York, Ohio, and other states.

The mushroom's structure includes a cap (the wide portion on top), gills (the numerous rows of paper-thin tissue seen underneath the cap when it opens), and a stem.

Look for: Young mushrooms that are small to medium in size. Caps should be either closed around the stem or moderately open with pink or light-tan gills. The surface of the cap should be white or creamy, or uniform light brown if of a brown type.

Avoid: Overripe mushrooms (shown by wide-open caps and dark, discolored gills underneath) and those with pitted or seriously discolored caps.

Onions. The many varieties of onions grown commercially fall into three general classes, distinguished by color: yellow, white, and red.

Onions are available year-round, either fresh or from storage.

Major onion-growing states are California, New York, Texas, Michigan, Colorado, Oregon, and Idaho.

Look for: Hard or firm onions that are dry and have small necks. They should be reasonably free from green sunburn spots or other blemishes.

Avoid: Onions with wet or very soft necks, which usually are immature or affected by decay. Also avoid onions with thick, hollow, woody centers in the neck or with fresh sprouts.

Onions (Green) and Leeks. Green onions and leeks (sometimes called scallions) are similar in appearance, but are somewhat different in nature. Green onions are ordinary onions harvested very young. They have very little or no bulb formation and their tops are tubular. Leeks have slight bulb formation and broad, flat, dark-green tops.

Sold in small tied bunches, they are all available to some extent throughout the entire year, but are most plentiful in spring and summer.

Look for: Bunches with fresh, crisp, green tops. They should have portions extending two or three inches up from the root end.

Avoid: Yellowing, wilted, discolored, or decayed tops (indicating flabby, tough, or fibrous condition of the edible portions). Bruised tops will not affect the eating quality of the bulbs if the tops are removed.

Peppers. Sweet green peppers are the most common variety and are available in varying amounts throughout the year, but most plentiful during late summer. (Fully matured peppers of the same type have a bright red color.) A variety of colored peppers is also available, including white, yellow, orange, red, and purple.

Look for: Peppers with deep, characteristic color, glossy sheen, relatively heavy weight, and firm walls or sides.

Avoid: Peppers with very thin walls (indicated by lightweight and flimsy sides), peppers that are wilted or flabby with cuts or punctures through the walls, and pepper with soft watery spots on the sides (evidence of decay).

Potatoes. For practical purposes, potatoes can be put into three groups, although the distinctions between them are not clear cut and there is much overlapping.

"New potatoes" is a term most frequently used to describe those potatoes freshly harvested and marketed during the late winter or early spring. The name is also widely used in later crop producing areas to designate freshly dug potatoes that are not fully matured. New potatoes are best used for boiling or in casseroles. They vary widely in size and shape, depending upon variety, but are likely to be affected by "skinning" or "feathering" of the outer layer of skin. Skinning usually affects only their appearance.

"General-purpose potatoes" include the great majority of supplies, both round and long types, offered for purchase. With the aid of air-cooled storage, they are amply available throughout the year. As the term implies, they are used for boiling, frying, and baking, although many of the common varieties are not considered to be best for baking.

Potatoes grown specifically for baking also are available. Variety and growing area are important factors affecting baking quality. A long variety with fine, scaly netting on the skin, such as the Russet Burbank, is commonly used for baking.

Look for: New potatoes that are firm and free from blemishes and sunburn (a green discoloration under the skin). Some amount of skinned surface is normal, but potatoes with large skinned and discolored areas are undesirable. For general-purpose and baking potatoes, look for reasonably smooth, firm potatoes free from blemishes, sunburn, and decay.

Avoid: Potatoes with large cuts, bruises, or decay, which will cause waste in peeling, and sprouted or shriveled potatoes. Also avoid green potatoes. The green portions, which contain the alkaloid **solanin**, may penetrate the flesh and cause bitter flavor.

Sweet Potatoes. Two types of sweet potatoes are available in varying amounts year-round. Moist sweet potatoes (sometimes called yams) are the most common type. They have orange-colored flesh and are very sweet. (The true yam is the root of a tropical vine that is not grown commercially in the United States.)

Dry sweet potatoes have pale-colored flesh and are low in moisture.

Most sweet potatoes are grown in the southern tier and some eastern states. California also is a major producer.

Look for: Firm sweet potatoes with smooth, bright, uniformly colored skins, free from signs of decay. Because they are more perishable than white potatoes, extra care should be used in selecting sweet potatoes.

Avoid: Sweet potatoes with worm holes, cuts, grub injury, or any other defects that penetrate the skin. These defects cause waste and can readily lead to decay. Even if the decayed portion is removed, the remainder of the potato flesh may have a bad taste.

Decay is the worst problem with sweet potatoes and is of three types: wet, soft decay; dry, firm decay that begins at the end of the potato, making it discolored and shriveled; and dry rot in the form of sunken, discolored areas on the sides of the potato.

Sweet potatoes should not be stored in the refrigerator.

Tomatoes. Extremely popular and nutritious, tomatoes are in moderate to liberal supply throughout the year. Florida, California, and a number of other states are major producers, but imports supplement domestic supplies.

The best flavor usually comes from locally grown tomatoes produced on nearby farms. This type of tomato is allowed to ripen completely before being picked. Many areas, however, now ship tomatoes that are picked right after the color has begun to change from green to pink.

If tomatoes need further ripening, store them at room temperature but not in direct sunlight. Unless they are fully ripened, do not store tomatoes in a refrigerator—the cold temperature might keep them from ripening later on and ruin the flavor.

Look for: Tomatoes that are smooth, well ripened, and reasonably free from blemishes.

For fully ripe fruit, look for an overall rich, red color and a slight softness. Softness is easily detected by gentle handling.

For tomatoes slightly less than fully ripe, look for firm texture and color ranging from pink to light red.

Avoid: Soft, overripe, or bruised tomatoes, and tomatoes with sunburn (green or yellow areas near the stem scar), and growth cracks (deep brown cracks around the stem scar). Also avoid decayed tomatoes which will have soft, water-soaked spots, depressed areas, or surface mold.

Fresh Produce Distribution Systems

Produce distributors vary in size and quality. There are two types of produce distributors—primary and secondary. The primary distributor in most markets purchases most of its produce from the source. The secondary distributors purchase most of their product from the primary distributors for resale.

Distribution

Deciding which type of produce distributor to use depends mostly on the size of the market. Large urban markets will likely have access to primary produce distributors. Smaller markets and areas distant from large cities will have to depend upon secondary produce distributors. The advantage of dealing with primary distributors is one of better prices and more selection. However, secondary distributors may be able to provide services, such as more frequent or smaller deliveries, that the primary distributor cannot.

Choosing a distributor will depend upon several factors, including purchasing volume, the type of produce needed, and the type of processing required. Developing a relationship with a distributor is critical when buying produce. Because produce is a seasonal commodity, the price and availability of different types of produce is always changing. Your produce distributor should keep you informed of changes in the market. Produce distributors, especially secondary distributors, can also be a good secondary source for other products. Many produce distribu-tors also handle dry goods, canned goods, processed produce, and cheese and dairy items.

Packaging

One concern with produce is inconsistency in packaging. Counts and weights may vary from one distributor to another. Many times produce will be repackaged by the secondary distributor. Produce items such as carrots, celery and broccoli can be cut to a specific size and packaged according to a buyer's specific needs. Buy-ers should understand how the items they are purchasing will be packaged and delivered to them before ordering and receiving the items. Items that are pack-aged by weight should be checked upon receipt to ensure that they are the correct weight. Items packaged by count should be counted for accuracy. Items that may vary according to the amount of fill in the case, flat, or box should be checked and compared to buyers' expectations according to the deal they have with their distributors.

Costs, Pricing, and Yield of Fresh Produce

Produce distributors purchase produce items in large quantities according to auction prices. The prices a buyer pays from the distributor, whether it be pri-mary or secondary, will be based on cost-plus markup pricing. The auction prices are usually available from various sources (*Nation's Restaurant News*, Cornell Cooperative Extension, *Food Institute Report*). These auction prices can be used for comparison purposes when receiving bids. It is wise for buyers to request weekly bids on their most popular and most used produce items. Be careful, however, to consider not only price, but also quality and service when determin-ing the best bid price.

Yields will vary for many types of produce based on the growing season for that product. For example, the yield for leafy produce will be less in the early part of the season than later in the season when the plants mature. Quality changes throughout the season will also affect an item's yield. Another important factor that affects produce yield and prices is the weather. Drastic weather changes in an important growing region can cause spikes in pricing and problems with product quality. Because produce must be shipped from growing regions to major markets, any disruption in the transportation system can affect quality and price.

Processed Fruits and Vegetables

Most fresh produce items can be processed into a form that makes them available for use later. Produce items can be canned, frozen, dried, or vacuum packaged to preserve them for later use. The type of processed produce item purchased will be determined by how the item will be used and the quality required. For the most part, canned fruits and vegetables are poorer quality than frozen fruits and veg-etables because the canning process requires the item be cooked. However, a canned product is the perfect solution for some uses. Vacuum packing has become popular because it can extend the life of an item while preserving the quality. Frozen products have long been popular because the quality is usually retained and the product is easy to utilize in recipes. Exhibit 5 provides a list of popular processed produce items along with their grades, growing seasons, and growing areas.

Grading, Specifications, and Quality

The Fruit and Vegetable Division of the USDA's Agricultural Marketing Service (AMS), along with the FDA, conducts regular mandatory inspections of processing facilities. The plant inspection ensures the wholesomeness of the processed product. However, U.S. grading of processed fruits and vegetables is a voluntary service that must be paid for by the processor. The U.S. grade shield indicates that the product has been "packed under the continuous inspection of the U.S. Department of Agriculture" (Exhibit 6). Grading standards have been established for canned, frozen, and dried products, as follows.

*   *Grade A (Fancy)*—the very best product with excellent color, uniform size, uniform weight, conforming shape, and few blemishes.

*   *Grade B (Extra Standard or Choice)*—slightly less perfect than Grade A

*   *Grade C (Standard)*—may contain some broken or non-conforming pieces. The flavor may fall below Grade A or Grade B standards. The color is not as attractive.

Processed fruit and vegetable specifications should include the product's:

*   Exact nature.

*   Intended use.

*   U.S. grade.

*   Brand name, if applicable.

*   Size (weight or volume).

*   Container size.

*   Packaging (can, jar, plastic bag).

*   Packaging procedure (vacuum packed, for example).

*   Product yield (drained weight).

*   Product form (whole, pieces, dried).

*   Packing medium (in juice, for example).

*   Color.

*   Special requirements (such as percentage of ingredients).

*   Handling procedures (refrigerated or frozen).

Exhibit 7 provides several sample specifications for processed produce products.

Exhibit 5   Processed Fruits and Vegetables—U.S. Grades, Packing Seasons, and Producing Areas

Product	U.S. Grades	Primary Packing Season	Primary Producing Area
Apples—Canned	A or Fancy (85) C or Standard (70)	October to December	Michigan, Washington, Virginia
Apples—Frozen	A or Fancy (85) C or Standard (75)	October to December	Michigan, Washington, Virginia
Apple Juice—Canned	A (90) B (80)	October to December	Michigan, Washington, Virginia
Applesauce—Canned	A or Fancy (90) B or Choice (80)	October to December	Michigan, Washington, Virginia
Apricots—Canned	A or Fancy (90) B or Choice (80) C or Standard (70)	June and July	California
Asparagus—Canned	A or Fancy (85) C or Standard (70)	April to July	California, New Jersey, Michigan
Asparagus—Frozen	A or Fancy B or X-Standard	April to July	California, New Jersey, Michigan
Beans, Green & Waxed—Canned	A or Fancy (90) B or X-Standard (80)	June to October	Northwest, Wisconsin
Beans, Green & Waxed—Frozen	A or Fancy (90) B or X-Standard (80) C or Standard (70)	June to October	Northwest, California
Beans, Lima—Canned	A or Fancy (90) B or X-Standard (80) C or Standard (70)	August to October	California, East Coast
Beans, Lima—Frozen	A or Fancy (90) B or X-Standard (80) C or Standard (70)	August to October	California, East Coast
Beets—Canned	A or Fancy (85) C or Standard (70)	August to December	California, Northwest, Michigan, New York
Berries—Frozen	A or Fancy (85) B or Choice (70)	June to August	Northwest, California
Broccoli—Frozen	A, B	June to August	California
Brussels Sprouts—Frozen	A, B, C	June to August	California
Carrots—Canned	A or Fancy (85) C or Standard (70)	August to May	California, Texas
Carrots—Frozen	A or Fancy (90) B or X-Standard (80)	July to October	California, Northwest, Texas
Cauliflower—Frozen	A or Fancy (85) B or X-Standard (70)	June to September	California
Cherries, Red—Frozen	A or Fancy (90) B or Choice (80) C or Standard (70)	June to July	New York, Pennsylvania, Michigan
Corn on Cob—Frozen	A or Fancy (90) B or X-Standard (80)	June to August	Northwest
Corn, Whole Kernel—Canned	A or Fancy (90) B or X-Standard (80) C or Standard (70)	August to October	Northwest, Wisconsin, Minnesota
Corn, Whole Kernel—Frozen	A or Fancy (90) B or X-Standard (80) C or Standard (70)	June to August	Northwest, Wisconsin, Minnesota
Cranberry Sauce—Canned	A or Fancy (85) C or Standard (70)	October to January	Massachusetts, New Jersey
Fruit Cocktail	A or Fancy (85) B or Choice (70)	June to September	California
Fruit Jelly	A (90) or B (80)	Year-round	California, Virginia, Michigan, Ohio
Fruit Preserves—Jam	A (85) or B (70)	Year-round	California, Virginia, Michigan, Ohio

Exhibit 5 *(continued)*

Product	U.S. Grades	Primary Packing Season	Primary Producing Area
Mushrooms—Canned	A or Fancy (90) B or X-Standard (80)	Year-round	Pennsylvania, North Carolina
Olives, Green—Canned	A or Fancy (90) B or X-Standard (80) C or Standard (70)	Year-round	California, Spain
Olives, Ripe—Canned	A or Fancy (90) B or X-Standard (80) C or Standard (70)	October to February	California
Onion Rings—Breaded Frozen	A or Fancy (85) B or X-Standard (70)	April to December	Various states
Onions—Canned	A or Fancy (85) C or Standard (70)	April to December	Various states
Peaches—Frozen	A (90) B (80) C (70)	July to September	California, Virginia, Pennsylvania, Georgia
Peaches, Clingstone—Canned	A, B, C	July to September	California
Peaches, Freestone—Canned	A, B, C	July to September	California
Pears—Canned	A or Fancy (90) B or Choice (80) C or Standard (70)	July to November	Northwest California
Peas—Canned	A or Fancy (90) B or X-Standard (80) C or Standard (70)	July to August	Wisconsin, Minnesota
Peas—Frozen	A or Fancy (90) B or X-Standard (80) C or Standard (70)	June to July	Northwest, Wisconsin, Minnesota
Peas & Carrots—Canned	A or Fancy (90) B or X-Standard (80) C or Standard (70)	June to August	Northwest, Wisconsin, Minnesota
Peas & Carrots—Frozen	A or Fancy (90) B or X-Standard (80) C or Standard (70)	June to July	Northwest, California
Pickles—Canned	A or Fancy (90) B or X-Standard (80)	Year-round	Michigan
Pineapple—Canned	A or Fancy (90) B or Choice (80) C or Standard (70)	January to September	Puerto Rico, Hawaii, Philippines
Pineapple—Frozen	A or Fancy (90) B or Choice (80) C or Standard (70)	January to September	Puerto Rico, Hawaii, Philippines
Pineapple Juice—Canned	A or Fancy (85) C or Standard (70)	January to September	Puerto Rico, Hawaii, Philippines
Plums—Canned	A or Fancy (90) B or Choice (80) C or Standard (70)	July to September	California, Northwest
Potatoes, French Fry—Frozen	A or Fancy (90) B or X-Standard (80)	September to May	Idaho, Washington, North Central, Maine
Potatoes, White—Canned	A (90) B (80)	September to March	Various states
Potatoes, Hash Brown—Frozen	A (90) B (80)	September to May	Northwest, North Central, Northeast
Sauerkraut—Canned	A or Fancy (90) B or X-Standard (80) C or Standard (70)	Year-round	New York, Pennsylvania
Spinach—Canned	A or Fancy B or X-Standard	June to October	California, Texas

(continued)

Exhibit 5 *(continued)*

Product	U.S. Grades	Primary Packing Season	Primary Producing Area
Spinach—Frozen	A or Fancy (90) B or X-Standard (80)	June to October	California
Strawberries—Frozen	A or Fancy (90) B or Choice (80) C or Standard (70)	May to July	California, Northwest, Mexico
Sweet Potatoes—Canned	A or Fancy (90) B or X-Standard (80)	July to March	Southeast
Tomatoes—Canned	A or Fancy (90) B or X-Standard (80) C or Standard (70)	July to November	California
Tomato Catsup—Canned	A or Fancy (85) B or X-Standard (85) C or Standard (70)	Year-round	California
Tomato Juice—Canned	A or Fancy (93) C or Standard (80)	July to February	California
Tomato Juice, Concentrate—Canned	A or Fancy (85) C or Standard (70)	July to February	California
Tomato Paste—Canned	A or Fancy (90) C or Standard (80)	July to November	California
Tomato Puree—Canned	A or Fancy (90) C or Standard (80)	July to November	California
Tomato Sauce—Canned	A or Fancy (85) C or Standard (70)	July to November	California
Vegetables, Mixed—Frozen	A or Fancy (90) B or X-Standard (80) C or Standard (70)	Year-round	California, Northwest

Distribution

Distribution of processed fruits and vegetables likely will be through a primary or secondary distributor. Most items will be associated with a major brand or will be labeled as a packer brand. Processed fruits and vegetables, much like fresh produce, are subject to changes in the market due to seasonal growing conditions and availability. However, drastic changes in availability or quality are unusual since processors plan for seasonal changes.

Pricing and Yield

The pricing of processed fruits and vegetables is closely aligned with the prices of fresh produce. The differences are the time lag between the prices of the fresh product as opposed to the processed product. The price of the fresh product will be reflected later in the price of the processed product. This can be used as an advantage if a processed product can be substituted for a fresh product. If the price of the fresh product increases drastically, a processed product can sometimes be purchased at a lower price as a hedge against the increasing price. Then, as the fresh price decreases and the processed price increases, the buyer can return to the fresh product.

Yield becomes an issue with different types and brands of processed products. Canned items should be compared using the drained weight of the product. Frozen,

Exhibit 6   USDA Inspection Shields for Processed Produce

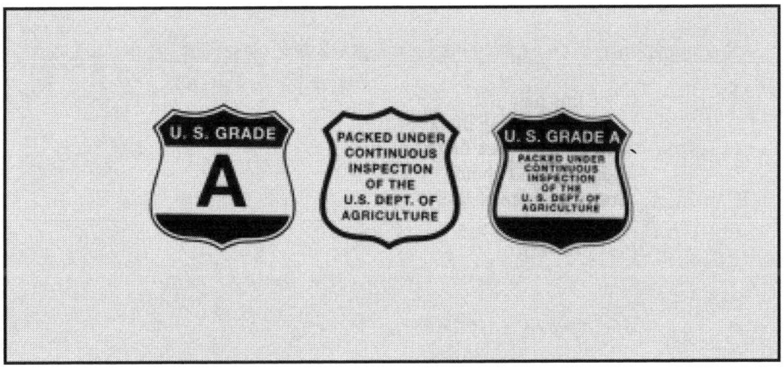

dried and vacuum-packed items should be inspected for quality and weight. The product purchase specifications should specifically state the expected yield of the product.

Produce Food Safety Issues

Buyers should understand that fresh fruits and vegetables and the processed products made from them are grown from the land. Soil contains certain natural and man-made hazards such as bacterial contaminants, parasites, and chemicals. Fresh fruits and vegetables should be purchased from reliable sources, inspected for contaminants, and thoroughly washed to remove any source of chemical or bacterial contamination. Processed products should be handled correctly to avoid contamination.

Management Considerations

Farm Fresh

A growing trend in the restaurant industry is opening a restaurant in a rural area where fresh produce can be grown on the property. This, of course, takes a very special restaurant concept on special property capable of raising crops. You do not need to move to a farm, however, to raise some of your own produce. Investigate using a piece of landscaped property next to the restaurant building to raise a few special crops. Good examples of easy-to-grow produce include herbs, peppers, baby greens, and heirloom tomatoes. Herbs can also be grown in window boxes. As long as there is available natural light, small crops can be raised.

Sustainability

Many food service organizations have begun to consider **sustainable practices** when purchasing fresh fruits and vegetables. One example of a sustainable practice may involve purchasing produce items from local farmers and providing the farmer with food waste that can be used for composting in exchange. This trade-off of services saves both parties money and provides a renewable resource. The

Exhibit 7   Sample Specifications for Processed Fruits and Vegetables

---

Specification #1 (Frozen Orange Juice Concentrate)

- U.S. Grade A (Fancy); minimum point score of 95
- 32-oz cans of 12 per case
- 3:1 concentrate; no sugar added
- Minimum of 50% Florida Valencia orange solids
- Pulp added, 4 to 8 grams per 6 oz (concentrate basis)
- Sugar/acid ratio—range from 14.5:1 to 16.5:1
- Brix—44.8 to 45.8 degrees
- Proof of grade required

Specification #2 (Frozen French Fry Potatoes)

- U.S. Grade A (Fancy)
- Blast frozen (-40° both F and C)
- Extra Long; $3/8'' \times 3/8''$ with at least 90% over 2″
- Minimum of 10% under 2″ pieces (measured per carton)
- Oil blanch; uniform color (no high sugars)
- From Russet Burbank variety; minimum of 32% solids
- 6 bags (4.5 lb each) per carton

Specification #3 (Canned Tomatoes)

- U.S. Grade B (Extra Standard); minimum point score of 85
- California 145 coreless variety; packed in natural juice
- 66 oz minimum drained weight measured by case
- Number 10 size cans, 6 per case
- Proof of grade required

Specification #4 (Canned Peach Halves)

- California clingstone; packed in heavy syrup
- Number 10 size cans, 6 per case; 35/40 count
- USDA Grade A; minimum point score of 9
- Minimum drained weight—65 oz per number 10 size can
- Good yellow color; minimum breakage; uniform size

Specification #5 (Frozen Peas)

- N.W. Pack—12 packages (2.5 lb each) per case
- USDA Grade A (Fancy); minimum point score of 94
- Less than 5% pieces; good green color
- 3 to 5 sieve size

---

downside of the practice is the time and commitment required to make the relationship successful.

 **Key Terms** ————————————————————————————

color added—A labeling requirement for fruit that has been artificially colored.

fancy—The highest quality grade given to the very best produce products.

ripening—The process by which produce matures and becomes suitable for eating.

solanin—A chemical found in green potatoes that causes a bitter flavor.

sustainable practices—Environmentally sound farming practices for produce (i.e., composting).

utility—The least desirable quality grade for fresh apples.

Review Questions

1. What are the major categories and varieties of fresh fruits?
2. What are the major categories and varieties of fresh vegetables?
3. How do the growing areas for fruits and vegetables affect their availability?
4. What are the factors important to quality in fruits?
5. What are the factors important to quality in vegetables?
6. Describe the distribution, processing and packaging options for fresh produce.
7. Explain the factors that affect yield for fresh produce and their effect on costs.
8. What are the requirements and content of purchasing specifications for fresh produce?
9. What are the market forms of processed fruits and vegetables?
10. What are the requirements and content of purchasing specifications for processed fruits and vegetables?
11. What are some of the sources of information availability in purchasing decisions for fresh and processed produce items?

Internet Sites

For more information, visit the following Internet sites. Remember that Internet addresses can change without notice. If the site is no longer there, you can use a search engine to look for additional sites.

Agricultural Marketing Service
www.ams.usda.gov

Chefs Collaborative
www.chefscollaborative.org

Cornell Cooperative Extension
http://scnyat.cce.cornell.edu/vegfruit/
prodprice.htm

Food Institute Report
www.foodinstitute.com/index.cfm

FoodRoutes
www.foodroutes.org

Nation's Restaurant News
www.nrn.com

Chapter 13 Outline

Baked Goods Production and Processing
Specifications for Baked Goods
Commodity Ingredients
    Grain Products
    Sugar and Other Sweeteners
    Fats and Oils
Dressings
Condiments and Spices
Other Grocery Items
Commodity and Grocery Item
    Specifications
Food Safety for Baked Goods and Grocery
    Items
Management Considerations
    Make-or-Buy Decisions

Competencies

1. Identify the major categories of baked goods. (p. 387)

2. Describe the content of specifications for baked goods. (p. 388)

3. Identify the different types of commodity ingredients important to baked goods. (pp. 388–390)

4. Describe the major categories and uses of fats and oils. (pp. 390–393)

5. Identify the types and characteristics of condiments and spices. (pp. 393–394)

6. Explain the requirements, content, and importance of specifications for commodity, condiment, and grocery items. (pp. 394–395)

7. Describe management considerations related to purchasing baked goods and grocery items. (pp. 395–396)

13

Baked Goods and Grocery Items

THE PURCHASING DECISIONS MADE FOR BAKED GOODS and grocery items can have considerable impact on a food service operation because they often supplement other food items, are used to prepare food items, or need to be included in other food items.

Baked Goods Production and Processing

Baked goods can be produced in food service operations using raw ingredients or purchased for service in the finished state. The decision whether to **make or buy** must be based on cost, convenience, and customer demand. The availability of equipment, space, and trained staff members can also influence the decision. Additionally, how the food service operation wants to market itself to the public is important to the make-or-buy decision. High-volume operations with equipment and expertise may find great value in preparing freshly baked goods on site. Small operators might do well to look for high-quality bakeries that can provide suitable baked products. Somewhere in between are cook-and-serve products that require only limited preparation by food service operators, but give the perception of a fresh product to the customer.

When purchasing baked goods, the major consideration is the type of item needed first, then selection of the best quality items for the best price. The traditional retail bakery produces goods for sale to retail and food service operations. A delivery person will check on the food service operator several times per week to deliver product. The delivery person, working with the operator, will establish a par stock to ensure adequate supplies and should exchange out-of-date items with fresh product.

Full-line distributors also may provide baked goods for food service operations. Baked goods are produced by manufacturers and supplied to distributors for sale to food service operators. These products are produced on a more limited basis with choices limited to what is popular in the marketplace. The advantages to these products are their availability and predictable pricing.

Specialty baked goods can be purchased from local bakeries. Local bakers often can provide high-quality specialized products like cakes, cheesecakes, gourmet breads, and pies. Availability of these products will vary according to the size of the market.

Specifications for Baked Goods

Specifications for baked goods will differ depending upon whether the product is a standard product in the market or a specialized product made to order for the food service operation. Most of the time, specifications will need to be written for each type of item. Standard specifications are likely not available. Standard baked goods, such as sandwich bread, hamburger buns, and hot dog buns, can have standard specifications. For example, a standard specification for sandwich bread would include details for the type of bread, the baked weight, the slice size, the number of slices per loaf, package type, and freshness requirements.

Specifications for such specialized products as cakes and pies would need to include the size and weight of the product, as well as the type and quality of the ingredients. Specifications for baked goods should be written specifically for the needs of the food service operation. Standard specifications based on government inspection or grading standards are not available for most baked products and are difficult to develop due to the different ingredients associated with specialized recipes. Specifications for baked goods should include the product's:

- Name.

- Intended use.

- U.S. grade (if applicable).

- Brand name.

- Size.

- Container size.

- Type of packaging.

- Weight.

- Form (fresh or frozen).

- Special requirements (deliver by date).

- Handling procedures.

Exhibit 1 is a sample specification for bread base mix.

Commodity Ingredients

The grain-based products used in baking typically are commodities easily available in the market. The issues are the type of commodity and the quality of the commodity ingredient. These commodity ingredients include wheat flour, rice, other grains (oats, barley, rye), and sugar.

Grain Products

Wheat Flour. The wheat kernel is composed of three parts—the bran, the germ, and the endosperm. White flour is made from the endosperm part of the kernel. Whole-wheat flour includes the whole kernel. Wheat can further be defined as

Exhibit 1   Sample Purchase Specification for Bread Base Mix

- Bread base mix used to make a standard white bread loaf and variety breads.
- General Mills, Pillsbury, or Cornerstone brands preferred.
- Bulk 50 lb moisture-resistant bag.
- Shelf life should be a minimum of 3 months, maximum of 6 months.
- Dry mix to store in a cool, dry place.
- Ingredients must be Kosher compliant.
- Bread base mix must not require more than 30 minutes of fermentation time.

hard spring wheat, hard winter wheat, or soft wheat. Hard spring wheat is higher in protein than soft wheat. High-protein flours are utilized for making breads because the higher percentage of protein allows for better gluten development (moisture and manipulation are used to create an elastic network of proteins). **Low-protein flours** are used for baked goods in which flakiness is important. **High-protein flours** are often referred to as bread flour, while low-protein flours are referred to as pastry flour. A combination of the two flour types produces **all-purpose flour**, which can be used for more general applications.

Another special wheat type is the hard durum wheat used in pasta and macaroni products. Durum wheat produces high-protein flour best suited for products that must hold their shape during cooking.

Rice. Rice is available in several forms for food service use. **Brown rice** is rice in its natural state. **White rice** has had the outer bran removed. Furthermore, rice can be of the short-grain, medium-grain, or long-grain variety. **Converted rice**, which is short-grain white rice that has been parboiled, is the most popular type of rice used in food service. **Parboiled rice** has been steamed to cook quicker and fluffier. The type of rice purchased depends on how it will be used in the food service operation.

Other Grain Products. Products such as cornmeal, oatmeal, barley, and rye can be purchased as commodity ingredients like flour and rice. Primary concerns are for the fineness of the milling and availability from distributors. How those grains will be used will determine how much should be purchased. Buyers should not purchase more of these grains than can be used in 30–45 days.

Sugar and Other Sweeteners

Sugar. Sugar is produced from sugar beets and sugar cane. There is no difference in the quality of the types of sugar. Sugar from cane is cheaper to produce than sugar from beets, but the price is not usually different in the market because of government subsidies and tariffs. As a commodity, sugar is readily available for purchase from distributors at stable prices.

Sugar may be classified as one of the following varieties:

- Course grain—most often used for decorating

- Sanding grade—most often used in decorating

- Standard granulated—table sugar, used for traditional baking

- Fine granulated—used in baking

- Superfine or very fine granulated—often used in beverages and for baking

- Powdered sugar or confectioner's sugar—sugar ground to a powder, most often used in decorating

- Brown sugar—sugar produced late in the refining process when it still contains a percentage of molasses. The amount of molasses determines if the sugar is classified as light, medium, or dark brown.

Corn Syrup. Corn syrup is a sweetener composed of dextrose, whereas sugar is composed of sucrose. Corn syrup has the advantage of being a more powerful sweetener than sugar by volume, which makes it less expensive. Corn syrup is used in many baking recipes and as a sweetener in soft drinks.

Non-Caloric or Artificial Sweeteners. Three primary artificial sweeteners dominate the market. **Saccharin**, **aspartame**, and **sucralose** all are packaged under several popular brand names, as well as private labels. Determining which products to buy depends upon how the product will be used and which product the customer demands. Many food service operators will carry all three types in order to satisfy all types of customer requests.

Honey. Honey is a natural form of pure sweetener. The USDA grades honey according to its color, clarity, flavor, and aroma. Honey is graded A or B. Honey is available from most distributors in jars or portion-control containers.

Jellies, Jams, Preserves, and Marmalades. Jellies, jams, preserves, and marmalades must be at least 45 percent fruit to 55 percent sweetener by weight or they must be labeled imitation. Based on color, flavor, and consistency, the USDA grades these products as Grade A or Grade B. These products are available in a variety of bulk packages such as cans and jars, as well as in portion-control packages.

Fats and Oils

Fats and oils are necessary for cooking, baking, and proper human nutrition. Shortenings provide tenderness in baked goods, oils provide cooking mediums for foods, and fat carries much of the flavor of food.

Types of Fats and Oils. In general, fats are produced from animal products, while oils are produced from plant products. Exhibit 2 lists terms used in fat and oil manufacturing. Fats are solid at room temperature, while oils are liquid at room temperature. There are eight primary types of fats and oils: soybean oil, cottonseed oil, corn oil, peanut oil, butterfat, lard, olive oil, and coconut oil. The type of oil purchased will depend upon how it will be used. Oils used for stovetop cooking have different requirements than those used for frying. Oils

Exhibit 2 Fat and Oil Manufacturing Terms

Purchasers should understand the meaning of terms used to describe various processes in the manufacture of fats and oils.

Refining—Removing various amounts of free fatty acids, gums, color pigments, and perhaps seed particles.

Bleaching—Removing some color pigments and minor amounts of cleansing agents remaining after the refining process. It is a physical process rather than a chemical one. The oil is heated, agitated, and then filtered.

Hydrogenation—Adding hydrogen to unsaturated fatty acids in the oil, done for two purposes: (1) to retard fat interaction with oxygen and thus reduce rancidity, and (2) to raise the melting point, changing liquid/solid properties.

Winterization—Removing fatty acids that are of high molecular weight and more saturated, so that the oil will remain fluid and not become cloudy at refrigerator temperatures.

Deodorization—Heating under pressure, injecting steam, and removing materials that could contribute objectionable flavor or odor. The oil is left bland and colorless.

Formulation—Altering the manufacturing process or using additives so that the end product is better suited for its intended use.

used to make dressings would have completely different requirements. Determinations should be based on quality and value. Better quality oils and fats will be more stable in the cooking process, but may be more expensive.

Fats for Baking. The type of fat or oil used in baking is determined by the needs of the recipe. Hydrogenated fats (hydrogen atoms are added to the fat to create an oil that is solid at room temperature) are often used in baked goods to provide tenderness and flakiness in the dough. Fats used in cakes give the cake a smooth texture.

Fats and Oils for Frying. Specialized products have been developed for frying purposes. Frying food requires that the fat or oil be stable at high temperatures. Frying fats and oils should have a high smoke point (the temperature at which the fat begins to break down). As a fat is reused, its smoke point decreases due to the deterioration of the fat. Frying fats and oils should not provide any off flavors or odors to the food being cooked in them. Good quality, highly stable frying fat and oil can be reused through several cooking cycles as long as it is properly filtered and cleaned. Exhibit 3 lists common problems with fats and oils used for frying.

The trend in food service has been toward using fats and oils low in saturated fats and **trans fatty acids** (trans fats). Most fats and oils used in food service are partially hydrogenated. Hydrogenated oils are shelf-stable, stand up well to repeated heating and give foods the texture and consistency needed, which is sometimes referred to as "mouth feel." The problem is that the hydrogenation process creates trans fatty acids, which have been found to contribute to cholesterol development in humans. Saturated fats do not contain trans fatty acids, but have been shown to

Exhibit 3   Common Frying Problems

Problem 1: Foods do not brown properly.
Check these factors:

- Breading—Improper breading can affect product color.
- Oil temperature—Is it too low?
- Recovery—Is basket overloaded, causing the temperature of oil to drop?
- Foaming—Oil could be breaking (decomposing). How long has it been in use?

Problem 2: Foods are too brown.
Check these factors:

- What types of foods have been fried? (For example, potatoes cause dark oil when sugar/starch is released into the oil and caramelizes.)
- Has the oil broken or been improperly filtered?

Problem 3: Objectionable fat flavor.
Check these factors:

- Does fresh oil (or food) have odor? What type of food (for example, fish) has been fried?
- Condition of oil in fryer—Is it old? Has it deteriorated? (For example, soy oil reverts unless treated, causing a beany or fishy flavor.)
- Has exhaust system dripped into the kettle?
- Were cleaning materials left in the kettle?

Problem 4: Excessive oil absorption.
Check these factors:

- Was food fried from thawed state?
- Improper drainage.
- Oil temperature—Is it too low?
- Was product incorrectly blanched by processor?
- Calibration of fryer.

Problem 5: Oil smoking or foaming.
Check these factors:

- Oil temperature—Is it too high?
- Was all gum/carbon removed from the kettle during cleaning?
- Has oil been freshly filtered?
- Excessive moisture in the raw material.

---

contribute to heart disease. Food service manufacturers are beginning to develop foods and oils that eliminate trans fats and saturated fats as ingredients. The problem is that these new products have been less than successful so far due to their instability during repeated heating, or have been very expensive to develop and are drawn from genetically modified (GMO) seeds, which creates new problems for buyers wishing to avoid GMO foods. As new products are developed buyers should be aware of the need to consider fats, oils, and products that are low in trans fats and **saturated fats** (fats that have as much hydrogen as they can hold). Look for products using **unsaturated fats** as ingredients and for products with no trans fatty acids. Purchase specifications for fats, oils, and food products should be written with this concern in mind (see Exhibit 4).[1]

Exhibit 4   Sample Specifications for Common Fats and Oils

Specification #1: Baking Fat

Solid fat index:	At 70° F (21° C), 20.5 to 22%
	At 80° F (27° C), 17 to 19%
	At 90° F (32° C), 14 to 16%
	At 104° F (40° C), 6 to 8%
Wiley melt point:	115–119° F (46–48° C)
Color:	As specified
Trans fatty acid:	0.0%
Minimum smoke point:	325° F (163° C)
Emulsifier:	2.9 to 3.1%
AOM stability:	100 hours minimum*
Either plasticized or liquid.	Packaging as specified.

Specification #2: Frying Fat

Solid fat index,	
Summer range:	At 70° F (21° C), 27 to 31%
	At 92° F (33° C), 13 to 16%
	At 104° F (40° C), 2%
Winter range:	At 70° F (21° C), 22 to 24%
	At 92° F (33° C), 6.5 to 8.5%
	At 104° F (40° C), 0 to .05%
Wiley melt point:	105–110° F (40–43° C)
Melt point:	106° F (41° C)
Congeal point:	86.5° F (30.3° C)
Minimum smoke point:	465° F (240° C)
Trans fatty acid:	0.0%
Flavor:	Neutral and bland
AOM stability:	180 hours minimum*
Either plasticized or liquid.	Packaging as specified.

Specification #3: Salad Oil

Oil:	Refined soybean oil
Trans fatty acid:	0.0%
Peroxide value:	1.5
Color:	Neutral
Flavor:	Bland
Chill test:	More than 100 hours at 32° F (0° C)

(All major oil suppliers make a "refined salad oil.")

Specification #4: Margarine

Fat:	80% minimum (soybean oil and/or cottonseed oil)
Moisture:	16.1 to 16.3%
Nonfat milk solids:	1.3% minimum
Solid fat index:	At 50° F (10° C), 28.5% ± 1.5%
	At 70° F (21° C), 17.5% ± 1.5%
	At 90° F (32° C), 4.2% ± 0.8%
Trans fatty acid:	0.0%
Salt:	2.4 to 2.6%

Fortified with vitamins as labeled.

*AOM stands for active oxygen method. It is a technique for measuring fat stability—how long before a fat becomes rancid.

Sources: Specifications #1 and #2 are modifications of specifications established by Lever Brothers Co., Industrial Division, 390 Park Ave., New York. A specification used by C & T Refinery, Inc., Richmond, VA, forms the basis of Specification #3. The U.S. Food and Drug Administration has established standards for margarine, essentially those shown in Specification #4.

Dressings

A primary commodity ingredient in most dressings is some type of vegetable oil (soybean, olive, corn, or cottonseed). Different types of oil are used for different dressings because of the characteristics they lend to the dressing. When purchasing prepared dressings, buyers should compare the percentage of oil to the other ingredients, the flavor ingredients, weight per gallon, and viscosity (thickness and weight) of the dressing. If an operator chooses to produce dressings on site, the total cost of the ingredients and the labor involved in the process should be calculated to compare against the cost of prepared dressings.

Condiments and Spices

Condiments and spices do not generally represent a large percentage of food service expenditures; however, their importance to recipes and customer satisfaction can be substantial. Spices, flavorings, and seasonings of various types are generally available from most food service distributors. Most spices used in food service can be purchased in various sizes. Care must be taken to only purchase spices in quantities that can be used within a few months. Spices purchased through distributors are usually brand-name products with reasonable and stable prices. Flavorings used in food service include salts, monosodium glutamate (MSG), vanilla, and other synthetic or natural flavors. Common salts include table salt for tabletop use and kosher or coarse salt for cooking purposes. More exotic salts, such as sea salt and black salt, can be purchased, depending upon the requirements and uses in the kitchen. MSG is often purchased as a flavor enhancer; however, MSG has been restricted by many food service operators. When purchasing flavorings such as vanilla, natural flavorings are usually the best quality because they are derived from the actual natural ingredients; however, synthetic flavorings may be a better value, depending on how they will be used.

Condiments, such as mustard, ketchup, and salsa, are very brand oriented. The quality of private-label condiments versus their brand-name competitors may not be much different when tested. However, the customer's perception of quality is what matters, and brand-name condiments are often seen as a better value. Mustards are available in different varieties, and choices should be made based on the operator's needs and the customer's expectations of variety and brand name. Ketchup used to be available in only one type; however, new types are now on the market that are spicier and even different colors. Salsa has replaced ketchup as the number-one condiment used by consumers. The type of salsa purchased should depend upon how it will be used and the customer's expectations. Salsa could involve a make-or-buy decision. Freshly made salsa can be produced quite inexpensively in terms of the ingredients, particularly when they are in season. However, the labor required to prepare the salsa needs to be included when comparing the value of fresh salsa to prepared salsa.

Other Grocery Items

There are a multitude of other canned and frozen grocery items that could be discussed, but the list is too large. Frozen grocery items should be selected according to their intended use. Frozen products are preferred for quality and freshness when available. The quality of frozen products should be comparable to that of fresh products. Products should be tested before selection.

Canned products have the advantage of long shelf life and easy storage. Newer aseptic packaging (sterilized packaging with a sterile food product within the confines of a hygienic environment) may be a good choice for some products. Canned products should be checked for quality and appearance. When evaluating canned products, buyers should check the drained weight of different products to ensure they are getting the best value.

Examples of grocery items include asparagus, beans, beets carrots, corn, green beans, mixed vegetables, peas, pickles, potatoes, spinach, zucchini, tomatoes, tomato sauce, various fruit and fruit mixtures, fruit and vegetable juices, condensed soups, meats, poultry, and seafood. All of these products are available as canned or frozen items.

Commodity and Grocery Item Specifications

Purchasing specifications for commodities and grocery items should be written based on the needs of the food service operation. Standard purchase specifications based on government inspection or grading standards are not available for most commodities or grocery items. Specifications for commodities and grocery items should include the product's:

- Name.
- Intended use.
- U.S. grade (if applicable).
- Brand name.
- Size.
- Container size.
- Type of packaging.
- Weight or drained weight
- Form.
- Special requirements.
- Handling procedures.

Exhibit 5 shows a sample specification for canned tomatoes, a common grocery item.

Food Safety for Baked Goods and Grocery Items

Most baked goods, commodity ingredients, and grocery items are not considered to be potentially hazardous foods. Any food safety concerns are usually caused by either chemical or physical contamination. Special care should be taken to check bulk commodities, such as flour and rice, for physical contamination with stones, pebbles, or insects. Bulk commodity products need to be stored in closed containers at least six inches off the floor. Canned products should be transferred to clean food-storage containers if the entire product is not utilized from the can.

Management Considerations

Make-or-Buy Decisions

Baked goods, dressings, and other grocery items offer great opportunities for operators to compare the value of making a product versus purchasing a comparable product. In many situations, given comparable products, the cost of labor to prepare a product will be the deciding factor in the decision. However, operators should also keep in mind the customer's expectations for value. If the customer feels strongly that the fresh product is a better value for their dining dollar, then management must honor this expectation. When considering make-or-buy decisions, distributors should be able to help find comparable products and make

Exhibit 5   Sample Purchase Specification for Canned Tomatoes

- Unit: case.
- Trade spec: extra or standard.
- U.S. grade: B.
- Brand: Heinz, Hunt's, or Red Gold preferred.
- Jersey, Michigan, or Midwestern pack preferred.
- Minimum drained weight per #10 can: 63.5–68 oz.
- Tomatoes to be 70% whole.
- Pack: 6 #10 cans per case.
- Special requirements: low sodium, less than 140 mg per #10 can.

comparisons between those products. Food service buyers should work with their distributor partners to determine the availability of and the best choices for the use of prepared products versus making an item from scratch. Distributors will have the best knowledge of the products available, while buyers will know best how the product will work in their food production systems.

Endnotes

1. Mike Buzalka, "A Not-So-Quick Oil Change," *Food Management* (February 2007), available on-line at www.food-management.com/article/16338/.

 # Key Terms

all-purpose flour—A mixture of high- and low-protein flours that is used for general applications.

aspartame—One of three predominant artificial sweeteners on the market.

brown rice—Rice in its natural state with the outer bran intact.

converted rice—Short-grain white rice that has been parboiled.

corn syrup—A sweetener composed of dextrose that is a stronger sweetener by volume than sugar.

high-protein flour—Flour used for making bread because the higher percentage of protein allows for better gluten development.

low-protein flour—Flour that is used in baked goods in which flakiness is an important quality.

make-or-buy decision—The decision whether to produce a product from raw ingredients or buy it ready to serve.

parboiled rice—Rice that has been partially cooked by boiling.

saccharin—One of three predominant artificial sweeteners on the market.

saturated fats—Fats that have as much hydrogen as they can hold and are usually solid at room temperature. These fats contribute to health problems in humans.

sucralose—One of three predominant artificial sweeteners on the market.

sugar—A natural sweetener produced from sugar beets or sugar cane.

trans fatty acids—Harmful acids that are created when hydrogen is added to a fat or oil.

unsaturated fats—Fats with open hydrogen bonds. They usually are found in plant products and are liquid at room temperature.

white rice—Rice with the outer bran removed.

 Review Questions

1. What are the major categories of baked goods?
2. What information should be included in a purchase specification for baked goods?
3. What are the different types of commodity ingredients important to baked goods?
4. What are the major categories of fats and oils?
5. What are the different types of condiments used in the food service industry?
6. What information should be included in a purchase specification for a grocery item?
7. Why are purchase specifications important for grocery items?
8. What would be a good source for information regarding a make or buy decision?

 Internet Sites

For more information, visit the following Internet sites. Remember that Internet addresses can change without notice. If the site is no longer there, you can use a search engine to look for additional sites.

American Heart Association Trans Fat Page
www.americanheart.org/presenter.jhtml?identifier=3045792#def_trans_fat

American Institute of Baking
www.aibonline.org/

Food Products Association
www.fpa-food.org/index.asp

National Frozen & Refrigerated Foods Association
www.nfraweb.org/

National Grain and Feed Association
www.ngfa.org/default.asp

U.S. FDA Trans Fat Initiatives
www.fda.gov/oc/initiatives/transfat/

Chapter 14 Outline

Types of Beverages
    Malt Beverages
    Spirits
    Wines
    Non-Alcoholic Beverages
Spirits
    Measures and Storage
    Market Types
    Judging the Quality of Spirits
Beer
    Beer Terminology
    Classes
    Alcohol Content
    Packaging
    Storage and Service
Wine Fundamentals
    Wine Terminology
    Types of Wine
    Wine Production
    Taste Talk
    Judging Wine
Non-Alcoholic Beverages
    Coffee
    Tea
    Cocoa
    Soft Drinks
    Bottled Water

Competencies

1. List the types of beverages offered in food service operations. (pp. 399–405)

2. Distinguish among the different categories of spirits, define terminology related to spirits, and describe the common forms of packaging for spirits. (pp. 405–417)

3. Distinguish among the different categories of beer, define terminology related to beer, and describe the common forms of packaging for beer. (pp. 417–424)

4. Distinguish among the different categories of wine, define terminology related to wine, and explain wine tasting and judging. (pp. 424–433)

5. Describe the varieties, quality standards, processing stages, and market forms for coffee. (pp. 433–437)

6. Describe the varieties, quality standards, processing stages, and market forms for tea. (pp. 437–439)

7. Describe the market forms for soft drinks and bottled water. (pp. 439–443)

8. Explain the requirements, content, and importance of specifications for beverages. (pp. 399, 435–443)

14

Beverages

BEVERAGE OPERATIONS ARE FOUND IN HOTELS AND RESTAURANTS. They are also free-standing and, of course, in other venues such as private clubs and on cruise ships. A number of factors make the purchase of beverages unique. Most beverages are purchased by brand, so the brand itself becomes the purchase specification. If food and beverage managers know their guests' preferences, they can specify the desired brands, reducing the time and effort required for purchasing activities.

The purchasing and marketing of beverages cannot be separated in most operations; because of this, the buyer may play a smaller role in the purchase of these items compared to other products. Therefore, this chapter emphasizes the marketing and operations aspects in great detail. The purpose is twofold: to highlight the need for line and purchasing staff to work cooperatively as beverage purchase decisions are made and, secondly, to focus on factors influencing the effectiveness of marketing decisions.

Types of Beverages

The types of beverages offered for sale in a beverage establishment are fundamentally determined by the guests' needs, wants, and expectations. The broad categories include malt beverages, spirits, wines, and non-alcoholic beverages.

Malt Beverages

Malt beverages contain 0.5 percent or more of alcohol, are brewed or produced wholly or in part from malt, and include beers, ales, stouts, and porters, as well as bock and sake. These beverages have malt barley as a main ingredient. Malt-beverage ingredients also include hops, water, yeast, adjuncts (e.g., corn, rice, wheat, soybean flakes, potato starch, and/or sugar), and additives (e.g., preservatives and/or enzymes). Beer varieties include:

- Pilsner—a light, rich, and mellow lager.

- Bavarian—light in body and darker than pilsner.

- Dortmunder—dark color and full body.

- Malt liquor—more pronounced malt flavor and slightly darker color than regular beer.

- Steam beer—high carbon dioxide content with a creamy foam.

Ale contains more hops than other beers, giving it a characteristic bitter taste. Porter is produced from malt roasted at high temperatures. Stout is higher in alcohol content with a more "hop-like" taste than porter. Bock is a German beer that is richer, darker, and higher in alcohol content than regular 3.2 percent beer. Sake is produced from rice. Near beers are non-alcoholic beverages produced with the same ingredients; however, the alcohol is removed prior to bottling.

Spirits

Spirits differ depending on what they are made from and what flavorings are added. For example, brandy is made from fruit, rum is made from sugar cane or molasses, and gin is made from grain and flavored with juniper berries. Spirits have higher alcohol content than malt beverages or wine. Some common types of spirits are:

- Gin.
- Vodka.
- Rum.
- Brandy.
- Tequila.
- Whiskey.
- Bitters.
- Liqueurs or cordials.
- Schnapps.
- Sherry.

Spirits are especially popular in many operations because they are used to make mixed drinks or cocktails. For example, a martini marries gin and vermouth and is typically garnished with an olive. A Long Island iced tea mixes equal parts of vodka, tequila, rum, gin, and triple sec with sweet and sour mix and cola.

Spirits and cordials are being combined into drinks that feature a rainbow of colors. When exotic and dramatic garnishes are added, the potential to increase beverage revenues and profits rises. Retro drinks, such as mai tais and grasshoppers, are also being introduced to a new generation of guests. All of these market trends affect purchasing.

Wines

Wines are produced by fermenting grapes. The basic wine classifications include table wines, natural and fortified wines, aperitif and dessert wines, and sparkling wines. **Table wine** is the largest category, and these wines are suitable to accompany food. They may be further classified based on color as red, white, or rosé. **Natural wines** include most table wines because the product is the result of grape fermentation without the addition of alcohol or sugar. In contrast,

fortified wines have added alcohol, usually in the form of a brandy distilled from wine and added during fermentation. This produces a sweeter wine higher in alcohol content. **Aperitif wines** are fortified, flavored with herb ingredients, and are usually served before a meal as an appetizer or cocktail. **Dessert wines** are fortified and are served as dessert or with dessert following a meal. **Sparkling wines** are usually produced by fermenting them a second time and trapping the carbon dioxide gas produced by a second fermentation to add the appealing effervescent bubbles.

Some beverage operators are promoting "undiscovered gems," that is, unknown wines from little known, unheralded wine-growing areas across the United States. These handcrafted, vibrant wines from younger American producers represent great value for guests, as well as the beverage establishment. Guests are also ordering more wines from around the world (merlots from Australia, for example). Other guests are willing to experiment and try new wines that offer value. All of these provide challenges in identifying and procuring these products.

Wines by the glass give the guest a higher perceived value provided that the wines are fairly priced. Some believe that a price of a glass of wine should not exceed the price of a premium beer. Some beverage establishments are featuring super-premium wines by the glass at remarkably low prices. Wine flights featuring two-ounce pours of a number of samples encourage the guests to experiment with expensive wines that they may not choose to purchase by the bottle. Half bottles of expensive wine are becoming a more popular option since they permit two guests to pair two or three wines with two or three separate food courses, as well as enjoy a variety of wines without over-consuming alcohol. Guests today are more often ordering the softer, easier to drink wines that pair well with food menu items, particularly fresh fish, in casual-dining establishments. Those responsible for purchasing must keep in tune with these evolving trends.

Another wine option is to develop and feature private-label wine selections, capitalizing on the power of the establishment's brand. These proprietary labels bear the visible and exclusive stamp of the beverage establishment in which they are being sold. The advantages to doing so include marketing opportunities, pricing freedom, enhanced perception of the brand by the guests, and the guests' perception that the wine is special and exclusive since they can only obtain it at the beverage establishment with the name on the brand. A proprietary wine label resulting from a collaborative effort on the part of the Musser family of the Grand Hotel on Mackinac Island, Michigan, and the Trinchero family of Napa Valley, California, is presented in Exhibit 1.

To effectively add value to the guests' experience, the private-label wines must be priced within the "comfort zone" of the guests. Guests who believe that the proprietary wines are too pricey—that is, that they do not represent value—simply will not order them.

Wine can help create an elegant dining atmosphere. The opportunities to improve the guest's experience and the unit's profitability concurrently are almost limitless. The purchaser must be knowledgeable about the product. Some distributors, distillers, and vintners (wine producers) offer special services, such as

Exhibit 1   Proprietary Wine Label from Grand Hotel, Mackinac Island, Michigan

---

Front of the label

The Trincheros of Trinchero Family Estates and the Musser Family of Grand Hotel together present this distinctive private label vintage bottled exclusively for Grand Hotel. Crafted from grapes grown in California's cool coastal climates, this distinctive collaboration proudly boasts the heritage and time-honored traditions of both families.

TRINCHERO   1999
Grand Hotel   Estate Bottled
              Petit Verdot
              Napa Valley

Back of the label

Welcome to the Wine Cellars of Grand Hotel. Each year Grand Hotel Chef Hans Burtscher and I research, study or taste over 500 wines from the world over, searching for the finest. A few of the wines we find are of such exceptional quality and value that we have them specifically bottled under our name through Grand hotel Cellars. Hopefully you will enjoy these wines, as we believe they are reflections of the standards we have set for all aspects of Grand Hotel.

Produced & Bottled by   (signed)
Trinchero Family Estates   R. D. Musser III
St. Helena, Napa County, CA 94574   President

Source: Lendal H. Kotschevar and Ronald F. Cichy, *Managing Beverage Service* (Lansing, Mich.: Educational Institute of the American Hotel & Lodging Association, 2004), p. 16.

constructing a wine list or training staff member in wine service. Operators should use training programs to teach purchasers about general information about wines.

With the improvement in the quality and variety of domestic products, increased wine consumption is likely to continue. Wine is now available in bulk containers (similar to those used for fluid milk). These containers allow wines to be dispensed at the bar through a tap system much like that used for beer. Regardless of whether wine is required for large banquet groups or more intimate dining applications, there truly are wine products for everyone's taste.

Thousands of grape varieties have evolved from all parts of the world. Buyers should be aware that wine from similar grape varieties may have different names according to the region or country in which the grapes are grown. Several common classic red and white wine grape varieties are shown in Exhibits 2 and 3, respectively.

Non-Alcoholic Beverages

Non-alcoholic beverages include designer teas, energy drinks, flavored bottled waters, fruit smoothies, gourmet coffees, and lemonade, among others. Fresh fruit and herbal sodas are popular summertime non-alcoholic beverage options. Alcohol-free refreshers such as ginger lemon, cherry, lemon verbena, passion fruit, and

Exhibit 2   Classic Red Wine Grapes

Cabernet Sauvignon
[ka-behr-NAY soh-vihn-YOHN]

Growing Areas
  Often called the "king of red grapes," Cabernet Sauvignon is produced throughout the world. The most famous growing area is Bordeaux, France. Needs slightly warmer growing conditions than many other grape varieties. Best growing sites are moderately warm, semi-arid regions with well-drained fields and long growing seasons.

Varietal/Blend
  Often blended with Merlot, Cabernet Franc, and Syrah.

Vinification
  Fermented in stainless steel or oak. Well rounded, high in tannin content and ages well. Aged in old or new oak. Ranges from medium-bodied to heavier full-bodied.

Flavors
  Black currant flavor with hint of mint and cedar.

Merlot
[mehr-LOH]

Growing Areas
  One of the world's most popular red grape varieties, Merlot is the most widely planted grape in the Bordeaux region of France and matures in regions cooler than those required for Cabernet Sauvignon. It is grown worldwide, particularly in Italy, Spain, South America, United States, South Africa, Australia, and New Zealand.

Varietal/Blend
  Used to soften Cabernet Sauvignon-based wines.

Vinification
  As with Cabernet Sauvignon, Merlot is fermented in stainless steel or oak. In some regions, it is cool-fermented when used as a varietal. Lower in tannic bitterness and higher in alcohol content than Cabernet Sauvignon. Also, slightly lower natural acidity than Cabernet Sauvignon and less astringency. Dry, fruity, and usually oak-aged.

Flavors
  Similar in flavor to Cabernet Sauvignon, Merlot tends to be softer and mellower with fruity flavors of black currant, black cherry, and mint.

Pinot Noir
[PEE-noh NWAHR]

Growing Areas
  One of the oldest grape varieties, Pinot Noir is the primary grape of France's Burgundy region. Difficult to grow, it thrives in a moderately cool climate with warm days and cool nights. Also produced in the United States, Australia, New Zealand, South Africa, Germany, Eastern Europe, and Italy.

Varietal/Blend
  Used in most red wines from Burgundy and in the bulk of Champagne production.

(continued)

Exhibit 2 *(continued)*

Vinification
One of the most difficult grapes to ferment, sometimes oak barrel-fermented. Neither acidic nor tannic, Pinot Noir has a soft, velvety texture. Usually oak-aged. Burgundies are always aged in new oak.

Flavors
Predominately raspberry, strawberry, and sometimes cherry flavors.

Syrah/Shiraz
[see-RAH]

Growing Areas
Grown mostly in France and Australia (named as Shiraz and Hermitage), but increasingly in the United States, Algeria, and South Africa.

Varietal/Blend
Used for blending in Châteauneuf-du-Pape and makes for a fine quality wine as a varietal.

Vinification
Traditionally fermented at up to 35 degrees Centigrade but now often fermented at cooler temperatures in stainless steel vats. Rich and tannic with a velvety texture. Dry, full, rarely oak-aged, except in Australia.

Flavors
Fruit flavored, particularly blackberry and raspberry with a peppery overtone.

Sanigiovese
[san-jaw-VAY-zeh]

Growing Areas
The primary grape of Tuscany, Italy. Thriving in a hot, dry climate, little is grown outside of Italy, with limited production in the United States, Australia, and Argentina.

Varietal/Blend
Rarely used as varietal, Sanigiovese is blended with most Tuscan red wines and is the basic blend of Chianti.

Vinification
Short fermentation (3 days) for Chianti. High natural acidity with moderate to high tannins and medium levels of alcohol, produces a spicy, smooth texture. Sweet and sour style, best drunk young and fresh. Usually oak-aged.

Flavors
Predominant flavors of black and red cherries.

Gamay
[ga-MAY]

Growing Areas
The Beaujolais grape of Burgundy, France. Virtually all production is in France where the grape flourishes on the granite hills of Burgundy.

Varietal/Blend
Used as a varietal, it is not blended with other wines.

Exhibit 2 *(continued)*

Vinification
Usually fermented using carbonic maceration to enhance fruitiness. Low in alcohol and relatively high in acidity with light tannins. Never oak-aged. Best drunk soon after bottling.

Flavors
Cherry flavors may dominate with hints of raspberries and strawberries.

Zinfandel
[ZIHN-fuhn-dehl]

Growing Areas
This specialty red wine grape of California is not widely grown in other parts of the world. Some production in Italy (known as Primitivo), South Africa, South America, and Australia.

Varietal/Blend
Used as a varietal and can be blended with a number of different wines. Also used as a base for sparkling wines.

Vinification
Modern technology and the lack of confining traditions creates conditions for producing sweetish "blush" wines as well as high-quality, rich reds. Sometimes, fermented using carbonic maceration to enhance fruitiness. Dry, full, usually oak-aged.

Flavors
Unique black fruit and raspberry flavors with spicy fruitiness.

Source: Lendal H. Kotschevar and Ronald F. Cichy, *Managing Beverage Service* (Lansing, Mich.: Educational Institute of the American Hotel & Lodging Association, 2004), pp. 225–227.

tarragon flavors can be more appealing choices than iced tea. They are usually produced by combining natural herb and fruit concentrates with sugar, resulting in a drink base that is added to soda when the drink is prepared immediately prior to service.

Spirits

Distilled spirits include any alcoholic beverage that is made by distillation rather than fermentation. **Fermentation** is a chemical process in which yeast is added to a sugar source to break the sugar down into alcohol, carbon dioxide gas, and heat. **Distillation** is a process in which a fermented liquid is heated to separate the alcohol from it. Both beers and wines are made through fermentation. All spirits start out colorless and completely clear—their browns and other hues show up in the aging process.

According to the Distilled Spirits Council of the United States, there are currently more than 4,000 brands of distilled spirits on the market in the United States. These spirits contribute more than $41.2 billion in economic activity and more than 620,000 jobs in the U.S. economy.

Exhibit 3   Classic White Wine Grapes

Chardonnay
[shar-dn-AY]

Growing Areas
>   Chardonnay, one of the most popular and versatile of all white grape varieties, is produced in most wine-producing countries throughout the world. The most famous growing area is Burgundy, France. This grape variety adapts to varying climates.

Varietal/Blend
>   A quality varietal, Chardonnay is also the major wine blended with Pinot Noir and Pinot Meunier to produce Champagne.

Vinification
>   Adaptable to different wine-making techniques: stainless steel fermentation, barrel fermentation, and malolactic fermentation. Different growing soils and varied wine-making techniques produce a range of styles and characteristics. Generally, smooth from a fine balance of sugar and acidity. Also, strong affinity with oak aging that adds depth and flavor.

Flavor
>   Often with hints of tropical fruits, with buttery, lemon, and sometimes nutty flavors.

Sauvignon Blanc
[SOH-vee-nyaw*n* BLAH*N*GK]

Growing Areas
>   After, Chardonnay, Sauvignon Blanc is the second most popular white wine. It is best grown in cool climates and native to France's Loire Valley region. Countries producing Sauvignon Blanc include: New Zealand, Australia, Chile, Austria, Italy, United States, and South Africa.

Varietal/Blend
>   A crisp and tart varietal in Loire, France, and in New Zealand. Often blended with Sémillon in Bordeaux, France, and in many regions around the world to produce elegant, dry wines. Also, a component of the sweet, rich wines of Sauternes and Barsac.

Vinification
>   Stainless steel fermentation and usually unoaked. Tangy and sharp when unblended. Softer styles from barrel-fermented Sémillon blends.

Flavor
>   Sunny climates produce rich, tropical fruit flavors; cool climates produce sharp, tangy gooseberry flavors with mineral overtones.

Riesling
[REEZ-ling]

Growing Areas
>   One of the world's great white wine grapes producing some of the very best white wines. Native of Germany, and suited to the coldest of wine-growing climates, Riesling is produced in Northern France, Northern Italy, Eastern Europe, South Africa, Australia, New Zealand, and the United States.

Varietal/Blend
>   Primarily a varietal, occasionally used in blending.

Exhibit 3 *(continued)*

Vinification
> Stainless steel fermented and varied from light and dry to rich and sweet; usually made in dry and semi-dry styles. German-style is sweet and tart; Alsatian-style is bone dry.

Flavor
> Often tastes as it smells. Spicy and fruity with hints of green apple, lime, peaches, apricot, and honey.

Sémillon
[seh-mee-YOHN]

Growing Areas
> Produced worldwide: Native to France's Bordeaux region and found also in Australia, South America, South Africa, eastern Europe, and the United States.

Varietal/Blend
> While mostly a varietal in Australia, Sémillon is blended with Savignon Blanc to produce many of the white wines from Bordeaux, France. Also used in the production of dessert wines.

Vinification
> Stainless steel fermentation and rarely oaked. Blended, produces dry wines or sweet wines.

Flavor
> Often tastes as it smells. Dry, wines have flavors of nectarine and lemon. Sweeter wines have flavors of peaches, apricots, and honey.

Viognier
[vee-oh-NYAY]

Growing Areas
> With limted acreage planted worldwide, Viognier is the primary grape of France's Rhone Valley and is also grown in the United States, Australia, and South America. Low yields and high susceptibility to vineyard diseases make Viognier wines difficult to find and relatively expensive.

Varietal/Blend
> Mainly produced as a varietal, but used as a blend in the United States with Chenin Blanc and Chardonnay. Sometimes used as a blend to add fragrance and soften Syrah.

Vinification
> Stainless steel fermentation, dry, rarely oaked. Dry wines with strong aromatics produce a soft, rich, and luscious style.

Flavor
> Produces rich floral aromatics with flavor hints of apricots, peaches, and pears.

Chenin Blanc
[SHEN-ihn BLAH*N*GK]

Growing Areas
> Native to the Loire Valley of France and widely grown in South Africa and the United States with some production also in Chile, Australia, and New Zealand.

(continued)

Exhibit 3   *(continued)*

Varietal/Blend
Used as a varietal and often blended with Chardonnay and Sauvignon Blanc. In South Africa, used for fortified wines.

Vinification
Varied depending on desired style—bone dry, semi-sweet, sweet, or sparkling. One of the most versatile of all wine grape varieties. Depending on the wine-making technique, Chenin Blanc is produced as crisp, dry table wines, light sparkling wines, dessert wines, and brandy. Usually stainless steel fermentation and unoaked.

Flavor
Often sweet and sour at the same time: floral and citrus aromas with apple and pear flavors.

Source: Lendal H. Kotschevar and Ronald F. Cichy, *Managing Beverage Service* (Lansing, Mich.: Educational Institute of the American Hotel & Lodging Association, 2004), pp. 228–230.

In the United States, the strength of alcohol is measured in terms of **proof.** The percentage of alcohol in a beverage is one-half the beverage's proof. For example, a 100-proof beverage contains 50 percent alcohol. Most liquors range between 80 and 86.9 proof, except for gin, which ranges from 90 to 94.6 proof. Not all brands of the same liquor have the same percentage of alcohol. For example, vodka may range from 80 proof to 100 proof, and some rum is 151 proof. United States law requires that all spirit labels state proof and that imported spirits be labeled in U.S. proof.

Distilled spirits are liquors obtained from the process of distillation. Distilled spirits include whiskeys, vodka, gin, rum, tequila, brandy, and others, or any dilution or mixtures of these, used for human consumption. Distilled spirits do not include mixtures that are half or more wine, such as wines fortified with brandy like sherry or dessert wines. Spirits are generally classified into five main groups:

*   Grain spirits
*   Plant liquors
*   Fruit liquors
*   Liqueurs
*   Bitters

Spirits made from grains include whiskey, vodka, and gin. Continuous-still products made from grain are called **grain neutral spirits.** Tasteless and colorless, they can be used to make vodka or flavored spirits such as liqueurs and types of gin. They are also used for blending. If a similar spirit is made from a non-grain mash, it must be labeled as a neutral spirit—the word "grain" cannot be used. Many plant liquors are produced around the world. However, most are consumed only locally or nationally and, even though they may be consumed by millions (as are Chinese distilled spirits made from sorghum or rice), they are not prominent worldwide. Rum and tequila are the only plant liquors to have attained this status. Brandies are the most important fruit liquors. **Liqueurs**, or cordials, are made from a base of grain, plant, or fruit spirits or their combination. Aromatic or fruit bitters are highly flavored spirits containing bitter substances such as quinine.

Measures and Storage

The metric system is now generally in use for the purchase of spirits and wine, but most properties still measure in the familiar ounce system. Distributors can usually provide conversion tables upon request.

Many types of automated dispensing devices are available to control the alcohol content (portion size) of prepared drinks. Using measured shots and interfacing automatic drink-preparation equipment with cash registers can help control beverage costs and track bar income. Use of these devices enables the operator to purchase in larger containers, which provides a savings in packaging costs.

Storeroom managers, who often act as purchasers, should establish storeroom par levels, maintain perpetual and physical inventories, and keep supporting records for liquor products. Sales should form the basis of par levels, to be exceeded only with proper authorization. If purchases exceed par levels but are warranted by discounts, documents should note the reason for excess purchase size and the length of time the supply should last.

Like other beverage products, liquor should be stored at the proper temperature—60° F (16° C) is ideal. Temperature extremes must be avoided. Inventory dollar levels and turnover standards for the storeroom must be set. These vary according to the purchasing policy, but they should be pre-established and regularly measured.

For example, some companies use a one-week inventory as standard, providing 52 turns per year; stated another way, the cost of liquor in storage, on the average, equals approximately one week's beverage cost.

Market Types

Liquor is identified by either "call" or "house" brands. **Call brands** (also known as "pour" brands) are those used when a guest requests a specific label such as Johnny Walker Black Label with soda or Canadian Club with water. When a guest orders "scotch and soda" or "whiskey and water" without requesting a specific brand, the establishment can supply any brand. Historically, **house brands** (also known as "well" brands) have been non-promoted labels purchased at lower cost than the call products. There may not be a difference in product quality, but the call brand costs more and receives greater recognition and status because of advertising and other distiller promotions. Acceptable, unadvertised brands can be used for guests without a brand preference. This is the operator's decision and it should be based upon quality, value, and guest satisfaction.

Spirits may be grouped according to the quality of the brand name. House or well brands are used when a guest does not ask for a specific alcohol brand. For example, if a customer orders a rum and cola, the bartender would use the well brand or use upselling and ask whether the guest prefers Bacardi or another premium rum. Well brands are the first quality level, with the lowest prices, minimal packaging and processing, and average-quality ingredients. Call brands are used when a customer specifies a brand by name, such as a Bacardi and cola. Call brands are usually of higher quality and price than well brands. **Premium brands** have the best taste, packaging, and ingredients. They are usually the highest priced of all brands. The establishment may have several levels of premium brands, including super premium, select premium, and the top level—ultra premium.

The trend today is toward greater use of recognized brands as a means of communicating quality to the customer. The cost differential is a cost-effective part of the marketing plan for many operators, who provide products of recognized labels at the bar in much the same manner that they supply condiments with familiar labels at the dining table.

Gin. Gin is a compounded spirit. There are basically two kinds of gin: dry and heavy. Dry gin is light in flavor and body. The term "dry" indicates a light, somewhat delicate spirit that mixes well with other substances. Dry gins are often labeled "dry," "extra dry," or "very dry," although there is no real variation among dry gins. Heavy gins are high in flavor and body and carry with them a slight suggestion of malt.

There are several sweet, flavored gins, including mint, orange, lime, or lemon gin. Old Tom is a sweet English gin. Sloe gin is not actually a gin—it is a heavy pink to reddish colored liqueur flavored with sloe berries.

Popular brands of gin include Beefeater, Bombay, Bombay Sapphire, Gilbey's, Gordon's, Schenley, Seagram's Extra Dry, Tanqueray, and Tanqueray 10. Popular drinks made with gin are Gibson, Gimlet, Gin Fizz, Gin and Tonic, Martini, Singapore Sling, and Tom Collins.

Vodka. Vodka is a neutral spirit that is distilled or treated after distillation (with charcoal and other materials) so as to be without distinctive character, aroma, taste, or color. Because it lacks flavor and has a soft, mellow character, it mixes better than any other alcohol product. The quality of a vodka depends upon the quality of the grain neutral spirit used to make it. Vodka is distilled at 190 proof. Water is then added and the spirit is bottled at between 80 and 110 proof.

Flavorings play an important role in vodka's popularity. Absolut, a Swedish brand, produces vodka with flavors such as citrus (Absolut Citron), jalapeno (Absolut Peppar), and black currant berries (Absolut Kurrant). Many new drinks call for specific flavors of vodka. Several sweetened vodkas are on the market, often flavored with orange, lemon, mint, grape, or other ingredients. These products are usually bottled at 70 proof.

Popular brands of vodka include Absolut, Belvedere, Finlandia, Grey Goose, Smirnoff, Stolichnaya, and Tanqueray Sterling. Popular drinks made with vodka are Black Russian, Bloody Mary, Cape Codder, Greyhound, Martini, Salty Dog, Screwdriver, Sea Breeze, and Vodka and Tonic.

Rum. Fermentation and distillation of molasses produces **rum**. Most rums are blends, ranging in body and flavor from heavy and pungent to slight and brandy-like, and in color from light to dark. Blending produces a rum distinctive in aroma, taste, body, and color. Rum is usually bottled at 80, 86, or 151 proof. Labels must indicate a rum's area of origin.

There are two basic kinds of rums, light-bodied and heavy-bodied, although there are many variations among them. Light rum (also known as silver or dry rum) is most popular in the United States. Light rums usually bear a white or silver label. They are mild and slightly sweet in flavor. Most light rums are aged for one year. Most light rums come from Puerto Rico. Cuba, the Dominican Republic, Haiti, Venezuela, Mexico, Hawaii, and the Philippines also produce light rum. Heavy-bodied, more pungent rums are produced in Jamaica, New England, and Guyana (Demerara, Trinidad, and Barbados). These rums have a heavy bouquet resulting from their basic ingredient: the rich skimmings from sugar boilers. Much of this rum is often sent to England and other countries for aging and consumption. The label and product are nearly as dark as molasses.

Popular brands of rum include Bacardi, Captain Morgan, Castillo, Myers, and Mt. Gay. Popular drinks made with run are Bahama Mama, Cuba Libre, Electric Lemonade, Hurricane, Long Beach Tea, Long Island Iced Tea, Mai Tai, Piña Colada, and Strawberry Daiquiri.

Brandy. Brandy is the primary liquor made from fruit. The word brandy (short for brandywine) comes from the Dutch word brandewijn meaning "burnt wine," referring to the fact that the wine was distilled with heat. Any distilled spirit made from fruit or fruit derivatives qualifies as a brandy. However, only a spirit distilled from grapes can be called just "brandy." If distilled from other fruit, the type of fruit must precede the word "brandy" ("pear brandy," for example). Cognac and Armagnac are famous brandies from France.

The character of a brandy is influenced by the kind of grapes it is made from, the climate and soil they are cultivated in, cultivation and harvesting methods, fermentation and distillation processes, aging, and blending. Each factor is important and all have an effect on the type and quality of a brandy.

Some brandy producers use special words or letters on labels to indicate quality and other product characteristics. In general, "E" means especial, "F" means fine, "V" means very, "O" means old, "S" means superior, "P" means pale, "X" means extra, and "C" means cognac. However, such designations are not used uniformly, so buyers need to learn producers' or districts' specific codes to understand their labels. For example, at one time the number of stars indicated quality, but some very poor brandies today carry three or four stars. Armagnacs and cognacs are generally labeled as shown in Exhibit 4. Popular brands of Cognac include Courvoisier, Hennessey, Martell, and Remy Martin. Popular brands of Armagnac include DeMontal, Janneau, Larressingle, and Sempe.

Tequila. Only Mexico produces **tequila**, a distinctive liquor distilled from the fermented juice of the blue variety of the agave plant (tequilon weber cactus). According to Mexican government regulations, the product may be called tequila only if it is produced in a designated region surrounding the town of Tequila in Jalisco, Mexico. The Mexican government regulates the making of tequila. A tequila label bears the letters DGN if the product conforms to these regulations.

When tequila is aged, it develops a gold color. White tequila is a new product shipped without aging; silver tequila is aged up to three years; gold tequila is aged in oak casks for two to four years and may carry the name *muy añejo* (very old). Some tequilas may be artificially colored, so buyers must know what they are buying. Some tequilas are aged quite long and are expensive. Popular brands of tequila include Don Julio, Herradura, Jose Cuervo, Patron, and Sauza. Popular

Exhibit 4   Labeling of Armagnac and Cognac

Armagnac:	
VO, VSOP, or Reserve	The youngest brandy in the blend is no less than 4¹/₂ years old.
XO, Reserve, Vielle Reserve, Extra, or Napoleon	The youngest brandy in the blend is no less than 5¹/₂ years old.
Vintage	Indicates the year distilled (not the year the grapes were grown). The product is not blended with brandies distilled in other years.
Cognac:	
VS or three stars	Average aging period of the brandies in the blend is less than 4¹/₂ years.
VSOP, VO, or Reserve	Average age of the blend ingredients is 12 to 20 years; the youngest brandy used is no less than 4¹/₂ years old.
Napoleon, VVSOP, XO, Cordon Bleu, Vielle Reserve, Royal, Vieux, or Grand Reserve	Most of the blend is aged 20 to 40 or more years and the youngest is at least 5¹/₂ years old.
Grande Fine Champagne or Grande Champagne	Made only from grapes grown in the Grande Champagne area.
Petite Champagne or Petite Fine Champagne	At least 50% of the grapes came from the Grande Champagne area with the remainder grown in the Petite Champagne area.
Vintage	None permitted.

Source: Lendal H. Kotschevar and Ronald F. Cichy, *Managing Beverage Service* (Lansing, Mich.: Educational Institute of the American Hotel & Lodging Association, 2004), p. 192.

drinks made with tequila are Brave Bull, Mexican Coffee, Margarita, Tequila Sunrise, and Tequila Sunset.

Whiskey. Whiskeys are grain spirits and vary depending on the source of grain, type of fermentation, distillation method, and processing after distillation. The sections that follow focus on the major whiskeys—Scotch, Irish, American, and Canadian. By convention, Scotch and Canadian varieties are whisky (no "e"), while others are whiskey.

Scotch whisky. While commonly referred to simply as "scotch," this product is actually a type of whisky. The U.S. government defines **scotch** as a distinctive spirit from Scotland manufactured in compliance with British laws. If the spirit is a mixture of Scotch whiskies; it must be labeled "Blended Scotch Whisky" or "Scotch—a blend;" unblended malt scotch is labeled "Single Malt Scotch Whisky." U.S. imports must be at least 80 proof (scotch is bottled at 80 to 115 proof).

Popular brands of single malt scotch include Glenfiddich, Glenlivet, Laphroaig, and Macallan. Popular blends include Chivas Regal, Dewar's, J&B, and Johnnie Walker. Popular drinks made with scotch include Rob Roy, Rusty Nail, scotch and soda, and scotch sour. Other drinks made with scotch can be found by visiting many of the Internet sites listed at the end of this chapter. It is essential that the individual purchasing these products know their guests' preferences, so the correct products can be available when ordered.

Irish whiskey. The Irish produce whiskey much the same as the Scots do. There are, however, some differences. The Irish use sprouted barley and other cereals to make wort (the liquid that results from fermentation), and the sprouts are dried in closed kilns, thus avoiding the smoky taste characteristic of scotch whisky. Also, **Irish whiskey** is pot-distilled three times, creating a final spirit that is light and delicate in character. Only the middle distillate is retained, producing a liquor that is very smooth and mellow. The mandatory aging time is three years, but the usual period is five to eight years in old sherry casks. Irish whiskeys are often blended to make them lighter. Blends are labeled "Irish Whiskey—a Blend" or "Blended Irish Whiskey." Popular brands include Bushmill's and Jameson. Popular drinks made with Irish Whiskey are: Irish Coffee, Tipperary, and Nutty Irishman (made with Bailey's Irish Cream, which is a combination of Irish whiskey, cream, and chocolate).

American whiskeys. The United States produces three different kinds of whiskey in addition to whiskey blends: bourbon, rye whiskey, and corn whiskey. Bourbon is by far the most extensively produced.

Bourbon is named for Bourbon County, Kentucky, where it originated. **Tennessee Whiskey** is a unique type of bourbon invented by the Jack Daniels' distillery. To carry the name "Tennessee Whiskey," the product must be distilled in Tennessee. Sour mash is a spirit made from a regular sweet mash brew mixed with some soured old mash brew in a ratio of about two regular to one sour. Federal regulations require that a whiskey labeled "sour mash" have at least one part sour to three parts regular mash. The sour mash gives a heavier body and finer flavor to the bourbon, lending it a bit of sweetness and delicacy. Most bourbons are sour mash, although their labels may not indicate it.

Bourbon has a rich body and the full, distinctive flavor of corn. Most of its color develops during aging, although color may be added. Bourbon is bottled as bottled-in-bond straight, a blend of straights, or a blend of straight bourbon and grain neutral spirits. "Straight" indicates an unblended whiskey of one distillation. Blends must be 20 percent or more straight whiskey. Bottled bourbon has an alcohol content of between 80 and 110 proof.

Popular brands include Early Times, Jack Daniels, Jim Beam, Old Crow, and Wild Turkey. Drinks made with bourbon are Bourbon Soda, Bourbon Sour, Old Fashioned, Manhattan, Mint Julep, Whiskey Collins, and Whiskey Sour.

Rye whiskey must be made from 51 percent or more rye grain. Like other American whiskeys, it must not come off distillation at more than 160 proof. Rye whiskey is produced by continuous distillation. It is usually bottled and sold at 80 to 110 proof, although some ryes are higher in alcohol content. Rye must be aged at least two years in new charred oak casks. Pennsylvania and Maryland produce the most rye whiskey.

A whiskey bearing the name "corn" must be made from a mash containing at least 80 percent corn. It is distilled by the continuous method. It need not be aged in charred oak casks and therefore may lack color. **Corn whiskey** must go into the aging cask (oak) at 125 proof or higher. Its flavor is definitely that of corn, and the body is light.

Canadian whisky is lighter in body and more delicate in flavor than American bourbon. Corn is the primary grain, usually mixed with additional fermentable products such as rye and barley malt. The Canadian government allows distillates to come off at 150 to 185 proof, resulting in a spirit light in flavor and body. Canadian whisky is aged primarily in old oak barrels, which help to produce a delicately flavored product. The normal aging time is six years. Canadian whiskies are blends of whisky and grain neutral spirits, modifying the flavor toward the lighter end. They are labeled "Blended Canadian Whisky" or "Canadian Whisky—A Blend." Popular brands include Canadian Club, Crown Royal, and Seagram's VO. Drinks made with Canadian whisky are Canadian Tea, Canadian Coffee, Crown Safari, and Royal Manhattan. More drinks made with Canadian whisky can be found by visiting some of the Internet sites listed at the end of this chapter.

Liqueurs, Aperitifs, and Bitters. Liqueurs, also known as cordials, are compounded spirits flavored in various ways. Liqueurs contain at least 2½ percent sugar usually added as syrup; most contain more syrup. The sugar content of a 2½ percent sugar liqueur is equivalent to about a half-teaspoon of sugar (eight calories) per two-ounce drink. Liqueurs are flavored with many different substances, including herbs, spices, fruits, mint, coffee, and licorice. The processing method, the quality of the flavorings, and the basic ingredients influence the final quality of each liqueur. Most liqueurs are made from grain-neutral spirits, but there are exceptions—bourbon is used for Southern Comfort, Scotch whisky for Drambuie, Irish whiskey for Irish Mist, and rum for Tia Maria. All liqueurs are usually aged so that the flavor, spirit, and flavorings can marry. Liqueurs are often used as after-dinner drinks. Some (such as Triple Sec) are used as flavoring ingredients for mixed drinks. Exhibit 5 lists many types of liqueurs. Note the variety of locales from which these products originate. Liqueurs listed without a country designation are generally produced by several countries and by multiple commercial distillers. Popular liqueurs include Amaretto, Baileys, Chambord, Cassis, Grand Marnier, Kahlua, Malibu, Peach Schnapps, Sloe Gin, Southern Comfort and Triple Sec. These more popular liqueurs are sorted by flavor in Exhibit 6.

Aperitifs are spirits consumed primarily as appetizers. They may also be mixed with other alcohol products. Many aperitifs, also called digestives, are flavored with ingredients that give them a bitter taste. Campari, an Italian liquor, is a well-known aperitif with a very sweet, bitter flavor. It is a rich red and lends a pleasing color to mixed drinks. Amer picon, a brandy, is a similar product produced in the Balkans; it is flavored with quinine, the same substance that gives tonic water its bitter flavor. When quinine was discovered to be a preventive against the malaria virus, it became a popular addition to many mixers, offering the option of enjoying a drink while taking your medicine. Amer picon also contains orange and is quite sweet. Fernet branca is another sweet, bitter spirit. It has a reputation of being a good remedy for hangovers. Some aperitifs, including vermouth, are fortified wines; dry vermouth is used in martinis and sweet vermouth in Manhattans. Vermouth is also consumed straight. The fortified wines of Dubonnet and Lillet are both used as mixers and served straight.

Exhibit 5   Types of Liqueurs

Amaretto—(Italy) Made from neutral alcohol, herbs, and apricot pulp kernels. Because the apricot is a relative of the almond, the seed imparts a distinctive almond taste.

Anisette—(Italy) Made from Anise, a dried, ripe fruit that has a definite licorice-like taste.

B&B—(France) Blended liqueur with half Benedictine and half brandy.

Campari—(France) Made from neutral spirits with added herbs, roots, and other aromatic ingredients.

Chartreuse—(France) Subtle blend of 130 different herbs; varieties include yellow and green.

Cassis—(France) Made from black currant berries grown near the Burgundy wine region of France.

Chambord—(France) Delicate and aromatic liqueur made from black raspberries; sweeter than Cassis.

Curacao—(Curacao) Made from the skins of small oranges; comes in red, blue, orange, or triple sec; colors are acquired with food coloring.

Cointreau—(Spain; West Indies) Brand name for one of the finest triple secs, an orange-flavored liqueur.

Crème de Banana—Bright yellow liqueur made by macerating ripe bananas in a pure spirit.

Crème de Cacao (White)—Colorless liqueur with the taste of chocolate; primary flavoring ingredient is the cocoa bean.

Crème de Cacao (Dark)—Dark liqueur that gets its color from percolation through cocoa beans.

Crème de Menthe (White)—Sweet liqueur derived from several varieties of mint, principally peppermint.

Crème de Menthe (Green)—Sweet mint-flavored liqueur made with green coloring.

Crème de Noyaux—Light liqueur that derives its flavor from fruit stones, resulting in an almond flavor.

Drambuie—(Scotland) Scotch-based liqueur with a variety of herbal ingredients; taste is tangy, heathery, and smooth.

Frangelico—(Italy) Hazelnut-based liqueur.

Galliano—(Italy) Honey-sweet liqueur that is bright yellow and packaged in a tall, tapered bottle; named after a military hero.

Grand Marnier—(France) Orange-flavored liqueur with Cognac as its base; blends bitter Haitian oranges with fine French Cognac.

Irish Mist—(Ireland) Blend of honey, herbal ingredients, and Irish whiskey.

Jagermeister—(Germany) Said to originally contain opium, this unusual tasting liqueur derives its flavor from herbs and roots.

Kahlua—(Mexico) Distinctly heavy and sweet; derived from Mexican coffee beans.

Licor 43—(Spain) Made in Spain from 43 different fruits; has a distinctive vanilla taste.

(continued)

Exhibit 5 *(continued)*

Malibu—(Canada) Rum-based spirit with coconut as its flavoring base.

Midori—(Japan) Bright-green melon liqueur with honeydew melons providing the primary flavor.

Peach Schnapps—Peach-flavored liqueur with peach kernel extracts added for a fuller flavor.

Peppermint Schnapps—Clear, pleasant liqueur with the light taste of candy canes; usually less sweet than crème de menthe.

Pernod—(France) Anise-flavored (licorice) liqueur that contains herbs, anise, parsley, coriander, and chamomile.

Sambuca—(Italy) Licorice-flavored liqueur deriving its taste from the fruit of the elder bush; a cousin to anisette.

Sloe Gin—Sweet-flavored and tinted with sloe berries, the fruits of the blackthorn tree; sugar is also added.

Southern Comfort—(America) Peach liqueur with Bourbon added; aged in oak barrels.

Strega—(Italy) Italina coffee liqueur with more than 70 herbs.

Tia Maria—(Jamica) Rum-based beverage flavored with Jamaican Blue Mountain coffee extracts; also has a delicate hint of chocolate flavor; somewhat like Kahlua, but drier and lighter.

Triple Sec—(Curacao) White, dry, orange-flavored liqueur with a distinctive three-stage production process; "Sec" means "dry" in French.

Tuaca—(Italy) Vanilla- and butterscotch-flavored liqueur.

Yukon Jack—(Canada) Close imitator of Southern Comfort; strong, sweetened whiskey with herbs added for flavoring.

Source: Lendal H. Kotschevar and Ronald F. Cichy, *Managing Beverage Service* (Lansing, Mich.: Educational Institute of the American Hotel & Lodging Association, 2004), p. 193.

Bitters are used only as flavoring ingredients; in many recipes, a dash or two produces just the right flavor. Bitters are usually made from roots, spices, bark, berries, fruit, or herbs steeped in or distilled with a neutral spirit. Bitters have a highly flavorful, aromatic, bitter taste. Some of the better known brands include Angostura, made in Trinidad from a very old secret formula; Abbot's Aged Bitters, made by the same family for years in Baltimore; Peychaud's Bitters, made in New Orleans; and Orange Bitters, made in England from the dried peel of bitter Seville oranges.

Judging the Quality of Spirits

Every type of spirit has its own distinguishing characteristics, and within types there are differences that clearly separate products. For example, some rums are light and delicate while others are heavy and robust. These differences are the reasons for consumer preferences. Some people like the smoky flavor of scotch; others

Exhibit 6   Popular Liqueurs Sorted by Flavor

Orange
        Curacao, Cointreau, Grand Marnier, Triple Sec

Peach
        Peach Schnapps, Southern Comfort

Chocolate/Cocoa Beans
        Baileys, Crème de Cacao (white), Crème de Cacao (dark)

Coffee
        Kahlua, Strega, Tia Maria

Mint/Peppermint
        Crème de Menthe (white), Crème de Menthe (green), Peppermint Schnapps

Almond
        Amaretto (also apricot), Crème de Noyaux

Licorice
        Anisette, Sambuca, Pernod

Berries
        Cassis, Chambord

Honey
        Galliano, Irish Mist

Source: Lendal H. Kotschevar and Ronald F. Cichy, *Managing Beverage Service* (Lansing, Mich.: Educational Institute of the American Hotel & Lodging Association, 2004), p. 195.

prefer vodka. Scotch drinkers may have a preference for one brand over another. Even vodka drinkers can be staunch advocates of one brand, although vodka is supposed to be colorless, odorless, and tasteless.

Evaluating spirit quality is not easy. Spirits are perhaps the most difficult to judge of all alcoholic beverages. A good judge must be able not only to identify the elusive factors that make up quality, but to remember these factors and compare them to a standard.

A glass used to judge spirits should be straight or have slightly outwardly sloping sides. Only a finger's depth of room-temperature spirit is poured into it.

While an expert judge may be able to taste as many as 400 spirits in a day, the average person should not try to taste more than four or five. An expert judge never swallows the spirit. Pure, tasteless, room-temperature water is used often to cleanse the palate. It can be non-sparkling spring water. Some judges also eat a low-salt or no-salt cracker to remove former flavors. Others say they should not be used. Items that have a flavor carryover should not be used to cleanse the palate.

Beer

Beer is one of the most popular alcoholic beverages consumed in bars, lounges, restaurants, hotels, and resorts around the world. It is also considered to be the oldest alcoholic beverage. About 13,000 years ago, Mesopotamians and Sumerians recorded on clay tablets a beer-making process. Beer is an alcoholic beverage obtained through the fermentation of grains. Modern beer is carbonated and flavored with hops. Today, there are many styles and numerous brands of beer, each made with a unique blend of basic ingredients and with brewing techniques that enhance the fundamental beer-making process.

Beer Terminology

Beer is a beverage made from fermented grain. It has the lowest alcohol content, the highest food value (i.e., the most calories other than from alcohol), and the shortest life span of the three types of alcoholic beverages. There are two classes of beer: ale, which is top-fermented at warmer temperatures and not aged, and lager, which is bottom-fermented and aged at colder temperatures.

Other beer terms that those who purchase beers need to know are:

- **Draft beer**—Beer drawn from a keg or a cask to a glass.
- **Dry beer**—Beer that is less sweet, with little or no aftertaste.
- **Light beer**—Beer with one-third to one-half fewer calories than regular beer.
- **Non-alcoholic beer**—Beer with few calories and less than 0.5 percent alcohol. The fermentation process is stopped before alcohol forms or the alcohol is removed after brewing.
- **Head**—The foam that forms at the top of a glass when beer is poured. The ideal head on a beer should be one-half to one inch thick.
- **Keg**—An aluminum or wooden container for storing beer.
- **Tap**—A faucet used to pour beer from a keg, or the process used to set up a beer keg for service.

There are many different categories of beer including light, premium, popular, super premium, and imports. Operations that purchase specialty beers must make sure that the purchasing personnel know the style, origin, and unique characteristics of each beer. Beer distributors are a good source of this information.

Classes

Quality in beer is determined largely by the quality of the components used in making it. The four basic ingredients from which most beer is made are water, malt, hops, and yeast. Each ingredient contributes to the beer-making process and to the overall flavor and appearance of the beer. The brewing process also has a major influence on the finished product. Beers with typical (bottom) fermentation can be classified into several groupings, including:

- Lager—Lager beer accounts for the majority of malt beverage production in the United States. Lager beers are light-bodied.
- Bock—This is a heavy, dark-colored beer, sweeter and richer in flavor than lager. Traditionally prepared to herald the arrival of spring, true bock beer is only available for about six weeks of the year.

- Dark beer—This beer is made from malt toasted to a darker color than normal. It is often confused with bock beer, but it does not have the sweetness of true bock.

- Pilsner—This is a beer of the style of Pilsen, Czechoslovakia. Pilsner has a pronounced flavor of hops, a light body, and a light color.

- Bavarian—Bavarian is also light in body and color. Bavarian-type hops are used, which gives the beer its own distinctive characteristic.

Other beer types are classified as top-fermentation because the yeasts that ferment the basic mixture rise to the surface instead of remaining on the bottom. Beverages in this category include:

- Ale—Ale is characterized by its more pronounced hops flavor, which makes it more bitter than lager beer. Ales are much favored by the English and Canadians.

- Porter—This is similar to ale, but is heavier and darker, with a rich and heavy foam. In flavor, it is sweeter, tastes less like hops, and possesses a distinctive malt character. Very dark malt is used in the brewing.

- Stout—This brew is closest to porter, but even darker and heavier, with more of a hops flavor.

- Weiss—Weiss is brewed from wheat malt and further differentiated by a second fermentation in the package.

Most beer can be defined as either lager or ale. Around the world, lager is by far the most popular style beer. Lagers are of a German tradition and were brewed in the Alpine caves of Bavaria and other parts of Europe where cooler temperatures prevailed. Ale was traditionally brewed in the British Isles.

Exhibit 7 shows some of the many distinct styles of beer within the ale and lager families. Pilsner is one of the most popular lager styles. Modern brands of lager include Budweiser, Miller, Sam Adams, and Coors. Porter and stout are popular styles of ale. Modern brands of ale include Bass, Red Hook, Sierra Nevada, and Anchor Steam. In addition, there are an increasing number of microbrews produced by relatively small breweries. Styles of both ale and lager beer vary in relation to color (from light to dark) and in the amount of alcohol by volume. The difference between lagers and ales is created by the type of yeast used in the brewing process and by the temperature of the fermentation. Bottom-fermenting yeast produces lagers; top-fermenting yeast produces ales.

Alcohol Content

Throughout this chapter, the alcohol content of beer is discussed in terms of its percentage by volume. Alcohol by volume is a measure of the space the alcohol in a beer takes up as a percentage of total space. Alcohol by weight is also a measure of the amount of alcohol content. Here the measure is the amount of weight the alcohol in a beer has as a percentage of total weight.

Today's popular beers generally contain alcohol levels of 3 percent to 7 percent alcohol by volume. There are also several brands of non-alcoholic beer on the

Exhibit 7   Lager and Ale Families of Beer

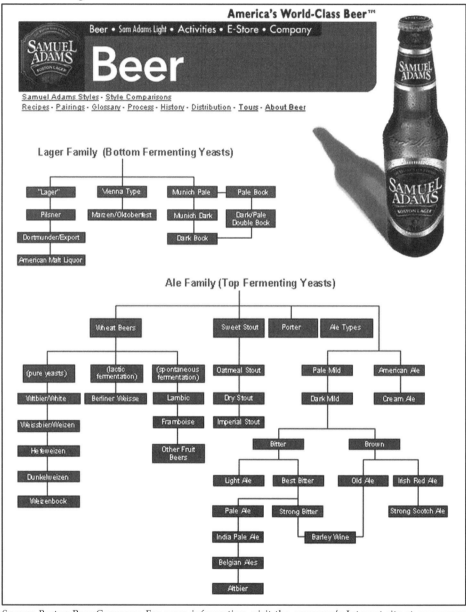

Source: Boston Beer Company. For more information, visit the company's Internet site at: www.sam adams.com.

market. Many people believe that these beers are called "non-alcoholic" because they do not contain alcohol. But actually, they do contain low levels of alcohol— usually 0.5 percent by weight, although the amount varies by brand.

Designations of "light" beer vary among countries. In the some countries, light beer is defined by a low amount of alcohol, usually between 2.6 percent and 4 percent alcohol by volume. In the United States, the number of calories defines a beer as "light." Light beers typically contain around 100 calories in a 12-ounce serving (compared to 135–170 calories for regular beer.) Light beer brewers use a special process to break down more sugars during fermentation, creating a beer with fewer calories but with alcohol content comparable to that of regular beer.

Ice beers contain 15–20 percent more alcohol by volume than traditionally brewed beers. Ice brewed beers are super-chilled before the final filtration at the end of the maturing stage. Lower than freezing temperatures can be used because of the high alcohol content of ice beer. Ice brewing clarifies the beer by removing unwanted proteins and also helps preserve freshness.

Packaging

Beer is a perishable product so it must be packaged and shipped to preserve its freshness Packaging beer in cans or in amber or brown bottles protects it from becoming light-struck. Overexposure to light gives beer a "skunky," sulphur-like aroma, destroying both the taste and aroma of the beer. Exposure to direct sunlight can affect the aroma of beer within minutes.

Beer that is to be canned or bottled is always pasteurized. **Pasteurization** heats the finished, filtered beer at 140° to 150° F (60° to 65.5° C) to kill bacteria that causes spoiling. The shelf life for most bottled and canned beer is between 110 and 120 days. All imported beers (bottled, canned, or kegged) must be pasteurized because of the lengthy time between shipping and service.

Domestic draft beer is not pasteurized, so it must be kept cool at all times. Storing temperatures for draft beer are 36° to 38° F (2° to 3° C). Higher temperatures may cause the beer to turn sour and become cloudy. Draft beer is packaged in metal kegs and sold directly to bars and restaurants. Full kegs hold 31 gallons, but half kegs are more popular.

Brewers mark their products with a freshness date, much like perishable food at a grocery store. This is helpful, but not all breweries use the same freshness labeling system. For example, some brewers use a born-on date. In this case, you may have to add 110 days to the date to determine if it is still fresh enough to serve. Other brewers use a standard expiration date, similar to most food products. Imported brands use a more complicated set of numbers known as the Julian Code, which is explained in Exhibit 8.

Keg beer is usually stored in a cooler located some distance from the tap where it is dispensed. Gas pressure (carbon dioxide) is applied to the top of the keg, forcing beer out a hose line at the bottom of the keg to the tap. Whenever the tap is opened, gas pressure drives beer out of the keg, through the hose line out the tap, and into a glass. The hook-up requires an assortment of connectors, hoses, taps, and fittings. Keg and tap systems are diagrammed in Exhibit 9.

The key to this system is setting the proper gas pressure. Too much or too little pressure can cause the beer to foam excessively at the tap. The proper amount of pressure varies with each keg hook-up. The diameter of the hose, the length of the line, the temperature of the beer, and the height of the tap are variables that determine

Exhibit 8   Julian Code

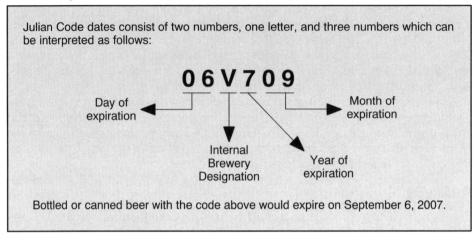

Source: Lendal H. Kotschevar and Ronald F. Cichy, *Managing Beverage Service* (Lansing, Mich.: Educational Institute of the American Hotel & Lodging Association, 2004), p. 157.

the proper amount of pressure to apply with a particular keg hook-up. Beer distributors service these systems when their products are purchased and sold. Distributor servicing of keg hook-ups involves cleaning the hoses and making sure the carbon dioxide pressure inside the line is appropriate. All keg hook-ups (single keg and multiple keg hook-ups) should be checked before the bar opens so that, if necessary, repair service can be called immediately.

Storage and Service

Some buyers make the mistake of assuming beer is a highly stable product. Quite the reverse is true—beer is a very perishable product. It is, in fact, a food product, being made from grains, yeasts, and hops, and should be treated as such. Finished and packaged beer leaving the brewery is at the peak of its flavor and aroma. It must be handled properly or it may deteriorate. Beer does not age after packaging, but it ages in lagering vats prior to packaging. Consequently, it must be kept fresh.

The sooner beer is served, the better its taste, so FIFO (first in, first out) stock rotation is very important. Cool storage temperatures are desired because a lower temperature prolongs the storage time. If beer is stored at too high a temperature, it can significantly reduce the time that the beer retains top quality. The storage temperature can range between 40° and 70° F (4° and 21° C). The storage area must be clean and dry. Dampness can cause carton damage and, in extreme cases, rust on bottle caps.

Light is an enemy of beer freshness. Light-struck beer has an undesirable taste and aroma. Storage rooms should not have natural sources of sunlight; electric lights should be turned off when not in use. Beer bottles are dark-colored for this reason. Canned beer is not subject to light damage, but sunlight can cause heat buildup which may also cause damage.

Exhibit 9   Keg and Tap Systems

Draft beer taps are connected to kegs that
are out of the view of guests. These connection lines can be quite long depending upon
the size of the bar.

Changing Out a Keg

As a bartender, you may need to change out a keg from time to time. Use these
instructions for practice.

ONE	**TWO**	**THREE**
Align lug locks on tavern head with lug housing in top of keg; insert tavern head.	Turn tavern head handle 1/4 turn clockwise; the tavern head is now secured to keg.	Rotate on/off valve handle 1/4 turn clockwise to open beer and CO_2 ports in keg. The keg is now tapped.

Multi-Keg Systems

Multi-keg draft systems are commonly used in high-volume service situations.
WIth several kegs attached to one line, interruptions in guest service are minimal.

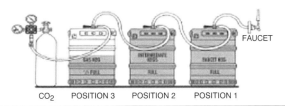

Source: Lendal H. Kotschevar and Ronald F. Cichy, *Managing Beverage Service* (Lansing, Mich.: Educational Institute of the American Hotel & Lodging Association, 2004), p. 158.

Because they are not pasteurized, draft beers are preferred by many consumers. Since they yield greater profits, they are also preferred by many operators. Modern kegs are easy to tap, and serving staff can be readily trained in the proper handling of the equipment. Whether serving canned, bottled, or draft beer, there are some fundamental procedures and rules to follow.

One fundamental condition that must be met is chilling to the proper temperature. Beer should be chilled to 36–38° F (2–3° C) before serving. Unpasteurized draft beer can spoil if held above 45° F (7° C). Canned or bottled beer will not spoil, but requires holding at that temperature in order to be served properly. Beer served too cold will be flat (the carbon dioxide is trapped) and perhaps cloudy. Beer served too warm will be "wild" and foam excessively.

Wine Fundamentals

Knowledge of wine is fundamental to beverage purchasing. Today's guests are more sophisticated and knowledgeable about wine than ever before, and they expect food service professionals to be knowledgeable as well. This chapter reviews various types of wines and describes the basic steps in making wine. **Viniculture,** the study or science of making wine, is a complex and intricate topic on which hundreds of books and thousands of articles have been written.

This section is an introduction to the major red and white grape varieties and describes the wines made from them. It also explores the often confusing language of taste and presents a practical wine-tasting vocabulary that buyers will find useful when purchasing wines.

Wine Terminology

Buyers must understand basic wine terminology. Some common terms applicable to wine purchasing are included here.

Vintages. Part of the wine mystique, **vintages** rate the quality and potential of the year's production. Historically, vintages primarily applied to France and Germany; however, wines from California and Italy now carry vintage information. Vintages had their origin in the past when quality varied substantially from year to year and region to region, depending on weather, processing procedures, and other factors.

Variations still occur but have been modified to some extent by modern production techniques. For the vast majority of wines sold, vintages have no application.

Varietals. This is a term often used in California that describes the primary grape variety in the bottle. Cabernet Sauvignon and Pinot Chardonnay are considered varietals. Some of this varietal production may carry vintage dates, which are the pride of the California vintners.

Generic. This is a term describing California wines merchandised as European types (Burgundy, Chablis, Chianti, and others). Some are quite good; lower grades are generally called "jug wines." A somewhat similar term in France is "vin ordinaire," which defines common (ordinary) wine, identified only as red, white, or rosé with no origin showed.

Exhibit 10   Wine Legs

A lot of myths have evolved about what the "legs," or more properly called "tears," observed in a glass of wine represent. They do not represent a wine's quality or its glycerol content. They represent a wine's alcohol content. The more alcohol, the more legs. However, wines would have to have about a five percent difference in alcohol level to notice a significant difference. Often the cleanliness of the glass can override this difference.

James Thompson, a British physicist, explained the formation of tears in 1855. His work was overlooked, however, and Marangoni, who published in 1871, is credited with the explanation, and tears are therefore called the Marangoni effect.

The forces involved in producing tears are:

- Surface Tension: The attractive forces between molecules of the liquid that hold the liquid together.

- Interfacial Tension: The attractive forces between molecules of the liquid and the molecules of a solid surface.

If the interfacial tension is greater than the surface tension, molecules of the liquid will adhere to the glass and continue to wet areas higher and higher on the surface until the weight of the clinging liquid equals the interfacial forces trying to lift more liquid. In a pure liquid, this action stops, a meniscus forms, and no tears develop.

Wine, however, is a mixture of alcohol and water. The alcohol evaporates faster and has a lower surface tension (about 1/3). As a film of wine climbs up the side of the glass, the alcohol evaporates faster from the film surface, increasing the water concentration and thereby the surface tension and the film is pushed higher.

This increased surface tension effect compensates by transferring more alcohol-laden wine to the rising film to lower the surface tension. More alcohol then evaporates and the water concentrated film is pushed ever higher until gravity takes over.

When gravity prohibits more wine from rising, the only way the liquid has to decrease its surface tension and energy state is by beading, whereby the surface water molecules are strongly pulled into the body of the water, aiming to achieve the lowest energy state, which is a spherical shape.

The beads grow until the forces of gravity are stronger than the interfacial forces holding the drop to the glass and it flows down the glass as tears.

Source: www.thewinemerchantinc.com/educational/LegsTears.html. Used with permission.

Blending. This practice involves combining different wines to achieve some purpose, usually to maintain consistency over time, but occasionally to utilize a product that otherwise might not be marketable. In California, most generics are blends.

Legs or Tears. Wine **legs** or tears represent a wine's alcohol content. The more alcohol present, the more legs or tears. Exhibit 10 has more detail on this characteristic of wine.

Types of Wine

Wine appreciation is an ancient art. Many guests may know a great deal about wine, while others are interested in learning more. Therefore, beverage purchasers need to know the basics of wines.

Wine is made from fermented grapes, other fruits, or flowers, and is usually classified according to color. Red wines have a purple color and are served at a cool room temperature. White wines have a pale color ranging from straw to gold and are served chilled. Blush wines (rosés) are pink and are served chilled. These three types of wine are also known as table wines. Generally speaking, cooler wines can mask imperfections while warmer wine allows for a better expression of any complex characteristics of an older or more expensive wine. Wine tends to warm at the rate of four degrees Fahrenheit or two degrees Celsius for every ten minutes left at room temperature, though the temperature of the room will affect this speed.

Many customers will want to know about the wines they order, so those who purchase beverages need to be familiar with the following terms that apply to wines:

- **Aging**—storing wines before bottling.

- **Aroma**—the odor of a young wine, usually fruity or flowery.

- **Bouquet**—the complex smell of a mature wine.

- **Body**—the feel and weight of a wine in the mouth.

- **Dry**—not sweet.

- **Vintage**—the year a wine's grapes were harvested and wine-making was begun.

- Aperitif wine—wine with spirits added and flavored with herbs and spices (vermouth, for example).

- Dessert wine—wine with spirits added, but with no herbs or spices. Port, sherry, and Madeira are dessert wines.

- Port—dessert wine that normally ages at least 20 years.

- Sparkling wine—wine containing carbon dioxide, which produces bubbles when the wine is poured. Champagne is a sparkling wine produced from grapes grown in Champagne, France.

- Still wine—wine with no carbon dioxide or bubbles.

- House wine—usually inexpensive wines the operation sells by the glass. They may be bought in large bottles, jugs, or plastic containers. Many restaurants limit their house wines to a Chablis, a Burgundy, and a rosé or blush wine.

While there are thousands of grape varieties, not all are used for making wine. In fact, there are only about 50 grape varieties that impart most of the flavor and taste to wines around the world. Wine is made from the juice of one variety of grape or from blending the juices of two or more varieties. A wine produced from a single grape variety is called a varietal wine. In some countries, such as France, a varietal wine must be made from 100 percent of the grape variety. In the United States, a wine may be identified as a varietal with only 75 percent of the grape variety actually used (with the choice of other grapes left to the winemaker). Examples of names of varietal wines are chardonnay, riesling, cabernet sauvignon, merlot, and pinot gris.

   The Internet sites listed at the end of this chapter provide more detailed information on these and on many more grape varieties and wines.

   Wine made from a blend of wines to resemble a particular wine of an established wine-producing region is called a generic wine. Many countries have treaty agreements that protect the names of important wine regions. Examples of names of generic wines are bordeaux, chablis, chianti, burgundy, beaujolais, and champagne. Blending is a common practice and generic wines are not necessarily inferior to varietals. In fact, a blended wine is often superior in taste to its components alone. French champagne is almost always a blend of grape varieties. Brand-name wines are usually blends that rely on the bottler's reputation for consistency, quality, price, and value. Mateus and Blue Nun are examples of brand-name wines.

   Basic wine classifications addressed in the sections that follow are:

- Table wines.

- Fortified wines.

- Aperitif and dessert wines.

- Sparkling wines.

Table Wines. Table wines make up the largest category of wine and, as the name suggests, include wines primarily suited to accompany food, but not limited to such purpose. Table wines are referred to as "still" wines. They are not bubbly. Although some table wines may be very slightly carbonated, the amount of carbon dioxide does not disqualify them as table wines. Most table wines are natural wines—the product of grape fermentation without the addition of alcohol or sugar (beyond a small amount allowed for certain wines under specified conditions). Natural fermentation stops when there is no more sugar to convert to alcohol or when the alcohol reaches a specified percentage by volume. In the United States, table wines may have an alcohol content no higher than 14 percent by volume.

   On a wine menu, table wines will be further classified by color as red, white, or rose. However, these colors are approximations: "reds" run from purple to slightly red-tinged brown to clear, light red; "whites" run from clear as water to green-tinged to varying shades of yellow through gold to light brown. Rosé wine is generally described by its rose color (light pink to light orange-red) and is made by leaving the skins of red grapes in the fermentation process for a short period, then removing them. Its taste characteristics (which vary widely), however, are more to the point. Color is an important distinction when wine with the same name comes in both red and white. A Graves is a famous white wine from the Bordeaux district in France; there is a red Graves, however, which is a fine wine but is neither well-known nor particularly important.

Fortified Wines. Fortified wines may range in alcohol content from 14 percent to 24 percent by volume. Alcohol—usually in the form of a brandy distilled from wine—is added to a wine during fermentation. Adding alcohol produces two results: the extra alcohol brings the alcohol content beyond what is naturally possible and the unfermented sugar stays in the wine to produce a sweet wine. Some fortified wines (such as sherry) allow for complete fermentation of the sugar, with the brandy (and often a sweetener) added after fermentation. Port, madeira, and vermouth are other examples of fortified wines.

Aperitif and Dessert Wines. Aperitif wines (from the French, aperitif, meaning "appetizer") are wines that are traditionally served before meals as an appetizer or cocktail. They are often fortified and herb-flavored (vermouth, for instance, is both fortified and flavored with herbal ingredients). Dry sherries are often included in this category.

Dessert wines, as the name implies, are meant to be served after dinner with dessert or *as* dessert. Dessert wines are often fortified—the sweet varieties of sherry (Cream and Oloroso, primarily) and port are examples. Madeira is another. Natural wines, such as some varieties of sauternes and many German wines classified as *Beerenauslese* or *Trochenbeerenauslese*, are sweet wines that are often used as dessert wines.

Sparkling Wines. The alcohol content of sparkling wines is typically 13 percent to 14 percent by volume. Basically, any wine can be made into a sparkling wine by adding carbon dioxide gas under pressure. However, sparkling wines are usually made by re-fermentation. An already fermented wine is fermented a second time by the addition of a small bit of yeast and sugar in a tightly sealed container. The carbon dioxide gas resulting from the fermentation is trapped inside and forced into the wine because of the pressure developed. In the classic champagne method, the second fermentation takes place in the bottle in which it is sold—a laborious and exacting process that accounts for the high price of the best champagne. Less expensive methods include the transfer process (the wine is transferred through a filter to another bottle) and the Charmat process (or bulk process), in which the second fermentation takes place in a vat and the wine is later filtered and bottled under pressure.

The most famous of the sparkling wines is, of course, champagne. Champagne, by law, can come only from the Champagne district of France. American "champagne" must be identified as "American champagne," "California champagne," or "New York State champagne." The Italian word for "sparkling" is *spumante*, and the German word is *schaumwein* or *sekt*.

Wine Production

The grape, of course, is the essence of wine. Not only do wine grapes provide a multitudinous variety of wines, but every part of the grape can have an effect on taste. For example, tannins produce a dry, sometimes puckery, sensation in the mouth and back of the throat. These astringent substances are found in the seeds, skins, and stems of grapes, as well as in oak storage barrels (especially new oak barrels). Tannins are important in the production of good red wines, providing flavor, texture, and preservative qualities to the wine. Although grapes may appear to be in a range of either red-purples or green-yellows, wine grapes are commonly referred to as either red or black *(noir)* or as green or white *(blanc)*, depending on the color of their skins at ripeness.

After a wine is aged, it is possible for wine experts to make a final judgment as to what the quality of the wine will be. Up to this point all indications may point to a great or a good year, but it is only after the wine is aged that the experts make their final determination. In some years, the aged wines may be described as *ordinary*; in a slightly better year, the wine may be said to be *medium*; in a better year, described as *good*; if still better, the wine is described as *great*, and the

Beverages **429**

Exhibit 11 Comparison of Vintages for the Wine-Growing Regions of France

VINTAGE	Red Bordeaux	White Bordeaux	Red Burgundy	White Burgundy	Côtes du Rhône Growths	Alsace	Pouilly-Loire Sancerre	Anjou Touraine	Beaujolais	Champagne
★ EXCEPTIONAL VINTAGES: 1921, 1928, 1929, 1945 ★										
1947	★	••••	••••		★			★		
1949	★	••••	★		••••			••••		
1955	★	••••	••••	•••	••••			••••		
1959	••••	••••	★	•••	•••	★		★		
1961	★	★	★	••••	••••	••••		•••		
1962	••••	••••	•••	•••	•••	••		•••		
1964	•••	••	••••	•••	•••	•••				
1966	••••	•••	••••	•••	••••	••••				
1967	•••	★	•••	•••	••••	••••				
1969	•	••	••••	••••	•••	•••		••••		
1970	★	•••	•••	★	★	•••		••••		
1971	••••	•••	••••	••••	••••	★		•••		
1973	•••	•••	••	••••		••••		••		
1974	••	•••	•••	•••		••		••		
1975	••••	••••	•	•••	••••	•••		•••		
1976	•••	••••	••••	••••	••••	★		••••		
1977	••	••	••	•••		••		••		
1978	••••	•••	★	••••	★	••		•••		
1979	••••	•••	•••	★	••••	••••		•••		
1980	••	••	•••	•••	•••	••	•••	••	•	
1981	••••	•••	••	•••	•••	••••	••	•••	•••	
1982	★	•••	•••	••••	••	•••	••••	•••	•••	
1983	••••	••••	••••	••••	•••	★	••••	••••	★	
1984	••	••	•••	•••	••	••	••••	•••	••	
1985	Abundant harvest of very fine quality									

Average vintage • Medium vintage •• Good vintage ••• Great vintage •••• Exceptional vintage ★

These appreciations are based on averages; the exception proves the rule.

Courtesy of Wines of France.

very best is said to be *exceptional*. Thus the vintage year shown on a label of such wines is important, because a buyer will have a basis for judging the quality and value of the wine without opening a bottle and tasting it. Vintage year indicates the year in which the wine was fermented. Exhibit 11 shows a vintage chart for wines of France. Note that the wine qualities do not stay the same in the same year between different areas. Thus, in 1982, the reds of Bordeaux were the only ones called "exceptional," while other areas obtained only a "medium" rating.

Taste Talk

To some people, the language of taste associated with wine is a confusing and seemingly endless list of highly subjective, ambiguous words sprinkled with occasional scientific-sounding terms, such as:

- Acidic.

- Balanced.

- Bouquet.

- Buttery.

- Chewy.

- Herbaceous.

- Oaky.

- Tannic.

The difficulty of describing the taste of wine arises from the deeper difficulty of language to communicate sensations. This more fundamental difficulty is compounded by the fact that our sense of taste is often dominated by our sense of smell. In fact, most of what we experience as taste is actually the result of our sense of smell. For proof, simply recall how your favorite foods tasted when you had a serious cold. The truth of the matter is that you will not taste what you cannot smell.

The tongue detects four primary flavors: sweet, sour, bitter, and salty. Every flavor experienced by taste in your mouth can be reduced to a combination of these four components. However, the nose knows no such limitation. You are capable of detecting thousands of scents. Putting these scents into words often feels cumbersome and inadequate to the actual sensation you experience. It is no wonder that taste talk seems, at times, forced and stilted—seemingly appropriate only for the secret society of wine connoisseurs. However, while taste is indeed personal and subjective, it can be communicated. A taste vocabulary has been developed to share sensations of flavors and aromas. The following sections address the look, smell, and taste of wine as well as how judges evaluate the taste of wines. These qualities are important to know when purchasing wines.

Look. The appearance of a wine is best viewed by looking at it against a plain, white background. Pour the wine into a clear wine glass until it is no more than one-third full and hold the glass by the stem. Holding the glass by the bowl will obstruct your full view of the wine and your fingerprints will dull and blur the color of the wine. Also, as wine connoisseurs know, the heat of your hand on the bowl will change the wine's temperature and affect your evaluation of its taste.

Tilt the glass to an approximately 45-degree angle. This enables you to look down on the wine and evaluate it in terms of clarity and color. The wine will have a deeper color in the middle of the glass than at the rim, but the clarity of the wine will stand out. When light passes through quality wines, they appear brilliant and sharp. **Clarity** is determined by the amount of matter you see floating in the wine and is usually a function of how much or how little the wine was refined during production. Both red and white wines should look clear and bright, never hazy or murky.

The color of a wine may be influenced by a number of factors such as the variety of grape from which the wine is made, growing conditions in the vineyard, wine-making techniques, aging, and maturing in the bottle. In general, white wines darken and red wines lighten with age. Young white wines may be nearly colorless or have a yellowish or greenish tinge to them. As they age, they become more typical with a yellow straw color and mature as gold or deep gold colors. White wines that appear as amber or brown are likely overly aged and poor tasting. Young red wines typically appear purple and age to rich red or ruby red. Red wines with mahogany or brown colors are likely past maturity and poor tasting. Young rosé wines are pink or pinkish red and mature to reddish orange. Amber colored rosé wines are likely poor tasting.

Swirling the wine in the glass will give you an indication of the wine's consistency or viscosity. Viscosity indicates levels of sugars and alcohol in wine and may range from thin and watery (low viscosity) to thick or syrupy (high viscosity). When swirled in a wine glass, wines with high viscosity tend to cling to the sides of the glass longer than those with low viscosity—developing "tears" or "legs" that drip back down the sides of the glass. Viscosity is a visual clue to the body of the wine, which is evaluated when experiencing the texture or weight of the wine in the mouth.

Smell. Swirl wine in the wine glass. This agitation releases the aromas. Close your eyes to concentrate on your sense of smell and smell deeply. You will find that wine does not always smell like grapes. In fact, the most common scents in wine are floral, fruity, spicy, vegetative, or wood odors. While the fruity aromas come from the grapes, the more complex fragrance, the bouquet of a wine, results from the fermentation process, aging techniques, and maturing time in the bottle. Hundreds of aromas have been identified and associated with wines. From smell alone, experts can identify not only the type of grape but also the wine-making methods used to produce a wine. The dominant grape used in a wine has distinct aroma and taste characteristics. For example, Pinot Noir typically smells of red fruits (cherries or strawberries), while Cabernet Sauvignon tends to have darker fruit aromas, like black cherries or plums.

Taste. While there are only four distinct flavors that the tongue is capable of tasting (sweet, sour, bitter, and salty), there are many taste sensations that you experience when tasting wine. Entire books have been written on tasting wine and on the factors contributing to the varied taste sensations. A basic, instructive, and easy-to-learn system for understanding the many aspects of wine tasting is offered by OregonWines.com. This organization identifies eight primary factors that contribute to taste sensations of wine:

- Sweetness—the amount of residual sugar in a wine, ranging from low (bone dry) to high (sweet).

- Acidity—the amount of citric, malic, and other acids in a wine, ranging from low (flat) to high (biting). A flat wine with too little acidity makes for a bland, uninspiring, flabby wine; too much acidity produces a predominant tart or sour flavor to the wine.

- Tannins—phenolic compounds, drawn from the skins and pips of grapes, which impart a sharp, bitter flavor to the wine. Signs of higher tannin content in a wine would be if the wine felt chalky or rough in your mouth or if the wine made your mouth pucker. A wine with too little tannin is said to be weak, with little structure. A wine with too much tannin produces a taste similar to over-steeped tea.

- Oak—the influence of compounds from oak barrels used to age the wine. Signs of oakiness would be if, when smelling the wine, you detected any aromas of vanilla, wood, or smoke and, if when tasting the wine, it imparted a buttery, rich flavor.

- Finish—the length and quality of a wine's aftertaste, ranging from brief to long.

- Complexity—how the wine's sweetness, acidity, tannins, and oak affect the wine's overall flavor, ranging from simple to complex.

- Body—how the wine's components affect the intensity and richness of the wine's overall flavor, ranging from weak to potent. Signs of a full-bodied wine would be a strong, potent, fully-developed flavor.

- Balance—how all the other factors balance out, ranging from unbalanced to well-balanced.

Judging Wine

The objective in judging a wine is to evaluate its quality, critical when purchasing wines. Judging wines relies on experience. As a buyer's experience in tasting wine grows, he or she learns to identify various aromatic and taste components of types of wines and to measure their value. The experienced judge knows how to identify the various sensations and to properly interpret their meaning. All judges should have specific standards by which they judge a specific wine. Each standard may have different elements appropriate to that wine. These elements are judged and their balance evaluated. If there are variations from the standard, these are recorded in the judge's evaluation and a final judgment obtained.

Usually, not more than six wines are judged at one time—more might result in tasting fatigue. Low-alcohol and the most delicate wines are selected for judging first. Water and low-salt crackers or bread are sometimes provided to cleanse the palate between judgments. The judging should be in a quiet and well-lighted room. Set a plain, white cloth on the table or surface to be used by the judge, so the wine can be viewed through the glass with the white cloth as backdrop. Use plain, clear, bell-shaped glasses with the top rim smaller than the bowl to help concentrate the bouquet as it rises from the wine. The opening of the glass should be large enough to allow the nose to get into the glass to smell the wine at close quarters. The glass should be large enough to adequately hold the wine and allow it to be swirled.

The amount of wine poured may vary. Some judges feel a small amount—an ounce or two—is enough, while others may desire more because they feel that they are better able to judge the depth of color and also have enough wine to build up a proper aroma in the glass. The wine should be served at a proper temperature.

When tasting the wine, judges will often suck it up with some aggressiveness so there is a spray that pervades the entire mouth. Before swallowing or spitting the wine out, most judges will draw a sharp intake of breath through the mouth over the surface of the wine. This important routine is practiced because the taste buds provide very limited sensations. The taste sensations combined simultaneously with the far more complex odors will offer a more precise record of wine's "taste." It is not necessary to take a lot of wine to obtain the proper taste sensations. A small amount is adequate. Many judges do not swallow; they spit the wine out after tasting. If the judge consumes some, he or she is doing so to get the throat sensations that can provide a clue to aftertaste.

Some wine experts describe tasting as first an attack, then an evolution or development, and finally a finish. Sweet sensations are evident in the attack, acid and salt in the evolution, and bitter in the finish. In tasting, the judge is looking for a balance between the sweet, the acidic, and the bitter components. If they are there in balance, along with proper odor, the wine is apt to be scored high. Variations from what the judge considers a desirable balance can downgrade the wine.

Non-Alcoholic Beverages

The remaining sections are devoted to the many non-alcoholic beverages that are required by food service operations. Coffee, tea, cocoa, and carbonated soft drinks are all very profitable items and, therefore, must be properly purchased and managed. Non-alcoholic beverages are generally formulated in the operation by special machines. Three factors usually affect quality: water (condition and temperature), ingredient formulas, and equipment condition.

Water is the major physical part of these drinks (approximately 97 percent in coffee and 85 percent in carbonated products). Cleanliness, sanitation, and temperature affect product quality. Water should be filtered to remove impurities. Many operators use activated carbon filters to remove chlorine and other chemicals. Soft water should be used, since hard water affects the flavor of beverages and impedes equipment performance with calcium buildup. Of the several types of water softeners, polyphosphate is one recommended choice for this purpose.

The proper ratio of beverage ingredient to water (or ice) must be maintained. Most coffee today is purchased in a prepackaged form to accommodate the quantity of water used. Carbonated drink formulas are usually metered automatically.

Coffee

Coffee is imported by the United States, since there is no domestic production of this product (with the minor exception of some Hawaiian coffee). Coffee supplies can be disrupted by weather (freezes), wars, and political upheaval. When these disruptions occur, they often cause dramatic price swings.

Background. Good quality coffee beans are a product of climate and cultivation. Better grades are grown 2,000 feet or more above sea level. Coffee plants need shade from the tropical sun, consistent amounts of moisture, and regular pruning. Picking must be done carefully to protect the unripe beans ("cherries") from damage and to exclude twigs or stones. Colombian coffees, since they meet quality concerns more closely, have long been considered the premium exportable coffee.

Varieties. The coffee bush or tree evolved in the Near East. Today, the Arabica variety forms the basis for the world coffee supply, having successfully adapted to other semi-tropical areas such as Brazil, Colombia, Venezuela, Mexico, and Central America. Two other independent varieties (Robusta and Liberacia) evolved in Africa. They are generally considered less desirable than the Arabica types, however. Each producing nation uses its own terminology to identify individual sub-varieties, which can confuse the coffee buyer. The discussion that follows applies to the primary exporting nations in South and Central America and Africa.

Buyers must understand some general terms:

- **Brazils**—coffees grown in the country of Brazil. They are named after the region in which they are grown or the port through which they are shipped. Santos coffees are shipped through the port of Santos.

- **Robusta**—coffees that largely come from Africa and are identified by country of origin (such as Uganda or Ivory Coast) or the district of growth.

- **Milds**—include all other varieties except Robustas and Brazils. Mild coffees are named after the country in which they are grown (e.g., Colombians, Mexicans, and Salvadors).

These terms are much misunderstood among both salespersons and consumers. Brazil, Robusta, and Mild do not describe flavor or quality. For example, a "mild" does not necessarily identify a coffee mild in flavor and lacking bitterness-it simply identifies the country of origin.

Quality and Blending. Two terms that do relate to quality are "rio" and "soft." Rio (river) identifies low-grown (river-grown) coffees which may be of the Arabica variety. Because of the climate in which they are grown, rios sometimes have a harsh flavor and lack other desirable quality factors. The term "soft" identifies fine-flavored coffees.

While these terms identify coffee characteristics, they do not guarantee good quality or even consistency. Coffee is a product of nature, so qualities vary from one growing season to the next. The length of time in storage also affects quality, since beans can lose moisture or develop mold. Blending beans from various sources is required to produce desirable coffee.

Commercial or nationally advertised brands are composed of several varieties of coffee. Blends may change annually or even more frequently depending upon the condition of the raw beans. An expert blender is needed to maintain a uniform blend flavor at all times even though the varieties composing the blend may undergo constant change. Coffees used in blends are selected for such characteristics as body, mellowness, sharpness, or filler (inexpensive coffee designed to reduce prices). "Body" is used to describe a brew that has a heavy flavor and aroma, while "thin" applies to a light, almost indistinct flavor and aroma. Sharpness is associated with acidity, which is typically a desirable characteristic in coffee.

Specifications. Roasting, grinding, and packaging specifications are important concerns. Each coffee has a definite character and purpose in the blend. Brazil is thin, sharp, and flavorful. Colombian has a fine coffee flavor and aroma, possessing both body and sharpness; it is mellow yet has noticeable, distinctive traits in comparison to the more bland Brazil. Centrals have much the same characteristics as Colombians, but are not as full-bodied. They are generally less expensive than Colombian and may be substituted for a cost savings. Robustas tend to have less flavor and aroma than American coffees; nonetheless, they do have high levels of soluble solids and are frequently used in vending and soluble coffee blends.

Grades. There is minimal regulation of coffee shipped into the United States. The New York Coffee and Sugar Exchange has established certain standards to qualify the "chops" (lots of 250 bags) for trading. The United States Food and Drug Administration (FDA) has responsibility for determining that the product is wholesome and is traded under its proper name. Grades have been established, but they relate only to allowable defects in the form of extraneous matter such as sticks, stones, and twigs:

Defects Allowed Within Grade	Grade
1–9	#1
10–21	#2
22–45	#3
46–90	#4
91–170	#5
171–348	#6
349–450	#7

For example, a specification calling for "Santos 3-4s" would have an average of approximately 45 defects per bag.

Roasting. Roasting develops flavor in the bean. It releases the volatile oils in the bean and caramelizes the carbohydrates. The type of roast used is determined by customer preference. It may be light, medium, heavy, or dark. Usually the roast length and temperature are timed electronically, but in some processing plants it is still done by appearance, with the roast compared to a standard sample for color. Many Americans prefer a light roast, while heavier roasts are more prevalent in other countries. The bean loses approximately 16 percent of its weight during roasting. When it reaches the proper color shade, the roast is "quenched" or "finished" by introducing water into the roast chamber to inhibit further cooking. The water vaporizes to steam and causes a more uniform color.

Grinding. Roasted whole beans may be purchased and ground at the property or operation. For practical purposes, however, it is generally best to have the coffee ground and packaged by the processor, whose equipment and procedures are better than those in most hospitality establishments. The specifications should state the grind requirements, which depend upon the type of urn to be used in making coffee.

Each grind contains particles of many sizes. Grinds differ only in the proportion of different particle sizes that they contain. These proportions are measured by shaking samples through a set of graded screens. Two screen sizes are used: 14 and 28 mesh (per inch). The percentages remaining on each screen and in the receptacle should be as follows:

	Regular	Drip	Fine
Remaining on:			
14 mesh screen	33%	7%	none
28 mesh screen	55%	73%	70%
Retained in receptacle:	12%	20%	30%

The finer grinds are used when coffee passes through the coffee bed once, while coarser grinds are used in recirculating urns. In either case, the grind should be uniform.

Brewing. High-yield or high-extraction coffee products are also available. These claim to yield 25 percent more brewed coffee per pound at a cost just slightly more than the regular product. A special roast and grind are used. Three basic methods may be used to make these types of products:

• Traditional system—A finer grind and a darker roast are used. The product is in traditional crystal form.

• Flake—Coffee crystals are flattened to increase the surface area exposed to the water and to increase extraction.

• Low density/fast roast—The traditional system is used, but the product volume is expanded by introducing water at a crucial point in the process.

How does a purchaser compare prices of high-yield coffees with regular coffee products? Coffee is traditionally brewed at approximately 50 cups per pound (2.5 ounces per 8-cup pot brewer). Suppose that by using a high-yield product, total output of brewed coffee is increased 25 percent. Assuming regular coffee at $10.00 per pound and high-yield coffee at $10.90, the cost comparison is as follows:

	Cost per lb.	Cups per lb.	Cost per cup
Regular	$10.00	50	$.20 ($10.00 ÷ 50)
High-Yield	$10.90	62.5*	$.17 ($10.90 ÷ 62.5)

*50 × 1.25 = 62.5 cups

In this example, better value is achieved by using the high-yield coffee. Of course, this assumes the products are of comparable quality.

Coffee Pricing. Large-volume coffee buyers can profit from a knowledge of market prices. As with other products, coffee prices can be estimated. Currently, the leading market service for coffee prices is Complete Coffee Coverage. Another force in the market is the International Coffee Organization (ICO), headquartered in London and engaged in quota assignments to producing nations and promotion to increase consumption. The following steps are suggested for buyers who want to obtain maximum value from coffee.

Determine a specification. If the volume used is large enough (2,000 to 3,000 pounds per week), some contract roasters are willing to experiment with buyers. Roasters agree to provide a specification that meets the buyers' needs, and sell on a contract basis. If this option is not selected, many commercial blends are available. Again, buyers should determine what best suits their needs and test one brand against another using sensory perception: smell first, look for bright sharp odor, sip the brew (black), and check for a flavor that is sharp and acidic, not burnt or bitter.

Establish a pricing system. There are two basic pricing systems. Buyers may use either a price list or a formula.

When using a roaster (or distributor) price list, buyers should realize that prices tend to change less frequently than the cost of raw coffee beans. It is best to have at least two distributors and to regularly take bids, awarding the business for a fixed period to the low bidder. If only one product is acceptable, the operator depends on the distributor to price fairly.

If a formula pricing system is selected, buyers should establish a spread between reported prices and quoted prices. A fairly sophisticated system was described previously for a large buyer. Smaller buyers can also use a variation of this system. *The Wall Street Journal* carries daily green (unroasted) coffee bean prices in the "Cash Price" section. The buyer can request that this spread be maintained by the distributor and that new prices be computed on the last Friday of each month for the following month's billing.

Control receiving and storage. Check incoming shipments for weight and quality. A sample from a previous shipment should be kept and compared to the quality of the new shipment. Always rotate stocks of coffee. Regardless of packaging, ground coffee should be consumed within two weeks of receipt. Use the FIFO system.

Manage the brewing process. Coffee should be brewed at 210° F (99° C) minimum and served at approximately 145° F (63° C). The urn and faucets should be clean. Coffee oils accumulate and become rancid, causing a bitter brew. The spray heads should be checked for proper water dispersal over the coffee bed. Water should be used at the recommended amount per pound of coffee and checked for condition; since hardness adversely effects quality, hard water should be treated with a softener.

Tea

Although tea is important in world commerce and ranks among the top ten internationally traded commodities, it is much less important than coffee as a beverage in the United States.

There are three types of tea:

- **Green**—The leaves have been withered, rolled, and fired immediately. These teas are primarily used by the Chinese and Japanese.

- **Black**—The leaves have been fermented or oxidized before firing. This class is of primary importance in world trade and is the product generally used in the

Exhibit 12 Tea Grade Designations

Term	Abbreviation	Description
Orange Pekoe	O.P.	Thin leaves; some tip leaf; pale liquor
Pekoe	P.E.K.	Shorter leaves; more liquor color
Souchong	S.O.V.	Flat, open leaf; pale liquor
Broken Orange Pekoe	B.O.P.	Broken grade; best quality; small leaves contain tip; liquor is strong; good color
Broken Pekoe	B.P.	Larger than B.O.P.; less color; used as filler
Broken Pekoe Souchong	B.P.S.	Larger than B.P.; less color; used as filler
Fannings	E.N.G.S.	Top grade for tea bag use; smaller than B.O.P.; good brew with good color
Dust	D	Smallest grade; quick brew; strong flavor; used in blends

United States. Major exporting sites are India, Ceylon, Pakistan, Indonesia, and Africa.

- **Oolong**—These leaves have been partially fermented and are used primarily in blending.

Development of tea bags and "instant" soluble tea (strictly American innovations) has led to some increase in consumption, but it still lags behind population increases. New specialty teas offer a wide range of flavors and are gaining acceptance.

Grades and Quality. There are two basic grades of tea within the classes mentioned—leaf and broken grades. The term "broken" does not denote lack of quality, but rather that the tea is smaller than leaf grades. Broken grades comprise the majority of the available supply, carry a higher price, and are generally preferred in the United States. Within the leaf and broken leaf grades, there are additional identifications such as Pekoe and Orange Pekoe.

Quality and flavor characteristics vary from one area to another depending upon growing conditions, moisture, cultivation, care in picking, and processing. It is necessary to blend various lots of tea to obtain a uniform, consistent brew. The major tea distributors in the United States have experts who buy from samples and perform this blending function. Some trade designations are explained in Exhibit 12.

Distribution. There are a few major companies in the United States that handle the bulk of tea distribution. Most of these companies import their own leaves and in some cases have buyers in the producing nations. The least expensive way to purchase tea is in 100-pound wooden crates. Blending, packing into bags, or converting to instant soluble tea all add to the price per pound. A buyer's decision regarding these alternatives must take into consideration the operation's volume and ability to brew.

Few companies in the United States have adequate volume to specify their own blend. Private labels are generally a standard acceptable blend, with the user company's tag. Sometimes, economic advantages can be gained by using private labels if the production costs are less. Generally, the processor passes any cost savings on to the buyer.

Pricing. Since tea is not a major U.S. product, pricing is difficult. The Wall Street Journal quotes prices on an irregular basis. Tea is quoted regularly on the London Exchange, but many American buyers do not have access to this information or are not in a position to use it. Buyers should perform taste tests and obtain competitive quotes. A broad range of prices exists because the spread between raw tea cost and tea bag price is wide. Tea is available pre-made in tanks, jugs, cans, and many other packaging. Another available form is soluble tea dispensed through machines. All of this convenience increases costs, and the buyer must determine cost per serving. Considering only product costs, the least expensive way to serve tea is to brew bulk tea at the operation.

Cocoa

Cocoa is a product of the cacao tree, which evolved in Central and South America. Of the many varieties of cacao trees, only two are commercially important. The criollo variety produces a "fine" or "flavor" cocoa. The foraserto variety yields a "base" or ordinary grade cocoa. Cacao trees flourish only in tropical climates. After harvest, the beans are dried, causing them to turn brown and lose nearly all of their moisture and about half their weight. Most cocoa imported into the United States is in this form.

The candy industry uses the majority of cocoa beans exported to the United States. Upon receipt in the United States, the processor cleans, blends, and roasts the beans; removes the shell; and leaves the meat. The meats are crushed, liquefying the cocoa butter (54 percent butter content) and forming a "chocolate liquor." In the manufacture of baking chocolate, this fat percentage is maintained. The manufacture of cocoa requires removal of some cocoa butter from the chocolate liquor.

There are generally accepted standards for the percentage of cocoa butter associated with common designations. Breakfast or high-fat cocoa should contain 22 percent cocoa fat. Cocoa or medium-fat cocoa should have 10–22 percent cocoa fat. Low-fat cocoa should be less than 10 percent cocoa fat. The cocoa butter removed during cocoa processing is later used to make milk chocolate and fudge topping.

The labeling of chocolate products is sometimes misleading, but, as a general rule, products labeled chocolate must be made from pure chocolate. A product made from cocoa may not be so labeled. For example, chocolate and cocoa are often used to flavor milk. When milk is flavored with chocolate, it may be labeled "chocolate milk." Milk or other dairy drinks made with cocoa should be labeled "chocolate flavored."

The cost of cocoa and chocolate products varies substantially depending on the amount of processing involved. There is no substitution for good specifications, healthy competition, and proper buying.

Soft Drinks

For hospitality operators, a major source of revenue is flavored **soft drinks**, both carbonated and non-carbonated. Colas dominate the flavored drink field.

Lemon-lime, orange, root beer, and ginger ale follow in popularity. Diet and decaffeinated products are very popular.

Historical Development. Carbonated drinks have their origins in naturally occurring springs of carbonated water. The Greeks and Romans believed that bathing in these waters was physically beneficial. By the late 1700s, carbonated water was being produced commercially.

The branded carbonated beverage business began in the United States with root beer. Charles Hires established his company in Philadelphia in 1876 and brand identification was born. In 1885 in Waco, Texas, a "Dr. Pepper," who was actually a pharmacist, introduced the drink that bears his name. Coca-Cola was first sold in Atlanta soda fountains in 1886 and, by 1899, the company began franchising, which formed the basis of its early growth. Pepsi-Cola began in New Bern, North Carolina. Another pharmacist developed its formula and the company began bottling operations in 1904.

The formulas for cola flavorings are closely guarded secrets and it is difficult to break down the components. Generally, these flavorings contain sweetener, caramel, acid, and extract from the cola nut. Cola trees are cultivated in Brazil, the West Indies, and west Africa. The nut is high in caffeine, smells like nutmeg, and looks like a horse chestnut.

Low-calorie drinks were introduced in 1952. At the end of the 1960s, Gatorade was marketed as the first product designed specifically to relieve thirst and restore energy by quickly replacing body liquids and salt lost as perspiration.

The use of concentrated syrups in food and beverage service operations grew from the original drug store soda fountains. Syrups were purchased by the gallon and combined with carbonated water. By the early 1950s, bottlers developed remote tank systems in conjunction with fountain equipment manufacturers.

Purchasing and Distribution. The carbonated beverage industry is dominated by several major companies. The hospitality purchaser can choose among three alternatives in setting carbonated beverage specifications: nationally branded and promoted products, regional or controlled-label products, and private-label products. The choice depends upon marketing philosophy. Most of the major hospitality chains serve nationally branded products because they believe that this is what the guest wants. The major retail chains offer both branded merchandise and their own private labels.

Syrups. Most food and beverage operations use concentrated syrup, which is reconstituted at one part syrup to at least five parts carbonated mix. Five-gallon containers are connected in tandem and directed to the fountain through a series of tubes, with carbonated water added at the fountain. Five-gallon premixed product is available from most bottlers. It is ready to use with carbonation and water added by the bottler, and is primarily used with mobile equipment.

Selection of syrup brand establishes the purchasing system used. Major brands maintain national price schedules for their distributors and certain classes of direct customers. These schedules are constructed to reflect the cost of performing required services and are available to any customer who meets a standard set of qualifications, which includes size of the shipment, ordering procedures, and payment terms.

Promotion is an important part of the cost structure of syrup manufacturers. Customer recognition and acceptance of these branded products is a major part of their stock in trade. To keep their name before the public, the major companies engage in extensive joint advertising and promotion activities with their syrup customers. Syrup is the most profitable way for the soft-drink companies to sell their heavily promoted products. Promotions vary from glass giveaways to menu or media advertising. The factors necessary to qualify for these programs are now standardized. The essential requirement is that value be received by both parties. Great care is taken so that these allowances are not construed as volume discounts in violation of the Robinson-Patman Act.

Equipment is offered on a lease basis from some syrup manufacturers, generally as part of a promotional package, that displays the name or logo of the company. Over the years, the syrup companies have increased their emphasis on promotion activities, which should be a major consideration in the operator's selection.

Ready-to-drink. Ready-to-drink products are of two types. They may be carbonated, then bottled or canned in a variety of sizes. Another form is pre-mixed (generally in five-gallon bulk containers). These products are usually sold on a competitive basis within the regional market. Ready-to-drink products are frequently manufactured by franchise bottlers, although syrup manufacturers operate some plants themselves in certain areas. Depending on the policies of the local franchises and competition, there may be substantial pricing variations by region.

Regional labels offer another alternative to the operator, particularly regarding ready-to-use products. They are generally less expensive than the branded products.

Private-label products. Private-label products offer beverage buyers still another option. Flavor and syrup manufacturers have offered their products in competition with national brands for years. For example, the Howard Johnson Company successfully sold its own "HOJO" products. From the viewpoint of product cost, the savings potential is significant. The major ingredient in beverage syrups is sweetener. Liquid sugar costs about $.40 per pound; corn sweeteners are even less expensive. Assuming five pounds of sugar per gallon of syrup, the major ingredient costs about $2.00 per gallon. The cost of syrup to the food and beverage operator can easily be three or four times higher than this figure. Buyers and operators should make their own cost comparisons if they feel private-label products are a reasonable alternative. While the above costs are only for illustration, a wide spread is likely. A decision has to be made as to how valuable brand identification is to the operation's customers.

Distribution. Distribution may be accomplished through manufacturers, franchised bottlers, or independent distributors. Usually, the size of the shipment determines the method. If purchased from the manufacturer or franchise bottler, the quoted price per gallon usually includes distribution costs. An independent distributor usually sells on a cost-plus basis. Buyers may find it to their advantage, however, to negotiate a fixed amount per tank or case rather than a percentage over cost.

If five-gallon tanks of syrup cost $60, a nominal markup of 10 percent would yield $6.00. This may be considered relatively high based on the distributor's cost to actually handle the product. Buyers might negotiate a fixed fee per tank for all of their syrup requirements. It should be understood that this negotiation is independent of the promotions sometimes offered by syrup manufacturers.

Bottled Water

Bottled water is very popular in the United States; both domestic and imported bottled waters are sold in a variety of food and beverage venues.

More than 20 years ago, bottled water consisted mostly of status-symbol brands like Perrier. After Jack Nicholson brought a bottle of Evian to the Academy Awards, sales of this French still water skyrocketed.

Types and Varieties. Water has "come of age" as a beverage of choice by frequent guests of food and beverage operations. Bottled water has captured the second place behind soft drinks in terms of per capita consumption ahead of beer, coffee, and milk. Water represents consumer trends toward wholesome products and health and fitness. Water comes in many different types and varieties, and varying quality standards make its selection somewhat of a challenge. However, once a particular brand of bottled water is selected, it is usually enough to simply supply a purchase specification that lists the product's name and the market form (or, in most cases, the bottle or container size).

The types and varieties of bottled water have expanded over the past five years as demand for this non-alcoholic beverage has increased. Bottled water may either be sparkling or **still. Sparkling water** can range from lightly bubbly to aggressively effervescent. Bottled mineral water is the fastest growing subcategory of bottled water. Spring bottled water must come from an underground opening from which it flows naturally. Glacial water must originate from a glacier source. Artesian bottled water flows from a natural source above the Earth's water table. Consumers are increasingly curious about the sources of the bottled water they drink, monitoring water sources more closely than soft drinks, juices, and teas.

When bottled water has been purified or is called "drinking water;" it is required to have been processed. Some bottled waters undergo active-carbon filtration, deionization, or reverse osmosis, all processes that filter water from a municipal source. About a quarter of all bottled water in the United States is municipal water. Increasingly, these waters are enhanced by infusing nutrients. Water is a popular beverage with both adults and children. Those who consume bottled water are more likely to pay more for additive-free foods, and are more likely to prefer diet food and beverages.

Flavored waters have shown growth in popularity with consumers, particularly those who seek low-carbohydrate drinks. Flavored waters are frequently lightly sweetened, multi-vitamin or energy enhanced, or have added soy isoflavones (i.e., plant hormones). Fruit flavors added to in these bottled waters include berry, citrus, grape, green apple, peach, tropical, and watermelon. Newer products include oxygenated water and water with added caffeine. Structured waters enhance cellular absorption and the body's oxygen uptake, while others have the acidity (pH) adjusted to buffer an acidic diet and flushing of waste from cells and the body.

Another category of non-alcoholic beverages is **energy drinks.** Although beyond the scope of this chapter, an example is N Motion energy drinks that contain taurine, rhodiola rosea, green tea extract, and caffeine. These beverages are designed to provide an energy boost.

Quality Standards. Bottled water appeals to guests who are interested in healthy product offerings in a food and beverage operation. Increased consumption is being driven by children, particularly five- to nine-year-olds. This is good news for parents and school systems that struggle with obesity issues related to high calorie beverages. Many children see mineral water as a "cool" drink.

Labeling for bottled water has come a long way, but still has some to go. While the traditional Nutrition Facts label (reporting calories, fats, proteins, carbohydrates) is meaningless, the consumer may benefit if the amounts of calcium, magnesium, potassium, and other minerals present are listed on the label.

The amount of dissolved minerals in bottled water affects the taste. Sparkling water has been said to go best with grilled fish, particularly oily fish. The bubbles assist in ridding the mouth of the aftertaste that often occurs with fish such as salmon. In contrast, beef and lamb call for a still water so the water does not dominate the flavor. Lemon-based desserts go well with a still water, while chocolate desserts are best with palate-washing sparkling waters. Of course, the main rule is to drink what you like with the food that you are eating. However, these may help servers suggest various forms of bottled water to enhance the quality of the guests' experience. Suggestive selling must be truly that approach, not a hard sell. Guests usually do not like it when servers "sneak up" and pour more water that has not been ordered.

Market Forms. Bottled water includes both convenience (individual) sizes, as well as bulk (over 1.5 liters) sizes.

Specifications. It is estimated that there are over 600 domestic and in excess of 300 imported brands of bottled water available on the market. Perhaps the easiest way to specify bottled water is with the brand name and the container size. Brand dominators include Coca-Cola, Group Danone, Nestlé, and PepsiCo. The brand popularity may vary by country. For example, in Great Britain the leader is Danone (which owns Evian and Volvic), Highland Spring, and Buxton (owned by Nestlé). In the United States, the dominant brand is Aquafina (owned by PepsiCo), followed by Dasani (owned by Coca-Cola), Poland Spring (owned by Nestlé), and Arrowhead. Sparkling water brands that dominate include Perrier, San Pelligrino, LaCroix, and Poland Spring.

Specifications must be based guest requirements. Different occasions may require different bottled waters. If bottled waters are going to be sold in the food and beverage operation, the operation simply needs to train all servers to be able to explain how bottled water, just as any other product or service offered, will contribute positively to the food and beverage experience.

 **Key Terms**

aging—Storing wines before bottling.

ale—A malt beverage that contains more hops than beer and has a characteristic bitter taste.

aperitif wine—A wine that is fortified, flavored with herb ingredients, and usually is served before a meal as an appetizer or cocktail.

aperitif—A spirit consumed primarily as an appetizer. It may be mixed with other alcohol products, and many are flavored with ingredients that give them a bitter taste.

aroma—The odor of a young wine, usually fruity or flowery.

beer—An alcoholic beverage made from fermented grains. It has the lowest alcohol content and highest food value among alcoholic beverages.

bitters—A type of spirit usually made from roots, spices, bark, berries, fruit, or other herbs steeped in or distilled with a neutral spirit and used primarily in mixed drinks.

black tea—Tea in which the leaves have been fermented or oxidized before firing.

blending—The practice of combining different wines to achieve some purpose. It is usually done to maintain consistency over time.

body—The feel and weight of a wine in the mouth.

bouquet—The complex fragrance of a wine resulting from the fermentation process, aging techniques, and maturing time in the bottle.

bourbon—An American whiskey produced from a grain mixture containing at least 51 percent corn.

brandy—Any distilled spirit made from fruit or fruit derivatives.

Brazils—Coffees grown in the country of Brazil. They are named after the region in which they are grown or the port through which they are shipped.

brewing—The process of preparing ground coffee for drinking. Brewing can be done by the traditional system or by using flake, low-density, or high-yield coffee.

call brand—A brand of liquor that is used when a customer specifically requests it.

Canadian whisky—Distinctive whisky of Canada, characteristically light, mild, and delicate; most are blended whiskys distilled from mashes of corn, rye, and malted barley.

clarity—A quality indicator for wine that is determined by the amount of matter that is floating in the wine.

cocoa—A product of the cacao tree that is used to make chocolate-flavored products.

corn whiskey—An American whiskey that must be made from a mash containing at least 80 percent corn.

dessert wine—A fortified wine that usually is served as dessert or with dessert after a meal.

distillation—A process in which a fermented liquid is heated to separate the alcohol from it.

draft beer—Beer drawn from a keg or a cask to a glass.

dry beer—Beer that is less sweet, with little or no aftertaste.

dry—Not sweet.

energy drink—A non-alcoholic beverage that contains additives designed to provide an energy boost to the consumer.

fermentation—A chemical process in which yeast is added to a sugar source to break the sugar down into alcohol, carbon dioxide gas, and heat.

fortified wine—Wine that contains added alcohol, usually in the form of brandy distilled from wine and added during fermentation.

generic—A California wine that is merchandised as a European type.

gin—A compounded spirit that is usually classified as dry or heavy. Dry gins are light in flavor and body, while heavy gins are more heavily flavored and full bodied.

grain neutral spirit—Any of a variety of tasteless and colorless spirits distilled from grain.

green tea—Tea in which the leaves have been withered, rolled, and fired immediately.

grinding—The process of preparing whole coffee beans for brewing. The type of grind needed will depend on the brewing method used.

head—The foam that forms at the top of a glass when beer is poured. The ideal head on a beer should be one-half to one inch thick.

house brand—A non-promoted label that is purchased at a lower cost than call brands.

Irish whiskey—Distinctive whiskey of Ireland made principally from barley, both malted and unmalted, together with oats, wheat, and sometimes a small proportion of rye.

keg—An aluminum or wooden container for storing beer.

legs—An indication of a wine's alcohol content. The more alcohol in a wine, the more legs or tears it has.

light beer—Beer with one-third to one-half fewer calories than regular beer.

liqueur—A flavored, usually sweet alcoholic beverage with an alcohol content higher than a fortified wine, but lower than most liquors. It is made from a base of grain, plant, or fruit spirits, or their combination.

malt beverage—A beverage that contains 0.5 percent or more of alcohol and is produced wholly or in part from malt. Malt beverages include beers, ales, stouts, porters, bock, and sake.

Milds—Coffees that include all other varieties except Robustas and Brazils. Mild coffees are named after the country in which they are grown.

natural wine—A wine category that includes wines produced by fermentation without the addition of alcohol or sugar.

non-alcoholic beer—Beer with few calories and less than 0.5 percent alcohol. The

oolong tea—Tea in which the leaves have been partially fermented.

pasteurization—The process of heating a liquid to a high temperature and maintaining the heat for a period of time to kill all bacteria and eliminate other impurities.

pilsner—A light, rich, mellow lager.

premium brand—A brand of liquor that has the best taste, packaging, and ingredients among its competitors. It usually also has the highest price.

proof—A measurement of a spirit's strength.

roasting—The process that develops flavor in coffee beans by releasing volatile oils and caramelizing carbohydrates.

Robustas—Coffees that largely come from Africa and are identified by country of origin (such as Uganda or Ivory Coast) or district of growth.

rum—A spirit distilled from fermented sugar cane juice or molasses juice.

rye whiskey—An American whiskey that must be made from 51 percent or more rye grain.

scotch—A distinctive whisky from Scotland with at least 80 proof alcohol content, manufactured in compliance with British laws.

soft drinks—Non-alcoholic flavored drinks that may be carbonated or non-carbonated.

sparkling water—Bottled water that is carbonated. It can range from lightly bubbly to aggressively effervescent.

sparkling wine—Wine that is produced by trapping the carbon dioxide produced in a second fermentation

spirit—An alcoholic beverage made from distillation, rather than fermentation.

still water—Bottled water that is not carbonated.

table wine—The largest category of wine, which includes wines primarily suited to accompany food.

tap—A beer faucet used to pour beer from a keg, or the process used to set up a beer keg for service.

Tennessee whiskey—Often called sour mash whiskey instead of bourbon; sour mash is a spirit made from a regular sweet mash brow mixed with some soured old mash brew in a ratio of about two regular to one sour.

tequila—A distinctive Mexican spirit distilled from the fermented juice of the blue variety of the agave plant.

varietal—A term often used in California that describes the primary grape variety in a bottle of wine.

viniculture—The study or science of making wine.

vintage—The year a wine's grapes were harvested and wine-making was begun, or a rating of the quality and potential of a year's wine production.

vodka—A clear, colorless, flavorless spirit made by passing highly refined neutral spirits through charcoal, by redistillation, or other government-approved processes.

wine—An alcoholic beverage that is produced by fermenting grapes.

 Review Questions

1. What are the different types and categories of liquor?

2. What are the different types and categories of beer?

3. What are the different types and categories of wine?

4. What are the common terms used for liquor, beer, and wine products?

5. What are the common forms of packaging for beer, liquor, and wine products?

6. What are the different varieties, quality standards, processing stages, and market forms for coffee?

7. What are the different varieties, quality standards, processing stages, and market forms for tea?

8. What are the different types, requirements, and market forms for soft drinks and bottled water?

9. Why are the requirements and content of specifications for alcoholic and non-alcoholic beverages important?

10. What sources of information can assist in purchasing decisions for alcoholic and non-alcoholic beverages?

 References

Condor, Bob. "Bottled Water to Be the No. 2 Drink." *Knight Ridder Tribune Business News.* (April 6, 2003): p. 1.

Kitty, K. *Beverage Industry New York* 95, no. 8 (August 2004): p. 16.

Kotschevar, Lendal H. and Ronald F. Cichy. *Managing Beverage Service* (Lansing, Mich.: Educational Institute of the American Hotel & Lodging Association), 2004.

"Profits Flow in Bottled Water." *Marketing Week* (February 17, 2005).

Scarpa, J. "Testing the Waters." *Restaurant Business* 102, no. 8 (May 1, 2003): p. 76.

U.S. Bottled Water 2004. Snapshots International Ltd. (October 2004).

Internet Sites

For more information, visit the following Internet sites. Remember that Internet addresses can change without notice. If the site is no longer there, you can use a search engine to look for additional sites.

Aboutwines.com
www.aboutwines.com

Adams Beverage Group Industry
  Links
www.beveragenet.net/links/links.asp

Ardent Spirits
www.ardentspirits.com

Bartender Magazine
www.bartender.com

Cellarnotes.net
www.cellarnotes.net

Champagne Magic
www.champagnemagic.com

Decanter Magazine
www.decanter.com

Distilled Spirits Council of the United
  States
www.discus.org

Good Cooking Beverage Guide
www.goodcooking.com/beverage.htm

iVodka.com
www.ivodka.com

International Sommelier Guild
www.internationalsommelier.com

Wine Label Regulations
www.internetwineguide.com/structure/
abwine/labelreg.htm

Malt Advocate Magazine
www.whiskeypages.com

Nightclub & Bar Magazine
www.nightclub.com

OregonWines.com
www.oregonwines.com

Professional Friends of Wine
www.winepros.org

The Scotch Whiskey Association
www.scotch-whisky.org.uk/

The Webtender
www.webtender.com/browse.html

Wine Labels
www.thewinedoctor.com/advisory/
labelinterpreter.shtml

Wine Enthusiast Magazine
www.winemag.com

Wine & Spirits Wholesalers of
  America, Inc.
www.wswa.org/public/

Wine Lovers' Page
www.wineloverspage.com/wines/

Wine Society of Texas
www.winesocietyoftexas.org/
virtual_classroom

Wine Spectator
www.winespectator.com

Wines of France
www.frenchwinesfood.com

Chapter 15 Outline

Capital Equipment
    Manufacturers and Distributors
Supplies and Smallware
    Supplies
    Smallware
Pricing Arrangements
Purchasing versus Leasing
Services

Competencies

1. List the sources of available information to assist in purchasing decisions for equipment, supplies, and services. (p. 451)

2. Define capital equipment, identify the factors that should be considered in its purchase, and describe the role of capital equipment manufacturers and distributors. (pp. 451–452)

3. Identify the categories of supplies and smallware, and describe the factors that should be considered in their purchase. (pp. 452–458)

4. Explain the requirements, content, and importance of specifications for equipment, supplies, and services. (pp. 452–458)

5. Identify the key factors to consider when deciding whether to purchase or lease equipment. (pp. 458–459)

15

Equipment, Supplies, and Services

FOOD SERVICE PURCHASING INVOLVES MORE THAN JUST FOOD AND BEVERAGES. There are many non-food items, equipment, smallware items, supplies, and services that buyers must purchase for food service operations. These items can have a great impact on expenses and on how effectively the operation functions. If the equipment and supplies are not available to prepare the food and beverages, the food and beverage products purchased cannot be put to use.

Capital Equipment

Items that have a useful life that can be depreciated or expensed over several years are considered to be **capital equipment.** Examples of capital equipment include refrigerators, freezers, ovens, ranges, ice machines, furniture and office equipment. Exhibit 1 gives a sample specification for a dishwashing machine.

In deciding what type of equipment to purchase, buyers should consider how the equipment will be used, where it will be used, how often it will be used, and what will be its expected useful life. When comparing pieces of equipment the question to ask is which piece of equipment will benefit the operation. Equipment specifications can be obtained from manufacturers and modified to meet the operator's needs. When possible, the manufacturer's specifications should be used. The standard specification will not require special modifications that will increase the cost of the item. If equipment must be designed specifically for an operation, it may be wise to work with a food service consultant who has specialized knowledge in the areas of design and equipment selection. Smallware includes the items needed to prepare foods and/or serve products to the customers. National and local trade shows, such as the National Restaurant Association Show (www.restaurant.org/show), or state restaurant shows are good sources of information because buyers often get the opportunity to sample the products and discuss their needs with a professional. Keep in mind that a buyer's best source for information may be a distributor in his or her local area.

Manufacturers and Distributors

When purchasing equipment, buyers will likely deal with food service equipment distributors to supply the items. Only very large organizations purchasing multiple pieces of equipment will deal directly with the manufacturer. Dealing with

Exhibit 1   Sample Capital Equipment Specification

Product Name:	Door type dishmachine
Manufacturer Name:	ABC Dishwashers, Inc.
Product ID:	ABC-5
Equivalents:	ABC-5A & 5B
Manufacturer Part Number:	ABC-5
Material:	Stainless Steel
Brand Name:	ABC-5 Restaurant Model Low Temperature
Vendor Description:	Dishmachine, door type, low temp. chemical sanitizing
Product Notes:	Dishmachine, door type, low temp, double rack, auto-start, top mount controls, built-in chemical dispensing, built-in scrap accumulator, 115 volt, 40 amp
Voltage:	115 volt, standard household current
Shipping Weight:	420 lb

an equipment distributor has the advantage of having a representative that can offer services like training, maintenance, and repair after the sale. Many distributors have developed into full-service organizations offering design, engineering, installation, and financing service in addition to equipment. Many of these full-service distributors also fabricate sheet metal items like shelves, tables, and counters. Buyers should be aware of discounts offered by the manufacturer through the distributor. Special promotions and allowances can offer opportunities for cost savings. Buyers should also be aware of warranties and service agreements available.

Supplies and Smallware

Supplies and smallware are items needed to do business and serve customers in food service operations. Some supplies are visible to the customer, and some are used only behind the scenes. **Supplies** are usually defined as items that will be consumed in the service of customers. **Smallware** includes the items needed to prepare foods and/or serve products to the customers. Exhibit 2 contains descriptions of the smallwares and supplies used in a beverage service operation. Exhibit 3 gives quantities of selected smallwares and supplies needed in a 100-seat restaurant.

Supplies

Paper Goods. Different types of food service operations will have different needs for paper goods. Typically, paper goods include paper napkins, cups, carry-out containers, paper towels, plastic film, and foil. Other items to consider are guest

Exhibit 2   Beverage Service Smallware and Supplies

Beverage servers and bartenders make use of a large variety of tools to execute excellent beverage service. They quickly learn how to use each piece of equipment to produce the best result. Equipment commonly found in beverage service establishments includes the following:

beverage tray—A small, round, plastic tray (often 12 inches in diameter), usually lined with rubber or cork, used to carry food and beverages.

bus tub—A large tub, usually plastic, in which soiled dishware is placed and taken to the dishwashing area.

chafer—A metal holder that keeps food hot using Sterno. Chafers are usually made of stainless steel, silver, or copper.

decoy system—Bus tubs and dish racks with one dirty dish, glass, and other tableware in them to show where to place dirty items.

drip bucket—A bucket that collects drips of water produced by ice melting in a food and beverage display.

glass froster—A cold storage unit, like a small refrigerator, that cools glasses so they are frosted when removed.

glassware—Tumblers, wine glasses, champagne flutes, beer steins, water glasses.

jigger—A measuring receptacle used to mix cocktails.

linen roll-up—Silverware rolled up in a linen napkin.

metal shaker—A metal cup that is placed over a mixing glass in order to shake cocktail ingredients with ice.

order pad (captain's pad)—A pad of paper, often with carbon copies, on which guest orders are written before they are entered into the pre-check machine or POS system.

oval tray (service tray)—A large plastic tray, usually lined with rubber or cork, used to carry food and beverages.

portable bar—A cabinet on rollers used to store and serve beverages, glassware, napkins, stirrers, and other supplies.

ramekin—A small receptacle used to hold butter and sauces.

speed rail—A rack that holds bottles of a restaurant's most popular brands of liquor and the restaurant's house brands.

tray jack—A wooden or metal stand that oval trays are placed on when serving food or drinks.

underliner—A plate set under teapots or condiments. Underliners may be covered with napkins or paper doilies.

checks, register tape, tissues, stationery, and copy paper. Typical paper goods can be purchased through full-time distributors or a specialty paper goods distributor. Other paper items may need to be ordered from specialized distributors or separate supply houses, particularly if a company logo or lettering is necessary.

   Selection factors. Selecting paper goods is a matter of investigating the possible options and making a decision based on customer expectations and cost weighed against value. An upscale casual-dining operation should not use the

Exhibit 3   Selected Smallware and Supply Requirements for a 100-Seat Restaurant

Dinnerware

20 doz.	dinner plates		8 doz.	coffee cups
20 doz.	salad plates		8 doz.	saucers
10 doz.	platters		8 doz.	18 oz. nappies
9 doz.	soup/salad bowls		20 doz.	bread and butter
10 doz.	bouillons		10 doz.	5 oz. ramekins
20 doz.	fruits		5 doz.	12 oz. rarebits

Glassware

15 doz.	14 oz. large beverage		12 doz.	5 oz. juice
20 doz.	10 oz. water		6 doz.	4 ½ oz. sherbet

Flatware

30 doz.	teaspoons		30 doz.	dinner forks
15 doz.	dessert/oval bowl spoons		15 doz.	salad forks
15 doz.	ice tea spoons		20 doz.	dinner knives
15 doz.	bouillon spoons			

Tabletop Accessories

84 each	salt and pepper shakers		36 each	sugar pack holder
24 each	ashtrays		36 each	table tents
60 each	bread baskets		12 each	oil and vinegar sets
12 each	12 oz. s/s creamers			

Entrance Lobby

1 each	sand urn		1 each	mint tray
1 each	menu board		60 each	menu covers
1 each	toothpick dispenser			

Bar Glasses

3 doz.	wine		12 doz.	collins
1 doz.	carafe		4 doz.	martini
12 doz.	beer		2 doz.	Irish coffee
1 doz.	pitchers		3 doz.	sour
6 doz.	rocks		2 doz.	champagne
4 doz.	double rocks			

General Cleaning Supplies

4 each	hand and nail brushes		144 each	hand towels
2 each	Hi-Lo brushes w/squeegee		2 each	mop buckets and wringer
1 each	drain brush		2 each	mops
1 each	steam kettle brush		2 each	wet floor signs
2 each	coffee decanter brush		1 each	counter brush
1 each	bake pan lip brush		2 each	floor brooms
2 each	coffee urn brushes		12 each	28 gal. trash can w/lids
1 each	stack oven brush		4 each	dollies for 28 gal. trash can
4 each	heavy duty hand brush		4 each	rectangular trash cans
12 each	16 ounce spray bottle			

Source: North American Association of Foodservice Equipment Manufacturers, www.nafem.org/resources/smallwares/restaurant100.cfm.

same type of paper napkin as a quick-service restaurant. Similar decisions must be made for all types of paper goods. For instance, when purchasing foil, the gauge of the foil is a determining factor in the cost. How the foil will be used should be the determining factor in the purchase decision.

Distribution systems. Distributors for paper goods are more varied than those of food and beverage supplies. Paper goods can be purchased from full-line distributors, local supply distributors, national or regional supply distributors, or specialized distributors. Full-line distributors can supply paper products along with food orders, providing one-stop shopping and simplifying the ordering process. However, product availability may be limited. Local distributors have the advantage of being able to provide personalized local service, but these local distributors may not be able to provide products at the lowest prices. National and regional supply distributors are large enough to carry a large selection at a low price, but deliveries may be limited by minimum shipping requirements. Specialized distributors may be able to cater to your specific needs, but may also require a guaranteed purchase contract.

Specifications. Specifications for paper goods should include all the information important to the needs of the operation, including the product's:

- Exact name.
- Brand name.
- Intended use.
- Form.
- Size.
- Packaging.
- Package size.
- Container type.
- Personalization or promotional requirements.
- Color.
- Type of material.
- Special requirements.

Chemicals and Cleaning Supplies. Chemicals and cleaning supplies are necessary to maintain, clean, and sanitize food service facilities. They can be dishwashing detergents, sanitizers, floor cleaning detergents, scouring powders, bathroom cleaners, and any materials used to apply or use the chemicals.

Selection factors. Chemicals and cleaning supplies should be selected based on the needs of the operation. Products that can be used for multiple cleaning tasks should be considered over single-use products. Products should be compared for performance or, in the case of supplies, durability. There is a growing concern for purchasing more environmentally friendly, or green, products. Many states and local jurisdictions have specific requirements for cleaning and chemical products. Refer to sites like Green Seal (www.greenseal.org) and the U.S. Environmental Protection

Agency Environmentally Preferable Purchasing website (www.epa.gov/oppt/epp) or contact your local state environmental agency for guidance. Buyers should consider the as-used cost (accounting for dilution), effectiveness, safety, training needs, odor, container size, and services provided by the supplier when making purchasing decisions for chemical products.

Distribution system. Chemical distributors are dominated by national companies with large product lines. Typically, these distributors are heavily oriented toward service. Products can be purchased through full-line or local distributors. Distributors typically provide services such as chemical training, quality control, and maintenance and repair on cleaning equipment (particularly dish machines). Care must be taken to fully investigate any purchasing contracts because they sometimes require minimum orders.

Specifications. Specifications for cleaning supplies and chemicals are typically based on brand. Information that should be included in a specification includes the product's:

- Type and exact name.
- Brand name.
- Intended use.
- Form.
- Size.
- Container size.
- Packaging.
- Safety concerns.
- Effectiveness requirements.
- Special requirements.

Exhibit 4 is a sample specification for a surface and floor cleaner.

Smallware

Types and Categories. Smallware includes china, glassware, and flatware used to serve guests, as well as utensils and pots and pans used to prepare food. China includes all manner of plates, dishes, and cups used to serve the customer.

Glassware comes in many shapes and sizes, depending on the operation's beverage needs. The actual size of glasses used varies from establishment to establishment, depending on guest preferences, standard pour sizes, and the prices charged. Flatware includes forks, spoons, table knives, steak knives, soup spoons, and any other special types of flatware needed to serve the customer. Utensils used in the kitchen fall into the categories of serving utensils and cooking utensils. The types needed depend upon the operation's needs and the types of food prepared.

Selection Factors. The selection of china is based on aesthetic factors, customer expectations, practicality, durability, and cost. Standard patterns are available,

Exhibit 4 Sample Chemical Product Specification

Product name:	Surface and floor cleaner
Brand name:	XYZ Super Cleaner
Intended use:	Used to clean nonporous surfaces
Form:	Concentrated liquid
Packaging:	4 one-gallon bottles per case; each bottle must be clearly labeled
Package size:	One gallon, 32:1 dilution factor
Special requirements:	United States Environmental Protection Agency (USEPA), Design for the Environment (DfE) approved; MSDS available.

making it easy to order and replace pieces as needed. Stoneware or earthenware may be acceptable substitutes for china depending upon the operation.

Glassware selection is based on the types of beverages served, customer expectations, practicality, durability, and cost. As with china, standard patterns and sizes make it easy to order and replace items as needed.

Flatware is available in a range of styles and prices, depending upon the type of material it is made from. Stainless steel and silver plating are the most popular types of materials used for flatware. Flatware should be selected for its aesthetic appeal and how it matches the china and tabletop. Other considerations include cost and availability for replacement.

The primary selection factors for utensils are the items' intended purpose, durability, and cost. The needs of the personnel using the utensils should be considered. If the utensil is not the correct tool for the task, money will be wasted because the utensil will not be used.

Distribution Systems. China, glassware, flatware, and utensils, much like paper goods, are available form a variety of distributors. Convenience is an advantage to working with full-line distributors, but they usually only carry a minimum number of patterns and product types. Local distributors often carry a larger line of products and can provide fast local service, but the cost may be higher because of the lower volume. National and regional distributors can provide a broad selection of items and patterns, but service and delivery may be limited and minimum order requirements may apply. Purchasing special-order products from specialized distributors could require minimum purchase contracts and additional costs for special requests.

Specifications. Specifications for china, glassware, flatware, and utensils should be based on standard manufacturer specifications with any special requirements added. Flatware may also include specifications for gauge of stainless steel; percentage of chrome, nickel, and steel for stainless steel; and weight for silver plating.

Specify the type of metal desired (stainless steel or aluminum) and gauge of metal where applicable for utensils.

Information that should be included in a smallware specification includes:

- Name or type of item.

- Intended use.

- Brand or manufacturer.

- Size.

- Form.

- Safety concerns.

- Color.

- Material used to make the item.

- Personalization or promotional requirements.

- Special requirements.

Pricing Arrangements

When purchasing equipment and supplies, care should be taken to ensure that the price paid for the product includes all of the costs included in acquiring and using the product. Product quality can be an important consideration. Inexpensive products priced below the market average may not have the same effectiveness or life span as more expensive products. Consider whether the product can be used as purchased or if other products, equipment or services will be required in order to properly use the product. Be sure to also consider not only the cost of the item, but also the delivery or freight expenses, installation costs, operating costs, potential savings expected from the item, and the projected salvage value of the item. When purchasing items on credit, make sure to consider the cost of the credit over the life of the financing in the overall cost of the item.

Suppliers may set prices based on how many items are purchased. For example a discount may be offered for cleaning supplies if the buyer purchases a full line of products or a certain amount of the product. Bulk discounts may be attractive, but keep in mind that larger quantities of a product will take up more storage space and may tie up cash that could be used for other purchases or operational activities.

Purchasing versus Leasing

Capital equipment can often be leased instead of purchased. When a food service organization lacks the capital to purchase equipment or is not sure how long the business will exist in a particular location, leasing equipment can be a viable alternative. Equipment distributors can set up leasing arrangements for the same types of equipment that can be purchased. Leased equipment must be selected from standard stock pieces and usually cannot be modified, but they will typically be covered with maintenance contracts. Leases can usually be established for two

5. **Print** the information requested below. Course name and number are found at the top of your exam. The **EXAM CONTROL NUMBER** must be filled in for the exam to be graded.

COURSE NAME: _____

COURSE NUMBER _____ EXAM DATE: _____

Completely blacken the letter on the answer sheet that corresponds to the answer you have chosen

EXAM CONTROL NO.

⓪ ⓪ ⓪ ⓪ ⓪ ⓪ ⓪
① ① ① ① ① ① ①
② ② ② ② ② ② ②
③ ③ ③ ③ ③ ③ ③
④ ④ ④ ④ ④ ④ ④
⑤ ⑤ ⑤ ⑤ ⑤ ⑤ ⑤
⑥ ⑥ ⑥ ⑥ ⑥ ⑥ ⑥
⑦ ⑦ ⑦ ⑦ ⑦ ⑦ ⑦
⑧ ⑧ ⑧ ⑧ ⑧ ⑧ ⑧
⑨ ⑨ ⑨ ⑨ ⑨ ⑨ ⑨

DO NOT USE INK

THE EXAM CONTROL NUMBER **MUST** BE FILLED IN FOR THE EXAM TO BE GRADED

1 (A) (B) (C) (D) (E)
2 (A) (B) (C) (D) (E)
3 (A) (B) (C) (D) (E)
4 (A) (B) (C) (D) (E)
5 (A) (B) (C) (D) (E)
6 (A) (B) (C) (D) (E)
7 (A) (B) (C) (D) (E)
8 (A) (B) (C) (D) (E)
9 (A) (B) (C) (D) (E)
10 (A) (B) (C) (D) (E)
11 (A) (B) (C) (D) (E)
12 (A) (B) (C) (D) (E)
13 (A) (B) (C) (D) (E)
14 (A) (B) (C) (D) (E)
15 (A) (B) (C) (D) (E)
16 (A) (B) (C) (D) (E)
17 (A) (B) (C) (D) (E)
18 (A) (B) (C) (D) (E)
19 (A) (B) (C) (D) (E)
20 (A) (B) (C) (D) (E)
21 (A) (B) (C) (D) (E)
22 (A) (B) (C) (D) (E)
23 (A) (B) (C) (D) (E)
24 (A) (B) (C) (D) (E)

25 (A) (B) (C) (D) (E)
26 (A) (B) (C) (D) (E)
27 (A) (B) (C) (D) (E)
28 (A) (B) (C) (D) (E)
29 (A) (B) (C) (D) (E)
30 (A) (B) (C) (D) (E)
31 (A) (B) (C) (D) (E)
32 (A) (B) (C) (D) (E)
33 (A) (B) (C) (D) (E)
34 (A) (B) (C) (D) (E)
35 (A) (B) (C) (D) (E)
36 (A) (B) (C) (D) (E)
37 (A) (B) (C) (D) (E)
38 (A) (B) (C) (D) (E)
39 (A) (B) (C) (D) (E)
40 (A) (B) (C) (D) (E)
41 (A) (B) (C) (D) (E)
42 (A) (B) (C) (D) (E)
43 (A) (B) (C) (D) (E)
44 (A) (B) (C) (D) (E)
45 (A) (B) (C) (D) (E)
46 (A) (B) (C) (D) (E)
47 (A) (B) (C) (D) (E)
48 (A) (B) (C) (D) (E)
49 (A) (B) (C) (D) (E)
50 (A) (B) (C) (D) (E)
51 (A) (B) (C) (D) (E)
52 (A) (B) (C) (D) (E)
53 (A) (B) (C) (D) (E)
54 (A) (B) (C) (D) (E)
55 (A) (B) (C) (D) (E)
56 (A) (B) (C) (D) (E)
57 (A) (B) (C) (D) (E)
58 (A) (B) (C) (D) (E)
59 (A) (B) (C) (D) (E)
60 (A) (B) (C) (D) (E)
61 (A) (B) (C) (D) (E)
62 (A) (B) (C) (D) (E)

63 (A) (B) (C) (D) (E)
64 (A) (B) (C) (D) (E)
65 (A) (B) (C) (D) (E)
66 (A) (B) (C) (D) (E)
67 (A) (B) (C) (D) (E)
68 (A) (B) (C) (D) (E)
69 (A) (B) (C) (D) (E)
70 (A) (B) (C) (D) (E)
71 (A) (B) (C) (D) (E)
72 (A) (B) (C) (D) (E)
73 (A) (B) (C) (D) (E)
74 (A) (B) (C) (D) (E)
75 (A) (B) (C) (D) (E)
76 (A) (B) (C) (D) (E)
77 (A) (B) (C) (D) (E)
78 (A) (B) (C) (D) (E)
79 (A) (B) (C) (D) (E)
80 (A) (B) (C) (D) (E)
81 (A) (B) (C) (D) (E)
82 (A) (B) (C) (D) (E)
83 (A) (B) (C) (D) (E)
84 (A) (B) (C) (D) (E)
85 (A) (B) (C) (D) (E)
86 (A) (B) (C) (D) (E)
87 (A) (B) (C) (D) (E)
88 (A) (B) (C) (D) (E)
89 (A) (B) (C) (D) (E)
90 (A) (B) (C) (D) (E)
91 (A) (B) (C) (D) (E)
92 (A) (B) (C) (D) (E)
93 (A) (B) (C) (D) (E)
94 (A) (B) (C) (D) (E)
95 (A) (B) (C) (D) (E)
96 (A) (B) (C) (D) (E)
97 (A) (B) (C) (D) (E)
98 (A) (B) (C) (D) (E)
99 (A) (B) (C) (D) (E)
100 (A) (B) (C) (D) (E)

553-8UN-C798

A T T E N T I O N

Keep the attached final examination answer sheet!

Read other side before detaching from answer sheet.

In order to earn a course completion certificate from the Educational Institute of the American Hotel & Lodging Association, you must use this sheet to record your final exam answers. This answer sheet cannot be replaced.

The textbook and final examination answer sheet are intended to be sold as a unit.

Returns will not be accepted if the original plastic shrink wrap is broken.

American Hotel & Lodging Educational Institute

A nonprofit educational foundation of the American Hotel & Lodging Association

3. ...have one yet, leave this section blank and one will be assigned.

Have you ever taken an Educational Institute Course before? ☐ Yes ☐ No

4. **BIRTH DATE:** Your birth date will help us to further identify your student record. Please fill in your birth date using a four-digit year, followed by a two-digit month, followed by a two-digit day. Example: A birthday of June 5, 1985, should be entered in the grid as 19850605. The first two digits of the year have been filled in for you.

BIRTH DATE

YEAR · MO · DAY

TF3574-slw (05/07)   0987654

to five years, depending upon the type of equipment. Sometimes, lease-purchase options can be agreed upon. The disadvantages to leasing are, of course, that the operator does not own the equipment and the lease agreement comes with a premium cost over purchasing the equipment outright. Leasing may also be a good way to try out equipment needed for a new menu item because the equipment can be returned if the item does not produce results.

Services

Many jobs performed in food service operations are performed by outside contractors. Outside contractors often have the expertise and equipment to best perform a particular job. Sometimes, the contractors are providing maintenance or repair expertise. Other contractors may provide services on a continuing basis. Still other services may be one-time jobs.

Examples of jobs that might be considered for outside service contractors include:

- Bookkeeping or payroll services.

- Heating, ventilation, and air conditioning maintenance and repair.

- Refrigeration maintenance and repair.

- Kitchen hood and duct cleaning.

- Pest control services.

- Landscaping.

- Snow removal.

- Money pick-up service.

- Office machine leasing, maintenance, and repair.

- Locksmith services.

- Roof repair.

- Driveway and parking lot maintenance and repair.

- Marketing and advertising.

- Cleaning.

Service suppliers should be selected based on their expertise in the area and their reputation. Before hiring a contractor for a service, check the contractor's background and record of service. Ask to see references from other clients, and to see their business license if applicable. Make sure the contractor has proof of proper insurance and is bonded, if necessary. Avoid unlicensed, uninsured service personnel. It might sound like a good idea to have an employee's husband mow the lawn, but if he is injured, it is the operation's responsibility if he is not properly insured to do the work. Operators should keep in mind that they are hiring contractors to complete a task or do some type of work. Reputable service providers should be able to complete the services on a timely basis.

 **Key Terms** ————————————————————————————

capital equipment— Items that have a useful life that can be depreciated or expensed over several years.

smallware—Items needed to prepare foods and/or serve products to the customers.

supplies—Items that will be consumed in the service of customers.

 Review Questions ————————————————————————

1. What is capital equipment, and what should food service operators consider when purchasing it?

2. What are the selection factors and specification requirements for paper goods?

3. What are the selection factors and specification requirements for chemicals and cleaning supplies?

4. What are the selection factors and specification requirements for small-wares?

5. What pricing factors must a buyer consider when purchasing equipment and supplies?

6. For what services might a food service operator use an outside contractor? What factors should be considered when choosing a contractor?

 Internet Sites ————————————————————————————

For more information, visit the following Internet sites. Remember that Internet addresses can change without notice. If the site is no longer there, you can use a search engine to look for additional sites.

Ecolab Cleaning and Sanitizing
www.ecolab.com

Enodis Equipment
www.enodisusa.com

Food Service Consultants Society
   International (FCSI)
www.fcsi.org

Foodservice Equipment Reports
   Magazine
www.fermag.com

Foodservice Equipment & Supplies
   Magazine
www.fesmag.com

Hobart Equipment
www.hobartcorp.com

North America Association of Food
   Equipment Manufacturers (NAFEM)
www.nafem.org

Vulcan-Hart Equipment
www.vulcanhart.com

Index